D0938969

The Penguin Book of Feminist Writing

THE
PENGUIN BOOK
of
FEMINIST WRITING

Edited by
HANNAH DAWSON

PENGUIN CLASSICS
an imprint of
PENGUIN BOOKS

PENGUIN CLASSICS

UK | USA | Canada | Ireland | Australia
India | New Zealand | South Africa

Penguin Books is part of the Penguin Random House group of companies
whose addresses can be found at global.penguinrandomhouse.com.

Penguin
Random House
UK

This selection first published 2021
001

Introduction and selection copyright © Hannah Dawson, 2021

The moral right of the introducer has been asserted

The permissions on pp. 643–50 constitute an extension of this copyright page

Every effort has been made to trace copyright holders and to obtain their permission for the use of copyright
material. The publisher apologises for any errors or omissions and would be grateful if notified of any corrections
that should be incorporated in future reprints or editions of this book.

Set in 11.25/14.75 pt Adobe Caslon Pro
Typeset by Jouve (UK), Milton Keynes
Printed and bound in Great Britain by Clays Ltd, Elcograf S.p.A.

The authorized representative in the EEA is Penguin Random House Ireland,
Morrison Chambers, 32 Nassau Street, Dublin D02 YH68

A CIP catalogue record for this book is available from the British Library

ISBN: 978–0–241–43286–0

www.greenpenguin.co.uk

MIX
Paper from
responsible sources
FSC® C018179

Penguin Random House is committed to a
sustainable future for our business, our readers
and our planet. This book is made from Forest
Stewardship Council® certified paper.

To my sister Rebecca, and her baby Joan

How far we women are more excellent then men. Our bodies are fruitefull, whereby the world encreaseth, and our care wonderful, by which man is preserved.

Jane Anger, 1589

That story tells us that if a husband kicks you, you should just smile at him and say, 'Don't do that, my lord and husband: you'll hurt your foot.'

Tarabai Shinde, 1882

The emancipation of women can only be completed when a fundamental transformation of living is effected.

Alexandra Kollontai, 1921

Oh Bondage Up Yours!

Poly Styrene, 1977

You have to git man off your eyeball, before you can see anything a'tall.

Alice Walker, 1982

There is a movement in the shadow of a sun that is old now. There, just there. Coming from the rim of the world. A disturbing disturbance that is not a hawk nor stormy weather, but a dark woman, of all things. My sister, my me – rustling, like life.

Toni Morrison, 1985

The world is not a safe place to live in.

Gloria Anzaldúa, 1987

In this society, safety and security will not be premised on violence or the threat of violence; it will be based on a collective commitment to guaranteeing the survival and care of all peoples.

INCITE! 2001

Contents

Contents

Contents

Contents

Contents

Contents

Contents

Contents

Contents

Contents

Introduction

I put hoops in my ears. I rubbed cream that smelt of geraniums onto my arms, and went out into the night to meet my friends. I had to go along a road that had a park on one side and empty buildings on the other. There was no one around. The liquid moon of a motorbike's headlamp appeared, far off on the opposite side of the road. As it came closer, it crossed over, and came straight at me. I put my head down, away from the light. I froze. The motorbike swerved and stopped, sort of side-on, blocking my path, gleaming purring metal. A voice said, 'What have you got for me darling?' I looked up and from deep within the helmet a man wearing the mask of a skull looked back at me, sharp teeth and jawbone coming out of the dark. I thought: he is going to hurt me. And then I smiled at him.

Why did I smile? I have asked myself this question many times. I have felt shame at my smile. It came involuntarily, as automatic as adrenalin. Does my training run that deep? Mary Wollstonecraft said that 'the mighty business of female life is to please'.[1] How to parse a woman's smile? Who can tell its secrets? In this instance I know that the texture of my smile was fear. I smiled because I was terrified, and this was how my body thought to protect me. Survivors of rape worry that they will not be believed, sometimes because they did not fight back, or try to escape. They are right to worry; juries acquit men on these grounds. But these acquittals, and the systematic suspicion of a woman's testimony, fail to comprehend the workings of violence. Silence, stillness, a smile: these are the last ditches of protection, the body's chronic attempts to circumvent an attack, rather than complicity with it. Indeed, complicity itself, often touted as consent, can be the evaporation of power.

Perhaps my smile did protect me, and disarm him. Or perhaps he thought twice when other people turned into the road. Or perhaps he only ever wanted to mess with my head. At any rate, he drove off. Nothing happened, not really. There was no harm done. Yet I tell this story because my fear at the edge of the cavernous park was one more jolt in everyday gendered reality: a hand between my thighs on a crowded train; the boy who was my friend who gave me a razor and told me to shave my legs; the driver who shouted out of his window 'do you want to die, bitch?'; earning less than men, for the same work; watching another woman assaulted on television, for entertainment; receiving another instruction to cheer up, calm down, eat more, eat less; seeing rooms of white men make decisions about women's bodies; hearing a President say that he could do anything to women. Grab 'em by the pussy.

Feminism only makes sense if you believe in sexism. Otherwise it has no object, no legitimate claim. And here we come to a precipice: many people do not believe in sexism, in the same way that many people do not believe in racism. They deny that these are structural realities. If they concede that there is a problem, it certainly does not exist in them. They are not sexist. Indeed, men might say that *they* are under attack, caught up in a kind of war – they love their military metaphors – a culture war, a war on free speech, a sex war that women are winning, wearing the trousers, victorious over redundant, henpecked men.

I met a man, a successful artist, who said he was worried that women now have an unfair advantage. He was sympathetic to feminism, he explained, but he thought it ran the risk of discriminating against men. He told me that he had been asked to speak on a panel where he was the only man. This upset him, he said. He felt like a token. I saw another man on the news, a Member of Parliament, say that he did not believe in feminism, but in equality for all. He simply would not put up with double standards (lower for women, higher for men). I heard another man on the radio, a judge this time, say that he disapproved of positive discrimination. The first priority, he insisted, in choosing a judge is that they should be a good judge, rather than come from a particular group of people. He was concerned that favouring a candidate on the basis of their identity would discourage those who felt that the dice were loaded against them. I have listened to many men say that the 'me too' movement feels like an assault on them. It has gone too far, they explain. Their hands are tied. They are not allowed to flirt anymore. There are some bad men, of course, but not them. Not all men. When is International Men's Day, they ask every year.

Privilege does not see itself as such. This is core to its operation. The way of the world passes for the way of justice. Male supremacy stipulates itself as a reflection of merit, rather than a contingent function of power. And if you are told that what you think you see – sexism, misogyny – is not really there, but just a figment of your imagination, you might start to doubt your eyes, your capacity to read the world. You might venture to say that one of the reasons why people did not vote for Hillary Clinton in the 2016 US Presidential election was because she was a woman. This might elicit outrage, or a smirk, followed by a list of 'real' reasons why she was not quite right. She was cold, unlikeable, too pleased with herself. As Rebecca Solnit put it, 'unconscious bias' was 'running for president'.[2]

You might complain when a man touches you, you might whisper that it is harassment – and then be told that it is just a bit of fun, don't be such a snowflake. And indeed, as your words fall through the air, they can seem like snowflakes, settling on nothing, vanishing into the tarmac. You are the offence, your complaint is the offence, rather than the offence that you are complaining about, and you are making everybody feel bad. A feminist is a killjoy, by definition, as Sara Ahmed explains; you kill joy by calling out sexism. 'To be willing to go against a social order, which is protected as a moral order, a happiness order, is to be willing to cause unhappiness'. You are the one who is 'difficult', and 'angry', and causing tension, not the man with his hand on your knee.[3]

In this perceptual rift, the women who speak up are painted as the assailants. When Clinton stood against Donald Trump, the crowd shouted 'Lock her up'. When Christine Blasey Ford alleged that US Supreme Court nominee Brett Kavanaugh had sexually assaulted her in high school, it was as though Zeus thundered back. The President called the accusation a 'trauma' for Kavanaugh; 'a man's life is in tatters'; what was happening to him was 'unfair'.[4] Kavanaugh shouted. He wept. He said that his name had been 'destroyed'. In fact, what happened was that he was confirmed in post while Blasey Ford received death threats and lived in hiding. Andrea Dworkin wrote: 'men often react to women's words – speaking and writing – as if they were acts of violence; sometimes men react to women's words with violence. So we lower our voices. Women whisper. Women apologize. Women shut up. Women trivialize what we know. Women shrink. Women pull back. Most women have experienced enough dominance from men – control, violence, insult, contempt – that no threat seems empty'.[5]

In the story of Medusa, a woman is angry and can turn men to stone. This cannot be borne, so Perseus cuts off her head. He decapitates a woman who has been raped and cast out of society. Or you could see it another way. You could say that he neutralizes a dangerous threat.[6]

From the perspective of gender, there are two ways of experience. One is flooded with light and runs along smooth lines. It feels well framed by language. Words like meritocracy and impartiality seem to touch something real. In this realm, the architecture of decision-making is constructed out of glass and steel. Shafts of objective reason shine through to the best candidate. Unbending principles of due process and the rule of law gird the halls. Here the best man wins. Here a man is innocent until proven guilty. To obstruct his path, to stop him from further ascent because of the whisperings of women would be prejudicial. He could lose his career. It would be a witch-hunt.

The very same place can feel like it is made of thorns. Due process, the rule of law, the proper channels – these bar your way; they can draw blood. The branches of the state – immigration, education, justice, healthcare – these tangle you up. You might know that you have been beaten, or are qualified for a particular job, or are ill – but the verdicts come back negative. Not guilty. Rejected. It is all in your head. Work – invisible, precarious, reproductive, emotional – does not feel like liberation. This does not feel like a land of equal opportunity. It does not feel like a safety net.

You might say quietly: if this is a witch-hunt, I am not the hunter. In the sixteenth century, it was said that you could find out whether someone was a witch by forcing them under water. If they floated back up, they were a witch. The king of Scotland, James VI, explained that this was because God made the pure water expel them. He (the king) went on to say that another way of ascertaining whether someone is a witch is seeing whether they can cry. Witches cannot cry. This is not a fail-safe method with women, however, because women can fake cry, 'dissemblingly like the Crocodiles'.[7] They can turn on the waterworks. It is impossible to know whether a woman is a witch, or just a woman.

Here, you are guilty until proven innocent. You cannot be trusted on the basis of your words, or your crocodile tears. Weep or don't weep; speak up or stay silent; you'll drown all the same.

To try and make people see what is right in front of their eyes: this is core to the history of feminism, as it has been to the history of all human rights struggles. It ran through the anti-slavery movement. 'Am I Not A Man And A Brother?' was the very basic question stamped on the halfpenny manufactured by Abolitionists in *c.* 1790. There is 'no truth more self-evident', wrote Frederick Douglass, than 'that every man is, and of right ought to be, the owner of his own body; and that no man can rightfully claim another man as his property'. But white people would not see it. Douglass identified the same problem with women's suffrage, for which he also campaigned. 'There are none so blind as those who will not see', he consoled in 1870, wondering at those who would not admit the truth of 'the right of woman . . . to have a voice in the Government under which she lives'.[8]

As Douglass knew in relation to American 'liberty', the most blinkered are the most proud of their panoramic vision. When the so-called enlightenment dawned over Europe at the end of the seventeenth century, the philosopher John Locke announced that men were not born subject to kings but, rather, were born equal and free. Mary Astell, also a philosopher, pointed out that Locke had a blind spot. 'If all men are born free', she asked, 'how is it that all women are born slaves?'[9] How could this be so blatant a fallacy to her, yet so perfect a syllogism to the person who was being lauded as the greatest thinker of the age? Under the system of coverture in English common law, a wife's identity and will were subsumed by her husband's. Her property became his, even the gifts he gave her. He was permitted to beat her, within reason, if she would not bend voluntarily to his command.[10] Astell had her own blind spot in brandishing the status of a slave on behalf of aristocratic white women when there were black women and men being bought and sold in London. As for Locke, he actively participated in the administration of the transatlantic slave trade, and had a hand in composing *The Fundamental Constitutions of Carolina* which declared in 1669 that 'every freeman of Carolina shall have absolute power and authority over his negro slaves'.[11]

More than a hundred years later, Mary Wollstonecraft gazed at the French Revolution, thrilled by its promise of liberty. Blithely assuming that she was one of the guys – like Thomas Paine, author of *The Rights of Man* – she wrote *A Vindication of the Rights of Men*, arguing that mankind should be free from tyranny. It turned out, however, when they were excluded from the Revolution, that women were not considered as part of mankind, and Wollstonecraft realized that she would have to write a follow-up: her masterpiece, *A Vindication of the Rights of Woman*, published in 1792.

When these ripples rolled into the eponymous waves of modern feminism, Emmeline Pankhurst was still trying to bring women into view. In her *Freedom or death* speech, delivered in Hartford, Connecticut in 1913, she took it that her task was simply to get people to see her for what she was – human. If, she thought, they could see – really see – this truth, then surely they would then see the legitimacy of suffragette violence? If she were a man, she said, a male taxpayer, standing in front of them, it would be obvious to them that he was entitled to take up arms. No taxation without representation: the maxim is clear. But in the upside-down of gender politics, truisms do not extend to the shadowlands of women. Pankhurst gave voice to the baffling difficulty of convincing men to use their eyes. 'We women,' she said, 'in trying to make our case clear, always have to make as part of our argument, and urge upon men in our audience the fact – a very simple fact – that women are human beings. It is quite evident you do not all realize we are human beings or it would not be necessary to argue with you that women may, suffering from intolerable injustice, be driven to adopt revolutionary methods'.[12]

The story of the four waves of feminism is deeply flawed.[13] It belies the differences between feminisms – and between women. It suggests progress on a succession of discrete fronts – from political equality at the beginning of the twentieth century, to personal liberation after the Second World War, to girl power in the 1990s, to . . . wherever we are now – without interrogating who 'we' are, nor ongoing oppression, nor the oppression that feminism itself has inflicted. Looking at feminism through the white, western tunnel of the four-waves narrative occludes the manifold global resistance to the injustices of gender that go back hundreds of years. In 42 BCE, a Roman woman, Hortensia, forced her way through the men in the forum to speak publicly against the taxation of women: 'Why should we pay taxes when we have no part in the honours, the commands, the state-craft, for which you contend against each other with such harmful results?'[14] In *c.* 1200, in

Japan, Shunzei kyō no musume wrote that 'there is nothing more deplorable than the fate of being a woman'.[15] In 1691, in what is now Mexico, Sor Juana Inés de la Cruz had had enough of men criticizing women, of the double bind that punishes a woman for saying yes *and* for saying no: 'if not willing, she offends, but willing, she infuriates'.[16]

The so-called first wave rose in the nineteenth century, but it did not rise first, as the tale is too often told, in Seneca Falls in 1848 with the Declaration of Sentiments – a response to the Declaration of Independence, which claimed the same rights for women that American men had so righteously claimed for themselves. The wave had already risen, for example, in Massachusetts in 1836 when the Lowell Factory Girls walked out in protest at pay cuts and degrading working conditions; they organized an Association to resist the 'aggressions' of 'ungenerous, illiberal and avaricious capitalists', and affirmed that 'union is power'. 'We feel it our imperative duty to stand by each other through weal and woe', they declared.[17]

Women also rose in the Feminist Congress in Argentina in 1910, in the Feminist Congress in Mexico in 1916 and in the Australia Women's Peace Army in the same year, in the Women's Suffrage League in Tokyo in 1924, in the All India Women's Conference in 1927, in the Pan-Arab Women's Congress in Damascus in 1930 – and in innumerable other spaces around the world. While some of these risings included the franchise in their demands, their concerns ranged more variously and specifically; they encompassed, for example, education, domestic violence, wages for housework and childcare, equal pay for equal work, dangerous employment, and the abolition of polygamy. The National Association of Colored Women's Clubs was founded in 1896 by African American women including Frances Harper, Ida B. Wells, Harriet Tubman, Margaret Murray Washington, and Mary Church Terrell. Its maxim was 'Lifting as we climb'. Among the resolutions of the Colored Women's Congress were reform of the 'evils . . . in the penal system', 'the equal enforcement of the law for all classes of American citizens', 'the same standard of morality for men as for women', better housing, professional training, and care for 'the orphans, the aged, and the infirm'.[18] The anarchist feminist Emma Goldman wrote in 1906 that she had little hope that the vote would bring 'true emancipation', and mocked the feminist shibboleth of a job as the route to 'Glorious Independence!' For 'the great mass of working girls and women', she objected, paid work only doubles their burden as they toil in a sweat-shop to make a pittance before returning to subordination in 'home, sweet home'.[19]

Even the vote, which only scratched the surface of women's needs, was not bestowed equally on all women. In the UK, only propertied women over thirty were given the vote in 1918; the rest had to wait until 1928. While 'women' were given the vote in Australia in 1902, indigenous women were excluded from the franchise until 1962. This fact is like a flashbulb on the iniquities and ahistoricism of the four-waves framework. The waves are endless and many of them crash women onto the rocks.

Some anglophone feminists in the 1960s saw themselves as part of a second wave, surging forward again after the momentum of the suffragettes had ebbed away. An insight that streamed through this time was that the personal is political. As Carol Hanisch, member of New York Radical Women and co-organizer of the 1968 Miss America protest, elucidated: 'Women are messed over, not messed up!'[20] What goes on behind closed doors, in bedrooms, kitchens and psyches, is shaped by relations of power. Problems that are labelled and experienced as 'personal' have shared and structural dimensions. Women organized consciousness-raising groups to make their realities known – to themselves as well as others. Suburban wives with perfect lives started to glimpse why it was that they felt like they were losing their minds. They began to articulate 'the problem that has no name', to voice 'the silent question "Is this all?"', as Betty Friedan put it in 1963 in *The Feminine Mystique*, the book that felt like 'a bolt of lightning' to many women and sold over 3 million copies.[21] 'All my childhood I remember my mother cleaning', writes Kate Zambreno, 'To be a housewife, in the old mold, was to live by the rule of erasure'. She points to Louise Bourgeois's *Femme Maison* paintings: 'the illustrated women with houses for heads'.[22] Zambreno writes about women 'vampirized' by 'genius' men.[23] Many women are still stranded in this netherworld. They often wash up there after having a baby.

Alongside domestic sacrifice, the second wave also surged around male violence, as in Susan Brownmiller's 1975 book *Against Our Will*, which argued that rape is 'a conscious process of intimidation by which *all men* keep *all women* in a state of fear'.[24]

While the second wave claimed to speak for all women, however, many were not included. bell hooks noted that Friedan's bestseller ignored 'the women who are most victimized by sexist oppression; women who are daily beaten down, mentally, physically, and spiritually – women who are powerless to change their condition in life'. When Friedan agitated for 'college-educated, middle- and upper-class, married white women' who wanted 'more', who did she think would look after their children and clean their homes while they were off pursuing their careers? Did she think about 'women without men, without children, without homes'? Did she think about 'non-white women and poor white women'? Did she think about the fulfilment of 'a maid, a babysitter, a factory worker, a clerk, or a prostitute'?[25] As with sexism, so with racism and classism, the line between thoughtlessness and cruelty is indistinct. Not thinking, not seeing, is not innocent. Bias is never too far below the surface of consciousness, and sometimes it is right on top. White, straight, feminism did – does – violence to millions of women at the borders of power, by exploiting them for personal advancement, by erasing and excluding them from the category of woman.

Sometimes the exclusion was explicit. Friedan called lesbian feminists 'the lavender menace'. Brownmiller did not pour oil on troubled waters when she wrote: 'a lavender herring, perhaps, but surely no clear and present danger'.[26] In response, Rita Mae Brown, Artemis March, Lois Hart, and Cynthia Funk, among others, wore T-shirts saying LAVENDER MENACE. They wrote the Radicalesbians Manifesto. It began: 'What is a lesbian? A lesbian is the rage of all women condensed to the point of explosion. She is the woman who, often beginning at an extremely early age, acts in accordance with her inner compulsion to be a more complete and freer human being than her society . . . cares to allow her'. 'In this sexist society', it went on, 'for a woman to be independent means she can't be a woman – she must be a dyke'.[27]

Not only were there strong rip currents in the second wave, but it surfaced – and surfaced differently – far beyond picket fences. As the Black Feminist Statement of the Combahee River Collective declared in 1977, 'Black, other Third World, and working women have been involved in the feminist movement from its start, but both outside reactionary forces and racism and elitism within the movement itself have served to obscure our participation'. The Collective turned their attention to 'sterilization abuse, abortion rights, battered women, rape and health care', and the psychological dispossession, as they phrased it, of Black women. They affirmed their 'origins in the historical reality of Afro-American women's continuous life-and-death struggle for survival and liberation'.[28]

Alice Walker elucidated racist-sexism in *The Color Purple*. Celie says she's given up on God. 'If he ever listened to poor colored women the world would be a different place', she says. But Shug says Celie's got the wrong idea of God – 'the one that's in the white folks' white bible'. Celie goes about 'trying to chase that old white man out of my head', but it is hard. 'You have to git man off your eyeball, before you can see anything a'tall'.[29]

In 1954, the Federation of South African Women issued their Women's Charter, testifying to the reality of the 'thousands of African women' who have to scrape a living for themselves and their children. They called for release from 'poverty, race and class discrimination, and the evils of the colourbar', and laws that stop wives owning property.[30] In 1971, the First National Conference of *Raza* Women demanded that Mexican American women – Chicanas – be heard, represented, and valued. They wanted an end to 'unbearable, inhumane' working conditions, abusive marriages, misogynistic religion, and the incarceration of women 'who are forced to prostitution'. They asked for education, equal pay, training, opportunities for promotion, safe and legal abortion, education, paid maternity leave, and childcare; 'Chicana motherhood', they said, 'should not preclude educational, political, social, and economic advancement'.[31]

In 1991, Anita Hill testified to the US Senate that Clarence Thomas, Supreme Court nominee, had harassed her. But the Senate, 98 per cent male, backed Thomas. Rebecca Walker saw this as a closing of the ranks against what was not even there – the *illusion* of equality between men and women, a backlash against the phantom of 'metaphoric castration'. It demonstrated that women were not permitted to speak out against male power, and were still 'under siege'. 'I will not be silenced', wrote Walker, daughter of Alice, 'I am not a postfeminism feminist. I am the Third Wave'.[32]

In some ways, then, the third wave explicitly renewed the energy of the second. There was also, however, within this next generation of feminists, a conscious challenge to their (fore)mothers. Rebecca Walker resisted 'a strictly defined and all-encompassing feminist identity'. She felt 'the guilt of betrayal' about the parts of herself that did not fit: her 'curiosity about pornography, attraction to a stable domestic partnership, a desire to start a business and pursue traditional individual power'. She wanted a feminism for a 'generation that has grown up transgender, bisexual, interracial', that centred 'difference', 'individuality and complexity', and deconstructed the polarities of female and male, oppressed and oppressor.[33]

While feminism has always been anti-essentialist, third wavers further queried the universalizing, binary tyranny of gender. ACT UP published Queer Nation Manifesto in 1990: 'Being queer is not about a right to privacy; it is about the freedom to be public, to just be who we are . . . Everyone of us is a world of infinite possibility. We are an army because we have to be. We are an army because we are so powerful'.[34] Emi Koyama's Transfeminist Manifesto of 2001 proposes two basic principles: everyone has the right to say who they are, and to make decisions about their own bodies.[35]

One manifestation of the third wave was Punk. 'The whole point of punk', wrote Virginie Despentes, 'is not doing what you're told to do'. Despentes is 'more King Kong than Kate Moss'. She wants it all, and she wants men to 'get fucked, with your condescension towards us, your ridiculous shows of group strength, of limited protection, and your manipulative whining about how hard it is to be a guy around emancipated women. What is really hard is actually to be a woman and have to listen to your shit'.[36] In the early 1990s, Riot Grrrls roared their rebel sisterhood in music and in zines. Olivia Laing remembers these 'lovingly handwritten or typed manifestos, full of collaged confessions, rants and recommendations, photocopied and disseminated at concerts or by post'. She describes 'the thrill of envelopes landing on the mat', being 'armed with Pritt Stick' in her teenage bedroom, and 'the intense pleasure of setting down my thoughts and sending them out; of being part of a community, a culture'.[37] 'DON'T EVER LET THEM SILENCE YOU girl', counselled the band Bikini Kill, 'you are sensational what you have to say is important it is relevant you are undeniable you are capable indescribable revolutionary YOU ARE FUCKING BEAUTIFUL'.[38]

There was a twist in optical ambitions. Rather than simply make sexism visible, some feminists confiscated it. They walked right into the male gaze and occupied it, turning themselves from objects into subjects. Kathleen Hanna wore the word SLUT on her body. Bitch and Animal released their Pussy Manifesto. 'I'm sick of my genitalia being an insult', Bitch sang, 'Let Pussy manifest! and let freedom sing!'[39] Inga Muscio wanted to create a Cuntlovin' universe.[40]

Internationally, women continued to agitate in their own ways for liberation from the particular hardships they faced. In Korea in 1982, Lee Tai-Young argued against the patriarchal family, in which the father had all the authority while the mother did all the work, and, in the event of divorce, the father had custody of the children.[41] Ellen Kuzwayo fought against apartheid in South Africa and wrote in her 1985 autobiography about the particular effects of colonialism on the experience of black women in her country – poverty, alcoholism, shattered community, and the 'ever-present' violence in Soweto, 'rape, theft, murder', that is rooted in state violence. In spite of all this, her commitment was 'to stand side by side with our men folk and our children in this long struggle to liberate ourselves and to bring about peace and justice for all in a country we love so deeply'.[42] In 1995, Winona LaDuke, a Native American from the Anishinaabe nation argued that indigenous nations should be recognized as such by the United Nations, and granted self-determination. Instead, their lives are determined by corporations who care neither for the land nor the people of the land. Indigenous women are 'prey', subject to 'discrimination, exploitation, sterilization'. LaDuke is clear, however, that hers is not the feminism of capitalists. 'This is not a struggle for women of the dominant society in so-called 'first world' countries to have equal pay and equal status if that pay and status continues to be based on a consumption model that is unsustainable. It is a struggle to recover our status as Daughters of the Earth'.[43]

We in the twenty-first century are splashing about in the fourth wave. Are we waving or drowning? Our moment is digital, viral, quasi-democratic and performatively at least – diverse. Frothing back and forth through global nodes, it insists that feminism must be indigenous, and attend to those most marginalized by overlapping structures of power. With a renewed structural understanding, feminism now is both keenly focused on differential oppression, as well as comfortable again with the juggernaut concept of patriarchy.

#metoo is a chastening demonstration of where we are. Founded in 2006 by Tarana Burke 'to help survivors of sexual violence, particularly Black women and girls, and other young women of color from low wealth communities, find pathways to healing', her movement subsequently swept the world.[44]

One might have thought that surely, at last, this would be the moment of truth. In a flash, on everyone's screens, people would see what feminists had been trying to show for centuries. Twitter lit up like an unpolluted night sky. Every woman had a horror to impart. And yet men, and women too, shrugged, or called bullshit. Harvey Weinstein was sent to prison for rape, but nothing much changed. Indeed, men doubled down. This *was* a moment of truth, but not the one feminists had longed for. The absence of action, of acknowledgement, after we had told our stories, felt like a slap in the face, a reminder of just how deeply some men feel entitled to women's bodies. It demonstrated yet again the basic, unfathomable refusal of people to see what is right in front of their eyes.

In part, sexism is hard to see because it is a structural phenomenon. It is, that is to say, a web of historic, economic, political, institutional and individual forces that operate on bodies and psyches, and that sustain an oppressive hierarchy based on gender. It exists in the connections between events as much as in the events themselves. It cannot always be read off the intentions of actors, but is legible in the patterns and outcomes of life. It is often inadvertent; indeed inadvertency is part of its mechanism. It is a bit like gravity; it cannot be seen, but its pull can be felt – in governments packed with men; in laws that permit domestic violence and ban abortion; in girls deprived of education and ostracised for menstruating; in female genital mutilation; in unpaid labour and low-paid exploitative and precarious work; in the flat-lining of careers – for those who are lucky enough to have one – after women have children; in gender-based murder; in the victimization of women in war; in forced sterilization; in the stripping of rights and safety from migrant women; in the fact that black women have a higher risk of dying from pregnancy-related complications than white women.

Sceptics of feminism can see individual incidents of harm as bad, but they will not admit a pattern. Indeed, trying to convince them of one is a sexist experience in itself. Nothing to see here. You are gaslit; you are a conspiracy theorist. It is only when the facts are admitted as linked that patriarchy comes into view. It is then that the little things – the things that we are told do not matter – can be understood as mattering. A wolf whistle matters, for example, because it *is* part of the grand scheme of things – because it reverberates amid the noise, as constant as traffic, of men judging, policing, and silencing women – because it recurs on a continuum that runs from the gender pay gap all the way through to femicide.

Seeing sexism as structural elucidates why there can be no such thing as reverse sexism, just like there can be no such thing as reverse racism. Racism and sexism and racist-sexism only make sense as descriptions of the systematic disadvantage and harm meted out to particular groups. An unwanted arm around your waist would not be a significant problem in itself, but it becomes one against the background power relations between men and women. Those who object to so-called positive discrimination, or political correctness, or identity politics, or 'the woman card', fail to see the discrimination, incorrectness, and privilege that routinely stacks the deck. Those who deny that sexism exists imagine that men and women exist on some mythical plain abstracted from time and culture, a level playing field where atomized individuals are free to make of their lives what they will, each giving as good as they get, like Beatrice and Benedict in their merry war in *Much Ado About Nothing*. This view ignores the ancient landscape that domination has sculpted, the earth it has cut away. To get a sense of the geography of this place, we might think of the answer Margaret Atwood got when she asked a man, 'Why do men feel threatened by women?' Because 'they're afraid women will laugh at them', he said. Then she asked women why they felt threatened by men. Because 'they're afraid of being killed', they said.[45]

Feminists have their own blind spots. Indeed, the fear of men, and the thirst for their incarceration, can itself be a blind spot. As abolition feminists point out, prisons do not solve the problem of male violence. The vast majority of reported rapes are never even prosecuted.[46] The system does not deliver justice. Nor does it deliver protection. 'Prisons and police', explains Mariame Kaba, make people feel 'that the scary, awful, monster people are kept at bay'.[47] But this is a fantasy, and a harmful one. It feeds and enforces precisely the kind of hierarchies and binaries that feminism has historically been committed to overthrowing and denaturalising. It feeds a 'them and us' mentality, and essentialises violence in particular kinds of bodies. When a white woman calls the police because she feels threatened by a black man who is minding his own business, what is it,

Introduction

exactly, that she is afraid of? In that moment, it is she who is possessed of lethal force.

The reality is that the state criminalizes the most vulnerable people in society. As Angela Davis says, 'Prisons are racism incarnate'.[48] You are disproportionately likely to be locked up if you are black, or trans, or poor, or queer, or homeless, or suffering from mental illness, for example.[49] The brokenness of the carceral impulse within feminism is perhaps most starkly revealed in the fact that most women in prison are themselves victims of domestic violence, and within prison endure further violence, in strip searches, for example, or – arguably to give them their more proper name – sexual assaults.[50] The guiding question for abolitionists is – as Ruth Wilson Gilmore puts it – 'What can we do about it so that there is less harm?'[51] The answer is not simply to dismantle the institutions that perpetuate violence but to invest in areas that would dissolve it – education, housing, mental and physical healthcare, and reparative justice. The answer is not to ignore or accept violence against women, but to pay true attention to their healing, and to build a place of actual safety.

I am white, middle class, cis, and more or less straight. That is a lot of privilege. There is a lot I do not see. It is my responsibility to look closer. It is my responsibility to listen, and to let that listening be transformative. I can still feel the change Angela Davis began in me when I first heard her talk, when she explained how the category of woman is internally racialized, how she was not a carceral feminist, nor a glass-ceiling feminist, how she used not to be a feminist at all but rather a revolutionary black woman – until black women redefined feminism.[52] Gender is not the only structure of domination. Race, class, sexuality, disability, noncitizenship, religion, age – these are also sites of oppression, often in overlapping ways. Slavery, empire, feudalism, capitalism, colonialism, nationalism, (neo)liberalism – these are historical and ongoing practices that favour some and crush others. Women have often lost the most in these global sagas, and they have been at the forefront of resistance – which is why the feminism of the most marginalized has often also been socialist, anti-racist, anti-imperial, and internationalist.

Women born on the precipitous side of the tracks, on the wrong side of the wire fence, face exceptional injustice. Claudia Jones, Black Nationalist, Communist Feminist, elucidated the compounding of disadvantage for particular groups of women in her 1949 theory of triple oppression;

'Negro women – as workers, as Negroes, and as women – are the most oppressed stratum of the whole population'.[53] The Combahee River Collective articulated the 'interlocking' systems of 'racial, sexual, heterosexual, and class oppression', and the need to dismantle 'capitalism and imperialism' if oppressed peoples are ever to be free.[54] Women – including 'feminist' women – have been, and continue to be, beneficiaries and perpetrators of systems of oppression, even if they – I – do not see it. As Reni Eddo-Lodge observes in *Why I'm No Longer Talking to White People About Race*, 'If feminism can understand the patriarchy, it's important to question why so many feminists struggle to understand whiteness as a political structure in the very same way'.[55]

Work on the self is critical feminist work. The personal is political, and this cuts many ways. 'Our emotional lives are very much informed by ideology', writes Davis, 'we ourselves often do the work of the state in and through our interior lives'.[56] Feminism is a struggle against oppression. It must therefore, to invoke Kimberlé Crenshaw's dynamizing analysis, be intersectional – to attend particularly to those who are *most* oppressed at the intersections of different axes of oppression.[57] By the same token, it must unearth and acknowledge its own role as oppressor. It must not shy away from Audre Lorde's question: 'What woman here is so enamoured of her own oppression that she cannot see her heelprint upon another woman's face?'[58] Feminists need to look inside themselves to see what tyrants reside there.

You can hear the slice of the double-edged sword of white feminism in the crystal clear diction of Elizabeth Cady Stanton when she declared in Seneca Falls that 'We hold these truths to be self-evident: that all men and women are created equal'.[59] Just as Stanton drew attention to what the Founding Fathers could not see – the wrongful exclusion of women from 'mankind' – so was she incapable of seeing the exclusions in her own idea of 'woman'. And when called out, she did not budge. On 26 December 1865, she wrote to the Editor of the *National Anti-Slavery Standard* to say that 'the black man is still, in a political point of view, far above the educated white women of the country', and now he had been emancipated, 'the representative women of the nation' ought to push for suffrage for women rather than for him – for fear that 'he, once entrenched in all his inalienable rights, may not be an added power to hold us at bay'?[60]

The negation of, the blindness towards, black women as women was pointed out by Sojourner Truth at the very beginning of the first wave. She was not invited to speak at a woman's rights convention in 1851 in Akron, Ohio, but she rose to her feet and asked 'ain't I a woman?'[61] This question has been a call to arms for those marginalized by feminism ever since. Anna Julia Cooper was born in 1858 in North Carolina. She was the daughter of an enslaved mother and a master father. Driven by the desire for education which runs like electricity through the history of feminism, Cooper trained to be a teacher. She had to give this up when she married in 1877, but after her husband's death a year later, she returned to educating both herself and other African Americans, doing a PhD at the Sorbonne in Paris, as well as adopting five children and writing groundbreaking philosophy. She wished that the 'mists' 'be cleared from the eyes' of the Woman's Movement. 'Is not woman's cause broader', she asked, 'and deeper, and grander, than a blue stocking debate or an aristocratic pink tea?' She described what it was like for a black woman to travel through the United States on her own, 'the feeling of slighted womanhood'. 'She thinks she is quiet and unobtrusive in her manner, simple and inconspicuous in her dress', but nonetheless the train conductor – whom she has seen help white women down from the high carriage onto a little stool, and from there onto the platform – folds his arms and turns his back when she comes to alight. Laying out a structural understanding of oppression, Cooper documents the subtle, lesser harms that work in concert with predation. She is interested in the hundred small ways each day that 'society hold[s] the leash'. At the station she sees two signs swinging over two rooms. One says, 'FOR LADIES', the other, 'FOR COLORED PEOPLE', and she wonders 'under which head I come'.[62] Where is her sign? She has fallen through the cracks. This invisibility, and the pressure of this invisibility, are evoked in the title of the classic 1982 text edited by Gloria T. Hull, Patricia Bell-Scott, and Barbara Smith: *All the Women are White, All the Blacks are Men, But Some of us are Brave*.[63]

The betrayals of feminism, and its entanglements with other political movements, have taken many forms around the globe. Huda Shaarawi was an Egyptian nationalist and feminist. She fought for independence from Britain, and then, when the men with whom she had fought and won denied her the vote, Shaarawi founded the Egyptian Feminist Union. In the uprising of 1919, in which peaceful protesters were shot or beaten by the British,

Shaarawi wrote to Lady Brunyate, the wife of a colonial official – a woman she had thought was her friend. She reminded her 'of the conversations we had last summer at my house in Ramleh. You assured me that Britain had taken part in the war to do service to the cause of justice and humanity, to protect the freedom of oppressed peoples and safeguard their rights. Would you kindly tell me if you remain convinced of this today?'[64] In 1947, Funmilayo Ransome-Kuti, Nigerian feminist nationalist, wrote 'We had Equality till Britain Came'. She detailed the degradation of life for Nigerian women and girls under colonialism, from fixed and exploitative wages, to being stripped in the street by tax collectors to determine if a girl is old enough to pay. She appealed 'to the women of Great Britain, in the name of the women of Nigeria and the Cameroons under British Mandate, to help free us from slavery, political, social and economic . . . Your country is responsible for the state of ours. Can you let this state of things continue?'[65]

The alignment of political struggles is often complex for women, torn between allegiances. bell hooks reflected in *Ain't I a Woman* on the way that black women were 'conditioned . . . to devalue our femaleness and to regard race as the only relevant label of identification. In other words, we were asked to deny a part of ourselves – and we did. Consequently, when the women's movement raised the issue of sexist oppression, we argued that sexism was insignificant in light of the harsher, more brutal reality of racism. We were afraid to acknowledge that sexism could be just as oppressive as racism'.[66]

In *Borderlands: La Frontera*, Gloria Anzaldúa discusses the particular kind of displacement that belongs to a queer Chicana. Alienated from her own Catholic home, she nonetheless carries home on her back like a turtle, defending it fiercely when 'non-*mexicanos*' denigrate it. 'Alienated from her mother culture, "alien" in the dominant culture, the woman of color does not feel safe within the inner life of her Self'. Anzaldúa will not compromise; she will make 'a new culture – *una cultura mestiza*'. 'Don't give me your tenets and your laws', she commands, 'Don't give me your lukewarm gods. What I want is an accounting with all three cultures – white, Mexican, Indian. I want the freedom to carve and chisel my own face, to staunch the bleeding with ashes, to fashion my own gods out of my entrails'.[67]

Feminism, if it is to be true to itself, does not ship in imperiously, foghorn blaring, dictating terms. Patricia Mohammed illuminates the importance of indigenous feminism. The white women's liberation movement is not a welcome import in the Caribbean. In a place scarred by slavery and colonization Mohammed finds a feminism that is gently, lovingly, coded in terms that are not easily communicable to the outsider. It is 'a nurturing one, a recognition of a shared condition, despite sexual difference and despite obvious inequalities'.[68] In *It's Not About the Burqa*, Mariam Khan brings together a diversity of Muslim women's voices. 'We've listened', she writes, 'to a lot of people talking about who Muslim women are without actually hearing Muslim women. So now, we are speaking. And now, it's your turn to listen'.[69]

Feminism's relation to class, and to capitalism, is deep and fraught. As with anti-racism, feminism has both united and vied with socialism. 'We are not convinced', A Black Feminist Statement avowed, 'that a socialist revolution that is not also a feminist and anti-racist revolution will guarantee our liberation'.[70] Women workers, so often in the vanguard of revolution, have many times felt taken for granted or even abused by the left. The 'worker' was coded male and the one enemy was capital. In 1969 Shulamith Firestone, Marilyn Webb, and others went to Washington to support the New Left's Counter-Inauguration when Richard Nixon was sworn in as President. When Webb began to speak, a man yelled back 'Take her off the stage and fuck her'. When Firestone tried to be heard, she too was shouted down. A few days later she published a letter. 'Fuck off, left', it said, 'You can examine your navel by yourself from now on. We're starting our own movement'.[71]

Marxism has always attracted feminists. Its insights into labour and alienation have made it a plenteous resource for women's liberation. In the *Manifesto of the Communist Party*, published in 1848, Karl Marx and Friedrich Engels called for the 'Aufhebung' – the transformation or, depending on how radical you are feeling as a translator, abolition – of the family. 'The bourgeois' husband, they elaborated, 'sees in his wife a mere instrument of production'.[72] Eleanor Marx, Karl's daughter, brought socialism into deeper dialogue with feminism in 'The Woman Question' in 1886. 'Women', she wrote, 'are the creatures of an organized tyranny of men, as the workers are the creatures of an organized tyranny of idlers'. Marriage is a transaction, the accumulation of human property that enslaves the wife in child-bearing, house-keeping, and 'obedience to her lord', closing 'the book of her life at its fairest page for ever', while the husband 'lives and loves according to his own bad pleasure'. Marx (Eleanor) despaired of England, France and Germany, and looked to 'the strange exception of Russia, where women are socially more free than in any other part of Europe'.[73] And indeed it was there, in and around the Revolution of 1917, that a revolution for women occurred.

One of its leaders was Alexandra Kollontai. Born in 1872 in St Petersburg, proponent of sexual liberation, co-organizer of the first International Women's Day on 8 March 1911, and an activist for the Socialist Movement of Women Workers, she then joined the Bolshevik government. She saw that women workers were doubly encumbered in the factory and in the home, victims of both capitalism and patriarchy. She sought 'to shift the burden of motherhood from the shoulders of women to those of the state'.[74] Communism initially gave a raft of rights to women – not just the vote, but university education, legal and free abortion, equal pay legislation, an equalizing of marriage, and an easing of divorce. The patriarchal equilibrium was soon rebalanced, however, as Stalin reinvested in the nuclear family and banned abortion – and in 2017 Putin decriminalized some forms of domestic violence.[75]

According to Marx, the capitalist exploits the worker by working them as long and as hard as possible, and paying them as little as he can get away with, creaming off the surplus labour value for his own profit. The worker becomes a wage-slave, 'degraded to the most miserable sort of commodity', alienated from their labour and themselves.[76] Women pointed out that they were not being paid at all for the work they did in the home; indeed, the consensus was that when they were at home they were not working. Their labour was invisible and unvalued. Beware the person who calls you 'invaluable', or who asks, 'do you work?' 'They say it is love', wrote Silvia Federici in 1975, 'We say it is unwaged work'.[77] Out of the International Feminist Collective in Italy, Federici helped organize the Wages for Housework Campaign around the world. In Britain, child benefit, conceived as wages for childcare, was introduced by the Labour government in 1977 and paid to mothers.

Selma James looked all the way down the rabbit hole. The capitalist is a thief. He wants as much unpaid labour as he can get, he gets it in exchange for wages, and this labour is produced by women – which he gets for free. 'First', James explains, labour power 'must be nine months in the womb, must be fed, clothed, and trained; then when it works its bed must be made, its floor swept, its lunchbox prepared, its sexuality not gratified but quietened, its dinner ready when it gets home, even if this is eight in the morning from the night shift. This is how labor power is produced and reproduced when it is daily consumed in the factory or the office. *To describe its basic production and reproduction is to describe women's work*.[78] The home, then, and the heteropatriarchal family, are sites of daylight – and night-time – robbery. It is the factory where the workers who make the workers have their labour priced at a big, pregnant, zero.

Just as some feminists drew on Marxism, so others made a bed with capitalism. As Dawn Foster explains, when Sheryl Sandberg advised women to 'Lean In' she turned sexism into a deficiency of women's will-power. If you lean in hard enough, the story goes, you can realize your ambitions. This lets businesses and governments, and men generally, off the hook for their role in blocking women. It suggests that women can choose their place in the world – that it is their fault if they are poor, or unpromoted, rather than the result of structural inequality. It disowns the vast majority of women who do not have the opportunity to lean in, and celebrates instead the 1 per cent clip-clopping over the glass ceiling, many of whom were privileged to start with and have leaned *on* other women to get there.[79] Liberalism – and liberal feminism – deifies individual freedom, as though everyone were equally furnished with options. As bell hooks says, however, 'being oppressed means the absence of choices'.[80]

Audre Lorde skewered the exploitative dynamic within feminism when she asked the question 'how do you deal with the fact that the women who clean your houses and tend your children while you attend conferences on feminist theory are, for the most part, poor women and women of Color? What is the theory behind racist feminism?'[81] Feminism forsakes itself when it loses sight of the divergent material realities of women's lives. As Johnnie Tillmon, the grassroots reformer of the US's vindictive welfare system said in 1972, 'for a lot of middle-class women in this country, Women's Liberation is a matter of concern. For women on welfare it's a matter of survival'.[82]

The lens of feminism must be wide, and constantly refocused to see those at the margins. There is a strain of feminism that says that trans-women are not women. This strikes me as a breach of sisterhood and a failure of feminist thinking. Feminism is the fight against the enforcement of one, rigid idea of what a woman is and ought to be; it is an insurrection against the discipline of gender, a liberation of selfhood – in all its ampleness and authenticity. It is the insistence that biology is not destiny, that, as The Xenofeminist Manifesto puts it, 'Nothing should be accepted as fixed, permanent, or "given" – neither material conditions nor social forms'. 'If nature is unjust, change nature!'[83]

Together with this mutiny against the regimes of gender, feminism is also rooted in an awareness of gender's enigmatic and inexhaustible power – the knowledge that, as Andrea Long Chu explains, 'you are not the central transit hub for meaning about yourself'.[84] 'I travel in a loop of gender', writes Katherine Angel.[85] In Bernadine Evaristo's *Girl, Woman, Other*, Megan who was becoming Morgan, 'who was attracted to a woman who'd once been a man, who was now saying gender was full of misguided expectations anyway', wonders at the sheer 'head fuckery' of it all.[86] Sex cannot be cleanly peeled away from gender, and even when you try and hold 'sex' up, alone, to the light, you find that it is a spectrum rather than a binary, that it cannot be encompassed within a simple or static definition, and that there is as much variety within sex classes as there is continuity between them. Bodies, in short, do not conform. In any case, it makes no sense – it is brutal – to force lived reality through conceptual dichotomies it does not fit. Trans people exist. To say otherwise is to deny a person their existence.

Black women taught feminism that it had to be intersectional, to see the effects of compound oppression. Transwomen face, at least, sexism and transphobia. Black women also taught feminism that alarm bells should ring out when feminists start to police the borders of womanhood. Angela Davis remembers fighting in the 1980s 'to expand the category "women" so that it could embrace Black women, Latina women, Native American women, and so forth'. She feels the same punitive energy now being directed against trans women, and invites us all, yet again, to self-reflect, to open ourselves to the productive potential of taxonomic rupture and surprise.[87] When your taxonomy causes harm, it is time to rethink your taxonomy. As Emi Koyama writes, 'there are as many ways of being a woman as there are women'.[88] If feminism has any DNA, it is anti-exclusionary. It rallies for all who suffer under the social impositions of gender. It should therefore rally for trans, nonbinary and intersex people.

Feminism is the insight that sexism exists, and the struggle against that oppression. The writers in this anthology tap into this insight and this struggle. They do so from all around the world, from the fifteenth century to the twenty-first, in myriad genres and with a cornucopia of ideas. Some charge towards patriarchy, such as the English author who went – fittingly – by the name of Jane Anger in 1589. 'Fie on the falsehood of men', she cries, 'whose minds go oft a-madding and whose tongues cannot so soon be wagging but straight they fall a-tattling! Was there ever any so abused, so slandered, so railed upon, or so wickedly handled undeservedly, as are we women?'[89] Other writers bring a cool gaze to the subordination of women. Raicho Hiratsuka, for example, a Bluestocking born in 1886 in Tokyo, wrote: 'We do not wish to become wives. Once our eyes have been opened, we cannot fall asleep again. We are alive. We are awake'.[90]

One danger with feminism is that it creates a narrative, and an identity, of victimhood. This is a conundrum because the basis of feminism is that women *are* victimized. If there were no sexism there would be no need for the movement. But the repetition of the point can itself be injurious to women. It can suggest that they have no agency, nor infinitely rich lives that transcend their gender. It can even encourage a doubling down of aggression, as Kate Manne has explained; 'misogyny is a self-masking phenomenon: trying to draw attention to the phenomenon is liable to give rise to more of it'. This is a catch-22 dilemma; as Manne ventures, 'there is no way around this'.[91] We cannot *not* name the problem.

But just as feminism is about calling out injustices, so is it a breaking free of them, a swimming away from abjection towards abundant selfhood and solidarity. It is about every girl everywhere who, in Denise Riley's words, 'is on fire with passion to achieve herself'.[92] It is the train that Simone de Beauvoir and Deborah Levy bought a ticket for. 'The destination', as Levy writes, 'was to head towards a freer life.'[93] It is the imagination of other possible worlds – the world, for example, dreamed up by Rokeya Sakhawat Hossain, a Muslim activist and educationalist, born in 1880 in Pairaband, in what is now Bangladesh. She created Ladyland, where men are shut indoors in purdah, while the women live in peace and plenitude, siphoning water from the clouds, and winning a war by harnessing the light of the sun, and without a drop of blood being shed.

This anthology begins with another utopia – this one by Christine de Pizan, a woman born in *c.* 1364 who earned a living as a writer in Paris when she was widowed with three children at the age of 25. Her pen became a shovel as she sat in her book-lined room and contemplated all the damning words that had been written about her sex. With the help of Lady Reason, Lady Rectitude and Lady Justice, she built The City of Ladies, constructed both with and for great women. Sisterhood runs like a mountain stream through this anthology. 'So clothe yourself in my dress', wrote Anna Akhmatova in 1912.[94]

There is also discord and desertion in these pages. The history of feminism is as much the history of conflict between feminists as it is the history of conflict against patriarchy – and if feminism is to move forward, if true solidarity is to emerge, it needs to reckon with its internal tensions. It needs, in Audre Lorde's words, to turn and face 'the cold winds of self-scrutiny'.[95] Navigating difference is challenging, especially perhaps for women, who tend *de facto* to be the world's experts on merging and connecting. In *Between Women*, Luise Eichenbaum and Susie Orbach discuss the 'enormous misunderstandings' that can exist between women. We need 'to unravel, uncover, and speak openly about these difficulties . . . the hurt, the envy, the competition, the unexpressed anger, the feelings of betrayal and the experience of abandonment'.[96]

We need to think about difference as inflected by power. Lorde reflects on how white women learnt to express anger against men but not how to respond to it from other women. 'My response to racism is anger', said Lorde in 1981, and the right response to that is change – not guilt or deflection or defensiveness.[97] But the change has not come, as Eddo-Lodge noted about white feminists in 2017. 'My speaking up about racism in feminism, to them, was akin to a violent attack on their very idea of themselves'.[98] There is a vast amount of psychological and practical work to be done. As Lorde says, 'no woman is responsible for altering the psyche of her oppressor, even when that psyche is embodied in another woman'. But Lorde also consoles: 'the strength of women lies in recognizing differences between us as creative'.[99] Mutual recognition is exhilarating, and inflexible self-righteousness will not get us there. Feminism is often associated with speaking up and speaking out, but it is as much about learning to hear. As Lola Olufemi writes, 'those who are and have always been the wrong kind of woman . . . they have cleared a space for us to understand the political possibilities that feminism offers us. We only have to listen for it to reveal itself'.[100]

When I agreed to do this anthology in the winter of 2016, it seemed manageable. I had taught the history of feminism, and thought I knew many of its contours. But I had inherited a story from the global north. The history of feminism is as big and complex as the history of patriarchy, which is to say that it is the history of the world. As the books thumped into my office, it became obvious that no one volume could do justice to this literature. What follows on these pages is the tiniest fraction of the flares that writers have sent up into the sky. They are pieces that changed me, and – not always the same thing – pieces that I love. What I hope is that you will find at least one piece here that you did not know before, and that you love. I hope that the glimpses I have gathered will open up for you the vistas of which they are a part. This is a beginning, not an end, and I am still travelling.

It is usual in anthologies to provide biographies of the authors, but in the end I decided not to do this. A woman writing struggles not to be reduced to her life. When she writes about something other than herself, she is asked 'is this about you'? And when she does write about herself, her work is read as small, domestic, narcissistic. Wollstonecraft wrote about freedom, just like Rousseau and Kant, but she is framed by her lovers and her broken heart. Even when men write explicitly about themselves, they are still allowed to be epic, to speak to the universal. Think of the reception of Karl Ove Knausgaard who wrote about changing his baby's nappy. And then think of Rachel Cusk who wrote about so much more. As Chris Kraus says, the world is divided into 'poet-men, presenters of ideas, and actress-women, presenters of themselves'.[101]

Of course, much feminist writing draws definitively on the personal, but this made me even less inclined to give potted biographies. I felt like I was writing obituaries, which as a genre seems to bend inexorably towards sexism. 'Wife, mother of two.' Insofar as the authors in this volume write about themselves, I want them to do so in their own words. I want to cut them free of the peculiar rope that ties a woman's words to her circumstances. I have noted the barest details of these writers' lives to locate them lightly in time and space, and then I have let them do the talking – to fix them in the canon of classics where they belong.

Hannah Dawson

Notes

1. Mary Wollstonecraft, *A Vindication of the Rights of Woman*, ed. Sylvana Tomaselli (Cambridge University Press, 1995), p. 282.
2. https://lithub.com/rebecca-solnit-unconscious-bias-is-running-for-president/
3. Sara Ahmed, 'Feminist Killjoys (And Other Willful Subjects)', *The Scholar and Feminist Online*, 8:3 (2010).
4. 'The trauma for a man: Male fury and fear rises in GOP in defense of Kavanaugh', *The Washington Post*, 2 October 2018; Trump: 'Scary and difficult time for young men' in US, BBC website, 3 October 2018.
5. Andrea Dworkin, *Intercourse* (Basic Books, 2007), p. xxxi.
6. Deborah Levy writes about the decapitation of female power in *The Cost of Living* (Hamish Hamilton, 2018), p. 110.
7. James VI and I, *Daemonologie* (Edinburgh, 1597), III, 6.
8. Frederick Douglass, 'Woman Suffrage Movement' in *The Portable Frederick Douglass*, ed. John Stauffer and Henry Louis Gates (Penguin Classics, 2016), pp. 491–4, 491, 492.
9. Mary Astell, *Reflections upon Marriage* in *Political Writings*, ed. Patricia Springborg (Cambridge University Press, 1996), pp. 7–80, 18.
10. Laura Gowing, *Gender Relations in Early Modern England* (Taylor & Francis, 2012), pp. 15, 37.
11. John Locke, 'The Fundamental Constitutions of Carolina' in *Political Essays*, ed. Mark Goldie (Cambridge University Press, 1997), pp. 161–181, 180.
12. Emmeline Pankhurst, *Freedom or death* (The Perfect Library, print on demand), p. 6.

13. For a wonderfully lucid philosophical account of the waves, see Susan James, 'Feminisms' in *The Cambridge History of Twentieth-Century Political Thought*, eds. Terence Ball and Richard Bellamy (Cambridge University Press, 2003), pp. 493–516. There is an ocean of historiography on feminism; I think the best place to dive in is the primary sources. In writing this Introduction and in compiling the anthology as a whole I am deeply indebted to the anthologies, and their editors, that have come before, especially *Feminist Writings from Ancient Times to the Modern World: A Global Sourcebook and History*, ed. Tiffany K. Wayne, 2 vols. (Greenwood, 2011); *A Feminist Reader: Feminist Thought from Sappho to Satrapi*, eds. Sharon M. Harris and Linda K. Hughes, 4 vols. (Cambridge University Press, 2013); *Feminist Manifestos: A Global Documentary Reader*, ed. Penny A. Weiss (New York University Press, 2018); *Burn It Down! Feminist Manifestos for the Revolution*, ed. Breanne Fahs (Verso, 2020).

14. Hortensia, 'Speech on Taxation without Representation' in *Feminist Writings*, vol. I, ed. Wayne, pp. 14–17, 15.

15. Shunzei kyō no musume, 'The Fate of being a woman' in *Feminist Writings*, vol. I, ed. Wayne, pp. 55–58, 56.

16. Sor Juana Inés de la Cruz, 'A Philosophical Satire' in *A Feminist Reader*, vol. I, ed. Harris and Hughes, pp. 99–102, 101.

17. Lowell Factory Girls Association, 'Constitution' in *Feminist Manifestos*, ed. Weiss, pp. 53–55.

18. The National Colored Woman's Congress and the National Association of Colored Women's Clubs, 'Resolutions and Objectives' in *Feminist Manifestos*, ed. Weiss, pp. 110–116.

19. Emma Goldman, 'The Tragedy of Woman's Emancipation' in *Anarchy and the Sex Question*, ed. Shawn P. Wilbur (PM Press, 2016), pp. 27–34, 29.

20. Carol Hanisch, 'The Personal Is Political', *News from the Second Year: Women's Liberation*, ed. Shulamith Firestone and Anne Koedt (1970).

21. Betty Friedan, *The Feminine Mystique* (Penguin Classics, 2010), pp. 5, 9. Louis Menand, 'Books as Bombs', *The New Yorker*, 17 January 2001.

22. Kate Zambreno, *Book of Mutter* (The MIT Press, 2017), p. 21.

23. Kate Zambreno, *Heroines* (Semiotext(e), 2012), p. 81.

24. Susan Brownmiller, *Against Our Will: Men, Women and Rape* (Fawcett Columbine, 1975), p. 15.

25. bell hooks, *Feminist Theory: From Margin to Center* (Pluto Press, second edition, 2000), pp. 1–2.

26. Susan Brownmiller, 'Sisterhood Is Powerful', *The New York Times*, 15 March 1970.

27. Radicalesbians, 'The Woman-Identified Woman' in *Feminist Manifestos*, ed. Weiss, pp. 221–6, 222, 223.

28. Combahee River Collective, 'A Black Feminist Statement' in *Feminist Manifestos*, ed. Weiss, pp. 269–277, 271, 274, 276.

29. Alice Walker, *The Color Purple* (Orion, 2014), pp. 173–177.

30. Federation of South African Women, 'Women's Charter' in *Feminist Writings*, II, ed. Wayne, pp. 568–72, 569.

31. First National Conference of *Raza* Women, 'Women of *La Raza* Unite!' in *Feminist Manifestos*, ed. Weiss, pp. 244–249, 248.

32. Rebecca Walker, 'Becoming the Third Wave', *Ms. Magazine*, 1992.

33. Rebecca Walker (ed.), *to be real: telling the truth and changing the face of feminism* (Anchor Books, 1995), pp. xxi, xxx, xxxiii.

34. Act Up, 'Queer Nation Manifesto: Queers Read This' in *Burn it Down!*, ed. Fahs, pp. 28–40, 28–9.

35. Emi Koyama, *The Transfeminist Manifesto* in *Burn it Down!*, ed. Fahs, pp. 86–97.

36. Virginie Despentes, *King Kong Theory* (Serpent's Tail, 2009), pp. 3, 104, 125, 126.

37. Olivia Laing, 'Riot grrl: when teen sisters were doing it for themselves', *Guardian*, 30 June 2013.

38. Bikini Kill, 'Riot Grrrl Manifesto' in *Feminist Manifestos*, ed. Weiss, pp. 329–32, 330.

39. Bitch and Animal, 'Pussy Manifesto' in *Burn it Down!*, ed. Fahs, pp. 445–7.

40. Inga Muscio, *Cunt: A Declaration of Independence* (Seal Press, 1998).

41. Lee Tai-Young, 'The Legal Status of Korean Women' in *Feminist Writings*, ed. Wayne, II, pp. 632–5.

42. Ellen Kuzwayo, 'Call Me Woman' in *Feminist Writings*, II, ed. Wayne, pp. 638–42, 639, 640.

43. Winona LaDuke, 'Mothers of Our Nations' in *Feminist Writings*, II, ed. Wayne, pp. 658–61, 659.

44. https://metoomvmt.org/

45. Margaret Atwood, 'Writing the Male Character' in *Second Words: Selected Critical Prose* (Beacon Press, 1984).

46. In England and Wales over 98% of reported rapes are never prosecuted, *Independent*, 17 September 2019

47. https://transformharm.org/towards-the-horizon-of-abolition-a-conversation-with-mariame-kaba/

48. Angela Davis, *Freedom is a Constant Struggle: Ferguson, Palestine, and the Foundations of a Movement* (Haymarket Books, 2016), p. 107.

49. For example, across the global north, prisons are filled disproportionately with people of colour: half the prisoners in New Zealand are Maori, whereas Maoris make up only 15 per cent of the population as a whole; African Americans in the US are five times more likely to be incarcerated than white people; over 40 per cent of young people in custody in the UK are from Black, Asian and Ethnic Minority backgrounds, The Lammy Review: An independent review into the treatment of, and outcomes for, Black, Asian and Minority Ethnic individuals in the Criminal Justice System (commissioned by the UK government, 2017), pp. 3–4; Ashley Nellis, *The Color of Justice: Racial and Ethnic Disparity in State Prisons* (sentencingproject.org, 2016).

50. http://www.prisonreformtrust.org.uk/PressPolicy/News/vw/1/ItemID/494; Angela Davis, *Are Prisons Obsolete?* (Seven Stories Press, 2003), pp. 60–83.

51. https://theintercept.com/2020/06/10/ruth-wilson-gilmore-makes-the-case-for-abolition/

52. That was in 2017 at the Women of the World Festival. Here she is in 2020, changing more minds as the Black Lives Matter movement energized the world after the murders of Breonna Taylor and George Floyd: https://www.youtube.com/watch?v=8ebWFn GWOaA

53. Claudia Jones, 'An End to the Neglect of the Problems of Negro women' in *Claudia Jones: Beyond Containment* (Ayebia Clarke Publishing, 2011), pp. 74–86, 75.

54. Combahee River Collective, 'Black Feminist Statement', pp. 270, 273.

55. Reni Eddo-Lodge, *Why I'm No Longer Talking to White People About Race* (Bloomsbury Circus, 2017), p. 168.

56. Angela Davis, *Freedom is a Constant Struggle*, p. 142.

57. Kimberlé Crenshaw, 'Demarginalizing the Intersection of Race and Sex: A Black Feminist Critique of Antidiscrimination Doctrine, Feminist Theory and Antiracist Politics', *University of Chicago Legal Forum*, 1 (1989), pp. 139–67.

58. Audre Lorde, 'The Uses of Anger: Women Responding to Racism' in *Sister Outsider: Essays and Speeches by Audre Lorde* (Crossing Press, 1984), pp. 124–133.

59. Woman's Rights Convention, Seneca Falls, 'Declaration of Sentiments' in *Feminist Manifestos*, ed. Weiss, pp. 75–81.

60. Elizabeth Cady Stanton, *The Selected Papers of Elizabeth Cady Stanton and Susan B. Anthony*, vol. I, ed. Ann D. Gordon (Rutgers University Press, 1997), p. 206.

61. Sojourner Truth, Speech at Women's Rights Convention, Akron, Ohio in *Feminist Manifestos*, ed. Weiss, p. 95.

62. Anna Julia Cooper, 'Woman Versus the Indian' in *A Feminist Reader*, II, ed. Harris and Hughes, pp. 420–444, 442–3, 425–6, 429.

63. *All the Women are White, All the Blacks are Men, But Some of us are Brave*, ed. Gloria T. Hull, Patricia Bell-Scott and Barbara Smith (The Feminist Press, 1982).

64. Huda Shaarawi, translated and edited by Margot Badran, *Harem Years: The Memoirs of an Egyptian Feminist (1879–1924)* (Virago, 1986), p. 117.

65. Funmilayo Ransome-Kuti, 'We Had Equality till Britain Came' in *Feminist Writings*, II, ed. Wayne, pp. 544–7, 546.

66. bell hooks, *Ain't I a Woman: Black Women and Feminism* (Pluto Press, 1981), p. 1.

67. Gloria Anzaldúa, *Borderlands: La Frontera: The New Mestiza* (aunt lute books, 1987), p. 44.

68. Patricia Mohammed, 'Towards Indigenous Feminist Theorizing in the Caribbean', *Feminist Review*, 59 (1998), p. 28.

69. Mariam Khan, *It's Not About the Burqa: Muslim Women on Faith, Feminism, Sexuality and Race* (Picador, 2019), p. 2.

70. Combahee River Collective, 'A Black Feminist Statement' in *Feminist Manifestos*, ed. Weiss, p. 273.

71. Susan Faludi, 'Death of a Revolutionary', *The New Yorker*, 8 April 2013.

72. Karl Marx and Friedrich Engels, *Manifesto of the Communist Party*, ed. Terrell Carver (Cambridge University Press, 1996), pp. 16, 17.

73. Eleanor Marx, 'The Woman Question', marxists.org/archive.

74. Alexandra Kollontai, 'The Labour of Women in the Evolution of the Economy', marxists.org/archive

75. On the patriarchal equilibrium, see Judith M. Bennett, *History Matters: Patriarchy and the Challenge of Feminism* (University of Pennsylvania Press, 2006).

76. Karl Marx, *Economic and Philosophical Manuscripts* in *Karl Marx: selected writings*, ed. David McLellan (Oxford University Press, 2000), pp. 83–120, p. 85.

77. Silvia Federici, 'Wages Against Housework' in *Revolution at Point Zero: Housework, Reproduction, and Feminist Struggle* (PM Press, 2012), pp. 15–22.

78. Selma James, 'The Power of Women and the Subversion of the Community' in *Sex, Race, and Class* (PM Press, 2012), pp. 43–59, 51.

79. Dawn Foster, *Lean Out* (Repeater Books, 2015).

80. bell hooks, *Feminist Theory: From Margin to Center* (Pluto Press, 2000), p. 5.

81. Audre Lorde, 'The Master's Tools Will Never Dismantle the Master's House' in *Sister Outsider*, pp. 110–13, 112.

82. Johnnie Tillmon, 'Welfare Is a Women's Issue' in *Feminist Writings*, II, ed. Wayne, pp. 598–601, 599.

83. Laboria Cuboniks, *The Xenofeminist Manifesto: A Politics for Alienation* (Verso, 2018), p. 15, 93.

84. Andrea Long Chu, *Females* (Verso, 2019), p. 38.

85. Katherine Angel, *Unmastered: A Book On Desire, Most Difficult To Tell* (Allen Lane, 2012), p. 110.

86. Bernadine Evaristo, *Girl, Woman, Other* (Hamish Hamilton, 2019), p. 321.

87. Angela Y. Davis, *Freedom is a Constant Struggle: Ferguson, Palestine, and the Foundations of a Movement* (Haymarket Books, 2016), p. 96, 98, 103.

88. Emi Koyama, *The Transfeminist Manifesto* in *Burn It Down!*, ed. Fahs, p. 87.

89. Jane Anger, *her Protection for Women* in *The Women's Sharp Revenge: Five Women's Pamphlets from the Renaissance*, ed. Simon Shepherd (St. Martin's Press, 1985), pp. 29–51, 32.

90. Raicho Hiratsuka, 'To the Women of the World' in *Feminist Writings*, II, ed. Wayne, pp. 447–450, p. 448.

91. Kate Manne, *Down Girl: The Logic of Misogyny* (Penguin, 2019), p. xix.

92. Denise Riley, 'In 1970' in *Selected Poems* (Reality Street Editions, 2000), p. 19.

93. Deborah Levy, *The Cost of Living*, p. 95.

94. Anna Akhmatova, 'Sister, I have come to take your place' in *An Anthology of Russian Women's Writing, 1777–1992* (Oxford University Press, 1994), pp. 224–5.

95. Audre Lorde, 'Uses of Anger' in *Sister Outsider*, p. 132.

96. Luise Eichenbaum and Susie Orbach, *Between Women: Love, Envy, and Competition in Women's Friendships* (Penguin, 1989), pp. xv–xvi.

97. Audre Lorde, 'Uses of Anger' in *Sister Outsider*, p. 124.

98. Reni Eddo-Lodge, *Why I'm No Longer Talking to White People About Race*, p. 165.

99. Audre Lorde, 'Uses of Anger' in *Sister Outsider*, p. 131, 133.

100. Lola Olufemi, *Feminism, Interrupted* (Pluto Press, 2020), p. 145.

101. Chris Kraus, *I Love Dick* (Tuskar Rock Press, 2015), pp. 161–2.

Note on the Text

This collection brings together voices from all around the world and deep into the past. Each text is of its place and time.

I will not trot out the warning that some readers may find aspects of this book offensive. Feminism is a struggle against oppression. Its objects *are* offensive. They are offences against women, against the social punishments of gender, and they are disturbing. This book bears witness to the violence and abuse, the racism and racist language, the exploitation and discrimination that is the history of patriarchy.

Interwoven with what feminists are fighting against is what they are fighting for, and beyond that, the worlds that they are making. All of life is in these texts, including sex and swearing, alongside – and sometimes within – philosophy, poetry, politics, confrontation, solidarity, joy and care.

Principles of transcription

While errors have been silently corrected, and the texts lightly standardized and sometimes modernized, the basic intention of this edition has been to remain faithful to the original sources.

CHRISTINE DE PIZAN

Born 1364, Republic of Venice
Died *c.* 1430, France

from *The Book of the City of Ladies*

1405

One day, I was sitting in my study surrounded by many books of different kinds, for it has long been my habit to engage in the pursuit of knowledge. My mind had grown weary as I had spent the day struggling with the weighty tomes of various authors whom I had been studying for some time. I looked up from my book and decided that, for once, I would put aside these difficult texts and find instead something amusing and easy to read from the works of the poets. As I searched around for some little book, I happened to chance upon a work which did not belong to me but was amongst a pile of others that had been placed in my safekeeping. I opened it up and saw from the title that it was by Matheolus. With a smile, I made my choice. Although I had never read it, I knew that, unlike many other works, this one was said to be written in praise of women. Yet I had scarcely begun to read it when my dear mother called me down to supper, for it was time to eat. I put the book to one side, resolving to go back to it the following day.

The next morning, seated once more in my study as is my usual custom, I remembered my previous desire to have a look at this book by Matheolus. I picked it up again and read on a little. But, seeing the kind of immoral language and ideas it contained, the content seemed to me likely to appeal only to those who enjoy reading works of slander and to be of no use whatsoever to anyone who wished to pursue virtue or to improve their moral standards. I therefore leafed through it, read the ending, and decided to switch to some more worthy and profitable work. Yet, having looked at this book, which I considered to be of no authority, an extraordinary thought became planted in my mind which made me wonder why on earth it was that so many men, both clerks and others, have said and continue to say and write such awful, damning things about women and their ways. I was at a loss as to how to explain it. It is not just a handful of writers who do this, nor only this Matheolus whose book is neither regarded as authoritative nor intended to be taken seriously. It is all manner of philosophers, poets and orators too numerous to mention, who all seem to speak with one voice and are unanimous in their view that female nature is wholly given up to vice.

As I mulled these ideas over in my mind again and again, I began to examine myself and my own behaviour as an example of womankind. In order to judge in all fairness and without prejudice whether what so many famous men have said about us is true, I also thought about other women I know, the many princesses and countless ladies of all different social ranks who have shared their private and personal thoughts with me. No matter which way I looked at it and no matter how much I turned the question over in my mind, I could find no evidence from my own experience to bear out such a negative view of female nature and habits. Even so, given that I could scarcely find a moral work by any author which didn't devote some chapter or paragraph to attacking the female sex, I had to accept their unfavourable opinion of women since it was unlikely that so many learned men, who seemed to be endowed with such great intelligence and insight into all things, could possibly have lied on so many different occasions. It was on the basis of this one simple argument that I was forced to conclude that, although my understanding was too crude and ill-informed to recognize the great flaws in myself and other women, these men had to be in the right. Thus I preferred to give more weight to what others said than to trust my own judgement and experience.

I dwelt on these thoughts at such length that it was as if I had sunk into a deep trance. My mind became flooded with an endless stream of names as I recalled all the authors who had written on this subject. I came to the conclusion that God had surely created a vile thing when He created woman. Indeed, I was astounded that such a fine craftsman could have wished to make such an appalling object which, as these writers would have it, is like a vessel in which all the sin and evil of the world has been collected and preserved. This thought inspired such a great sense of disgust and sadness in me that I began to despise myself and the whole of my sex as an aberration in nature.

With a deep sigh, I called out to God: 'Oh Lord, how can this be? Unless I commit an error of faith, I cannot doubt that you, in your infinite wisdom and perfect goodness, could make anything that wasn't good. Didn't you yourself create woman especially and then endow her with all the qualities that you wished her to have? How could you possibly have made a mistake in anything? Yet here stand women not simply accused, but already judged, sentenced and condemned! I just cannot understand this contradiction. If it is true, dear Lord God, that women are guilty of such horrors as so many men seem to say, and as you yourself have said that the testimony of two or more witnesses is conclusive, how can I doubt their word? Oh God, why wasn't I born a male so that my every desire would be to serve you, to do right in all things, and to be as perfect a creature as man claims to be? Since you chose not to show such grace to me, please pardon and forgive me, dear Lord, if I fail to serve you as well as I should, for the servant who receives fewer rewards from his lord is less obligated to him in his service.'

Sick at heart, in my lament to God I uttered these and many other foolish words since I thought myself very unfortunate that He had given me a female form.

Sunk in these unhappy thoughts, my head bowed as if in shame and my eyes full of tears, I sat slumped against the arm of my chair with my cheek resting on my hand. All of a sudden, I saw a beam of light, like the rays of the sun, shine down into my lap. Since it was too dark at that time of day for the sun to come into my study, I woke with a start as if from a deep sleep. I looked up to see where the light had come from and all at once saw before me three ladies, crowned and of majestic appearance, whose faces shone with a brightness that lit up me and everything else in the place. As you can imagine, I was full of amazement that they had managed to enter a room whose doors and windows were all closed. Terrified at the thought that it might be some kind of apparition come to tempt me, I quickly made the sign of the cross on my forehead.

With a smile on her face, the lady who stood at the front of the three addressed me first: 'My dear daughter, don't be afraid, for we have not come to do you any harm, but rather, out of pity on your distress, we are here to comfort you. Our aim is to help you get rid of those misconceptions which have clouded your mind and made you reject what you know and believe in fact to be the truth just because so many other people have come out with the opposite opinion. You're acting like that fool in the joke who falls asleep in the mill and whose friends play a trick on him by dressing him up in women's clothing. When he wakes up, they manage to convince him that he is a woman despite all evidence to the contrary! My dear girl, what has happened to your sense? Have you forgotten that it is in the furnace that gold is refined, increasing in value the more it is beaten and fashioned into different shapes? Don't you know that it's the very finest things which are the subject of the most intense discussion? Now, if you turn your mind to the very highest realm of all, the realm of abstract ideas, think for a moment whether or not those philosophers whose views against women you've been citing have ever been proven wrong. In fact, they are all constantly correcting each other's opinions, as you yourself should know from reading Aristotle's *Metaphysics* where he discusses and refutes both their views and those of Plato and other philosophers. Don't forget the Doctors of the Church either, and Saint Augustine in particular, who all took issue with Aristotle himself on certain matters, even though he is considered to be the greatest of all authorities on both moral and natural philosophy. You seem to have accepted the philosophers' views as articles of faith and thus as irrefutable on every point.

'As for the poets you mention, you must realize that they sometimes wrote in the manner of fables which you have to take as saying the opposite of what they appear to say. You should therefore read such texts according to the grammatical rule of *antiphrasis*, which consists of interpreting something that is negative in a positive light, or vice versa. My advice to you is to read those passages where they criticize women in this way and to turn them to your advantage, no matter what the author's original intention was. It could be that Matheolus is also meant to be read like this because there are some passages in his book which, if taken literally, are just out-and-out heresy. As for what these authors – not just Matheolus but also the more authoritative writer of the *Romance of the Rose* – say about the God-given, holy state of matrimony, experience should tell you that they are completely wrong when they say that marriage is insufferable thanks to women. What husband ever gave his wife the power over him to utter the kind of insults and obscenities which

4

these authors claim that women do? Believe me, despite what you've read in books, you've never actually *seen* such a thing because it's all a pack of outrageous lies. My dear friend, I have to say that it is your naivety which has led you to take what they come out with as the truth. Return to your senses and stop worrying your head about such foolishness. Let me tell you that those who speak ill of women do more harm to themselves than they do to the women they actually slander.'

On receiving these words from the distinguished lady, I didn't know which of my senses was the more struck by what she said: whether it was my ears as I took in her stirring words, or my eyes as I admired her great beauty and dress, her noble bearing and face. It was the same for the other ladies too: my gaze darted back and forth from one to the other since they were all so alike that you could hardly tell them apart. All except for the third lady, who was no less imposing than the other two. This lady had such a stern face that whoever glanced into her eyes, no matter how brazen they were, would feel afraid of committing some misdeed since she seemed to threaten punishment to all wrongdoers. Out of respect for the ladies' noble appearance, I stood up before them but was far too dumbfounded to utter a single word. I was extremely curious to know who they were and would have dearly loved to dare ask them their names, where they were from, why they had come, and what the priceless symbols were that each of them held like a sceptre in her right hand. Yet I didn't think myself worthy to put these questions to such honourable ladies as these, so I held my tongue and carried on gazing at them. Though still frightened, I was also in part reassured, for the lady's words had already begun to assuage my fears.

Presently, the wise lady who had addressed me first seemed to read my mind and began to answer my unspoken questions with these words: 'My dear daughter, you should know that it is by the grace of God, who foresees and ordains all things, that we, celestial creatures though we may be, have been sent down to earth in order to restore order and justice to those institutions which we ourselves have set up at God's command. All three of us are His daughters, for it was He who created us. My task is to bring back men and women when they drift away from the straight and narrow. Should they go astray but yet have the sense to know me when they see me, I come to them in spirit and speak to their conscience, instructing

5

them in the error of their ways and showing them how exactly it is that they have done wrong. Then I teach them to follow the correct road and to avoid doing what is undesirable. Because it is my role to light their way to the true path and to teach both men and women to acknowledge their flaws and weaknesses, you see me here holding up a shining mirror like a sceptre in my right hand. You can be sure that whoever looks into this mirror, no matter who they may be, will see themselves as they truly are, such is its great power. Not for nothing is it encrusted with precious stones, as you can see. With the help of this mirror, I can determine the nature, quantity and essence of all things and can take full measure of them. Without this mirror, nothing can come to good. Since you obviously want to know what function my two sisters perform, each of them will shortly speak to you in turn and will add her weight to my words by giving you a clear explanation of both her name and her powers.

'First, however, I will tell you exactly why we are here. I want you to know that, as we do nothing without good reason, our appearance here today has a definite purpose. Though we do not attempt to be known in all places, since not everyone strives to acquaint themselves with us, we have none the less come to visit you, our dear friend. Because you have long desired to acquire true knowledge by dedicating yourself to your studies, which have cut you off from the rest of the world, we are now here to comfort you in your sad and dejected state. It is your own efforts that have won you this reward. You will soon see clearly why it is that your heart and mind have been so troubled.

'Yet we also have a further, more important reason for coming to visit you, which we'll now go on to tell you about. Our wish is to prevent others from falling into the same error as you and to ensure that, in future, all worthy ladies and valiant women are protected from those who have attacked them. The female sex has been left defenceless for a long time now, like an orchard without a wall, and bereft of a champion to take up arms in order to protect it. Indeed, this is because those trusty knights who should by right defend women have been negligent in their duty and lacking in vigilance, leaving womankind open to attack from all sides. It's no wonder that women have been the losers in this war against them since the envious slanderers and vicious traitors who criticize them have been allowed to aim all manner of weapons at their defenceless targets. Even the strongest city will fall if there is no one to defend it, and even the most undeserving case will win if there is no one to testify against it. Out of the goodness and simplicity of their hearts, women have trusted in God and have patiently endured the countless verbal and written assaults that have been unjustly and shamelessly launched upon them. Now, however, it is time for them to be delivered out of the hands of Pharaoh. For this reason, we three ladies whom you see before you have been moved by pity to tell you that you are to construct a building in the shape of a walled city, sturdy and impregnable. This has been decreed by God, who has chosen you to do this with our help and guidance. Only ladies who are of good reputation and worthy of praise will be admitted into this city. To those lacking in virtue, its gates will remain forever closed.'

2

JANE ANGER

We do not know the author of this pamphlet,
but they went by the name of Jane Anger
Sixteenth century, England

from *Her Protection for Women*

1589

To all Women in general, and gentle Reader whatsoever

Fie on the falsehood of men, whose minds go oft a madding and whose tongues cannot so soon be wagging, but straight they fall a tattling! Was there ever any so abused, so slandered, so railed upon, or so wickedly handled undeservedly, as are we women? Will the gods permit it, the goddesses stay their punishing judgments, and we ourselves not pursue their undoings for such devilish practises? O Paul's steeple and Charing Cross! A halter hold all such persons. Let the streams of the channels in London streets run so swiftly, as they may be able alone to carry them from that sanctuary. Let the stones be as ice, the soles of their shoes as glass, the ways steep like Etna, and every blast a whirlwind puffed out of Boreas his long throat, that these may hasten their passage to the Devil's haven. Shall surfeiters rail on our kindness, you stand still and say naught, and shall not Anger stretch the veins of her brains, the strings of her fingers, and the lists of her modesty, to answer their surfeitings? Yes truly. And herein I conjure all you to aid and assist me in defence of my willingness, which shall make me rest at your commands. Fare you well.

Your friend,
Ja. A.

[...]

If we will not suffer them to smell on our smocks, they will snatch at our petticoats: but if our honest natures cannot away with that uncivil kind of jesting, then we are coy. Yet if we bear with their rudeness, and be somewhat modestly familiar with them, they will straight make matter of nothing, blazing abroad that they have surfeited with love; and then their wits must be shown in telling the manner how.

[. . .]

If we stand fast, they strive: if we totter, (though but a little), they will never leave till they have overturned us.

[. . .]

Our good toward them is the destruction of ourselves, we being well formed, are by them foully deformed. Of our true meaning they make mocks, rewarding our loving follies with disdainful flouts. We are the grief of man, in that we take all the grief from man: we languish when they laugh, we lie sighing when they sit singing, and sit sobbing when they lie slugging and sleeping.

[. . .]

For by men are we confounded though they by us are sometimes crossed. Our tongues are light because earnest in reproving men's filthy vices, and our good counsel is termed nipping injury in that it accords not with their foolish fancies. Our boldness rash for giving noddies nipping answers, our disposition naughty for not agreeing with their vile minds and our fury dangerous because it will not bear with their knavish behaviours [. . .] The viper stormeth when his tail is trodden on, and may not we fret when all our body is a foot-stool to their vile lust?

3.

SOR JUANA INÉS DE LA CRUZ

Born *c.* 1648, San Miguel Nepantla, New Spain, now Mexico
Died 1695, Mexico City, New Spain, now Mexico

from *A Philosophical Satire*
1691

Misguided men, who will chastise
a woman when no blame is due,
oblivious that it is you
who prompted what you criticize;

If your passions are so strong
that you elicit their disdain,
how can you wish that they refrain
when you incite them to their wrong?

You strive to topple their defense,
and then, with utmost gravity,
you credit sensuality
for what was won with diligence.

Your daring must be qualified,
your sense is no less senseless
than the child who calls the bogeyman,
then weeps when he is terrified.

Your mad presumption knows no bounds,
though for a wife you want Lucrece,
in lovers you prefer Thais,
thus seeking blessings to compound.

If knowingly one clouds a mirror
– was ever humor so absurd
or good counsel so obscured? –
can he lament that it's not clearer?

From either favor or disdain
the selfsame purpose you achieve,
if they love, they are deceived,
if they love not, hear you complain.

There is no woman suits your taste,
though circumspection be her virtue:
ungrateful, she who does not love you,
yet she who does, you judge unchaste.

You men are such a foolish breed,
appraising with a faulty rule,
the first you charge with being cruel,
the second, easy, you decree.

So how can she be temperate,
the one who would her love expend?
if not willing, she offends,
but willing, she infuriates.

Amid the anger and torment
your whimsy causes you to bear,
one may be found who does not care:
how quickly then is grievance vent.

So lovingly you inflict pain
that inhibitions fly away;
how, after leading them astray,
can you wish them without stain?

Who does the greater guilt incur
when a passion is misleading?
She who errs and heeds his pleading,
or he who pleads with her to err?

Whose is the greater guilt therein
when either's conduct may dismay:
she who sins and takes the pay,
or he who pays her for the sin?

Why, for sins you're guilty of,
do you, amazed, your blame debate?
Either love what you create
or else create what you can love.

Were not it better to forbear,
and thus, with finer motivation,
obtain the unforced admiration
of her you plotted to ensnare?

But no, I deem you still will revel
in your arms and arrogance,
and in promise and persistence
adjoin flesh and world and devil.

4.

MARY ASTELL

Born 1666, Newcastle upon Tyne, England
Died 1731, London, Great Britain

from *Some Reflections Upon Marriage*

1700
(the following is from the Preface to the 1706 edition)

If Mankind had never sinn'd, Reason wou'd always have been obey'd, there wou'd have been no struggle for Dominion, and Brutal Power wou'd not have prevail'd. But in the laps'd State of Mankind, and now that Men will not be guided by their Reason but by their Appetites, and do not what they *ought* but what they *can*, the Reason, or that which stands for it, the Will and Pleasure of the Governor is to be the Reason of those who will not be guided by their own, and must take place for Order's sake, altho' it shou'd not be conformable to right Reason. Nor can there be any Society great or little, from Empires down to private Families, without a last Resort, to determine the Affairs of that Society by an irresistible Sentence. Now unless this Supremacy be fix'd somewhere, there will be a perpetual Contention about it, such is the love of Dominion, and let the Reason of things be what it may, those who have least Force, or Cunning to supply it, will have the Disadvantage. So that since Women are acknowledg'd to have least Bodily strength, their being commanded to obey is in pure kindness to them and for their Quiet and Security, as well as for the Exercise of their Vertue. But does it follow that Domestic Governors have more Sense than their Subjects, any more than that other Governors have? We do not find that any Man thinks the worse of his own Understanding because another has superior Power; or concludes himself less capable of a Post of Honour and Authority, because he is not Prefer'd to it. How much time wou'd lie on Men's hands, how empty wou'd the Places of Concourse be, and how silent

13

most Companies did Men forbear to Censure their Governors, that is in effect to think themselves Wiser. Indeed Government wou'd be much more desirable than it is, did it invest the Possessor with a superior Understanding as well as Power. And if mere Power gives a Right to Rule, there can be no such thing as Usurpation; but a Highway-Man so long as he has strength to force, has also a Right to require our Obedience.

Again, if Absolute Sovereignty be not necessary in a State, how comes it to be so in a Family? Or if in a Family why not in a State; since no Reason can be alledg'd for the one that will not hold more strongly for the other? If the Authority of the Husband so far as it extends, is sacred and inalienable, why not of the Prince? The Domestic Sovereign is without Dispute Elected, and the Stipulations and Contract are mutual, is it not then partial in Men to the last degree, to contend for, and practise that Arbitrary Dominion in their Families, which they abhor and exclaim against in the State? For if Arbitrary Power is evil in itself, and an improper Method of Governing Rational and Free Agents it ought not to be Practis'd any where; Nor is it less, but rather more mischievous in Families than in Kingdoms, by how much 100000 Tyrants are worse than one. What tho' a Husband can't deprive a Wife of Life without being responsible to the Law, he may however do what is much more grievous to a generous Mind, render Life miserable, for which she has no Redress, scarce Pity which is afforded to every other Complainant. It being thought a Wife's Duty to suffer everything without Complaint. If *all Men are born free*, how is it that all Women are born slaves? As they must be if the being subjected to the *inconstant, uncertain, unknown, arbitrary Will* of Men, be the *perfect Condition of Slavery*? And if the Essence of Freedom consists, as our Masters say it does, in having a *standing rule to live by*? And why is Slavery so much condemn'd and strove against in one Case, and so highly applauded and held so necessary and so sacred in another?

'is true that GOD told *Eve* after the Fall that *her husband shou'd Rule over her*. And so it is that he told *Esau* by mouth of *Isaac* his Father, that he shou'd serve his *younger brother*, and shou'd in time, and when he was strong enough to do it, *break the Yoke from off his Neck*. Now why one Text shou'd be a Command any more than the other, and not both of them be

Predictions only; or why the former shou'd prove *Adam's* natural Right to Rule, and much less every Man's, any more than the latter is a Proof of *Jacob's* Right to Rule, and of *Esau's* to Rebel, one is yet to learn? The Text in both Cases foretelling what wou'd be; but, neither of them determining what ought to be.

5

BELINDA SUTTON

Born near the Volta river in what is now Ghana, probably of Fante or
Anlo-Ewe descent, eighteenth century
Died, Massachusetts, United States of America

The Petition of Belinda an African, to the Legislature of Massachusetts

1783

The Petition of Belinda an African, humbly shews: that seventy years have rolled away, since she on the banks of the Rio de Valta received her existence – the mountains Covered with spicy forests, the valleys loaded with the richest fruits, spontaneously produced; joined to that happy temperature of air to exclude excess; would have yielded her the most complete felicity, had not her mind received early impressions of the cruelty of men, whose faces were like the moon, and whose Bows and Arrows were like the thunder and the lightning of the Clouds – The idea of these, the most dreadful of all Enemies, filled her infant slumbers with horror, and her noontide moments with evil apprehensions! – But her affrighted imagination, in its most alarming extension, never represented distresses equal to what she hath since really experienced – for before she had Twelve years enjoyed the fragrance of her native groves, and ever she realized, that Europeans placed their happiness in the yellow dust which she carelessly marked with her infant footsteps – even when she, in a sacred grove, with each hand in that of a tender Parent, was paying her devotions to the great Orisa who made all things – an armed band of white men, driving many of her Countrymen in Chains, ran into the hallowed shade! – could the Tears, the sighs and supplications, bursting from Tortured Parental affection, have blunted the keen edge of Avarice, she might have been rescued from Agony, which many of her Country's Children have felt, but which none hath ever described, – in vain she lifted her supplicating voice to an insulted father, and her guiltless hands to a dishonoured Deity! She was ravished from the bosom of her Country, from the arms of her friends – while the advanced age of her Parents, rendering them unfit for servitude, cruelly separated her from them forever!

Scenes which her imagination never conceived of – a floating World – the sporting Monsters of the deep – and the familiar meetings of Billows and clouds, strove, but in vain to divert her melancholy attention, from three hundred Africans in chains, suffering the most excruciating torments; and some of them rejoicing, that the pangs of death came like a balm to their wounds.

Once more her eyes were blest with a Continent – but alas! how unlike the Land where she received her being! here all things appeared unpropitious – she learned to catch the Ideas, marked by the sounds of language only to know that her doom was Slavery, from which death alone was to emancipate her. – What did it avail her, that the walls of her Lord were hung with splendor, and that the dust trodden underfoot in her native Country, crowded his Gates with sordid worshipers – the Laws had rendered her incapable of receiving property – and though she was a free moral agent, accountable for her actions, yet she never had a moment at her own disposal!

Fifty years her faithful hands have been compelled to ignoble servitude for the benefit of an Isaac Royall, until, as if Nations must be agitated, and the world convulsed for the preservation of that freedom which the Almighty Father intended for all the human Race, the present war was Commenced – The terror of men armed in the Cause of freedom, compelled her master to fly – and to breathe away his Life in a Land, where, Lawless domination sits enthroned – pouring bloody outrage and cruelty on all who dare to be free.

The face of your Petitioner, is now marked with the furrows of time, and her frame feebly bending under the oppression of years, while she, by the Laws of the Land, is denied the enjoyment of one morsel of that immense wealth, apart whereof hath been accumilated by her own industry, and the whole augmented by her servitude.

WHEREFORE, casting herself at the feet of your honours, as to a body of men, formed for the extirpation of vassalage, for the reward of Virtue, and the just return of honest industry – she prays, that such allowance may be made her out of the estate of Colonel Royall, as will prevent her and her more infirm daughter from misery in the greatest extreme, and scatter comfort over the short and downward path of their Lives.

the mark of Belinda

6.

JUDITH SARGENT MURRAY

Born 1751, Gloucester, Massachusetts, United States of America
Died 1820, Natchez, Mississippi, United States of America

from *On the Equality of the Sexes*
1790

Is it upon mature consideration we adopt the idea, that nature is thus
partial in her distributions? Is it indeed a fact, that she hath yielded to
one half of the human species so unquestionable a mental superiority? I
know that to both sexes elevated understandings, and the reverse, are
common. But, suffer me to ask, in what the minds of females are so
notoriously deficient, or unequal. May not the intellectual powers be
ranged under these four heads – imagination, reason, memory and judgment. The province of imagination hath long since been surrendered up
to us, and we have been crowned undoubted sovereigns of the regions of
fancy. Invention is perhaps the most arduous effort of the mind; this
branch of imagination hath been particularly ceded to us, and we have
been time out of mind invested with that creative faculty. Observe the
variety of fashions (here I bar the contemptuous smile) which distinguish
and adorn the female world; how continually are they changing, insomuch
that they almost render the wise man's assertion problematical, and we
are ready to *say, there is something new under the sun*. Now what a playful-
ness, what an exuberance of fancy, what strength of inventive imagination,
doth this continual variation discover? Again, it hath been observed, that
if the turpitude of the conduct of our sex, hath been observed, that if the
turpitude of the ever so enormous, so extremely ready are we, that the very
first thought presents us with an apology, so plausible, as to produce our
actions even in an amiable light. Another instance of our creative powers,
is our talent for slander; how ingenious are we at inventive scandal? what
a formidable story can we in a moment fabricate merely from the force of

a prolifick imagination? how many reputations, in the fertile brain of a female, have been utterly despoiled? how industrious are we at improving a hint? suspicion how easily do we convert into conviction, and conviction, embellished by the power of eloquence, stalks abroad to the surprise and confusion of unsuspecting innocence.

Perhaps it will be asked if I furnish these facts as instances of excellency in our sex. Certainly not; but as proofs of a creative faculty, of a lively imagination. Assuredly great activity of mind is thereby discovered, and was this activity properly directed, what beneficial effects would follow. Is the needle and kitchen sufficient to employ the operations of a soul thus organized? I should conceive not. Nay, it is a truth that those very departments leave the intelligent principle vacant, and at liberty for speculation. Are we deficient in reason? we can only reason from what we know, and if an opportunity of acquiring knowledge hath been denied us, the inferiority of our sex cannot fairly be deduced from thence. Memory, I believe, will be allowed us in common, since every one's experience must testify, that a loquacious old woman is as frequently met with, as a communicative old man; their subjects are alike drawn from the fund of other times, and the transactions of their youth, or of maturer life, entertain, or perhaps fatigue you, in the evening of their lives. 'But our judgment is not so strong – we do not distinguish so well.'

Yet it may be questioned, from what doth this superiority, in this determining faculty of the soul, proceed. May we not trace its source in the difference of education, and continued advantages? Will it be said that the judgment of a male of two years old, is more sage than that of a female's of the same age? I believe the reverse is generally observed to be true. But from that period what partiality! how is the one exalted, and the other depressed, by the contrary modes of education which are adopted! the one is taught to aspire, and the other is early confined and limited. As their years increase, the sister must be wholly domesticated, while the brother is led by the hand through all the flowery paths of science. Grant that their minds are by nature equal, yet who shall wonder at the *apparent* superiority, if indeed custom becomes *second nature*; nay if it taketh place of nature, and that it doth the experience of each day will evince.

At length arrived at womanhood, the uncultivated fair one feels a void, which the employments allotted her are by no means capable of filling. What can she do? to books she may not apply; or if she doth, *to those only of the novel kind,* lest she merit the appellation of a *learned lady;* and what ideas have been affixed to this term, the observation of many can testify. Fashion, scandal, and some-times what is still more reprehensible, are then called in to her relief; and who can say to what lengths the liberties she takes may proceed. Meantime she herself is most unhappy; she feels the want of a cultivated mind. Is she single, she in vain seeks to fill up time from sexual employments or amusements. Is she united to a person whose soul nature made equal to her own, education hath set him so far above her, that in those entertainments which are productive of such rational felicity, she is not qualified to accompany him. She experiences a mortifiying consciousness of inferiority, which embitters every enjoyment. Doth the person to whom her adverse fate hath consigned her, possess a mind incapable of improvement, she is equally wretched, in being so closely connected with an individual whom she cannot but despise.

Now, was she permitted the same instructors as her brother, (with an eye however to their particular departments) for the employment of a rational mind an ample field would be opened. In astronomy she might catch a glimpse of the immensity of the Deity, and thence she would form amazing conceptions of the august and supreme Intelligence. In geography she would admire Jehovah in the midst of his benevolence; thus adapting this globe to the various wants and amusements of its inhabitants. In natural philosophy she would adore the infinite majesty of heaven, clothed in condescension; and as she traversed the reptile world, she would hail the goodness of a creating God. A mind, thus filled, would have little room for the trifles with which our sex are, with too much justice, accused of amusing themselves, and they would thus be rendered fit companions for those, who should one day wear them as their crown. Fashions, in their variety, would then give place to conjectures, which might perhaps conduce to the improvement of the literary world: and there would be no leisure for slander or detraction. Reputation would not then be blasted, but serious speculations would occupy the lively imaginations of the sex. Unnecessary visits would be precluded, and that custom would only be indulged by way of relaxation, or to answer the demands of consanguinity and friendship. Females would become discreet, their judgments would be invigorated, and their partners for life being circumspectly chosen, an unhappy Hymen would then be as rare, as is now the reverse.

Will it be urged that those acquirements would supersede our domestick duties? I answer that every requisite in female economy is easily attained; and, with truth I can add, that when once attained, they require no further *mental attention*. Nay, while we are pursuing the needle, or the superintendency of the family, I repeat, that our minds are at full liberty for reflection; that imagination may exert itself in full vigor; and that if a just foundation is early laid, our ideas will then be worthy of rational beings. If we were industrious we might easily find time to arrange them upon paper, or should avocations press too hard for such an indulgence, the hours allotted for conversation would at least become more refined and rational. Should it still be vociferated, 'Your domestick employments are sufficient' – I would calmly ask, is it reasonable, that a candidate for immortality, for the joys of heaven, an intelligent being, who is to spend an eternity in contemplating the works of Deity, should at present be so degraded, as to be allowed no other ideas, then those which are suggested by the mechanism of a pudding, or the sewing the seams of a garment? Pity that all such censurers of female improvement do not go one step further, and deny their future existence; to be consistent they surely ought.

Yes, ye lordly, ye haughty sex, our souls are by nature *equal* to yours; the same breath of God animates, enlivens, and invigorates us; and that we are not fallen lower than yourselves, let those witness who have greatly towered above the various discouragements by which they have been so heavily oppressed; and though I am unacquainted with the list of celebrated characters on either side, yet from the observations I have made in the contracted circle in which I have moved, I dare confidently believe, that from the commencement of time to the present day, there hath been as many females, as males, who, by the *mere force of natural powers*, have merited the crown of applause; who, *thus unassisted*, have seized the wreath of fame. I know there are who assert, that as the animal powers of the one sex are superiour, of course their mental faculties also must be stronger; thus attributing strength of mind to the transient organization of this earth born tenement. But if this reasoning is just, man must be content to yield the palm [to] many of the brute creation, since by not a few of his brethren of the field, he is far surpassed in bodily strength.

Moreover, was this argument admitted, it would prove too much, for occular demonstration evinceth, that there are many robust masculine ladies, and effeminate gentlemen. Yet I fancy that Mr Pope, though clogged with an enervated body, and distinguished by a diminutive stature, could nevertheless lay claim to greatness of soul; and perhaps there are many other instances which might be adduced to combat so unphilosophical an opinion. Do we not often see, that when the clay built tabernacle is well nigh dissolved, when it is just ready to mingle with the parent soil, the immortal inhabitant aspires to, and even attaineth heights the most sublime, and which were before wholly unexplored. Besides, were we to grant that animal strength proved any thing, taking into consideration the accustomed impartiality of nature, we should be induced to imagine, that she had invested the female mind with superior strength as an equivalent for the bodily powers of man. But waving this however palpable advantage, for *equality only*, we wish to contend.

7.

OLYMPE DE GOUGES

Born 1748, Montauban, France
Executed 1793, Paris, France

from *Declaration of the Rights of Woman and of the Female Citizen*

1791

The Rights of Woman

Man, are you capable of being just? It is a woman who poses the question, you will not deprive her of that right at least. Tell me, what gives you sovereign empire to oppress my sex? Your strength? Your talents? Observe the Creator in his wisdom, survey in all her grandeur that nature with whom you seem to want to be in harmony, and give me, if you dare, an example of this tyrannical empire. Go back to animals, consult the elements, study plants, finally glance at all the modifications of organic matter, and surrender to the evidence when I offer you the means; search, probe, and distinguish, if you can, the sexes in the administration of nature. Everywhere you will find them mingled; everywhere they cooperate in harmonious togetherness in this immortal masterpiece.

Man alone has raised his exceptional circumstances to a principle. Bizarre, blind, bloated with science and degenerated – in a century of enlightenment and wisdom – into the crassest ignorance, he wants to command as a despot a sex which is in full possession of its intellectual faculties; he pretends to enjoy the Revolution and to claim his rights to equality in order to say nothing more about it.

Declaration of the Rights of Woman and the Female Citizen For the National Assembly to decree in its last sessions, or in those of the next legislature:

Preamble

Mothers, daughters, sisters [and] representatives of the nation demand to be constituted into a national assembly. Believing that ignorance, omission, or scorn for the rights of woman are the only causes of public misfortunes and of the corruption of governments, [the women] have resolved to set forth in a solemn declaration the natural, inalienable, and sacred rights of woman in order that this declaration, constantly exposed before all the members of the society, will ceaselessly remind them of their rights and duties; in order that the authoritative acts of women and the authoritative acts of men may be at any moment compared with and respectful of the purpose of all political institutions; and in order that citizens' demands, henceforth based on simple and incontestable principles, will always support the constitution, good morals, and the happiness of all.

Consequently, the sex that is as superior in beauty as it is in courage during the suffering of maternity recognized and declares in the presence and under the auspices of the Supreme Being, the following Rights of Woman and of Female Citizens.

Article I

Woman is born free and lives equal to man in her rights. Social distinctions can be based only on the common utility.

[...]

Postscript

Woman, wake up; the alarm bell of reason is being heard throughout the whole universe; discover your rights. The powerful empire of nature is no longer surrounded by prejudice, fanaticism, superstition, and lies. The flame of truth has dispersed all the clouds of folly and usurpation. Enslaved man has multiplied his strength and needs recourse to yours to break his chains. Having become free, he has become unjust to his companion. Oh, women, women! When will you cease to be blind? What advantage have you received from the Revolution? A more pronounced scorn, a more marked disdain. In the centuries of corruption you ruled only over the weakness of men. The reclamation of your patrimony, based on the wise decrees of nature – what have you to dread from such a fine undertaking? The *bon mot* of the legislator of the marriage of Cana? Do you fear that our French legislators, correctors of that morality, long ensnared by political practices now out of date, will only say again to you: women, what is there in common between you and us? Everything, you will have to answer. If they persist in their weakness in putting this non sequitur in contradiction to their principles, courageously oppose the force of reason to the empty pretensions of superiority; unite yourselves beneath the standards of philosophy; deploy all the energy of your character, and you will soon see these haughty men, not grovelling at your feet as servile adorers, but proud to share with you the treasures of the Supreme Being. Regardless of what barriers confront you, it is in your power to free yourselves; you have only to want to. Let us pass not to the shocking tableau of what you have been in society; and since national education is in question at this moment, let us see whether our wise legislators will think judiciously about the education of women.

Women have done more harm than good. Constraint and dissimulation have been their lot. What force has robbed them of, ruse returned to them; they had recourse to all the resources of their charms, and the most irreproachable persons did not resist them. Poison and the sword were both subject to them; they commanded in crime as in fortune. The French government, especially, depended throughout the centuries on the nocturnal administrations of women; the cabinet kept no secret from their indiscretion; ambassadorial post, command, ministry, presidency, pontificate, college of cardinals; finally, anything which characterizes the folly of men, profane and sacred, all have been subject to the cupidity and ambition of this sex, formerly contemptible and respected, and since the revolution, respectable and scorned.

In this sort of contradictory situation, what remarks could I not make! I have but a moment to make them, but this moment will fix the attention of the remotest posterity. Under the Old Regime, all was vicious, all was guilty; but could not the amelioration of conditions be perceived even in the substance of vices? A woman only had to be beautiful or amiable; when she possessed these two advantages, she saw a hundred fortunes at her feet. If she did not profit from them, she had a bizarre character or a rare philosophy which made her scorn wealth; then she was deemed to be like a crazy woman; the most indecent made herself respected with gold; commerce in women was a kind of industry in the first class [of society], which, henceforth, will have no more credit. If it still had it, the revolution would be lost, and under the new relationships we would always be corrupted; however, reason can always be deceived [into believing] that any other road to fortune is closed to the woman whom a man buys, like the slave on the African coasts. The difference is great; that is known. The slave is commanded by the master; but if the master gives her liberty without recompense, and at an age when the slave has lost all her charms, what will become of this unfortunate woman? the victim of scorn, even the doors of charity are closed to her; she is poor and old, they say; why did she not know how to make her fortune? Reason finds other examples that are even more touching. A young, inexperienced woman, seduced by a man whom she loves, will abandon her parents to follow him; the ingrate will leave her after a few years, and the older she has become with him, the more inhuman is his inconstancy; if she has children, he will likewise abandon them. If he is rich, he will consider himself excused from sharing his fortune with his noble victims. If some involvement binds him to his duties, he will deny them, trusting that the laws will support him. If he is married, any other obligation loses its rights. Then what laws remain to extirpate vice all the way to its root? The law of dividing wealth and public administration between men and women. It can easily be seen that one who is born into a rich family gains very much from such equal sharing. But the one born into a poor family with merit and virtue - what is her lot? Poverty and opprobrium. If she does not precisely excel in music or painting, she cannot be admitted to any public function when she has all the capacity for it. I do not want to give only a sketch of things; I will go more deeply into this in the new edition of all my political writings, with notes, which I propose to give to the public in a few days.

I take up my text again on the subject of morals. Marriage is the tomb of trust and love. The married woman can with impunity give bastards to her husband, and also give them the wealth which does not belong to them. The woman who is unmarried has only one feeble right; ancient and inhuman laws refuse to her for her children the right to the name and the wealth of their father; no new laws have been made in this matter. If it is considered a paradox and an impossibility on my part to try to give my sex an honorable and just consistency, I leave it to men to attain glory for dealing with this matter; but while we wait, the way can be prepared through national education, the restoration of morals, and conjugal conventions.

8.

MARY WOLLSTONECRAFT

Born 1759, London, Great Britain
Died 1797, London, Great Britain

from *A Vindication of the Rights of Woman*
1792

Consider, I address you as a legislator, whether, when men contend for their freedom, and to be allowed to judge for themselves respecting their own happiness, it be not inconsistent and unjust to subjugate women, even though you firmly believe that you are acting in the manner best calculated to promote their happiness? Who made man the exclusive judge, if woman partake with him the gift of reason?

In this style, argue tyrants of every denomination, from the weak king to the weak father of a family; they are all eager to crush reason; yet always assert that they usurp its throne only to be useful. Do you not act a similar part, when you *force* all women, by denying them civil and political rights, to remain immured in their families groping in the dark? for surely, Sir, you will not assert, that a duty can be binding which is not founded on reason? If indeed this be their destination, arguments may be drawn from reason: and thus augustly supported, the more understanding women acquire, the more they will be attached to their duty comprehending it for unless they comprehend it, unless their morals be fixed on the same immutable principle as those of man, no authority can make them discharge it in a virtuous manner. They may be convenient slaves, but slavery will have its constant effect, degrading the master and the abject dependent.

But, if women are to be excluded, without having a voice, from a participation of the natural rights of mankind, prove first, to ward off the charge of injustice and inconsistency, that they want reason else this flaw in your NEW CONSTITUTION will ever shew that man must, in some shape, act like a tyrant, and tyranny, in whatever part of society it rears its brazen front, will ever undermine morality.

I have repeatedly asserted, and produced what appeared to me irrefragable arguments drawn from matters of fact, to prove my assertion, that women cannot, by force, be confined to domestic concerns; for they will, however ignorant, intermeddle with more weighty affairs, neglecting private duties only to disturb, by cunning tricks, the orderly plans of reason which rise above their comprehension.

Besides, whilst they are only made to acquire personal accomplishments, men will seek for pleasure in variety, and faithless husbands will make faithless wives; such ignorant beings, indeed, will be very excusable when, not taught to respect public good, nor allowed any civil rights, they attempt to do themselves justice by retaliation.

The box of mischief thus opened in society, what is to preserve private virtue, the only security of public freedom and universal happiness?

Let there be then no coercion *established* in society, and the common law of gravity prevailing, the sexes will fall into their proper places. And, now that more equitable laws are forming your citizens, marriage may become more sacred: your young men may choose wives from motives of affection, and your maidens allow love to root out vanity.

The father of a family will not then weaken his constitution and debase his sentiments, by visiting the harlot, nor forget, in obeying the call of appetite, the purpose for which it was implanted. And, the mother will not neglect her children to practise the arts of coquetry, when sense and modesty secure her the friendship of her husband.

But, till men become attentive to the duty of a father, it is vain to expect women to spend that time in their nursery which they, wise in their generation, choose to spend at their glass; for this exertion of cunning is only an instinct of nature to enable them to obtain indirectly a little of that power of which they are unjustly denied a share: for, if women are not permitted to enjoy legitimate rights, they will render both men and themselves vicious, to obtain illicit privileges.

I wish, Sir, to set some investigations of this kind afloat in France; and should they lead to a confirmation of my principles, when your constitution is revised the Rights of Woman may be respected, if it be fully proved that reason calls for this respect, and loudly demands JUSTICE for one half of the human race.

I am, Sir,
Yours respectfully,
M. W.

[. . .]

Introduction

After considering the historic page, and viewing the living world with anxious solicitude, the most melancholy emotions of sorrowful indignation have depressed my spirits, and I have sighed when obliged to confess, that either nature has made a great difference between man and man, or that the civilization which has hitherto taken place in the world has been very partial. I have turned over various books written on the subject of education, and patiently observed the conduct of parents and the management of schools; but what has been the result? – a profound conviction that the neglected education of my fellow-creatures is the grand source of the misery I deplore; and that women, in particular, are rendered weak and wretched by a variety of concurring causes, originating from one hasty conclusion. The conduct and manners of women, in fact, evidently prove that their minds are not in a healthy state; for, like the flowers which are planted in too rich a soil, strength and usefulness are sacrificed to beauty; and the flaunting leaves, after having pleased a fastidious eye, fade, disregarded on the stalk, long before the season when they ought to have arrived at maturity. – One cause of this barren blooming I attribute to a false system of education, gathered from the books written on this subject by men who, considering females rather as women than human creatures, have been more anxious to make them alluring mistresses than affectionate wives and rational mothers; and the understanding of the sex has been so bubbled by this specious homage, that the civilized women of the present century, with a few exceptions, are only anxious to inspire love, when they ought to cherish a nobler ambition, and by their abilities and virtues exact respect.

[. . .]

My own sex, I hope, will excuse me, if I treat them like rational creatures, instead of flattering their *fascinating* graces, and viewing them as if they were in a state of perpetual childhood, unable to stand alone. I earnestly wish to point out in what true dignity and human happiness consists – I wish to persuade women to endeavour to acquire strength, both of mind and body, and to convince them that the soft phrases, susceptibility of heart, delicacy of sentiment, and refinement of taste, are almost synonymous with epithets of weakness, and that those beings who are only the objects of pity and that kind of love, which has been termed its sister, will soon become objects of contempt.

Dismissing then those pretty feminine phrases, which the men condescendingly use to soften our slavish dependence, and despising that weak elegancy of mind, exquisite sensibility, and sweet docility of manners, supposed to be the sexual characteristics of the weaker vessel, I wish to shew that elegance is inferior to virtue, that the first object of laudable ambition is to obtain a character as a human being, regardless of the distinction of sex; and that secondary views should be brought to this simple touchstone.

[. . .]

The Prevailing Opinion of a Sexual Character Discussed

[. .] To preserve personal beauty, woman's glory! the limbs and faculties are cramped with worse than Chinese bands, and the sedentary life which they are condemned to live, whilst boys frolic in the open air, weakens the muscles and relaxes the nerves. – As for Rousseau's remarks, which have since been echoed by several writers, that they have naturally, that is from their birth, independent of education, a fondness for dolls, dressing, and talking – they are so puerile as not to merit a serious refutation. That a girl, condemned to sit for hours together listening to the idle chat of weak nurses, or to attend at her mother's toilet, will endeavour to join the conversation, is, indeed, very natural; and that she will imitate her mother or aunts, and amuse herself by adorning her lifeless doll, as they do in dressing her, poor innocent babe! is undoubtedly a most natural consequence. For men of the greatest abilities have seldom had sufficient strength to rise above the surrounding atmosphere; and, if the pages of genius have always been blurred by the prejudices of the age, some allowance should be made for a sex, who, like kings, always see things through a false medium.

Pursuing these reflections, the fondness for dress, conspicuous in women, may be easily accounted for, without supposing it the result of a desire to please the sex on which they are dependent. The absurdity, in short, of supposing that a girl is naturally a coquette, and that a desire connected with the impulse of nature to propagate the species, should appear even before an improper education has, by heating the imagination, called it forth prematurely, is so unphilosophical, that such a sagacious observer as Rousseau would not have adopted it, if he had not been accustomed to make reason give way to his desire of singularity, and truth to a favourite paradox.

Yet thus to give a sex to mind was not very consistent with the principles of a man who argued so warmly, and so well, for the immortality of the soul. – But what a weak barrier is truth when it stands in the way of an hypothesis! Rousseau respected – almost adored virtue – and yet he allowed himself to love with sensual fondness. His imagination constantly prepared inflammable fuel for his inflammable senses; but, in order to reconcile his respect for self-denial, fortitude, and those heroic virtues, which a mind like his could not coolly admire, he labours to invert the law of nature, and broaches a doctrine pregnant with mischief and derogatory to the character of supreme wisdom.

His ridiculous stories, which tend to prove that girls are *naturally* attentive to their persons, without laying any stress on daily example, are below contempt. – And that a little miss should have such a correct taste as to neglect the pleasing amusement of making O's, merely because she perceived that it was an ungraceful attitude, should be selected with the anecdotes of the learned pig.*

---

* 'I once knew a young person who learned to write before she learned to read, and began to write with her needle before she could use a pen. At first, indeed, she took it

I have, probably, had an opportunity of observing more girls in their infancy than J. J. Rousseau I can recollect my own feelings, and I have looked steadily around me; yet, so far from coinciding with him in opinion respecting the first dawn of the female character, I will venture to affirm, that a girl, whose spirits have not been damped by inactivity, or innocence tainted by false shame, will always be a romp, and the doll will never excite attention unless confinement allows her no alternative. Girls and boys, in short, would play harmlessly together, if the distinction of sex was not inculcated long before nature makes any difference. I will go further, and affirm, as an indisputable fact, that most of the women, in the circle of my observation, who have acted like rational creatures, or shewn any vigour of intellect, have accidentally been allowed to run wild – as some of the elegant formers of the fair sex would insinuate.

The baneful consequences which flow from inattention to health during infancy, and youth, extend further than is supposed – dependence of body naturally produces dependence of mind; and how can she be a good wife or mother, the greater part of whose time is employed to guard against or endure sickness? Nor can it be expected that a woman will resolutely endeavour to strengthen her constitution and abstain from enervating indulgencies, if artificial notions of beauty, and false descriptions of sensibility, have been early entangled with her motives of action. Most men are sometimes obliged to bear with bodily inconveniencies, and to endure, occasionally, the inclemency of the elements; but genteel women are, literally speaking, slaves to their bodies, and glory in their subjection.

I once knew a weak woman of fashion, who was more than commonly proud of her delicacy and sensibility. She thought a distinguishing taste and puny appetite the height of all human perfection, and acted accordingly. – I have seen this weak sophisticated being neglect all the duties of life, yet recline with self-complacency on a sofa, and boast of her want of appetite

---

into her head to make no other letter than the O: this letter she was constantly making of all sizes, and always the wrong way. Unluckily, one day, as she was intent on this employment, she happened to see herself in the looking-glass; when, taking a dislike to the constrained attitude in which she sat while writing, she threw away her pen, like another Pallas, and determined against the O any more. Her brother was also equally averse to writing: it was the confinement, however, and not the constrained attitude, that most disgusted him.' Rousseau's *Emilius*.

as a proof of delicacy that extended to, or, perhaps, arose from, her exquisite sensibility: for it is difficult to render intelligible such ridiculous jargon. Yet, at the moment, I have seen her insult a worthy old gentlewoman, whom unexpected misfortunes had made dependent on her ostentatious bounty, and who, in better days, had claims on her gratitude. Is it possible that a human creature could have become such a weak and depraved being, if, like the Sybarites, dissolved in luxury, everything like virtue had not been worn away, or never impressed by precept, a poor substitute, it is true, for cultivation of mind, though it serves as a fence against vice?

Such a woman is not a more irrational monster than some of the Roman emperors, who were depraved by lawless power. Yet, since kings have been more under the restraint of law, and the curb, however weak, of honour, the records of history are not filled with such unnatural instances of folly and cruelty, nor does the despotism that kills virtue and genius in the bud, hover over Europe with that destructive blast which desolates Turkey, and renders the men, as well as the soil, unfruitful.

Women are every where in this deplorable state; for, in order to preserve their innocence, as ignorance is courteously termed, truth is hidden from them, and they are made to assume an artificial character before their faculties have acquired any strength. Taught from their infancy that beauty is woman's sceptre, the mind shapes itself to the body, and, roaming round its gilt cage, only seeks to adorn its prison. Men have various employments and pursuits which engage their attention, and give a character to the opening mind; but women, confined to one, and having their thoughts constantly directed to the most insignificant part of themselves, seldom extend their views beyond the triumph of the hour. But were their understanding once emancipated from the slavery to which the pride and sensuality of man and their short-sighted desire, like that of dominion in tyrants, of present sway, has subjected them, we should probably read of their weaknesses with surprise. I must be allowed to pursue the argument a little farther.

Perhaps, if the existence of an evil being were allowed, who, in the allegorical language of scripture, went about seeking whom he should devour, he could not more effectually degrade the human character than by giving a man absolute power.

This argument branches into various ramifications. – Birth, riches, and every extrinsic advantage that exalt a man above his fellows, without any mental exertion, sink him in reality below them. In proportion to his weakness, he is played upon by designing men, till the bloated monster has lost all traces of humanity. And that tribes of men, like flocks of sheep, should quietly follow such a leader, is a solecism that only a desire of present enjoyment and narrowness of understanding can solve. Educated in slavish dependence, and enervated by luxury and sloth, where shall we find men who will stand forth to assert the rights of man; – or claim the privilege of moral beings, who should have but one road to excellence? Slavery to monarchs and ministers, which the world will be long in freeing itself from, and whose deadly grasp stops the progress of the human mind, is not yet abolished.

Let not men then in the pride of power, use the same arguments that tyrannic kings and venal ministers have used, and fallaciously assert that woman ought to be subjected because she has always been so. But, when man, governed by reasonable laws, enjoys his natural freedom, let him despise woman, if she do not share it with him; and, till that glorious period arrives, in descanting on the folly of the sex, let him not overlook his own.

9.

MARY HAYS

Born 1759, London, Great Britain
Died 1843, London, United Kingdom

from *Appeal to the Men of Great Britain on Behalf of Women*

1798

A Brother and Sister were one day going to market with some eggs, and other country provisions to sell. 'Dear Jacky,' said the sister, after a good deal of consideration, and not a little proud of her powers of calculation, – 'Dear Jacky, you have somehow made a very unfair division of our eggs, of which you know it was intended that we should have equal shares; so pray give me two dozen of yours, and I shall then have as many as you have.' 'No,' says John, – John Bull as likely as any John, – 'that would never do; but dear, sweet, pretty sister Peg, give me one dozen of yours, and then I shall have five times as many as you have; which you know will be quite the same as if you had them yourself, or indeed better; as I shall save you the trouble of carrying them, shall protect you and the rest of your property, and shall besides give you many fine things when we get to the fair – Bless me, Margaret! what is the matter with you? How frightful you always are when in a passion! And how horribly ugly you look whenever you contradict me! I wish poor Ralph the miller saw you just now, I'm sure he'd never look at you again. Besides, sister of mine, since you force me to it, and provoke me beyond all bearing, I must tell you, that as I am stronger than you, I can take them whether you will or no.' The thing was no sooner said than done, and poor Peg, found herself obliged to submit to something much more convincing than her brother's logic.

On they jogged however together, Peg pouting all the way, and John not a bit the civiler for having got what he knew in his heart he had no title to; and when they got to the fair, poor Peg's property, of which he was to have been the faithful guardian, and careful steward; went with his own, to purchase baubles and gin for his worthless favorite. But then, had not Peg pretended to put herself upon a footing of equality with him; or had she even after all, but calmly and quietly given up her own rights without murmuring, – nothing so easy as that, till it comes home to a man's own case, – he swore manfully that there should not have been a word between them.

Thus goes the world!

10.

CHARLOTTE BRONTË

Born 1816, Thornton, Yorkshire, United Kingdom
Died 1855, Haworth, Yorkshire, United Kingdom

from *Jane Eyre: An Autobiography*
1847

It is in vain to say human beings ought to be satisfied with tranquillity: they must have action; and they will make it if they cannot find it. Millions are condemned to a stiller doom than mine, and millions are in silent revolt against their lot. Nobody knows how many rebellions besides political rebellions ferment in the masses of life which people earth. Women are supposed to be very calm generally: but women feel just as men feel; they need exercise for their faculties, and a field for their efforts as much as their brothers do; they suffer from too rigid a restraint, too absolute a stagnation, precisely as men would suffer; and it is narrow-minded in their more privileged fellow-creatures to say that they ought to confine them-selves to making puddings and knitting stockings, to playing on the piano and embroidering bags. It is thoughtless to condemn them, or laugh at them, if they seek to do more or learn more than custom has pronounced necessary for their sex.

II

SENECA FALLS CONVENTION

Women's Rights Convention, July 1848, Seneca Falls, New York, United
States of America. Drafted by Elizabeth Cady Stanton, Martha
C. Wright, Lucretia Mott, and Mary Ann McClintock around Wright's
dinner table, the Declaration was then read out by Stanton at the
Convention and signed by participants there.

from *Declaration of Sentiments*
1848

When, in the course of human events, it becomes necessary for one portion of the family of man to assume among the people of the earth a
position different from that which they have hitherto occupied, but one
to which the laws of nature and of nature's God entitle them, a decent
respect to the opinions of mankind requires that they should declare the
causes that impel them to such a course.

We hold these truths to be self-evident: that all men and women are
created equal; that they are endowed by their Creator with certain inalienable rights; that among these are life, liberty, and the pursuit of
happiness; that to secure these rights governments are instituted, deriving
their just powers from the consent of the governed. Whenever any form
of government becomes destructive of these ends, it is the right of those
who suffer from it to refuse allegiance to it, and to insist upon the institution of a new government, laying its foundation on such principles, and
organizing its powers in such form, as to them shall seem most likely to
effect their safety and happiness. Prudence, indeed, will dictate that governments long established should not be changed for light and transient
causes; and accordingly all experience hath shown that mankind are more
disposed to suffer, while evils are sufferable, than to right themselves by
abolishing the forms to which they are accustomed. But when a long train
of abuses and usurpations, pursuing invariably the same object, evinces a

design to reduce them under absolute despotism, it is their duty to throw off such government, and to provide new guards for their future security. Such has been the patient sufferance of the women under this government, and such is now the necessity which constrains them to demand the equal station to which they are entitled. The history of mankind is a history of repeated injuries and usurpations on the part of man toward woman, having in direct object the establishment of an absolute tyranny over her. To prove this, let facts be submitted to a candid world.

He has never permitted her to exercise her inalienable right to the elective franchise.

He has compelled her to submit to laws, in the formation of which she had no voice.

He has withheld from her rights which are given to the most ignorant and degraded men – both natives and foreigners.

Having deprived her of this first right of a citizen, the elective franchise, thereby leaving her without representation in the halls of legislation, he has oppressed her on all sides.

He has made her, if married, in the eye of the law, civilly dead.

He has taken from her all right in property, even to the wages she earns.

He has made her, morally, an irresponsible being, as she can commit many crimes with impunity, provided they be done in the presence of her husband. In the covenant of marriage, she is compelled to promise obedience to her husband, he becoming, to all intents and purposes, her master – the law giving him power to deprive her of her liberty, and to administer chastisement.

He has so framed the laws of divorce, as to what shall be the proper causes, and in case of separation, to whom the guardianship of the children shall be given, as to be wholly regardless of the happiness of women – the law, in all cases, going upon a false supposition of the supremacy of man, and giving all power into his hands.

After depriving her of all rights as a married woman, if single, and the owner of property, he has taxed her to support a government which recognizes her only when her property can be made profitable to it.

He has monopolized nearly all the profitable employments, and from those she is permitted to follow, she receives but a scanty remuneration. He closes against her all the avenues to wealth and distinction which he considers most honorable to himself. As a teacher of theology, medicine, or law, she is not known.

He has denied her the facilities for obtaining a thorough education, all colleges being closed against her.

He allows her in church, as well as state, but a subordinate position, claiming apostolic authority for her exclusion from the ministry, and, with some exceptions, from any public participation in the affairs of the church.

He has created a false public sentiment by giving to the world a different code of morals for men and women, by which moral delinquencies which exclude women from society, are not only tolerated, but deemed of little account in man.

He has usurped the prerogative of Jehovah himself, claiming it as his right to assign for her a sphere of action, when that belongs to her conscience and to her God.

He has endeavored, in every way that he could, to destroy her confidence in her own powers, to lessen her self-respect, and to make her willing to lead a dependent and abject life.

Now, in view of this entire disfranchisement of one-half the people of this country, their social and religious degradation – in view of the unjust laws above mentioned, and because women do feel themselves aggrieved, oppressed, and fraudulently deprived of their most sacred rights, we insist that they have immediate admission to all the rights and privileges which belong to them as citizens of the United States.

12

SOJOURNER TRUTH

Born 1797, Rosendale, New York, United States of America
Died 1883, Battle Creek, Michigan, United States of America

Ain't I A Woman?

1851

Well, children, where there is so much racket there must be something out of kilter. I think that 'twixt the negroes of the South and the women at the North, all talking about rights, the white men will be in a fix pretty soon. But what's all this here talking about?

That man over there says that women need to be helped into carriages, and lifted over ditches, and to have the best place everywhere. Nobody ever helps me into carriages, or over mud-puddles, or gives me any best place! And ain't I a woman? Look at me! Look at my arm! I have ploughed and planted, and gathered into barns, and no man could head me! And ain't I a woman? I could work as much and eat as much as a man – when I could get it – and bear the lash as well! And ain't I a woman? I have borne thirteen children, and seen most all sold off to slavery, and when I cried out with my mother's grief, none but Jesus heard me! And ain't I a woman?

Then they talk about this thing in the head; what's this they call it? [member of audience whispers, 'intellect'] That's it, honey. What's that got to do with women's rights or negroes' rights? If my cup won't hold but a pint, and yours holds a quart, wouldn't you be mean not to let me have my little half measure full?

Then that little man in black there, he says women can't have as much rights as men, 'cause Christ wasn't a woman! Where did your Christ come from? Where did your Christ come from? From God and a woman! Man had nothing to do with Him.

If the first woman God ever made was strong enough to turn the world upside down all alone, these women together ought to be able to turn it back, and get it right side up again! And now they is asking to do it, the men better let them.

Obliged to you for hearing me, and now old Sojourner ain't got nothing more to say.

13

ELIZABETH BARRETT BROWNING

Born 1806, County Durham, United Kingdom
Died 1861, Florence, Italy

from *Aurora Leigh*
1856

I read a score of books on womanhood
To prove, if women do not think at all,
They may teach thinking, (to a maiden aunt
Or else the author) – books demonstrating
Their right of comprehending husband's talk
When not too deep, and even of answering
With pretty 'may it please you,' or 'so it is,' –
Their rapid insight and fine aptitude,
Particular worth and general missionariness,
As long as they keep quiet by the fire
And never say 'no' when the world says 'ay,'
For that is fatal, – their angelic reach
Of virtue, chiefly used to sit and darn,
And fatten household sinners – their, in brief,
Potential faculty in everything
Of abdicating power in it: she owned
She liked a woman to be womanly,
And English women, she thanked God and sighed,
(Some people always sigh in thanking God)
Were models to the universe. And last
I learnt cross-stitch, because she did not like
To see me wear the night with empty hands,
A- doing nothing. So, my shepherdess

Was something after all, (the pastoral saints
Be praised for't) leaning lovelorn with pink eyes
To match her shoes, when I mistook the silks;
Her head uncrushed by that round weight of hat
So strangely similar to the tortoise-shell
Which slew the tragic poet.
                    By the way,
The works of women are symbolical.
We sew, sew, prick our fingers, dull our sight,
Producing what? A pair of slippers, sir,
To put on when you're weary – or a stool
To tumble over and vex you . . . 'curse that stool!'
Or else at best, a cushion where you lean
And sleep, and dream of something we are not,
But would be for your sake. Alas, alas!
This hurts most, this . . . that, after all, we are paid
The worth of our work, perhaps.

14.

JOHN STUART MILL AND HARRIET TAYLOR

Mill: Born 1806, London, United Kingdom;
Died 1873, Avignon, France.
Taylor (née Hardy): Born 1807, London, United Kingdom;
Died 1858, Avignon, France. Mill said his writings were
'the joint product' of them both.

from *The Subjection of Women*
1869

Some will object, that a comparison cannot fairly be made between the government of the male sex and the forms of unjust power which I have adduced in illustration of it, since these are arbitrary, and the effect of mere usurpation, while it on the contrary is natural. But was there ever any domination which did not appear natural to those who possessed it? There was a time when the division of mankind into two classes, a small one of masters and a numerous one of slaves, appeared, even to the most cultivated minds, to be a natural, and the only natural, condition of the human race. No less an intellect, and one which contributed no less to the progress of human thought, than Aristotle, held this opinion without doubt or misgiving; and rested it on the same premises on which the same assertion in regard to the dominion of men over women is usually based, namely that there are different natures among mankind, free natures, and slave natures; that the Greeks were of a free nature, the barbarian races of Thracians and Asiatics of a slave nature. But why need I go back to Aristotle? Did not the slaveowners of the Southern United States maintain the same doctrine, with all the fanaticism with which men cling to the theories that justify their passions and legitimate their personal interests? Did they not call heaven and earth to witness that the dominion of the white man over the black is natural, that the black race is by nature incapable of freedom, and marked out for slavery? some even going so far as to say that the freedom of manual labourers is an unnatural order of things anywhere. Again, the theorists of absolute monarchy have always affirmed it to be the only natural form of government; issuing from the patriarchal, which was the primitive and spontaneous form of society, framed on the model of the paternal, which is anterior to society itself, and, as they contend, the most natural authority of all. Nay, for that matter, the law of force itself, to those who could not plead any other, has always seemed the most natural of all grounds for the exercise of authority. Conquering races hold it to be Nature's own dictate that the conquered should obey the conquerors, or, as they euphoniously paraphrase it, that the feebler and more unwarlike races should submit to the braver and manlier. The smallest acquaintance with human life in the middle ages, shows how supremely natural the dominion of the feudal nobility over men of low condition appeared to the nobility themselves, and how unnatural the conception seemed, of a person of the inferior class claiming equality with them, or exercising authority over them. It hardly seemed less so to the class held in subjection. The emancipated serfs and burgesses, even in their most vigorous struggles, never made any pretension to a share of authority; they only demanded more or less of limitation to the power of tyrannizing over them. So true is it that unnatural generally means only uncustomary, and that everything which is usual appears natural. The subjection of women to men being a universal custom, any departure from it quite naturally appears unnatural. But how entirely, even in this case, the feeling is dependent on custom, appears by ample experience. Nothing so much astonishes the people of distant parts of the world, when they first learn anything about England, as to be told that it is under a queen: the thing seems to them so unnatural as to be almost incredible. To Englishmen this does not seem in the least degree unnatural, because they are used to it; but they do feel it unnatural that women should be soldiers or members of parliament. In the feudal ages, on the contrary, war and politics were not thought unnatural to women, because not unusual; it seemed natural that women of the privileged classes should be of manly character, inferior in nothing but bodily strength to their husbands and fathers. The independence of women seemed rather less unnatural to the Greeks than to other ancients, on account of the fabulous Amazons (whom they believed to be historical), and the partial example afforded by the Spartan women; who, though no less subordinate by law than in other Greek states, were more free in fact, and being trained to bodily exercises in the same manner with men, gave ample proof that they were not naturally disqualified for them. There can be little doubt that Spartan experience suggested to Plato, among many other of his doctrines, that of the social and political equality of the two sexes.

But, it will be said, the rule of men over women differs from all these others in not being a rule of force: it is accepted voluntarily; women make no complaint, and are consenting parties to it. In the first place, a great number of women do not accept it. Ever since there have been women able to make their sentiments known by their writings (the only mode of publicity which society permits to them), an increasing number of them have recorded protests against their present social condition: and recently many thousands of them, headed by the most eminent women known to the public, have petitioned Parliament for their admission to the Parliamentary Suffrage. The claim of women to be educated as solidly, and in the same branches of knowledge, as men, is urged with growing intensity, and with a great prospect of success; while the demand for their admission into professions and occupations hitherto closed against them, becomes every year more urgent. Though there are not in this country, as there are in the United States, periodical Conventions and an organized party to agitate for the Rights of Women, there is a numerous and active Society organized and managed by women, for the more limited object of obtaining the political franchise. Nor is it only in our own country and in America that women are beginning to protest, more or less collectively, against the disabilities under which they labour. France, and Italy, and Switzerland, and Russia now afford examples of the same thing. How many more women there are who silently cherish similar aspirations, no one can possibly know; but there are abundant tokens how many would cherish them, were they not so strenuously taught to repress them as contrary to the proprieties of their sex. It must be remembered, also, that no enslaved class ever asked for complete liberty at once. When Simon de Montfort called the deputies of the commons to sit for the first time in Parliament, did any of them dream of demanding that an assembly, elected by their constituents, should make and destroy ministries, and dictate to the king in affairs of state? No such thought entered into the imagination of the most ambitious of them. The nobility had already these pretensions; the commons pretended to nothing but to be exempt from arbitrary taxation, and from the gross individual oppression of the king's officers. It is a political law of nature that those who are under any power of ancient origin, never begin by complaining of the power itself, but only of its oppressive exercise. There is never any want of women who complain of ill usage by their husbands. There would be infinitely more, if complaint were not the greatest of all provocatives to a repetition and increase of the ill usage. It is this which frustrates all attempts to maintain the power but protect the woman against its abuses. In no other case (except that of a child) is the person who has been proved judicially to have suffered an injury, replaced under the physical power of the culprit who inflicted it. Accordingly wives, even in the most extreme and protracted cases of bodily ill usage, hardly ever dare avail themselves of the laws made for their protection: and if, in a moment of irrepressible indignation, or by the interference of neighbours, they are induced to do so, their whole effort afterwards is to disclose as little as they can, and to beg off their tyrant from his merited chastisement.

All causes, social and natural, combine to make it unlikely that women should be collectively rebellious to the power of men. They are so far in a position different from all other subject classes, that their masters require something more from them than actual service. Men do not want solely the obedience of women, they want their sentiments. All men, except the most brutish, desire to have, in the woman most nearly connected with them, not a forced slave but a willing one, not a slave merely, but a favour-ite. They have therefore put everything in practice to enslave their minds. The masters of all other slaves rely, for maintaining obedience, on fear; either fear of themselves, or religious fears. The masters of women wanted more than simple obedience, and they turned the whole force of education to effect their purpose. All women are brought up from the very earliest years in the belief that their ideal of character is the very opposite to that of men; not self-will, and government by self-control, but submission, and yielding to the control of others. All the moralities tell them that it is the duty of women, and all the current sentimentalities that it is their nature, to live for others; to make complete abnegation of themselves, and to have no life but in their affections. And by their affections are meant the only ones they are allowed to have – those to the men with whom they are connected, or to the children who constitute an additional and indefeasible tie between them and a man. When we put together three things – first, the natural attraction between opposite sexes; secondly, the wife's entire dependence on the husband, every privilege or pleasure she has being either his gift, or depending entirely on his will; and lastly, that the principal object of human pursuit, consideration, and all objects of social ambition, can in general be sought or obtained by her only through him, it would be a miracle if the object of being attractive to men had not become the polar star of feminine education and formation of character. And, this great means of influence over the minds of women having been acquired, an instinct of selfishness made men avail themselves of it to the utmost as a means of holding women in subjection, by representing to them meekness, submissiveness, and resignation of all individual will into the hands of a man, as an essential part of sexual attractiveness. Can it be doubted that any of the other yokes which mankind have succeeded in breaking, would have subsisted till now if the same means had existed, and had been as sedulously used, to bow down their minds to it? If it had been made the object of the life of every young plebeian to find personal favour in the eyes of some patrician, of every young serf with some seigneur; if domestication with him, and a share of his personal affections, had been held out as the prize which they all should look out for, the most gifted and aspiring being able to reckon on the most desirable prizes; and if, when this prize had been obtained, they had been shut out by a wall of brass from all interests not centering in him, all feelings and desires but those which he shared or inculcated; would not serfs and seigneurs, plebeians and patricians, have been as broadly distinguished at this day as men and women are? and would not all but a thinker here and there, have believed the distinction to be a fundamental and unalterable fact in human nature?

The preceding considerations are amply sufficient to show that custom, however universal it may be, affords in this case no presumption, and ought not to create any prejudice, in favour of the arrangements which place women in social and political subjection to men. But I may go farther, and maintain that the course of history, and the tendencies of progressive human society, afford not only no presumption in favour of this system of inequality of rights, but a strong one against it; and that, so far as the whole course of human improvement up to this time, the whole stream of modern tendencies, warrants any inference on the subject, it is, that this relic of the past is discordant with the future, and must necessarily disappear.

For, what is the peculiar character of the modern world – the difference which chiefly distinguishes modern institutions, modern social ideas, modern life itself, from those of times long past? It is, that human beings are no longer born to their place in life, and chained down by an inexorable bond to the place they are born to, but are free to employ their faculties, and such favourable chances as offer, to achieve the lot which may appear to them most desirable. Human society of old was constituted on a very different principle. All were born to a fixed social position, and were mostly kept in it by law, or interdicted from any means by which they could emerge from it. As some men are born white and others black, so some were born slaves and others freemen and citizens; some were born patricians, others plebeians; some were born feudal nobles, others commoners and roturiers. A slave or serf could never make himself free, nor, except by the will of his master, become so. In most European countries it was not till towards the close of the middle ages, and as a consequence of the growth of regal power, that commoners could be ennobled. Even among nobles, the eldest son was born the exclusive heir to the paternal possessions, and a long time elapsed before it was fully established that the father could disinherit him. Among the industrious classes, only those who were born members of a guild, or were admitted into it by its members, could lawfully practise their calling within its local limits; and nobody could practise any calling deemed important, in any but the legal manner – by processes authoritatively prescribed. Manufacturers have stood in the pillory for presuming to carry on their business by new and improved methods. In modern Europe, and most in those parts of it which have participated most largely in all other modern improvements, diametrically opposite doctrines now prevail. Law and government do not undertake to prescribe by whom any social or industrial operation shall or shall not be conducted, or what modes of conducting them shall be lawful. These things are left to the unfettered choice of individuals. Even the laws which required that workmen should serve an apprenticeship, have in this country been repealed: there being ample assurance that in all cases in which an apprenticeship is necessary, its necessity will suffice to enforce it. The old theory was, that the least possible should be left to the choice of the individual agent; that all he had to do should, as far as practicable, be laid down for him by superior wisdom. Left to himself he was sure to go wrong. The modern conviction, the fruit of a thousand years of experience, is, that things in which the individual is the person directly interested, never go right but as they are left to his own discretion; and that any regulation of them by authority, except to protect the rights of others, is sure to be mischievous. This conclusion, slowly arrived at, and not adopted until almost every possible application of the contrary theory had been made with disastrous result, now (in the industrial department) prevails universally in the most advanced countries, almost universally in all that have pretensions to any sort of advancement. It is not that all processes are supposed to be equally good, or all persons to be equally qualified for everything; but that freedom of individual choice is now known to be the only thing which procures the adoption of the best processes, and throws each operation into the hands of those who are best qualified for it. Nobody thinks it necessary to make a law that only a strong-armed man shall be a blacksmith. Freedom and competition suffice to make blacksmiths strong-armed men, because the weak-armed can earn more by engaging in occupations for which they are more fit. In consonance with this doctrine, it is felt to be an overstepping of the proper bounds of authority to fix beforehand, on some general presumption, that certain persons are not fit to do certain things. It is now thoroughly known and admitted that if some such presumptions exist, no such presumption is infallible. Even if it be well grounded in a majority of cases, which it is very likely not to be, there will be a minority of exceptional cases in which it does not hold: and in those it is both an injustice to the individuals, and a detriment to society, to place barriers in the way of their using their faculties for their own benefit and for that of others. In the cases, on the other hand, in which the unfitness is real, the ordinary motives of human conduct will on the whole suffice to prevent the incompetent person from making, or from persisting in, the attempt.

If this general principle of social and economical science is not true; if individuals, with such help as they can derive from the opinion of those who know them, are not better judges than the law and the government, of their own capacities and vocation; the world cannot too soon abandon this principle, and return to the old system of regulations and disabilities. But if the principle is true, we ought to act as if we believed it, and not to ordain that to be born a girl instead of a boy, any more than to be born black instead of white, or a commoner instead of a nobleman, shall decide the person's position through all life.

15.

TARABAI SHINDE

Born 1850, Buldhana, Berar Province, India
Died 1910, India

from *A Comparison Between Women and Men*
1882

God brought this amazing universe into being; and he it was also who created men and women both. So is it true that only women's bodies are home to all kinds of wicked vices? Or have men got just the same faults as we find in women? I wanted this to be shown absolutely clearly, and that's the reason I've written this small book, to defend the honour of all my sister countrywomen. I'm not looking at particular castes or families here. It's a comparison just between women and men.

[...]

These days the newspapers are always writing about poor helpless women and the wicked things they do. Why won't any of you come forward and put a stop to these great calamities?

Just look now, how the custom of not remarrying widows has spread – in so many places, to so many castes, like a great sickness. It's hard to imagine the bitter despair all these hundreds and thousands of widows must suffer. And how many disasters come out of it. Because stridharma hasn't ever been saved just by making people sit at home and control their thoughts. What they do with their minds and eyes can make them just as guilty. Where does it get you if you snatch away all the happy signs of a woman's marriage, if you chop off one woman's hair and wipe off another's kumkum from her forehead? Women still have the same hearts inside, the same thoughts of good and evil. You can strip the outside till it's naked, but you can't do the same to the inside, can you? In fact, what does stridharma

54

really mean? It means always obeying orders from your husband and doing everything he wants. He can kick you and swear at you, keep his whores, get drunk, gamble with dice and bawl he's lost all his money, steal, commit murder, be treacherous, slander people, rob peoples' treasures or squeeze them for bribes. He can do all this, but when he comes home, stridharma means women are meant to think, 'Oh, Who's this coming now but our little lord Krishna, who's just stolen the milkmaids' curds and milk and tried to blame Chandravali for it'. And then smile at him and offer their devotion, stand ready at his service as if he was Paramatma himself. But how can people go on believing this idea of stridharma once they've begun to think about what's good and bad? They'd change their ideas straightway, wouldn't they? A man can run off with someone else's wife, but that's not against the rule of pativrata. In fact, there are thousands of reasons for breaking the rule. You're supposed to worship your husband as if he were a god. But who is there nowadays that really does? There's that story of Savitri' which sets out an example of pativrata. Would any woman now try to follow it all to the letter? Go on then, can you show us even one?

That story tells us that if a husband kicks you, you should just smile at him and say, 'Don't do that, my lord and husband: you'll hurt your foot'. And so saying, you should sit down and promptly start massaging his foot. You're not to cry if he lets you have it with his fist, even if he beats you with a stick. No, you've got to smile, fetch fresh butter and rub it into his hands for him, saying, 'My lord, the palm of your hand must be burning from those blows'. And if there's no butter in the house, use the neighbour's, and if she's got none, run and get some from the market. But who'd do any of this nowadays? Far from stroking his hand, she'd more likely tell him to shove it in the stove. If he dislikes a particular sort of food, she's meant to avoid it too. It's just the opposite though – he throws it down and she picks it up straight. It's got to be something sweet though! If it's some ordinary old vegetable like carrots or gourd, then fine, she'll avoid them for life! But if it's mangoes the husband won't eat, will she give them up? Not a bit! If the husband asks for water, she's not standing ready with a clean brass vessel. Instead the lady will tell him, 'Oh yes, I'm dying for some water, there's some in that pot over there, get yourself some, and get me some while you're at it! What am I supposed to do? This child here just won't let me get up'.

The husband's only got to mention his bath and she's meant to lay out the stool, get a bucket of hot water and stand ready to scrub his feet. But actually she just calls out, 'Anyone out here? Come in here, Ramya boy, he wants to have a bath, fetch him water and fold his dhoti for him. If he asks for me, tell him I'm having me tea'. As soon as her husband comes in for dinner, she's meant to bring a stool, lay out vessels for drinking, serve him his favourite foods, then sit wasting her time entertaining him with talk till he's finished his feast. But nowadays he'll be saying, 'Have you finished in there or not? Come on, serve it up, it's nine o'clock!' And the answer comes from her: 'All right, I'm coming, it's nearly ready. Can't you even wait till the vegetables and lentils are done? What, do you want me to serve you uncooked rice? What a chore this business is, every bloody day at nine o'clock! Every day the same hurry!' Then comes the subject of his roll of betel nut, and off they go again. He calls out, 'Make me some betel, will you? The dish is in that niche in the wall over there. No, no, not like that – can't you even roll betel nut properly? You take all the ingredients together in your hand, like this'. So the lord and master goes over to the dish and looks inside, only to find there's no lime. 'Look, there's no lime', he says. 'Go and get some, will you?' But all he gets out of her is, 'There's some supari nut in a little bag in that box up there. You eat your betel and get one of those out for me. Ugh – doesn't your mouth feel nasty when you finish eating?' Well now – isn't this much closer to the truth?

This is what pativrata means these days. If I was to tell you the whole of it from start to finish, it'd take a whole separate book. Who on earth really follows the shastras to the letter or expects anyone else to? If the husband is really to be like a god to the wife then shouldn't he behave like one? And if wives are to worship them like true devotees, shouldn't husbands have a tender love for them in return, and care about their joys and pains like a real god would? When the gods see those who worship them, they feel happy and satisfied. Shouldn't husbands be the same? When husbands find virtues or faults in people devoted to them, shouldn't they take a proper account of them, accept their shortcomings and correct them with love? What woman could really treat her husband like a god, no matter how nasty he was?

16.

KISHIDA TOSHIKO

Born 1863, Kyoto, Japan
Died 1901, Japan

from *Daughters in Boxes*
1883

But, to turn to the topic of this evening's lecture, the expression 'daughters in boxes' is a popular one, heard with frequency in the regions of Kyoto and Osaka. It is the daughters of middle-class families and above who are often referred to as such. Why such an expression? Because these girls are like creatures kept in a box. They may have hands and feet and a voice – but all to no avail, because their freedom is restricted. Unable to move, their hands and feet are useless. Unable to speak, their voice has no purpose. Hence the expression.

It is only for daughters that such boxes are constructed. Parents who make these boxes do not mean to restrict their daughters' freedom. Rather, they hope to guide their daughters along the correct path toward acquiring womanly virtues. Therefore it is out of love for their daughters that these parents construct these boxes. Or so we are told, but, if we look at the situation more closely, we cannot help questioning whether it is truly love that these parents have for their daughters. For do they not cause their daughters to suffer? I should like to gather a few students – perhaps only two or three – and make of them true daughters in a box. But the box I would construct would not be a box with walls. Rather, it would be a formless box. For a box with walls visible to the human eye is cramped and does not allow one to cultivate truly bright and healthy children. Sisters crowd each other, competing for space, and end up developing warped personalities. And so I intend to create a box without walls.

A box without walls is one that allows its occupants to tread wherever their feet might lead and stretch their arms as wide as they wish. Some may object and say: is your box not one that encourages dissipation and willfulness? No, it is not so at all. My box without walls is made of heaven and earth – its lid I would fashion out of the transparent blue of the sky and at its bottom would be the fathomless depths of the earth upon which we stand. My box would not be cramped, allowing its occupants such a tiny space that whenever they attempt to move, their arms and legs strike against one another, causing them to suffer. It may seem biased to say so, but constructing this box is above all a woman's task and an important task at that. A hastily made box will not do. A woman should carry with her into marriage a box filled with a good education. Upon giving birth to a daughter, she should raise her in the box she has herself carefully constructed. Thus she will nurture a bright daughter of good character. But if she forces her daughter into a box she has hastily constructed, the child will chafe at the narrowness of the structure and resent being placed inside. Far better to build the box before the birth of the child, for indeed a woman's ability to produce good children for the propagation of the family and to encourage domestic harmony depends on how carefully she has built this box.

17.

ELEANOR MARX

Born 1855, London, United Kingdom
Died 1898, London, United Kingdom

from *The Woman Question*
1886

Society is morally bankrupt, and in nothing does this gruesome moral bankruptcy come out with a more hideous distinctness than in the relation between men and women. Efforts to postpone the crash by drawing bills upon the imagination are useless. The facts have to be faced.

One of these facts of the most fundamental importance is not, and never has been, fairly confronted by the average man or woman in considering these relations. It has not been understood even by those men and women above the average who have made the struggle for the greater freedom of women the very business of their lives. This fundamental fact is, that the question is one of economics. The position of women rests, as everything in our complex modern society rests, on an economic basis. Had Bebel done nothing but insist upon this, his work would have been valuable. The woman question is one of the organisation of society as a whole. For those who have not grasped this conception, we may quote Bacon in the first book of the *Advancement of Learning*. 'Another error . . . is that, after the distribution of particular Arts and Sciences, men have abandoned universality . . . which cannot but cease and stop all progression . . . Neither is it possible to discover the more remote and deeper parts of any science if you stand but upon the level of the same science and ascend not to a higher.' This error, indeed, when 'men (and women) have abandoned universality,' is something more than a 'peccant humour.' It is a disease. Or, to use an illustration possibly suggested by the passage and the phrase just quoted, those who attack the present treatment of women without seeking for the cause of this in the economics of our latter-day society are like doctors who treat a local infection without inquiring into the general bodily health.

This criticism applies not alone to the commonplace person who makes a jest of any discussion into which the element of sex enters. It applies to those higher natures, in many cases earnest and thoughtful, who see that women are in a parlous state, and are anxious that something should be done to better their condition. These are the excellent and hard-working folk who agitate for that perfectly just aim, women's suffrage; for the repeal of the Contagious Diseases Act, a monstrosity begotten of male cowardice and brutality; for the higher education of women; for the opening to them of universities, the learned professions, and all callings, from that of teacher to that of bagman. In all this work – good as far as it goes – three things are especially notable. First, those concerned in it are of the well-to-do classes, as a rule. With the single and only partial exception of the Contagious Disease agitation, scarcely any of the women taking a prominent part in these various movements belong to the working class. We are prepared for the comment that something very like this may be said, as far as concerns England, of the larger movement that claims our special efforts. Certainly, Socialism is at present in this country little more than a literary movement. It has but a fringe of working men on its border. But we can answer to this criticism that in Germany this is not the case, and that even here Socialism is now beginning to extend among the workers.

The second point is that all these ideas of our *advanced* women are based either on property, or on sentimental or professional questions. Not one of them gets down through these to the bedrock of the economic basis, not only of these three, but of society itself. This fact is not astonishing to those who note the ignorance of economics characteristic of most of those that labour for the enfranchisement of women. Judging from the writings and speeches of the majority of women's advocates, no attention has been given by them to the study of the evolution of society. Even the orthodox political economy, which is, as we think, misleading in its statements and inaccurate in its conclusions, does not appear to have been mastered generally.

The third point grows out of the second. The school of whom we speak make no suggestion that is outside the limits of the society of today. Hence their work is, always from our point of view, of little value. We will support all women, not only those having property, enabled to vote; the Contagious Diseases Act repealed; every calling thrown open to both sexes. The actual position of women in respect to men would not be very vitally touched. (We are not concerned at present with the results of the increased competition and more embittered struggle for existence.) For not one of these things, save indirectly the Contagious Diseases Act, touches them in their sex relations. Nor should we deny that, with the gain of each or all of these points, the tremendous change that is to come would be more easy of attainment. But it is essential to keep in mind that ultimate change, only to come about when the yet more tremendous social change whose corollary it will be has taken place. Without that larger social change women will never be free.

The truth, not fully recognised even by those anxious to do good to woman, is that she, like the labour-classes, is in an oppressed condition; that her position, like theirs, is one of merciless degradation. Women are the creatures of an organised tyranny of men, as the workers are the creatures of an organised tyranny of idlers. Even where this much is grasped, we must never be weary of insisting on the non-understanding that for women, as for the labouring classes, no solution of the difficulties and problems that present themselves is really possible in the present condition of society. All that is done, heralded with no matter what flourish of trumpets, is palliative, not remedial. Both the oppressed classes, women and the immediate producers, must understand that their emancipation will come from themselves. Women will find allies in the better sort of men, as the labourers are finding allies among the philosophers, artists, and poets. But the one has nothing to hope from man as a whole, and the other has nothing to hope from the middle class as a whole.

The truth of this comes out in the fact that, before we pass to the consideration of the condition of women, we have to speak this word of warning. To many, that which we have to say of the Now will seem exaggerated; much that we have to say of the Hereafter, visionary, and perhaps all that is said, dangerous. To cultured people, public opinion is still that of man alone, and the customary is the moral. The majority still lays stress upon the occasional sex-helplessness of woman as a bar to her even consideration with man. It still descants upon the *natural calling* of the female. As to the former, people forget that sex-helplessness at certain times is largely exaggerated by the unhealthy conditions of our modern life, if, indeed, it is not wholly due to these. Given rational conditions, it would largely, if not completely, disappear. They forget also that all this about which the talk is so glib when women's freedom is under discussion is conveniently ignored when the question is one of women's enslavement. They forget that by capitalist employers this very sex-helplessness of woman is only taken into account with the view of lowering the general rate of wages. Again, there is no more a *natural calling* of woman than there is a natural law of capitalistic production, or a *natural* limit to the amount of the labourer's product that goes to him for means of subsistence. That in the first case, woman's *calling* is supposed to be only the tending of children, the maintenance of household conditions, and a general obedience to her lord; that, in the second, the production of surplus value is a necessary preliminary to the production of capital; that, in the third, the amount the labourer receives for his means of subsistence is so much as will keep him only just above starvation point: these are not natural laws in the same sense as are the laws of motion. They are only certain temporary conventions of society, like the convention that French is the language of diplomacy.

To treat the position of women at the present time in detail is to repeat a thousand-times-told tale. Yet, for our purpose, we must re-emphasise some familiar points, and perhaps mention one or two less familiar. And first, a general idea that has to do with all women. The life of woman does not coincide with that of man. Their lives do not intersect; in many cases do not even touch. Hence the life of the race is stunted. According to Kant, 'a man and woman constitute, when united, the whole and entire being; one sex completes the other.' But when each sex is incomplete, and the one incomplete to the most lamentable extent, and when, as a rule, neither of them comes into real, thorough, habitual, free contact, mind to mind, with the other, the being is neither whole nor entire.

Second, a special idea that has to do with only a certain number, but that a large one, of women. Every one knows the effect that certain callings, or habits of life, have on the *physique* and on the face of those that follow them. The horsy man, the drunkard are known by gait, physiognomy. How many of us have ever paused, or dared to pause, upon the serious fact that in the streets and public buildings, in the friend-circle, we can, in a moment, tell the unmarried women, if they are beyond a certain age which lively writers call, with a delicate irony peculiarly their own, *uncertain?* But we cannot tell a man that is unmarried from one that is wedded. Before the question that arises out of this fact is asked, let us call to mind the terrible proportion of women that are unmarried. For example, in England, in the year 1870, 41 per cent of the women were in this condition. The question to which all this leads is a plain one, a legitimate one, and is only an unpleasant one because of the answer that must be given. How is it that our sisters bear upon their brows this stamp of lost instincts, stifled affections, a nature in part murdered? How is it that their *more fortunate brothers* bear no such mark? Here, assuredly, no *natural law* obtains. This licence for the man, this prevention of legions of noble and holy unions that does not affect him, but falls heavily on her, are the inevitable outcome of our economic system. Our marriages, like our morals, are based upon commercialism. Not to be able to meet one's business engagements is a greater sin than the slander of a friend, and our weddings are business transactions.

Whether we consider women as a whole, or only that sad sisterhood wearing upon its melancholy brows the stamp of eternal virginity, we find alike a want of ideas and of ideals. The reason of this is again the economic position of dependency upon man. Women, once more like the labourers, have been expropriated as to their rights as human beings, just as the labourers were expropriated as to their rights as producers. The method in each case is the only one that makes expropriation at any time and under any circumstances possible – and that method is force.

In Germany at the present day the woman is a minor with regard to man. A husband *of low estate* may chastise a wife. All decisions as to the children rest with him, even to the fixing of the date of weanings. Whatever fortune the wife may have he manages. She may not enter into agreements without his consent; she may not take part in political associations. It is unnecessary for us to point out how much better, within the last few years, these things have been managed in England, or to remind our readers that the recent changes were due to the action of women themselves. But it is necessary to remind them that with all these added civil rights English women, married and unmarried alike, are morally dependent on man, and are badly treated by him. The position is little better in other civilised lands, with the strange exception of Russia, where women are socially more free than in any other part of Europe. In France, the women of the upper middle class are more unhappily situated than in England. Those of the lower middle and working classes are better off than either in England or Germany. But two consecutive paragraphs in the *Code Civil*, 340 and 341, show that injustice to women is not only Teutonic. *La recherche de la paternité est interdité* and *La recherche de la maternité est admise*.

Every one who refuses to blink facts knows that Demosthenes words of the Athenians are true of our English middle and upper classes today, 'We marry in order to obtain legitimate children and a faithful warder of the house; we keep concubines as servants for our daily attendance, but we seek the Hetairai for love's delight.' The wife is still the child-bearer, the housewarder. The husband lives and loves according to his own bad pleasure. Even those who admit this will possibly join issue with us when we suggest as another wrong to women the rigorous social rule that from man only must come the first proffer of affection, the proposal for marriage. This may be on the principle of compensation. After marriage the proffers come generally from the woman, and the reserve is the man's. That this is no natural law our Shakespeare has shown. Miranda, untrammelled by society, tenders herself to Ferdinand. 'I am your wife if you will marry me: if not I'll die your maid;' and Helena, in *All's Well that Ends Well*, with her love for Bertram, that carries her from Rousillon to Paris and Florence, is, as Coleridge has it, *Shakespeare's loveliest character*.

We have said that marriage is based upon commercialism. It is a barter transaction in many cases, and in all, under the condition of things today, the question of ways and means plays of necessity a large part. Among the upper classes the business is carried on quite unblushingly. The Sir Gorgius Midas pictures in *Punch* testify to this. The nature of the periodical in which they appear reminds us that all the horrors they reveal are only regarded as foibles, not as sins. In the lower middle class many a man denies himself the joy of home life until he grows out of the longing for it; many a woman closes the book of her life at its fairest page for ever, because of the dread *rerum angustarum domi* [*of the narrow confines of domestic life*].

Another proof of the commercial nature of our marriage system is afforded by the varying times at which wedlock is customary in the varying grades of society. The time is in no sense regulated, as it ought to be, by the time of life. Some favoured individuals, kings, princes, aristocrats, marry, or are married, at the age to which Nature points as fitting. Many of the working class marry young – that is, at the natural period. The virtuous capitalist who at that age makes a habitual use of prostitution dilates unctuously upon the improvidence of the artisan. The student of physiology and economics notes the fact as interesting evidence that not even the frightful capitalistic system has crushed out a normal and right-eous instinct. But, with the stratum of society wedged in between these two, unions, as we have just seen, cannot take place as a rule until years after the heyday of youth is passed and passion is on the wane.

All this tells far more on the women than on the men. Society provides, recognises, legalises for the latter the means of gratifying the sex instinct. In the eyes of that same society an unmarried woman who acts after the fashion habitual to her unmarried brothers and the men that dance with her at balls, or work with her in the shop, is a pariah. And even with the working classes who marry at the normal time, the life of the woman under the present system is the more arduous and irksome of the two. The old promise of the legend, *in sorrow shalt thou bring forth children*, is not only realised, but extended. She has to bring them up through long years, unrelieved by rest, unbrightened by hope, in the same atmosphere of perennial labour and sorrow. The man, worn out as he may be by labour, has the evening in which to do nothing. The woman is occupied until bedtime comes. Often with young children her toil goes far into, or all through, the night.

When marriage has taken place all is in favour of the one and is adverse to the other. Some wonder that John Stuart Mill wrote, *Marriage is at the present day the only actual form of serfdom recognised by law*. The wonder to us is that he never saw this serfdom as a question, not of sentiment, but of economics, the result of our capitalistic system. After marriage, as before, the woman is under restraint, and the man is not. Adultery in her is a crime, in him a venial offence. He can obtain a divorce, she cannot, on the ground of adultery. She must prove that *cruelty* (i.e. of a physical kind) has been shown. Marriages thus arranged, thus carried out, with such an attendant train of circumstances and of consequences, seem to us let us say it with all deliberation worse than prostitution. To call them sacred or moral is a desecration.

In connexion with the subject of divorce we may note an instance of the self-deception, not only of society and its constituent classes but of individuals. The clergy are ready and willing to marry anybody and everybody, age to youth, vice to virtue, *and no questions asked,* as a certain class of advertisements put it. Yet the clergy set their faces most sternly against divorce. To protest against such discordant unions as they again and again ratify would be an *interference with the liberty of the subject.* But to oppose anything that facilitates divorce is a most serious interference with the liberty of the subject. The whole question of divorce, complex in any case, is made more complicated by the fact that it has to be considered, first in relation to the present conditions, second in relation to the socialistic conditions of the future. Many advanced thinkers plead for greater facility of divorce now. They contend that divorce ought to be made at least as easy as marriage; that an engagement entered into by people who have had little or no opportunity of knowing one another ought not to be irrevocably, or even stringently binding; that incompatibility of temper, non-realisation of deep-rooted hopes, actual dislike, should be sufficient grounds for separation; finally, and most important of all, that the conditions of divorce should be the same for the two sexes. All this is excellent, and would be not only feasible but just, if – but mark the if – the economic positions of the two sexes were the same. They are not the same. Hence, whilst agreeing with every one of these ideas theoretically, we believe that they would, practically applied under our present system, result, in the majority of cases, in yet further injustice to women. The man would be able to take advantage of them; the woman would not, except in the rare instances where she had private property or some means of livelihood. The annulling of the union would be to him freedom; to her, starvation for herself and her children.

18

PANDITA RAMABAI SARASVATI

Born 1858, Karnataka, India
Died 1922, Bombay Presidency, India

from *The High Caste Hindu Woman*
1887

In no other country is the mother so laden with care and anxiety on the approach of childbirth as in India. In most cases her hope of winning her husband to herself hangs solely on her bearing sons.

Women of the poorest as well as of the richest families, are almost invariably subjected to this trial. Many are the sad and heart-rending stories heard from the lips of unhappy women who have lost their husband's favor by bringing forth daughters only, or by having no children at all. Never shall I forget a sorrowful scene that I witnessed in my childhood. When about thirteen years of age I accompanied my mother and sister to a royal harem where they had been invited to pay a visit. The Prince had four wives, three of whom were childless. The eldest having been blessed with two sons, was of course the favorite of her husband, and her face beamed with happiness.

We were shown into the nursery and the royal bed-chamber, where signs of peace and contentment were conspicuous. But oh! what a contrast to this brightness was presented in the apartments of the childless three. Their faces were sad and careworn; there seemed no hope for them in this world, since their lord was displeased with them, on account of their misfortune.

A lady friend of mine in Calcutta told me that her husband had warned her not to give birth to a girl, the first time, or he would never see her face again, but happily for this wife and for her husband also, she had two sons before the daughter came. In the same family there was another woman, the sister-in-law of my friend, whose first-born had been a daughter. She longed unceasingly to have a son, in order to win her husband's favor, and when I went to the house, constantly besought me to foretell whether this time she should have a son! Poor woman! she had been notified by her husband that if she persisted in bearing daughters she should be superseded by another wife, have coarse clothes to wear and scanty food to eat, should have no ornaments, save those which are necessary to show the existence of a husband, and she should be made the drudge of the whole household. Not unfrequently, it is asserted, that bad luck attends a girl's advent, and poor superstitious mothers in order to avert such a catastrophe, attempt to convert the unborn child into a boy, if unhappily it be a girl.

Rosaries used by mothers of sons are procured to pray with; herbs and roots celebrated for their virtue are eagerly and regularly swallowed; trees and son-giving gods are devoutly worshipped. There is a curious ceremony, honored with the name of 'sacrament,' which is administered to the mother between the third and the fourth month of her pregnancy for the purpose of converting the embryo into a boy.

In spite of all these precautions girls will come into Hindu households as ill-luck, or rather nature, will have it. After the birth of one or more sons girls are not unwelcome, and under such circumstances, mothers very often long to have a daughter. And after her birth both parents lavish love and tenderness upon her, for natural affection, though modified and blunted by cruel custom, is still strong in the parent's heart. Especially may this be the case with the Hindu mother. That maternal affection, sweet and strong, before which 'there is neither male nor female,' asserts itself not unfrequently in Hindu homes, and overcomes selfishness and false fear of popular custom. A loving mother will sacrifice her own happiness by braving the displeasure of her lord, and will treat her little daughter as the best of all treasures. Such heroism is truly praiseworthy in a woman; any country might be proud of her. But alas! the dark side is too conspicuous to be passed over in silence.

In a home shadowed by adherence to cruel custom and prejudice, a child is born into the world; the poor mother is greatly distressed to learn that the little stranger is a daughter, and the neighbors turn their noses in all directions to manifest their disgust and indignation at the occurrence of such a phenomenon. The innocent babe is happily unconscious of all that is going on around her, for a time at least. The mother, who has lost the favor of her husband and relatives because of the girl's birth, may selfishly avenge herself by showing disregard to infantile needs and slighting babyish requests. Under such a mother the baby soon begins to feel her misery, although she does not understand how or why she is caused to suffer this cruel injustice.

19

FRANCISCA SENHORINHA DA MOTTA DINIZ

Born 1859, São João del Rei, Brazil
Died 1897, Campanha, Brazil

from *Equality of Rights*

1890

Men, in their youth, are prepared for professions, and marriage is not considered as the grand feature in their lives; whilst women, on the contrary, have no other scheme to sharpen their faculties. It is not business, extensive plans, or any of the excursive flights of ambition, that engross their attention; no, their thoughts are not employed in rearing such noble structures. To rise in the world, and have the liberty of running from pleasure to pleasure, they must marry advantageously, and to this object their time is sacrificed, and their persons often legally prostituted [. . .]

If girls were allowed to take sufficient exercise, and not confined in close rooms till their muscles are relaxed, and their powers of digestion destroyed [. . .] if fear in girls, instead of being cherished, perhaps, created, were treated in the same manner as cowardice in boys, we should quickly see women with more dignified aspects. It is true, they could not then with equal propriety be termed the sweet flowers that smile in the walk of man; but they would be more respectable members of society, and discharge the important duties of life by the light of their own reason. 'Educate women like men,' says Rousseau, 'and the more they resemble our sex the less power will they have over us.' This is the very point I aim at. I do not wish them to have power over men; But over themselves.

[. . .] We believe, with the strong faith noble causes inspire, that an ideal state will soon be here, when educated women free from traditional prejudices and superstitions will banish from their education the oppression and false beliefs besetting them and will fully develop their physical, moral, and intellectual attributes. Then, linked arm in arm with the steps of light to have their ephemeral physical beauty crowned with the immortal diadem of true beauty, of science and creativity. In the full light of the new era of redemption we shall battle for the restoration of equal rights and our cause – the Emancipation of women.

[. . .] We are not daunted by such hypocrisy as men's treating us like queens only to give us the sceptre of the kitchen, or the procreation machine, etc. We are considered nothing but objects of indispensable necessity! We are cactus flowers and nothing more.

Women's emancipation through education is the bright torch which can dispel the darkness and bring us to the august temple of science and to a proper life in a civilized society.

In short, we want women to be fully aware of their own worth and of what they can achieve with their bodies as well as through their moral beauty and the force of their intellects. We want the lords of the stronger sex to know that although under their laws they can execute us for our political ideas, as they owe us the justice of equal rights. And that includes the right to vote and to be elected to office.

By right we should not be denied expression in Parliament. We should not continue to be mutilated in our moral and mental personality. The right to vote is an attribute of humanity because it stems from the power of speech. Women are human beings, too.

We Brazilian, Italian, French, and other women of diverse nationalities do not request the vote under the restrictions currently imposed on English women, but with the full rights of republican citizens. We live in a generous and marvellous country recognized as a world leader in liberal ideas and in the ability to throw off old prejudices.

Our ideas are not utopian but instead great and noble, and they will induce humanity to advance toward justice.

This is our political program.

20

ANNA JULIA COOPER

Born 1858, Raleigh, North Carolina, United States of America
Died 1964, Washington, D.C., United States of America

from *A Voice from the South by a Black Woman of the South*

1892

In the National Woman's Council convened at Washington in February 1891, among a number of thoughtful and suggestive papers read by eminent women, was one by the Rev. Anna Shaw, bearing the above title.

That Miss Shaw is broad and just and liberal in principal is proved beyond contradiction. Her noble generosity and womanly firmness are unimpeachable. The unwavering stand taken by herself and Miss Anthony in the subsequent color ripple in Wimodaughsis ought to be sufficient to allay forever any doubts as to the pure gold of these two women.

Of Wimodaughsis (which, being interpreted for the uninitiated, is a woman's culture club whose name is made up of the first few letters of the four words wives, mothers, daughters, and sisters) Miss Shaw is president, and a lady from the Blue Grass State was secretary.

Pandora's box is opened in the ideal harmony of this modern Eden without an Adam when a colored lady, a teacher in one of our schools, applies for admission to its privileges and opportunities.

The Kentucky secretary, a lady zealous in good works and one who, I can't help imagining, belongs to that estimable class who daily thank the Lord that He made the earth that they may have the job of superintending its rotations, and who really would like to help 'elevate' the colored people (in her own way of course and so long as they understand their places) is filled with grief and horror that any persons of Negro extraction should aspire to learn type-writing or languages or to enjoy any other advantages offered in the sacred halls of Wimodaughsis. Indeed, she had not calculated that there were any wives, mothers, daughters, and sisters, except white ones; and, she is really convinced that Whimodaughsis would sound just as well, and then it need mean just white mothers, daughters and sisters. In fact, so far as there is anything in a name, nothing would be lost by omitting for the sake of euphony, from this unique mosaic, the letters that represent wives. Whiwimodaughsis might be a little startling, and on the whole wives would better yield to white; since clearly all women are not wives, while surely all wives are daughters. The daughters therefore could represent the wives and this immaculate assembly for propagating liberal and progressive ideas and disseminating a broad and humanizing culture might be spared the painful possibility of the sight of a black man coming in the future to escort from an evening class this solitary cream-colored applicant. Accordingly the Kentucky secretary took the cream-colored applicant aside, and, with emotions befitting such an epoch-making crisis, told her, 'as kindly as she could,' that colored people were not admitted to the classes, at the same time refunding the money which said cream-colored applicant had paid for lessons in type-writing.

When this little incident came to the knowledge of Miss Shaw, she said firmly and emphatically, NO. As a minister of the gospel and as a Christian woman, she could not lend her influence to such unreasonable and uncharitable discrimination; and she must resign the honor of president of Wimodaughsis if persons were to be proscribed solely on account of their color.

To the honor of the board of managers, be it said, they sustained Miss Shaw; and the Kentucky secretary, and those whom she succeeded in inoculating with her prejudices, resigned.

'Twas only a ripple, – some bewailing of lost opportunity on the part of those who could not or would not seize God's opportunity for broadening and enlarging their own souls – and then the work flowed on as before.

Susan B. Anthony and Anna Shaw are evidently too noble to be held in thrall by the provincialisms of women who seem never to have breathed the atmosphere, beyond the confines of their grandfathers' plantations. It is only from the broad plateau of light and love that one can see petty prejudice and narrow priggishness in their true perspective; and it is on this high ground, as I sincerely believe, these two grand women stand.

As leaders in the woman's movement, of to-day, they have need of

73

clearness of vision as well as firmness of soul in adjusting recalcitrant forces, and wheeling into line the thousand and one none-such, never-to-be-modified, won't-be-dictated-to banners of their somewhat mottled array.

The black woman and the southern woman, I imagine, often got them into the predicament of the befuddled man who had to take singly across a stream a bag of corn, a fox and a goose. There was no one to help, and to leave the goose with the fox was death – with the corn, destruction. To re-christen the animals, the lion could not be induced to lie down with the lamb unless the lamb would take the inside berth.

The black woman appreciates the situation and can even sympathize with the actors in the serio-comic dilemma.

But, may it not be that, as women, the very lessons which seem hardest to master now, are possibly the ones most essential for our promotion to a higher grade of work?

We assume to be leaders of thought and guardians of society. Our country's manners and morals are under our tutoring. Our standards are law in our several little worlds. However tenaciously men may guard some prerogatives, they are our willing slaves in that sphere which they have always conceded to be woman's. Here, no one dares demur when her fiat has gone forth. The man would be mad who presumed, however inexplicable and past finding out any reason for her action might be, to attempt to open a door in her kingdom officially closed and regally sealed by her.

The American woman of to-day not only gives tone directly to her immediate world, but, her tiniest pulsation ripples out and out, down and down, till the outermost circles and the deepest layers of society feel the vibrations. It is pre-eminently an age of organizations. The 'leading woman,' the preacher, the reformer, the organizer 'enthuses' her lieutenants and captains, the literary women, the thinking women, the strong, earliest, irresistible women' these in turn touch their myriads of church clubs, social clubs, culture clubs, pleasure clubs and charitable clubs, till the same lecture has been duly administered to every married man in the land (not to speak of sons and brothers) from the President in the White House to the stone-splitter of the ditches. And so woman's lightest whisper is heard as in Dionysius' ear, by quick relays and endless reproductions, through every recess and cavern as well as on every hilltop and mountain in her vast domain. And her mandates are obeyed. When she says 'thumbs up,' woe to the luckless thumb that falters in its rising. They may be little things, the amenities of life, the little nothing which cost nothing and come to nothing, and yet can make a sentient being so comfortable or so miserable in this life, the oil of social machinery, which we call the courtesies of life, all are under the magic key of woman's permit.

The American woman then is responsible for American manners. Not merely the right ascension and declination of the satellites of her own drawing room; but the rising and the setting of the pestilential or life-giving orbs which seem to wander afar in space, all are governed almost wholly through her magnetic polarity. The atmosphere of street cars and parks and boulevards, of cafes and hotels and steamboats is charged and surcharged with her sentiments and restrictions. Shop girls and serving maids, cashiers and accountant clerks, scribblers and drummers, whether wage earner, salaried toiler, or proprietress, whether laboring to instruct minds, to save souls, to delight fancies, or to win bread, – the working women of America in whatever station or calling they may be found, are subjects, officers, or rulers of a strong centralized government, and bound together by a system of codes and countersigns, which, though unwritten, forms a network of perfect subordination and unquestioning obedience as marvelous as that of the Jesuits. At the head and center in this regime stands the Leading Woman in the principality. The one talismanic word that plays along the wires from palace to cook-shop, from imperial Congress to the distant plain, is Caste. With all her vaunted independence, the American woman of to-day is as fearful of losing caste as a Brahmin in India. That is the law under which she lives, the precepts which she binds as frontlets between her eyes and writes on the door-posts of her homes, the lesson which she instils into her children with their first baby breakfasts, the injunction she lays upon husband and lover with direst penalties attached.

The queen of the drawing room is absolute ruler under this law. Her pose gives the cue. The microscopic angle at which her pencilled brows are elevated, signifies who may be recognized and who are beyond the pale. The delicate intimation is, quick as electricity, telegraphed down. Like the wonderful transformation in the House that Jack Built (or regions thereabouts) when the rat began to gnaw the rope, the rope to hang the butcher, the butcher to kill the ox, the ox to drink the water, the water to quench the fire, the fire to burn the stick, the stick to beat the dog, and the dog to worry the cat, and on, and on, – when miladi causes the inner arch over her match-less orbs to ascend the merest trifle, presto! the Miss at the notions counter grows curt and pert, the dress goods clerk becomes indifferent and taciturn, hotel waiters and ticket dispensers look the other way, the Irish street laborer snarles and scowls, conductors, policemen and park superintendents jostle and push and threaten, and society suddenly seems transformed into a band of organized adders, snapping, and striking and hissing just because they like it on general principles. The tune set by the head singer, sung through all keys and registers, with all qualities of tone, – the smooth, flowing, and gentle, the creaking, whizzing, grating, screeching, growling – according to ability, taste, and temperament of the singers. Another application of like master, like man. In this case, like mistress, like nation.

It was the good fortune of the Black Woman of the South to spend some weeks, not long since, in a land over which floated the Union Jack. The Stars and Stripes were not the only familiar experiences missed. A uniform, matter-of-fact courtesy, a genial kindliness, quick perception of opportunities for rendering any little manly assistance, a readiness to give information to strangers, – a hospitable, thawing-out atmosphere everywhere – in shops and waiting rooms, on cars and in the streets, actually seemed to her chilled little soul to transform the commonest boor in the service of the public into one of nature's noblemen, and when the old whipped-cur feeling was taken up and analyzed she could hardly tell whether it consisted mostly of self pity for her own wounded sensibilities, or of shame for her country and mortification that her countrymen offered such an unfavorable contrast.

Some American girls, I noticed recently, in search of novelty and adventure, were taking an extended trip through our country unattended by gentleman friends; their wish was to write up for a periodical or lecture the ease and facility, the comfort and safety of American travel, even for the weak and unprotected, under our well-nigh perfect railroad systems and our gentlemanly and efficient corps of officials and public servants. I have some material I could furnish these young ladies, though possibly it might not be just on the side they wish to have illuminated. The Black Woman of the South has to do considerable travelling in this country, often unattended.

She thinks she is quiet and unobtrusive in her manner, simple and inconspicuous in her dress, and can see no reason why in any chance assemblage of ladies, or even a promiscuous gathering of ordinarily well-bred and dignified individuals, she should be signaled out for any marked consideration. And yet she has seen these same 'gentlemanly and efficient' railroad conductors, when their cars had stopped at stations having no raised platforms, making it necessary for passengers to take the long and trying leap from the car step to the stool, thence to the ground, or else relieving her of satchels and bags and enabling her to make the descent easily, deliberately fold their arms and turn round when the Black Woman's turn came to alight – bearing her satchel, and bearing besides another unnamable burden inside the heaving bosom and tightly compressed lips. The feeling of slighted womanhood is unlike every other emotion of the soul. Happily for the human family, it is unknown to many and indescribable to all. Its poignancy, compared with which even Juno's *spretae injuria formae* is earthly and vulgar, is holier than that of jealousy, deeper than indigation, tenderer than rage. Its first impulse of wrathful protest and proud self-vindication is checked and shamed by the consciousness that self-assertion would outrage still further the same delicate instinct. Were there a brutal attitude of hate or of ferocious attack, the feminine response of fear or repulsion is simple and spontaneous. But when the keen sting comes through the finer sensibilities, from a hand which, by all known traditions and ideals of propriety, should have been trained to reverence and respect them, the condemnation of man's inhumanity to woman is increased and embittered by the knowledge of personal identity with a race of beings so fallen.

I purposely forbear to mention instances of personal violence to colored women travelling in less civilized sections of our country, where women have been forcibly ejected from cars, thrown out of seats, their garments rudely torn, their person wantonly and cruelly injured. America is large and must for some time yet endure its out-of-the-way jungles of barbarism as Africa its uncultivated tracts of marsh and malaria. There are murderers and thieves and villains in both London and Paris. Humanity from the first has had its vultures and sharks, and representatives of the fraternity who prey upon mankind may be expected no less in America than elsewhere. That this virulence breaks out most readily and commonly against colored persons in this country, is due of course to the fact that they are, generally speaking, weak and can be imposed upon with impunity. Bullies are always cowards at heart and may be credited with a pretty safe instinct in scenting their prey. Besides, society, where it has not exactly said to its dogs 's-s-sik him!' has at least engaged to be looking in another direction or studying the rivers on Mars. It is not of the dogs and their doings, but of society holding the leash that I shall speak. It is those subtle exhalations of atmospheric odors for which woman is accountable, the indefinable, unplaceable aroma which seems to exude from the very pores in her finger tips like the delicate sachet so dexterously hidden and concealed in her linens; the essence of her teaching, guessed rather than read, so adroitly is the lettering and wording manipulated; it is the undertones of the picture laid finely on by woman's own practiced hand, the reflection of the lights and shadows on her own brow; it is, in a word, the reputation of our nation for general politeness and good manners and of our fellow citizens to be somewhat more than cads or snobs that shall engage our present study. There can be no true test of national courtesy without travel. Impressions and conclusions based on provincial traits and characteristics can thus be modified and generalized. Moreover, the weaker and less influential the experimenter, the more exact and scientific the deductions. Courtesy 'for revenue only' is not politeness, but diplomacy. Any rough can assume civility toward those of 'his set,' and does not hesitate to carry it even to servility toward those in whom he recognizes a possible patron or his master in power, wealth, rank, or influence. But, as the chemist prefers distilled H_2O in testing solutions to avoid complications and unwarranted reactions, so the Black Woman holds that her femininity linked with the impossibility of popular affinity or unexpected attraction through position and influence in her case makes her a touchstone of American courtesy exceptionally pure and singularly free from extraneous modifiers. The man who is courteous to her is so, not because of anything he hopes or fears or sees, but because he is a gentleman.

I would eliminate also from the discussion all uncharitable reflections upon the orderly execution of laws existing in certain states of this Union, requiring persons known to be colored to ride in one car, and persons supposed to be white in another. A good citizen may use his influence to have existing laws and statutes changed or modified, but a public servant must not be blamed for obeying orders. A railroad conductor is not asked to dictate measures, nor to make and pass laws. His bread and butter are conditioned on his managing his part of the machinery as he is told to do. If, therefore, I found myself in that compartment of a train designated by the sovereign law of the state for presumable Caucasians, and for colored persons only when traveling in the capacity of nurses and maids, should a conductor inform me, as a gentleman might, that I had made a mistake, and offer to show me the proper car for black ladies; I might wonder at the expensive arrangements of the company and of the state in providing special and separate accommodations for the transportation of the various hues of humanity, but I certainly could not take it as a want of courtesy on the conductor's part that he gave the information. It is true, public sentiment precedes and begets all laws, good or bad; and on the ground I have taken, our women are to be credited largely as teachers and moulders of public sentiment. But when a law has passed and received the sanction of the land, there is nothing for our officials to do but enforce it till repealed; and I for one, as a loyal American citizen, will give those officials cheerful support and ready sympathy in the discharge of their duty. But when a great burly six feet of masculinity with sloping shoulders and unkempt beard swaggers in, and, throwing a roll of tobacco into one corner of his jaw, growls out at me over the paper I am reading, 'Here gurl,' (I am past thirty) 'you better git out 'n dis kyar 'f yer don't, I'll put yer out,' – my mental annotation is Here's an American citizen who has been badly trained. He is sadly lacking in both 'sweetness' and 'light'; and when in the same section of our enlightened and progressive country, I see from the car window, working on private estates, convicts from the state penitentiary, among them squads of boys from fourteen to eighteen years of age in a chain-gang, their feet chained together and heavy blocks attached – not in 1850, but in 1890, '91 and '92, I make a note on the flyleaf of my memorandum, The women in this section should organize a Society for the Prevention of Cruelty to Human Beings, and disseminate civilizing tracts, and send throughout the region apostles of anti-barbarism for the propagation of humane and enlightened ideas. And when farther on in the same section our train stops at a dilapidated station, rendered yet more unsightly by dozens of loafers with their hands in their pockets while a productive soil and inviting climate beckon in vain to industry; and when, looking a little more closely, I see two dingy little rooms with, 'FOR LADIES' swinging over one and 'FOR COLORED PEOPLE' over the other; while wondering under which head I come, I notice a little way off the only hotel proprietor of the place whittling a pine stick as he sits with one leg thrown across an empty goods box; and as my eye falls on a sample room next door which seems to be driving the only wide-awake and popular business of the commonwealth, I cannot help ejaculating under my breath, 'What a field for the missionary woman.' I know that if by any fatality I should be obliged to lie over at that station, and, driven by hunger, should be compelled to seek refreshments or the bare necessaries of life at the only public accommodation in the town, that same stick-whittler would coolly inform me, without looking up from his pine splinter, 'We doan uccommodate no niggers hyur.' And yet we are so scandalized at Russia's barbarity and cruelty to the Jews! We pay a man a thousand dollars a night just to make us weep, by a recital of such heathenish inhumanity as is practiced on Sclavonic soil.

A recent writer on Eastern nations says: 'If we take through the earth's temperate zone, a belt of country whose northern and southern edges are determined by certain limiting isotherms, not more than half the width of the zone apart, we shall find that we have included in a relatively small extent of surface almost all the nations of note in the world, past or present. Now, if we examine this belt and compare the different parts of it with one another, we shall be struck by a remarkable fact. The peoples inhabiting it grow steadily more personal as we go west. So unmistakable is this gradation, that one is almost tempted to ascribe it to cosmical rather than to human causes. It is as marked as the change in color of the human complexion observable along any meridian, which ranges from black, at the equator to blonde toward the pole. In like manner the sense of self grows more intense as we follow in the wake of the setting sun, and fades steadily as we advance into the dawn. America, Europe, the Levant, India, Japan, each is less personal than the one before . . . That politeness should be one of the most marked results of impersonality may appear surprising, yet a slight examination will show it to be a fact. Considered a priori, the connection is not far to seek. Impersonality by lessening the interest in one's self, induces one to take an interest in others. Looked at a posteriori, we find that where the one trait exists the other is most developed, while an absence of the second seems to prevent the full growth of the first. This is true both in general and in detail. Courtesy increases as we travel eastward round the world, coincidently with a decrease in the sense of self. Asia is more courteous than Europe, Europe than America. Particular races show the same concomitance of characteristics. France, the most impersonal nation of Europe, is at the same time the most polite.' And by inference, Americans, the most personal, are the least courteous nation on the globe.

The Black Woman had reached this same conclusion by an entirely different route; but it is gratifying to vanity, nevertheless, to find one's self sustained by both science and philosophy in a conviction, wrought in by hard experience, and yet too apparently audacious to be entertained even as a stealthy surmise. In fact the Black Woman was emboldened some time since by a well put and timely article from an Editor's Drawer on the 'Mannerless Sex,' to give the world the benefit of some of her experience with the 'Mannerless Race'; but since Mr Lowell shows so conclusively that the entire Land of the West is a mannerless continent, I have determined to plead with our women, the mannerless sex on this mannerless continent, to institute a reform by placing immediately in our national curricula a department for teaching GOOD MANNERS.

Now, am I right in holding the American Woman responsible? Is it true that the exponents of woman's advancement, the leaders in woman's thought, the preachers and teachers of all woman's reforms, can teach this nation to be courteous, to be pitiful, having compassion one of another, not rendering evil for inoffensiveness, and railing in proportion to the improbability of being struck back; but contrariwise, being all of one mind, to love as brethren?

I think so.

It may require some heroic measures, and like all revolutions will call for a determined front and a courageous, unwavering, stalwart heart on the part of the leaders of the reform.

The 'all' will inevitably stick in the throat of the Southern woman. She must be allowed, please, to except the 'darkey' from the 'all'; it is too bitter a pill with black people in it. You must get the Revised Version to put it, 'love all white people as brethren.' She really could not enter any society on earth, or in heaven above, or in – the waters under the earth, on such unpalatable conditions.

The Black Woman has tried to understand the Southern woman's difficulties; to put herself in her place, and to be as fair, as charitable, and as free from prejudice in judging her antipathies, as she would have others in regard to her own. She has honestly weighed the apparently sincere excuse, 'But you must remember that these people were once our slaves'; and that other, 'But civility towards the Negroes will bring us on social equality with them.'

These are the two bugbears; or rather, the two humbugbears: for, though each is founded on a most glaring fallacy, one would think they were words to conjure with, so potent and irresistible is their spell as an argument at the North as well as in the South.

One of the most singular facts about the unwritten history of this country is the consummate ability with which Southern influence, Southern ideas and Southern ideals, have from the very beginning even up to the present day, dictated to and domineered over the brain and sinew of this nation. Without wealth, without education, without inventions, arts, sciences, or industries, without well-nigh every one of the progressive ideas and impulses which have made this country great, prosperous and happy, personally indolent and practically stupid, poor in everything but bluster and self-esteem, the Southerner has nevertheless with Italian finesse and exquisite skill, uniformly and invariably, so manipulated Northern sentiment as to succeed sooner or later in carrying his point and shaping the policy of this government to suit his purposes. Indeed, the Southerner is a magnificent manager of men, a born educator. For two hundred and fifty years he trained to his hand a people whom he made absolutely his own, in body, mind, and sensibility. He so insinuated differences and distinctions among them, that their personal attachment for him was stronger than for their own brethren and fellow sufferers. He made it a crime for two or three of them to be gathered together in Christ's name without a white man's supervision, and a felony for one to teach them to read even the Word of Life; and yet they would defend his interest with their life blood; his smile was their happiness, a pat on the shoulder from him their reward. The slightest difference among themselves in condition, circumstances, opportunities, became barriers of jealousy and disunion. He sowed his blood broadcast among them, then pitted mulatto against black, bond against free, house slave against plantation slave, even the slave of one clan against like slave of another clan; till, wholly oblivious of their ability for mutual succor and defense, all became centers of myriad systems of repellent forces, having but one sentiment in common, and that their entire subjection to that master hand.

And he not only managed the black man, he also hoodwinked the white man, the tourist and investigator who visited his lordly estates. The slaves were doing well, in fact couldn't be happier, – plenty to eat, plenty to drink, comfortably housed and clothed – they wouldn't be free if they could; in short, in his broad brimmed plantation hat and easy aristocratic smoking gown, he made you think him a veritable patriarch in the midst of a lazy, well fed, good natured, over-indulged tenantry.

Then, too, the South represented blood – not red blood, but blue blood. The difference is in the length of the stream and your distance from its source. If your own father was a pirate, a robber, a murderer, his hands are dyed in red blood, and you don't say very much about it. But if your great great great grandfather's grandfather stole and pillaged and slew, and you can prove it, your blood has become blue and you are at great pains to establish the relationship. So the South had neither silver nor gold, but she had blood; and she paraded it with so much gusto that the substantial little Puritan maidens of the North, who had been making bread and canning currants and not thinking of blood the least bit, began to hunt up the records of the Mayflower to see if some of the passengers thereon could not claim the honor of having been one of William the Conqueror's brigands, when he killed the last of the Saxon kings and, red-handed, stole his crown and his lands. Thus, the ideal from out the Southland brooded over the nation and we sing less lustily than of yore

> 'Kind hearts are more than coronets
> And simple faith than Norman blood.'

In politics, the two great forces, commerce and empire, which would otherwise have shaped the destiny of the country, have been made to pander and cater to Southern notions. 'Cotton is King' meant the South must be allowed to dictate or there would be no fun. Every statesman from 1830 to 1860 exhausted his genius in persuasion and compromises to smooth out her ruffled temper and gratify her petulant demands. But like a sullen younger sister, the South has pouted and sulked and cried: 'I won't play with you now; so there!' and the big brother at the North has coaxed and compromised and given in, and – ended by letting her have her way. Until 1860 she had as her pet an institution which it was death by the law to say anything about, except that it was divinely instituted, inaugurated by Noah, sanctioned by Abraham, approved by Paul, and just ideally perfect in every way. And when, to preserve the autonomy of the family arrangements, in '61,'62 and '63, it became necessary for the big brother to administer a little wholesome correction and set the obstreperous Miss vigorously down in her seat again, she assumed such an air of injured innocence, and melted away so lugubriously, the big brother has done nothing since but try to sweeten and pacify and laugh her back into a companionable frame of mind.

Father Lincoln did all he could to get her to repent of her petulance and behave herself. He even promised she might keep her pet, so disagreeable to all the neighbors and hurtful even to herself, and might manage it at home to suit herself, if she would only listen to reason and be just tolerably nice. But, no – she was going to leave and set up for herself; she didn't propose to be meddled with; and so, of course, she had to be spanked. Just a little at first – didn't mean to hurt, merely to teach her who was who. But she grew so ugly, and kicked and fought and scratched so outrageously, and seemed so determined to smash up the whole business, the head of the family got red in the face, and said: 'Well, now, he couldn't have any more of that foolishness. Arabella must just behave herself or take the consequences.' And after the spanking, Arabella sniffed and whimpered and pouted, and the big brother bit his lip, looked half ashamed, and said: 'Well, I didn't want to hurt you. You needn't feel so awfully bad about it, I only did it for your good. You know I wouldn't do anything to displease you if I could help it; but you would insist on making the row, and so I just had to. Now, there – there – let's be friends!' and he put his great strong arms about her and just dared anybody to refer to that little unpleasantness – he'd show them a thing or two. Still Arabella sulked, – till the rest of the family decided she might just keep her pets, and manage her own affairs and nobody should interfere.

So now, if one intimates that some clauses of the Constitution are a dead letter at the South and that only the name and support of that pet institution are changed while the fact and essence, minus the expense and responsibility, remain, he is quickly told to mind his own business and informed that he is waving the bloody shirt.

Even twenty-five years after the fourteenth and fifteenth amendments to our Constitution, a man who has been most unequivocal in his out-spoken condemnation of the wrongs regularly and systematically heaped on the oppressed race in this country, and on all even most remotely connected with them – a man whom we had thought our staunchest friend and most noble champion and defender – after a two weeks' trip in Georgia and Florida immediately gives signs of the fatal inception of the virus. Not even the chance traveller from England or Scotland escapes. The arch-manipulator takes him under his special watch-care and training, uses up his stock arguments and gives object lessons with his choicest specimens of Negro depravity and worthlessness; takes him through what, in New York, would be called 'the slums,' and would predicate there nothing but the duty of enlightened Christians to send out their light and emulate their Master's aggressive labors of love; but in Georgia is denominated 'our terrible problem, which people of the North so little understand, yet vouchsafe so much gratuitous advice about.' With an injured air he shows the stupendous and atrocious mistake of reasoning about these people as if they were just ordinary human beings, and amenable to the tenets of the Gospel; and not long after the inoculation begins to work, you hear this old-time friend of the oppressed delivering himself something after this fashion: 'Ah, well, the South must be left to manage the Negro. She is most directly concerned and must understand her problem better than outsiders. We must not meddle. We must be very careful not to widen the breaches. The Negro is not worth a feud between brothers and sisters.'

Lately a great national and international movement characteristic of this age and country, a movement based on the inherent right of every soul to its own highest development, I mean the movement making for Woman's full, free, and complete emancipation, has, after much courting, obtained the gracious smile of the Southern woman – I beg her pardon – the Southern lady.

She represents blood, and of course could not be expected to leave that out; and firstly and foremostly she must not, in any organization she may design to grace with her presence, be asked to associate with 'these people who were once her slaves.'

Now the Southern woman (I may be pardoned, being one myself) was never renowned for her reasoning powers, and it is not surprising that just a little picking will make her logic fall to pieces even here.

In the first place she imagines that because her grandfather had slaves who were black, all the blacks in the world of every shade and tint were once in the position of her slaves. This is as bad as the Irishman who was about to kill a peaceable Jew in the streets of Cork, – having just learned that Jews slew his Redeemer. The black race constitutes one-seventh the known population of the globe; and there are representatives of it here as else-where who were never in bondage at any time to any man, – whose blood is as blue and lineage as noble as any, even that of the white lady of the South. That her slaves were black and she despises her slaves, should no more argue antipathy to all dark people and peoples, than that Guiteau, an assassin, was white, and I hate assassins, should make me hate all persons more or less white. The objection shows a want of clear discrimination.

The second fallacy in the objection grows out of the use of an ambiguous middle, as the logicians would call it, or assigning a double signification to the term 'Social equality.'

Civility to the Negro implies social equality. I am opposed to associating with dark persons on terms of social equality. Therefore, I abrogate civility to the Negro. This is like

> Light is opposed to darkness.
> Feathers are light.
> Ergo, Feathers are opposed to darkness.

The 'social equality' implied by civility to the Negro is a very different thing from forced association with him socially. Indeed it seems to me that the mere application of a little cold common sense would show that uncongenial social environments could by no means be forced on any one. I do not, and cannot be made to associate with all dark persons, simply on the ground that I am dark; and I presume the Southern lady can imagine some whose faces are white, with whom she would no sooner think of chatting unreservedly than, were it possible, with a veritable 'darkey.' Such things must and will always be left to individual election. No law, human or divine, can legislate for or against them. Like seeks like; and I am sure with the Southern lady's antipathies at their present temperature, she might enter ten thousand organizations besprinkled with colored women without being any more deflected by them than by the proximity of a stone. The social equality scare then is all humbug, conscious or unconscious, I know not which. And were it not too bitter a thought to utter here, I might add that the overtures for forced association in the past history of these two races were not made by the manacled black man, nor by the silent and suffering black woman!

When I seek food in a public café or apply for first-class accommodations on a railway train, I do so because my physical necessities are identical with those of other human beings of like constitution and temperament, and crave satisfaction, I go because I want food, or I want comfort – not because I want association with those who frequent these places; and I can see no more 'social equality' in buying lunch at the same restaurant, or riding in a common car, than there is in paying for dry goods at the same counter or walking on the same street.

The social equality which means forced or unbidden association would be as much deprecated and as strenuously opposed by the circle in which I move as by the most hide-bound Southerner in the land. Indeed I have been more than once annoyed by the inquisitive white interviewer, who, with spectacles on nose and pencil and note-book in hand, comes to get some 'points' about 'your people.'

My 'people' are just like other people – indeed, too like for their own good. They hate, they love, they attract and repel, they climb or they grovel, struggle or drift, aspire or despair, endure in hope or curse in vexation, exactly like all the rest of unregenerate humanity. Their likes and dislikes are as strong; their antipathies – and prejudices too I fear, are as pronounced as you will find anywhere; and the entrance to the inner sanctuary of their homes and hearts is as jealously guarded against profane intrusion.

What the dark man wants then is merely to live his own life, in his own world, with his own chosen companions, in whatever of comfort, luxury, or emoluments his talent or his money can in an impartial market secure. Has he wealth, he does not want to be forced into inconvenient or unsanitary sections of cities to buy a home and rear his family. Has he art, he does not want to be cabined and cribbed into emulation with the few who merely happen to have his complexion. His talent aspires to study without proscription the masters of all ages and to rub against the broadest and fullest movements of his own day.

Has he religion, he does not want to be made to feel that there is a white Christ and a black Christ, a white Heaven and a black Heaven, a white Gospel and a black Gospel, – but the one ideal of perfect manhood and womanhood, the one universal longing for development and growth, the one desire for being, and being better, the one great yearning, aspiring, outreaching, in all the heartthrobs of humanity in whatever race or clime.

A recent episode in the Corcoran art gallery at the American capital is to the point. A colored woman who had shown marked ability in drawing and coloring, was advised by her teacher, himself an artist of no mean rank, to apply for admission to the Corcoran school in order to study the models and to secure other advantages connected with the organization. She accordingly sent a written application accompanied by specimens of her drawings, the usual modus operandi in securing admission.

The drawings were examined by the best critics and pronounced excellent, and a ticket of admission was immediately issued together with a highly complimentary reference to her work.

The next day my friend, congratulating her country and herself that at least in the republic of art no caste existed, presented her ticket of admission in propria persona. There was a little preliminary side play in Delsarte pantomime, – aghast – incredulity – wonder; then the superintendent told her in plain unartistic English that of course he had not dreamed a colored person could do such work, and had he suspected the truth of admission; that, to be right frank, the ticket would have to be cancelled, – she could under no condition be admitted to the studio.

Can it be possible that even art in America is to be tainted by this shrivelling caste spirit? If so, what are we coming to? Can any one conceive a Shakespeare, a Michael Angelo, or a Beethoven putting away any fact of simple merit because the thought, or the suggestion, or the creation emanated from a soul with an unpleasing exterior?

What is it that makes the great English bard pre-eminent as the photographer of the human soul? Where did he learn the universal language, so that Parthians, Medes and Elamites, and the dwellers in Mesopotamia, in Egypt and Libya, in Crete and Arabia do hear every one in our own tongue the wonderful revelations of this myriad mind? How did he learn our language? Is it not that his own soul was infinitely receptive to Nature, the dear old nurse, in all her protean forms? Did he not catch and reveal her own secret by his sympathetic listening as she 'would constantly sing a more wonderful song or tell a more marvellous tale' in the souls he met around him?

'Stand off! I am better than thou!' has never yet painted a true picture, nor written a thrilling song, nor given a pulsing, a soul-burning sermon. 'Tis only sympathy, another name for love, – that one poor word which, as George Eliot says, 'expresses so much of human insight' – that can interpret either man or matter.

It was Shakespeare's own all-embracing sympathy, that infinite receptivity of his, and native, all-comprehending appreciation, which proved a key to unlock and open every soul that came within his radius. And he received as much as he gave. His own stores were infinitely enriched thereby. For it is decreed

> Man like the vine supported lives,
> The strength he gains is from th' embrace he gives.

It is only through clearing the eyes from bias and prejudice, and becoming one with the great all pervading soul of the universe that either art or science can 'Read what is still unread in the manuscripts of God.' No true artist can allow himself to be narrowed and provincialized by deliberately shutting out any class of facts or subjects through prejudice against externals. And American art, American science, American literature can never be founded in truth, the universal beauty; can never learn to speak a language intelligible in all climes and for all ages, till this paralyzing grip of caste prejudice is loosened from its vitals, and the healthy sympathetic eye is taught to look out on the great universe as holding no favorites and no black beasts, but bearing in each plainest or loveliest feature the handwriting of its God.

And this is why, as it appears to me, woman in her lately acquired vantage ground for speaking an earnest helpful word, can do this country no deeper and truer and more lasting good than by bending all her energies to thus broadening, humanizing, and civilizing her native land.

'Except ye become as little children' is not a pious precept, but an inexorable law of the universe. God's kingdoms are all sealed to the seedy, moss-grown mind of self-satisfied maturity. Only the little child in spirit, the simple, receptive, educable mind can enter. Preconceived notions, blinding prejudices, and shrivelling antipathies must be wiped out, and the cultivable soul made a tabula rasa for whatever lesson great Nature has to teach.

This, too, is why I conceive the subject to have been unfortunately worded which was chosen by Miss Shaw at the Woman's Council and which stands at the head of this chapter.

Miss Shaw is one of the most powerful of our leaders, and we feel her voice should give no uncertain note. Woman should not, even by inference, or for the sake of argument, seem to disparage what is weak. For woman's cause is the cause of the weak; and when all the weak shall have received their due consideration, then woman will have her 'rights,' and the Indian will have his rights, and the Negro will have his rights, and all the strong will have learned at last to deal justly, to love mercy, and to walk humbly; and our fair land will have been taught the secret of universal courtesy which is after all nothing but the art, the science and the religion of regarding one's neighbor as one's self, and to do for him as we would, were conditions swapped, that he do for us.

It cannot seem less than a blunder, whenever the exponents of a great reform or the harbingers of a noble advance in thought and effort allow themselves to seem distorted by a narrow view of their own aims and principles. All prejudices, whether of race, sect or sex, class pride and caste distinctions are the belittling inheritance and badge of snobs and prigs.

The philosophic mind seem that its own 'rights' are the rights of humanity. That in the universe of God nothing trivial is or mean; and the recognition it seeks is not through the robber and wild beast adjustment of the survival of the bullies but through the universal application ultimately of the Golden Rule.

Not unfrequently has it happened that the impetus of a mighty thought wave has done the execution meant by its Creator in spite of the weak and distorted perception of its human embodiment. It is not strange if reformers, who, after all, but think God's thoughts after him, have often 'builded

90

more wisely than they knew;' and while fighting consciously for only a narrow gateway for themselves, have been driven forward by that irresistible 'Power not ourselves which makes for righteousness' to open a high road for humanity. It was so with our sixteenth century reformers. The fathers of the Reformation had no idea that they were inciting an insurrection of the human mind against all domination. None would have been more shocked than they at our nineteenth century deductions from their sixteenth century premises. Emancipation of mind and freedom of thought would have been as appalling to them as it was distasteful to the pope. They were right, they argued, to rebel against Romish absolutism – because Romish preaching and Romish practicing were wrong. They denounced popes for hacking heretics and forthwith began themselves to roast witches. The Spanish Inquisition in the hands of Philip and Alva was an institution of the devil; wielded by the faithful, it would become quite another thing. The only 'rights' they were broad enough consciously to fight for was the right to substitute the absolutism of their conceptions, their party, their 'ism' for an authority whose teaching they conceived to be corrupt and vicious. Persecution for a belief was wrong only when the persecutors were wrong and the persecuted right. The sacred prerogative of the individual to decide on matters of belief they did not dream of maintaining. Universal tolerance and its twin, universal charity, were not conceived yet. The broad foundation stone of all human rights, the great democratic principle 'A man's a man, and his own sovereign for a' that' they did not dare enunciate. They were incapable of drawing up a Declaration of Independence for humanity. The Reformation to the Reformers meant one bundle of authoritative opinions vs. another bundle of authoritative opinions. Justification by faith, vs. justification by ritual. Submission to Calvin vs. submission to the Pope. English and Germans vs. the Italians.

To our eye, viewed through a vista of three centuries, it was the death wrestle of the principle of thought enslavement in the throttling grasp of personal freedom; it was the great Emancipation Day of human belief, man's intellectual Independence Day, prefiguring and finally compelling the world-wide enfranchisement of his body and all its activities. Not Protestant vs. Catholic, then; not Luther vs. Leo, not Dominicans vs. Augustinians, nor Geneva vs. Rome; – but humanity rationally free, vs. the clamps of tradition and superstition which had manacled and muzzled it.

The cause of freedom is not the cause of a race or a sect, a party or a class, – it is the cause of human kind, the very birthright of humanity. Now unless we are greatly mistaken the Reform of our day, known as the Woman's Movement, is essentially such an Embodiment, if its pioneers could only realize it, of the universal good. And specially important is it that there be no confusion of ideas among its leaders as to its scope and universality. All mists must be cleared from the eyes of woman if she is to be a teacher of morals and manners: the former strikes its roots in the individual and its training and pruning may be accomplished by classes; but the latter is to lubricate the joints and minimize the friction of society, and it is important and fundamental that there be no chromatic or other aberration when the teacher is settling the point, 'Who is my neighbor?'

It is not the intelligent woman vs. the ignorant woman; nor the white woman vs. the black, the brown, and the red, – it is not even the cause of woman vs. man. Nay, 'tis woman's strongest vindication for speaking that the world needs to hear her voice. It would be subversive of every human interest that the cry of one-half the human family be stifled. Woman in stepping from the pedestal of statue-like inactivity in the domestic shrine, and daring to think and move and speak, – to undertake to help shape, mold, and direct the thought of her age, is merely completing the circle of the world's vision. Here is every interest that has lacked an interpreter and a defender. Her cause is linked with that of every agony that has been dumb – every wrong that needs a voice.

It is no fault of man's that he has not been able to see truth from her standpoint. It does credit both to his head and heart that no greater mistakes have been committed or even wrongs perpetrated while she sat making tatting and snipping paper flowers. Man's own innate chivalry and the mutual interdependence of their interests have insured his treating her cause, in the main at least, as his own. And he is pardonably surprised and even a little chagrined, perhaps, to find his legislation not considered 'perfectly lovely' in every respect. But in any case his work is only impoverished by her remaining dumb. The world has had to limp along with the wobbling gait and one-sided hesitancy of a man with one eye. Suddenly the bandage is removed from the other eye and the whole body is filled with light. It sees a circle where before it saw a segment. The darkened eye restored, every member rejoices with it.

What a travesty of its case for this eye to become plaintiff in a suit, Eye vs. Foot. 'There is that dull clod, the foot, allowed to roam at will, free and untrammelled; while I, the source and medium of light, brilliant and beautiful, am fettered in darkness and doomed to desuetude.' The great burly black man, ignorant and gross and depraved, is allowed to vote; while the franchise is withheld from the intelligent and refined, the pure-minded and lofty souled white woman. Even the untamed and untamable Indian of the prairie, who can answer nothing but 'ugh' to great economic and civic questions is thought by some worthy to wield the ballot which is still denied the Puritan maid and the first lady of Virginia.

Is not this hitching our wagon to something much lower than a star? Is not woman's cause broader, and deeper, and grander, than a blue stock-ing debate or an aristocratic pink tea? Why should woman become plaintiff in a suit versus the Indian, or the Negro or any other race or class who have been crushed under the iron heel of Anglo-Saxon power and selfishness? If the Indian has been wronged and cheated by the puissance of this American government, it is woman's mission to plead with her country to cease to do evil and to pay its honest debts. If the Negro has been deceitfully cajoled or inhumanly cuffed according to selfish expedi-ency or capricious antipathy, let it be woman's mission to plead that he be met as a man and honestly given half the road. If woman's own happiness has been ignored or misunderstood in our country's legislating for bread winners, for rum sellers, for property holders, for the family relations, for any, or all the interests that touch her vitally, let her rest her plea, not on Indian inferiority, nor on Negro depravity, but on the obligation of legisla-tors to do for her as they would have others do for them were relations reversed. Let her try to teach her country that every interest in this world is entitled at least to a respectful hearing, that every sentiency is worthy of its own gratification, that a helpless cause should not be trampled down, nor a bruised reed broken; and when the right of the individual is made sacred, when the image of God in human form, whether in marble or in clay, whether in alabaster or in ebony, is consecrated and inviolable, when men have been taught to look beneath the rags and grime, the pomp and pageantry of mere circumstance and have regard unto the celestial kernel uncontaminated at the core, – when race, color, sex, condition, are realized to be the accidents, not the substance of life, and consequently as not obscuring or modifying the inalienable title to life, liberty, and pursuit of happiness, – then is mastered the science of politeness, the art of courteous contact, which is naught but the practical application of the principal of benevolence, the back bone and marrow of all religion; then woman's lesson is taught and woman's cause is won – not the white woman nor the black woman nor the red woman, but the cause of every man or woman who has writhed silently under a mighty wrong. The pleading of the American woman for the right and the opportunity to employ the American method of influencing the disposal to be made of herself, her property, her children in civil, economic, or domestic relations is thus seen to be based on a principle as broad as the human race and as old as human society. Her wrongs are thus indissolubly linked with all undefended woe, all helpless suffering, and the plenitude of her 'rights' will mean the final triumph of all right over might, the supremacy of the moral forces of reason and justice and love in the government of the nation.

God hasten the day.

21

CHARLOTTE PERKINS GILMAN

Born 1860, Hartford, Connecticut, United States of America
Died 1935, Pasadena, California, United States of America

The Yellow Wall-paper
1892

It is very seldom that mere ordinary people like John and myself secure ancestral halls for the summer.

A colonial mansion, a hereditary estate, I would say a haunted house, and reach the height of romantic felicity – but that would be asking too much of fate!

Still I will proudly declare that there is something queer about it.

Else, why should it be let so cheaply? And why have stood so long untenanted?

John laughs at me, of course, but one expects that in marriage.

John is practical in the extreme. He has no patience with faith, an intense horror of superstition, and he scoffs openly at any talk of things not to be felt and seen and put down in figures.

John is a physician, and *perhaps* – (I would not say it to a living soul, of course, but this is dead paper and a great relief to my mind –) *perhaps* that is one reason I do not get well faster.

You see he does not believe I am sick!

And what can one do?

If a physician of high standing, and one's own husband, assures friends and relatives that there is really nothing the matter with one but temporary nervous depression – a slight hysterical tendency – what is one to do?

My brother is also a physician, and also of high standing, and he says the same thing.

So I take phosphates or phosphites – whichever it is, and tonics, and journeys, and air, and exercise and am absolutely forbidden to 'work' until I am well again.

Personally, I disagree with their ideas.

Personally, I believe that congenial work, with excitement and change, would do me good.

But what is one to do?

I did write for a while in spite of them; but it *does* exhaust me a good deal – having to be so sly about it, or else meet with heavy opposition.

I sometimes fancy that in my condition if I had less opposition and more society and stimulus – but John says the very worst thing I can do is to think about my condition, and I confess it always makes me feel bad.

So I will let it alone and talk about the house.

The most beautiful place! It is quite alone, standing well back from the road, quite three miles from the village. It makes me think of English places that you read about, for there are hedges and walls and gates that lock, and lots of separate little houses for the gardeners and people.

There is a *delicious* garden! I never saw such a garden – large and shady, full of box-bordered paths, and lined with long grape-covered arbors with seats under them.

There were greenhouses, too, but they are all broken now.

There was some legal trouble, I believe, something about the heirs and co-heirs; anyhow, the place has been empty for years.

That spoils my ghostliness, I am afraid, but I don't care – there is something strange about the house – I can feel it.

I even said so to John one moonlight evening, but he said what I felt was a *draught*, and shut the window.

I get unreasonably angry with John sometimes. I'm sure I never used to be so sensitive. I think it is due to this nervous condition.

But John says if I feel so, I shall neglect proper self-control; so, I take pains to control myself – before him, at least, and that makes me very tired.

I don't like our room a bit. I wanted one downstairs that opened on the piazza and had roses all over the window, and such pretty old-fashioned chintz hangings! but John would not hear of it.

He said there was only one window and not room for two beds, and no near room for him if he took another.

He is very careful and loving, and hardly lets me stir without special direction.

I have a schedule prescription for each hour in the day; he takes all care from me, and so I feel basely ungrateful not to value it more.

He said we came here solely on my account, that I was to have perfect rest and all the air I could get. 'Your exercise depends on your strength, my dear,' said he, 'and your food somewhat on your appetite; but air you can absorb all the time.' So we took the nursery at the top of the house.

It is a big, airy room, the whole floor nearly, with windows that look all ways, and air and sunshine galore. It was nursery first and then play-room and gymnasium, I should judge; for the windows are barred for little children, and there are rings and things in the walls.

The paint and paper look as if a boys' school had used it. It is stripped off – the paper – in great patches all around the head of my bed, about as far as I can reach, and in a great place on the other side of the room low down. I never saw a worse paper in my life.

One of those sprawling flamboyant patterns committing every artistic sin.

It is dull enough to confuse the eye in following, pronounced enough to constantly irritate and provoke study, and when you follow the lame uncertain curves for a little distance they suddenly commit suicide – plunge off at outrageous angles, destroy themselves in unheard of contradictions.

The color is repellant, almost revolting; a smouldering unclean yellow, strangely faded by the slow-turning sunlight.

It is a dull yet lurid orange in some places, a sickly sulphur tint in others.

No wonder the children hated it! I should hate it myself if I had to live in this room long.

There comes John, and I must put this away, – he hates to have me write a word.

We have been here two weeks, and I haven't felt like writing before, since that first day.

I am sitting by the window now, up in this atrocious nursery, and there is nothing to hinder my writing as much as I please, save lack of strength.

John is away all day, and even some nights when his cases are serious.

I am glad my case is not serious!

But these nervous troubles are dreadfully depressing.

John does not know how much I really suffer. He knows there is no *reason* to suffer, and that satisfies him.

Of course it is only nervousness. It does weigh on me so not to do my duty in any way!

I meant to be such a help to John, such a real rest and comfort, and here I am a comparative burden already!

Nobody would believe what an effort it is to do what little I am able, – to dress and entertain, and order things.

It is fortunate Mary is so good with the baby. Such a dear baby!

And yet I *cannot* be with him, it makes me so nervous.

I suppose John never was nervous in his life. He laughs at me so about this wall-paper!

At first he meant to repaper the room, but afterwards he said that I was letting it get the better of me, and that nothing was worse for a nervous patient than to give way to such fancies.

He said that after the wall-paper was changed it would be the heavy bedstead, and then the barred windows, and then that gate at the head of the stairs, and so on.

'You know the place is doing you good,' he said, 'and really, dear, I don't care to renovate the house just for a three months' rental.'

'Then do let us go downstairs,' I said, 'there are such pretty rooms there.'

Then he took me in his arms and called me a blessed little goose, and said he would go down to the cellar, if I wished, and have it whitewashed into the bargain.

But he is right enough about the beds and windows and things.

It is an airy and comfortable room as any one need wish, and, of course, I would not be so silly as to make him uncomfortable just for a whim.

I'm really getting quite fond of the big room, all but that horrid paper.

Out of one window I can see the garden, those mysterious deep-shaded arbors, the riotous old-fashioned flowers, and bushes and gnarly trees.

Out of another I get a lovely view of the bay and a little private wharf belonging to the estate. There is a beautiful shaded lane that runs down there from the house. I always fancy I see people walking in these numerous paths and arbors, but John has cautioned me not to give way to fancy in the least. He says that with my imaginative power and habit of story-making, a nervous weakness like mine is sure to lead to all manner of excited fancies, and that I ought to use my will and good sense to check the tendency. So I try.

I think sometimes that if I were only well enough to write a little it would relieve the press of ideas and rest me.

But I find I get pretty tired when I try.

It is so discouraging not to have any advice and companionship about my work. When I get really well, John says we will ask Cousin Henry and Julia down for a long visit; but he says he would as soon put fireworks in my pillow-case as to let me have those stimulating people about now.

I wish I could get well faster.

But I must not think about that. This paper looks to me as if it *knew* what a vicious influence it had!

There is a recurrent spot where the pattern lolls like a broken neck and two bulbous eyes stare at you upside down.

I get positively angry with the impertinence of it and the everlastingness. Up and down and sideways they crawl, and those absurd, unblinking eyes are everywhere. There is one place where two breadths didn't match, and the eyes go all up and down the line, one a little higher than the other.

I never saw so much expression in an inanimate thing before, and we all know how much expression they have! I used to lie awake as a child and get more entertainment and terror out of blank walls and plain furniture than most children could find in a toy-store.

I remember what a kindly wink the knobs of our big, old bureau used to have, and there was one chair that always seemed like a strong friend.

I used to feel that if any of the other things looked too fierce I could always hop into that chair and be safe.

The furniture in this room is no worse than inharmonious, however, for we had to bring it all from downstairs. I suppose when this was used as a playroom they had to take the nursery things out, and no wonder! I never saw such ravages as the children have made here.

The wall-paper, as I said before, is torn off in spots, and it sticketh closer than a brother – they must have had perseverance as well as hatred.

Then the floor is scratched and gouged and splintered, the plaster itself is dug out here and there, and this great heavy bed which is all we found in the room, looks as if it had been through the wars.

But I don't mind it a bit – only the paper.

There comes John's sister. Such a dear girl as she is, and so careful of me! I must not let her find me writing.

She is a perfect and enthusiastic housekeeper, and hopes for no better profession. I verily believe she thinks it is the writing which made me sick!

But I can write when she is out, and see her a long way off from these windows.

There is one that commands the road, a lovely shaded winding road, and one that just looks off over the country. A lovely country, too, full of great elms and velvet meadows.

This wall-paper has a kind of subpattern in a different shade, a particularly irritating one, for you can only see it in certain lights, and not clearly then.

But in the places where it isn't faded and where the sun is just so – I can see a strange, provoking, formless sort of figure, that seems to skulk about behind that silly and conspicuous front design.

There's sister on the stairs!

Well, the Fourth of July is over! The people are all gone and I am tired out. John thought it might do me good to see a little company, so we just had mother and Nellie and the children down for a week.

Of course I didn't do a thing. Jennie sees to everything now.

But it tired me all the same.

John says if I don't pick up faster he shall send me to Weir Mitchell in the fall.

But I don't want to go there at all. I had a friend who was in his hands once, and she says he is just like John and my brother, only more so!

Besides, it is such an undertaking to go so far.

I don't feel as if it was worth while to turn my hand over for anything, and I'm getting dreadfully fretful and querulous.

I cry at nothing, and cry most of the time.

Of course I don't when John is here, or anybody else, but when I am alone.

And I am alone a good deal just now. John is kept in town very often by serious cases, and Jennie is good and lets me alone when I want her to.

So I walk a little in the garden or down that lovely lane, sit on the porch under the roses, and lie down up here a good deal.

I'm getting really fond of the room in spite of the wall-paper. Perhaps *because* of the wall-paper.

It dwells in my mind so!

I lie here on this great immovable bed – it is nailed down, I believe – and follow that pattern about by the hour. It is as good as gymnastics, I assure you. I start, we'll say, at the bottom, down in the corner over there where it has not been touched, and I determine for the thousandth time that I *will* follow that pointless pattern to some sort of a conclusion.

I know a little of the principle of design, and I know this thing was not arranged on any laws of radiation, or alternation, or repetition, or symmetry, or anything else that I ever heard of.

It is repeated, of course, by the breadths, but not otherwise.

Looked at in one way each breadth stands alone, the bloated curves and flourishes a kind of 'debased Romanesque' with *delirium tremens* go waddling up and down in isolated columns of fatuity.

But, on the other hand, they connect diagonally, and the sprawling outlines run off in great slanting waves of optic horror, like a lot of wallowing seaweeds in full chase.

The whole thing goes horizontally, too, at least it seems so, and I exhaust myself in trying to distinguish the order of its going in that direction.

They have used a horizontal breadth for a frieze, and that adds wonderfully to the confusion.

There is one end of the room where it is almost intact, and there, when the crosslights fade and the low sun shines directly upon it, I can almost fancy radiation after all, the interminable grotesques seem to form around a common centre and rush off in headlong plunges of equal distraction.

It makes me tired to follow it. I will take a nap I guess.

I don't know why I should write this.

I don't want to.

I don't feel able.

And I know John would think it absurd. But I *must* say what I feel and think in some way it is such a relief!

But the effort is getting to be greater than the relief.

Half the time now I am awfully lazy, and lie down ever so much.

John says I mustn't lose my strength, and has me take cod liver oil and lots of tonics and things, to say nothing of ale and wine and rare meat.

Dear John! He loves me very dearly, and hates to have me sick. I tried to have a real earnest reasonable talk with him the other day, and tell him how I wish he would let me go and make a visit to Cousin Henry and Julia.

But he said I wasn't able to go, nor able to stand it after I got there; and I did not make out a very good case for myself, for I was crying before I had finished.

It is getting to be a great effort for me to think straight.

Just this nervous weakness I suppose.

And dear John gathered me up in his arms, and just carried me upstairs and laid me on the bed, and sat by me and read to me till it tired my head.

He said I was his darling and his comfort and all he had, and that I must take care of myself for his sake, and keep well.

He says no one but myself can help me out of it, that I must use my will and self-control and not let any silly fancies run away with me.

There's one comfort, the baby is well and happy, and does not have to occupy this nursery with the horrid wall-paper.

If we had not used it, that blessed child would have!

What a fortunate escape! Why, I wouldn't have a child of mine, an impressionable little thing, live in such a room for worlds.

I never thought of it before, but it is lucky that John kept me here after all, I can stand it so much easier than a baby, you see.

Of course I never mention it to them any more I am too wise, but I keep watch of it all the same.

There are things in that paper that nobody knows but me, or ever will.

Behind that outside pattern the dim shapes get clearer every day.

It is always the same shape, only very numerous.

And it is like a woman stooping down and creeping about behind that pattern. I don't like it a bit. I wonder I begin to think I wish John would take me away from here!

It is so hard to talk with John about my case, because he is so wise, and because he loves me so.

But I tried it last night.

It was moonlight. The moon shines in all around just as the sun does.

I hate to see it sometimes, it creeps so slowly, and always comes in by one window or another.

John was asleep and I hated to waken him, so I kept still and watched the moonlight on that undulating wall-paper till I felt creepy.

The faint figure behind seemed to shake the pattern, just as if she wanted to get out.

I got up softly and went to feel and see if the paper *did* move, and when I came back John was awake.

'What is it, little girl?' 'he said. Don't go walking about like that – you'll get cold.'

I thought it was a good time to talk, so I told him that I really was not gaining here, and that I wished he would take me away.

'Why, darling!' said he, 'our lease will be up in three weeks, and I can't see how to leave before.

'The repairs are not done at home, and I cannot possibly leave town just now. Of course if you were in any danger, I could and would, but you really are better, dear, whether you can see it or not. I am a doctor, dear, and I know. You are gaining flesh and color, your appetite is better, I feel really much easier about you.'

'I don't weigh a bit more,' said I, 'nor' as much; and my appetite may be better in the evening when you are here, but it is worse in the morning when you are away!'

'Bless her little heart!' said he with a big hug, 'she shall be as sick as she pleases! But now let's improve the shining hours by going to sleep, and talk about it in the morning!'

'And you won't go away?' I asked gloomily.

'Why, how can I, dear? It is only three weeks more and then we will take a nice little trip of a few days while Jennie is getting the house ready. Really, dear, you are better!'

'Better in body perhaps –' I began, and stopped short, for he sat up straight and looked at me with such a stern, reproachful look that I could not say another word.

'My darling,' said he, 'I beg of you, for my sake and for our child's sake, as well as for your own, that you will never for one instant let that idea enter your mind! There is nothing so dangerous, so fascinating, to temperament like yours. It is a false and foolish fancy. Can you not trust me as a physician when I tell you so?'

So of course I said no more on that score, and we went to sleep before long. He thought I was asleep first, but I wasn't, and lay there for hours trying to decide whether that front pattern and the back pattern really did move together or separately.

On a pattern like this, by daylight, there is a lack of sequence, a defiance of law, that is a constant irritant to a normal mind.

The color is hideous enough, and unreliable enough, and infuriating enough, but the pattern is torturing.

You think you have mastered it, but just as you get well underway in following, it turns a back-somersault and there you are. It slaps you in the face, knocks you down, and tramples upon you. It is like a bad dream.

The outside pattern is a florid arabesque, reminding one of a fungus. If you can imagine a toadstool in joints, an interminable string of toadstools, budding and sprouting in endless convolutions – why, that is something like it.

That is, sometimes!

There is one marked peculiarity about this paper, a thing nobody seems to notice but myself, and that is that it changes as the light changes.

When the sun shoots in through the east window – I always watch for that first long, straight ray – it changes so quickly that I never can quite believe it.

That is why I watch it always.

By moonlight the moon shines in all night when there is a moon I wouldn't know it was the same paper.

At night in any kind of light, in twilight, candlelight, lamplight, and worst of all by moonlight, it becomes bars! The outside pattern I mean, and the woman behind it is as plain as can be.

I didn't realize for a long time what the thing was that showed behind, that dim sub-pattern, but now I am quite sure it is a woman.

By daylight she is subdued, quiet. I fancy it is the pattern that keeps her so still. It is so puzzling. It keeps me quiet by the hour.

I lie down ever so much now. John says it is good for me, and to sleep all I can.

Indeed he started the habit by making me lie down for an hour after each meal.

It is a very bad habit I am convinced, for you see I don't sleep.

And that cultivates deceit, for I don't tell them I'm awake – O no!

The fact is I am getting a little afraid of John.

He seems very queer sometimes, and even Jennie has an inexplicable look.

It strikes me occasionally, just as a scientific hypothesis, that perhaps it is the paper!

I have watched John when he did not know I was looking, and come into the room suddenly on the most innocent excuses, and I've caught him several times *looking at the paper!* And Jennie too. I caught Jennie with her hand on it once.

She didn't know I was in the room, and when I asked her in a quiet, a very quiet voice, with the most restrained manner possible, what she was doing with the paper – she turned around as if she had been caught stealing, and looked quite angry – asked me why I should frighten her so!

Then she said that the paper stained everything it touched, that she had found yellow smooches on all my clothes and John's, and she wished we would be more careful!

Did not that sound innocent? But I know she was studying that pattern, and I am determined that nobody shall find it out but myself!

Life is very much more exciting now than it used to be. You see I have something more to expect, to look forward to, to watch. I really do eat better, and am more quiet than I was.

John is so pleased to see me improve! He laughed a little the other day, and said I seemed to be flourishing in spite of my wall-paper.

I turned it off with a laugh. I had no intention of telling him it was *because* of the wall-paper – he would make fun of me. He might even want to take me away.

I don't want to leave now until I have found it out. There is a week more, and I think that will be enough.

I'm feeling ever so much better! I don't sleep much at night, for it is so interesting to watch developments; but I sleep a good deal in the daytime.

In the daytime it is tiresome and perplexing.

There are always new shoots on the fungus, and new shades of yellow all over it. I cannot keep count of them, though I have tried conscientiously.

It is the strangest yellow, that wall-paper! It makes me think of all the yellow things I ever saw – not beautiful ones like buttercups, but old foul, bad yellow things.

But there is something else about that paper the smell! I noticed it the moment we came into the room, but with so much air and sun it was not bad. Now we have had a week of fog and rain, and whether the windows are open or not, the smell is here.

It creeps all over the house.

I find it hovering in the dining-room, skulking in the parlor, hiding in the hall, lying in wait for me on the stairs.

It gets into my hair.

Even when I go to ride, if I turn my head suddenly and surprise it – there is that smell!

Such a peculiar odor, too! I have spent hours in trying to analyze it, to find what it smelled like.

It is not bad – at first, and very gentle, but quite the subtlest, most enduring odor I ever met.

In this damp weather it is awful, I wake up in the night and find it hanging over me.

It used to disturb me at first. I thought seriously of burning the house – to reach the smell.

But now I am used to it. The only thing I can think of that it is like is the *color* of the paper! A yellow smell.

There is a very funny mark on this wall, low down, near the mopboard. A streak that runs round the room. It goes behind every piece of furniture, except the bed, a long, straight, even *smooch*, as if it had been rubbed over and over.

I wonder how it was done and who did it, and what they did it for. Round and round and round – round and round and round – it makes me dizzy!

I really have discovered something at last.

Through watching so much at night, when it changes so, I have finally found out.

The front pattern *does* move – and no wonder! The woman behind shakes it!

Sometimes I think there are a great many women behind, and sometimes only one, and she crawls around fast, and her crawling shakes it all over.

Then in the very bright spots she keeps still, and in the very shady spots she just takes hold of the bars and shakes them hard.

And she is all the time trying to climb through. But nobody could climb through that pattern – it strangles so; I think that is why it has so many heads.

They get through, and then the pattern strangles them off and turns them upside down, and makes their eyes white!

If those heads were covered or taken off it would not be half so bad.

I think that woman gets out in the daytime!

And I'll tell you why privately I've seen her!

I can see her out of every one of my windows!

It is the same woman, I know, for she is always creeping, and most women do not creep by daylight.

I see her in that long shaded lane, creeping up and down. I see her in those dark grape arbors, creeping all around the garden.

I see her on that long road under the trees, creeping along, and when a carriage comes she hides under the blackberry vines.

I don't blame her a bit. It must be very humiliating to be caught creeping by daylight!

I always lock the door when I creep by daylight. I can't do it at night, for I know John would suspect something at once.

And John is so queer now, that I don't want to irritate him. I wish he would take another room! Besides, I don't want anybody to get that woman out at night but myself.

I often wonder if I could see her out of all the windows at once.

But, turn as fast as I can only see out of one at one time.

And though I always see her, she *may* be able to creep faster than I can turn!

I have watched her sometimes away off in the open country, creeping as fast as a cloud shadow in a high wind.

*

If only that top pattern could be gotten off from the under one! I mean to try it, little by little.

I have found out another funny thing, but I shan't tell it this time! It does not do to trust people too much.

There are only two more days to get this paper off, and I believe John is beginning to notice. I don't like the look in his eyes.

And I heard him ask Jennie a lot of professional questions about me. She had a very good report to give.

She said I slept a good deal in the daytime.

John knows I don't sleep very well at night, for all I'm so quiet!

He asked me all sorts of questions, too, and pretended to be very loving and kind.

As if I couldn't see through him!

Still, I don't wonder he acts so, sleeping under this paper for three months.

It only interests me, but I feel sure John and Jennie are secretly affected by it.

Hurrah! This is the last day, but it is enough. John is to stay in town over night, and won't be out until this evening.

Jennie wanted to sleep with me – the sly thing! but I told her I should undoubtedly rest better for a night all alone.

That was clever, for really I wasn't alone a bit! As soon as it was moon-light and that poor thing began to crawl and shake the pattern, I got up and ran to help her.

I pulled and she shook, I shook and she pulled, and before morning we had peeled off yards of that paper.

A strip about as high as my head and half around the room.

And then when the sun came and that awful pattern began to laugh at me, I declared I would finish it to-day!

We go away to-morrow, and they are moving all my furniture down again to leave things as they were before.

Jennie looked at the wall in amazement, but I told her merrily that I did it out of pure spite at the vicious thing.

She laughed and said she wouldn't mind doing it herself, but I must not get tired.

How she betrayed herself that time!

But I am here, and no person touches this paper but me, – not *alive!*

She tried to get me out of the room it was too patent!

But I said it was so quiet and empty and clean now that I believed I would lie down again and sleep all I could; and not to wake me even for dinner – I would call when I woke.

So now she is gone, and the servants are gone, and the things are gone, and there is nothing left but that great bedstead nailed down, with the canvas mattress we found on it.

We shall sleep downstairs to-night, and take the boat home tomorrow.

I quite enjoy the room, now it is bare again.

How those children did tear about here!

This bedstead is fairly gnawed!

But I must get to work.

I have locked the door and thrown the key down into the front path.

I don't want to go out, and I don't want to have anybody come in, till John comes.

I want to astonish him.

I've got a rope up here that even Jennie did not find. If that woman does get out, and tries to get away, I can tie her!

But I forgot I could not reach far without anything to stand on!

This bed will *not* move!

I tried to lift and push it until I was lame, and then I got so angry I bit off a little piece at one corner – but it hurt my teeth.

Then I peeled off all the paper I could reach standing on the floor. It sticks horribly and the pattern just enjoys it! All those strangled heads and bulbous eyes and waddling fungus growths just shriek with derision!

I am getting angry enough to do something desperate. To jump out of the window would be admirable exercise, but the bars are too strong even to try.

Besides I wouldn't do it. Of course not. I know well enough that a step like that is improper and might be misconstrued.

I don't like to *look* out of the windows even – there are so many of those creeping women, and they creep so fast.

I wonder if they all come out of that wall-paper as I did?

But I am securely fastened now by my well-hidden rope – you don't get *me* out in the road there!

I suppose I shall have to get back behind the pattern when it comes night, and that is hard!

It is so pleasant to be out in this great room and creep around as I please!

I don't want to go outside. I won't, even if Jennie asks me to.

For outside you have to creep on the ground, and everything is green instead of yellow.

But here I can creep smoothly on the floor, and my shoulder just fits in that long smooch around the wall, so I cannot lose my way.

Why there's John at the door!

It is no use, young man, you can't open it!

How he does call and pound!

Now he's crying for an axe.

It would be a shame to break down that beautiful door!

'John dear!' said I in the gentlest voice, 'the key is down by the front steps, under a plantain leaf!'

That silenced him for a few moments.

Then he said – very quietly indeed, 'Open the door, my darling!'

'I can't,' said I. 'The key is down by the front door under a plantain leaf!'

And then I said it again, several times, very gently and slowly, and said it so often that he had to go and see, and he got it of course, and came in. He stopped short by the door.

'What is the matter?' he cried. 'For God's sake, what are you doing!'

I kept on creeping just the same, but I looked at him over my shoulder.

'I've got out at last,' said I, 'in spite of you and Jane! And I've pulled off most of the paper, so you can't put me back!'

Now why should that man have fainted? But he did, and right across my path by the wall, so that I had to creep over him every time!

22.

EMMA GOLDMAN

Born 1869, Kaunas, Lithuania
Died 1940, Toronto, Canada

Anarchy and the Sex Question
1896

The workingman, whose strength and muscles are so admired by the pale, puny off-springs of the rich, yet whose labour barely brings him enough to keep the wolf of starvation from the door, marries only to have a wife and house-keeper, who must slave from morning till night, who must make every effort to keep down expenses. Her nerves are so tired by the continual effort to make the pitiful wages of her husband support both of them that she grows irritable and no longer is successful in concealing her want of affection for her lord and master, who, alas! soon comes to the conclusion that his hopes and plans have gone astray, and so practically begins to think that marriage is a failure.

The Chain Grows Heavier and Heaver

As the expenses grow larger instead of smaller, the wife, who has lost all of the little strength she had at marriage, likewise feels herself betrayed, and the constant fretting and dread of starvation consumes her beauty in a short time after marriage. She grows despondent, neglects her household duties, and as there are no ties of love and sympathy between herself and her husband to give them strength to face the misery and poverty of their lives, instead of clinging to each other, they become more and more estranged, more and more impatient with each other's faults.

The man cannot, like the millionaire, go to his club, but he goes to a saloon and tries to drown his misery in a glass of beer or whiskey. The unfortunate partner of his misery, who is too honest to seek forgetfulness in the arms of a lover, and who is too poor to allow herself any legitimate recreation or amusement, remains amid the squalid, half-kept surroundings shc calls home, and bitterly bemoans the folly that made her a poor man's wife.

Yet there is no way for them to part from each other.

But They Must Wear It

However galling the chain which has been put around their necks by the law and Church may be, it may not be broken unless those two persons decide to permit it to be severed.

Should the law be merciful enough to grant them liberty, every detail of their private life must be dragged to light. The woman is condemned by public opinion and her whole life is ruined. The fear of this disgrace often causes her to break down under the heavy weight of married life without daring to enter a single protest against the outrageous system that has crushed her and so many of her sisters.

The rich endure it to avoid scandal – the poor for the sake of their children and the fear of public opinion. Their lives are one long continuation of hypocrisy and deceit.

The woman who sells her favours is at liberty to leave the man who purchases them at any time, while the respectable wife cannot free herself from a union which is galling to her.

All unnatural unions which are not hallowed by love are prostitution, whether sanctioned by the Church and society or not. Such unions cannot have other than a degrading influence both upon the morals and health of society.

The System Is to Blame

The system which forces women to sell their womanhood and independence to the highest bidder is a branch of the same evil system which gives to a few the right to live on the wealth produced by their fellow-men, 99 percent of whom must toil and slave early and late for barely enough to keep soul and body together, while the fruits of their labour are absorbed by a few idle vampires who are surrounded by every luxury wealth can purchase.

Look for a moment at two pictures of this nineteenth century social system.

Look at the homes of the wealthy, those magnificent palaces whose costly furnishings would put thousands of needy men and women in comfortable circumstances. Look at the dinner parties of these sons and daughters of wealth, a single course of which would feed hundreds of starving ones to whom a full meal of bread washed down by water is a luxury. Look upon these votaries of fashion as they spend their days devising new means of selfish enjoyment – theatres, balls, concerts, yachting, rushing from one part of the globe to another in their mad search for gaiety and pleasure. And then turn a moment and look at those who produce the wealth that pays for these excessive, unnatural enjoyments.

The Other Picture

Look at them herded together in dark, damp cellars, where they never get a breath of fresh air, clothed in rags, carrying their loads of misery from the cradle to the grave, their children running around the streets, naked, starved, without anyone to give them a loving word or tender care, growing up in ignorance and superstition, cursing the day of their birth.

Look at these two startling contrasts, you moralists and philanthropists, and tell me who is to be blamed for it! Those who are driven to prostitution, whether legal or otherwise, or those who drive their victims to such demoralization?

The cause lies not in prostitution, but in society itself; in the system of inequality of private property and in the State and Church. In the system of legalized theft, murder and violation of the innocent women and helpless children.

The Cure for the Evil

Not until this monster is destroyed will we get rid of the disease which exists in the Senate and all public offices; in the houses of the rich as well as in the miserable barracks of the poor. Mankind must become conscious of their strength and capabilities, they must be free to commence a new life, a better and nobler life.

Prostitution will never be suppressed by the means employed by the Rev. Dr Parkhurst and other reformers. It will exist as long as the system exists which breeds it.

When all these reformers unite their efforts with those who are striving to abolish the system which begets crime of every description and erect one which is based upon perfect equity – a system which guarantees every member, man, woman or child, the full fruits of their labour and a perfectly equal right to enjoy the gifts of nature and to attain the highest knowledge – woman will be self-supporting and independent. Her health no longer crushed by endless toil and slavery no longer will she be the victim of man, while man will no longer be possessed of unhealthy, unnatural passions and vices.

An Anarchist's Dream

Each will enter the marriage state with physical strength and moral confidence in each other. Each will love and esteem the other, and will help in working not only for their own welfare, but, being happy themselves, they will desire also the universal happiness of humanity. The offspring of such unions will be strong and healthy in mind and body and will honour and respect their parents, not because it is their duty to do so, but because the parents deserve it. They will be instructed and cared for by the whole community and will be free to follow their own inclinations, and there will be no necessity to teach them sycophancy and the base art of preying upon their fellow-beings. Their aim in life will be, not to obtain power over their brothers, but to win the respect and esteem of every member of the community.

Anarchist Divorce

Should the union of a man and woman prove unsatisfactory and distasteful to them they will in a quiet, friendly manner, separate and not debase the several relations of marriage by continuing an uncongenial union.

If, instead of persecuting the victims, the reformers of the day will unite their efforts to eradicate the cause, prostitution will no longer disgrace humanity.

To suppress one class and protect another is worse than folly. It is criminal. Do not turn away your heads, you moral man and woman.

Do not allow your prejudice to influence you: look at the question from an unbiased standpoint.

Instead of exerting your strength uselessly, join hands and assist to abolish the corrupt, diseased system.

If married life has not robbed you of honour and self-respect, if you have love for those you call your children, you must, for your own sake as well as theirs, seek emancipation and establish liberty. Then, and not until then, will the evils of matrimony cease.

23.

ROKEYA SAKHAWAT HOSSAIN

Born 1880, Pairaband, Rangpur District, in what is now Bangladesh
Died 1932, Kolkata, India

Sultana's Dream

1905

One evening I was lounging in an easy chair in my bedroom and thinking lazily of the condition of Indian womanhood. I am not sure whether I dozed off or not. But, as far as I remember, I was wide awake. I saw the moonlit sky sparkling with thousands of diamond-like stars, very distinctly.

All on a sudden a lady stood before me; how she came in, I do not know. I took her for my friend, Sister Sara.

'Good morning,' said Sister Sara. I smiled inwardly as I knew it was not morning, but starry night. However, I replied to her, saying, 'How do you do?'

'I am all right, thank you. Will you please come out and have a look at our garden?'

I looked again at the moon through the open window, and thought there was no harm in going out at that time. The men-servants outside were fast asleep just then, and I could have a pleasant walk with Sister Sara.

I used to have my walks with Sister Sara, when we were at Darjeeling. Many a time did we walk hand in hand and talk light-heartedly in the botanical gardens there. I fancied, Sister Sara had probably come to take me to some such garden and I readily accepted her offer and went out with her.

When walking I found to my surprise that it was a fine morning. The town was fully awake and the streets alive with bustling crowds. I was feeling very shy, thinking I was walking in the street in broad daylight, but there was not a single man visible.

Some of the passers-by made jokes at me. Though I could not

understand their language, yet I felt sure they were joking. I asked my friend, 'What do they say?'

'The women say that you look very mannish.'

'Mannish?' said I, 'What do they mean by that?'

'They mean that you are shy and timid like men.'

'Shy and timid like men?' It was really a joke. I became very nervous, when I found that my companion was not Sister Sara, but a stranger. Oh, what a fool had I been to mistake this lady for my dear old friend, Sister Sara.

She felt my fingers tremble in her hand, as we were walking hand in hand.

'What is the matter, dear?' she said affectionately. 'I feel somewhat awkward,' I said in a rather apologizing tone, 'as being a purdahnishin woman I am not accustomed to walking about unveiled.'

'You need not be afraid of coming across a man here. This is Ladyland, free from sin and harm. Virtue herself reigns here.'

By and by I was enjoying the scenery. Really it was very grand. I mistook a patch of green grass for a velvet cushion. Feeling as if I were walking on a soft carpet, I looked down and found the path covered with moss and flowers.

'How nice it is,' said I.

'Do you like it?' asked Sister Sara. (I continued calling her 'Sister Sara,' and she kept calling me by my name).

'Yes, very much; but I do not like to tread on the tender and sweet flowers.'

'Never mind, dear Sultana; your treading will not harm them; they are street flowers.'

'The whole place looks like a garden,' said I admiringly. 'You have arranged every plant so skillfully.'

'Your Calcutta could become a nicer garden than this if only your countrymen wanted to make it so.'

'They would think it useless to give so much attention to horticulture, while they have so many other things to do.'

'They could not find a better excuse,' said she with smile.

I became very curious to know where the men were. I met more than a hundred women while walking there, but not a single man.

'Where are the men?' I asked her.

'In their proper places, where they ought to be.'

'Pray let me know what you mean by "their proper places".'

'O, I see my mistake, you cannot know our customs, as you were never here before. We shut our men indoors.'

'Just as we are kept in the zenana?'

'Exactly so.'

'How funny,' I burst into a laugh. Sister Sara laughed too.

'But dear Sultana, how unfair it is to shut in the harmless women and let loose the men.'

'Why? It is not safe for us to come out of the zenana, as we are naturally weak.'

'Yes, it is not safe so long as there are men about the streets, nor is it so when a wild animal enters a marketplace.'

'Of course not.'

'Suppose, some lunatics escape from the asylum and begin to do all sorts of mischief to men, horses and other creatures; in that case what will your countrymen do?'

'They will try to capture them and put them back into their asylum.'

'Thank you! And you do not think it wise to keep sane people inside an asylum and let loose the insane?'

'Of course not!' said I laughing lightly.

'As a matter of fact, in your country this very thing is done! Men, who do or at least are capable of doing no end of mischief, are let loose and the innocent women, shut up in the zenana! How can you trust those untrained men out of doors?'

'We have no hand or voice in the management of our social affairs. In India man is lord and master, he has taken to himself all powers and privileges and shut up the women in the zenana.'

'Why do you allow yourselves to be shut up?'

'Because it cannot be helped as they are stronger than women.'

'A lion is stronger than a man, but it does not enable him to dominate the human race. You have neglected the duty you owe to yourselves and you have lost your natural rights by shutting your eyes to your own interests.'

'But my dear Sister Sara, if we do everything by ourselves, what will the men do then?'

'They should not do anything, excuse me; they are fit for nothing. Only catch them and put them into the zenana.'

'But would it be very easy to catch and put them inside the four walls?' said I. 'And even if this were done, would all their business – political and commercial – also go with them into the zenana?'

Sister Sara made no reply. She only smiled sweetly. Perhaps she thought it useless to argue with one who was no better than a frog in a well.

By this time we reached Sister Sara's house. It was situated in a beautiful heart-shaped garden. It was a bungalow with a corrugated iron roof. It was cooler and nicer than any of our rich buildings. I cannot describe how neat and how nicely furnished and how tastefully decorated it was.

We sat side by side. She brought out of the parlour a piece of embroidery work and began putting on a fresh design.

'Do you know knitting and needle work?'

'Yes; we have nothing else to do in our zenana.'

'But we do not trust our zenana members with embroidery!' she said laughing, 'as a man has not patience enough to pass thread through a needlehole even!'

'Have you done all this work yourself?' I asked her pointing to the various pieces of embroidered teapoy cloths.

'Yes.'

'How can you find time to do all these? You have to do the office work as well? Have you not?'

'Yes. I do not stick to the laboratory all day long. I finish my work in two hours.'

'In two hours! How do you manage? In our land the officers, – magistrates, for instance – work seven hours daily.'

'I have seen some of them doing their work. Do you think they work all the seven hours?'

'Certainly they do!'

'No, dear Sultana, they do not. They dawdle away their time in smoking. Some smoke two or three choroots during the office time. They talk much about their work, but do little. Suppose one choroot takes half an hour to burn off, and a man smokes twelve choroots daily; then you see, he wastes six hours every day in sheer smoking.'

We talked on various subjects, and I learned that they were not subject to any kind of epidemic disease, nor did they suffer from mosquito bites as we do. I was very much astonished to hear that in Ladyland no one died in youth except by rare accident.

'Will you care to see our kitchen?' she asked me.

'With pleasure,' said I, and we went to see it. Of course the men had been asked to clear off when I was going there. The kitchen was situated in a beautiful vegetable garden. Every creeper, every tomato plant was itself an ornament. I found no smoke, nor any chimney either in the kitchen – it was clean and bright; the windows were decorated with flower gardens. There was no sign of coal or fire.

'How do you cook?' I asked.

'With solar heat,' she said, at the same time showing me the pipe, through which passed the concentrated sunlight and heat. And she cooked something then and there to show me the process.

'How did you manage to gather and store up the sun-heat?' I asked her in amazement.

'Let me tell you a little of our past history then. Thirty years ago, when our present Queen was thirteen years old, she inherited the throne. She was Queen in name only, the Prime Minister really ruling the country.

'Our good Queen liked science very much. She circulated an order that all the women in her country should be educated. Accordingly a number of girls' schools were founded and supported by the government. Education was spread far and wide among women. And early marriage also was stopped. No woman was to be allowed to marry before she was twenty-one. I must tell you that, before this change we had been kept in strict purdah.'

'How the tables are turned,' I interposed with a laugh.

'But the seclusion is the same,' she said. 'In a few years we had separate universities, where no men were admitted.

'In the capital, where our Queen lives, there are two universities. One of these invented a wonderful balloon, to which they attached a number of pipes. By means of this captive balloon which they managed to keep afloat above the cloud-land, they could draw as much water from the atmosphere as they pleased. As the water was incessantly being drawn by the university people no cloud gathered and the ingenious Lady Principal stopped rain and storms thereby.'

'Really! Now I understand why there is no mud here!' said I. But I could not understand how it was possible to accumulate water in the pipes. She explained to me how it was done, but I was unable to understand her, as my scientific knowledge was very limited. However, she went on, 'When the other university came to know of this, they became exceedingly jealous and tried to do something more extraordinary still. They invented an instrument by which they could collect as much sun-heat as they wanted. And they kept the heat stored up to be distributed among others as required.

'While the women were engaged in scientific research, the men of this country were busy increasing their military power. When they came to know that the female universities were able to draw water from the atmosphere and collect heat from the sun, they only laughed at the members of the universities and called the whole thing "a sentimental nightmare"!'

'Your achievements are very wonderful indeed! But tell me, how you managed to put the men of your country into the zenana. Did you entrap them first?'

'No.'

'It is not likely that they would surrender their free and open air life of their own accord and confine themselves within the four walls of the zenana! They must have been overpowered.'

'Yes, they have been!'

'By whom? By some lady-warriors, I suppose?'

'No, not by arms.'

'Yes, it cannot be so. Men's arms are stronger than women's. Then?'

'By brain.'

'Even their brains are bigger and heavier than women's. Are they not?'

'Yes, but what of that? An elephant also has got a bigger and heavier brain than a man has. Yet man can enchain elephants and employ them, according to their own wishes.'

'Well said, but tell me please, how it all actually happened. I am dying to know it!'

'Women's brains are somewhat quicker than men's. Ten years ago, when the military officers called our scientific discoveries "a sentimental nightmare," some of the young ladies wanted to say something in reply to those remarks. But both the Lady Principals restrained them and said, they should reply not by word, but by deed, if ever they got the opportunity.' And they had not long to wait for that opportunity.'

'How marvellous!' I heartily clapped my hands. 'And now the proud gentlemen are dreaming sentimental dreams themselves.'

'Soon afterwards certain persons came from a neighbouring country and took shelter in ours. They were in trouble having committed some political offense. The king who cared more for power than for good government asked our kind-hearted Queen to hand them over to his officers. She refused, as it was against her principle to turn out refugees. For this refusal the king declared war against our country.

'Our military officers sprang to their feet at once and marched out to meet the enemy. The enemy however, was too strong for them. Our soldiers fought bravely, no doubt. But in spite of all their bravery the foreign army advanced step by step to invade our country.

'Nearly all the men had gone out to fight; even a boy of sixteen was not left home. Most of our warriors were killed, the rest driven back and the enemy came within twenty-five miles of the capital.

'A meeting of a number of wise ladies was held at the Queen's palace to advise as to what should be done to save the land. Some proposed to fight like soldiers; others objected and said that women were not trained to fight with swords and guns, nor were they accustomed to fighting with any weapons. A third party regretfully remarked that they were hopelessly weak of body.

"If you cannot save your country for lack of physical strength," said the Queen, "try to do so by brain power."

'There was a dead silence for a few minutes. Her Royal Highness said again, "I must commit suicide if the land and my honour are lost."

'Then the Lady Principal of the second university (who had collected sun-heat), who had been silently thinking during the consultation, remarked that they were all but lost, and there was little hope left for them. There was, however, one plan which she would like to try, and this would be her first and last efforts; if she failed in this, there would be nothing left but to commit suicide. All present solemnly vowed that they would never allow themselves to be enslaved, no matter what happened.

'The Queen thanked them heartily, and asked the Lady Principal to try her plan. The Lady Principal rose again and said, "before we go out the men must enter the zenanas. I make this prayer for the sake of purdah." "Yes, of course," replied Her Royal Highness.

'On the following day the Queen called upon all men to retire into zenanas for the sake of honour and liberty. Wounded and tired as they were, they took that order rather for a boon! They bowed low and entered the zenanas without uttering a single word of protest. They were sure that there was no hope for this country at all.

'Then the Lady Principal with her two thousand students marched to the battle field, and arriving there directed all the rays of the concentrated sunlight and heat towards the enemy.

'The heat and light were too much for them to bear. They all ran away panic-stricken, not knowing in their bewilderment how to counteract that scorching heat. When they fled away leaving their guns and other ammunitions of war, they were burnt down by means of the same sun-heat. Since then no one has tried to invade our country any more.'

'And since then your countrymen never tried to come out of the zenana?'

'Yes, they wanted to be free. Some of the police commissioners and district magistrates sent word to the Queen to the effect that the military officers certainly deserved to be imprisoned for their failure; but they never neglected their duty and therefore they should not be punished and they prayed to be restored to their respective offices.

'Her Royal Highness sent them a circular letter intimating to them that if their services should ever be needed they would be sent for, and that in the meanwhile they should remain where they were. Now that they are accustomed to the purdah system and have ceased to grumble at their seclusion, we call the system "Mardana" instead of "zenana".'

'But how do you manage,' I asked Sister Sara, 'to do without the police or magistrates in case of theft or murder?'

'Since the "Mardana" system has been established, there has been no more crime or sin; therefore we do not require a policeman to find out a culprit, nor do we want a magistrate to try a criminal case.'

'That is very good, indeed. I suppose if there was any dishonest person, you could very easily chastise her. As you gained a decisive victory without shedding a single drop of blood, you could drive off crime and criminals too without much difficulty!'

'Now, dear Sultana, will you sit here or come to my parlour?' she asked me.

'Your kitchen is not inferior to a queen's boudoir!' I replied with a pleasant smile, 'but we must leave it now; for the gentlemen may be cursing me for keeping them away from their duties in the kitchen so long.' We both laughed heartily.

'How my friends at home will be amused and amazed, when I go back and tell them that in the far-off Ladyland, ladies rule over the country and control all social matters, while gentlemen are kept in the Mardanas to mind babies, to cook and to do all sorts of domestic work; and that cooking is so easy a thing that it is simply a pleasure to cook!'

'Yes, tell them about all that you see here.'

'Please let me know, how you carry on land cultivation and how you plough the land and do other hard manual work.'

'Our fields are tilled by means of electricity, which supplies motive power for other hard work as well, and we employ it for our aerial conveyances too. We have no rail road nor any paved streets here.'

'Therefore neither street nor railway accidents occur here,' said I. 'Do not you ever suffer from want of rainwater?' I asked.

'Never since the "water balloon" has been set up. You see the big balloon and pipes attached thereto. By their aid we can draw as much rainwater as we require. Nor do we ever suffer from flood or thunderstorms. We are all very busy making nature yield as much as she can. We do not find time to quarrel with one another as we never sit idle. Our noble Queen is exceedingly fond of botany; it is her ambition to convert the whole country into one grand garden.'

'The idea is excellent. What is your chief food?'

'Fruits.'

'How do you keep your country cool in hot weather? We regard the rainfall in summer as a blessing from heaven.'

'When the heat becomes unbearable, we sprinkle the ground with plentiful showers drawn from the artificial fountains. And in cold weather we keep our room warm with sun-heat.'

She showed me her bathroom, the roof of which was removable. She could enjoy a shower bath whenever she liked, by simply removing the roof (which was like the lid of a box) and turning on the tap of the shower pipe.

'You are a lucky people!' ejaculated I. 'You know no want. What is your religion, may I ask?'

'Our religion is based on Love and Truth. It is our religious duty to love one another and to be absolutely truthful. If any person lies, she or he is . . .'

'Punished with death?'

'No, not with death. We do not take pleasure in killing a creature of God, especially a human being. The liar is asked to leave this land for good and never to come to it again.'

'Is an offender never forgiven?'

'Yes, if that person repents sincerely.'

'Are you not allowed to see any man, except your own relations?'

'No one except sacred relations.'

'Our circle of sacred relations is very limited; even first cousins are not sacred.'

'But ours is very large; a distant cousin is as sacred as a brother.'

'That is very good. I see purity itself reigns over your land. I should like to see the good Queen, who is so sagacious and far-sighted and who has made all these rules.'

'All right,' said Sister Sara.

Then she screwed a couple of seats onto a square piece of plank. To this plank she attached two smooth and well-polished balls. When I asked her what the balls were for, she said they were hydrogen balls and they were used to overcome the force of gravity. The balls were of different capacities to be used according to the different weights desired to be overcome. She then fastened to the air-car two wing-like blades, which, she said, were worked by electricity. After we were comfortably seated she touched a knob and the blades began to whirl, moving faster and faster every moment. At first we were raised to the height of about six or seven feet and then off we flew. And before I could realize that we had commenced moving, we reached the garden of the Queen.

My friend lowered the air-car by reversing the action of the machine, and when the car touched the ground the machine was stopped and we got out.

I had seen from the air-car the Queen walking on a garden path with her little daughter (who was four years old) and her maids of honour.

'Halloo! You here!' cried the Queen addressing Sister Sara. I was introduced to Her Royal Highness and was received by her cordially without any ceremony.

I was very much delighted to make her acquaintance. In the course of the conversation I had with her, the Queen told me that she had no objection to permitting her subjects to trade with other countries. 'But,' she continued, 'no trade was possible with countries where the women were kept in the zenanas and so unable to come and trade with us. Men, we find, are rather of lower morals and so we do not like dealing with them. We do not covet other people's land, we do not fight for a piece of diamond though it may be a thousand-fold brighter than the Koh-i-Noor, nor do we grudge a ruler his Peacock Throne. We dive deep into the ocean of knowledge and try to find out the precious gems, which nature has kept in store for us. We enjoy nature's gifts as much as we can.'

After taking leave of the Queen, I visited the famous universities, and was shown some of their manufactories, laboratories and observatories.

After visiting the above places of interest we got again into the air-car, but as soon as it began moving, I somehow slipped down and the fall startled me out of my dream. And on opening my eyes, I found myself in my own bedroom still lounging in the easy-chair!

24.

QIU JIN

Born 1875, Shanyin, Zhejiang, China
Executed 1907, Zhejiang, China

A Song: Promoting Women's Rights
1906

Our generation yearns to be free;
To all who struggle: one more cup of the Wine of Freedom!
Male and female equality was by Heaven endowed,
So why should women lag behind?
Let's struggle to pull ourselves up,
To wash away the filth and shame of former days.
United we can work together,
And restore this land with our soft white hands.

Most humiliating is the old custom,
Of treating women no better than cows and horses.
When the light of dawn shines on our civilization,
We must rise to head the list.
Let's tear out the roots of servitude,
Gain knowledge, learning and practice what we know.
Take responsibility on our shoulders,
Never to fail or disappoint, our citizen heroines!

25.

SAROJINI NAIDU

Born 1879, Hyderabad, India
Died 1949, Lucknow, India

Education of Indian Women
1906

It seems to me a paradox, at once touched with humour and tragedy, that on the very threshold of the twentieth century, it should still be necessary for us to stand upon public platforms and pass resolutions in favour of what is called female education in India – in all places in India, which, at the beginning of the first century was already ripe with civilisation and had contributed to the world's progress radiant examples of women of the highest genius and widest culture. But as by some irony of evolution the paradox stands to our shame, it is time for us to consider how best we can remove such a reproach, how we can best achieve something more fruitful than the passing of empty resolutions in favour of female education from year to year. At this great moment of stress and striving, when the Indian races are seeking for the ultimate unity of a common national ideal, it is well for us to remember that the success of the whole movement lies centred in what is known as the woman question. It is not you but we who are the true nation-builders. But it seems to me that there is not even an unanimous acceptance of the fact that the education of women is an essential factor in the process of nation-building.

Many of you will remember that, some years ago, when Mrs Sathianadhan first started 'The Indian Ladies' Magazine,' a lively correspondence went on as to whether we should or should not educate our women. The women themselves with one voice pleaded their own cause most eloquently, but when it came to the man there was division in the camp. Many men doubtless proved themselves true patriots by proving themselves the true friends of education for the mothers of the people. But others there were who took fright at the very word. 'What,' they cried, 'educate our women? What, then, will become of the comfortable domestic ideals as exemplified by the luscious "halwa" and the savoury "omelette"?' Others again were neither 'for Jove nor for Jehovah,' but were for compromise, bringing forward a whole syllabus of compromises. 'Teach this,' they said, 'and not that.'

But, my friends, in the matter of education you cannot say *thus far and no further*. Neither can you say to the winds of Heaven 'Blow not where ye list,' nor forbid the waves to cross their boundaries, nor yet the human soul to soar beyond the bounds of arbitrary limitations. The word education is the worst misunderstood word in any language. The Italians, who are an imaginative people, with their subtle instinct for the inner meaning of words have made a positive difference between *instruction* and *education* and we should do well to accept and acknowledge that difference. *Instruction* being merely the accumulation of knowledge might, indeed, lend itself to conventional definition, but *education* is an immeasurable, beautiful, indispensable atmosphere in which we live and move and have our being. Does one man dare to deprive another of his birthright to God's pure air which nourishes his body? How, then, shall a man dare to deprive a human soul of its immemorial inheritance of liberty and life? And yet, my friends, man has so dared in the case of Indian women. That is why you men of India are to-day what you are: because your fathers, in depriving your mothers of that immemorial birthright, have robbed you, their sons, of your just inheritance. Therefore, I charge you, restore to your women their ancient rights, for, as I have said it is we, and not you, who are the real national-builders, and without our active co-operation at all points of progress all your Congresses and Conferences are in vain. Educate your women and the nation will take care of itself, for it is true to-day as it was yesterday and will be to the end of human life that the hand that rocks the cradle is the power that rules the world.

26.

TEFFI

Born 1872, Saint Petersburg, Russia
Died 1952, Paris, France

from *The Woman Question*

1907

Scene I

[A *drawing-room. Against the wall stands a big, old-fashioned couch. Evening. Lamps are burning.* Through the open door can be seen a table set for dinner. MOTHER *is wiping the tea-cups with a cloth.* VANYA *is sitting at the table reading.* KOLYA *is stretched out in a rocking chair, wearing a cycling cap.* KATYA *is pacing round the room.*]

KATYA [agitatedly]. That's outrageous! Really outrageous! As if a woman weren't the same as a man!

KOLYA. That's just it. She isn't.

KATYA. But lots of countries do have equal rights for women, and no one there thinks that things are any the worse for that. Why can't we manage?

KOLYA. We just can't.

KATYA. But why not?

KOLYA. We just can't, and that's it.

KATYA. That's it – because you're a fool.

MOTHER [*from the dining room*]. Not fighting *again?* Do stop it! You ought to be ashamed of yourselves!

KATYA. He does it on purpose to tease me. You know how hard it is for me. I've dedicated my life . . . [*Starts crying*]

KOLYA. Ha, ha! [*sings*] She's dedicated her life, and she's been victimized! [*A bell is heard*]

MOTHER. Will you stop that, you two! That's someone at the door.
[*Enter Father*]

FATHER. Well, here I am. What on earth is this? What's Katya
bawling about?

KOLYA. She's dedicated her life, and she's been victimized.

MOTHER. Oh, for heaven's sake hold your tongues! Father's just got
back, and he's tired . . . Instead of . . .

FATHER [*with a frown*]. Good God, whatever next! Your father
rushes round all day like a mad dog, but he can't count on a
moment's peace when he gets home. It's all your fault, Mother.
You let things get out of hand. Katerina spends all day, every
day running off to meetings, and this blockhead does nothing
but loll about at home. Take off that hat! You're not in a stable.
Father works like a horse, slaving over papers all day, and instead
of . . .

MOTHER. Shurochka, dear, how about a nice glass of tea?

FATHER. I'm coming, Shurochka. I only want one, though. I've got
to run again.

MOTHER [*passing him the glass, which he drinks down on his feet*].
You've got to run?

FATHER [*Irritably*]. Yes, of course. Quite simple really. It's hardly
the first time, is it? I spend my life running round like a mouse
in a treadmill, and all for your sakes. The fact is, we've got a meeting this evening. Oh, yes, I nearly forgot what I dropped by for!
Let me congratulate you, darling. Uncle Petya was promoted to
general today. We must put on a dinner for him tomorrow. You'll
arrange things, won't you? I'll buy the wine myself, of course.

MOTHER. So you're not coming home till late tonight?

FATHER. There's feminine logic for you! Well, of course not.

[*He picks up the briefcase by the wrong end, and out flutter papers and a
long pink ribbon.*]

KOLYA. Papa – you've dropped a ribbon.

FATHER [*stuffing the ribbon back hastily*]. Yes, yes, of course. Oh! The
ribbon! That's a business matter! Well, goodbye, then, Shurochka
[*pinching her cheek*]. Sleep well, Mama.

MOTHER [*Sighing*]. Oh, the poor dear. He's such a hard worker.

KOLYA. Hmmm, the ribbon – that's a business matter. Well, of course, if he says so.

MOTHER. What?

KATYA. I'm so bored, I think I'm going off my head.

MOTHER. That's because you never do anything, my dear. If you found yourself something to do, like sewing, or a little reading, or even helping your mother do the housework, then you wouldn't be bored, would you?

KOLYA. I'm off. I've decided to help Mother with the housework.

[*Exits through dining-room. Can be seen taking a spoon and eating jam directly from the pot.*]

KATYA. I don't want to help. I'm not a cook. Perhaps *I'd* like to work in an office too. Yes, sir. And may be *I'd* like to go to meetings in the evenings.

[KOLYA *guffaws.* KATYA *jumps, then threatens him with her fist.*]

I hate you all! No, I've changed my mind. I don't want equal rights any more. What good would they do me? No! I'd like to see the men in our shoes for a while, then we women would boss them around like they boss us. *Then* we'd see what kind of tune they'd sing.

VANYA. You think that would be better?

KATYA. Better? Yes, we women would turn the whole world upside down . . .

VANYA. You've said enough! If you want a new life, invent a new breed of human beings. If people stay the same, so does every-thing else.

KATYA. That's not true! You're lying! You're saying that on purpose to spite me! And in any case, you can tell your Andrei Nikolaevich that I'm not going to marry him. I haven't the slightest intention of doing it. We'd get married, and the very next day he'd ask me what was for dinner. No, not for anything! I'd rather shoot myself.

VANYA. Now you really have gone off your rocker!

KATYA. I'll finish school, I'll train as a doctor, and then I'll have him as a wife myself. He'd better not dare do anything – except a little light housework. No need to worry, I can support the family on my own.

VANYA. But surely that's just the same?

KATYA. Of course it isn't. Life would be quite different if we were in charge. We women aren't the same as you men, you know; we're exactly the opposite.

VANYA. Which is to say, what? What do you mean, 'exactly the opposite'?

KATYA. Everything about us is exactly the opposite. You're all lunatics. You've gone insane from all that power. Take your Andrei Nikolaevich, for instance. How he dotes on that Professor Petukhov. Oh, what a scholar! Oh, how sweet, how absent-minded! Petukhov's nothing but an old dodderer, and he never takes a bath either. You all fawn on each other. You cheat on your wives, you play cards all day and night if you feel like it, and everything turns out just as you want. Could a woman get away with it?

MOTHER'S VOICE. Katya! I'm going to lie down for a while. If you hear Father ring the bell, wake Glasha up – you know how soundly she sleeps!

KATYA. All right! I won't sleep a wink all night in any case.

[VANYA *exits and locks his door*]

KATYA [*banging on his door with her fist*]. So tell him I won't have him! Do you hear? I won't have him! [*Sits down on couch and starts crying*] Poor Andryusha . . . and poor me! . . . So what, we'll wait until everything's been turned upside down . . . I will be a lady doctor, Andrusha . . . [*lies on the couch*] I believe that everything will come true . . . won't it be wonderful? . . . [*yawns*] I'l show him. It would be so nice . . . [*falls asleep*].

[*The lights dim slowly. For a few moments it is completely dark. Then immediately daylight blazes.* KATYA *is sitting at the table going through some papers.* KOLYA *is on the couch embroidering some slippers.* FATHER *is washing cups in the dining room.*]

Scene 2

KOLYA [*on a whining note*]. Bother, I've got to rip all this out! I'm a cross-stitch short again!

KATYA. Quiet, you're bothering me.

VANYA [*enters, animated, throws his hat on a chair.*]

VANYA. What an amazing day! I've come straight here from Parliament House. I sat up in the gallery; It was terribly stuffy. Deputy Ovchina was discussing the man question. She said some amazing things. Men are humans too, she said! And a man's brain, in spite of its excessive weight and overabundance of grey matter, is a real human brain all the same. She cited history. In bygone days, men were allowed to hold extremely responsible jobs . . .

FATHER. That's all very interesting. But you'd better help me with the dishes.

VANYA. She cited examples of new experiments they're doing. For instance, if men work as cooks and nannies, why . . .

KATYA. Shut up, Vanya, you're bothering me. [*A bell rings*] Oh, that must be Mama.

FATHER [*bustling about*]. Oh, Heavens, Styopka didn't hear it again. I'll have to open the door myself.

[*Runs out*]

MOTHER [*coming in with* FATHER]. Really, my sweet, you shouldn't do it! Leave opening doors to the servants – that's what they're there for! Listen, children, I have some wonderful news! Aunt Masha has been promoted to general.

FATHER. What an impressive woman she is!

KATYA. Pooh! She's done nothing all her life except steal the regimental oats.

FATHER. Katya, really!

KATYA. She drinks like a fish and chases every pair of trousers in sight.

FATHER. Kolya, leave the room. Katya, you mustn't talk like that in front of the boy!

MOTHER [*to* FATHER]. Well, Shurochka, you'll have to organize a dinner for Aunt Masha today. Try not to let us down, won't you? I'll buy the wine myself, of course. But you're in charge of the food and so on. Kolya and Vanya, be sure to help your father!

FATHER [*timidly*]. Mightn't it be possible to postpone the dinner until tomorrow? It's a teeny bit short notice . . .

MOTHER. Wonderful There's masculine logic for you! I invite guests for dinner today, and he says he'll serve it tomorrow! [*Exit*]

27.

ROSA LUXEMBURG

Born 1871, Zamosc, Poland
Died 1919, Berlin, Germany

Women's Suffrage and Class Struggle
1912

'Why are there no organizations for working women in Germany? Why do we hear so little about the working women's movement?' With these questions, Emma Ihrer, one of the founders of the proletarian women's movement of Germany, introduced her 1898 essay, Working Women in the Class Struggle. Hardly fourteen years have passed since, but they have seen a great expansion of the proletarian women's movement. More than a hundred fifty thousand women are organized in unions and are among the most active troops in the economic struggle of the proletariat. Many thousands of politically organized women have rallied to the banner of Social Democracy: the Social Democratic women's paper [*Die Gleichheit*, edited by Clara Zetkin] has more than one hundred thousand subscribers; women's suffrage is one of the vital issues on the platform of Social Democracy.

Exactly these facts might lead you to underrate the importance of the fight for women's suffrage. You might think: even without equal political rights for women we have made enormous progress in educating and organizing women. Hence, women's suffrage is not urgently necessary. If you think so, you are deceived. The political and syndical awakening of the masses of the female proletariat during the last fifteen years has been magnificent. But it has been possible only because working women took a lively interest in the political and parliamentary struggles of their class in spite of being deprived of their rights. So far, proletarian women are sustained by male suffrage, which they indeed take part in, though only indirectly. Large masses of both men and women of the working class already consider the election campaigns a cause they share in common.

In all Social Democratic electoral meetings, women make up a large segment, sometimes the majority. They are always interested and passionately involved. In all districts where there is a firm Social Democratic organization, women help with the campaign. And it is women who have done invaluable work distributing leaflets and getting subscribers to the Social Democratic press, this most important weapon in the campaign.

The capitalist state has not been able to keep women from taking on all these duties and efforts of political life. Step by step, the state has indeed been forced to grant and guarantee them this possibility by allowing them union and assembly rights. Only the last political right is denied women: the right to vote, to decide directly on the people's representatives in legislature and administration, to be an elected member of these bodies. But here, as in all other areas of society, the motto is: 'Don't let things get started!' But things have been started. The present state gave in to the women of the proletariat when it admitted them to public assemblies, to political associations. And the state did not grant this voluntarily, but out of necessity, under the irresistible pressure of the rising working class. It was not least the passionate pushing ahead of the proletarian women themselves which forced the Prusso-German police state to give up the famous 'women's section' in gatherings of political associations and to open wide the doors of political organizations to women. This really set the ball rolling. The irresistible progress of the proletarian class struggle has swept working women right into the whirlpool of the political life. Using their right of union and assembly, proletarian women have taken a most active part in parliamentary life and in election campaigns. It is only the inevitable consequence, only the logical result of the movement that today millions of proletarian women call defiantly and with self-confidence: Let us have suffrage!

Once upon a time, in the beautiful era of pre-1848 absolutism, the whole working class was said not to be 'mature enough' to exercise political rights. This cannot be said about proletarian women today, because they have demonstrated their political maturity. Everybody knows that without them, without the enthusiastic help of proletarian women, the Social Democratic Party would not have won the glorious victory of January 12, [1912], would not have obtained four and a quarter million votes. At any rate, the working class has always had to prove its maturity for political freedom by a successful revolutionary uprising of the masses. Only when Divine Right on the throne and the best and noblest men of the nation actually felt the calloused fist of the proletariat on their eyes and its knee on their chests, only then did they feel confidence in the political 'maturity' of the people, and felt it with the speed of lightning. Today, it is the proletarian woman's turn to make the capitalist state conscious of her maturity. This is done through a constant, powerful mass movement which has to use all the means of proletarian struggle and pressure.

Women's suffrage is the goal. But the mass movement to bring it about is not a job for women alone, but is a common class concern for women and men of the proletariat. Germany's present lack of rights for women is only one link in the chain of the reaction that shackles the people's lives. And it is closely connected with the other pillar of the reaction: the monarchy. In advanced capitalist, highly industrialized, twentieth-century Germany, in the age of electricity and airplanes, the absence of women's political rights is as much a reactionary remnant of the dead past as the reign by Divine Right on the throne. Both phenomena – the instrument of heaven as the leading political power, and woman, demure by the fireside, unconcerned with the storms of public life, with politics and class struggle – both phenomena have their roots in the rotten circumstances of the past, in the times of serfdom in the country and guilds in the towns. In those times, they were justifiable and necessary. But both monarchy and women's lack of rights have been uprooted by the development of modern capitalism, have become ridiculous caricatures. They continue to exist in our modern society, not just because people forgot to abolish them, not just because of the persistence and inertia of circumstances. No, they still exist because both – monarchy as well as women without rights – have become powerful tools of interests inimical to the people. The worst and most brutal advocates of the exploitation and enslavement of the proletariat are entrenched behind throne and altar as well as behind the political enslavement of women. Monarchy and women's lack of rights have become the most important tools of the ruling capitalist class.

In truth, our state is interested in keeping the vote from working women and from them alone. It rightly fears they will threaten the traditional institutions of class rule, for instance militarism (of which no thinking proletarian woman can help being a deadly enemy), monarchy, the systematic robbery of duties and taxes on groceries, etc. Women's suffrage is a horror and abomination for the present capitalist state because behind it stand millions of women who would strengthen the enemy within, i.e., revolutionary Social Democracy. If it were a matter of bourgeois ladies voting the capitalist state could expect nothing but effective support for the reaction. Most of those bourgeois women who act like lionesses in the struggle against 'male prerogatives' would trot like docile lambs in the camp of conservative and clerical reaction if they had suffrage. Indeed, they would certainly be a good deal more reactionary than the male part of their class. Aside from the few who have jobs or professions, the women of the bourgeoisie do not take part in social production. They are nothing but co-consumers of the surplus value their men extort from the proletariat. They are parasites of the parasites of the social body. And consumers are usually even more rabid and cruel in defending their 'right' to a parasite's life than the direct agents of class rule and exploitation. The history of all great revolutionary struggles confirms this in a horrible way. Take the great French Revolution. After the fall of the Jacobins, when Robespierre was driven in chains to the place of execution the naked whores of the victory-drunk bourgeoisie danced in the streets, danced a shameless dance of joy around the fallen hero of the Revolution. And in 1871, in Paris, when the heroic workers' Commune was defeated by machine guns, the raving bourgeois females surpassed even their bestial men in their bloody revenge against the suppressed proletariat. The women of the property-owning classes will always fanatically defend the exploitation and enslavement of the working people by which they indirectly receive the means for their socially useless existence.

Economically and socially, the women of the exploiting classes are not an independent segment of the population. Their only social function is to be tools of the natural propagation of the ruling classes. By contrast, the women of the proletariat are economically independent. They are productive for society like the men. By this I do not mean their bringing up children or their housework which helps men support their families on scanty wages. This kind of work is not productive in the sense of the present capitalist economy no matter how enormous an achievement the sacrifices and energy spent, the thousand little efforts add up to. This is but the private affair of the worker, his happiness and blessing, and for this reason nonexistent for our present society. As long as capitalism and the wage system rule, only that kind of work is considered productive which produces surplus value, which creates capitalist profit. From this point of view, the music-hall dancer whose legs sweep profit into her employer's pocket is a productive worker, whereas all the toil of the proletarian women and mothers in the four walls of their homes is considered unproductive. This sounds brutal and insane, but corresponds exactly to the brutality and insanity of our present capitalist economy. And seeing this brutal reality clearly and sharply is the proletarian woman's first task.

For, exactly from this point of view, the proletarian women's claim to equal political rights is anchored in firm economic ground. Today, millions of proletarian women create capitalist profit like men – in factories, workshops, on farms, in home industry, offices, stores. They are therefore productive in the strictest scientific sense of our present society. Every day enlarges the hosts of women exploited by capitalism. Every new progress in industry or technology creates new places for women in the machinery of capitalist profiteering. And thus, every day and every step of industrial progress adds a new stone to the firm foundation of women's equal political rights. Female education and intelligence have become necessary for the economic mechanism itself. The narrow, secluded women of the patriarchal 'family circle' answers the needs of industry and commerce as little as those of politics. It is true, the capitalist state has neglected its duty even in this respect. So far, it is the unions and the Social Democratic organizations that have done most to awaken the minds and moral sense of women. Even decades ago, the Social Democrats were known as the most capable and intelligent German workers. Likewise, unions and Social Democracy have today lifted the women of the proletariat out of their stuffy, narrow existence, out of the miserable and petty mindlessness of household managing. The proletarian class struggle has widened their horizons, made their minds flexible, developed their thinking, shown them great goals for their efforts. Socialism has brought about the mental rebirth of the mass of proletarian women – and thereby has no doubt also made them capable productive workers for capital.

Considering all this, the proletarian woman's lack of political rights is a vile injustice, and the more so for being by now at least half a lie. After all, masses of women take an active part in political life. However, Social

Democracy does not use the argument of 'injustice.' This is the basic difference between us and the earlier sentimental, utopian socialism. We do not depend on the justice of the ruling classes, but solely on the revolutionary power of the working masses and on the course of social development which prepares the ground for this power. Thus, injustice by itself is certainly not an argument with which to overthrow reactionary institutions. If, however, there is a feeling of injustice in large segments of society – says Friedrich Engels, the co-founder of scientific socialism – it is always a sure sign that the economic bases of the society have shifted considerably, that the present conditions contradict the march of development. The present forceful movement of millions of proletarian women who consider their lack of political rights a crying wrong is such an infallible sign, a sign that the social bases of the reigning system are rotten and that its days are numbered.

A hundred years ago, the Frenchman Charles Fourier, one of the first great prophets of socialist ideals, wrote these memorable words: In any society, the degree of female emancipation is the natural measure of the general emancipation. This is completely true of our present society. The current mass struggle for women's political rights is only an expression and a part of the proletariat's general struggle for liberation. In this lies its strength and its future. Because of the female proletariat, general, equal, direct suffrage for women would immensely advance and intensify the proletarian class struggle. This is why bourgeois society abhors and fears women's suffrage. And this is why we want and will achieve it. Fighting for women's suffrage, we will also hasten the coming of the hour when the present society falls in ruins under the hammer strokes of the revolutionary proletariat.

28.

ANNA AKHMATOVA

Born 1889, Odesa, Ukraine
Died 1966, Domodedovo, USSR

sister I have come to take your place

1912

'Sister, I have come to take your place
At the high bonfire standing in the forest.

Your hair has long turned grey. Your eyes
Are dimmed, turned misty, by your tears.

You cannot understand what the birds sing,
You do not see the stars or summer lightning.

Time has stilled your rattling tambourine,
I know you fear the silence of the trees.

Sister, I have come to take your place
At the high bonfire standing in the forest.'

'Have you come to bury me, then?
But where is your shovel, your spade?
You have only a flute in your hands.
Yet you are not to blame.
I must lament that my voice
Fell silent for good, long since.

So clothe yourself in my dress,
Forget the disquiet I feel,
Let the wind play in your hair.
You smell like the lilac smells,
The path you have walked is steep,
You have stepped into radiance.'

The first sister walked away,
The second took the first's place.
Stumbling as though she were blind
She went down the strange narrow path.

She sees the flame still before her,
Feels the tambourine still in her hand.
For the one is a snow-white banner,
For the one is a lighthouse ablaze.

29.

EMMELINE PANKHURST

Born 1858, Manchester, United Kingdom
Died 1928, London, United Kingdom

from *Freedom or death*

1913

Mrs Hepburn, ladies and gentlemen:

Many people come to Hartford to address meetings as advocates of some reform. Tonight it is not to advocate a reform that I address a meeting in Hartford. I do not come here as an advocate, because whatever position the suffrage movement may occupy in the United States of America, in England, it has passed beyond the realm of advocacy and it has entered into the sphere of practical politics. It has become the subject of revolution and civil war, and so tonight I am not here to advocate woman suffrage. American suffragists can do that very well for themselves.

I am here as a soldier who has temporarily left the field of battle in order to explain – it seems strange it should have to be explained – what civil war is like when civil war is waged by women. I am not only here as a soldier temporarily absent from the field at battle; I am here – and that, I think, is the strangest part of my coming – I am here as a person who, according to the law courts of my country, it has been decided, is of no value to the community at all: and I am adjudged because of my life to be a dangerous person, under sentence of penal servitude in a convict prison. So you see there is some special interest in hearing so unusual a person address you. I dare say, in the minds of many of you – you will perhaps forgive me this personal touch – that I do not look either very like a soldier or very like a convict, and yet I am both.

Now, first of all I want to make you understand the inevitableness of revolution and civil war, even on the part of women, when you reach a certain stage in the development of a community's life. It is not at all difficult if revolutionaries come to you from Russia, if they come to you from China, or from any other part of the world, if they are men, to make you understand revolution in five minutes, every man and every woman to understand revolutionary methods when they are adopted by men.

Many of you have expressed sympathy, probably even practical sympathy, with revolutionaries in Russia. I dare say you have followed with considerable interest the story of how the Chinese revolutionary, Sun Yat-sen, conducted the Chinese revolution from England. And yet I find in American newspapers there is a great deal of misunderstanding of the fact that one of the chief minds engaged in conducting with the women's revolution is, for purposes of convenience, located in Paris. It is quite easy for you to understand – it would not be necessary for me to enter into explanations at all – the desirability of revolution if I were a man, in any of these countries, even in a part of the British Empire known to you as Ireland. If an Irish revolutionary had addressed this meeting, and many have addressed meetings all over the United States during the last twenty or thirty years, it would not be necessary for that revolutionary to explain the need of revolution beyond saying that the people of his country were denied – and by people, meaning men – were denied the right of self-government. That would explain the whole situation. If I were a man and I said to you, 'I come from a country which professes to have representative institutions and yet denies me, a taxpayer, an inhabitant of the country, representative rights,' you would at once understand that the human being, being a man, was justified in the adoption of revolutionary methods to get representative institutions. But since I am a woman it is necessary in the twentieth century to explain why women have adopted revolutionary methods in order to win the rights of citizenship.

You see, in spite of a good deal that we hear about revolutionary methods not being necessary for American women, because American women are so well off, most of the men of the United States quite calmly acquiesce in the fact that half of the community are deprived absolutely of citizen rights, and we women, in trying to make our case clear, always have to make as part of our argument, and urge upon men in our audience the fact – a very simple fact – that women are human beings. It is quite evident you do not all realize we are human beings or it would not be necessary to argue with you that women may, suffering from intolerable injustice, be driven to adopt revolutionary methods. We have, first of all to convince you we are human beings, and I hope to be able to do that in the course of the evening before I sit down, but before doing that, I want to put a few political arguments before you – not arguments for the suffrage, because I said when I opened, I didn't mean to do that – but arguments for the adoption of militant methods in order to win political rights.

A great many of you have been led to believe, from the somewhat meagre accounts you get in the newspapers, that in England there is a strange manifestation taking place, a new form of hysteria being swept across part of the feminist population of those Isles, and this manifestation takes the shape of irresponsible breaking of windows, burning of letters, general inconvenience to respectable, honest business people who want to attend to their business. It is very irrational you say: even if these women had sufficient intelligence to understand what they were doing, and really did want the vote, they have adopted very irrational means for getting the vote. 'How are they going to persuade people that they ought to have the vote by breaking their windows?' you say. Now, if you say that, it shows you do not understand the meaning of our revolution at all, and I want to show you that when damage is done to property it is not done in order to convert people to woman suffrage at all. It is a practical political means, the only means we consider open to voteless persons to bring about a political situation, which can only be solved by giving women the vote

[. . .]

Well now, I want to argue with you as to whether our way is the right one: I want to explain all these things that you have not understood: I want to make you understand exactly what our plan of campaign has been because I have always felt that if you could only make people understand most people's hearts are in the right place and most people's understandings are sound and most people are more or less logical – if you could only make them understand.

Now, I want to come back to the point where I said, if the men of Hartford had a grievance and had no vote to get their redress, if they felt that grievance sufficiently, they would be forced to adopt other methods. That brings me to an explanation of these methods that you have not been able to understand. I am going to talk later on about the grievances, but I want to first of all make you understand that this civil war carried on by women is not the hysterical manifestation which you thought it was, but was carefully and logically thought out, and I think when I have finished you will say, admitted the grievance, admitted the strength of the cause, that we could not do anything else, that there was no other way, that we had either to submit to intolerable injustice and let the woman's movement go back and remain in a worse position than it was before we began, or we had to go on with these methods until victory was secured; and I want also to convince you that these methods are going to win, because when you adopt the methods of revolution there are two justifications which I feel are necessary or to be desired. The first is, that you have good cause for adopting your methods in the beginning, and secondly that you have adopted methods which when pursued with sufficient courage and determination are bound, in the long run, to win.

Now, it would take too long to trace the course of militant methods as adopted by women, because it is about eight years since the word militant was first used to describe what we are doing; it is about eight years since the first militant action was taken by women. It was not militant at all, except that it provoked militancy on the part of those who were opposed to it. When women asked questions in political meetings and failed to get answers, they were not doing anything militant. To ask questions at political meetings is an acknowledged right of all people who attend public meetings; certainly in my country, men have always done it, and I hope they do it in America, because it seems to me that if you allow people to enter your legislatures without asking them any questions as to what they are going to do when they get there you are not exercising your citizen rights and your citizen duties as you ought. At any rate in Great Britain it is a custom, a time-honoured one, to ask questions of candidates for parliament and ask questions of members of the government. No man was ever put out of a public meeting for asking a question until Votes for Women came onto the political horizon. The first people who were put out of a political meeting for asking questions, were women; they were brutally ill-used; they found themselves in jail before twenty-four hours had expired.

But instead of the newspapers, which are largely inspired by the politicians, putting militancy and the reproach of militancy, if reproach there is, on the people who had assaulted the women, they actually said it was the women who were militant and very much to blame. How different the reasoning is that men adopt when they are discussing the cases of men and those of women. Had they been men who asked the questions, and had those men been brutally ill-used, you would have heard a chorus of reprobation on the part of the people toward those who refused to answer those questions. But as they were women who asked the questions, it was not the speakers on the platform who would not answer them, who were to blame, or the ushers at the meeting; it was the poor women who had their bruises and their knocks and scratches, and who were put into prison for doing precisely nothing but holding a protest meeting in the street after it was all over. However, we were called militant for doing that, and we were quite willing to accept the name, because militancy for us is time-honoured; you have the church militant, and in the sense of spiritual militancy we were very militant indeed. We were determined to press this question of the enfranchisement of women to the point where we were no longer to be ignored by the politicians as had been the case for about fifty years, during which time women had patiently used every means open to them to win their political enfranchisement.

We found that all the fine phrases about freedom and liberty were entirely for male consumption, and that they did not in any way apply to women. When it was said taxation without representation is tyranny, when it was 'Taxation of men without representation is tyranny,' everybody quite calmly accepted the fact that women had to pay taxes and even were sent to prison if they failed to pay them – quite right. We found that 'Government of the people, by the people and for the people,' which is also a time-honoured Liberal principle, was again only for male consumption; half of the people were entirely ignored; it was the duty of women to pay their taxes and obey the laws and look as pleasant as they could under the circumstances. In fact, every principle of liberty enunciated in any civilized country on earth, with very few exceptions, was intended entirely for men, and when women tried to force the putting into practice of these principles, for women, then they discovered they had to come into a very, very unpleasant situation indeed.

Now, I am going to pass rapidly over all the incidents that happened after the two first women went to prison for asking questions of cabinet ministers, and come right up to the time when our militancy became real militancy, when we organized ourselves on an army basis, when we determined, if necessary, to fight for our rights just as our forefathers had fought for their rights. Then people began to say that while they believed they had no criticism of militancy, as militancy, while they thought it was quite justifiable for people to revolt against intolerable injustice, it was absurd and ridiculous for women to attempt it because women could not succeed. After all the most practical criticism of our militancy coming from men has been the argument that it could not succeed. They would say, 'We would be with you if you could succeed but it is absurd for women who are the weaker sex, for women who have not got the control of any large interests, for women who have got very little money, who have peculiar duties as women, which handicaps them extremely – for example, the duty of caring for children – it is absurd for women to think they can ever win their rights by fighting; you had far better give it up and submit because there it is, you have always been subject and you always will be.' Well now, that really became the testing time. Then we women determined to show the world, that women, handicapped as women are, can still fight and can still win, and now I want to show you how this plan of ours was carefully thought out, even our attacks on private property, which has been so much misunderstood. I have managed in London to make audiences of business men who came into the meetings very, very angry with us indeed, some of whom had their telephonic communication cut off for several hours and had not been able to even get telegrams from their stock-brokers in cities far distant, who naturally came to our meetings in a very angry frame of mind, understand the situation: and if it has been possible to make them understand, if some of them even get fairly enthusiastic about our methods, it ought to be possible, Mrs Hepburn, for me to explain the situation to an audience in Hartford, who, after all, are far enough off to be able to see, unlike men in our own country who are not able to see wood for trees.

I would like to suggest that if later on, while I am explaining these matters to you, there comes into the mind of any man or woman in the audience some better plan for getting what we want out of an obstinate government, I would be thankful and grateful if that person, man or woman, would tell me of some better plan than ours for dealing with the situation.

Here we have a political system where no reforms can get onto the statute book of the old country unless it is initiated by the government of the country, by the cabinet, by the handful of people who really govern the country. It doesn't matter whether you have practically every member of parliament on your side, you cannot get what you want unless the cabinet initiate legislation, a situation by which the private member has become almost of no account at all, the ordinary private member of parliament. He may introduce bills, but he knows himself that he is only registering a pious opinion of a certain number of electors in his constituency; it may be his own; but that pious opinion will never find its way onto the statute book of his country until the government in power, the prime minister and his colleagues, introduces a government measure to carry that reform. Well then, the whole problem of people who want reform is, to bring enough political pressure to bear upon the government to lead them to initiate, to draft a bill, and introduce it in the first instance, into the House of Commons, force it through the House of Commons, press it through the House of Lords, and finally land it safely, having passed through the shoals and rapids of the parliamentary river, safely on the statute book as an Act of Parliament. Well, combinations of voters have tried for generations, even with the power of the vote, to get their reforms registered in legislation, and have failed. You have to get your cause made a first class measure; you have to make the situation in the country so urgent and so pressing that it has become politically dangerous for the government to neglect that question any longer, so politically expedient for them to do it that they realize they cannot present themselves to the country at the next general election unless it has been done.

Well, that was the problem we had to face, and we faced it, a mere handful of women. Well, whether you like our methods or not, we have succeeded in making woman suffrage one of the questions which even cabinet ministers now admit cannot indefinitely be neglected. It must be dealt with within a very short period of time. No other methods than ours would have brought about that result. You may have sentimental articles in magazines by the chancellor of the exchequer who seems to be able to spare time from his ordinary avocations to write magazine articles telling you that militancy is a drag on the movement for woman suffrage. But our answer to that is, methinks our gentlemen doth protest too much, because until militancy became to be known neither Mr Lloyd George nor any statesman, no, nor any member of parliament, ever thought it was necessary to mention the subject of woman suffrage at all. Now they mention it constantly, to tell us what damage we have done to our cause. They are all urging us to consider the serious position into which we have brought the cause of woman suffrage.

30

MARGARET SANGER

Born 1879, Corning, New York, United States of America
Died 1966, Tucson, Arizona, United States of America

'Birth Control – A parents' problem or woman's?' from *Woman and the New Race*

1920

The problem of birth control has arisen directly from the effort of the feminine spirit to free itself from bondage. Woman herself has wrought that bondage through her reproductive powers and while enslaving herself has enslaved the world. The physical suffering to be relieved is chiefly woman's. Hers, too, is the love life that dies first under the blight of too prolific breeding. Within her is wrapped up the future of the race – it is hers to make or mar. All of these considerations point unmistakably to one fact – it is woman's duty as well as her privilege to lay hold of the means of freedom. Whatever men may do, she cannot escape the responsibility. For ages she has been deprived of the opportunity to meet this obligation. She is now emerging from her helplessness. Even as no one can share the suffering of the overburdened mother, so no one can do this work for her. Others may help, but she and she alone can free herself.

The basic freedom of the world is women's freedom. A free race cannot be born of slave mothers. A woman enchained cannot choose but give a measure of that bondage to her sons and daughters. No woman can call herself free who does not own and control her body. No woman can call herself free until she can choose consciously whether she will or will not be a mother.

It does not greatly alter the case that some women call themselves free because they earn their own livings, while others profess freedom because they defy the conventions of sex relationship. She who earns her own living gains a sort of freedom that is not to be undervalued, but in quality and in quantity it is of little account beside the untrammeled choice of mating or not mating, of being a mother or not being a mother. She gains food and clothing and shelter, at least without submitting to the charity of her companion, but the earning of her own living does not give her the development of her inner sex urge, far deeper and more powerful in its outworking than any of these externals. In order to have that development, she must still meet and solve the problem of motherhood.

With the so-called 'free' woman, who chooses a mate in defiance of convention, freedom is largely a question of character and audacity. If she does attain to an unrestricted choice of a mate, she is still in a position to be enslaved through her reproductive powers. Indeed, the pressure of law and custom upon the woman not legally married is likely to make her more of a slave than the woman fortunate enough to marry the man of her choice.

Look at it from any standpoint you will, suggest any solution you will, conventional or unconventional, sanctioned by law or in defiance of law, woman is in the same position, fundamentally, until she is able to determine for herself whether she will be a mother and to fix the number of her offspring. This unavoidable situation is alone enough to make birth control, first of all, a woman's problem. On the very face of the matter, voluntary motherhood is chiefly the concern of the woman.

It is persistently urged, however, that since sex expression is the act of two, the responsibility of controlling the results should not be placed upon woman alone. Is it fair, it is asked, to give her, instead of the man, the task of protecting herself when she is, perhaps, less rugged in physique than her mate, and has, at all events, the normal, periodic inconveniences of her sex?

We must examine this phase of her problem in two lights – that of the ideal, and of the conditions working toward the ideal. In an ideal society, no doubt, birth control would become the concern of the man as well as the woman. The hard, inescapable fact which we encounter to-day is that man has not only refused any such responsibility, but has individually and collectively sought to prevent woman from obtaining knowledge by which she could assume this responsibility for herself. She is still in the position of a dependent to-day because her mate has refused to consider her as an individual apart from his needs. She is still bound because she has in the past left the solution of the problem to him. Having left it to him, she finds that instead of rights, she has only such privileges as she has gained by petitioning, coaxing and cozening. Having left it to him, she is exploited, driven and enslaved to his desires.

While it is true that he suffers many evils as the consequence of this situation, she suffers vastly more. While it is true that he should be awakened to the cause of these evils, we know that they come home to her with crushing force every day. It is she who has the long burden of carrying, bearing and rearing the unwanted children. It is she who must watch beside the beds of pain where lie the babies who suffer because they have come into overcrowded homes. It is her heart that the sight of the deformed, the subnormal, the undernourished, the overworked child smites first and oftenest and hardest. It is her love life that dies first in the fear of undesired pregnancy. It is her opportunity for self expression that perishes first and most hopelessly because of it.

Conditions, rather than theories, facts, rather than dreams, govern the problem. They place it squarely upon the shoulders of woman. She has learned that whatever the moral responsibility of the man in this direction may be, he does not discharge it. She has learned that, lovable and considerable as the individual husband may be, she has nothing to expect from men in the mass, when they make laws and decree customs. She knows that regardless of what ought to be, the brutal, unavoidable fact is that she will never receive her freedom until she takes it for herself.

Having learned this much, she has yet something more to learn. Women are too much inclined to follow in the footsteps of men, to try to think as men think, to try to solve the general problems of life as men solve them. If after attaining their freedom, women accept conditions in the spheres of government, industry, art, morals and religion as they find them, they will be but taking a leaf out of man's book. The woman is not needed to do man's work. She is not needed to think man's thoughts. She need not fear that the masculine mind, almost universally dominant, will fail to take care of its own. Her mission is not to enhance the masculine spirit, but to express the feminine; here is not to preserve a man-made world, but to create a human world by the infusion of the feminine element into all of its activities.

Woman must not accept; she must challenge. She must not be awed by that which has been built up around her; she must reverence that within her which struggles for expression. Her eyes must be less upon what is and more clearly upon what should be. She must listen only with a frankly questioning attitude to the dogmatized opinions of man-made society. When she chooses her new, free course of action, it must be in the light of her own opinion – of her own intuition. Only so can she give play to the feminine spirit. Only thus can she free her mate from the bondage which he wrought for himself when he wrought hers. Only thus can she restore to him that of which he robbed himself in restricting her. Only thus can she remake the world.

The world is, indeed, hers to remake, it is hers to build and to recreate. Even as she has permitted the suppression of her own feminine element and the consequent impoverishment of industry, art, letters, science, morals, religions and social intercourse, so it is hers to enrich all these.

Woman must have her freedom – the fundamental freedom of choosing whether or not she shall be a mother and how many children she will have. Regardless of what man's attitude may be, that problem is hers – and before it can be his, it is hers alone.

She goes through the vale of death alone, each time a babe is born. As it is the right neither of man nor the state to coerce her into this ordeal, so it is her right to decide whether she will endure it. That right to decide imposes upon her the duty of clearing the way to knowledge by which she may make and carry out the decision.

Birth control is woman's problem. The quicker she accepts it as hers and hers alone, the quicker will society respect motherhood. The quicker, too, will the world be made a fit place for her children to live.

31

ALEXANDRA KOLLONTAI

Born 1872, Saint Petersburg, Russia
Died 1952, Moscow, USSR

from *Sexual Relations and the Class Struggle*

1921

What are the roots of this unforgivable indifference to one of the essential tasks of the working class? How can we explain to ourselves the hypocritical way in which 'sexual problems' are relegated to the realm of 'private matters' that are not worth the effort and attention of the collective? Why has the fact been ignored that throughout history one of the constant features of social struggle has been the attempt to change relationships; and that the way personal relationships are organised in a certain social group has had a vital influence on the outcome of the struggle between hostile social classes?

The tragedy of our society is not just that the usual forms of behaviour and the principles regulating this behaviour are breaking down, but that a spontaneous wave of new attempts at living is developing from within the social fabric, giving man hopes and ideals that cannot yet be realised.

We are people living in the world of property relationships, a world of sharp class contradictions and of an individualistic morality. We still live and think under the heavy hand of an unavoidable loneliness of spirit. Man experiences this 'loneliness' even in towns full of shouting noise and people, even in a crowd of close friends and work-mates. Because of their loneliness men are apt to cling in a predatory and unhealthy way to illusions about finding a soul mate from among the members of the opposite sex. They see sly Eros as the only means of charming away, if only for a time, the gloom of inescapable loneliness.

People have perhaps never in any age felt spiritual loneliness as deeply and persistently as at the present time. People have probably never become so depressed and fallen so fully under the numbing influence of this loneliness.

It could hardly be otherwise. The darkness never seems so black as when there's a light shining just ahead.

The individualists, who are only loosely organised into a collective with other individuals, now have the chance to change their sexual relationships so that they are based on the creative principle of friendship and togetherness rather than on something blindly physiological. The individualistic property morality of the present day is beginning to seem very obviously paralysing and oppressive. In criticising the quality of sexual relationships modern man is doing so far more than rejecting the outdated forms of behaviour of the current moral code. His lonely soul is seeking the regeneration of the very essence of these relationships. He moans and pines for 'great love', for a situation of warmth and creativity which alone has the power to disperse the cold spirit of loneliness from which present day 'Individualists' suffer.

If the sexual crisis is three quarters the result of external socioeconomic relationships, the other quarter hinges on our 'refined individualistic psyche', fostered by the ruling bourgeois ideology. The 'potential for loving' of people today is, as the German writer Meisel-Hess puts it, at a low ebb. Men and women seek each other in the hope of finding for themselves, through another person, a means to a larger share of spiritual and physical pleasure. It makes no difference whether they are married to the partner or not, they give little thought to what's going on in the other person, to what's happening to their emotions and psychological processes.

The 'crude individualism' that adorns our era is perhaps nowhere as blatant as in the organisation of sexual relationships. A person wants to escape from his loneliness and naively imagines that being 'in love' gives him the right to the soul of the other person – the right to warm himself in the rays of that rare blessing of emotional closeness and understanding. We individualists have had our emotions spoiled in the persistent cult of the 'ego'. We imagine that we can reach the happiness of being in a state of 'great love' with those near to us, without having to 'give' up anything of ourselves.

The claims we make on our 'contracted partner' are absolute and undivided. We are unable to follow the simplest rule of love – that another person should be treated with great consideration. New concepts of the relationships between the sexes are already being outlined. They will teach us to achieve relationships based on the unfamiliar ideas of complete freedom, equality and genuine friendship. But in the meantime mankind has to sit in the cold with its spiritual loneliness and can only dream about the 'better age' when all relationships between people will be warmed by the rays of 'the sun god', will experience a sense of togetherness, and will be educated in the new conditions of living.

The sexual crisis cannot be solved unless there is a radical reform of the human psyche, and unless man's potential for loving is increased. And a basic transformation of the socio-economic relationships along communist lines is essential if the psyche is to be re-formed. This is an 'old truth' but there is no other way out.

The sexual crisis will in no way be reduced, whatever kind of marriage or personal relationships people care to try.

History has never seen such a variety of personal relationships – indissoluble marriage with its 'stable family', 'free unions', secret adultery; a girl living quite openly with her lover in a so-called 'wild marriage'; pair marriage, marriage in threes and even the complicated marriage of four people – not to talk of the various forms of commercial prostitution. You get the same two moral codes existing side by side in the peasantry as well – a mixture of the old tribal way of life and the developing bourgeois family. Thus you get the permissiveness of the girls' house side by side with the attitude that fornication, or men sleeping with their daughters-in-law, is a disgrace.

It's surprising that, in the face of the contradictory and tangled forms of present-day personal relationships, people are able to preserve a faith in moral authority, and are able to make sense of these contradictions and thread their way through these mutually destructive and incompatible moral codes. Even the usual justification – 'I live by the new morality' – doesn't help anyone, since the new morality is still only in the process of being formed. Our task is to draw out from the chaos of present-day contradictory sexual norms the shape, and make clear the principles, of a morality that answers the spirit of the progressive and revolutionary class.

Besides the already mentioned inadequacies of the contemporary psyche – extreme individuality, egoism that has become a cult – the 'sexual crisis' is made worse by two characteristics of the psychology of modern man:

1. The idea of 'possessing' the married partner;
2. The belief that the two sexes are unequal, that they are of unequal worth in every way, in every sphere, including the sexual sphere.

Bourgeois morality, with its introverted individualistic family based entirely on private property, has carefully cultivated the idea that one partner should completely 'possess' the other. It has been very successful. The idea of 'possession' is more pervasive now than under the patrimonial system of marriage relationships.

During the long historical period that developed under the aegis of the 'tribe', the idea of a man possessing his wife (there has never been any thought of a wife having undisputed possession of her husband) did not go further than a purely physical possession. The wife was obliged to be faithful physically – her soul was her own. Even the knights recognised the right of their wives to have *chichesbi* (platonic friends and admirers) and to receive the 'devotion' of other knights and minnesingers. It is the bourgeoisie who have carefully tended and fostered the ideal of absolute possession of the 'contracted partner's' emotional as well as physical 'I', thus extending the concept of property rights to include the right to the other person's whole spiritual and emotional world. Thus the family structure was strengthened and stability guaranteed in the period when the bourgeoisie were struggling for domination. This is the ideal that we have accepted as our heritage and have been prepared to see as an unchangeable moral absolute!

The idea of 'property' goes far beyond the boundaries of 'lawful marriage'. It makes itself felt as an inevitable ingredient of the most 'free' union of love. Contemporary lovers with all their respect for freedom are not satisfied by the knowledge of the physical faithfulness alone of the person they love. To be rid of the eternally present threat of loneliness, we 'launch an attack' on the emotions of the person we love with a cruelty and lack of delicacy that will not be understood by future generations. We demand the right to know every secret of this person's being. The modern lover would forgive physical unfaithfulness sooner than 'spiritual' unfaithfulness. He sees any emotion experienced outside the boundaries of the 'free' relationship as the loss of his own personal treasure.

People 'in love' are unbelievably insensitive in their relations to a third person. We have all no doubt observed this strange situation: two people who love each other are in a hurry, before they have got to know each other properly, to exercise their rights over all the relationships that the other person has formed up till that time, to look into the innermost corners of their partner's life. Two people who yesterday were unknown to each other, and who come together in a single moment of mutual erotic feeling, rush to get at the heart of the other person's being. They want to feel that this strange and incomprehensible psyche, with its past experience that can never be suppressed, is an extension of their own self.

The idea that the married pair are each other's property is so accepted that when a young couple who were yesterday each living their own separate lives are today opening each other's correspondence without a blush, and making common property of the words of a third person who is a friend of only one of them, this hardly strikes us as something unnatural. But this kind of 'intimacy' is only really possible when people have been working out their lives together for a long period of time. Usually a dishonest kind of closeness is substituted for this genuine feeling, the deception being fostered by the mistaken idea that a physical relationship between two people is a sufficient basis for extending the rights of possession to each other's emotional being.

The 'inequality' of the sexes – the inequality of their rights, the unequal value of their physical and emotional experience – is the other significant circumstance that distort the psyche of contemporary man and is a reason for the deepening of the 'sexual crisis'. The 'double morality' inherent in both patrimonial and bourgeois society has, over the course of centuries, poisoned the psyche of men and women. These attitudes are so much a part of us that they are more difficult to get rid of than the ideas about possessing people that we have inherited only from bourgeois ideology.

The idea that the sexes are unequal, even in the sphere of physical and emotional experience, means that the same action will be regarded differently according to whether it was the action of a man or a woman. Even the most 'progressive' member of the bourgeoisie, who has long ago rejected the whole code of current morality, easily catches himself out at this point since he too in judging a man and a different woman for the same behaviour will pass different sentences.

One simple example is enough.

Imagine that a member of the middle-class intelligentsia who is learned, involved in politics and social affairs – who is in short a 'personality', even a 'public figure' – starts sleeping with his cook (a not uncommon thing to happen) and even becomes legally married to her. Does bourgeois society change its attitude to this man, does the event throw even the tiniest shadow of doubt as to his moral worth?

Of course not. Now imagine another situation. A respected woman of bourgeois society – a social figure, a research student, a doctor, or a writer, it's all the same – becomes friendly with her footman, and to complete the scandal marries him. How does bourgeois society react to the behaviour of the hitherto 'respected' woman? They cover her with 'scorn', of course! And remember, it's so much the worse for her if her husband, the footman, is good-looking or possesses other 'physical qualities'. 'It's obvious what she's fallen for', will be the sneer of the hypocritical bourgeoisie.

If a woman's choice has anything of an 'individual character' about it she won't be forgiven by bourgeois society. This attitude is a kind of throwback to the traditions of tribal times. Society still wants a woman to take into account, when she is making her choice, rank and status and the instructions and interests of her family. Bourgeois society cannot see a woman as an independent person separate from her family unit and outside the isolated circle of domestic obligations and virtues.

Contemporary society goes even further than the ancient tribal society in acting as woman's trustee, instructing her not only to marry but to fall in love only with those people who are 'worthy' of her.

We are continually meeting men of considerable spiritual and intellectual qualities who have chosen as their friend-for-life a worthless and empty woman, who in no way matches the spiritual worth of the husband. We accept this as something normal and we don't think twice about it. At the most friends might pity Ivan Ivanovich for having landed himself with such an unbearable wife. But if it happens the other way round, we flap our hands and exclaim with concern. 'How could such an outstanding woman as Maria Petrovna fall for such a nonentity? I begin to doubt the worth of Maria Petrovna.'

Where do we get this double criterion from? What is the reason for it? The reason is undoubtedly that the idea of the sexes being of 'different value' has become, over the centuries, a part of man's psychological make-up. We are used to evaluating a woman not as a personality with individual qualities and failing irrespective of her physical and emotional experience, but only as an appendage of a man. This man, the husband or the lover, throws the light of his personality over the woman, and it is this reflection and not the woman herself that we consider to be the true definition of her emotional and moral make-up. In the eyes of society the personality of a man can be more easily separated from his actions in the sexual sphere. The personality of a woman is judged almost exclusively in terms of her sexual life. This type of attitude stems from the role that women have played in society over the centuries, and it is only now that a re-evaluation of these attitudes is slowly being achieved, at least in outline.

Only a change in the economic role of woman, and her independent involvement in production, can and will bring about the weakening of these mistaken and hypocritical ideas.

The three basic circumstances distorting the modern psyche – extreme egoism, the idea that married partners possess each other, and the acceptance of the inequality of the sexes in terms of physical and emotional experience – must be faced if the sexual problem is to be settled. People will find the 'magic key' with which they can break out of their situation only when their psyche has a sufficient store of 'feelings of consideration', when their ability to love is greater, when the idea of freedom in personal relationships becomes fact and when the principle of 'comradeship' triumphs over the traditional idea of inequality' and submission. The sexual problems cannot be solved without this radical re-education of our psyche.

32

ALEXANDRA KOLLONTAI

Born 1872, Saint Petersburg, Russia
Died 1952, Moscow, USSR

The Labour of Women in the Evolution of the Economy

1921

In its search for new forms of economy and of living which meet the interests of the proletariat, the Soviet republic has inevitably committed a number of mistakes, and has a number of times had to alter and correct its line. But in the sphere of social upbringing and the protection of motherhood, the labour republic from the first months of its existence has marked out the right direction for developments to take. And in this sphere a deep and fundamental revolution in morals and attitudes is being achieved. In this country, where private property has been abolished and where politics is dictated by the desire to raise the level of the general economy, we can now deal in our stride with problems that were insoluble under the bourgeois system.

Soviet Russia has approached the question of protecting motherhood by keeping in view the solution to the basic problem of the labour republic – the development of the productive forces of the country, the raising and restoration of production. In order to carry out the job in hand it is necessary, in the first place, to tap the tremendous forces engaged in unproductive labour and use all available resources effectively; and, in the second place, to guarantee the labour republic an uninterrupted flow of fresh workers in the future, i.e. to guarantee the normal increase in population.

As soon as one adopts this point of view, the question of the emancipation of women from the burden of maternity solves itself. A labour state establishes a completely new principle: care of the younger generation is not a private family affair, but a social-state concern. Maternity is protected and provided for not only in the interests of the woman herself, but still more in the interests of the tasks before the national economy during the transition to a socialist system: it is necessary to save women from an unproductive expenditure of energy on the family so that this energy can be used efficiently in the interests of the collective; it is necessary to protect their health in order to guarantee the labour republic a flow of healthy workers in the future. In the bourgeois state it is not possible to pose the question of maternity in this way: class contradictions and the lack of unity between the interests of private economies and the national economy hinder this. In a labour republic, on the other hand, where the individual economies are dissolving into the general economy and where classes are disintegrating and disappearing, such a solution to the question of maternity is demanded by life, by necessity. The labour republic sees woman first and foremost as a member of the labour force, as a unit of living labour; the function of maternity is seen as highly important, but as a supplementary task and as a task that is not a private family matter but a social matter.

> 'Our policy on the protection of maternity and childhood,' as Vera Pavlovna Lebedeva correctly notes, 'is based on the picture of woman in the work process, which we keep constantly before our mind's eye.'

But in order to give woman the possibility of participating in productive labour without violating her nature or breaking with maternity, it is necessary to take a second step; it is necessary for the collective to assume all the cares of motherhood that have weighed so heavily on women, thus recognising that the task of bringing up children ceases to be a function of the private family and becomes a social function of the state. Maternity begins to be seen in a new light. Soviet power views maternity as a social task. Soviet power, basing itself on this principle, has outlined a number of measures to shift the burden of motherhood from the shoulders of women to those of the state. Soviet power takes responsibility for the care of the baby and the material provision of the child, through the sub-department of the Protection of Motherhood and Childhood (headed by comrade V.P. Lebedeva) and the section of Narkompros (the Commissariat of Education) which deals with social upbringing.

The principle that Soviet power accepts in tackling the problem is that the mother be relieved of the cross of motherhood, and be left with the smile of joy which arises from the contact of the woman with her child. Of course, this principle is far from having been realised. In practice we lag behind our intentions. In our attempts to construct new forms of life and living, to emancipate the labouring woman from family obligations, we are constantly running up against the same obstacles; our poverty, and the devastation of the economy. But a foundation has been laid, the signposts are in place; our task is to follow the directions firmly and decisively.

The labour republic does not limit itself to financial provisions for motherhood and the distribution of benefits. It aims, above all, to transform the conditions of life in order to make it fully possible for a woman to combine motherhood and social labour and to preserve the baby for the republic, surrounding it with the necessary care and attention. From the very first months of the existence of the dictatorship of the proletariat in Russia, worker and peasant power has been striving to cover the country with a network of institutions for the protection of motherhood and the social upbringing of children. The mother and the child became a special object of concern in Soviet politics. During the first months of the revolution, when I held the position of People's Commissar of Social Welfare, I considered it to be my main task to chart the course that the labour republic should adopt in the sphere of protecting the interests of woman as a labour unit and as a mother.

It was at this time that the board which deals with the protection of motherhood was set up and began to organise model 'palaces of motherhood'. Since then, comrade Vera Pavlovna Lebedeva has worked ably and energetically, and the cause of the protection of motherhood has flourished and established firm roots. From the early stages of the working woman's pregnancy, she receives the assistance of Soviet power. Consultation centres for pregnant and nursing mothers are now to be found across the length and breadth of Russia. In tsarist times only six consultation centres existed; now we have about two hundred such centres, and a hundred and thirty-eight milk kitchens.

But of course, the most important task is to relieve the working mother of the unproductive labour involved in ministering to the physical needs of the child. Maternity does not in the least mean that one must oneself change the nappies, wash the baby or even be by the cradle. The social obligation of the mother is above all to give birth to a healthy baby. The labour republic must therefore provide the pregnant woman with the most favourable possible conditions; and the woman for her part must observe all the rules of hygiene during her pregnancy, remembering that in these months she no longer belongs to herself, she is serving the collective, 'producing' from her own flesh and blood a new unit of labour, a new member of the labour republic. The woman's second obligation is to *breast-feed her baby*; only when she has done this does the woman have the right to say that she has fulfilled her obligations. The other tasks involved in caring for the younger generation can be carried out by the collective; of course the maternal instinct is strong, and there is no need to stifle it. But why should this instinct be narrowly limited to the love and care of one's own child? Why not allow this instinct, which for the labour republic has valuable potential, the opportunity to develop vigorously and to reach its highest stage, where the woman not only cares for her own children but has a tender affection for all children?

The slogan advanced by the labour republic, 'Be a mother not only to your child, but to all the children of the workers and peasants,' must show the working woman a new approach to motherhood. There have been instances where a mother, even a communist mother, refuses to breast-feed a baby that is suffering from a lack of milk, only because it is not 'her' baby. Is such behaviour permissible? Future society, with its communist emotion and understanding, will be as amazed at such egoistic and anti-social acts as we are when we read of the woman in prehistoric society who loved her own child but found the appetite to eat the child of another tribe. Or to take another case, examples of which abound: a mother deprives her baby of milk in order to save herself the bother of caring for it. And can we allow the number of foundlings in Soviet Russia to continue growing at the present rate?

These problems, it is true, derive from the fact that the question of motherhood is being tackled but has not yet been completely solved. In this difficult transition period there are hundreds of thousands of women who are exhausted by the dual burden of hired labour and maternity. There are not enough creches, children's homes and maternity homes, and the financial provisions do not keep pace with the price rises of goods on the free market. Consequently working women are afraid of motherhood and abandon their children. The growth in the number of foundlings, however, is also evidence that not all women in the labour republic have yet grasped the fact that motherhood is *not a private matter but a social obligation*. You who work amongst women will have to discuss this question and explain to working women, peasant women and office workers the obligations of motherhood in the new situation of the labour republic. At the same time, we obviously have to step up the work of developing the system of maternity protection and social upbringing. The easier it becomes for mothers to combine work and maternity, the fewer foundlings there will be.

We have already pointed out that maternity does not involve the mother always being with the child or devoting herself entirely to its physical and moral education. The obligation of the mother to her children is to ensure that a healthy and normal atmosphere is provided for their growth and development. In bourgeois society we always find that it is the children of the well-to-do classes who are healthy and flourishing, and never the children of the poor. How do we explain this? Is it because bourgeois mothers devoted themselves entirely to the education of their children? Not at all. Bourgeois mammas were very willing to place their children in the care of hired labourers: nannies and governesses. Only in poor families do mothers themselves bear all the hardships of maternity; the children are with their mothers, but they die like flies. There can be no question of a normal upbringing: the mother does not have the time, and so the children are educated on the street. Every mother of the bourgeois class hurries to shift at least a part of child-care on to society; she sends the child to a kindergarten, to school or to a summer camp. The sensible mother knows that social education gives the child something that the most exclusive maternal love cannot give, in the prosperous circles of bourgeois society, where great significance is attached to giving the children a proper education in the bourgeois spirit, parents give their children into the care of trained nannies, doctors and pedagogues. Hired personnel take over the role of the mother in supervising the physical care and moral education of the child, and the mother is left with the one natural and inalienable right: to give birth to the child.

The labour republic does not take children away from their mothers by force as the bourgeois countries have made out in tales about the horrors of the 'Bolshevik regime'; on the contrary, the labour republic tries to create institutions which would give all women, and not just the rich, the opportunity to have their children brought up in a healthy, joyful atmosphere. Instead of the mother anxiously thrusting her child into the care of a hired nanny, Soviet Russia wants the working or peasant woman to be able to go to work, calm in the knowledge that her child is safe in the expert hands of a creche, a kindergarten or a children's home.

In order to protect woman as the reproducer of the race, the labour republic has created 'maternity homes' and has tried to open them wherever they are particularly needed. In 1921 we had a hundred and thirty-five such homes. These homes not only provide a refuge for the single woman in this most serious period of her life, but allow the married women to get away from home and family and the petty cares of the domestic round and to devote all her attention to regaining strength after the birth and to looking after her child in the first, most important weeks. Later on the mother is not essential to the child, but in the first weeks there is still, as it were, a physiological tie between mother and child, and during this period the separation of mother and child is not advisable. You know yourselves, comrades, how willingly working women and even the wives of important functionaries take advantage of the maternity homes, where they find loving attention and peace. We do not have to use agitational methods to persuade women to use the maternity homes. Our problem is that the material resources of Russia are so limited; we are poor, and this makes it difficult for us to extend our network to cover the entire area of labour Russia with such 'aid stations' for working women and peasant women. There are, unfortunately, still no maternity homes at all in the rural regions, and in general we have done least of all to help the peasant mothers. In fact, all we have done for them is to organise summer creches. This makes it easier for the peasant mother to work in the fields without her baby suffering in any way. In the course of 1921, 689 such creches, providing for 32,180 children, were opened. For mothers working in factories and offices, creches have been set up at factories and institutions, and also at a district and town level. I do not have to emphasise the great significance of these creches for the mothers. The trouble is that we do not have enough of them, and we cannot satisfy even a tenth of the demand for such aid centres.

The network of social education organisations which relieve mothers of the hard work involved in caring for children includes, apart from the creches and the children's homes which cater for orphans and foundlings up to the age of three, kindergartens for the three to seven year olds, children's 'hearths' for children of school age, children's clubs, and finally children's house communes and children's work colonies. The social educational system also includes free meals for children of pre-school and school age. Vera Velichkina (Bonch-Bruyevich), a revolutionary to the end of her life, fought very hard for this measure, the introduction of which has as you know helped us a great deal in the hard years of the civil war, and has saved many children of the proletariat from emaciation and death from starvation. The concern of the state for children is also manifest in the provision of free milk, special food rations for the young, and clothes and footwear for children in need. All these projects are far from having been realised in full; in practice we have covered only a narrow section of the population. However, we have so far failed to relieve the couple from all the difficulties of bringing up children, not because we have taken the wrong course but because our poverty prevents us from fulfilling all that Soviet power has planned. The general direction of the policy on maternity is correct. But our lack of resources hinders us. So far, experiments have only been carried out at a fairly modest level. Even so, they have given results and have revolutionised family life, introducing fundamental changes in the relationships between the sexes. This is a question we will discuss in the following talk.

The task of Soviet power is thus to provide conditions for the woman where her labour will not be spent on non-productive work about the home and looking after children but on the creation of new wealth for the state, for the labour collective. At the same time, it is important to preserve not only the interests of the woman but also the life of the child, and this is to be done by giving the woman the opportunity to combine labour and maternity. Soviet power tries to create a situation where a woman does not have to cling to a man she has grown to loathe only because she has nowhere else to go with her children, and where a woman alone does not have to fear her life and the life of her child. In the labour republic it is not the philanthropists with their humiliating charity but the workers and peasants, fellow-creators of the new society, who hasten to help the working woman and strive to lighten the burden of motherhood. The woman who bears the trials and tribulations of reconstructing the economy on an equal footing with the man, and who participated in the civil war, has a right to demand that in this most important hour of her life, at the moment when she presents society with a new member, the labour republic, the collective, should take upon itself the job of caring for the future of the new citizen.

Russia now has 524 protection of motherhood and social education sections. This is, nevertheless, insufficient. The transitional nature of the dictatorship places women in a particularly difficult situation; the old is destroyed but the new has not yet been created. The party and Soviet power must during this period pay increasing attention to the problem of maternity and the methods of solving it. If correct answers are found to these questions, not only women but also the national economy will gain.

I would like to say a few words about a question which is closely connected with the problem of maternity – the question of abortion, and Soviet Russia's attitude to it. On 20 November 1920 the labour republic issued a law abolishing the penalties that had been attached to abortion. What is the reasoning behind this new attitude? Russia, after all, suffers not from an overproduction of living labour but rather from a lack of it. Russia is thinly, not densely populated. Every unit of labour power is precious. Why then have we declared abortion to be no longer a criminal offence? Hypocrisy and bigotry are alien to proletarian politics. Abortion is a problem connected with the problem of maternity, and likewise derives from the insecure position of women (we are not speaking here of the bourgeois class, where abortion has other reasons – the reluctance to 'divide' an inheritance, to suffer the slightest discomfort, to spoil one's figure or miss a few months of the season etc.)

Abortion exists and flourishes everywhere, and no laws or punitive measures have succeeded in rooting it out. A way round the law is always found. But 'secret help' only cripples women; they become a burden on the labour government, and the size of the labour force is reduced. Abortion, when carried out under proper medical conditions, is less harmful and dangerous, and the woman can get back to work quicker. Soviet power realises that the need for abortion will only disappear on the one hand when Russia has a broad and developed network of institutions protecting motherhood and providing social education, and on the other hand when women understand that *childbirth is a social obligation;* Soviet power has therefore allowed abortion to be performed openly and in clinical conditions.

Besides the large-scale development of motherhood protection, the task of labour Russia is to strengthen in women the healthy instinct of motherhood, to make motherhood and labour for the collective compatible and thus do away with the need for abortion. This is the approach of the labour republic to the question of abortion, which still faces women in the bourgeois countries in all its magnitude. In these countries women are exhausted by the dual burden of hired labour for capital and motherhood. In Soviet Russia the working woman and peasant woman are helping the Communist Party to build a new society and to undermine the old way of life that has enslaved women. As soon as woman is viewed as being essentially a labour unit, the key to the solution of the complex question of maternity can be found. In bourgeois society, where housework complements the system of capitalist economy and private property creates a stable basis for the isolated form of the family, there is no way out for the working woman. The emancipation of women can only be completed when a fundamental transformation of living is effected; and life-styles will change only with the fundamental transformation of all production and the establishment of a communist economy. The revolution in everyday life is unfolding before our very eyes, and in this process the liberation of women is being introduced in practice.

33.

VIRGINIA WOOLF

Born 1882, London, United Kingdom
Died 1941, River Ouse, Sussex, United Kingdom

from *A Room of One's Own*

1929

All I could do was to offer you an opinion upon one minor point – a woman must have money and a room of her own if she is to write fiction; and that, as you will see, leaves the great problem of the true nature of woman and the true nature of fiction unsolved. I have shirked the duty of coming to a conclusion upon these two questions – women and fiction remain, so far as I am concerned, unsolved problems. But in order to make some amends I am going to do what I can to show you how I arrived at this opinion about the room and the money. I am going to develop in your presence as fully and freely as I can the train of thought which led me to think this. Perhaps if I lay bare the ideas, the prejudices, that lie behind this statement you will find that they have some bearing upon women and some upon fiction. At any rate, when a subject is highly controversial – and any question about sex is that – one cannot hope to tell the truth. One can only show how one came to hold whatever opinion one does hold. One can only give one's audience the chance of drawing their own conclusions as they observe the limitations, the prejudices, the idiosyncrasies of the speaker. Fiction here is likely to contain more truth than fact. Therefore I propose, making use of all the liberties and licences of a novelist, to tell you the story of the two days that preceded my coming here – how, bowed down by the weight of the subject which you have laid upon my shoulders, I pondered it, and made it work in and out of my daily life. I need not say that what I am about to describe has no existence; Oxbridge is an invention; so is Fernham; 'I' is only a convenient term for somebody who has no real being. Lies will flow from my lips, but there may perhaps be some truth mixed up with them; it is for you to seek out this truth and to decide whether any part of it is worth keeping. If not, you will of course throw the whole of it into the waste-paper basket and forget all about it.

Here then was I (call me Mary Beton, Mary Seton, Mary Carmichael or by any name you please – it is not a matter of any importance) sitting on the banks of a river a week or two ago in fine October weather, lost in thought. That collar I have spoken of, women and fiction, the need of coming to some conclusion on a subject that raises all sorts of prejudices and passions, bowed my head to the ground. To the right and left bushes of some sort, golden and crimson, glowed with the colour, even it seemed burnt with the heat, of fire. On the further bank the willows wept in perpetual lamentation, their hair about their shoulders. The river reflected whatever it chose of sky and bridge and burning tree, and when the undergraduate had oared his boat through the reflections they closed again, completely, as if he had never been. There one might have sat the clock round lost in thought.

Thought to call it by a prouder name than it deserved – had let its line down into the stream. It swayed, minute after minute, hither and thither among the reflections and the weeds, letting the water lift it and sink it, until – you know the little tug – the sudden conglomeration of an idea at the end of one's line: and then the cautious hauling of it in, and the careful laying of it out? Alas, laid on the grass how small, how insignificant this thought of mine looked; the sort of fish that a good fisherman puts back into the water so that it may grow fatter and be one day worth cooking and eating. I will not trouble you with that thought now, though if you look carefully you may find it for yourselves in the course of what I am going to say.

But however small it was, it had, nevertheless, the mysterious property of its kind – put back into the mind, it became at once very exciting, and important; and as it darted and sank, and flashed hither and thither, set up such a wash and tumult of ideas that it was impossible to sit still. It was thus that I found myself walking with extreme rapidity across a grass plot. Instantly a man's figure rose to intercept me. Nor did I at first under-stand that the gesticulations of a curious-looking object, in a cut-away coat and evening shirt, were aimed at me. His face expressed horror and indignation. Instinct rather than reason came to my help; he was a Beadle; I was a woman. This was the turf; there was the path. Only the Fellows and Scholars are allowed here; the gravel is the place for me. Such thoughts were the work of a moment. As I regained the path the arms of the Beadle sank, his face assumed its usual repose, and though turf is better walking than gravel, no very great harm was done. The only charge I could bring against the Fellows and Scholars of whatever the college might happen to be was that in protection of their turf, which has been rolled for 300 years in succession, they had sent my little fish into hiding.

[...]

Be that as it may, I could not help thinking, as I looked at the works of Shakespeare on the shelf, that the bishop was right at least in this; it would have been impossible, completely and entirely, for any woman to have written the plays of Shakespeare in the age of Shakespeare. Let me imagine, since facts are so hard to come by, what would have happened had Shakespeare had a wonderfully gifted sister called Judith, let us say. Shakespeare himself went, very probably – his mother was an heiress – to the grammar school, where he may have learnt Latin – Ovid, Virgil, and Horace – and the elements of grammar and logic. He was, it is well known, a wild boy who poached rabbits, perhaps shot a deer, and had, rather sooner than he should have done, to marry a woman in the neighbourhood, who bore him a child rather quicker than was right. That escapade sent him to seek his fortune in London. He had, it seemed, a taste for the theatre; he began by holding horses at the stage door. Very soon he got work in the theatre, became a successful actor, and lived at the hub of the universe, meeting everybody, knowing everybody, practising his art on the boards, exercising his wits in the streets, and even getting access to the place of the queen. Meanwhile his extraordinarily gifted sister, let us suppose, remained at home. She was as adventurous, as imaginative, as agog to see the world as he was. But she was not sent to school. She had no chance of learning grammar and logic, let alone of reading Horace and Virgil. She picked up a book now and then, one of her brother's perhaps, and read a few pages. But then her parents came in and told her to mend the stockings or mind the stew and not moon about with books and papers. They would have spoken sharply but kindly, for they were substantial people who knew the conditions of life for a woman and loved their daughter – indeed, more likely than not she was the apple of her father's eye. Perhaps she scribbled some pages up in an apple loft on the sly, but was careful to hide them or set fire to them. Soon, however, before she was out of her teens, she was to be betrothed to the son of a neighbouring wool-stapler. She cried out that marriage was hateful to her, and for that she was severely beaten by her father. Then he ceased to scold her. He begged her instead not to hurt him, not to shame him in this matter of her marriage. He would give her a chain of beads or a fine petticoat, he said; and there were tears in his eyes. How could she disobey him? How could she break his heart? The force of her own gift alone drove her to it. She made up a small parcel of her belongings, let herself down by a rope one summer's night and took the road to London. She was not seventeen. The birds that sang in the hedge were not more musical than she was. She had the quickest fancy, a gift like her brother's, for the tune of words. Like him, she had a taste for the theatre. She stood at the stage door; she wanted to act, she said. Men laughed in her face. The manager – a fat, loose-lipped man – guffawed. He bellowed something about poodles dancing and women acting – no woman, he said, could possibly be an actress. He hinted – you can imagine what. She could get no training in her craft. Could she even seek her dinner in a tavern or roam the streets at midnight? Yet her genius was for fiction and lusted to feed abundantly upon the lives of men and women and the study of their ways. At last – for she was very young, oddly like Shakespeare the poet in her face, with the same grey eyes and rounded brows – at last Nick Greene the actor-manager took pity on her; she found herself with child by that gentleman and so – who shall measure the heat and violence of the poet's heart when caught and tangled in a woman's body? – killed herself one winter's night and lies buried at some cross-roads where the omnibuses now stop outside the Elephant and Castle.

That, more or less, is how the story would run, I think, if a woman in Shakespeare's day had had Shakespeare's genius. But for my part, I agree with the deceased bishop, if such he was – it is unthinkable that any woman in Shakespeare's day should have had Shakespeare's genius. For genius like Shakespeare's is not born among labouring, uneducated, servile people. It was not born in England among the Saxons and the Britons. It is not born today among the working classes. How, then, could it have been born among women whose work began, according to Professor Trevelyan, almost before they were out of the nursery, who were forced to it by their parents and held to it by all the power of law and custom? Yet genius of a sort must have existed among women as it must have existed among the working classes. Now and again an Emily Brontë or a Robert Burns blazes out and proves its presence. But certainly it never got itself on to paper. When, however, one reads of a witch being ducked, of a woman possessed by devils, of a wise woman selling herbs, or even of a very remarkable man who had a mother, then I think we are on the track of a lost novelist, a suppressed poet, of some mute and inglorious Jane Austen, some Emily Brontë who dashed her brains out on the moor or mopped and mowed about the highways crazed with the torture that her gift had put her to. Indeed, I would venture to guess that Anon, who wrote so many poems without signing them, was often a woman. It was a woman, Edward Fitzgerald, I think, suggested, who made the ballads and the folk-songs, crooning them to her children, beguiling her spinning with them, or the length of the winter's night.

This may be true or it may be false – who can say? – but what is true in it, so it seemed to me, reviewing the story of Shakespeare's sister as I had made it, is that any woman born with a great gift in the sixteenth century would certainly have gone crazed, shot herself, or ended her days in some lonely cottage outside the village, half witch, half wizard, feared and mocked at. For it needs little skill in psychology to be sure that a highly gifted girl who had tried to use her gift for poetry would have been so thwarted and hindered by other people, so tortured and pulled asunder by her own contrary instincts, that she must have lost her health and sanity to a certainty. No girl could have walked to London and stood at a stage door and forced her way into the presence of actor-managers without doing herself a violence and suffering an anguish which may have been irrational for chastity may be a fetish invented by certain societies for unknown reasons – but were none the less inevitable. Chastity had then, it has even now, a religious importance in a woman's life, and has so wrapped itself round with nerves and instincts that to cut it free and bring it to the light of day demands courage of the rarest. To have lived a free life in London in the sixteenth century would have meant for a woman who was poet and playwright a nervous stress and dilemma which might well have killed her. Had she survived, whatever she had written would have been twisted and deformed, issuing from a strained and morbid imagination. And undoubtedly, I thought, looking at the shelf where there are no plays by women, her work would have gone unsigned. That refuge she would have sought certainly. It was the relic of the sense of chastity that dictated anonymity to women even so late in the nineteenth century. Currer Bell, George Eliot, George Sand, all the victims of inner strife as their writings prove, sought ineffectively to veil themselves by using the name of a man. Thus they did homage to the convention, which if not implanted by the other sex was liberally encouraged by them (the chief glory of a woman is not to be talked of, said Pericles, himself a much-talked-of man) that publicity in women is detestable. Anonymity runs in their blood. The desire to be veiled still possesses them.

34.

VIRGINIA WOOLF

Born 1882, London, United Kingdom
Died 1941 River Ouse, Sussex, United Kingdom

from *Professions for Women*

1931

What could be easier than to write articles and to buy Persian cats with the profits? But wait a moment. Articles have to be about something. Mine, I seem to remember, was about a novel by a famous man. And while I was writing this review, I discovered that if I were going to review books I should need to do battle with a certain phantom. And the phantom was a woman, and when I came to know her better I called her after the heroine of a famous poem, The Angel in the House. It was she who used to come between me and my paper when I was writing reviews. It was she who bothered me and wasted my time and so tormented me that at last I killed her. You who come of a younger and happier generation may not have heard of her – you may not know what I mean by the Angel in the House. I will describe her as shortly as I can. She was intensely sympathetic. She was immensely charming. She was utterly unselfish. She excelled in the difficult arts of family life. She sacrificed herself daily. If there was chicken, she took the leg; if there was a draught she sat in it – in short she was so constituted that she never had a mind or a wish of her own, but preferred to sympathise always with the minds and wishes of others. Above all – I need not say it – she was pure. Her purity was supposed to be her chief beauty – her blushes, her great grace. In those days – the last of Queen Victoria – every house had its Angel. And when I came to write I encountered her with the very first words. The shadow of her wings fell on my page; I heard the rustling of her skirts in the room. Directly, that is to say, I took my pen in my hand to review that novel by a famous man, she slipped behind me and whispered: 'My dear, you are a young woman. You are writing about a book that has been written by a man. Be sympathetic; be tender; flatter; deceive; use all the arts and wiles of our sex. Never let anybody guess that you have a mind of your own. Above all, be pure.' And she made as if to guide my pen. I now record the one act for which I take some credit to myself, though the credit rightly belongs to some excellent ancestors of mine who left me a certain sum of money – shall we say five hundred pounds a year? – so that it was not necessary for me to depend solely on charm for my living. I turned upon her and caught her by the throat. I did my best to kill her. My excuse, if I were to be had up in a court of law, would be that I acted in self-defence. Had I not killed her she would have killed me. She would have plucked the heart out of my writing. For, as I found, directly I put pen to paper, you cannot review even a novel without having a mind of your own, without expressing what you think to be the truth about human relations, morality, sex. And all these questions, according to the Angel of the House, cannot be dealt with freely and openly by women; they must charm, they must conciliate, they must – to put it bluntly – tell lies if they are to succeed. Thus, whenever I felt the shadow of her wing or the radiance of her halo upon my page, I took up the inkpot and flung it at her. She died hard. Her factitious nature was of great assistance to her. It is far harder to kill a phantom than a reality. She was always creeping back when I thought I had dispatched her. Though I flatter myself that I killed her in the end, the struggle was severe; it took much time that had better have been spent upon learning Greek grammar; or in roaming the world in search of adventures. But it was a real experience; it was an experience that was bound to befall all women writers at that time. Killing the Angel in the House was part of the occupation of a woman writer.

35

VIRGINIA WOOLF

Born 1882, London, United Kingdom
Died 1941 River Ouse, Sussex, United Kingdom

from *Three Guineas*

1938

In other words, sir, I take you to mean that the world as it is at present is divided into two services; one the public and the other the private. In one world the sons of educated men work as civil servants, judges, soldiers and are paid for that work; in the other world, the daughters of educated men work as wives, mothers, daughters but are they not paid for that work? Is the work of a mother, of a wife, of a daughter, worth nothing to the nation in solid cash? That fact, if it be a fact, is so astonishing that we must confirm it by appealing once more to the impeccable Whitaker. Let us turn to his pages again. We may turn them, and turn them again. It seems incredible, yet it seems undeniable. Among all those offices there is no such office as a mother's; among all those salaries there is no such salary as a mother's. The work of an archbishop is worth £15,000 a year to the State; the work of a judge is worth £5,000 a year; the work of a permanent secretary is worth £3,000 a year; the work of an army captain, of a sea captain, of a sergeant of dragoons, of a policeman, of a postman all these works are worth paying out of the taxes, but wives and mothers and daughters who work all day and every day, without whose work the State would collapse and fall to pieces, without whose work your sons, sir, would cease to exist, are paid nothing whatever. Can it be possible? Or have we convicted Whitaker, the impeccable, of errata?

[. . .]

When he says, as history proves that he has said, and may say again, 'I am fighting to protect our country' and thus seeks to rouse her patriotic emotion, she will ask herself, 'What does "our country" mean to me an outsider?' To decide this she will analyse the meaning of patriotism in her own case. She will inform herself of the position of her sex and her class in the past. She will inform herself of the amount of land, wealth and property in the possession of her own sex and class in the present – how much of 'England' in fact belongs to her. From the same sources she will inform herself of the legal protection which the law has given her in the past and now gives her. And if he adds that he is fighting to protect her body, she will reflect upon the degree of physical protection that she now enjoys when the words 'Air Raid Precaution' are written on blank walls. And if he says that he is fighting to protect England from foreign rule, she will reflect that for her there are no 'foreigners', since by law she becomes a foreigner if she marries a foreigner. And she will do her best to make this a fact, not by forced fraternity, but by human sympathy. All these facts will convince her reason (to put it in a nutshell) that her sex and class has very little to thank England for in the past; not much to thank England for in the present; while the security of her person in the future is highly dubious.

36.

RASHID JAHAN

Born 1905, Aligarh, India
Died 1952, Moscow, USSR

Man and Woman

c. 1940

Woman: Arre, you have come again?
Man: Yes.
Woman: But weren't you to be married yesterday?
Man: Yes.
Woman: Then?
Man: Then what?
Woman: I mean, where is your bride?
Man: You really want my life to be ruined.
Woman: But when did I say anything of the sort?
Man: Then what do you mean by troubling me so?
Woman: Meaning?
Man: Why do you pretend? You know exactly what I mean.
Woman: I see. But I have been ready to marry you for over a year; you are the one who declines.
Man: Oh, you mean you are ready to get married? But what about your job?
Woman: That will remain, too.
Man: But I cannot accept that my wife should go about working for others. And instead of looking after the house or her children, she should charge off every morning.
Woman: Won't you also leave for work every morning? Am I supposed to sit at home all day and swat flies?
Man: There are always enough chores to do in the house, such as housekeeping, etc.

180

Woman: Right . . . so while you go to your office I should spend the day peering into every corner of our home.

Man: I didn't say that but surely there is enough to do in the house.

Woman: Such as?

Man: You know, looking after the house . . . After all, our mothers did that, didn't they?

Woman: You mean I should keep the hearth going?

Man: I didn't say that.

Woman: Then what do you mean by looking after the house?

Man: Look here, I don't know. You have made it a habit to pull my leg whenever I come to meet you.

Woman: All right, if you don't like the sound of my voice, I will stay quiet then . . . Tell me, are you really getting married or did you say that just to impress me?

Man: I will get married one day; after all, your highness is not the only woman in the world. Tell me, why are you so worried about me?

Woman: Because I love you very dearly.

Man: Well said! If you really loved me, would you have been so adamant for a year and would you have argued with me? . . . 'I won't leave my job' . . . After all, what is so special about your precious job? It isn't as though you are earning a thousand rupees. All you earn is a hundred rupees, no more.

Woman: Maybe, but these few rupees hold the key to my independence.

Man: You mean your independence lies in a mere hundred rupees?

Woman: Hundred, two hundred . . . that's not the point. The real test of independence is the ability to stand on your own two feet.

Man: You don't have the slightest faith in me. You think I will give you no money.

Woman: Not at all, but I wouldn't have earned that money by my hard work.

Man: How does it make a difference who earns it – a man or a woman.

Woman: Oh, of course it makes a big difference. You must have heard that old folk song: the male sparrow bought a grain of rice, the female bought a grain of daal and together they made khichdi.

Man: I don't want your grain of daal.

Woman: I won't be able to eat plain rice.

Man: Indeed, you will want chutney, papad, pickles.

Woman: Indeed, I will.

Man: Whenever I see you, you are surrounded by a flock of admirers like moths to a flame.

Woman: Obviously, you will not let them enter the house.

Man: Never.

Woman: But you know they are my friends.

Man: Yes, indeed, very dear friends.

Woman: Does that mean they will not be able to come and meet me?

Man: I hate them intensely.

Woman: Can I ask why?

Man: Each one has his or her own temperament.

Woman: So why don't you make sure I sit in parda?

Man: I wish I could do that, but will you agree?

Woman: There are many other things that I wouldn't agree to either.

Man: Anyhow, you may or may not agree to other things, but I will not be able to tolerate the flock of your admirers.

Woman: So, who will be permitted to visit our home?

Man: Only common friends, that is, those who are common to both of us.

Woman: Hmm, Mr and Mrs Sethi and Mr Safdar.

Man: Why? Why can't they come?

Woman: Because I can't stand them.

Man: But why? Why do you dislike them?

Woman: I just do.

Man: Surely there has to be a reason?

Woman: Each one has his or her own temperament.

Man: You talk like a child.

Woman: And you?

Man: I always talk sensibly and rationally.

Woman: Yes, of course you do. According to your argument, you hate my friends so they cannot enter our house but if I hate your friends . . . too bad! They will come and go without restraint.

Man: All right, Bibi Saheba, you work from morning to evening and when I come home tired after a long day and want to enjoy a moment with you, you find that your wife returned home with a drove of friends. So this is the map of married life you have in mind?

Woman: Can I ask what sort of map you have in mind of our life after marriage? In the morning when you are setting out for work, your wife should get you ready all dressed up like a doll! Then, after you have gone, she should stay home turning the beads of a rosary, taking your name and do the housework. This life of forced imprisonment is called 'looking after the house'. And, then, when you return home, tired and irritable, your wife should please you and later fawn over Safdar sahib and Mrs Sethi.

Man: I didn't say anything of the sort.

Woman: Then what did you say?

Man: All I meant was that you should stay home like all the other women and look after the house . . .

Woman: Again, 'look after the house'?

Man: Yes, look after the house.

Woman: I cannot quit my work and sell my freedom.

Man: Your freedom?

Woman: Yes, my freedom.

Man: Indeed! While you draw deep gulps of your freedom, your children will suffer.

Woman: It is not as though the children will be born immediately after marriage.

Man: Well, they will be born some day; unless, of course, you even object to their birth.

Woman: No, I have no such objection.

Man: Will you quit your job when the children are born?

Woman: No, not even then.

Man: Can I ask you, then, who will look after the children?

Woman: You and I, together.

Man: A woman's first duty is towards her children.

Woman: And a man's first duty is to be deserving of children.

Man: What do you mean?

Woman: I mean a woman is always being ordered to raise children, but who do the children belong to?

Man: The father.

Woman: Then why should I raise them? He should raise them who owns them.

Man: You say the strangest of things!

Woman: What's so strange about this?

Man: What isn't strange about this? Now you are refusing to even raise children.

Woman: I may or may not refuse to do so; you clearly are refusing to do it.

Man: My job is not to raise children; my job is to earn money.

Woman: I will earn money, too.

Man: Hmm . . . Such pride over a measly hundred rupees! God alone knows the havoc you would have created had you earned more.

Woman: All right, for the sake of argument, imagine that your salary is a hundred rupees and mine is eight hundred. In that case, who should leave the job? You or me?

Man: You.

Woman: Why?

Man: Because I am a man.

Woman: You mean you consider yourself superior, no matter what the situation?

Man: I am not the only one who thinks so; the universe has created me superior.

Woman: I don't think you are better than me. You should get married to a woman who worships you day and night.

Man: Yes, I will. After all, you are not the only woman in the world.

Woman: Then, go your own way. Why do you come here every day and bother me?

Man (*after a moment's silence*): You claim to set much store by love.

Woman: So do you.

Man (*after another silence*): So, tell me, when will you marry me?

Woman: Whenever you say, but I won't leave my job.

37.
DING LING

Born 1904, Changde, China
Died 1986, Beijing, China

Thoughts on March 8

1942

When will it no longer be necessary to attach special weight to the word 'woman' and raise it specially?

Each year this day comes round. Every year on this day, meetings are held all over the world where women muster their forces. Even though things have not been as lively these last two years in Yan'an as they were in previous years, it appears that at least a few people are busy at work here. And there will certainly be a congress, speeches, circular telegrams, and articles.

Women in Yan'an are happier than women elsewhere in China. So much so that many people ask enviously: 'How come the women comrades get so rosy and fat on millet?' It doesn't seem to surprise anyone that women make up a big proportion of the staff in the hospitals, sanatoria and clinics, but they are inevitably the subject of conversation, as a fascinating problem, on every conceivable occasion.

Moreover, all kinds of women comrades are often the target of deserved criticism. In my view these reproaches are serious and justifiable.

People are always interested when women comrades get married, but that is not enough for them. It is virtually impossible for women comrades to get onto friendly terms with a man comrade, and even less likely for them to become friendly with more than one. Cartoonists ridicule them: 'A departmental head getting married too?' The poets say, 'All the leaders in Yan'an are horsemen, and none of them are artists. In Yan'an it's impossible for an artist to find a pretty sweetheart.' But in other situations, they are lectured: 'Damn it, you look down on us old cadres and say we're country bumpkins. But if it weren't for us country bumpkins, you wouldn't be coming to Yan'an to eat millet!' But women invariably want to get married. (It's even more of a sin not to be married, and single women are even more of a target for rumors and slanderous gossip.) So they can't afford to be choosy, anyone will do: whether he rides horses or wears straw sandals, whether he's an artist or a supervisor. They inevitably have children. The fate of such children is various. Some are wrapped in soft baby wool and patterned felt and looked after by governesses. Others are wrapped in soiled cloth and left crying in their parents' beds, while their parents consume much of the child allowance. But for this allowance (twenty-five yuan a month, or just over three pounds of pork), many of them would probably never get a taste of meat. Whoever they marry, the fact is that those women who are compelled to bear children will probably be publicly derided as 'Noras who have returned home.' Those women comrades in a position to employ governesses can go out once a week to a prim get-together and dance. Behind their backs there will also be the most incredible gossip and whispering campaigns, but as soon as they go somewhere, they cause a great stir and all eyes are glued to them. This has nothing to do with our theories, our doctrines, and the speeches we make at meetings. We all know this to be a fact, a fact that is right before our eyes, but it is never mentioned.

It is the same with divorce. In general there are three conditions to pay attention to when getting married: (1) political purity; (2) both parties should be more or less the same age and comparable in looks; (3) mutual help. Even though everyone is said to fulfill these conditions – as for point 1, there are no open traitors in Yan'an; as for point 3, you can call anything 'mutual help,' including darning socks, patching shoes, and even feminine comfort – everyone nevertheless makes a great show of giving thoughtful attention to them. And yet the pretext for divorce is invariably the wife's political backwardness. I am the first to admit that it is a shame when a man's wife is not progressive and retards his progress. But let us consider to what degree they are backward. Before marrying, they were inspired by the desire to soar in the heavenly heights and lead a life of bitter struggle. They got married partly because of physiological necessity and partly as a response to sweet talk about 'mutual help.' Thereupon they are forced to toil away and become 'Noras returned home.' Afraid of being thought 'backward,' those who are a bit more daring rush around begging nurseries to take their children. They ask for abortions and risk punishment and even death by secretly swallowing potions to produce abortions. But the answer comes back: 'Isn't giving birth to children also work? You're just after an easy life; you want to be in the limelight. After all, what indispensable political work have you performed? Since you are so frightened of having children and are not willing to take responsibility once you have had them, why did you get married in the first place? No one forced you to.' Under these conditions, it is impossible for women to escape this destiny of 'backwardness.' When women capable of working sacrifice their careers for the joys of motherhood, people always sing their praises. But after ten years or so, they have no way of escaping the tragedy of 'backwardness.' Even from my point of view, as a woman, there is nothing attractive about such 'backward' elements. Their skin is beginning to wrinkle, their hair is growing thin, and fatigue is robbing them of their last traces of attractiveness. It should be self-evident that they are in a tragic situation. But whereas in the old society they would probably have been pitied and considered unfortunate, nowadays their tragedy is seen as something self-inflicted, as their just deserts. Is it not so that there is a discussion going on in legal circles as to whether divorces should be granted simply on the petition of one party or on the basis of mutual agreement? In the great majority of cases, it is the husband who petitions for divorce. For the wife to do so, she must be leading an immoral life, and then of course she deserves to be cursed.

I myself am a woman, and I therefore understand the failings of women better than others. But I also have a deeper understanding of what they suffer. Women are incapable of transcending the age they live in, of being perfect, or of being hard as steel. They are incapable of resisting all the temptations of society or all the silent oppression they suffer here in Yan'an. They each have their own past written in blood and tears; they have experienced great emotions – in elation as in depression, whether engaged in the lone battle of life or drawn into the humdrum stream of life. This is even truer of the women comrades who come to Yan'an, and I therefore have much sympathy for those fallen and classified as criminals. What is more, I hope that men, especially those in top positions, as well as women themselves, will consider the mistakes women commit in their social context. It would be better if there were less empty theorizing and more talk about real problems, so that theory and practice would not be divorced, and better if all Communist Party members were more responsible for their own moral conduct. But we must also hope for a little more from our women comrades, especially those in Yan'an. We must urge ourselves on and develop our comradely feeling.

People without ability have never been in a position to seize everything. Therefore, if women want equality, they must first strengthen themselves. There is no need to stress this point, since we all understand it. Today there are certain to be people who make fine speeches bragging about the need to acquire political power first. I would simply mention a few things that any frontliner, whether a proletarian, a fighter in the war of resistance, or a woman, should pay attention to in his or her everyday life:

1. Don't allow yourself to fall ill. A wild life can at times appear romantic, poetic, and attractive, but in today's conditions it is inappropriate. You are the best keeper of your life. There is nothing more unfortunate nowadays than to lose your health. It is closest to your heart. The only thing to do is keep a close watch on it, pay careful attention to it, and cherish it.

2. Make sure you are happy. Only when you are happy can you be youthful, active, fulfilled in your life, and steadfast in the face of all difficulties; only then will you see a future ahead of you and know how to enjoy yourself. This sort of happiness is not a life of contentment, but a life of struggle and of advance. Therefore we should all do some meaningful work each day and some reading, so that each of us is in a position to give something to others. Loafing about simply encourages the feeling that life is hollow, feeble, and in decay.

3. Use your brain, and make a habit of doing so. Correct any tendency not to think and ponder, or to swim with the current. Before you say or do anything, think whether what you are saying is right, whether that is the most suitable way of dealing with the problem, whether it goes against your own principles, whether you feel you can take responsibility for it. Then you will have no cause to regret your actions later. This is what is known as acting rationally. It is the best way of avoiding the pitfalls of sweet words and honeyed

phrases, of being sidetracked by petty gains, of wasting our emotions and wasting our lives.

4. Resolution in hardship, perseverance to the end. Aware, modern women should identify and cast off all their rosy illusions. Happiness is to take up the struggle in the midst of the raging storm and not to pluck the lute in the moonlight or recite poetry among the blossoms. In the absence of the greatest resolution, it is very easy to falter in mid-path. Not to suffer is to become degenerate. The strength to carry on should be nurtured through the quality of 'perseverance.' People without great aims and ambitions rarely have the firmness of purpose that does not covet petty advantages or seek a comfortable existence. But only those who have aims and ambitions for the benefit, not of the individual, but of humankind as a whole can persevere to the end.

Postscript. On rereading this article, it seems to me that there is much room for improvement in the passage on what we should expect from women, but because I have to meet a deadline with the manuscript, I have no time to revise it. But I also feel that there are some things that, if said by a leader before a big audience, would probably evoke satisfaction. But when they are written by a woman, they are more than likely to be demolished. But since I have written it, I offer it as I always intended, for the perusal of those people who have similar views.

38.

HUDA SHAARAWI

Born 1879, Minya, Egypt
Died 1947, Cairo, Egypt

'Pan-Arab Feminism', delivered at the inaugural conference of the Arab Feminist Union

1944

The opening speech

Ladies and Gentlemen, The Arab woman who is equal to the man in duties and obligations will not accept, in the twentieth century, the distinctions between the sexes that the advanced countries have done away with. The Arab woman will not agree to be chained in slavery and to pay for the consequences of men's mistakes with respect to her country's rights and the future of her children. The woman also demands with her loudest voice to be restored her political rights, rights granted to her by the *Sharia* and dictated to her by the demands of the present. The advanced nations have recognised that the man and the woman are to each other like the brain and heart are to the body; if the balance between these two organs is upset the system of the whole body will be upset. Likewise, if the balance between the two sexes in the nation is upset it will disintegrate and collapse. The advanced nations, after careful examination into the matter, have come to believe in the equality of sexes in all rights even though their religious and secular laws have not reached the level Islam has reached in terms of justice towards the woman. Islam has given her the right to vote for the ruler and has allowed her to give opinions on questions of jurisprudence and religion. The woman, given by the Creator the right to vote for the successor of the Prophet, is deprived of the right to vote for a deputy in a circuit or district election by a (male) being created by God. At the same time, this right is enjoyed by a man who might have less education and experience than the woman. And she is the mother who has given birth to the man and has raised him and guided him. The *Sharia* gave her the right to education, to take part in the *hijra* (referring to the time of the Prophet Muhhamad and his flight from Mecca to Medina), and to fight in the ranks of warriors and has made her equal to the man in all rights and responsibilities, even in the crimes that either sex can commit. However, the man who alone distributes rights, has kept for himself the right to legislate and rule, generously turning over to his partner his own share of responsibilities and sanctions without seeking her opinion about the division. The woman today demands to regain her share of rights that have been taken from her and gives back to the man the responsibilities and sanctions he has given to her. Gentlemen, this is justice and I do not believe that the Arab man who demands that the others give him back his usurped rights would be avaricious and not give the woman back her own lawful rights, all the more so since he himself has tasted the bitterness of deprivation and usurped rights.

Whenever the woman has demanded her rights in legislation and ruling to participate with the man in all things that bring good and benefit to her nation and her children, he claims he wants to spare the woman the perils of election battles, *forgetting* that she is more zealous about the election of deputies than men and that she already participates in election battles, quite often influencing the results. It is strange that in these cases she becomes the subject of his respect and kindness but when the election battle subsides he denies her what she has brought about.

If the man is sincere in what he says let him prove this by first giving the woman her political rights without her having to go through cruel political battles. In our parliamentary life there is wide opportunity for that in the elections of the governorates and municipality councils, and family affairs councils and in being appointed a member of the senate. Gentlemen, I leave room for the conferees to defend the rights of the woman in all areas.

The closing speech

In this final session of the conference please allow me, on behalf of myself and the conference organisers, to thank you for honouring us with your sustained presence during the four days of this conference despite the length of the sessions dealing with issues men are often ill at ease with. I thank you for the concern you have expressed on these matters and for the attention you have given to our objectives, a successful step on the road towards realising our demands. We are proud of this step which signals, thanks be to God, that we have gained the confidence of male intellectuals and reformers in the demonstrated abilities of women in effectively carrying out different kinds of work in the service of country and nation. There are some who still hesitate to give us this confidence and do not understand the benefits that accrue to the nation when women enjoy their political rights. Others fear that the women will compete with them in work. Let me assure you all that if depriving women of the political and civil rights they demand, and that men oppose, would benefit the country, or would increase men's rights, we would relinquish them with pleasure, but, unfortunately, they would be lost rights that men could not use for themselves or for the country. These rights, buried alive, are of no benefit to society. Every woman who does not stand up for her legitimate rights would be considered as not standing up for the rights of her country and the future of her children and society. Every man who is pushed by his selfishness to trespass on the legitimate rights of women is robbing the rights of others and bringing harm to his country. He is an obstacle preventing the country from benefiting from the abilities and efforts of half the nation or more. He is impeding the advancement of his country and preventing it from being placed in the position it deserves – among the advanced nations whose civilisation was built on the shoulders of women and men together, just as Arab civilisation at the beginning of Islam was built on the co-operation and equality of the two sexes. Now after this feminist conference and the presentation of the cause of women to the public and the placing of its documents in a historical archive, it is incumbent upon man to record on his own page in the historical record that which will honour him and justify his stand before God, the nation, and future generations.

39

SIMONE DE BEAUVOIR

Born 1908, Paris, France
Died 1986, Paris, France

from *The Second Sex*

1949

I hesitated a long time before writing a book on woman. The subject is irritating, especially for women; and it is not new. Enough ink has flowed over the quarrel about feminism; it is now almost over: let's not talk about it any more. Yet it is still being talked about. And the volumes of idiocies churned out over this past century do not seem to have clarified the problem. Besides, is there a problem? And what is it? Are there even women? True, the theory of the eternal feminine still has its followers; they whisper, 'Even in Russia, *women* are still very much women'; but other well-informed people – and also at times those same ones – lament, 'Woman is losing herself, woman is lost.' It is hard to know any longer if women still exist, if they will always exist, if there should be women at all, what place they hold in this world, what place they should hold. 'Where are the women?' asked a short-lived magazine recently.* But first, what is a woman? '*Tota mulier in utero*: she is a womb,' some say. Yet speaking of certain women, the experts proclaim, 'They are not women', even though they have a uterus like the others. Everyone agrees there are females in the human species; today, as in the past, they make up about half of humanity; and yet we are told that 'femininity is in jeopardy'; we are urged, 'Be women, stay women, become women.' So not every female human being is necessarily a woman; she must take part in this mysterious and endangered reality known as femininity. Is femininity secreted by the ovaries? Is it enshrined in a Platonic heaven? Is a frilly petticoat

---

* Out of print today, entitled *Franchise*.

enough to bring it down to earth? Although some women zealously strive to embody it, the model has never been patented. It is typically described in vague and shimmering terms borrowed from a clairvoyant's vocabulary. In St Thomas's time it was an essence defined with as much certainty as the sedative quality of a poppy. But conceptualism has lost ground: biological and social sciences no longer believe there are immutably determined entities that define given characteristics like those of the woman, the Jew or the black; science considers characteristics as secondary reactions to a *situation*. If there is no such thing today as femininity, it is because there never was. Does the word 'woman', then, have no content? It is what advocates of Enlightenment philosophy, rationalism or nominalism vigorously assert: women are, among human beings, merely those who are arbitrarily designated by the word 'woman'; American women in particular are inclined to think that woman as such no longer exists. If some backward individual still takes herself for a woman, her friends advise her to undergo psychoanalysis to get rid of this obsession. Referring to a book – a very irritating one at that – *Modern Woman: The Lost Sex*, Dorothy Parker wrote: 'I cannot be fair about books that treat women as women. My idea is that all of us, men as well as women, whoever we are, should be considered as human beings.' But nominalism is a doctrine that falls a bit short; and it is easy for anti-feminists to show that women *are* not men. Certainly woman like man is a human being; but such an assertion is abstract; the fact is that every concrete human being is always uniquely situated. Rejecting the notions of the eternal feminine, the black soul or the Jewish character is not to deny that there are today Jews, blacks or women: this denial is not a liberation for those concerned, but an inauthentic flight. Clearly, no woman can claim without bad faith to be situated beyond her sex. A few years ago, a well-known woman writer refused to have her portrait appear in a series of photographs devoted specifically to women writers. She wanted to be included in the men's category; but to get this privilege, she used her husband's influence. Women who assert they are men still claim masculine consideration and respect. I also remember a young Trotskyite standing on a platform during a stormy meeting, about to come to blows in spite of her obvious fragility. She was denying her feminine frailty; but it was for the love of a militant man she wanted to be equal to. The defiant position that American women occupy proves they are haunted by the feeling of their own femininity. And the truth is that anyone can clearly see that humanity is split into two categories of individuals with manifestly different clothes, faces, bodies, smiles, movements, interests and occupations; these differences are perhaps superficial; perhaps they are destined to disappear. What is certain is that for the moment they exist in a strikingly obvious way.

If the female function is not enough to define woman, and if we also reject the explanation of the 'eternal feminine', but if we accept, even temporarily, that there are women on the earth, we then have to ask: what is a woman?

Merely stating the problem suggests an immediate answer to me. It is significant that I pose it. It would never occur to a man to write a book on the singular situation of males in humanity.* If I want to define myself, I first have to say, 'I am a woman'; all other assertions will arise from this basic truth. A man never begins by positing himself as an individual of a certain sex: that he is a man is obvious. The categories 'masculine' and 'feminine' appear as symmetrical in a formal way on town hall records or identification papers. The relation of the two sexes is not that of two electrical poles: the man represents both the positive and the neuter to such an extent that in French *hommes* designates human beings, the particular meaning of the word *vir* being assimilated into the general meaning of the word 'homo'. Woman is the negative, to such a point that any determination is imputed to her as a limitation, without reciprocity. I used to get annoyed in abstract discussions to hear men tell me: 'You think such and such a thing because you're a woman.' But I know my only defence is to answer, 'I think it because it is true,' thereby eliminating my subjectivity; it was out of the question to answer, 'And you think the contrary because you are a man,' because it is understood that being a man is not a particularity; a man is in his right by virtue of being man; it is the woman who is in the wrong. In fact, just as for the ancients there was an absolute vertical that defined the oblique, there is an absolute human type that is masculine. Woman has ovaries and a uterus; such are the particular conditions that lock her in her subjectivity; some even say she

* The Kinsey Report, for example, confines itself to defining the sexual characteristics of the American man, which is completely different.

thinks with her hormones. Man vainly forgets that his anatomy also includes hormones and testicles. He grasps his body as a direct and normal link with the world that he believes he apprehends in all objectivity, whereas he considers woman's body an obstacle, a prison, burdened by everything that particularises it. 'The female is female by virtue of a certain *lack* of qualities,' Aristotle said. 'We should regard women's nature as suffering from natural defectiveness.' And St Thomas in his turn decreed that woman was an 'incomplete man', an 'incidental' being. This is what the Genesis story symbolises, where Eve appears as if drawn from Adam's 'supernumerary' bone, in Bossuet's words. Humanity is male, and man defines woman, not in herself, but in relation to himself; she is not considered an autonomous being. 'Woman, the relative being,' writes Michelet. Thus Monsieur Benda declares in *Uriel's Report*: 'A man's body has meaning by itself, disregarding the body of the woman, whereas the woman's body seems devoid of meaning without reference to the male. Man thinks himself without woman. Woman does not think herself without man.' And she is nothing other than what man decides; she is thus called 'the sex', meaning that the male sees her essentially as a sexed being; for him she is sex, so she is it in the absolute. She determines and differentiates herself in relation to man, and he does not in relation to her; she is the inessential in front of the essential. He is the Subject; he is the Absolute. She is the Other.*

---

* This idea has been expressed in its most explicit form by E. Levinas in his essay on *Time and the Other*. He expresses it like this: 'Is there not a situation where alterity would be borne by a being in a positive sense, as essence? What is the alterity that does not purely and simply enter into the opposition of two species of the same genus? I think that the absolutely contrary contrary, whose contrariety is in no way affected by the relationship that can be established between it and its correlative, the contrariety that permits its terms to remain absolutely other, is the feminine. Sex is not some specific difference . . . Neither is the difference between the sexes a contradiction . . . Neither is the difference between the sexes the duality of two complementary terms, for two complementary terms presuppose a preexisting whole . . . [A]lterity is accomplished in the feminine. The term is on the same level as, but in meaning opposed to, consciousness.' I suppose Mr Levinas is not forgetting that woman also is consciousness for herself. But it is striking that he deliberately adopts a man's point of view, disregarding the reciprocity of the subject and the object. When he writes that woman is mystery, he assumes that she is mystery for man. So this apparently objective description, is in fact an affirmation of masculine privilege.

The category of *Other* is as original as consciousness itself. The duality between Self and Other can be found in the most primitive societies, in the most ancient mythologies; this division did not always fall into the category of the division of the sexes, it was not based on any empirical given: this comes out in works like Granet's on Chinese thought, and Dumézil's on India and Rome. In couples such as VarunaMitra, Uranos-Zeus, SunMoon, DayNight, no feminine element is involved at the outset; neither in GoodEvil, auspicious and inauspicious, left and right, God and Lucifer; alterity is the fundamental category of human thought. No group ever defines itself as One without immediately setting up the Other opposite itself. It only takes three travellers brought together by chance in the same train compartment for the rest of the travellers to become vaguely hostile 'others.' Village people view anyone not belonging to the village as suspicious 'others'. For the native of a country, inhabitants of other countries are viewed as 'foreigners'; Jews are the 'others' for anti-Semites, blacks for racist Americans, indigenous people for colonists, proletarians for the propertied classes. After studying the diverse forms of primitive society in depth, Lévi-Strauss could conclude: 'The passage from the state of Nature to the state of Culture is defined by man's ability to think biological relations as systems of oppositions; duality, alternation, opposition, and symmetry, whether occurring in defined or less clear form, are not so much phenomena to explain as fundamental and immediate givens of social reality.'* These phenomena could not be understood if human reality were solely a *Mitsein* based on solidarity and friendship. On the contrary, they become clear if, following Hegel, a fundamental hostility to any other consciousness is found in consciousness itself; the subject posits itself only in opposition; it asserts itself as the essential and sets up the other as inessential, as the object.

But the other consciousness has an opposing reciprocal claim: travelling, a local is shocked to realise that in neighbouring countries locals view him as a foreigner; between villages, clans, nations and classes there are wars, potlatches, agreements, treaties and struggles that remove the

---

* See Claude Lévi-Strauss, The Elementary Structures of Kinship. I thank Claude Lévi-Strauss for sharing the proofs of his thesis that I drew on heavily, particularly in the second part, pp. 78–92.

absolute meaning from the idea of the Other and bring out its relativity; whether one likes it or not, individuals and groups have no choice but to recognise the reciprocity of their relation. How is it, then, that between the sexes this reciprocity has not been put forward, that one of the terms has been asserted as the only essential one, denying any relativity in regard to its correlative, defining the latter as pure alterity? Why do women not contest male sovereignty? No subject posits itself spontaneously and at once as the inessential from the outset; it is not the Other who, defining itself as Other, defines the One; the Other is posited as Other by the One positing itself as One. But in order for the Other not to turn into the One, the Other has to submit to this foreign point of view. Where does this submission in woman come from?

[. . .]

Childhood

One is not born, but rather becomes, woman. No biological, psychical or economic destiny defines the figure that the human female takes on in society; it is civilisation as a whole that elaborates this intermediary product between the male and the eunuch that is called feminine. Only the mediation of another can constitute an individual as an *Other*. Inasmuch as he exists for himself, the child would not grasp himself as sexually differentiated. For girls and boys, the body is first the radiation of a subjectivity, the instrument that brings about the comprehension of the world: they apprehend the universe through their eyes and hands, and not through their sexual parts. The drama of birth and weaning takes place in the same way for infants of both sexes; they have the same interests and pleasures; sucking is the first source of their most pleasurable sensations; they then go through an anal phase in which they get their greatest satisfactions from excretory functions common to both; their genital development is similar; they explore their bodies with the same curiosity and the same indifference; they derive the same uncertain pleasure from the clitoris and the penis; insofar as their sensibility already needs an object, it turns towards the mother: it is the soft, smooth, supple feminine flesh that arouses sexual desires and these desires are prehensile; the girl like the boy kisses, touches and caresses her mother in an aggressive manner; they feel the same jealousy at the birth of a new child; they show it with the same behaviour: anger, sulking, urinary problems; they have recourse to the same coquetry to gain the love of adults. Up to twelve, the girl is just as sturdy as her brothers; she shows the same intellectual aptitudes; she is not barred from competing with them in any area. If well before puberty and sometimes even starting from early childhood she already appears sexually specified, it is not because mysterious instincts immediately destine her to passivity, coquetry or motherhood but because the intervention of others in the infant's life is almost originary, and her vocation is imperiously breathed into her from the first years of her life.

40

CLAUDIA JONES

Born 1915, Belmont, Port of Spain, Trinidad and Tobago
Died 1964, London, United Kingdom

An End to the Neglect of the Problems of the Negro Women

1949

An outstanding feature of the present stage of the Negro liberation move-ment is the growth in the militant participation of Negro women in all aspects of the struggle for peace, civil rights, and economic security. Symptomatic of this new militancy is the fact that Negro women have become symbols of many present-day struggles of the Negro people. This growth of militancy among Negro women has profound meaning, both for the Negro liberation movement and for the emerging anti-fascist, anti-imperialist coalition.

To understand this militancy correctly, to deepen and extend the role of Negro women in the struggle for peace and for all interests of the work-ing class and the Negro people, means primarily to overcome the gross neglect of the special problems of Negro women. This neglect has too long permeated the ranks of the labor movement generally, of Left-progressives, and also of the Communist Party. The most serious assessment of these shortcomings by progressives, especially by Marxist-Leninists, is vitally necessary if we are to help accelerate this development and integrate Negro women in the progressive and labor movement and in our own Party.

The bourgeoisie is fearful of the militancy of the Negro woman, and for good reason. The capitalists know, far better than many progressives seem to know, that once Negro women undertake action, the militancy of the whole Negro people, and thus of the anti-imperialist coalition, is greatly enhanced.

Historically, the Negro woman has been the guardian, the protector, of the Negro family. From the days of the slave traders down to the present, the Negro woman has had the responsibility of caring for the needs of the family, of militantly shielding it from the blows of Jim-Crow insults, of rearing children in an atmosphere of lynch terror, segregation, and police brutality, and of fighting for an education for the children. The intensified oppression of the Negro people, which has been the hallmark of the postwar reactionary offensive, cannot therefore but lead to an acceleration of the militancy of the Negro woman. As mother, as Negro, and as worker, the Negro woman fights against the wiping out of the Negro family, against the Jim-Crow ghetto existence which destroys the health, morale, and very life of millions of her sisters, brothers, and children.

Viewed in this light, it is not accidental that the American bourgeoisie has intensified its oppression, not only of the Negro people in general, but of Negro women in particular. Nothing so exposes the drive to fascization in the nation as the callous attitude which the bourgeoisie displays and cultivates toward Negro women. The vaunted boast of the ideologists of Big Business – that American women possess 'the greatest equality' in the world is exposed in all its hypocrisy when one sees that in many parts of the world, particularly in the Soviet Union, the New Democracies and the formerly oppressed land of China, women are attaining new heights of equality. But above all else, Wall Street's boast stops at the water's edge where Negro and working-class women are concerned. Not equality, but degradation and super-exploitation: this is the actual lot of Negro women!

Consider the hypocrisy of the Truman Administration, which boasts about 'exporting democracy throughout the world' while the state of Georgia keeps a widowed Negro mother of twelve children under lock and key. Her crime? She defended her life and dignity – aided by her two sons – from the attacks of a 'white supremacist.' Or ponder the mute silence with which the Department of Justice has greeted Mrs Amy Mallard, widowed Negro school-teacher, since her husband was lynched in Georgia because he had bought a new Cadillac and become, in the opinion of the 'white supremacists,' 'too uppity.' Contrast this with the crocodile tears shed by the U.S. delegation to the United Nations for Cardinal Mindszenty, who collaborated with the enemies of the Hungarian People's Republic and sought to hinder the forward march to fuller democracy by the formerly oppressed workers and peasants of Hungary. Only recently, President

Truman spoke solicitously in a Mother's Day Proclamation about the manifestation of 'our love and reverence' for all mothers of the land. The so-called 'love and reverence' for the mothers of the land by no means includes Negro mothers who, like Rosa Lee Ingram, Amy Mallard, the wives and mothers of the Trenton Six, or the other countless victims, dare to fight back against lynch law and 'white supremacy' violence.

ECONOMIC HARDSHIPS

Very much to the contrary, Negro women – as workers, as Negroes, and as women – are the most oppressed stratum of the whole population.

In 1940, two out of every five Negro women, in contrast to two out of every eight white women, worked for a living. By virtue of their majority status among the Negro people, Negro women not only constitute the largest percentage of women heads of families, but are the main bread-winners of the Negro family. The large proportion of Negro women in the labor market is primarily a result of the low-scale earnings of Negro men. This disproportion also has its roots in the treatment and position of Negro women over the centuries.

Following emancipation, and persisting to the present day, a large percentage of Negro women – married as well as single – were forced to work for a living. But despite the shift in employment of Negro women from rural to urban areas, Negro women are still generally confined to the lowest-paying jobs. The Women's Bureau, U.S. Department of Labor, *Handbook of Facts for Women Workers* (1948, Bulletin 225), shows white women workers as having median earnings more than twice as high as those of non-white women, and non-white women workers (mainly Negro women) as earning less than $500 a year! In the rural South, the earnings of women are even less. In three large Northern industrial communities, the median income of white families ($1,720) is almost 60 percent higher than that of Negro families ($1,095). The super-exploitation of the Negro woman worker is thus revealed not only in that she receives, as woman, less than equal pay for equal work with men, but in that the majority of Negro women get less than half the pay of white women. Little wonder, then, that in Negro communities the conditions of ghetto-living – low salaries, high rents, high prices, etc. – virtually become an iron curtain hemming in the lives of Negro children and undermining their health and spirit! Little wonder that the maternity death rate for Negro women is triple that of white women! Little wonder that one out of every ten Negro children born in the United States does not grow to manhood or womanhood!

The low scale of earnings of the Negro woman is directly related to her almost complete exclusion from virtually all fields of work except the most menial and underpaid, namely, domestic service. Revealing are the following data given in the report of 1945, *Negro Women War Workers* (Women's Bureau, U.S. Department of Labor, Bulletin 205): Of a total 7½ million Negro women, over a million are in domestic and personal service. The overwhelming bulk – about 918,000 – of these women workers are employed in private families, and some 98,000 are employed as cooks, waitresses, and in like services in other than private homes. The remaining 60,000 workers in service trades are in miscellaneous personal service occupations (beauticians, boarding-house and lodging-house keepers, charwomen, janitors, practical nurses, housekeepers, hostesses, and elevator operators).

The next largest number of Negro women workers are engaged in agricultural work. In 1940, about 245,000 were agricultural workers. Of them, some 128,000 were unpaid family workers.

Industrial and other workers numbered more than 96,000 of the Negro women reported. Thirty-six thousand of these women were in manufacturing, the chief groups being 11,300 in apparel and other fabricated textile products, 11,000 in tobacco manufactures, and 5,600 in food and related products.

Clerical and kindred workers in general numbered only 13,000. There were only 8,300 Negro women workers in civil service.

The rest of the Negro women who work for a living were distributed along the following lines: teachers, 50,000; nurses and student nurses, 6,700; social and welfare workers, 1,700; dentists, pharmacists, and veterinarians, 120; physicians and surgeons, 129; actresses, 200; authors, editors, and reporters, 100; lawyers and judges, 39; librarians, 400; and other categories likewise illustrating the large-scale exclusion of Negro women from the professions.

During the anti-Axis war, Negro women for the first time in history had an opportunity to utilize their skills and talents in occupations other than domestic and personal service. They became trail blazers in many fields. Since the end of the war, however, this has given way to growing unemployment, to the wholesale firing of Negro women, particularly in basic industry.

This process has been intensified with the development of the economic crisis. Today, Negro women are being forced back into domestic work in great numbers. In New York State, for example, this trend was officially confirmed recently when Edward Corsi, Commissioner of the State Labor Department, revealed that for the first time since the war, domestic help is readily obtainable. Corsi in effect admitted that Negro women are not voluntarily giving up jobs, but rather are being systematically pushed out of industry. Unemployment, which has always hit the Negro woman first and hardest, plus the high cost of living, is what compels Negro women to re-enter domestic service today. Accompanying this trend is an ideological campaign to make domestic work palatable. Daily newspaper advertisements which base their arguments on the claim that most domestic workers who apply for jobs through U.S.E.S. 'prefer this type of work to work in industry,' are propagandizing the 'virtues' of domestic work, especially of 'sleepin positions.'

Inherently connected with the question of job opportunities where the Negro woman is concerned, is the special oppression she faces as Negro, as woman, and as worker. She is the victim of the white chauvinist stereotype as to where her place should be. In the film, radio, and press, the Negro woman is not pictured in her real role as breadwinner, mother, and protector of the family, but as a traditional 'mammy' who puts the care of children and families of others above her own. This traditional stereotype of the Negro slave mother, which to this day appears in commercial advertisements, must be combatted and rejected as a device of the imperialists to perpetuate the white chauvinist ideology that Negro women are 'backward,' 'inferior,' and the 'natural slaves' of others.

HISTORICAL ASPECTS

Actually, the history of the Negro woman shows that the Negro mother under slavery held a key position and played a dominant role in her own family grouping. This was due primarily to two factors: the conditions of slavery, under which marriage, as such, was non-existent, and the Negro's social status was derived from the mother and not the father; and the fact that most of the Negro people brought to these shores by the slave traders came from West Africa where the position of women, based on active participation in property control, was relatively higher in the family than that of European women.

Early historians of the slave trade recall the testimony of travelers indicating that the love of the African mother for her child was unsurpassed in any part of the world. There are numerous stories attesting to the self-sacrificial way in which East African mothers offered themselves to the slave traders in order to save their sons and Hottentot women refused food during famines until after their children were fed.

It is impossible within the confines of this article to relate the terrible sufferings and degradation undergone by Negro mothers and Negro women generally under slavery. Subject to legalized rape by the slaveowners, confined to slave pens, forced to march for eight to fourteen hours with loads on their backs and to perform back-breaking work even during pregnancy, Negro women bore a burning hatred for slavery, and undertook a large share of the responsibility for defending and nurturing the Negro family.

The Negro mother was mistress in the slave cabin, and despite the interference of master or overseer, her wishes in regard to mating and in family matters were paramount. During and after slavery, Negro women had to support themselves and the children. Necessarily playing an important role in the economic and social life of her people, the Negro woman became schooled in self-reliance, in courageous and selfless action.*

There is documentary material of great interest which shows that Negro family life and the social and political consciousness of Negro men and women underwent important changes after emancipation. One freedom observed, during the Civil War, that many men were exceedingly jealous of their newly acquired authority in family relations and insisted upon a recognition of their superiority over women. After the Civil War, the slave rows were broken up and the tenant houses scattered all over the plantation in order that each family might carry on an independent existence. The

---

* Today, in the rural sections of the South, especially on the remnants of the old plantations, one finds households where old grandmothers rule their daughters, sons, and grandchildren with a matriarchal authority.

new economic arrangement, the change in the mode of production, placed the Negro man in a position of authority in relation to his family. Purchase of homesteads also helped strengthen the authority of the male.

Thus, a former slave, who began life as a freedman on a 'one-horse' farm, with his wife working as a laundress, but who later rented land and hired two men, recalls the pride which he felt because of his new status: 'In my humble palace on a hill in the woods beneath the shade of towering pines and sturdy oaks, I felt as a king whose supreme commands were "law and gospel" to my subjects.'

One must see that a double motive was operative here. In regard to his wife and children, the Negro man was now enabled to assume economic and other authority over the family; but he also could fight against violation of women of his group where formerly he was powerless to interfere.

The founding of the Negro church, which from the outset was under the domination of men, also tended to confirm the man's authority in the family. Sanction for male ascendancy was found in the Bible, which for many was the highest authority in such matters.

Through these and other methods, the subordination of Negro women developed. In a few cases, instead of legally emancipating his wife and children, the husband permitted them to continue in their status of slaves. In many cases, state laws forbade a slave emancipated after a certain date to remain in the state. Therefore, the only way for many Negro wives and children to remain in the state was to become 'enslaved' to their relatives. Many Negro owners of slaves were really relatives of their slaves.

In some cases, Negro women refused to become subject to the authority of the men. In defiance of the decisions of their husbands to live on the places of their former masters, many Negro women took their children and moved elsewhere.

NEGRO WOMEN IN MASS ORGANIZATIONS

This brief picture of some of the aspects of the history of the Negro woman, seen in the additional light of the fact that a high proportion of Negro women are obliged today to earn all or part of the bread of the family, helps us understand why Negro women play a most active part in the economic, social, and political life of the Negro community today. Approximately 2,500,000 Negro women are organized in social, political, and fraternal clubs and organizations. The most prominent of their organizations are the National Association of Negro Women, the National Council of Negro Women, the National Federation of Women's Clubs, the Women's Division of the Elk's Civil Liberties Committee, the National Association of Colored Beauticians, National Negro Business Women's League, and the National Association of Colored Graduate Nurses. Of these, the National Association of Negro Women, with 75,000 members, is the largest membership organization. There are numerous sororities, church women's committees of all denominations, as well as organizations among women of West Indian descent. In some areas, N.A.A.C.P. chapters have Women's Divisions, and recently the National Urban League established a Women's Division for the first time in its history.

Negro women are the real active forces – the organizers and workers – in all the institutions and organizations of the Negro people. These organizations play a many-sided role, concerning themselves with all questions pertaining to the economic, political, and social life of the Negro people, and particularly of the Negro family. Many of these organizations are intimately concerned with the problems of Negro youth, in the form of providing and administering educational scholarships, giving assistance to schools and other institutions, and offering community service. The fight for higher education in order to break down Jim Crow in higher institutions, was symbolized last year, by the brilliant Negro woman student, Ada Lois Sipuel Fisher of Oklahoma. The disdainful attitudes which are sometimes expressed – that Negro women's organizations concern themselves *only* with 'charity' work – must be exposed as of chauvinist derivation, however subtle, because while the same could be said of many organizations of white women, such attitudes fail to recognize the *special character* of the role of Negro women's organizations. This approach fails to recognize the special function which Negro women play in these organizations, which, over and above their particular function, seek to provide social services denied to Negro youth as a result of the Jim-Crow lynch system in the U.S.

THE NEGRO WOMAN WORKER

The negligible participation of Negro women in progressive and trade-union circles is thus all the more startling. In union after union, even in those unions where a large concentration of workers are Negro women, few Negro women are to be found as leaders or active workers. The outstanding exceptions to this are the Food and Tobacco Workers' Union and the United Office and Professional Workers' Union.

But why should these be exceptions? Negro women are among the most militant trade unionists. The sharecroppers' strikes of the '30's were spark-plugged by Negro women. Subject to the terror of the landlord and white supremacist, they waged magnificent battles together with Negro men and white progressives in that struggle of great tradition led by the Communist Party. Negro women played a magnificent part in the pre-C.I.O. days in strikes and other struggles, both as workers and as wives of workers, to win recognition of the principle of industrial unionism, in such industries as auto, packing, steel, etc. More recently, the militancy of Negro women unionists is shown in the strike of the packing-house workers, and even more so, in the tobacco workers' strike – in which such leaders as Moranda Smith and Velma Hopkins emerged as outstanding trade unionists. The struggle of the tobacco workers led by Negro women later merged with the political action of Negro and white which led to the election of the first Negro in the South (in Winston-Salem, N. C.) since Reconstruction days.

It is incumbent on progressive unionists to realize that in the fight for equal rights for Negro workers, it is necessary to have a special approach to Negro women workers, who, far out of proportion to other women workers, are the main breadwinners in their families. The fight to retain the Negro woman in industry and to upgrade her on the job, is a major way of struggling for the basic and special interests of the Negro woman worker. Not to recognize this feature is to miss the special aspects of the effects of the growing economic crisis, which is penalizing Negro workers, with special severity.

THE DOMESTIC WORKER

One of the crassest manifestations of trade-union neglect of the problems of the Negro woman worker has been the failure, not only to fight against relegation of the Negro woman to domestic and similar menial work, but to *organize* the domestic worker. It is merely lip-service for progressive unionists to speak of organizing the unorganized without turning their eyes to the serious plight of the domestic worker, who, unprotected by union standards, is also the victim of exclusion from all social and labor legislation. Only about one in ten of all Negro women workers is covered by present minimum-wage legislation, although about one-fourth of all such workers are to be found in states having minimum-wage laws. All of the arguments heretofore projected with regard to the real difficulties of organizing the domestic workers – such as the 'casual' nature of their employment, the difficulties of organizing day workers, the problem of organizing people who work in individual households, etc., – must be overcome forthwith. There is a danger that Social-Democratic forces may enter this field to do their work of spreading disunity and demagogy, unless progressives act quickly.

The lot of the domestic worker is one of unbearable misery. Usually, she has no definition of tasks in the household where she works. Domestic workers may have 'thrown in,' in addition to cleaning and scrubbing, such tasks as washing windows, caring for the children, laundering, cooking, etc., and all at the lowest pay. The Negro domestic worker must suffer the additional indignity, in some areas, of having to seek work in virtual 'slave markets' on the streets where bids are made, as from a slave block, for the hardiest workers. Many a domestic worker, on returning to her own household, must begin housework anew to keep her own family together.

Who was not enraged when it was revealed in California, in the heinous case of Dora Jones, that a Negro woman domestic was enslaved for more than 40 years in 'civilized' America? Her 'employer' was given a minimum sentence of a few years and complained that the sentence was for 'such a long period of time.' But could Dora Jones, Negro domestic worker, be repaid for more than 40 years of her life under such conditions of exploitation and degradation? And how many cases, partaking in varying degrees of the condition of Dora Jones, are still tolerated by progressives themselves!

Only recently, in the New York State Legislature, legislative proposals were made to 'fingerprint' domestic workers. The Martinez Bill did not see the light of day, because the reactionaries were concentrating on other repressive legislative measures; but here we see clearly the imprint of the African 'pass' system of British imperialism (and of the German Reich in relation to the Jewish people!) being attempted in relation to women domestic workers.

It is incumbent on the trade unions to assist the Domestic Workers' Union in every possible way to accomplish the task of organizing the exploited domestic workers, the majority of whom are Negro women. Simultaneously, a legislative fight for the inclusion of domestic workers under the benefits of the Social Security Law is vitally urgent and necessary. Here, too, recurrent questions regarding 'administrative problems' of applying the law to domestic workers should be challenged and solutions found.

The continued relegation of Negro women to domestic work has helped to perpetuate and intensify chauvinism directed against all Negro women. Despite the fact that Negro women may be grandmothers or mothers, the use of the chauvinist term 'girl' for adult Negro women is a common expression. The very economic relationship of Negro women to white women, which perpetuates 'madam-maid' relationships, feeds chauvinist attitudes and makes it incumbent on white women progressives, and particularly Communists, to fight consciously against all manifestations of white chauvinism, open and subtle.

Chauvinism on the part of progressive white women is often expressed in their failure to have close ties of friendship with Negro women and to realize that this fight for equality of Negro women is in their own self-interest, inasmuch as the super-exploitation and oppression of Negro women tends to depress the standards of all women. Too many progressives, and even some Communists, are still guilty of exploiting Negro domestic workers, of refusing to hire them through the Domestic Workers' Union (or of refusing to help in its expansion into those areas where it does not yet exist), and generally of participating in the vilification of 'maids' when speaking to their bourgeois neighbors and their own families. Then, there is the expressed 'concern' that the exploited Negro domestic worker does not 'talk' to, or is not 'friendly' with, her employer, or the habit of assuming that the duty of the white progressive employer is to 'inform' the Negro woman of her exploitation and her oppression which she undoubtedly knows quite intimately. Persistent challenge to every chauvinist remark as concerns the Negro woman is vitally necessary, if we are to break down the understandable distrust on the part of Negro women who are repelled by the white chauvinism they often find expressed in progressive circles.

MANIFESTATIONS OF WHITE CHAUVINISM

Some of the crassest expressions of chauvinism are to be found at social affairs, where, all too often, white men and women and Negro men participate in dancing, but Negro women are neglected. The acceptance of white ruling-class standards of 'desirability' for women (such as light skin), the failure to extend courtesy to Negro women and to integrate Negro women into organizational leadership, are other forms of chauvinism.

Another rabid aspect of the Jim-Crow oppression of the Negro women is expressed in the numerous laws which are directed against her as regards property rights, inter-marriage (originally designed to prevent white men in the South from marrying Negro women), – and laws which hinder and deny the right of choice, not only to Negro women, but Negro and white men and women.

For white progressive women and men, and especially for Communists, the question of social relations with Negro men and women is above all a question of strictly adhering to social equality. This means ridding ourselves of the position which sometimes finds certain progressives and Communists fighting on the economic and political issues facing the Negro people, but 'drawing the line' when it comes to social intercourse or inter-marriage. To place the question as a 'personal' and not a political matter, when such questions arise, is to be guilty of the worst kind of Social-Democratic, bourgeois-liberal thinking as regards the Negro question in American life; it is to be guilty of imbibing the poisonous white-chauvinist 'theories' of a Bilbo or a Rankin. Similarly, too, with regard to guaranteeing the 'security' of children. This security will be enhanced only through the struggle for the liberation and equality of all nations and peoples, and not by shielding children from the knowledge of this struggle. This means ridding ourselves of the bourgeois-liberal attitudes which 'permit' Negro and white children of progressives to play together at camps when young, but draw the line when the children reach teen-age and establish boy-girl relationships.

The bourgeois ideologists have not failed, of course, to develop a special ideological offensive aimed at degrading Negro women, as part and parcel of the general reactionary ideological offensive against women of 'kitchen, church, and children.' They cannot, however, with equanimity or credibility, speak of the Negro woman's 'place' as in the home; for Negro women are in other peoples' kitchens. Hence, their task has been to intensify their theories of male 'superiority' as regards the Negro woman by developing introspective attitudes which coincide with the 'new school' of 'psychological inferiority' of women. The whole intent of a host of articles, books, etc., has been to obscure the main responsibility for the oppression of Negro women by spreading the rotten bourgeois notion about a 'battle of the sexes' and 'ignoring' the fight of both Negro men and women – the whole Negro people – against their common oppressors, the white ruling class.

Chauvinist expressions also include paternalistic surprise when it is learned that Negroes are professional people. Negro professional women workers are often confronted with such remarks as 'Isn't your family proud of you?' Then, there is the reverse practice of inquiring of Negro women professionals whether 'someone in the family' would like to take a job as a domestic worker.

The responsibility for overcoming these special forms of white chauvinism rests, not with the 'subjectivity' of Negro women, as it is often put, but squarely on the shoulders of white men and white women. Negro men have a special responsibility particularly in relation to rooting out attitudes of male superiority as regards women in general. There is need to root out all 'humanitarian' and patronizing attitudes toward Negro women. In one community, a leading Negro trade unionist, the treasurer of her Party section, would be told by a white progressive woman after every social function: 'Let me have the money; something may happen to you.' In another instance, a Negro domestic worker who wanted to join the Party was told by her employer, a Communist, that she was 'too backward' and 'wasn't ready' to join the Party. In yet another community, which since the war has been populated in the proportion of sixty percent Negro to forty percent white, white progressive mothers maneuvered to get their children out of the school in this community. To the credit of the initiative of the Party section organizer, a Negro woman, a struggle was begun which forced a change in arrangements which the school principal, yielding to the mothers' and to his own prejudices, had established. These arrangements involved a special class in which a few white children were isolated with 'selected Negro kids' in what was termed an 'experimental class in race relations.'

These chauvinist attitudes, particularly as expressed toward the Negro woman, are undoubtedly an important reason for the grossly insufficient participation of Negro women in progressive organizations and in our Party as members and leaders.

The American bourgeoisie, we must remember, is aware of the present and even greater potential role of the masses of Negro women, and is therefore not loathe to throw plums to Negroes who betray their people and do the bidding of imperialism.

Faced with the exposure of their callous attitude to Negro women, faced with the growing protests against unpunished lynchings and the legal lynchings 'Northern style,' Wall Street is giving a few token positions to Negro women. Thus, Anna Arnold Hedgeman, who played a key role in the Democratic National Negro Committee to Elect Truman, was rewarded with the appointment as Assistant to Federal Security Administrator Ewing. Thus, too, Governor Dewey appointed Irene Diggs to a high post in the New York State Administration.

Another straw in the wind showing attempts to whittle down the militancy of Negro women was the State Department's invitation to a representative of the National Council of Negro Women – the only Negro organization so designated – to witness the signing of the Atlantic Pact.

KEY ISSUES OF STRUGGLE

There are many key issues facing Negro women around which struggles can and must be waged.

But none so dramatizes the oppressed status of Negro womanhood as does the case of Rosa Lee Ingram, widowed Negro mother of fourteen children – two of them dead – who faces life imprisonment in a Georgia jail for the 'crime' of defending herself from the indecent advances of a 'white supremacist.' The Ingram case illustrates the landless, Jim-Crow, oppressed status of the Negro family in America. It illumines particularly the degradation of Negro women today under American bourgeois democracy moving to fascism and war. It reflects the daily insults to which Negro women are subjected in public places, no matter what their class, status, or position. It exposes the hypocritical alibi of the lynchers of Negro manhood who have historically hidden behind the skirts of white women when they try to cover up their foul crimes with the 'chivalry' of 'protecting white womanhood.' But white women, to-day, no less than their sisters in the abolitionist and suffrage movements, must rise to challenge this lie and the whole system of Negro oppression.

American history is rich is examples of the cost – to the democratic rights of both women and men – of failure to wage this fight. The suffragists, during their first jailings, were purposely placed on cots next to Negro prostitutes to 'humiliate' them. They had the wisdom to understand that the intent was to make it so painful, that no women would dare to fight for her rights if she had to face such consequences. But it was the historic shortcoming of the women's suffrage leaders, predominantly drawn as they were from the bourgeoisie and the petty-bourgeoisie, that they failed to link their own struggles to the struggles for the full democratic rights of the Negro people following emancipation.

A developing consciousness on the woman question today, therefore, must not fail to recognize that the Negro question in the United States is *prior* to, and not equal to, the woman question; that only to the extent that we fight all chauvinist expressions and actions as regards the Negro people and fight for the full equality of the Negro people, can women as a whole advance their struggle for equal rights. For the progressive women's movement, the Negro woman, who combines in her status the worker, the Negro, and the woman, is the vital link to this heightened political consciousness. To the extent, further, that the cause of the Negro woman worker is promoted, she will be enabled to take her rightful place in the Negro proletarian leadership of the national liberation movement, and by her active participation contribute to the entire American working class, whose historic mission is the achievement of a Socialist America – the final and full guarantee of woman's emancipation.

The fight for Rosa Lee Ingram's freedom is a challenge to all white women and to all progressive forces, who must begin to ask themselves: How long shall we allow this dastardly crime against all womenhood, against the Negro people, to go unchallenged! Rosa Lee Ingram's plight and that of her sisters also carries with it a challenge to progressive cultural workers to write and sing of the Negro woman in her full courage and dignity.

The recent establishment of the National Committee to Free the Ingram Family fulfills a need long felt since the early movement which forced commutation to life imprisonment of Mrs Ingram's original sentence of execution. This National Committee, headed by Mary Church Terrell, a founder of the National Association of Colored Women, includes among its leaders such prominent women, Negro and white, as Therese Robinson, National Grand Directoress of the Civil Liberties Committee of the Elks, Ada B. Jackson, and Dr Gene Weltfish.

One of the first steps of the Committee was the visit of a delegation of Negro and white citizens to this courageous, militant Negro mother imprisoned in a Georgia cell. The measure of support was so great that the Georgia authorities allowed the delegation to see her unimpeded. Since that time, however, in retaliation against the developing mass movement, the Georgia officials have moved Mrs Ingram, who is suffering from a severe heart condition, to a worse penitentiary, at Reedsville.

Support to the work of this committee becomes a prime necessity for all progressives, particularly women. President Truman must be stripped of his pretense of 'know-nothing' about the Ingram case. To free the Ingrams, support must be rallied for the success of the million-signatures campaign, and for U.N. action on the Ingram brief soon to be filed.

The struggle for jobs for Negro women is a prime issue. The growing economic crisis, with its mounting unemployment and wage-cuts and increasing evictions, is making its impact felt most heavily on the Negro masses. In one Negro community after another, Negro women, the last to be hired and the first to be fired, are the greatest sufferers from unemployment. Struggles must be developed to win jobs for Negro women in basic industry, in the white-collar occupations, in the communities, and in private utilities.

The successful campaign of the Communist Party in New York's East Side to win jobs for Negro women in the five-and-dime stores has led to the hiring of Negro women throughout the city, even in predominantly white communities. This campaign has extended to New England and must be waged elsewhere.

Close to 15 government agencies do not hire Negroes at all. This policy gives official sanction to, and at the same time further encourages, the pervasive Jim-Crow policies of the capitalist exploiters. A campaign to win jobs for Negro women here would thus greatly advance the whole struggle for jobs for Negro men and women. In addition, it would have a telling effect in exposing the hypocrisy of the Truman Administration's 'Civil Rights' program.

A strong fight will also have to be made against the growing practice of the United States Employment Service to shunt Negro women, despite their qualifications for other jobs, only into domestic and personal service work.

Where consciousness of the special role of Negro women exists, successful struggle can be initiated which will win the support of white workers. A recent example was the initiative taken by white Communist garment workers in a shop employing 25 Negro women where three machines were idle. The issue of upgrading Negro women workers became a vital one. A boycott movement has been initiated and the machines stand unused as of this writing, the white workers refusing to adhere to strict seniority at the expense of Negro workers. Meanwhile, negotiations are continuing on this issue. Similarly, in a Packard U.A.W. local in Detroit, a fight for the maintenance of women in industry and for the upgrading of 750 women, the large majority of whom were Negro, was recently won.

THE STRUGGLE FOR PEACE

Winning the Negro women for the struggle for peace is decisive for all other struggles. Even during the anti-Axis war, Negro women had to weep for their soldier-sons, lynched while serving in a Jim-Crow army. Are they, therefore, not interested in the struggle for peace?

The efforts of the bipartisan war-makers to gain the support of the women's organizations in general, have influenced many Negro women's organizations, which, at their last annual conventions, adopted foreign-policy stands favoring the Marshall Plan and Truman Doctrine. Many of these organizations have worked with groups having outspoken anti-imperialist positions.

That there is profound peace sentiment among Negro women which can be mobilized for effective action is shown, not only in the magnificent response to the meetings of Eslande Goode Robeson, but also in the position announced last year by the oldest Negro women's organization, under the leadership of Mrs Christine C. Smith, in urging a national mobilization of American Negro women in support of the United Nations. In this connection, it will be very fruitful to bring to our country a consciousness of the magnificent struggles of women in North Africa, who, though lacking in the most elementary material needs, have organized a strong movement for peace and thus stand united against a Third World War, with 81 million women in 57 nations, in the Women's International Democratic Federation.

Our Party, based on its Marxist-Leninist principles, stands foursquare on a program of full economic, political, and social equality for the Negro people and of equal rights for women. Who, more than the Negro woman, the most exploited and oppressed, belongs in our Party? Negro women can and must make an enormous contribution to the daily life and work of the Party. Concretely, this means prime responsibility lies with white men and women comrades. Negro men comrades, however, must participate in this task. Negro Communist women must everywhere now take their rightful place in Party leadership on all levels.

The strong capacities, militancy and organizational talents of Negro women, can, if well utilized by our Party, be a powerful lever for bringing forward Negro workers – men and women – as the leading forces of the Negro people's liberation movement, for cementing Negro and white unity in the struggle against Wall Street imperialism, and for rooting the Party among the most exploited and oppressed sections of the working class and its allies.

In our Party clubs, we must conduct an intensive discussion of the role of the Negro women, so as to equip our Party membership with clear understanding for undertaking the necessary struggles in the shops and communities. We must end the practice, in which many Negro women who join our Party, and who, in their churches, communities and fraternal groups are leaders of masses, with an invaluable mass experience to give to our Party, suddenly find themselves viewed in our clubs, not as leaders, but as people who have 'to get their feet wet' organizationally. We must end this failure to create an atmosphere in our clubs in which new recruits – in this case Negro women – are confronted with the 'silent treatment' or with attempts to 'blueprint' them into a pattern. In addition to the white chauvinist implications in such approaches, these practices confuse the basic need for Marxist-Leninist understanding which our Party gives to all workers, and which enhances their political understanding, with chauvinist disdain for the organizational talents of new Negro members, or for the necessity to promote them into leadership.

To win the Negro women for full participation in the anti-fascist, anti-imperialist coalition, to bring her militancy and participation to even greater heights in the current and future struggles against Wall Street imperialism, progressives must acquire political consciousness as regards her special oppressed status.

It is this consciousness, accelerated by struggles, that will convince increasing thousands that only the Communist Party, as the vanguard of the working class, with its ultimate perspective of Socialism, can achieve for the Negro women – for the entire Negro people – the full equality and dignity of their stature in a Socialist society in which contributions to society are measured, not by national origin, or by color, but a society in which men and women contribute according to ability, and ultimately under Communism receive according to their needs.

41.

JAHAN ARA SHAHNAWAZ

Born 1896, Lahore, India
Died 1979, Pakistan

Charter of Women's Rights

1954

The final meeting of the [Pakistan] Constituent Assembly took place just the day before we left for China. Jubilant speeches were delivered and the Charter of Women's Rights, with 3 per cent reservation of seats for women, both in the Central and Provincial Assemblies, was passed unanimously by the House. I had asked for a Charter of Women's Rights to include:

1. Equality of status
2. Equal opportunities
3. Equal pay for equal work
4. For Muslim women, all the rights given to them by the Islamic Personal Law of Shariat.

Just before the meeting, I met the members of the Assembly belonging to the minority communities and the young Muslim members of the Committee and I discussed the Charter with them. I said that adult suffrage had been accepted and they had better be careful in voting on the rights of women, which were being discussed by the Committee the next day, for women would surely come to know who had advocated their cause and who had opposed it. I told them also that the Charter framed by me had the backing of all the women's organizations in the country. The next day, when I spoke about it in the Committee, while Sir Zafrullah was presiding and Nishtar was piloting the draft of the report, the President said to me:

Begum Sahiba, Islam recognizes equality in civic rights, and we gladly concede the right given by religion to our women, but for an infant state like Pakistan it is not possible to incorporate the rights asked for as justiciable fundamental rights.

I pointed out that if Islam had given such rights, they could not be denied to the women citizens of an Islamic State. Was there any difference in the Holy Quran between *jaza* and *saza*? Even for the worst crime that a married man or a married woman could commit, both were to be put to death, and similarity in provisions for reward, punishment, and other provisions of different types, the words used were for both men and women. Sir Zafrullah said that even in Great Britain, Prime Minister Winston Churchill had refused to accept a bill for equal pay for equal work and had asked for a vote of confidence from the House. I replied that, as far as Great Britain was concerned, it had been one of the most conservative states with regard to the right of equality for women citizens and many of the rights accepted by other progressive countries were still denied to British women, therefore the citing of that example was no argument at all. After my speech, each one of the minority members spoke in support of me. Then the Muslim members went on in the same strain, one after the other. When it came to Sardar Bahadur Khan's turn, he supported the full Charter for Women's Rights. Sardar Abdur Rab Nishtar exclaimed: 'Even you are supporting it!' Sardar Bahadur let the cat out of the bag by saying that, in future, they had to face an equal number of women's electorate, and therefore he had to support it. The result was that both the President and Abdur Rab Nishtar yielded and the Charter for Women's Rights was passed unanimously. I returned to the hotel with tears of joy in my eyes.

42.

SUSAN SONTAG

Born 1933, New York City, New York, United States of America
Died 2004, New York City, New York, United States of America

from *Reborn: Early Diaries*
1947–1963
Edited by David Rieff

2/14/57

In marriage, I have suffered a certain loss of personality – at first the loss was pleasant, easy; now it aches and stirs up my general disposition to be malcontented with a new fierceness.

[...]

1/2/58

I am scared, numbed from the marital wars – that deadly, deadening combat which is the opposite, the antithesis of the sharp painful struggles of lovers. Lovers fight with knives and whips, husbands and wives with poisoned marshmallows, sleeping pills, and wet blankets.

[...]

2/15/58

Marriage is a sort of tacit hunting in couples. The world all in couples, each couple in its own little house, watching its own little interests +

stewing in its own little privacy – it's the most repulsive thing in the world. One's got to get rid of the *exclusiveness* of married love.

[. . .]

7/14/58

P sends me letters filled with hate and despair and self-righteousness. He speaks of my crime, my folly, my stupidity, my self-indulgence. He tells me how David is suffering, weeping, lonely – how I am causing him to suffer.

I shall never forgive him for having tormented David, for having staged this year so that my baby must suffer more than he had to. But I don't feel guilt, I feel sure these wounds to David are not too grave. Baby, sweet boy, forgive me! I shall make it up to you, I shall keep you with me and make you happy – in a right way, without being possessive or fearful or living vicariously in you.

Philip is contemptible. There will be a war to the death between us – over David. I accept that now, I won't give in to pity, for it is his life or mine.

His letters are one howl of pain and self-pity. The basic plea is a threat, the same threat advanced by the old Jewish mother (his mother with Marty [*Philip Rieff's younger brother*]) to the captive son or daughter: Leave me – or, marry that shikseh [*Martin Rieff married a Catholic woman*] – and I'll have a heart attack, or I'll kill myself. P writes: 'You are not you. You are us . . .' Then follows a catalogue of his wretched physical state – weeping, insomnia, colitis. 'I shall die before I am forty.'

Exactly! If I go back to him, I am not I. He could not have put the issue more sharply. Our marriage is a sequence of alternating self-immolations, he in me, I in him, we both in David. Our marriage, marriage, the institution of the family which is 'objective, right, natural, inevitable.'

[. . .]

11/19/59

The coming of the orgasm has changed my life. I am liberated, but that's not the way to say it. More important: it has narrowed me, it has closed off possibilities, it has made alternatives clear and sharp. I am no longer unlimited, i.e., nothing.

Sexuality is the paradigm. Before, my sexuality was horizontal, an infinite line capable of being infinitely subdivided. Now it is vertical; it is up and over, or nothing.

*

The orgasm focuses. I lust to write. The coming of the orgasm is not the salvation but, more, the birth of my ego. I cannot write until I find my ego. The only kind of writer [I] could be is the kind who exposes himself . . . To write is to spend oneself, to gamble oneself. But up to now I have not even liked the sound of my own name. To write, I must love my name. The writer is in love with himself . . . and makes his books out of that meeting and that violence.

11/20/59

I have never been as demanding of anyone as I am of I. I am jealous of everyone she sees, I hurt every minute she goes away from me. But not when I leave her, and know she is there. My love wants to incorporate her totally, to eat her. My love is selfish.

[. . .]

12/18/60

(1) [Ibsen's play] *Hedda Gabler*: As I. identifies with the pure female victim [as in D. W. Griffith's film] *Broken Blossoms*), I've always identified with the Lady Bitch Who Destroys Herself.

The stars I've liked – Bette Davis, Joan Crawford, Katharine Hepburn, Arletty, Ida Lupino, Valerie Hobson – especially as a child.

This woman is above all else a lady. She is tall, dark, proud. She is nervous, restless, frustrated, bored. She has a cruel tongue and she uses men badly.

Hedda [Gabler] is really very passive. She wants to be trapped. She crosses off her possibilities as they vanish. She draws the net in on all sides and then she strangles herself.

She is young, so she waits to be old. She is marriageable, so she waits to find herself married. She is suicidal, so she waits to find herself committing suicide.

Her imperiousness is a masquerade.

(2) Hedda is profoundly conventional. She trembles before the idea of scandal. All her seeming unconventionality – e.g., her smoking, her revolvers – stems from what [she] thinks she, being a *lady* (her father's daughter, etc.) can do.

*

Hedda wants to be given continual reasons (rewards) to live. She cannot supply the reasons herself. For all who cannot supply her with reasons she feels contempt. Contempt is her habitual attitude toward others, but her self-contempt is more severe.

Self-contempt and vanity. Detachment + conventionality.

[. . .]

9/14–9/15/61

1. Not to repeat myself
2. Not to try to be amusing
3. To smile less, talk less. Conversely, and most important, to mean it when I smile, and to believe what I say + say only what I believe
4. To sew on my buttons (+ button my lip)
5. To try to repair things which don't work
6. To take a bath every day, and wash my hair every ten days. Same for D.
7. To think about why I bite my nails in the movies
8. Not to make fun of people, be catty, criticize other people's looks, etc. (all this is vulgar and vain)
9. To be more economical (because the carefree way I spend money makes me more dependent on earning this much money)

[Undated in the notebook]

I. is right. I must give everything up, or I will always have bile instead of blood, skin instead of flesh.

It doesn't matter. Think of death. Don't try to 'appear.' I am so self-indulgent: I know nothing of the will.

Think: 'It doesn't matter.'

Think of Blake. He didn't smile for others.

I don't possess myself. I musn't try to possess anyone else; it's hopeless, for I'm too clumsy.

Don't smile so much, sit up straight, bathe every day, and above all Don't Say It, all those sentences that come ready-to-say on the tickertape at the back of my tongue.

'Do not long,' etc.

I must [go] *farther* even than this, which has thus far been too difficult for me.

Beware of anything that you hear yourself saying often.

E.g., the French girl on the train:

She: 'And my sister over there' – (pointing to sister, round adolescent face, sleeping in ungainly position)

I: 'Oh, is that your sister?'

She: 'Yes. We don't resemble each other at all, do we?' Think how many thousands of times she must have said that, and what feelings lie behind those words – hardened, strengthened, confirmed each time she says them.

[. . .]

3/3/62

The number my mother taught me:

 – formality ('please,' 'thank you,' 'excuse me,' 'sorry,' 'may I')
 – any division of attention is disloyalty
 – 'the Chinese family'

I wasn't my mother's child – I was her subject (subject, companion, friend, consort. I sacrificed my childhood – my honesty – to please her). My habit of 'holding back' – which makes all my activities and identities seem somewhat unreal to me – is loyalty to my mother. My intellectualism reinforces this – is an instrument for the detachment from my own feelings which I practice in the service of my mother.

I thought the root was fear – fear of growing up, as if I would, by growing up, relinquish my only claim to not being left, not being taken care of.

I thought this was why I can't give myself steadily (or at all) to sex, work, being a mother, etc. For if I did I would be naming myself an adult.

But I wasn't ever really a child!

The reason I'm not good in bed (haven't 'caught on' sexually) is that *I don't see myself* as someone who can satisfy another person sexually. – I don't see myself as free.

I see myself as 'someone who tries.' I try to please, but of course I never succeed.

I invite my own unhappiness because it's evidence for the other that I'm trying. Behind 'I'm so good that it hurts' lies: 'I'm trying to be good. Don't you see how hard it is. Be patient with me.'

From this, a will to failure that often – except in sex – my talents frustrate. So then I devalue my successes (fellowships, the novel, jobs). These become unreal to me. I feel I am masquerading, pretending.

43.

DORIS LESSING

Born 1919, Kermanshah, Iran
Died 2013, London, United Kingdom

from *The Golden Notebook*
1962

Anna meets her friend Molly in the summer of 1957 after a separation . . .

The two women were alone in the London flat.

'The point is,' said Anna, as her friend came back from the telephone on the landing, 'the point is, that as far as I can see, everything's cracking up.'

Molly was a woman much on the telephone. When it rang she had just enquired: 'Well, what's the gossip?' Now she said, 'That's Richard, and he's coming over. It seems today's his only free moment for the next month. Or so he insists.'

'Well I'm not leaving,' said Anna.

'No, you stay just where you are.'

Molly considered her own appearance – she was wearing trousers and a sweater, both the worse for wear. 'He'll have to take me as I come,' she concluded, and sat down by the window. 'He wouldn't say what it's about – another crisis with Marion, I suppose.'

'Didn't he write to you?' asked Anna, cautious.

'Both he and Marion wrote – ever such *bonhomous* letters. Odd, isn't it?'

This *odd, isn't it?* was the characteristic note of the intimate conversations they designated gossip. But having struck the note, Molly swerved off with: 'It's no use talking now, because he's coming right over, he says.'

'He'll probably go when he sees me here,' said Anna, cheerfully, but slightly aggressive. Molly glanced at her, keenly, and said: 'Oh, but why?'

It had always been understood that Anna and Richard disliked each other; and before, Anna had always left when Richard was expected. Now

Molly said: 'Actually I think he rather likes you, in his heart of hearts. The point is, he's committed to liking me, on principle – he's such a fool he's always got to either like or dislike someone, so all the dislike he won't admit he has for me gets pushed off on to you.'

'It's a pleasure,' said Anna. 'But do you know something? I discovered while you were away that for a lot of people you and I are practically interchangeable.'

'You've only just understood *that*?' said Molly, triumphant as always when Anna came up with – as far as she was concerned – facts that were self-evident.

In this relationship a balance had been struck early on: Molly was altogether more worldly-wise than Anna who, for her part, had a superiority of talent.

Anna held her own private views. Now she smiled, admitting that she had been very slow.

'When we're so different in every way,' said Molly, 'it's odd. I suppose because we both live the same kind of life – not getting married and so on. That's all they see.'

'Free women,' said Anna, wryly. She added, with an anger new to Molly, so that she earned another quick scrutinizing glance from her friend: 'They still define us in terms of relationships with men, even the best of them.'

'Well, *we* do, don't we?' said Molly, rather tart. 'Well, it's awfully hard not to,' she amended, hastily, because of the look of surprise Anna now gave her. There was a short pause, during which the women did not look at each other but reflected that a year apart was a long time, even for an old friendship.

Molly said at last, sighing: 'Free. Do you know, when I was away, I was thinking about us, and I've decided that we're a completely new type of woman. We must be, surely?'

'There's nothing new under the sun,' said Anna, in an attempt at a German accent. Molly, irritated – she spoke half a dozen languages well – said: 'There's nothing new under the sun,' in a perfect reproduction of a shrewd old woman's voice, German accented.

Anna grimaced, acknowledging failure. She could not learn languages, and was too self-conscious ever to become somebody else: for a moment

Molly had even looked like Mother Sugar, otherwise Mrs Marks, to whom both had gone for psycho-analysis. The reservations both had felt about the solemn and painful ritual were expressed by the pet name, 'Mother Sugar'; which, as time passed, became a name for much more than a person, and indicated a whole way of looking at life – traditional, rooted, conservative, in spite of its scandalous familiarity with everything amoral. *In spite of* – that was how Anna and Molly, discussing the ritual, had felt it; recently Anna had been feeling more and more it was *because of*; and this was one of the things she was looking forward to discussing with her friend.

But now Molly, reacting as she had often done in the past, to the slightest suggestion of a criticism from Anna of Mother Sugar, said quickly: 'All the same, she was wonderful and I was in much too bad a shape to criticize.'

'Mother Sugar used to say, "You're Electra", or "You're Antigone", and that was the end, as far as she was concerned,' said Anna.

'Well, not quite the end,' said Molly, wryly insisting on the painful probing hours both had spent.

'Yes,' said Anna, unexpectedly insisting, so that Molly, for the third time, looked at her curiously. 'Yes. Oh I'm not saying she didn't do me all the good in the world. I'm sure I'd never have coped with what I've had to cope with without her. But all the same . . . I remember quite clearly one afternoon, sitting there – the big room, and the discreet wall lights, and the Buddha and the pictures and the statues.'

'*Well?*' said Molly, now very critical.

Anna, in the face of this unspoken but clear determination not to discuss it, said: 'I've been thinking about it all during the last few months . . . no, I'd like to talk about it with you. After all, we both went through it, and with the same person . . .'

'*Well?*'

Anna persisted: 'I remember that afternoon, knowing I'd never go back. It was all that damned art all over the place.'

Molly drew in her breath, sharp. She said, quickly: 'I don't know what you mean.' As Anna did not reply, she said, accusing: 'And have you written anything since I've been away?'

'No.'

'I keep telling you,' said Molly, her voice shrill, 'I'll never forgive you if you throw that talent away. I mean it. I've done it, and I can't stand watching you I've messed with painting and dancing and acting and scribbling, and now . . . you're so talented, Anna. *Why?* I simply don't understand.'

'How can I ever say why, when you're always so bitter and accusing?'

Molly even had tears in her eyes, which were fastened in the most painful reproach on her friend. She brought out with difficulty: 'At the back of my mind I always thought, well, I'll get married, so it doesn't matter my wasting all the talents I was born with: Until recently I was even dreaming about having more children – yes I know it's idiotic but it's true. And now I'm forty and Tommy's grown up. But the point is, if you're not writing simply because you're thinking about getting married . . .'

'But we both want to get married,' said Anna, making it humorous; the tone restored reserve to the conversation; she had understood, with pain, that she was not, after all, going to be able to discuss certain subjects with Molly.

44.

SYLVIA PLATH

Born 1932, Boston, Massachusetts, United States of America
Died 1963, London, United Kingdom

Daddy

1962 (published posthumously in *Ariel* in 1965)

You do not do, you do not do
Any more, black shoe
In which I have lived like a foot
For thirty years, poor and white,
Barely daring to breathe or Achoo.

Daddy, I have had to kill you.
You died before I had time —
Marble-heavy, a bag full of God,
Ghastly statue with one gray toe
Big as a Frisco seal

And a head in the freakish Atlantic
Where it pours bean green over blue
In the waters off beautiful Nauset.
I used to pray to recover you.
Ach, du.

In the German tongue, in the Polish town
Scraped flat by the roller
Of wars, wars, wars.
But the name of the town is common.
My Polack friend

Says there are a dozen or two.
So I never could tell where you
Put your foot, your root,
I never could talk to you.
The tongue stuck in my jaw.

It stuck in a barb wire snare.
Ich, ich, ich, ich,
I could hardly speak.
I thought every German was you.
And the language obscene

An engine, an engine
Chuffing me off like a Jew.
A Jew to Dachau, Auschwitz, Belsen.
I began to talk like a Jew.
I think I may well be a Jew.

The snows of the Tyrol, the clear beer of Vienna
Are not very pure or true.
With my gipsy ancestress and my weird luck
And my Taroc pack and my Taroc pack
I may be a bit of a Jew.

I have always been scared of you,
With your Luftwaffe, your gobbledygoo.
And your neat mustache
And your Aryan eye, bright blue.
Panzer-man, panzer-man, O You —

Not God but a swastika
So black no sky could squeak through.
Every woman adores a Fascist,
The boot in the face, the brute
Brute heart of a brute like you.

You stand at the blackboard, daddy,
In the picture I have of you,
A cleft in your chin instead of your foot
But no less a devil for that, no not
Any less the black man who

Bit my pretty red heart in two.
I was ten when they buried you.
At twenty I tried to die
And get back, back, back to you.
I thought even the bones would do.

But they pulled me out of the sack,
And they stuck me together with glue.
And then I knew what to do.
I made a model of you,
A man in black with a Meinkampf look

And a love of the rack and the screw.
And I said I do, I do.
So daddy, I'm finally through.
The black telephone's off at the root,
The voices just can't worm through.

If I've killed one man, I've killed two —
The vampire who said he was you
And drank my blood for a year,
Seven years, if you want to know.
Daddy, you can lie back now.

There's a stake in your fat black heart
And the villagers never liked you.
They are dancing and stamping on you.
They always *knew* it was you.
Daddy, daddy, you bastard, I'm through.

45.

BETTY FRIEDAN

Born 1921, Peoria, Illinois, United States of America
Died 2006, Washington, D.C., United States of America

from *The Feminine Mystique*
1963

The Problem that Has No Name

The problem lay buried, unspoken, for many years in the minds of American women. It was a strange stirring, a sense of dissatisfaction, a yearning that women suffered in the middle of the twentieth century in the United States. Each suburban wife struggled with it alone. As she made the beds, shopped for groceries, matched slip-cover material, ate peanut butter sandwiches with her children, chauffeured Cub Scouts and Brownies, lay beside her husband at night, she was afraid to ask even of herself the silent question: 'Is this all?'

For over fifteen years there was no word of this yearning in the millions of words written about women, for women, in all the columns, books and articles by experts telling women their role was to seek fulfilment as wives and mothers. Over and over women heard in voices of tradition and of Freudian sophistication that they could desire no greater destiny than to glory in their own femininity. Experts told them how to catch a man and keep him, how to breastfeed children and handle their toilet training, how to cope with sibling rivalry and adolescent rebellion; how to buy a dish washer, bake bread, cook gourmet snails, and build a swimming pool with their own hands; how to dress, look, and act more feminine and make marriage more exciting; how to keep their husbands from dying young and their sons from growing into delinquents. They were taught to pity the neurotic, unfeminine, unhappy women who wanted to be poets or physicists or presidents. They learned that truly feminine women do not want careers, higher education, political rights – the independence and the opportunities that the old-fashioned feminists fought for. Some women, in their forties and fifties, still remembered painfully giving up those dreams, but most of the younger women no longer even thought about them. A thousand expert voices applauded their femininity, their adjustment, their new maturity. All they had to do was devote their lives from earliest girlhood to finding a husband and bearing children.

By the end of the 1950s, the average marriage age of women in America dropped to twenty, and was still dropping, into the teens. Fourteen million girls were engaged by seventeen. The proportion of women attending college in comparison with men dropped from 47 per cent in 1920 to 35 per cent in 1958. A century earlier, women had fought for higher education; now girls went to college to get a husband. By the mid fifties, 60 per cent dropped out of college to marry, or because they were afraid too much education would be a marriage bar. Colleges built dormitories for 'married students', but the students were almost always the husbands. A new degree was instituted for the wives – 'PhT' (Putting Husband Through).

Then American girls began getting married in high school. And the women's magazines, deploring the unhappy statistics about these young marriages, urged that courses on marriage, and marriage counsellors, be installed in the high schools. Girls started going steady at twelve and thirteen, in junior high. Manufacturers put out brassières with false bosoms of foam rubber for little girls of ten. And an advertisement for a child's dress, sizes 3–6x, in the *New York Times* in the fall of 1960, said: 'She Too Can Join the Man-Trap Set.'

By the end of the fifties, the United States birthrate was overtaking India's. Statisticians were especially astounded at the fantastic increase in the number of babies among college women. Where once they had two children, now they had four, five, six. Women who had once wanted careers were now making careers out of having babies. So rejoiced *Life* magazine in a 1956 paean to the movement of American women back to the home.

In a New York hospital, a woman had a nervous breakdown when she found she could not breastfeed her baby. In other hospitals, women dying of cancer refused a drug which research had proved might save their lives: its side effects were said to be unfeminine. 'If I have only one life, let me live it as a blonde', a larger-than-life-sized picture of a pretty, vacuous woman proclaimed from newspaper, magazine, and drugstore ads. And across America, three out of every ten women dyed their hair blonde. They ate a chalk called Metrecal, instead of food, to shrink to the size of the thin young models. Department-store buyers reported that American women, since 1939, had become three and four sizes smaller. 'Women are out to fit the clothes, instead of vice versa,' one buyer said.

Interior decorators were designing kitchens with mosaic murals and original paintings, for kitchens were once again the centre of women's lives. Home sewing became a million-dollar industry. Many women no longer left their homes, except to shop, chauffeur their children, or attend a social engagement with their husbands. Girls were growing up in America without ever having jobs outside the home. In the late fifties, a sociological phenomenon was suddenly remarked: a third of American women now worked, but most were no longer young and very few were pursuing careers. They were married women who held part-time jobs, selling or secretarial, to put their husbands through school, their sons through college, or to help pay the mortgage. Or they were widows supporting families. Fewer and fewer women were entering professional work. The shortages in the nursing, social work, and teaching professions caused crises in almost every American city. Concerned over the Soviet Union's lead in the space race, scientists noted that America's greatest source of unused brainpower was women. But girls would not study physics: it was 'unfeminine'. A girl refused a science fellowship at Johns Hopkins to take a job in a real-estate office. All she wanted, she said, was what every other American girl wanted – to get married, have four children, and live in a nice house in a nice suburb.

The suburban housewife – she was the dream image of the young American women and the envy, it was said, of women all over the world. The American housewife – freed by science and labour-saving appliances from the drudgery, the dangers of childbirth, and the illnesses of her grandmother. She was healthy, beautiful, educated, concerned only about her husband, her children, her home. She had found true feminine fulfilment. As a housewife and mother, she was respected as a full and equal partner to man in his world. She was free to choose automobiles, clothes, appliances, supermarkets; she had everything that women ever dreamed of.

In the fifteen years after the Second World War, this mystique of feminine fulfilment became the cherished and self-perpetuating core of contemporary American culture. Millions of women lived their lives in the image of those pretty pictures of the American suburban housewife, kissing their husbands good-bye in front of the picture window, depositing their station wagonsful of children at school, and smiling as they ran the new electric waxer over the spotless kitchen floor. They baked their own bread, sewed their own and their children's clothes, kept their new washing machines and dryers running all day. They changed the sheets on the beds twice a week instead of once, took the rug-hooking class in adult education, and pitied their poor frustrated mothers, who had dreamed of having a career. They gloried in their role as women, and wrote proudly on the census blank: 'Occupation: housewife'.

For over fifteen years, the words written for women, and the words women used when they talked to each other, while their husbands sat on the other side of the room and talked shop or politics or septic tanks, were about problems with their children, or how to keep their husbands happy, or improve their children's school, or cook chicken, or make slip-covers. Nobody argued whether women were inferior or superior to men; they were simply different. Words like 'emancipation' and 'career' sounded strange and embarrassing; no one had used them for years. When a Frenchwoman named Simone de Beauvoir wrote a book called *The Second Sex*, an American critic commented that she obviously 'didn't know what life was all about', and besides, she was talking about French women. The 'woman problem' in America no longer existed.

If a woman had a problem in the 1950s and 1960s, she knew that something must be wrong with her marriage, or with herself. Other women were satisfied with their lives, she thought. What kind of a woman was she if she did not feel this mysterious fulfilment waxing the kitchen floor? She was so ashamed to admit her dissatisfaction that she never knew how many other women shared it. If she tried to tell her husband, he didn't understand what she was talking about. She did not really understand it herself. For over fifteen years women in America found it harder to talk about this problem than about sex. 'I don't know what's wrong with women today,' a suburban psychiatrist said uneasily. 'I only know something is wrong because most of my patients happen to be women. And their problem isn't sexual.' Most women with this problem did not go to see a psychoanalyst, however. 'There's nothing wrong really,' they kept telling themselves. 'There isn't any problem.'

But on an April morning in 1959, I heard a mother of four, having coffee with four other mothers in a suburban development fifteen miles from New York, say in a tone of quiet desperation, 'the problem'. And the others knew, without words, that she was not talking about a problem with her husband, or her children, or her home. Suddenly they realized they all shared the same problem, the problem that has no name. They began, hesitantly, to talk about it. Later, after they had picked up their children at nursery school and taken them home to nap, two of the women cried, in sheer relief, just to know they were not alone.

Gradually I came to realize that the problem that has no name was shared by countless women in America. As a magazine writer I often interviewed women about problems with their children, or their marriages, or their houses, or their communities. But after a while I began to recognize the tell-tale signs of this other problem. I saw the same signs in suburban ranch houses and split-levels on Long Island and in New Jersey and Westchester County; in colonial houses in a small Massachusetts town; on patios in Memphis; in suburban and city apartments; in living-rooms in the Midwest. Sometimes I sensed the problem, not as a reporter, but as a suburban housewife, for during this time I was also bringing up my own three children in Rockland County, New York. The groping words I heard from other women, on quiet afternoons when children were at school or on quiet evenings when husbands worked late, I think I understood first as a woman long before I understood their larger social and psychological implications.

Just what was this problem that has no name? What were the words women used when they tried to express it? Sometimes a woman would say, 'I feel empty somehow . . . incomplete.' Or she would say, 'I feel as if I don't exist.' Sometimes she blotted out the feeling with a tranquillizer. Sometimes she thought the problem was with her husband, or her children, or that what she really needed was to redecorate her house, or move to a better neighbourhood, or have an affair, or another baby. Sometimes, she went to a doctor with symptoms she could hardly describe: 'A tired feeling . . . I get so angry with the children it scares me . . . I feel like crying without any reason.' (A Cleveland doctor called it 'the housewife's syndrome'.) A number of women told me about great bleeding blisters that break out on their hands and arms. 'I call it the housewife's blight,' said a family doctor in Pennsylvania. 'I see it so often lately in these young women with four, five, and six children, who bury themselves in their dishpans. But it isn't caused by detergent and it isn't cured by cortisone.'

Sometimes a woman would tell me that the feeling gets so strong she runs out of the house and walks through the streets. Or she stays inside her house and cries. Or her children tell her a joke, and she doesn't laugh because she doesn't hear it. I talked to women who had spent years on the analyst's couch, working out their 'adjustment to the feminine role', their blocks to 'fulfilment as a wife and mother'. But the desperate tone in these women's voices, and the look in their eyes, was the same as the tone and the look of other women, who were sure they had no problem, even though they did have a strange feeling of desperation.

A mother of four who left college at nineteen to get married told me:

> I've tried everything women are supposed to do – hobbies, gardening, pickling, canning, being very social with my neighbours, joining committees, running PTA [Parent–Teacher Association] teas. I can do it all, and I like it, but it doesn't leave you anything to think about – any feeling of who you are. I never had any career ambitions. All I wanted was to get married and have four children. I love the kids and Bob and my home. There's no problem you can even put a name to. But I'm desperate. I begin to feel I have no personality. I'm a server of food and a putter-on of pants and a bedmaker, somebody who can be called on when you want something. But who am I?

[...]

A New Life Plan for Women

[. . .] The identity crisis in men and women cannot be solved by one generation for the next; in our rapidly changing society, it must be faced continually, solved only to be faced again in the span of a single lifetime.

A life plan must be open to change, as new possibilities open, in society and in oneself.

In the light of woman's long battle for emancipation, the recent sexual counter-revolution in America has been perhaps a final crisis, a strange breath-holding interval before the larva breaks out of the shell into maturity – a moratorium during which many millions of women put themselves on ice and stopped growing. American women lately have been living much longer than men – walking through their leftover lives like living dead women. Perhaps men may live longer in America when women carry more of the burden of the battle with the world, instead of being a burden themselves. I think their wasted energy will continue to be destructive to their husbands, to their children, and to themselves until it is used in their own battle with the world. But when women as well as men emerge from biological living to realize their human selves, those left-over halves of life may become their years of greatest fulfilment.

When their mothers' fulfilment makes girls sure they want to be women, they will not have to 'beat themselves down' to be feminine; they can stretch and stretch until their own efforts will tell them who they are. They will not need the regard of boy or man to feel alive. And when women do not need to live through their husbands and children, men will not fear the love and strength of women, nor need another's weakness to prove their own masculinity. They can finally see each other as they are. And this may be the next step in human evolution.

Who knows what women can be when they are finally free to become themselves? Who knows what women's intelligence will contribute when it can be nourished without denying love? Who knows of the possibilities of love when men and women share not only children, home, and garden, not only the fulfilment of their biological roles, but the responsibilities and passions of the work that creates the human future. It has barely begun, the search of women for themselves. But the time is at hand when the voices of the feminine mystique can no longer drown out the inner voice that is driving women on to become complete.

46.

VALERIE SOLANAS

Born 1936, Ventnor City, New Jersey, United States of America
Died 1988, San Francisco, California, United States of America

from *S.C.U.M. Manifesto*

1968

Life in this society being, at best, an utter bore and no aspect of society being at all relevant to women, there remains to civic-minded, responsible, thrill-seeking females only to overthrow the government, eliminate the money system, institute complete automation and destroy the male sex.

It is now technically feasible to reproduce without the aid of males (or, for that matter, females) and to produce only females. We must begin immediately to do so. Retaining the male has not even the dubious purpose of reproduction. The male is a biological accident: the **Y** (male) gene is an incomplete **X** (female) gene, that is, it has an incomplete set of chromosomes. In other words, the male is an incomplete female, a walking abortion, aborted at the gene stage. To be male is to be deficient, emotionally limited; maleness is a deficiency disease and males are emotional cripples.

The male is completely egocentric, trapped inside himself, incapable of empathizing or identifying with others, of love, friendship, affection, of tenderness. He is a completely isolated unit, incapable of rapport with anyone. His responses are entirely visceral, not cerebral; his intelligence is a mere tool in the services of his drives and needs; he is incapable of mental passion, mental interaction; he can't relate to anything other than his own physical sensations. He is a half-dead, unresponsive lump, incapable of giving or receiving pleasure or happiness; consequently, he is at best an utter bore, an inoffensive blob, since only those capable of absorption in others can be charming. He is trapped in a twilight zone halfway between humans and apes, and is far worse off than the apes because, unlike the apes, he is capable of a large array of negative feelings – hate, jealousy, contempt, disgust, guilt, shame, doubt and moreover, he is *aware* of what he is and what he isn't.

Although completely physical, the male is unfit even for stud service. Even assuming mechanical proficiency, which few men have, he is, first of all, incapable of zestfully, lustfully, tearing off a piece, but instead is eaten up with guilt, shame, fear and insecurity, feelings rooted in male nature, which the most enlightened training can only minimize; second, the physical feeling he attains is next to nothing; and third, he is not empathizing with his partner, but is obsessed with how he's doing, turning in an A performance, doing a good plumbing job. To call a man an animal is to flatter him; he's a machine, a walking dildo. It's often said that men use women. Use them for what? Surely not pleasure.

Eaten up with guilt, shame, fears and insecurities and obtaining, if he's lucky, a barely perceptible physical feeling, the male is, nonetheless, obsessed with screwing; he'll swim through a river of snot, wade nostril-deep through a mile of vomit, if he thinks there'll be a friendly pussy awaiting him. He'll screw a woman he despises, any snaggle-toothed hag, and furthermore, pay for the opportunity. Why? Relieving physical tension isn't the answer, as masturbation suffices for that. It's not ego satisfaction; that doesn't explain screwing corpses and babies.

Completely egocentric, unable to relate, empathize or identify, and filled with a vast, pervasive, diffuse sexuality, the male is pyschically passive. He hates his passivity, so he projects it onto women, defines the male as active, then sets out to prove that he is ('prove that he is a Man'). His main means of attempting to prove it is screwing (Big Man with a Big Dick tearing off a Big Piece). Since he's attempting to prove an error, he must 'prove' it again and again. Screwing, then, is a desperate compulsive attempt to prove he's not passive, not a woman; but he is passive and does want to be a woman.

Being an incomplete female, the male spends his life attempting to complete himself, to become female. He attempts to do this by constantly seeking out, fraternizing with and trying to live through and fuse with the female, and by claiming as his own all female characteristics – emotional strength and independence, forcefulness, dynamism, decisiveness, coolness, objectivity, assertiveness, courage, integrity, vitality, intensity, depth of character, grooviness, etc – and projecting onto women all male traits – vanity, frivolity, triviality, weakness, etc. It should be said, though, that the male has one glaring area of superiority over the female – public relations. (He has done a brilliant job of convincing millions of women that men are women and women are men). The male claim that females find fulfillment through motherhood and sexuality reflects what males think they'd find fulfilling if they were female.

Women, in other words, don't have penis envy; men have pussy envy. When the male accepts his passivity, defines himself as a woman (males as well as females think men are women and women are men), and becomes a transvestite he loses his desire to screw (or to do anything else, for that matter; he fulfills himself as a drag queen) and gets his dick chopped off. He then achieves a continuous diffuse sexual feeling from 'being a woman'. Screwing is, for a man, a defense against his desire to be female. He is responsible for:

WAR

The male's normal compensation for not being female, namely, getting his Big Gun off, is grossly inadequate, as he can get it off only a very limited number of times; so he gets it off on a really massive scale, and proves to the entire world that he's a 'Man'. Since he has no compassion or ability to empathize or identify, proving his manhood is worth an endless amount of mutilation and suffering and an endless number of lives, including his own his own life being worthless, he would rather go out in a blaze of glory than to plod grimly on for fifty more years.

NICENESS, POLITENESS, AND 'DIGNITY'

Every man, deep down, knows he's a worthless piece of shit. Overwhelmed by a sense of animalism and deeply ashamed of it; wanting, not to express himself, but to hide from others his total physicality, total egocentricity, the hate and contempt he feels for other men, and to hide from himself the hate and contempt he suspects other men feel for him;

having a crudely constructed nervous system that is easily upset by the least display of emotion or feeling, the male tries to enforce a 'social' code that ensures perfect blandness, unsullied by the slightest trace or feeling or upsetting opinion. He uses terms like 'copulate', sexual congress', 'have relations with' (to men sexual relations is a redundancy), overlaid with stilted manners; the suit on the chimp.

47.

RADICALESBIANS

Formed in 1970, New York City, New York, United States of America

The Woman-Identified Woman

1970

What is a lesbian? A lesbian is the rage of all women condensed to the point of explosion. She is the woman who, often beginning at an extremely early age, acts in accordance with her inner compulsion to be a more complete and freer human being than her society – perhaps [not] then, but certainly later – cares to allow her. These needs and actions, over a period of years, bring her into painful conflict with people, situations, the accepted ways of thinking, feeling and behaving, until she is in a state of continual war with everything around her, and usually with her self. She may not be fully conscious of the political implications of what for her began as personal necessity, but on some level she has not been able to accept the limitations and oppression laid on her by the most basic role of her society – the female role. The turmoil she experiences tends to induce guilt proportional to the degree to which she feels she is not meeting social expectations, and/or eventually drives her to question and analyze what the rest of her society more or less accepts. She is forced to evolve her own life pattern, often living much of her life alone, learning usually much earlier than her 'straight' (heterosexual) sisters about the essential aloneness of life (which the myth of marriage obscures) and about the reality of illusions. To the extent that she cannot expel the heavy socialization that goes with being female, she can never truly find peace with herself. For she is caught somewhere between accepting society's view of her – in which case she cannot accept herself – and coming to understand what this sexist society has done to her and why it is functional and necessary for it to do so. Those of us who work that through find ourselves on the other side of a tortuous journey through a night that may have been decades long. The perspective gained from that journey, the liberation of the self, the inner peace, the real love of self and of all women, is something to be shared with all women – because we are all women.

It should first be understood that lesbianism, like male homosexuality, is a category of behavior possible only in a sexist society characterized by rigid sex roles and dominated by male supremacy. Those sex roles dehumanize women by defining us as a supportive/serving caste in relation to the master caste of men, and emotionally cripple men by demanding that they be alienated from their own bodies and emotions in order to perform their economic/political/military functions effectively. Homosexuality is a by-product of a particular way of setting up roles (or approved patterns of behavior) on the basis of sex; as such it is an inauthentic (not consonant with 'reality') category. In a society in which men do not oppress women, and sexual expression is allowed to follow feelings, the categories of homosexuality and heterosexuality would disappear.

But lesbianism is also different from male homosexuality, and serves a different function in the society. 'Dyke' is a different kind of put-down from 'faggot,' although both imply you are not playing your socially assigned sex role . . . are not therefore a 'real woman' or a 'real man'. The grudging admiration felt for the tomboy, and the queasiness felt around a sissy boy point to the same thing: the contempt in which women – or those who play a female role – are held. And the investment in keeping woman in that contemptuous role is very great. Lesbian is a word, the label, the condition that holds women in line. When a woman hears this word tossed her way, she knows she is stepping out of line. She knows that she has crossed the terrible boundary of her sex role. She recoils, she protests, she reshapes her actions to regain approval. Lesbian is a label invented by the Man to throw at any woman who dares to be his equal, who dares to challenge his prerogatives (including that of all women as part of the exchange medium among men), who dares to assert the primacy of her own needs. To have the label applied to people active in women's liberation is just the most recent instance of a long history; older women will recall that not so long ago, any woman who was successful, independent, nor orientating her whole life about a man, would hear this word. For in this sexist society, for a woman to be independent means she can't be a woman – she must be a dyke. That in itself should tell us where women are at. It says as clearly as can be said: women and person are contradictory terms. For a lesbian is not considered a 'real woman'. And yet, in popular thinking, there is really only one essential difference between a lesbian and other women: that of sexual orientation – which is to say, when you strip off all the packaging, you must finally realize that the essence of being a 'woman' is to get fucked by men.

'Lesbian' is one of the sexual categories by which men have divided up humanity. While all women are dehumanized as sex objects, as the objects of men they are given certain compensations: identification with his power, his ego, his status, his protection (from other males), feeling like a 'real woman,' finding social acceptance by adhering to her role, etc. Should a woman confront herself by confronting another woman, there are fewer rationalizations, fewer buffers by which to avoid the stark horror of her dehumanized condition. Herein we find the overriding fear of many women toward being used as a sexual object by a woman, which not only will bring her no male-connected compensations, but also will reveal the void which is woman's real situation. This dehumanization is expressed when a straight woman learns that a sister is a lesbian; she begins to relate to her lesbian sister as a potential sex object, laying a surrogate male role on the lesbian. This reveals her heterosexual conditioning to make herself into an object when sex is potentially involved in a relationship, and it denies the lesbian her full humanity. For women, especially those in the movement, to perceive their lesbian sisters through this male grid of role definitions is to accept this male cultural conditioning and to oppress their sisters much as they themselves have been oppressed by men. Are we going to continue the male classification system of defining all females in sexual relation to some other category of people? Affixing the label lesbian not only to a woman who aspires to be a person, but also to any situation of real love, real solidarity, real primacy among women, is a primary form of divisiveness among women: it is the condition which keeps women within the confines of the feminine role, and it is the debunking/scare term that keeps women from forming any primary attachments, groups, or associations among ourselves.

Women in the movement have in most cases gone to great lengths to avoid discussion and confrontation with the issue of lesbianism. It puts people up-tight. They are hostile, evasive, or try to incorporate it into some 'broader issue.' They would rather not talk about it. If they have to, they try to dismiss it as a 'lavender herring.' But it is no side issue. It is absolutely essential to the success and fulfilment of the women's liberation movement that this issue be dealt with. As long as the label 'dyke' can be used to frighten women into a less militant stand, keep her separate from her sisters, keep her from giving primacy to anything other than men and family – then to that extent she is controlled by the male culture. Until women see in each other the possibility of a primal commitment which includes sexual love, they will be denying themselves the love and value they readily accord to men, thus affirming their second-class status. As long as male acceptability is primary – both to individual movement and to the movement as a whole – the term lesbian will be used effectively against women. Insofar as women want only more privileges within the system, they do not want to antagonize male power. They instead seek acceptability for women's liberation, and the most crucial aspect of the acceptability is to deny lesbianism – i.e., to deny any fundamental challenge to the basis of the female. It should also be said that some younger, more radical women have honestly begun to discuss lesbianism, but so far it has been primarily as a sexual 'alternative' to men. This, however, is still giving primacy to men, both because the idea of relating more completely to women occurs as a negative reaction to men, and because the lesbian relationship is being characterized simply by sex, which is divisive and sexist. On one level, which is both personal and political, women may withdraw emotional and sexual energies from men, and work out various alternatives for those energies in their own lives. On a different political/ psychological level, it must be understood that what is crucial is that women begin disengaging from male-defined response patterns. In the privacy of our own psyches, we must cut those cords to the core. For irrespective of where our love and sexual energies flow, if we are male-identified in our heads, we cannot realize our autonomy as human beings.

But why is it that women have related to and through men? By virtue of having been brought up in a male society, we have internalized the male culture's definition of ourselves. That definition consigns us to sexual and family functions, and excludes us from defining and shaping the terms of our lives. In exchange for our psychic servicing and for performing society's non-profit-making functions, the man confers on us just one thing: the slave status which makes us legitimate in the eyes of the society in which we live. This is called 'femininity' or 'being a real woman' in our cultural lingo. We are authentic, legitimate, real to the extent that we are the property of some man whose name we bear. To be a woman who belongs to no man is to be invisible, pathetic, inauthentic, unreal. He confirms his image of us – of what we have to be in order to be acceptable by him – but not our real selves; he confirms our womanhood – as he defines it, in relation to him – but cannot confirm our personhood, our own selves as absolutes. As long as we are dependent on the male culture for this definition, for this approval, we cannot be free.

The consequence of internalizing this role is an enormous reservoir of self-hate. This is not to say the self-hate is recognized or accepted as such; indeed most women would deny it. It may be experienced as discomfort with her role, as feeling empty, as numbness, as restlessness, as a paralyzing anxiety at the center. Alternatively, it may be expressed in shrill defensiveness of the glory and destiny of her role. But it does exist, often beneath the edge of her consciousness, poisoning her existence, keeping her alienated from herself, her own needs, and rendering her a stranger to other women. They try to escape by identifying with the oppressor, living through him, gaining status and identity from his ego, his power, his accomplishments. And not by identifying with other 'empty vessels' like themselves. Women resist relating on all levels to other women who will reflect their own oppression, their own secondary status, their own self-hate. For to confront another woman is finally to confront one's self – the self we have gone to such lengths to avoid. And in that mirror we know we cannot really respect and love that which we have been made to be.

As the source of self-hate and the lack of real self-love are rooted in our male-given identity, we must create a new sense of self. As long as we cling to the idea of 'being a woman,' we will sense some conflict with that incipient self, that sense of I, that sense of a whole person. It is very difficult to realize and accept that being 'feminine' and being a whole person are irreconcilable. Only women can give to each other a new sense of self. That identity we have to develop with reference to ourselves, and not in relation to men. This consciousness is the revolutionary force from which all else will follow, for ours is an organic revolution. For this we must be available and supportive to one another, give our commitment and our love, give the emotional support necessary to sustain the movement. Our energies must flow toward our sisters, not backward toward our oppressors. As long as women's liberation tries to free women without facing the basic heterosexual structure that binds us in one-to-one relationship with our oppressors, tremendous energies will continue to flow into trying to straighten up each particular relationship with a man, into finding how to get better sex, how to turn his head around – into trying to make the 'new man' out of him, in the delusion that this will allow us to be the 'new woman.' This obviously splits our energies and commitments, leaving us unable to be committed to the construction of the new patterns which will liberate us.

It is the primacy of women relating to women, of women creating a new consciousness of and with each other, which is at the heart of women's liberation, and the basis for the cultural revolution. Together we must find, reinforce, and validate our authentic selves. As we do this, we confirm in each other that struggling, incipient sense of pride and strength, the divisive barriers begin to melt, we feel this growing solidarity with our sisters. We see ourselves as prime, find our centers inside of ourselves. We find receding the sense of alienation, of being cut off, of being behind a locked window, of being unable to get out what we know is inside. We feel a realness, feel at last that we are coinciding with ourselves. With that real self, with that consciousness, we begin a revolution to end the imposition of all coercive identifications, and to achieve maximum autonomy in human expression.

48.

SHULAMITH FIRESTONE

Born 1945, Ottawa, Canada
Died 2012, New York City, New York, United States of America

from *The Dialectic of Sex: The Case for Feminist Revolution*

1970

Sex class is so deep as to be invisible. Or it may appear as a superficial inequality, one that can be solved by merely a few reforms, or perhaps by the full integration of women into the labour force. But the reaction of the common man, woman, and child – '*That?* Why you can't change *that!* You must be out of your mind!' is the closest to the truth. We are talking about something every bit as deep as that. This gut reaction – the assumption that, even when they don't know it, feminists are talking about changing a fundamental biological condition – is an honest one. That so profound a change cannot be easily fitted into traditional categories of thought, e.g., 'political', is not because these categories do not apply but because they are not big enough: radical feminism bursts through them. If there were another word more all-embracing than *revolution* we would use it.

Until a certain level of evolution had been reached and technology had achieved its present sophistication, to question fundamental biological conditions was insanity. Why should a woman give up her precious seat in the cattle car for a bloody struggle she could not hope to win? But, for the first time in some countries, the preconditions for feminist revolution exist – indeed, the situation is beginning to *demand* such a revolution.

The first women are fleeing the massacre, and, shaking and tottering, are beginning to find each other. Their first move is a careful joint observation, to resensitize a fractured consciousness. This is painful: no matter how many levels of consciousness one reaches, the problem always goes deeper. It is everywhere. The division yin and yang pervades all culture, history, economics, nature itself; modern Western versions of sex discrimination are only the most recent layer. To so heighten one's sensitivity to sexism presents problems far worse than the black militant's new awareness of racism: feminists have to question, not just all of *Western* culture, but the organization of culture itself, and further, even the very organization of nature. Many women give up in despair: if *that's* how deep it goes they don't want to know. Others continue strengthening and enlarging the movement, their painful sensitivity to female oppression existing for a purpose: eventually to eliminate it.

Before we can act to change a situation, however, we must know how it has arisen and evolved, and through what institutions it now operates. Engels's '[We must] examine the historic succession of events from which the antagonism has sprung in order to discover in the conditions thus created the means of ending the conflict.' For feminist revolution we shall need an analysis of the dynamics of sex war as comprehensive as the Marx–Engels analysis of class antagonism was for the economic revolution. More comprehensive. For we are dealing with a larger problem, with an oppression that goes back beyond recorded history to the animal kingdom itself.

[. . .]

There is a level of reality that does not stem directly from economics.

The assumption that, beneath economics, reality is psychosexual is often rejected as ahistorical by those who accept a dialectical materialist view of history because it seems to land us back where Marx began: groping through a fog of utopian hypotheses, philosophical systems that might be right, that might be wrong (there is no way to tell), systems that explain concrete historical developments by *a priori* categories of thought; historical materialism, however, attempted to explain 'knowing' by 'being' and not vice versa.

But there is still an untried third alternative: we can attempt to develop a materialist view of history based on sex itself.

The early feminist theorists were to a materialist view of sex what Fourier, Bebel, and Owen were to a materialist view of class. By and large, feminist theory has been as inadequate as were the early feminist attempts to correct sexism. This was to be expected. The problem is so immense that, at first try, only the surface could be skimmed, the most blatant inequalities described. Simone de Beauvoir was the only one who came close to – who perhaps has done – the definitive analysis. Her profound work *The Second Sex* – which appeared as recently as the early fifties to a world convinced that feminism was dead – for the first time attempted to ground feminism in its historical base. Of all feminist theorists De Beauvoir is the most comprehensive and far-reaching, relating feminism to the best ideas in our culture.

It may be this virtue is also her one failing: she is almost too sophisticated, too knowledgeable. Where this becomes a weakness – and this is still certainly debatable – is in her rigidly existentialist interpretation of feminism (one wonders how much Sartre had to do with this). This, in view of the fact that all cultural systems, including existentialism, are themselves determined by the sex dualism. She says:

> 'Man never thinks of himself without thinking of the Other; he views the world under the sign of duality *which is not in the first place sexual in character*. But being different from man, who sets himself up as the Same, it is naturally to the category of the Other that woman is consigned; the Other includes woman. (Italics mine.)'

Perhaps she has overshot her mark: Why postulate a fundamental Hegelian concept of Otherness as the final explanation – and then carefully document the biological and historical circumstances that have pushed the class 'women' into such a category – when one has never seriously considered the much simpler and more likely possibility that this fundamental dualism sprang from the sexual division itself? To posit *a priori* categories of thought and existence – 'Otherness', 'Transcendence', 'Immanence' – into which history then falls may not be necessary. Marx and Engels had discovered that these philosophical categories themselves grew out of history.

Before assuming such categories, let us first try to develop an analysis in which biology itself – procreation – is at the origin of the dualism. The immediate assumption of the layman that the unequal division of the sexes is 'natural' may be well-founded. We need not immediately look beyond this. Unlike economic class, sex class sprang directly from a biological reality: men and women were created different, and not equal. Although, as De Beauvoir points out, this difference of itself did not necessitate the development of a class system – the domination of one group by another – the reproductive *functions* of these differences did. The biological family is an inherently unequal power distribution. The need for power leading to the development of classes arises from the psychosexual formation of each individual according to this basic imbalance, rather than, as Freud, Norman O. Brown, and others have, once again over-shooting their mark, postulated, some irreducible conflict of Life against Death, Eros vs. Thanatos.

The *biological family* – the basic reproductive unit of male/female/infant, in whatever form of social organization – is characterized by these fundamental – if not immutable – facts:

(1) That women throughout history before the advent of birth control were at the continual mercy of their biology – menstruation, menopause, and 'female ills', constant painful childbirth, wetnursing and care of infants, all of which made them dependent on males (whether brother, father, husband, lover, or clan, government, community-at-large) for physical survival.

(2) That human infants take an even longer time to grow up than animals, and thus are helpless and, for some short period at least, dependent on adults for physical survival.

(3) That a basic mother/child interdependency has existed in some form in every society, past or present, and thus has shaped the psychology of every mature female and every infant.

(4) That the natural reproductive difference between the sexes led directly to the first division of labour at the origins of class, as well as furnishing the paradigm of caste (discrimination based on biological characteristics).

These biological contingencies of the human family cannot be covered over with anthropological sophistries. Anyone observing animals mating, reproducing, and caring for their young will have a hard time accepting the 'cultural relativity' line. For no matter how many tribes in Oceania you can find where the connection of the father to fertility is not known, no matter how many matrilineages, no matter how many cases of sex-role reversal, male housewifery, or even empathic labour pains, these facts prove only one thing: the amazing *flexibility* of human nature. But human nature is adaptable *to* something, it is, yes, determined by its environmental conditions. And the biological family that we have described has existed everywhere throughout time. Even in matriarchies where woman's fertility is worshipped, and the father's role is unknown or unimportant, if perhaps not on the genetic father, there is still some dependence of the female and the infant on the male. And though it is true that the nuclear family is only a recent development, one which, as I shall attempt to show, only intensifies the psychological penalties of the biological family, though it is true that throughout history there have been many variations on this biological family, the contingencies I have described existed in all of them, causing specific psychosexual distortions in the human personality.

But to grant that the sexual imbalance of power is biologically based is not to lose our case. We are no longer just animals. And the kingdom of nature does not reign absolute. As Simone de Beauvoir herself admits:

'The theory of historical materialism has brought to light some important truths. Humanity is not an animal species, it is a historical reality. Human society is an antiphysis – in a sense it is against nature; it does not passively submit to the presence of nature but rather takes over the control of nature on its own behalf. This arrogation is not an inward, subjective operation; it is accomplished objectively in practical action.'

Thus the 'natural' is not necessarily a 'human' value. Humanity has begun to transcend Nature: we can no longer justify the maintenance of a discriminatory sex class system on grounds of its origins in nature. Indeed, for pragmatic reasons alone it is beginning to look as if we *must* get rid of it.

The problem becomes political, demanding more than a comprehensive historical analysis, when one realizes that, though man is increasingly capable of freeing himself from the biological conditions that created his tyranny over women and children, he has little reason to want to give this tyranny up. As Engels said, in the context of economic revolution:

'It is the law of division of labour that lies at the basis of the division into classes. [Note that this division itself grew out of a fundamental biological division.] But this does not prevent the ruling class, once having the upper hand, from consolidating its power at the expense of the working class, from turning its social leadership into an intensified exploitation of the masses.'

Though the sex class system may have originated in fundamental biological conditions, this does not guarantee once the biological basis of their oppression has been swept away that women and children will be freed. On the contrary, the new technology, especially fertility control, may be used against them to reinforce the entrenched system of exploitation.

So that just as to assure elimination of economic classes requires the revolt of the underclass (the proletariat) and, in a temporary dictatorship, their seizure of the means of *production*, so to assure the elimination of sexual classes requires the revolt of the underclass (women) and the seizure of control of *reproduction*: not only the full restoration to women of ownership of their own bodies, but also their (temporary) seizure of control of human fertility – the new population biology as well as all the social institutions of child-bearing and child-rearing. And just as the end goal of socialist revolution was not only the elimination of the economic class *privilege* but of the economic class *distinction* itself, so the end goal of feminist revolution must be, unlike that of the first feminist movement, not just the elimination of male *privilege* but of the sex *distinction* itself: genital differences between human beings would no longer matter culturally. (A reversion to an unobstructed *pansexuality* – Freud's 'polymorphous perversity' – would probably supersede hetero/homo/bi-sexuality.) The reproduction of the species by one sex for the benefit of both would be replaced by (at least the option of) artificial reproduction: children would be born to both sexes equally, or independently of either, however one chooses to look at it; the dependence of the child on the mother (and vice versa) would give way to a greatly shortened dependence on a small group of others in general, and any remaining inferiority to adults in physical strength would be compensated for culturally. The division of labour would be ended by the elimination of labour altogether (through cybernetics). The tyranny of the biological family would be broken.

And with it the psychology of power. As Engels claimed for strictly socialist revolution: 'The existence of not simply this or that ruling class but of any ruling class at all [will have] become an obsolete anachronism.' That socialism has never come near achieving this predicated goal is not only the result of unfulfilled or misfired economic preconditions, but also because the Marxian analysis itself was insufficient: it did not dig deep enough to the psychosexual roots of class. Marx was on to something more profound than he knew when he observed that the family contained within itself in embryo all the antagonisms that later develop on a wide scale within the society and the state. For unless revolution uproots the basic social organization, the biological family – the vinculum through which the psychology of power can always be smuggled – the tapeworm of exploitation will never be annihilated. We shall need a sexual revolution much larger than – inclusive of – a socialist one to truly eradicate all class systems.

49.

YOUNG LORDS WOMEN'S CAUCUS

Formed in the summer of 1970,
New York City, New York, United States of America

Young Lords Party Position Paper on Women

1970

Puerto Rican, Black, and other Third World (colonized) women are becoming more aware of their oppression in the past and today. They are suffering three different types of oppression under capitalism. First, they are oppressed as Puerto Ricans or Blacks. Second, they are oppressed as women. Third, they are oppressed by their own men. The Third World woman becomes the most oppressed person in the world today.

Economically, Third World women have always been used as a cheap source of labor and as sexual objects. Puerto Rican and Black women are used to fill working class positions in factories, mass assembly lines, hospitals and all other institutions. Puerto Rican and black women are paid lower wages than whites and kept in the lowest positions within society. At the same time, giving Puerto Rican and Black women jobs means the Puerto Rican and Black man is kept from gaining economic independence, and the family unit is broken down. Capitalism defines manhood according to money and status; the Puerto Rican and Black man's manhood is taken away by making the Puerto Rican and Black woman the breadwinner. This situation keeps the Third World man divided from his woman. The Puerto Rican and Black man either leaves the household or he stays and becomes economically dependent on the woman, undergoing psychological damage. He takes out all of his frustrations on his woman, beating her, repressing and limiting her freedom. Because this society produces these conditions, our major enemy is capitalism rather than our own oppressed men.

Third World Women have an integral role to play in the liberation of all oppressed people as well as in the struggle for the liberation of women. Puerto Rican and Black women make up over half of the revolutionary army, and in the struggle for national liberation they must press for the equality of women; the woman's struggle is the revolution within the revolution. Puerto Rican women will be neither behind nor in front of their brothers but always alongside them in mutual respect and love.

historical

In the past women were oppressed by several institutions, one of which was marriage. When a woman married a man she became his property and lost her last name. A man could have several wives in order to show other men what wealth he had and enhance his position in society. In Eastern societies, men always had several wives and a number of women who were almost prostitutes, called concubines, purely sexual objects. Women had no right to own anything, not even their children; they were owned by her husband. This was true in places all over the world.

In many societies, women had no right to be divorced, and in India it was the custom of most of the people that when the husband died, all his wives became the property of his brother.

In Latin America and Puerto Rico, the man had a wife and another woman called la corteja. This condition still exists today. The wife was there to be a homemaker, to have children and to maintain the family name and honor. She had to be sure to be a virgin and remain pure for the rest of her life, meaning she could never experience sexual pleasure. The wife had to have children in order to enhance the man's concept of virility and his position within the Puerto Rican society. La corteja became his sexual instrument. The man could have set her up in another household, paid her rent, bought her food, and paid her bills. He could have children with this woman, but they are looked upon as by-products of a sexual relationship. Both women had to be loyal to the man. Both sets of children grew up very confused and insecure and developed negative attitudes about the role.

Women have always been expected to be wives and mothers only. They are respected by the rest of the community for being good cooks, good housewives, good mothers, but never for being intelligent, strong, educated, or militant. In the past, women were not educated, only the sons got an education, and mothers were respected for the number of sons they had, not daughters. Daughters were worthless and the only thing they could do was marry early to get away from home. At home the role of the daughter was to be a nursemaid for the other children and kitchen help for her mother.

The daughter was guarded like a hawk by her father, brothers, and uncles to keep her a virgin. In Latin America, the people used 'duenas' or old lady watchdogs to guard the purity of the daughters. The husband must be sure that his new wife has never been touched by another man because that would ruin the 'merchandise.' When he marries her, her purpose is to have sons and keep his home but not to be a sexual partner.

Sex was a subject that was never discussed, and women were brainwashed into believing that the sex act was dirty and immoral, and its only function was for the making of children. In Africa, many tribes performed an operation on young girls to remove the clitoris so they would not get any pleasure out of sex and would become better workers.

the double standard, machismo, and sexual fascism

Capitalism sets up standards that are applied differently to Puerto Rican and Black men from the way they are applied to Puerto Rican and Black women. These standards are also applied differently to Third World peoples than they are applied to whites. These standards must be understood since they are created to divide oppressed people in order to maintain an economic system that is racist and oppressive.

Puerto Rican and Black men are looked upon as rough, athletic and sexual, but not as intellectuals. Puerto Rican women are not expected to know anything except about the home, kitchen and bedroom. All that they are expected to do is look pretty and add a little humor. The Puerto Rican man sees himself as superior to his woman, and his superiority, he feels, gives him license to do many things – curse, drink, use drugs, beat women, and run around with many women. As a matter of fact these things are considered natural for a man to do, and he must do them to be considered a man. A woman who curses, drinks, and runs around with a lot of men is considered dirty scum, crazy, and a whore.

Today Puerto Rican men are involved in a political movement. Yet the majority of their women are home taking care of the children. The Puerto Rican sister that involves herself is considered aggressive, castrating, hard and unwomanly. She is viewed by the brothers as sexually accessible because what else is she doing outside the home. The Puerto Rican man tries to limit the woman's role because they feel the double standard is threatened; they feel insecure without it as a crutch.

Machismo has always been a very basic part of Latin American and Puerto Rican culture. Machismo is male chauvinism and more. Machismo means 'mucho macho' or a man who puts himself selfishly at the head of everything without considering the woman. He can do whatever he wants because his woman is an object with certain already defined roles – wife, mother, and good woman.

Machismo means physical abuse, punishment and torture. A Puerto Rican man will beat his woman to keep her in place and show her who's boss. Most Puerto Rican men do not beat women publicly because in the eyes of other men that is a weak thing to do. So they usually wait until they're home. All the anger and violence of centuries of oppression which should be directed against the oppressor is directed at the Puerto Rican woman. The aggression is also directed at daughters. The daughters hear their fathers saying 'the only way a woman is going to do anything or listen is by hitting her.' The father applies this to the daughter, beating her so that she can learn 'respeto.' The daughters grow up with messed up attitudes about their role as women and about manhood. They grow to expect that men will always beat them.

Sexual fascists are very sick people. Their illness is caused in part by this system which mouths puritanical attitudes and laws and yet exploits the human body for profit.

Sexual Fascism is tied closely to the double standard and machismo. It means that a man or woman thinks of the opposite sex solely as sexual objects to be used for sexual gratification and then discarded. A sexual fascist does not consider people's feelings; all they see everywhere is a pussy or a dick. They will use any rap, especially political, to get sex.

prostitution

Under capitalism, Third World women are forced to compromise themselves because of their economic situation. The facts that her man cannot get a job and that the family is dependent on her support mean she hustles money by any means necessary. Black and Puerto Rican sisters are put into a situation where jobs are scarce or nonexistent and are forced to compromise body, mind, and soul; they are then called whores or prostitutes.

Puerto Rican and Black sisters are made to prostitute themselves in many other ways. The majority of these sisters on the street are also hard-core drug addicts, taking drugs as an escape from oppression. These sisters are subjected to sexual abuse from dirty old men who are mainly white racists who view them as the ultimate sexual objects. Also he has the attitude that he cannot really prove his manhood until he has slept with a Black or Puerto Rican woman. The sisters also suffer abuse from the pimps, really small time capitalists, who see the women as private property that must produce the largest possible profit.

Because this society controls and determines the economic situation of Puerto Rican and Black women, sisters are forced to take jobs at the lowest wages; at the same time take insults and other indignities in order to keep the job. In factories, our men are worked like animals and cannot complain because they will lose their jobs – their labor is considered abundant and cheap. In hospitals, our women comprise the majority of the nurse's aides, kitchen workers, and clerks. These jobs are unskilled, the pay is low, and there is no chance for advancement. In offices, our positions are usually as clerks, typists and no-promotion jobs. In all of these jobs, our sisters are subjected to racial slurs, jokes, and others indignities such as being leered at, manhandled, propositioned, and assaulted. Our sisters are expected to prostitute themselves and take abuse of any kind or lose these subsistence jobs.

Everywhere our sisters are turned into prostitutes. The most obvious example is the sisters hustling their bodies on the streets, but the other forms of prostitution are also types of further exploitation of the Third World women. The only way to eliminate prostitution is to eliminate this society which creates the need. Then we can establish a socialist society that meets the economic needs of all the people.

birth control, abortion,
sterilization = genocide

We have no control over our bodies, because capitalism finds it necessary to control the woman's body to control population size. The choice of motherhood is being taken out of the mother's hands. She is sterilized to prevent her from having children, or she has a child because she cannot get an abortion.

Third World sisters are caught up in a complex situation. On one hand, we feel that genocide is being committed against our people. We know that Puerto Ricans will not be around on the face of the earth very long if Puerto Rican women are sterilized at the rate they are being sterilized now. The practice of sterilization in Puerto Rico goes back to the 1930's when doctors pushed it as the only means of contraception. In 1947-48, 7% of the women were sterilized; between 1953-54, 4 out of every 25; and by 1965, the number had increased to about 1 out of every 3 women. In many cases our sisters are told that their tubes are going to be 'tied,' but are never told that the 'tying' is really 'cutting' and that the tubes can never be 'untied.'

Part of this genocide is also the use of birth control pills which were tested for 15 years on Puerto Rican sisters (guinea pigs) before being sold on the market in the U.S. Even now many doctors feel that these pills cause cancer and death from blood clotting.

Abortions in hospitals that are butcher shops are little better than the illegal abortions our women used to get. The first abortion death in NYC under the new abortion law was Carman Rodriguez, a Puerto Rican sister who died in Lincoln Hospital. Her abortion was legal, but the conditions in the hospital were deadly.

On the other hand, we believe that abortions should be legal if they are community controlled, if they are safe, if our people are educated about the risks and if doctors do not sterilize our sisters while performing abortions. We realize that under capitalism our sisters and brothers cannot support large families and the more children we have the harder it is to support them. We say, change the system so that women can freely be allowed to have as many children as they want without suffering any consequences.

day care centers

One of the main reasons why many sisters are tied to the home and cannot work or become revolutionaries is the shortage of day care centers for children. The centers that already exist are over-crowded, expensive, and are only super-baby-sitting centers. Day care centers should be free, should be open 24 hours a day, and should be centers where children are taught their revolutionary history and culture.

Many sisters leave their children with a neighbor, or the oldest child is left to take care of the younger ones. Sometimes they are left alone, and all of us have read the tragic results in the newspapers of what happens to children left alone – they are burned to death in fires, or they swallow poison, or fall out of windows to their death.

revolutionary women

Throughout history, women have participated and been involved in liberation struggles. But the writers of history have never given full acknowledgement to the role of revolutionary women. At the point of armed struggle for national liberation, women have proved themselves as revolutionaries.

MARIANA BRACETTI was a Puerto Rican woman who together with her husband fought in the struggle for independence in Lares. She was called 'el brazo de oro' [golden arm] because of her unlimited energy. For her role in the struggle, she was imprisoned. She sewed the first flag of El Grito de Lares.

Another nationalist woman was LOLA RODRIGUEZ DE TIO, a poet who expressed the spirit of liberty and freedom in 'La Borinquena.' Besides being a nationalist, she was a fighter for women's rights. She refused to conform to the traditional customs concerning Puerto Rican women and at one point cut her hair very short.

Only recently, a 19 year old coed, ANTONIA MARTINEZ, was killed in Puerto Rico in a demonstration against the presence of amerikkkan military recruiting centers. She was murdered when she yelled 'Viva Puerto Rico Libre!'

SOJOURNER TRUTH was born a slave in New York around 1800. She traveled in the north speaking out against slavery, and for women's right. She was one of the most famous black orators in history.

KATHLEEN CLEAVER is a member of the Central Committee of the Black Panther Party. The Black Panthers are the vanguard of the Black liberation struggle in the united states. Another Panther sister, ERICA HUGGINS, is imprisoned in Connecticut for supposedly being a member of a conspiracy. She was forced to have her child in prison, and was given no medical attention while she was pregnant. Her child was later taken away from her because of her political beliefs.

ANGELA DAVIS is a Black revolutionary sister who is being hunted by the f.b.i. and is on their 10 most wanted list because she always defended her people's right to armed self-defense and because of her Marxist-Leninist philosophy.

In other parts of the world, women are fighting against imperialism and foreign invasion. Our sisters in Vietnam have struggled alongside their brothers for 25 years, first against the French colonizer, then against the japanese invaders, and now against the amerikkkan aggressors. Their military capability and efficiency has been demonstrated in so many instances that a women's brigade was formed in the National Liberation Front of the North Vietnamese Army.

BLANCA CANALES was one of the leaders of the revolution in Jayuya in 1950.

LOLITA LEBRON, together with three other patriots, opened fire on the House of Representative in an armed attack in 1954, bringing the attention of the world on the colonial status of Puerto Rico. She emptied a 45 automatic from the balcony of the Congress on to the colonial legislators. She then draped herself in the Puerto Rican flag and cried 'Viva Puerto Rico Libre.' The result was 5 legislators shot, and one critically wounded. She was imprisoned in a federal penitentiary and sentenced to 50 years. She is still in prison for this heroic act of nationalism.

LA THI THAM was born in a province which was constantly

bombarded by U.S. planes. After her fiance was killed in action, she sought and got a job with a time bomb detecting team. She scanned the sky with field glasses and when the enemy dropped bombs along the countryside, she would locate those which had not exploded and her teammates would go and open them and clear the road for traffic.

KAN LICH, another Vietnamese sister, fought under very harsh and dangerous conditions. She became a brilliant commander, decorated many times for her military ability. Her practice to 'hit at close quarters, hit hard, withdraw quickly' proved to be valid.

The Central Committee of the Young Lords Party has issued this position paper to explain and to educate our brothers and sisters about the role of sisters in the past and how we see sisters in the struggle now and in the future. We criticize those brothers who are 'machos' and who continue to treat our sisters as less than equals. We criticize sisters who remain passive, who do not join in the struggle against our oppression.

We are fighting every day within our PARTY against male chauvinism because we want to make a revolution of brothers and sisters – together – in love and respect for each other.

FORWARD SISTERS IN THE STRUGGLE!
ALL POWER TO THE PEOPLE!

50.

GERMAINE GREER

Born 1939, Melbourne, Australia

from *The Female Eunuch*

1970

'The World has lost its soul, and I my sex'
(Toller, *Hinkemann*)

This book is a part of the second feminist wave. The old suffragettes, who served their prison term and lived on through the years of gradual admission of women into professions which they declined to follow, into parliamentary freedoms which they declined to exercise, into academies which they used more and more as shops where they could take out degrees while waiting to get married, have seen their spirit revive in younger women with a new and vital cast. Mrs Hazel Hunkins-Hallinan, leader of the Six Point Group, welcomed the younger militants and even welcomed their sexual frankness. 'They're young,' she said to Irma Kurtz, 'and utterly unsophisticated politically, but they're full of beans. The membership of our group until recently has been far too old for my liking.'* After the ecstasy of direct action, the militant ladies of two generations ago settled down to work of consolidation in hosts of small organizations, while the main force of their energy filtered away in post-war retrenchments and the revival of frills, corsets and femininity after the permissive twenties, through the sexual sell of the fifties, ever dwindling, ever more respectable. Evangelism withered into eccentricity.

The new emphasis is different. Then genteel middleclass ladies clamoured for reform, now ungenteel middle-class women are calling for revolution. For many of them the call for revolution came before the call for the

---

* 'Boadicea Rides Again', *Sunday Times Magazine*, 21.9.1969.

liberation of women. The New Left has been the forcing house for most movements, and for many of them liberation is dependent upon the coming of the classless society and the withering away of the state. The difference is radical, for the faith that the suffragettes had in the existing political systems and their deep desire to participate in them have perished. In the old days ladies were anxious to point out that they did not seek to disrupt society or to unseat God. Marriage, the family, private property and the state were threatened by their actions, but they were anxious to allay the fears of conservatives, and in doing so the suffragettes betrayed their own cause and prepared the way for the failure of emancipation. Five years ago it seemed clear that emancipation had failed: the number of women in Parliament had settled at a low level; the number of professional women had stabilized as a tiny minority; the pattern of female employment had emerged as underpaid, menial and supportive. The cage door had been opened but the canary had refused to fly out. The conclusion was that the cage door ought never to have been opened because canaries are made for captivity; the suggestion of an alternative had only confused and saddened them.

There are feminist organizations still in existence which follow the reforming tracks laid down by the suffragettes. Betty Friedan's National Organization for Women is represented in congressional committees, especially the ones considered to be of special relevance to women. Women politicians still represent female interests, but they are most often the interests of women as dependants, to be protected from easy divorce and all sorts of Casanova's charters. Mrs Hunkins-Hallinan's Six Point Group is a respected political entity. What is new about the situation is that such groups are enjoying new limelight. The media insist upon exposing women's liberation weekly, even daily. The change is that suddenly everyone is interested in the subject of women. They may not be in favour of the movements that exist, but they are concerned about the issues. Among young women in universities the movement might be expected to find strong support. It is not surprising that exploited women workers might decide to hold the government to ransom at last. It is surprising that women who seem to have nothing to complain about have begun to murmur. Speaking to quiet audiences of provincial women decently hatted and dressed, I have been surprised to find that the most radical ideas are gladly entertained, and the most telling criticisms and sharpest protests are uttered. Even the suffragettes could not claim the grass-roots support that the new feminism gains day by day.

We can only speculate about the causes of this new activity. Perhaps the sexual sell was oversell. Perhaps women have never really believed the account of themselves which they were forced to accept from psychologists, religious leaders, women's magazines and men. Perhaps the reforms which did happen eventually led them to the position from which they could at last see the whole perspective and begin to understand the rationale of their situation. Perhaps because they are not enmeshed in unwilling childbirth and heavy menial labour in the home, they have had time to think. Perhaps the plight of our society has become so desperate and so apparent that women can no longer be content to leave it to other people. The enemies of women have blamed such circumstances for female discontent. Women must prize this discontent as the first stirring of the demand for life; they have begun to speak out and to speak to each other. The sight of women talking together has always made men uneasy; nowadays it means rank subversion. 'Right on!'

> We may safely assert that the knowledge that men can acquire of women, even as they have been and are, without reference to what they might be, is wretchedly imperfect and superficial and will always be so until women themselves have told all that they have to tell.
>
> John Stuart Mill

The organized liberationists are a well-publicized minority; the same faces appear every time a feminist issue is discussed. Inevitably they are presented as the leaders of a movement which is essentially leaderless. They are not much nearer to providing a revolutionary strategy than they ever were; demonstrating, compiling reading lists and sitting on committees are not themselves liberated behaviour, especially when they are still embedded in a context of housework and feminine wiles. As means of educating the people who must take action to liberate themselves, their effectiveness is limited. The concept of liberty implied by such liberation is vacuous; at worst it is defined by the condition of men, themselves unfree, and at best it is left undefined in a world of very limited possibilities. On the one hand, feminists can be found who serve the notion of equality, 'social, legal, occupational, economic, political and moral', whose enemy is discrimination, whose means are competition and demand. On the other hand there are those who cherish an ideal of a better life, which will follow when a better life is assured for all by the correct political means. To women disgusted with conventional political methods, whether constitutional or totalitarian or revolutionary, neither alternative can make much appeal. The housewife who must wait for the success of world revolution for her liberty might be excused for losing hope, while conservative political methods can invent no way in which the economically necessary unit of the one-man family could be diversified. But there is another dimension in which she can find motive and cause for action, although she might not find a blueprint for Utopia. She could begin not by changing the world, but by re-assessing herself.

It is impossible to argue a case for female liberation if there is no certainty about the degree of inferiority or natural dependence which is unalterably female. That is why this book begins with the Body. We know what we are, but know not what we may be, or what we might have been. The dogmatism of science expresses the status quo as the ineluctable result of law: women must learn how to question the most basic assumptions about feminine normality in order to reopen the possibilities for development which have been successively locked off by conditioning. So, we begin at the beginning, with the sex of cells. Nothing much can be made of chromosomal difference until it is manifested in development, and development cannot take place in a vacuum: from the outset our observation of the female is consciously and unconsciously biassed by assumptions that we cannot help making and cannot always identify when they have been made. The new assumption behind the discussion of the body is that everything that we may observe *could be otherwise*. In order to demonstrate some of the aspects of conditioning a discussion follows of the effects of behaviour upon the skeleton. From *Bones* we move to *Curves*, which is still essential to assumptions about the female sex, and then to *Hair*, for a long time considered a basic secondary sexual characteristic.

Female sexuality has always been a fascinating topic; this discussion of it attempts to show how female sexuality has been masked and deformed by most observers, and never more so than in our own time. The conformation of the female has already been described in terms of a particular type of conditioning, and now the specific character of that conditioning begins to emerge. What happens is that the female is considered as a sexual object for the use and appreciation of other sexual beings, men. Her sexuality is both denied and misrepresented by being identified as passivity. The vagina is obliterated from the imagery of femininity in the same way that the signs of independence and vigour in the rest of her body are suppressed. The characteristics that are praised and rewarded are those of the castrate – timidity, plumpness, languor, delicacy and preciosity. *Body* ends with a look at the way in which female reproduction is thought to influence the whole organism in the operations of the *Wicked Womb*, source of hysteria, menstrual depression, weakness, and unfitness for any sustained enterprise.

The compound of induced characteristics of soul and body is the myth of the Eternal Feminine, nowadays called the *Stereotype.* This is the dominant image of femininity which rules our culture and to which all women aspire. Assuming that the goddess of consumer culture is an artefact, we embark on an examination of how she comes to be made, the manufacture of the *Soul*. The chief element in this process is like the castration that we saw practised upon the body, the suppression and deflection of *Energy*. Following the same simple pattern, we begin at the beginning with Baby, showing how of the greater the less is made. The *Girl* struggles to reconcile her schooling along masculine lines with her feminine conditioning until *Puberty* resolves the ambiguity and anchors her safely in the feminine posture, if it works. When it doesn't she is given further conditioning as a corrective, especially by psychologists, whose assumptions and prescriptions are described as the *Psychological Sell*.

Because so many assumptions about the sex of mind cloud the issue of female mental ability, there follows a brief account of the failure of fifty years of thorough and diversified testing to discover any pattern of differentiation in male and female intellectual powers, called *The Raw Material*. Because the tests have been irrelevant to the continuing conviction that women are illogical, subjective and generally silly, *Womanpower* takes a coherent expression of all such prejudice, Otto Weininger's *Sex and Character*, and turns all the defects which it defines into advantages, by rejecting Weininger's concepts of virtue and intelligence and espousing those of Whitehead and others. As a corrective to such a theoretical view of how valuable such female minds might be, *Work* provides a factual account of the patterns that the female contribution actually takes and how it is valued.

> Draw near, woman, and hear what I have to say. Turn your curiosity for once towards useful objects, and consider the advantages which nature gave you and society ravished away. Come and learn how you were born the companion of man and became his slave; how you grew to like the condition and think it natural; and finally how the long habituation of slavery so degraded you that you preferred its sapping but convenient vices to the more difficult virtues of freedom and repute. If the picture I shall paint leaves you in command of yourselves, if you can contemplate it without emotion, then go back to your futile pastimes; 'there is no remedy; the vices have become the custom.'
>
> Choderlos de Laclos, 'On the Education of Women', 1783

The castration of women has been carried out in terms of a masculine-feminine polarity, in which men have commandeered all the energy and streamlined it into an aggressive conquistatorial power, reducing all heterosexual contact to a sadomasochistic pattern. This has meant the distortion of our concepts of *Love*. Beginning with a celebration of an *Ideal, Love* proceeds to describe some of the chief perversions, *Altruism, Egotism, and Obsession.* These distortions masquerade under various mythic guises, of which two follow – *Romance*, an account of the fantasies on which the appetent and the disappointed woman is nourished, and *The Object of Male Fantasy*, which deals with the favourite ways in which women are presented in specifically male literature. *The middle-class Myth of Love and Marriage* records the rise of the most commonly accepted mutual fantasy of heterosexual love in our society, as a prelude to a discussion of the normal form of life as we understand it, the *Family*. The nuclear family of our time is severely criticized, and some vague alternatives are suggested, but the chief function of this part, as of the whole book, is mostly to suggest the possibility and the desirability of an alternative. The chief bogy of those who fear freedom is insecurity, and so *Love* ends with an animadversion on the illusoriness of *Security*, the ruling deity of the welfare state, never more insubstantial than it is in the age of total warfare, global pollution and population explosion.

Because love has been so perverted, it has in many cases come to involve a measure of hatred. In extreme cases it takes the form of *Loathing and Disgust* occasioned by sadism, fastidiousness and guilt, and inspires hideous crimes on the bodies of women, but more often it is limited to *Abuse* and ridicule, expressed by casual insult and facetiousness. Rather than dwell upon the injustices suffered by women in their individual domestic circumstances, these parts deal with more or less public occasions in which the complicated patterns of mutual exploitation do not supply any ambiguous context. There are many subjective accounts of suffering to be found in feminist literature, so *Misery* deals with the problem on a broader scale, showing how much objective evidence there is that women are not happy even when they do follow the blueprint set out by sentimental and marriage guidance counsellors and the system that they represent. Although there is no pattern of female assault on men to parallel their violence to women, there is plenty of evidence of the operation of *Resentment* in bitter, non-physical sexual conflict, usually enacted as a kind of game, a ritualized situation in which the real issues never emerge. This unconscious vindictiveness has its parallels in more organized and articulate female *Rebellion*, in that it seeks to characterize men as the enemy and either to compete with or confront or attack them. In so far as such movements *demand* of men, or *force* men to grant their liberty, they perpetuate the estrangement of the sexes and their own dependency.

Revolution ought to entail the correction of some of the false perspectives which our assumptions about womanhood, sex, love and society have combined to create. Tentatively it gestures towards the re-deployment of energy, no longer to be used in repression, but in desire, movement and creation. Sex must be rescued from the traffic between powerful and powerless, masterful and mastered, sexual and neutral, to become a form of communication between potent, gentle, tender people, which cannot be accomplished by denial of heterosexual contact. The Ultra-feminine must refuse any longer to countenance the self-deception of the

Omnipotent Administrator, not so much by assailing him as freeing her-self from the desire to fulfil his expectations. It might be expected that men would resist female liberation because it threatens the foundations of phallic narcissism, but there are indications that men themselves are seeking a more satisfying role. If women liberate themselves, they will perforce liberate their oppressors: men might well feel that as sole custo-dians of sexual energy and universal protectors of women and children they have undertaken the impossible, especially now that their misdirected energies have produced the ultimate weapon. In admitting women to male-dominated areas of life, men have already shown a willingness to share responsibility, even if the invitation has not been taken up. Now that it might be construed that women are to help carry the can full of the mess that men have made, it need not be surprising that women have not leapt at the chance. If women could think that civilization would come to maturity only when they were involved in it wholly, they might feel more optimism in the possibilities of change and new development. The spiritual crisis we are at present traversing might be just another growing pain.

Revolution does little more than 'peep to what it would'. It hints that women ought not to enter into socially sanctioned relationships, like mar-riage, and that once unhappily in they ought not to scruple to run away. It might even be thought to suggest that women should be deliberately promiscuous. It certainly maintains that they should be self-sufficient and consciously refrain from establishing exclusive dependencies and other kinds of neurotic symbioses. Much of what it points to is sheer irrespon-sibility, but when the stake is life and freedom, and the necessary condition is the recovery of a will to live, irresponsibility might be thought a small risk. It is almost a hundred years since Nora asked Helmer 'What do you consider is my most sacred duty?' and when he answered 'Your duty to your husband and children', she demurred.

> I have another duty, just as sacred . . . My duty to myself . . . I believe that before everything else I'm a human being – just as much as you are . . . or at any rate I shall try to become one. I know quite well that most people would agree with you, Torvald, and that you have a warrant for it in books; but I can't be satisfied any longer with what most people

say, and with what's in books. I must think things out for myself and try to understand them.*

The relationships recognized by our society, and dignified with full privileges, are only those which are binding, symbiotic, economically determined. The most generous, tender, spontaneous relationship deliquesces into the approved mould when it avails itself of the approved buttresses, legality, security, permanence. Marriage cannot be a *job* as it has become. Status ought not to be measured for women in terms of attracting and snaring a man. The woman who realizes that she is bound by a million Lilliputian threads in an attitude of impotence and hatred masquerading as tranquillity and love has no option but to run away, if she is not to be corrupted and extinguished utterly. Liberty is terrifying but it is also exhilarating. Life is not easier or more pleasant for the Noras who have set off on their journey to awareness, but it is more interesting, nobler even. Such counsel will be called encouragement of irresponsibility, but the woman who accepts a way of life which she has not knowingly chosen, acting out a series of contingencies falsely presented as destiny, is truly irresponsible. To abdicate one's own moral understanding, to tolerate crimes against humanity, to leave everything to someone else, the father-ruler-king-computer, is the only irresponsibility. To deny that a mistake has been made when its results are chaos visible and tangible on all sides, that is irresponsibility. What oppression lays upon us is not responsibility but guilt.

The revolutionary woman must know her enemies, the doctors, psychiatrists, health visitors, priests, marriage counsellors, policemen, magistrates and genteel reformers, all the authoritarians and dogmatists who flock about her with warnings and advice. She must know her friends, her sisters, and seek in their lineaments her own. With them she can discover cooperation, sympathy and love. The end cannot justify the means: if she finds that her revolutionary way leads only to further discipline and continuing incomprehension, with their corollaries of bitterness and diminution, no matter how glittering the objective which would justify it, she must understand that it is a wrong way and an illusory end.

* Ibsen, *A Doll's House*, Act III.

The struggle which is not joyous is the wrong struggle. The joy of the struggle is not hedonism and hilarity, but the sense of purpose, achievement and dignity which is the reflowering of etiolated energy. Only these can sustain her and keep the flow of energy coming. The problems are only equalled by the possibilities: every mistake made is redeemed when it is understood. The only ways in which she can feel such joy are radical ones: the more derided and maligned the action that she undertakes, the more radical.

The way is unknown, just as the sex of the uncastrated female is unknown. However far we can see it is not far enough to discern the contours of what is ultimately desirable. And so no ultimate strategy can be designed. To be free to start out, and to find companions for the journey is as far as we need to see from where we stand. The first exercise of the free woman is to devise her own mode of revolt, a mode which will reflect her own independence and originality. The more clearly the forms of oppression emerge in her understanding, the more clearly she can see the shape of future action. In the search for political awareness there is no substitute for confrontation. It would be too easy to present women with yet another form of self-abnegation, more opportunities for appetence and forlorn hope, but women have had enough bullying. They have been led by the nose and every other way until they have to acknowledge that, like everyone else, they are lost. A feminist elite might seek to lead uncomprehending women in another arbitrary direction, training them as a task force in a battle that might, that ought never to eventuate. If there is a pitched battle women will lose, because the best man never wins; the consequences of militancy do not disappear when the need for militancy is over. Freedom is fragile and must be protected. To sacrifice it, even as a temporary measure, is to betray it. It is not a question of telling women what to do next, or even what to want to do next. The hope in which this book was written is that women will discover that they have a will; once that happens they will be able to tell us how and what they want.

The fear of freedom is strong in us. We call it chaos or anarchy, and the words are threatening. We live in a true chaos of contradicting authorities, an age of conformism without community, of proximity without communication. We could only fear chaos if we imagined that it was unknown to us, but in fact we know it very well. It is unlikely that the techniques of liberation spontaneously adopted by women will be in such fierce conflict as exists between warring self-interests and conflicting dogmas, for they will not seek to eliminate all systems but their own. However diverse they may be, they need not be utterly irreconcilable, because they will not be conquistatorial.

Hopefully, this book is subversive. Hopefully, it will draw fire from all the articulate sections of the community. The conventional moralist will find much that is reprehensible in the denial of the Holy Family, in the denigration of sacred motherhood, and the inference that women are not by nature monogamous. The political conservatives ought to object that by advocating the destruction of the patterns of consumption carried out by the chief spenders, the housewives, the book invites depression and hardship. This is tantamount to admitting that the depression of women is necessary to the maintenance of the economy, and simply ratifies the point. If the present economic structure can change only by collapsing, then it had better collapse as soon as possible. The nation that acknowledges that all labourers are worthy of their hire and then withholds payment from 19.5 million workers cannot continue. Freudians will object that by setting aside the conventional account of the female psyche, and relying upon a concept of woman which cannot be found to exist, the book is mere metaphysics, forgetting the metaphysical basis of their own doctrine. The reformers will lament that the image of womanhood is cheapened by the advocacy of delinquency, so that women are being drawn further away from the real centres of power. In the computer kingdom the centres of political power have become centres of impotence, but even so, nothing in the book precludes the use of the political machine, although reliance on it may be contra-indicated. The most telling criticisms will come from my sisters of the left, the Maoists, the Trots, the IS, the SDS, because of my fantasy that it might be possible to leap the steps of revolution and arrive somehow at liberty and communism without strategy or revolutionary discipline. But if women are the true proletariat, the truly oppressed majority, the revolution can only be drawn nearer by their withdrawal of support for the capitalist system. The weapon that I suggest is that most honoured of the proletariat, withdrawal of labour. Nevertheless it is clear that I do not find the factory the real heart of civilization or the re-entry of women into industry as the necessary condition of liberation. Unless the concepts of work and play and reward for work change absolutely, women must continue to provide cheap labour, and even more, free labour exacted of right by an employer possessed of a contract for life, made out in his favour.

This book represents only another contribution to a continuing dialogue between the wondering woman and the world. No questions have been answered but perhaps some have been asked in a more proper way than heretofore. If it is not ridiculed or reviled, it will have failed of its intention. If the most successful feminine parasites do not find it offensive, than it is innocuous. What they can tolerate is intolerable for a woman with any pride. The opponents of female suffrage lamented that woman's emancipation would mean the end of marriage, morality and the state; their extremism was more clear-sighted than the woolly benevolence of liberals and humanists, who thought that giving women a measure of freedom would not upset anything. When we reap the harvest which the unwitting suffragettes sowed we shall see that the anti-feminists were after all right.

51.

ALICE WALKER

Born 1944, Eatonton, Georgia, United States of America

"'Women of Color' Have Rarely Had The Opportunity To Write About Their Love Affairs"
(a found poem: *The New York Review of Books*, Nov. 30, 1972)

Since he had few intimate friends, and little
is known
about his private life,
it is of interest that Shirley Graham,
his second wife,
has now published an account
of their life together
in *His Truth Is Marching On*.

Unfortunately, however, her version of Du Bois's
career
is perhaps more revealing of herself
than of her late husband.
The gaps in Mrs Du Bois's memoir
are more instructive
than her recollections.

She has nothing to say
about the internal drama
of the NAACP's birth.
She mentions Du Bois's conflict with

Washington
only in passing
and his debates with
Garvey
              not at all.

Instead she clutters her narrative
with lengthy accounts
of her father's
work
in the NAACP,
the food
    Du Bois liked,
and the international celebrities
she was able to meet
                              because she was married
to Du Bois.

'Women of Color' have rarely had
the opportunity to write about their love
affairs.
There are no black legends comparable to
that of Heloise
and Abelard
or even of Bonnie
and Clyde.

Mrs Du Bois (who was known as a writer
before she married)
seems to have wanted to fill this gap.

Her recollections, unfortunately, are a cloying
intrusion
into any serious effort
to understand
Du Bois.

She assumes her romance
with Du Bois
to be as interesting as any other aspect
of his career.

52.

AUDRE LORDE

Born 1934, New York City, New York, United States of America
Died 1992, Christiansted, U.S. Virgin Islands

Who Said It Was Simple

1973

There are so many roots to the tree of anger
that sometimes the branches shatter
before they bear.

Sitting in Nedicks
the women rally before they march
discussing the problematic girls
they hire to make them free.
An almost white counterman passes
a waiting brother to serve them first
and the ladies neither notice nor reject
the slighter pleasures of their slavery.
But I who am bound by my mirror
as well as my bed
see causes in color
as well as sex

and sit here wondering
which me will survive
all these liberations.

53.

RACHEL ADLER

Born 1943, Chicago, Illinois, United States of America

The Jew Who Wasn't There

1973

It is not unusual for committed Jewish women to be uneasy about their position as Jews. It was to cry down our doubts that rabbis developed their pre-packaged orations on the nobility of motherhood; the glory of childbirth; and modesty, the crown of Jewish womanhood. I have heard them all. I could not accept those answers for two reasons. First of all, the answers did not accept me as a person. They only set rigid stereotypes which defined me by limiting the directions in which I might grow. Second, the answers were not really honest ones. Traditional scholars agree that all philosophies of Judaism must begin with an examination of Jewish law, Halacha, since, in the Halacha are set down the ways in which we are expected to behave, and incontestably our most deeply engrained attitudes are those which we reinforce by habitual action.

Yet scholars do not discuss female status in terms of Halacha – at least not with females. Instead, they make lyrical exegeses on selected Midrashim and Agadot which, however complimentary they may be, do not really reflect the way in which men are expected to behave toward women by Jewish law. I think we are going to have to discuss it, if we are to build for ourselves a faith which is not based on ignorance and self-deception. That is why I would like to offer some hypotheses on the history and nature of the 'woman problem' in Halacha.

Ultimately our problem stems from the fact that we are viewed in Jewish law and practice as peripheral Jews. The category in which we are generally placed includes women, children, and Canaanite slaves. Members of this category are exempt from all positive commandments which occur within time limits.* These commandments would include hearing the sholar on Rosh HaShanah, eating in the Sukkah, praying with the lulav, praying the three daily services, wearing tallit and I'fillin, and saying Sh'ma.† In other words, members of this category have been 'excused' from most of the positive symbols which, for the male Jew, hallow time, hallow his physical being, and inform both his myth and his philosophy.

Since most of the mitzvot not restricted by time are negative, and since women, children and slaves are responsible to fulfill all negative mitzvot, including the negative time-bound mitzvot, it follows that for members of this category, the characteristic posture of their Judaism is negation rather than affirmation.‡ They must not, for example, eat non-kosher food, violate the Shabbat, eat chametz on Pesach, fail to fast on fast days, steal, murder, or commit adultery. That women, children, and slaves have limited credibility in Jewish law is demonstrated by the fact that their testimony is inadmissible in a Jewish court.§ The minyan – the basic unit of the Jewish community – excludes them, implying that the community is presumed to be the Jewish males to whom they are adjuncts. Torah study is incumbent upon them only insofar as it relates to 'their' mitzvot. Whether women are even permitted to study further is debated.¶

All of the individuals in this tri-partite category I have termed peripheral Jews. Children, if male, are full Jews *in potentio*. Male Canaanite slaves, if freed, become full Jews, responsible for all the mitzvot and able to count in a minyan.** Even as slaves, they have the b'rit mila, the covenant of circumcision, that central Jewish symbol, from which women are anatomically excluded. It is true that in Jewish law women are slightly more respected than slaves, but that advantage is outweighed by the fact that only women can never grow up, or be freed, or otherwise leave the category. The peripheral Jew is excused and sometimes barred from the

---

* Kiddushin 29a.
† Ibid., but see also Mishna Sukkah and Mishna Brachot 3:3.
‡ Kiddushin 29a.
§ Sh'vuot 30a. See also Rosh HaShanah 22a.
¶ Sotah 20a.
** It must be admitted that Canaanite slaves were only to be freed if some overriding mitzvah would be accomplished thereby. The classic case in which Rabbi Eliezer frees his slave in order to complete a minyan is given in Gittin 38b.

acts and symbols which are the lifeblood of the believing community, but this compliance with the negative mitzvot is essential, since, while he cannot be permitted to participate fully in the life of the Jewish people, he cannot be permitted to undermine it either.

To be a peripheral Jew is to be educated and socialized toward a peripheral commitment. This, I think, is what happened to the Jewish woman. Her major mitzvot aid and reinforce the life-style of the community and the family, but they do not cultivate the relationship between the individual and God. A woman keeps kosher because both she and her family must have kosher food. She lights the Shabbat candles so that there will be light, and hence, peace, in the household. She goes to the mikva so that her husband can have intercourse with her and she bears children so that, through her, he can fulfill the exclusively male mitzvah of increasing and multiplying.*

Within these narrow confines, there have been great and virtuous women, but in several respects the tzidkaniol (saintly women) have been unlike the tzaddikim, Beruria, the scholarly wife of Rabbi Meir, the Talmudic sage, and a few exceptional women like her stepped outside the limits of the feminine role, but legend relates how Beruria came to a bad end, implying that her sin was the direct result of her 'abnormal' scholarship.† There is no continuous tradition of learned women in Jewish history. Instead there are many tzidkaniot, some rationalists, some mystics, some joyous, some oscetic, singers, dancers, poets, halachists, all bringing to God the service of a singular, inimitable self.

How is it that the tzaddikim seem so individualized and the tzidkeniot so generalized? I would advance two reasons. First of all, the mitzvot of the tzadeket are mainly directed toward serving others. She is a tzadeket to the extent that she sacrifices herself in order that others may actualize themselves spiritually. One has no sense of an attempt to cultivate a religious self built out of the raw materials of a unique personality. The model for the tzadeket is Rachel, the wife of Rabbi Akiva, who sold her hair and sent her husband away to study for twenty-four years, leaving herself beggared and without means of support; or the wife of Rabbi Menachem

* Mikva is not itself a mitzvah. It is a prerequisite to a permitted activity, just as shechita is prerequisite to the permitted activity of eating meat. See Sefer HaChinuch, Mitzvah 175.
† Avoda Zara 18b. See Rashi.

Mendel of Rymanov (her name incidentally, goes unremembered) who sold her share in the next world to buy her husband bread.

Frequently there is a kind of masochism manifest in the accounts of the acts of tzidkaniot. I recall the stories held up to me as models to emulate, of women who chopped holes in icy streams to perform their monthly immersions. A lady in the community I came from, who went into labor on Shabbat and walked to the hospital rather than ride in a taxi, was acting in accordance with this model. Implicit is the assumption that virtue is to be achieved by rejecting and punishing the hated body which men every morning thank God is not theirs.*

Second, as Hillel says, 'an ignoramus cannot be a saint.'† He may have the best of intentions, but he lacks the disciplined creativity, the sense of continuity with his people's history and thought, and the forms in which to give Jewish expression to his religious impulses. Since it was traditional to give women cursory religious educations, they were severely limited in their ways of expressing religious commitment. Teaching, the fundamental method of the Jewish people for transmitting religious insights, was closed to women – those who do not learn, do not teach.‡ Moreover, expressions of spiritual creativity by women seem to have been severely limited. Religious music written by women is virtually non-existent. There are no prayers written by women in the liturgy, although there were prayers written in Yiddish by women for women who were unable to pray in Hebrew.

It was, perhaps, most damaging that the woman's meager mitzvot are, for the most part, closely connected to some physical goal or object. A woman's whole life revolved around physical objects and physical experiences – cooking, cleaning, childbearing, meeting the physical needs of children. Without any independent spiritual life to counterbalance the materialism of her existence, the mind of the average woman was devoted to physical considerations; marriages, deaths, dinners, clothes and money. It was, thus, natural that Jewish men should have come to identify women with *gashmiut* (physicality) and men with *ruchniut* (spirituality).

---

* In the Traditional Prayerbook see the morning blessing, Blessed are You, Lord our God, King of the universe, who has not created me a woman.
† Avot 2:6.
‡ Exactly this impression is used in Kiddushin 29b, where it is asserted that the mitzvah of teaching one's own offspring the Torah applies to men and not to women.

The Talmudic sages viewed the female mind as frivolous and the female sexual appetite as insatiable.* Unless strictly guarded and given plenty of busywork, all women were potential adulteresses.† In the Jewish view, all physical objects and experiences are capable of being infused with spiritual purpose; yet it is equally true that the physical, unredeemed by spiritual use, is a threat. It is therefore easy to see how women came to be regarded as semi-demonic in both Talmud and Kabbalah. Her sexuality presented a temptation, or perhaps a threat which came to be hedged ever more thickly by law and custom.‡ Conversing with women was likely to result in gossip or lewdness.§ Woman are classed as inadmissible witnesses in the same category with gamblers, pigeon-racers and other individuals of unsavory repute.¶

Make no mistake; for centuries, the lot of the Jewish woman was infinitely better than that of her non-Jewish counterpart. She had rights which other women lacked until a century ago. A Jewish woman could not be married without her consent. Her ketubah (marriage document) was a legally binding contract which assured that her husband was responsible for her support (a necessity in a world in which it was difficult for a woman to support herself), and that if divorced, she was entitled to a monetary settlement. Her husband was not permitted to abstain from sex for long periods of time without regard to her needs and her feelings.** In its time, the Talmud's was a very progressive view. The last truly revolutionary ruling for women, however, was the Edict of Rabbenu Gershom forbidding polygamy to the Jews of the Western world. That was in 1000 c.e. The problem is that very little has been done since then to ameliorate the position of Jewish women in observant Jewish society.

All of this can quickly be rectified if one steps outside of Jewish tradition

---

* Kiddushin 80b contains the famous statement, 'The rational faculty of women weighs lightly upon them.' Interestingly enough, the Tossafot illustrate this with an ancient misogynistic fabliau whose written source is the Satrycion of Petronius Arbiter. See also Sotah 20a.
† Mishna Ketubot 5:5.
‡ This is the context in which one may understand the statement of the Kitzur Shulchan Aruch, 'A man should be careful not to walk between two women, two dogs, or two swine.' Ganzfried, Rabbi Solomon, Code of Jewish Law I, trans. Hyman E. Goldin, second ed., New York: 1961, p.7.
§ Avot 1:5, see also the commentaries of Rashi, Rambam, and Rabbenu Yonah.
¶ Rosh HaShanah 22a.
** Mishna Ketubot 5:6.

and Halacha. The problem is how to attain some justice and some growing room for the Jewish woman if one is committed to remaining *within* Halacha. Some of these problems are more easily solved than others. For example, there is ample precedent for decisions permitting women to study Talmud, and it should become the policy of Jewish day schools to teach their girls Talmud. It would not be difficult to find a basis for giving women aliyot to the Torah. Moreover, it is both feasible and desirable for the community to begin educating women to take on the positive time-bound mitzvot from which they are now excused; in which case, those mitzvot would eventually become incumbent upon women. The more difficult questions are those involving minyan and mechitza (segregation at prayers). There are problems concerning the right of women to be rabbis, witness in Jewish courts, judges and leaders of religious services. We need decisions on these problems which will permit Jewish women to develop roles and role models in which righteousness springs from self-actualization, in contrast to the masochistic, self-annihilating model of the post-Biblical tzadeket. The halachic scholars must examine our problem anew, right now, with open minds and with empathy. They must make it possible for women to claim their share in the Torah and begin to do the things a Jew was created to do. If necessary we must agitate until the scholars are willing to see us as Jewish souls in distress rather than as tools with which men do mitzvot. If they continue to turn a deaf ear to us, the most learned and halachically committed among us must make halachic decisions for the rest. That is a move to be saved for desperate straits, for even the most learned of us have been barred from acquiring the systematic halachic knowledge which a rabbi has. But, to paraphrase Hillel, in a place where there are no menschen, we may have to generate our own menschlichkeit. There is no time to waste. For too many centuries, the Jewish woman has been a golem, created by Jewish society. She cooked and bore and did her master's will, and when her tasks were done, the Divine Name was removed from her mouth. It is time for the golem to demand a soul.*

---

* There is a famous folk tale that the scholar Rabbi Loewe of Prague created a golem, or robot, using the Kabbalah. The robot, formed from earth, came to life and worked as a servant when a tablet engraved with the Divine Name was placed in its mouth. When the tablet was removed, the golem reverted to mindless clay.

54.

JAN MORRIS

Born 1926, Clevedon, United Kingdom
Died 2020, Nant Gwynant, United Kingdom

from *Conundrum*

1974

Our children were safely growing; I felt I had, so far as I could, honoured the responsibilities of my marriage; rather than go mad, or kill myself, or worst of all perhaps infect everyone around me with my profoundest melancholy, I would accept Dr Benjamin's last resort, and have my body altered.

Nobody in the history of human kind has changed from a true man to a true woman, if we class a man or a woman purely by physical concepts. Hermaphrodites may have shifted the balance of their ambiguity, but nobody has been born with one complete body and died with the other. When I say, then, that I now began a change of sex, I speak in shorthand. What was about to happen was that my body would be made as female as science could contemplate or nature permit, to reset (as I saw it) the pointer of my sex more sensibly and accurately along the scale of my gender. Doctors, whose conception of these matters is often simplistic to the degree of obscurantism, have devised many tests for the determination of sex, and divided the concept into several categories. There is anatomical sex, the most obvious: breasts, vagina, womb and ovaries for the female, penis and testicles for the male. There is chromosomal sex, the most fundamental: the nuclear composition of the body, which need not necessarily conform to the anatomy, but which is accepted as a convenient rule of thumb for such purposes as international sport. There is hormonal sex, the chemical balance of male and female. There is psychological sex, the way people respond to the world, and feel themselves to be.

I was not much interested in these criteria, for I regarded sex merely as the tool of gender, and I believed that for me as for most people the interplay between the two lay very close to personality, not to be measured by blood tests or Freudian formulae. All I wanted was liberation, or reconciliation – to live as myself, to clothe myself in a more proper body, and achieve Identity at last. I would not hurry. First I would discover if it were feasible. Slowly, carefully, with infinite precaution against betrayal, I began the chemical experiments by which I would lose many of my male characteristics, and acquire some of the female: then, if all went well, several years later I would take the last step, and have the change completed by surgery.

To myself I had been woman all along, and I was not going to change the truth of me, only discard the falsity. But I *was* about to change my form and apparency – my status too, perhaps my place among my peers, my attitudes no doubt, the reactions I would evoke, my reputation, my manner of life, my prospects, my emotions, possibly my abilities. I was about to adapt my body from a male conformation to a female, and I would shift my public role altogether, from the role of a man to the role of a woman. It is one of the most drastic of all human changes, unknown until our own times, and even now experienced by very few: but it seemed only natural to me, and I embarked upon it only with a sense of thankfulness, like a lost traveller finding the right road at last.

55.

MARIAROSA DALLA COSTA

Born 1943, Treviso, Italy

A General Strike

1974

Today the feminist movement in Italy is opening the campaign for Wages for Housework. As you have heard from the songs, as you have seen from the photograph exhibition, as you have read on the placards, the questions we are raising today are many: the barbarous conditions in which we have to face abortion, the sadism we are subjected to in obstetric and gynaecological clinics, our working conditions – in jobs outside the home our conditions are always worse than men's, and at home we work without wages – the fact that social services either don't exist or are so bad that we are afraid to let our children use them, and so on.

Now at some point people might ask, what is the connection between the campaign we are opening today, the campaign for Wages for Housework, and all these things that we have raised today, that we have exposed and are fighting against? All these things that we have spoken about, that we have made songs about, that we have shown in our exhibitions and films?

We believe that the weakness of all women – that weakness that's behind our being crossed out of all history, that's behind the fact that when we leave the home we must face the most revolting, underpaid and insecure jobs – this weakness is based on the fact that all of us women, whatever we do, are wearied and exhausted at the very outset by the 13 hours of housework that no-one has ever recognized, that no-one has ever paid for.

We all do housework; it is the only thing all women have in common, it is the only base on which we can gather our power, the power of millions of women.

It is no accident that reformists of every stripe have always carefully avoided the idea of our organizing on the basis of housework. They have always refused to recognize housework as work, precisely because it is the only work that we all have in common. It is one thing to confront two or three hundred women workers in a shoe factory, and quite another to confront millions of housewives. And since all women factory workers are housewives, it is still another matter to confront these two or three hundred factory workers united with millions of housewives.

But this is what we are putting on the agenda today in this square. This is the first moment of organization. We have decided to organize ourselves around the work that we all do, in order to have the power of millions of women.

For us, therefore, the demand for wages for housework is a direct demand for power, because housework is what millions of women have in common.

If we can organize ourselves in our millions on this demand – and already there are quite a lot of us in this square – we can get so much power that we need no longer be in a position of weakness when we go out of the home. We can bring about new working conditions in house-work itself – if I have money of my own in my pocket I can even buy a dishwasher without feeling guilty and without having to beg my husband for it for months on end while he, who doesn't do the washing-up, considers a dishwasher unnecessary.

We want to say something else. For a long time – particularly strongly in the past 10 years, but let's say always – male workers have come out to struggle against their hours of work and for more money, and have gathered in this square.

In the factories of Porto Marghera there have been many strikes, many struggles. We well remember the marches of male workers who started in Porto Marghera, crossed the Mestre Bridge and arrived here in this square.

But let's make this clear. No strike has ever been a general strike. When half the working population is at home in the kitchens, while the others are on strike, it's not a general strike.

We've never seen a general strike. We've only seen men, generally men from the big factories, come out on the streets, while their wives, daughters, sisters, mothers, went on cooking in the kitchens.

Today in this square, with the opening of our mobilisation for Wages for Housework, we put on the agenda our working hours, our holidays, our strikes and our money.

When we win a level of power that enables us to reduce our 13 or more working hours a day to eight hours or even less than eight, when at the same time we can put on the agenda our holidays – because it's no secret to anyone that on Sundays and during vacation time women never have a holiday – then, perhaps, we'll be able to talk for the first time of a 'general' strike of the working class.

56.

SILVIA FEDERICI

Born 1942, Parma, Italy

from *Wages Against Housework*
1975

'A labour of love'

It is important to recognise that when we speak of housework we are not speaking of a job as other jobs, but we are speaking of the most pervasive manipulation, the most subtle and mystified violence that capitalism has ever perpetrated against any section of the working class. True, under capitalism every worker is manipulated and exploited and his/her relation to capital is totally mystified. The wage gives the impression of a fair deal: you work and you get paid, hence you and your boss are equal; while in reality the wage, rather than paying for the work you do, hides all the unpaid work that goes into profit. But the wage at least recognises that you are a worker, and you can bargain and struggle around and against the terms and the quantity of that wage, the terms and the quantity of that work. To have a wage means to be part of a social contract, and there is no doubt concerning its meaning: you work, not because you like it, or because it comes naturally to you, but because it is the only condition under which you are allowed to live. But exploited as you might be, *you are not that work.* Today you are a postman, tomorrow a cabdriver. All that matters is how much of that work you have to do and how much of that money you can get.

But in the case of housework the situation is qualitatively different. The difference lies in the fact that not only has housework been imposed on women, but it has been transformed into a natural attribute of our female physique and personality, an internal need, an aspiration, supposedly coming from the depth of our female character. Housework had to be transformed into a natural attribute rather than be recognised as a social contract because from the beginning of capital's scheme for women this work was destined to be unwaged. Capital had to convince us that it is a natural, unavoidable and even fulfilling activity to make us accept our unwaged work. In its turn, the unwaged condition of housework has been the most powerful weapon in reinforcing the common assumption that *housework is not work*, thus preventing women from struggling against it, except in the privatised kitchen-bedroom quarrel that all society agrees to ridicule, thereby further reducing the protagonist of a struggle. We are seen as nagging bitches, not workers in struggle.

Yet just how natural it is to be a housewife is shown by the fact that it takes at least twenty years of socialisation – day-to-day training, performed by an unwaged mother – to prepare a woman for this role, to convince her that children and husband are the best she can expect from life. Even so, it hardly succeeds. No matter how well trained we are, few are the women who do not feel cheated when the bride's day is over and they find themselves in front of a dirty sink. Many of us still have the illusion that we marry for love. A lot of us recognise that we marry for money and security; but it is time to make it clear that while the love or money involved is very little, the work which awaits us is enormous. This is why older women always tell us 'Enjoy your freedom while you can, buy whatever you want now . . .' But unfortunately it is almost impossible to enjoy any freedom if from the earliest days of life you are trained to be docile, subservient, dependent and most important to *sacrifice yourself* and even to get pleasure from it. If you don't like it, it is your problem, your failure, your guilt, your abnormality.

We must admit that capital has been very successful in hiding our work. It has created a true masterpiece at the expense of women. By denying housework a wage and transforming it into an act of love, capital has killed many birds with one stone. First of all, it has got a hell of a lot of work almost for free, and it has made sure that women, far from struggling against it, would seek that work as the best thing in life (the magic words: 'Yes, darling, you are a real woman'). At the same time, it has disciplined the male worker also; by making his woman dependent on his work and his wage, and trapped him in this discipline by giving him a servant after he himself has done so much serving at the factory or the office. In fact, our role as women is to be the unwaged but happy, and most of all loving, servants of the 'working class', i.e. those strata of the proletariat to which capital was forced to grant more social power. In the same way as god created Eve to give pleasure to Adam, so did capital create the housewife to service the male worker physically, emotionally and sexually – to raise his children, mend his socks, patch up his ego when it is crushed by the work and the social relations (which are relations of loneliness) that capital has reserved for him. It is precisely this peculiar combination of physical, emotional and sexual services that are involved in the role women must perform for capital that creates the specific character of that servant which is the housewife, that makes her work so burdensome and at the same time invisible. It is not an accident that most men start thinking of getting married as soon as they get their first job. This is not only because now they can afford it, but because having somebody at home who takes care of you is the only condition not to go crazy after a day spent on an assembly line or at a desk. Every woman knows that this is what she should be doing to be a true woman and have a 'successful' marriage. And in this case too, the poorer the family the higher the enslavement of the woman, and not simply because of the monetary situation. In fact capital has a dual policy, one for the middle class and one for the proletarian family. It is no accident that we find the most unsophisticated machismo in the working class family: the more blows the man gets at work the more his wife must be trained to absorb them, the more he is allowed to recover his ego at her expense. You beat your wife and vent your rage against her when you are frustrated or overtired by your work or when you are defeated in a struggle (to go into a factory is itself a defeat). The more the man serves and is bossed around, the more he bosses around. A man's home is his castle . . . and his wife has to learn to wait in silence when he is moody, to put him back together when he is broken down and swears at the world, to turn around in bed when he says 'I'm too tired tonight,' or when he goes so fast at love-making that, as one woman put it, he might as well make it with a mayonnaise jar. (Women have always found ways of fighting back, or getting back at them, but always in an isolated and privatised way. The problem, then, becomes how to bring this struggle out of the kitchen and bedroom and into the streets.)

This fraud that goes under the name of love and marriage affects all of us, even if we are not married, because *once housework was totally natural-ised and sexualised*, once it became a feminine attribute, all of us as females are characterised by it. If it is natural to do certain things, then all women are expected to do them and even like doing them – even those women who, due to their social position, could escape some of that work or most of it (their husbands can afford maids and shrinks and other forms of relaxation and amusement). We might not serve one man, but we are all in a servant relation with respect to the whole male world. This is why to be called a female is such a putdown, such a degrading thing. ('Smile, honey, what's the matter with you?' is something every man feels entitled to ask you, whether he is your husband, or the man who takes your ticket, or your boss at work.)

57.

AUDRE LORDE

Born 1934, New York City, New York, United States of America
Died 1992, Christiansted, U.S. Virgin Islands

Love Poem

1975

Speak earth and bless me with what is richest
make sky flow honey out of my hips
rigid as mountains
spread over a valley
carved out by the mouth of rain.

And I knew when I entered her I was
high wind in her forests hollow
fingers whispering sound
honey flowed
from the split cup
impaled on a lance of tongues
on the tips of her breasts on her navel
and my breath
howling into her entrances
through lungs of pain.

Greedy as herring-gulls
or a child
I swing out over the earth
over and over
again.

58

ADRIENNE RICH

Born 1929, Baltimore, Maryland, United States of America
Died 2012, Santa Cruz, California, United States of America

from *Of Woman Born*
1976

All human life on the planet is born of woman. The one unifying, incontrovertible experience shared by all women and men is that months-long period we spent unfolding inside a woman's body. Because young humans remain dependent upon nurture for a much longer period than other mammals, and because of the division of labor long established in human groups, where women not only bear and suckle but are assigned almost total responsibility for children, most of us first know both love and disappointment, power and tenderness, in the person of a woman.

We carry the imprint of this experience for life, even into our dying. Yet there has been a strange lack of material to help us understand and use it. We know more about the air we breathe, the seas we travel, than about the nature and meaning of motherhood. In the division of labor according to gender, the makers and sayers of culture, the namers, have been the sons of the mothers. There is much to suggest that the male mind has always been haunted by the force of the idea of *dependence on a woman for life itself*, the son's constant effort to assimilate, compensate for, or deny the fact that he is 'of woman born.'

Women are also born of women. But we know little about the effect on culture of that fact, because women have not been makers and sayers of patriarchal culture. Woman's status as childbearer has been made into a major fact of her life. Terms like 'barren' or 'childless' have been used to negate any further identity. The term 'nonfather' does not exist in any realm of social categories.

Because the fact of physical motherhood is so visible and dramatic, men recognized only after some time that they, too, had a part in generation. The meaning of 'fatherhood' remains tangential, elusive. To 'father' a child suggests above all to beget, to provide the sperm which fertilizes the ovum. To 'mother' a child implies a continuing presence, lasting at least nine months, more often for years. Motherhood is earned, first through an intense physical and psychic rite of passage – pregnancy and childbirth – then through learning to nurture, which does not come by instinct.

A man may beget a child in passion or by rape, and then disappear; he need never see or consider child or mother again. Under such circumstances, the mother faces a range of painful, socially weighted choices: abortion, suicide, abandonment of the child, infanticide, the rearing of a child branded 'illegitimate,' usually in poverty, always outside the law. In some cultures she faces murder by her kinsmen. Whatever her choice, her body has undergone irreversible changes, her mind will never be the same, her future as a woman has been shaped by the event.

Most of us were raised by our mothers, or by women who for love, necessity, or money took the place of our biological mothers. Throughout history women have helped birth and nurture each other's children. Most women have been mothers in the sense of tenders and carers for the young, whether as sisters, aunts, nurses, teachers, foster-mothers, stepmothers. Tribal life, the village, the extended family, the female networks of some cultures, have included the very young, very old, unmarried, and infertile women in the process of 'mothering.' Even those of us whose fathers played an important part in our early childhood rarely remember them for their patient attendance when we were ill, their doing the humble tasks of feeding and cleaning us; we remember scenes, expeditions, punishments, special occasions. For most of us a woman provided the continuity and stability – but also the rejections and refusals – of our early lives, and it is with a woman's hands, eyes, body, voice, that we associate our primal sensations, our earliest social experience.

2

Throughout this book I try to distinguish between two meanings of motherhood, one superimposed on the other: the *potential relationship* of any woman to her powers of reproduction and to children; and the *institution*, which aims at ensuring that that potential – and all women – shall remain under male control. This institution has been a keystone of the most diverse social and political systems. It has withheld over one-half the human species from the decisions affecting their lives; it exonerates men from fatherhood in any authentic sense; it creates the dangerous schism between 'private' and 'public' life; it calcifies human choices and potentialities. In the most fundamental and bewildering of contradictions, it has alienated women from our bodies by incarcerating us in them. At certain points in history, and in certain cultures, the idea of woman-as-mother has worked to endow all women with respect, even with awe, and to give women some say in the life of a people or a clan. But for most of what we know as the 'mainstream' of recorded history, motherhood as institution has ghettoized and degraded female potentialities.

The power of the mother has two aspects: the biological potential or capacity to bear and nourish human life, and the magical power invested in women by men, whether in the form of Goddess-worship or the fear of being controlled and overwhelmed by women. We do not actually know much about what power may have meant in the hands of strong, prepatriarchal women. We do have guesses, longings, myths, fantasies, analogues. We know far more about how, under patriarchy, female possibility has been literally massacred on the site of motherhood. Most women in history have become mothers without choice, and an even greater number have lost their lives bringing life into the world.

Women are controlled by lashing us to our bodies. In an early and classic essay, Susan Griffin pointed out that 'rape is a form of mass terrorism, for the victims of rape are chosen indiscriminately, but the propagandists for male supremacy broadcast that it is women who cause rape by being unchaste or in the wrong place at the wrong time – in essence, by behaving as though they were free . . . The fear of rape keeps women off the streets at night. Keeps women at home. Keeps women passive and modest for fear that they be thought provocative.'* In a later development of Griffin's analysis, Susan Brownmiller suggests that

* 'Rape: The All-American Crime,' in Jo Freeman, ed., *Women: A Femimist Perspective* (Stanford, Calif.: Mayfield Publishing, 1975).

enforced, indentured motherhood may originally have been the price paid by women to the men who became their 'protectors' (and owners) against the casual violence of other men.* If rape has been terrorism, motherhood has been penal servitude. *It need not be.*

This book is not an attack on the family or on mothering, *except as defined and restricted under patriarchy.* Nor is it a call for a mass system of state-controlled child-care. Mass child-care in patriarchy has had but two purposes: to introduce large numbers of women into the labor force, in a developing economy or during a war, and to indoctrinate future citizens.† It has never been conceived as a means of releasing the energies of women into the mainstream of culture, or of changing the stereotypic gender-images of both women and men.

3

I told myself that I wanted to write a book on motherhood because it was a crucial, still relatively unexplored, area for feminist theory. But I did not choose this subject; it had long ago chosen me.

This book is rooted in my own past, tangled with parts of my life which

* *Against Our Will: Men, Women and Rape* (New York: Simon and Schuster, 1975). Reviewing Brownmiller's book, a feminist newsletter commented: 'It would be extreme and contentious . . . to call mothers rape victims in general; probably only a small percentage are. But rape is the crime that can be committed because women are vulnerable in a special way; the opposite of "vulnerable" is "impregnable." Pregnability, to coin a word, has been the basis of female identity, the limit of freedom, the futility of education, the denial of growth.' ('Rape Has Many Forms,' review in *The Spokeswoman*, Vol. 6, No. 5 [November 15, 1975].)

† To these American capitalism is adding a third: the profit motive. Franchised, commercially operated child-care centers have become 'big business.' Many such centers are purely custodial; overcrowding limits physical and educational flexibility and freedom; the centers are staffed almost entirely by women, working for a minimum salary. Operated under giant corporations such as Singer, Time Inc., and General Electric, these profit-making preschools can be compared to commercial nursing homes in their exploitation of human needs and of the most vulnerable persons in the society. See Georgia Sassen, Cookie Arvin, and the Corporations and Child Care Research Project, 'Corporate Child Care,' *The Second Wave: A Magazine of the New Feminism*, Vol. 3, No. 3, pp. 21-23, 38–43.

stayed buried even while I dug away at the strata of early childhood, adolescence, separation from parents, my vocation as a poet; the geographies of marriage, spiritual divorce, and death, through which I entered the open ground of middle age. Every journey into the past is complicated by delusions, false memories, false naming of real events. But for a long time, I avoided this journey back into the years of pregnancy, childbearing, and the dependent lives of my children, because it meant going back into pain and anger that I would have preferred to think of as long since resolved and put away. I could not begin to think of writing a book on motherhood until I began to feel strong enough, and unambivalent enough in my love for my children, so that I could dare to return to a ground which seemed to me the most painful, incomprehensible, and ambiguous I had ever traveled, a ground hedged by taboos, mined with false-namings.

I did not understand this when I started to write the book. I only knew that I had lived through something which was considered central to the lives of women, fulfilling even in its sorrows, a key to the meaning of life; and that I could remember little except anxiety, physical weariness, anger, self-blame, boredom, and division within myself: a division made more acute by the moments of passionate love, delight in my children's spirited bodies and minds, amazement at how they went on loving me in spite of my failures to love them wholly and selflessly.

It seemed to me impossible from the first to write a book of this kind without being often autobiographical, without often saying 'I.' Yet for many months I buried my head in historical research and analysis in order to delay or prepare the way for the plunge into areas of my own life which were painful and problematical, yet from the heart of which this book has come. I believe increasingly that only the willingness to share private and sometimes painful experience can enable women to create a collective description of the world which will be truly ours. On the other hand, I am keenly aware that any writer has a certain false and arbitrary power. It is her version, after all, that the reader is reading at this moment, while the accounts of others – including the dead – may go untold.

This is in some ways a vulnerable book. I have invaded various professional domains, broken various taboos. I have used the scholarship available to me where I found it suggestive, without pretending to make myself into a specialist. In so doing, the question, *But what was it like for women?* was always in my mind, and I soon began to sense a fundamental perceptual difficulty among male scholars (and some female ones) for which 'sexism' is too facile a term. It is really an intellectual defect, which might be named 'patrivincialism' or 'patriochialism': the assumption that women are a subgroup, that 'man's world' is the 'real' world, that patriarchy is equivalent to culture and culture to patriarchy, that the 'great' or 'liberalizing' periods of history have been the same for women as for men, that generalizations about 'man,' 'humankind,' 'children,' 'Blacks,' 'parents,' 'working class' hold true for women, mothers, daughters, sisters, wet-nurses, infant girls, and can include them with no more than a glancing reference here and there, usually to some specialized function like breastfeeding. The new historians of 'family and childhood,' like the majority of theorists on child-rearing, pediatricians, psychiatrists, are male. In their work, the question of motherhood as an institution or as an idea in the heads of grown-up male children is raised only where 'styles' of mothering are discussed and criticized. Female sources are rarely cited (yet these sources exist, as the feminist historians are showing); there are virtually no primary sources from women-as-mothers; and all this is presented as objective scholarship.

It is only recently that feminist scholars such as Gerda Lerner, Joan Kelly, and Carroll Smith-Rosenberg have begun to suggest that, in Lerner's words: 'the key to understanding women's history is in accepting – painful though it may be – that it is the history of the *majority* of mankind . . . History, as written and perceived up to now, is the history of a minority, who may well turn out to be the "subgroup."'

I write with a painful consciousness of my own Western cultural perspective and that of most of the sources available to me: painful because it says so much about how female culture is fragmented by the male cultures, boundaries, groupings in which women live. However, at this point any broad study of female culture can be at best partial, and what any writer hopes – and knows – is that others like her, with different training, background, and tools, are putting together other parts of this immense half-buried mosaic in the shape of a woman's face.

[. . .]

ANGER AND TENDERNESS

> . . . to understand is always an ascending movement; that is why compre-
> hension ought always to be concrete. (One is never got out of the cave, one
> comes out of it.)
>
>   – Simone Weil, *First and Last Notebooks*

Entry from my journal, November 1960

My children cause me the most exquisite suffering of which I have any
experience. It is the suffering of ambivalence: the murderous alternation
between bitter resentment and raw-edged nerves, and blissful gratification
and tenderness. Sometimes I seem to myself, in my feelings toward these
tiny guiltless beings, a monster of selfishness and intolerance. Their voices
wear away at my nerves, their constant needs, above all their need for
simplicity and patience, fill me with despair at my own failures, despair
too at my fate, which is to serve a function for which I was not fitted. And
I am weak sometimes from held-in rage. There are times when I feel only
death will free us from one another, when I envy the barren woman who
has the luxury of her regrets but lives a life of privacy and freedom.

And yet at other times I am melted with the sense of their helpless,
charming and quite irresistible beauty – their ability to go on loving and
trusting – their staunchness and decency and unselfconsciousness. I love
them. But it's in the enormity and inevitability of this love that the sufferings lie.

April 1961

A blissful love for my children engulfs me from time to time and
seems almost to suffice – the aesthetic pleasure I have in these little,
changing creatures, the sense of being loved, however dependently, the
sense too that I'm not an utterly unnatural and shrewish mother – much
though I am!

May 1965

To suffer with and for and against a child – maternally, egotistically,
neurotically, sometimes with a sense of helplessness, sometimes with the

illusion of learning wisdom – but always, everywhere, in body and *soul, with* that child – because that child is a piece of oneself.

To be caught up in waves of love and hate, jealousy even of the child's childhood; hope and fear for its maturity; longing to be free of responsibility, tied by every fibre of one's being.

That curious primitive reaction of protectiveness, the beast defending her cub, when anyone attacks or criticizes him – And yet no one more hard on him than I!

September 1965

Degradation of anger. Anger at a child. How shall I learn to absorb the violence and make explicit only the caring? Exhaustion of anger. Victory of will, too dearly bought – far too dearly!

March 1966

Perhaps one is a monster – anti-woman – something driven and without recourse to the normal and appealing consolations of love, motherhood, joy in others . . .

Unexamined assumptions: First, that a 'natural' mother is a person without further identity, one who can find her chief gratification in being all day with small children, living at a pace tuned to theirs; that the isolation of mothers and children together in the home must be taken for granted; that maternal love is, and should be, quite literally selfless; that children and mothers are the 'causes' of each other's suffering. I was haunted by the stereotype of the mother whose love is 'unconditional'; and by the visual and literary images of motherhood as a single-minded identity. If I knew parts of myself existed that would never cohere to those images, weren't those parts then abnormal, monstrous? And – as my eldest son, now aged twenty-one, remarked on reading the above passages: 'You seemed to feel you ought to love us all the time. But there *is* no human relationship where you love the other person at every moment.' Yes, I tried to explain to him, but women – above all, mothers – have been supposed to love that way.

From the fifties and early sixties, I remember a cycle. It began when I had picked up a book or began trying to write a letter, or even found myself on the telephone with someone toward whom my voice betrayed eagerness, a rush of sympathetic energy. The child (or children) might be absorbed in busyness, in his own dreamworld; but as soon as he felt me gliding into a world which did not include him, he would come to pull at my hand, ask for help, punch at the typewriter keys. And I would feel his wants at such a moment as fraudulent, as an attempt moreover to defraud me of living even for fifteen minutes as myself. My anger would rise; I would feel the futility of any attempt to salvage myself, and also the inequality between us: my needs always balanced against those of a child, and always losing. I could love so much better, I told myself, after even a quarter-hour of selfishness, of peace, of detachment from my children. A few minutes! But it was as if an invisible thread would pull taut between us and break, to the child's sense of inconsolable abandonment, if I moved – not even physically, but in spirit – into a realm beyond our tightly circumscribed life together. It was as if my placenta had begun to refuse him oxygen. Like so many women, I waited with impatience for the moment when their father would return from work, when for an hour or two at least the circle drawn around mother and children would grow looser, the intensity between us slacken, because there was another adult in the house.

I did not understand that this circle, this magnetic field in which we lived, was not a natural phenomenon.

Intellectually, I must have known it. But the emotion-charged, tradition-heavy form in which I found myself cast as the Mother seemed, then, as ineluctable as the tides. And, because of this form – this micro-cosm in which my children and I formed a tiny, private emotional cluster, and in which (in bad weather or when someone was ill) we sometimes passed days at a time without seeing another adult except for their father – there was authentic need underlying my child's invented claims upon me when I seemed to be wandering away from him. He was reassuring himself that warmth, tenderness, continuity, solidity were still there for him, in my person. My singularity, my uniqueness in the world as *his mother* – perhaps more dimly also as Woman – evoked a need vaster than any single human being could satisfy, except by loving continuously, unconditionally, from dawn to dark, and often in the mid-dle of the night.

2

In a living room in 1975, I spent an evening with a group of women poets, some of whom had children. One had brought hers along, and they slept or played in adjoining rooms. We talked of poetry, and also of infanticide, of the case of a local woman, the mother of eight, who had been in severe depression since the birth of her third child, and who had recently murdered and decapitated her two youngest, on her suburban front lawn. Several women in the group, feeling a direct connection with her desperation, had signed a letter to the local newspaper protesting the way her act was perceived by the press and handled by the community mental health system. Every woman in that room who had children, every poet, could identify with her. We spoke of the wells of anger that her story cleft open in us. We spoke of our own moments of murderous anger at our children, because there was no one and nothing else on which to discharge anger. We spoke in the some-times tentative, sometimes rising, sometimes bitterly witty, unrhetorical tones and language of women who had met together over our common work, poetry, and who found another common ground in an unacceptable, but undeniable anger. The words are being spoken now, are being written down; the taboos are being broken, the masks of motherhood are cracking through.

For centuries no one talked of these feelings. I became a mother in the family-centered, consumer-oriented, Freudian-American world of the 1950s. My husband spoke eagerly of the children we would have; my parents-in-law awaited the birth of their grandchild. I had no idea of what *I* wanted, what *I* could or could not choose. I only knew that to have a child was to assume adult womanhood to the full, to prove myself, to be 'like other women.'

To be 'like other women' had been a problem for me. From the age of thirteen or fourteen, I had felt I was only acting the part of a feminine creature. At the age of sixteen my fingers were almost constantly ink-stained. The lipstick and high heels of the era were difficult-to-manage disguises. In 1945 I was writing poetry seriously, and had a fantasy of going to postwar Europe as a journalist, sleeping among the ruins in bombed cities, recording the rebirth of civilization after the fall of the Nazis. But also, like every other girl I knew, I spent hours trying to apply lipstick more adroitly, straightening the wandering seams of stockings, talking about 'boys.' There were two different compartments, already, to my life. But writing poetry, and my fantasies of travel and self-sufficiency, seemed more real to me; I felt that as an incipient 'real woman' I was a fake. Particularly was I paralyzed when I encountered young children. I think I felt men could be – wished to be – conned into thinking I was truly 'feminine'; a child, I suspected, could see through me like a shot. This sense of acting a part created a curious sense of guilt, even though it was a part demanded for survival.

I have a very clear, keen memory of myself the day after I was married: I was sweeping a floor. Probably the floor did not really need to be swept; probably I simply did not know what else to do with myself. But as I swept that floor I thought: 'Now I am a woman. This is an age-old action, this is what women have always done.' I felt I was bending to some ancient form, too ancient to question. *This is what women have always done.*

As soon as I was visibly and clearly pregnant, I felt, for the first time in my adolescent and adult life, not-guilty. The atmosphere of approval in which I was bathed – even by strangers on the street, it seemed – was like an aura I carried with me, in which doubts, fears, misgivings, met with absolute denial. *This is what women have always done.*

Two days before my first son was born, I broke out in a rash which was tentatively diagnosed as measles, and was admitted to a hospital for contagious diseases to await the onset of labor. I felt for the first time a great deal of conscious fear, and guilt toward my unborn child, for having 'failed' him with my body in this way. In rooms near mine were patients with polio; no one was allowed to enter my room except in a hospital gown and mask. If during pregnancy I had felt in any vague command of my situation, I felt now totally dependent on my obstetrician, a huge, vigorous, paternal man, abounding with optimism and assurance, and given to pinching my cheek. I had gone through a healthy pregnancy, but as if tranquilized or sleep-walking. I had taken a sewing class in which I produced an unsightly and ill-cut maternity jacket which I never wore; I had made curtains for the baby's room, collected baby clothes, blotted out as much as possible the woman I had been a few months earlier. My second book of poems was in press, but I had stopped writing poetry, and read little except household magazines and books on child-care. I felt myself perceived by the world simply as a pregnant woman, and it seemed easier, less disturbing, to perceive myself so. After my child was born the 'measles' were diagnosed as an allergic reaction to pregnancy.

Within two years, I was pregnant again, and writing in a notebook:

November 1956

Whether it's the extreme lassitude of early pregnancy or something more fundamental, I don't know; but of late I've felt, toward poetry, – both reading and writing it – nothing but boredom and indifference. Especially toward my own and that of my immediate contemporaries. When I receive a letter soliciting mss., or someone alludes to my 'career', I have a strong sense of wanting to deny all responsibility for and interest in that person who writes – or who wrote.

If there is going to be a real break in my writing life, this is as good a time for it as any. I have been dissatisfied with myself, my work, for a long time.

My husband was a sensitive, affectionate man who wanted children and who – unusual in the professional, academic world of the fifties – was willing to 'help.' But it was clearly understood that this 'help' was an act of generosity; that *his* work, his professional life, was the real work in the family; in fact, this was for years not even an issue between us. I understood that my struggles as a writer were a kind of luxury, a peculiarity of mine; my work brought in almost no money: it even cost money, when I hired a household helper to allow me a few hours a week to write. 'Whatever I ask he tries to give me,' I wrote in March 1958, 'but always the initiative has to be mine.' I experienced my depressions, bursts of anger, sense of entrapment, as burdens my husband was forced to bear because he loved me; I felt grateful to be loved in spite of bringing him those burdens.

But I was struggling to bring my life into focus. I had never really given up on poetry, nor on gaining some control over my existence. The life of a Cambridge tenement backyard swarming with children, the repetitious cycles of laundry, the night-wakings, the interrupted moments of peace or of engagement with ideas, the ludicrous dinner parties at which young wives, some with advanced degrees, all seriously and intelligently dedicated to their children's welfare and their husbands' careers, attempted to reproduce the amenities of Brahmin Boston, amid French recipes and the pretense of effortlessness – above all, the ultimate lack of seriousness with which women were regarded in that world – all of this defied analysis at that time, but I knew I had to remake my own life. I did not then understand that we – the women of that academic community – as in so many middle-class communities of the period – were expected to fill both the part of the Victorian cook, scullery maid, laundress, governess, and nurse. I only sensed that there were false distractions sucking at me, and I wanted desperately to strip my life down to what was essential.

June 1958

These months I've been all a tangle of irritations deepening to anger: bitterness, disillusion with society and with myself; beating out at the world, rejecting out of hand. What, if anything, has been positive? Perhaps the attempt to remake my life, to save it from mere drift and the passage of time . . .

The work that is before me is serious and difficult and not at all clear even as to plan. Discipline of mind and spirit, uniqueness of expression, ordering of daily existence, the most effective functioning of the human self – these are the chief things I wish to achieve. So far the only beginning I've been able to make is to waste less time. That is what some of the rejection has been all about.

By July of 1958 I was again pregnant. The new life of my third – and, as I determined, my last – child, was a kind of turning for me. I had learned that my body was not under my control; I had not intended to bear a third child. I knew now better than I had ever known what another pregnancy, another new infant, meant for my body and spirit. Yet, I did not think of having an abortion. In a sense, my third son was more actively chosen than either of his brothers; by the time I knew I was pregnant with him, I was not sleepwalking any more.

August 1958 (Vermont)

I write this as the early rays of the sun light up our hillside and eastern windows. Rose with [the baby] at 5:30 A.M. and have fed him and breakfasted. This is one of the few mornings on which I haven't felt terrible mental depression and physical exhaustion.

. . . I have to acknowledge to myself that I would not have chosen to have more children, that I was beginning to look to a time, not too far off, when I should again be free, no longer so physically tired, pursuing a more or less intellectual and creative life . . . The *only* way I can develop now is through much harder, more continuous, connected work than my present life makes possible. Another child means postponing this for some years longer – and years at my age are significant, not to be tossed lightly away.

And yet, somehow, something, call it Nature or that affirming fatalism of the human creature, makes me aware of the inevitable as already part of me, not to be contended against so much as brought to bear as an additional weapon against drift, stagnation and spiritual death. (For it is really death that I have been fearing – the crumbling to death of that scarcely-born physiognomy which my whole life has been a battle to give birth to – a recognizable, autonomous self, a creation in poetry and in life.)

If more effort has to be made then I will make it. If more despair has to be lived through, I think I can anticipate it correctly and live through it.

Meanwhile, in a curious and unanticipated way, we really do welcome the birth of our child.

There was, of course, an economic as well as a spiritual margin which allowed me to think of a third child's birth not as my own death-warrant but as an 'additional weapon against death.' My body, despite recurrent flares of arthritis, was a healthy one; I had good prenatal care; we were not living on the edge of malnutrition; I knew that all my children would be fed, clothed, breathe fresh air; in fact it did not occur to me that it could be otherwise. But, in another sense, beyond that physical margin, I knew I was fighting for my life through, against, and with the lives of my children, though very little else was clear to me. I had been trying to give birth to myself; and in some grim, dim way I was determined to use even pregnancy and parturition in that process.

Before my third child was born I decided to have no more children, to be sterilized. (Nothing is removed from a woman's body during this operation; ovulation and menstruation continue. Yet the language suggests a cutting – or burning – away of her essential womanhood, just as the old word 'barren' suggests a woman eternally empty and lacking.) My husband, although he supported my decision, asked whether I was sure it would not leave me feeling 'less feminine.' In order to have the operation at all, I had to present a letter, counter-signed by my husband, assuring the committee of physicians who approved such operations that I had already produced three children, and stating my reasons for having no more. Since I had had rheumatoid arthritis for some years, I could give a reason acceptable to the male panel who sat on my case; my own judgment would not have been acceptable. When I awoke from the operation, twenty-four hours after my child's birth, a young nurse looked at my chart and remarked coldly: 'Had yourself spayed, did you?'

The first great birth-control crusader, Margaret Sanger, remarks that of the hundreds of women who wrote to her pleading for contraceptive information in the early part of the twentieth century, all spoke of wanting the health and strength to be better mothers to the children they already had; or of wanting to be physically affectionate to their husbands without dread of conceiving. None was refusing motherhood altogether, or asking for an easy life. These women – mostly poor, many still in their teens, all with several children – simply felt they could no longer do 'right' by their families, whom they expected to go on serving and rearing. Yet there always has been, and there remains, intense fear of the suggestion that women shall have the final say as to how our bodies are to be used. It is as if the suffering of the mother – the primary identification of woman *as* the mother – were so necessary to the emotional grounding of human society that the mitigation, or removal, of that suffering, that identification, must be fought at every level, including the level of refusing to question it at all.

59

URSULA K. LE GUIN

Born 1929, Berkeley, California, United States of America
Died 2018, Portland, Oregon, United States of America

The Space Crone

1976

The menopause is probably the least glamorous topic imaginable; and this is interesting, because it is one of the very few topics to which cling some shreds and remnants of taboo. A serious mention of menopause is usually met with uneasy silence; a sneering reference to it is usually met with relieved sniggers. Both the silence and the sniggering are pretty sure indications of taboo.

Most people would consider the old phrase 'change of life' a euphemism for the medical term 'menopause,' but I, who am now going through the change, begin to wonder if it isn't the other way round. 'Change of life' is too blunt a phrase, too factual. 'Menopause,' with its chime-suggestion of a mere pause after which things go on as before, is reassuringly trivial.

But the change is not trivial, and I wonder how many women are brave enough to carry it out wholeheartedly. They give up their reproductive capacity with more or less of a struggle, and when it's gone they think that's all there is to it. Well, at least I don't get the Curse any more, they say, and the only reason I felt so depressed sometimes was hormones. Now I'm myself again. But this is to evade the real challenge, and to lose, not only the capacity to ovulate, but the opportunity to become a Crone.

In the old days women who survived long enough to attain the menopause more often accepted the challenge. They had, after all, had practice. They had already changed their life radically once before, when they ceased to be virgins and became mature women/wives/matrons/mothers/mistresses/whores/etc. This change involved not only the physiological alterations of puberty – the shift from barren childhood to fruitful maturity – but a socially recognized alteration of being: a change of condition from the sacred to the profane.

With the secularization of virginity now complete, so that the once awesome term 'virgin' is now a sneer or at best a slightly dated word for a person who hasn't copulated yet, the opportunity of gaining or regaining the dangerous/sacred condition of being at the Second Change has ceased to be apparent.

Virginity is now a mere preamble or waiting room to be got out of as soon as possible; it is without significance. Old age is similarly a waiting room, where you go after life's over and wait for cancer or a stroke. The years before and after the menstrual years are vestigial: the only meaningful condition left to women is that of fruitfulness. Curiously, this restriction of significance coincided with the development of chemicals and instruments that make fertility itself a meaningless or at least secondary characteristic of female maturity. The significance of maturity now is not the capacity to conceive but the mere ability to have sex. As this ability is shared by pubescents and by postclimacterics, the blurring of distinctions and elimination of opportunities is almost complete. There are no rites of passage because there is no significant change. The Triple Goddess has only one face: Marilyn Monroe's, maybe. The entire life of a woman from ten or twelve through seventy or eighty has become secular, uniform, changeless. As there is no longer any virtue in virginity, so there is no longer any meaning in menopause. It requires fanatical determination now to become a Crone.

Women have thus, by imitating the life condition of men, surrendered a very strong position of their own. Men are afraid of virgins, but they have a cure for their own fear and the virgin's virginity: fucking. Men are afraid of crones, so afraid of them that their cure for virginity fails them; they know it won't work. Faced with the fulfilled Crone, all but the bravest men wilt and retreat, crestfallen and cockadroop.

Menopause Manor is not merely a defensive stronghold, however. It is a house or household, fully furnished with the necessities of life. In abandoning it, women have narrowed their domain and impoverished their souls. There are things the Old Woman can do, say, and think that the Woman cannot do, say, or think. The Woman has to give up more than her menstrual periods before she can do, say, or think them. She has got to change her life.

The nature of that change is now clearer than it used to be. Old age is not virginity but a third and new condition; the virgin must be celibate, but the Crone need not. There was a confusion there, which the separation of female sexuality from reproductive capacity, via modern contraceptives, has cleared up. Loss of fertility does not mean loss of desire and fulfillment. But it does entail a change, a change involving matters even more important – if I may venture a heresy – than sex.

The woman who is willing to make that change must become pregnant with herself, at last. She must bear herself, her third self, her old age, with travail and alone. Not many will help her with that birth. Certainly no male obstetrician will time her contractions, inject her with sedatives, stand ready with forceps, and neatly stitch up the torn membranes. It's hard even to find an old-fashioned midwife, these days. That pregnancy is long, that labor is hard. Only one is harder, and that's the final one, the one that men also must suffer and perform.

It may well be easier to die if you have already given birth to others or yourself, at least once before. This would be an argument for going through all the discomfort and embarrassment of becoming a Crone. Anyhow it seems a pity to have a built-in rite of passage and to dodge it, evade it, and pretend nothing has changed. That is to dodge and evade one's womanhood, to pretend one's like a man. Men, once initiated, never get the second chance. They never change again. That's their loss, not ours. Why borrow poverty?

Certainly the effort to remain unchanged, young, when the body gives so impressive a signal of change as the menopause, is gallant; but it is a stupid, self-sacrificial gallantry, better befitting a boy of twenty than a woman of forty-five or fifty. Let the athletes die young and laurel-crowned. Let the soldiers earn the Purple Hearts. Let women die old, white-crowned, with human hearts.

If a space ship came by from the friendly natives of the fourth planet of Altair, and the polite captain of the space ship said, 'We have room for one passenger; will you spare us a single human being, so that we may converse at leisure during the long trip back to Altair and learn from an exemplary person the nature of the race?' – I suppose what most people would want to do is provide them with a fine, bright, brave young man, highly educated and in peak physical condition. A Russian cosmonaut would be ideal (American astronauts are mostly too old). There would surely be hundreds, thousands of volunteers, just such young men, all worthy. But I would not pick any of them. Nor would I pick any of the young women who would volunteer, some out of magnanimity and intellectual courage, others out of a profound conviction that Altair couldn't possibly be any worse for a woman than Earth is.

What I would do is go down to the local Woolworth's, or the local village marketplace, and pick an old woman, over sixty, from behind the costume jewelry counter or the betel-nut booth. Her hair would not be red or blonde or lustrous dark, her skin would not be dewy fresh, she would not have the secret of eternal youth. She might, however, show you a small snapshot of her grandson, who is working in Nairobi. She is a bit vague about where Nairobi is, but extremely proud of the grandson. She has worked hard at small, unimportant jobs all her life, jobs like cooking, cleaning, bringing up kids, selling little objects of adornment or pleasure to other people. She was a virgin once, a long time ago, and then a sexually potent fertile female, and then went through menopause. She has given birth several times and faced death several times – the same times. She is facing the final birth/death a little more nearly and clearly every day now. Sometimes her feet hurt something terrible. She never was educated to anything like her capacity, and that is a shameful waste and a crime against humanity, but so common a crime should not and cannot be hidden from Altair. And anyhow she's not dumb. She has a stock of sense, wit, patience, and experiential shrewdness, which the Altaireans might, or might not, perceive as wisdom. If they are wiser than we, then of course we don't know how they'd perceive it. But if they are wiser than we, they may know how to perceive that inmost mind and heart which we, working on mere guess and hope, proclaim to be humane. In any case, since they are curious and kindly, let's give them the best we have to give.

The trouble is, she will be very reluctant to volunteer. 'What would an old woman like me do on Altair?' she'll say. 'You ought to send one of those scientist men, they can talk to those funny-looking green people. Maybe Dr Kissinger should go. What about sending the Shaman?' It will be very hard to explain to her that we want her to go because only a person who has experienced, accepted, and acted the entire human condition – the essential quality of which is Change – can fairly represent humanity. 'Me?' she'll say, just a trifle slyly. 'But I never did anything.'

But it won't wash. She knows, though she won't admit it, that Dr Kissinger has not gone and will never go where she has gone, that the scientists and the shamans have not done what she has done. Into the space ship, Granny.

60.

ANDREA DWORKIN

Born 1946, Camden, New Jersey, United States of America
Died 2005, Washington, D.C., United States of America

from *Our Blood*
1976

What, then, are the root causes of rape?

Rape is the direct consequence of our polar definitions of men and women. Rape is *congruent* with these definitions; rape *inheres* in these definitions. Remember, rape is not committed by psychopaths or deviants from our social norms – rape is committed by *exemplars* of our social norms. In this male-supremacist society, men are defined as one order of being over and against women who are defined as another, opposite, entirely different order of being. Men are defined as aggressive, dominant, powerful. Women are defined as passive, submissive, powerless. Given these polar gender definitions, it is the very nature of men to aggress sexually against women. Rape occurs when a man, who is dominant by definition, takes a woman who, according to men and all the organs of their culture, was put on this earth for his use and gratification. Rape, then, is the logical consequence of a system of definitions of what is normative. Rape is no excess, no aberration, no accident, no mistake – it embodies sexuality as the culture defines it. As long as these definitions remain intact – that is, as long as men are defined as sexual aggressors and women are defined as passive receptors lacking integrity – men who are exemplars of the norm will rape women.

In this society, the norm of masculinity is phallic aggression. Male sexuality is, by definition, intensely and rigidly phallic. A man's identity is located in his conception of himself as the possessor of a phallus; a man's worth is located in his *pride* in phallic identity. The main characteristic of phallic identity is that *worth* is entirely contingent on the possession of a phallus. Since men have no other criteria for worth, no other notion of identity, those who do not have phalluses are not recognized as fully human.

61.

NAWAL EL SAADAWI

Born 1931 Kafr Tahlah, Egypt

from *The Hidden Face of Eve: Women in the Arab World*
1977

The Question that No One Would Answer

I was six years old that night when I lay in my bed, warm and peaceful in that pleasurable state which lies halfway between wakefulness and sleep, with the rosy dreams of childhood flitting by, like gentle fairies in quick succession. I felt something move under the blankets, something like a huge hand, cold and rough, fumbling over my body, as though looking for something. Almost simultaneously another hand, as cold and as rough and as big as the first one, was clapped over my mouth, to prevent me from screaming.

They carried me to the bathroom. I do not know how many of them there were, nor do I remember their faces, or whether they were men or women. The world to me seemed enveloped in a dark fog which prevented me from seeing. Or perhaps they put some kind of a cover over my eyes. All I remember is that I was frightened and that there were many of them, and that something like an iron grasp caught hold of my hand and my arms and my thighs, so that I became unable to resist or even to move. I also remember the icy touch of the bathroom tiles under my naked body, and unknown voices and humming sounds interrupted now and again by a rasping metallic sound which reminded me of the butcher when he used to sharpen his knife before slaughtering a sheep for *Eid*.

My blood was frozen in my veins. It looked to me as though some thieves had broken into my room and kidnapped me from my bed. They were getting ready to cut my throat which was always what happened with disobedient girls like myself in the stories that my old rural grandmother was so fond of telling me.

I strained my ears trying to catch the rasp of the metallic sound. The moment it ceased, it was as though my heart stopped beating with it. I was unable to see, and somehow my breathing seemed also to have stopped. Yet I imagined the thing that was making the rasping sound coming closer and closer to me. Somehow it was not approaching my neck as I had expected but another part of my body. Somewhere below my belly, as though seeking something buried between my thighs. At that very moment I realized that my thighs had been pulled wide apart, and that each of my lower limbs was being held as far away from the other as possible, gripped by steel fingers that never relinquished their pressure. I felt that the rasping knife or blade was heading straight down towards my throat. Then suddenly the sharp metallic edge seemed to drop between my thighs and there cut off a piece of flesh from my body.

I screamed with pain despite the tight hand held over my mouth, for the pain was not just a pain, it was like a searing flame that went through my whole body. After a few moments, I saw a red pool of blood around my hips.

I did not know what they had cut off from my body, and I did not try to find out. I just wept, and called out to my mother for help. But the worst shock of all was when I looked around and found her standing by my side. Yes, it was her, I could not be mistaken, in flesh and blood, right in the midst of these strangers, talking to them and smiling at them, as though they had not participated in slaughtering her daughter just a few moments ago.

They carried me to my bed. I saw them catch hold of my sister, who was two years younger, in exactly the same way they had caught hold of me a few minutes earlier. I cried out with all my might. No! No! I could see my sister's face held between the big rough hands. It had a deathly pallor and her wide black eyes met mine for a split second, a glance of dark terror which I can never forget. A moment later and she was gone, behind the door of the bathroom where I had just been. The look we exchanged seemed to say: 'Now we know what it is. Now we know where lies our tragedy. We were born of a special sex, the female sex. We are destined in advance to taste of misery, and to have a part of our body torn away by cold, unfeeling cruel hands.'

My family was not an uneducated Egyptian family. On the contrary, both my parents had been fortunate enough to have a very good education, by the standards of those days. My father was a university graduate and that year (1937) had been appointed General Controller of Education for the Province of Menoufia in the Delta region to the North of Cairo. My mother had been taught in French schools by her father who was Director-General of Army Recruitment. Nevertheless, the custom of circumcising girls was very prevalent at the time, and no girl could escape having her clitoris amputated, irrespective of whether her family lived in a rural or an urban area. When I returned to school after having recovered from the operation, I asked my classmates and friends about what had happened to me, only to discover that all of them without exception had been through the same experience, no matter what social class they came from (upper class, middle or lower-middle class).

In rural areas, among the poor peasant families, all the girls are circumcised as I later on found out from my relatives in Kafr Tahla. This custom is still very common in the villages, and even in the cities a large proportion of families believe it is necessary. However, the spread of education and a greater understanding among parents is making increasing numbers of fathers and mothers abstain from circumcising their daughters.

The memory of circumcision continued to track me down like a nightmare. I had a feeling of insecurity, of the unknown waiting for me at every step I took into the future. I did not even know if there were new surprises being stored up for me by my mother and father, or my grandmother, or the people around me. Society had made me feel, since the day that I opened my eyes on life, that I was a girl, and that the word *Bint* (girl) when pronounced by anyone is almost always accompanied by a frown.

Even when I had grown up and graduated as a doctor in 1955, I could not forget the painful incident that had made me lose my childhood once and for all, and that deprived me during my youth and for many years of married life from enjoying the fullness of my sexuality and the completeness of life that can only come from all-round psychological equilibrium. Nightmares of a similar nature followed me throughout the years, especially during the period when I was working as a medical doctor in the rural areas. There I very often had to treat young girls who had come to the out-patients clinic bleeding profusely after a circumcision. Many of them used to lose their lives as a result of the inhuman and primitive way in which the operation, savage enough in itself, was performed. Others were afflicted with acute or chronic infections from which they sometimes suffered for the rest of their days. And most of them, if not all, became the victims later on of sexual or mental distortions as a result of this experience.

My profession led me, at one stage, to examine patients coming from various Arab countries. Among them were Sudanese women. I was horrified to observe that the Sudanese girl undergoes an operation for circumcision which is ten times more cruel than that to which Egyptian girls are subjected. In Egypt it is only the clitoris which is amputated, and usually not completely. But in the Sudan, the operation consists in the complete removal of all the external genital organs. They cut off the clitoris, the two major outer lips (*labia majora*) and the two minor inner lips (*labia minora*). Then the wound is repaired. The outer opening of the vagina is the only portion left intact, not however without having ensured that, during the process of repairing, some narrowing of the opening is carried out with a few extra stitches. The result is that on the marriage night it is necessary to widen the external opening by slitting one or both ends with a sharp scalpel or razor so that the male organ can be introduced. When a Sudanese woman is divorced, the external opening is narrowed once more to ensure that she cannot have sexual relations. If she remarries, widening is done again.

My feeling of anger and rebellion used to mount up as I listened to these women explaining to me what happens during the circumcision of a Sudanese girl. My anger grew tenfold when in 1969 I paid a visit to the Sudan only to discover that the practice of circumcision was unabated, whether in rural areas, or even in the cities and towns.

Despite my medical upbringing and my education, in those days I was not able to understand why girls were made to undergo this barbaric procedure. Time and again I asked myself the question: 'Why? Why?' But I could never get an answer to this question which was becoming more and more insistent, just as I was never able to get an answer to the questions that raced around in my mind the day that both my sister and I were circumcised.

This question somehow seemed to be linked to other things that puzzled me. Why did they favour my brother as regards food, and the freedom to go out of the house? Why was he treated better than I was in all these matters? Why could my brother laugh at the top of his voice, move his legs freely, run and play as much as he wished, whereas I was not supposed to look into people's eyes directly, but was meant to drop my glance whenever I was confronted with someone? If I laughed, I was expected to keep my voice so low that people could hardly hear me or, better, confine myself to smiling timidly. When I played, my legs were not supposed to move freely, but had to be kept politely together. My duties were primarily to help in cleaning the house and cooking, in addition to studying since I was at school. The brothers, however, the boys, were not expected to do anything but study.

My family was educated and therefore differentiation between the boys and girls, especially as my father was himself a teacher, never reached the extent which is so common in other families. I used to feel very sorry for my young girl relatives when they were forced out of school in order to get married to an old man just because he happened to own some land, or when their younger brothers would humiliate and beat them for no reason at all, except that as boys they could afford to act superior to their sisters.

My brother tried to dominate me, in turn, but my father was a broad-minded man and tried as best he could to treat his children without discriminating between the boys and the girls. My mother, also, used to say that a girl is equal to a boy, but I used to feel that in practice this was often not the case.

Whenever this differentiation occurred I used to rebel, sometimes violently, and would ask my mother and father why it was that my brother was accorded privileges that were not given to me, despite the fact that I was doing better than him at school. My father and mother, however, never had any answer to give me except: 'It is so . . .' I would retort: 'Why should it be so?' And back would come the answer again, unchanged: 'Because it is so . . .' If I was in an obstinate mood, I would repeat the question again. Then, at the end of their patience, they would say almost in the same voice: 'He is a boy, and you are a girl.'

Perhaps they thought that this answer would be enough to convince me, or at least to keep me quiet. But on the contrary it always made me persist more than ever. I would ask: 'What is the difference between a boy and a girl?'

At this point my old grandmother, who very often paid us a visit, would intervene in the discussion, which she always described as being an 'infringement of good manners', and scold me sharply: 'I have never in all my life seen a girl with such a long tongue as you. Of course you are not like your brother. Your brother is a boy, a boy, do you hear? I wish you had been born a boy like him!'

No one in the family was ever able to give me a convincing answer to my question. So the question continued to turn around restlessly in my mind, and would jump to the forefront every time something happened that would emphasize the fact that the male is treated everywhere and at all times as though he belongs to a species which is superior to that of the female.

When I started to go to school, I noticed that the teachers would write my father's name on my notebooks, but never that of my mother. So I asked my mother why, and again she answered, 'It is so.' My father, however, explained that children are named after their father, and when I sought to find out the reason he repeated the phrase that I knew well by now: 'It is so.' I summoned up all my courage and said: 'Why is it so?' But this time I could see from my father's face that he really did not know the answer. I never asked him the question again, except later on when my search for the truth led me to ask him many other questions, and to talk to him about many other things that I was discovering on the way.

However from that day onwards I realized that I had to find my own answer to the question that no one would answer. From that day also extends the long path that has led to this book.

62.

COMBAHEE RIVER COLLECTIVE

Formed in 1974 in Boston, Massachussetts, United States of America

A Black Feminist Statement

1977

We are a collective of Black feminists who have been meeting together since 1974. During that time we have been involved in the process of defining and clarifying our politics, while at the same time doing political work within our own group and in coalition with other progressive organizations and movements. The most general statement of our politics at the present time would be that we are actively committed to struggling against racial, sexual, heterosexual, and class oppression, and see as our particular task the development of integrated analysis and practice based upon the fact that the major systems of oppression are interlocking. The synthesis of these oppressions creates the conditions of our lives. As Black women we see Black feminism as the logical political movement to combat the manifold and simultaneous oppressions that all women of color face.

We will discuss four major topics in the paper that follows: (1) the genesis of contemporary Black feminism; (2) what we believe, i.e., the specific province of our politics; (3) the problems in organizing Black feminists, including a brief herstory of our collective; and (4) Black feminist issues and practice.

1. The Genesis of Contemporary Black Feminism

Before looking at the recent development of Black feminism we would like to affirm that we find our origins in the historical reality of Afro-American women's continuous life-and-death struggle for survival and liberation. Black women's extremely negative relationship to the American political system (a system of white male rule) has always been determined by our membership in two oppressed racial and sexual castes. As Angela Davis points out in 'Reflections on the Black Woman's Role in the Community of Slaves,' Black women have always embodied, if only in their physical manifestation, an adversary stance to white male rule and have actively resisted its inroads upon them and their communities in both dramatic and subtle ways. There have always been Black women activists – some known, like Sojourner Truth, Harriet Tubman, Frances E. W. Harper, Ida B. Wells Barnett, and Mary Church Terrell, and thousands upon thousands unknown – who have had a shared awareness of how their sexual identity combined with their racial identity to make their whole life situation and the focus of their political struggles unique. Contemporary Black feminism is the outgrowth of countless generations of personal sacrifice, militancy, and work by our mothers and sisters.

A Black feminist presence has evolved most obviously in connection with the second wave of the American women's movement beginning in the late 1960s. Black, other Third World, and working women have been involved in the feminist movement from its start, but both outside reactionary forces and racism and elitism within the movement itself have served to obscure our participation. In 1973, Black feminists, primarily located in New York, felt the necessity of forming a separate Black feminist group. This became the National Black Feminist Organization (NBFO).

Black feminist politics also have an obvious connection to movements for Black liberation, particularly those of the 1960s and 1970s. Many of us were active in those movements (Civil Rights, Black nationalism, the Black Panthers), and all of our lives were greatly affected and changed by their ideologies, their goals, and the tactics used to achieve their goals. It was our experience and disillusionment within these liberation movements, as well as experience on the periphery of the white male left, that led to the need to develop a politics that was anti-racist, unlike those of white women, and anti-sexist, unlike those of Black and white men.

There is also undeniably a personal genesis for Black Feminism, that is, the political realization that comes from the seemingly personal experiences of individual Black women's lives. Black feminists and many more Black women who do not define themselves as feminists have all experienced sexual oppression as a constant factor in our day-to-day existence. As children we realized that we were different from boys and that we were treated differently. For example, we were told in the same breath to be quiet both for the sake of being 'ladylike' and to make us less objectionable in the eyes of white people. As we grew older we became aware of the threat of physical and sexual abuse by men. However, we had no way of conceptualizing what was so apparent to us, what we knew was really happening.

Black feminists often talk about their feelings of craziness before becoming conscious of the concepts of sexual politics, patriarchal rule, and most importantly, feminism, the political analysis and practice that we women use to struggle against our oppression. The fact that racial politics and indeed racism are pervasive factors in our lives did not allow us, and still does not allow most Black women, to look more deeply into our own experiences and, from that sharing and growing consciousness, to build a politics that will change our lives and inevitably end our oppression. Our development must also be tied to the contemporary economic and political position of Black people. The post World War II generation of Black youth was the first to be able to minimally partake of certain educational and employment options, previously closed completely to Black people. Although our economic position is still at the very bottom of the American capitalistic economy, a handful of us have been able to gain certain tools as a result of tokenism in education and employment which potentially enable us to more effectively fight our oppression.

A combined anti-racist and anti-sexist position drew us together initially, and as we developed politically we addressed ourselves to heterosexism and economic oppression under capitalism.

2. What We Believe

Above all else, our politics initially sprang from the shared belief that Black women are inherently valuable, that our liberation is a necessity not as an adjunct to somebody else's but because of our need as human persons for autonomy. This may seem so obvious as to sound simplistic, but it is apparent that no other ostensibly progressive movement has ever considered our specific oppression as a priority or worked seriously for the ending of that oppression. Merely naming the pejorative stereotypes attributed to Black women (e.g. mammy, matriarch, Sapphire, whore, bulldagger), let alone cataloguing the cruel, often murderous, treatment we receive, indicates how little value has been placed upon our lives during four centuries of bondage in the Western hemisphere. We realize that the only people who care enough about us to work consistently for our liberation are us. Our politics evolve from a healthy love for ourselves, our sisters and our community which allows us to continue our struggle and work.

This focusing upon our own oppression is embodied in the concept of identity politics. We believe that the most profound and potentially most radical politics come directly out of our own identity, as opposed to working to end somebody else's oppression. In the case of Black women this is a particularly repugnant, dangerous, threatening, and therefore revolutionary concept because it is obvious from looking at all the political movements that have preceded us that anyone is more worthy of liberation than ourselves. We reject pedestals, queenhood, and walking ten paces behind. To be recognized as human, levelly human, is enough.

We believe that sexual politics under patriarchy is as pervasive in Black women's lives as are the politics of class and race. We also often find it difficult to separate race from class from sex oppression because in our lives they are most often experienced simultaneously. We know that there is such a thing as racial-sexual oppression which is neither solely racial nor solely sexual, e.g., the history of rape of Black women by white men as a weapon of political repression.

Although we are feminists and Lesbians, we feel solidarity with progressive Black men and do not advocate the fractionalization that white women who are separatists demand. Our situation as Black people necessitates that we have solidarity around the fact of race, which white women of course do not need to have with white men, unless it is their negative solidarity as racial oppressors. We struggle together with Black men against racism, while we also struggle with Black men about sexism.

We realize that the liberation of all oppressed peoples necessitates the destruction of the political-economic systems of capitalism and imperialism as well as patriarchy. We are socialists because we believe that work must be organized for the collective benefit of those who do the work and create the products, and not for the profit of the bosses. Material resources must be equally distributed among those who create these resources. We are not convinced, however, that a socialist revolution that is not also a feminist and anti-racist revolution will guarantee our liberation. We have arrived at the necessity for developing an understanding of class relationships that takes into account the specific class position of Black women who are generally marginal in the labor force, while at this particular time some of us are temporarily viewed as doubly desirable tokens at white-collar and professional levels. We need to articulate the real class situation of persons who are not merely raceless, sexless workers, but for whom racial and sexual oppression are significant determinants in their working/ economic lives. Although we are in essential agreement with Marx's theory as it applied to the very specific economic relationships he analyzed, we know that his analysis must be extended further in order for us to understand our specific economic situation as Black women.

A political contribution which we feel we have already made is the expansion of the feminist principle that the personal is political. In our consciousness-raising sessions, for example, we have in many ways gone beyond white women's revelations because we are dealing with the implications of race and class as well as sex. Even our Black women's style of talking/testifying in Black language about what we have experienced has a resonance that is both cultural and political. We have spent a great deal of energy delving into the cultural and experiential nature of our oppression out of necessity because none of these matters has ever been looked at before. No one before has ever examined the multilayered texture of Black women's lives. An example of this kind of revelation/conceptualization occurred at a meeting as we discussed the ways in which our early intellectual interests had been attacked by our peers, particularly Black males. We discovered that all of us, because we were 'smart' had also been considered 'ugly,' i.e., 'smart-ugly.' 'Smart-ugly' crystallized the way in which most of us had been forced to develop our intellects at great cost to our 'social' lives. The sanctions in the Black and white communities against Black women thinkers is comparatively much higher than for white women, particularly ones from the educated middle and upper classes.

As we have already stated, we reject the stance of Lesbian separatism because it is not a viable political analysis or strategy for us. It leaves out far too much and far too many people, particularly Black men, women, and children. We have a great deal of criticism and loathing for what men have been socialized to be in this society: what they support, how they act, and how they oppress. But we do not have the misguided notion that it is their maleness, per se – i.e., their biological maleness – that makes them what they are. As Black women we find any type of biological determinism a particularly dangerous and reactionary basis upon which to build a politic. We must also question whether Lesbian separatism is an adequate and progressive political analysis and strategy, even for those who practice it, since it so completely denies any but the sexual sources of women's oppression, negating the facts of class and race.

3. Problems in Organizing Black Feminists

During our years together as a Black feminist collective we have experienced success and defeat, joy and pain, victory and failure. We have found that it is very difficult to organize around Black feminist issues, difficult even to announce in certain contexts that we are Black feminists. We have tried to think about the reasons for our difficulties, particularly since the white women's movement continues to be strong and to grow in many directions. In this section we will discuss some of the general reasons for the organizing problems we face and also talk specifically about the stages in organizing our own collective.

The major source of difficulty in our political work is that we are not just trying to fight oppression on one front or even two, but instead to address a whole range of oppressions. We do not have racial, sexual, heterosexual, or class privilege to rely upon, nor do we have even the minimal access to resources and power that groups who possess any one of these types of privilege have.

The psychological toll of being a Black woman and the difficulties this presents in reaching political consciousness and doing political work can never be underestimated. There is a very low value placed upon Black women's psyches in this society, which is both racist and sexist. As an early group member once said, 'We are all damaged people merely by virtue of being Black women.' We are dispossessed psychologically and on every other level, and yet we feel the necessity to struggle to change the condition of all Black women. In 'A Black Feminist's Search for Sisterhood,' Michele Wallace arrives at this conclusion:

> We exist as women who are Black who are feminists, each stranded for the moment, working independently because there is not yet an environment in this society remotely congenial to our struggle – because, being on the bottom, we would have to do what no one else has done: we would have to fight the world.

Wallace is pessimistic but realistic in her assessment of Black feminists' position, particularly in her allusion to the nearly classic isolation most of us face. We might use our position at the bottom, however, to make a clear leap into revolutionary action. If Black women were free, it would mean that everyone else would have to be free since our freedom would necessitate the destruction of all the systems of oppression.

Feminism is, nevertheless, very threatening to the majority of Black people because it calls into question some of the most basic assumptions about our existence, i.e., that sex should be a determinant of power relationships. Here is the way male and female roles were defined in a Black nationalist pamphlet from the early 1970s:

> We understand that it is and has been traditional that the man is the head of the house. He is the leader of the house/nation because his knowledge of the world is broader, his awareness is greater, his understanding is fuller and his application of this information is wiser . . . After all, it is only reasonable that the man be the head of the house because he is able to defend and protect the development of his home . . . Women cannot do the same things as men – they are made by nature to function differently. Equality of men and women is something that cannot happen even in the abstract world. Men are not equal to other men, i.e. ability, experience or even understanding. The value of men and women can be seen as in the value of gold and silver – they are not equal but both have great value. We must realize that men and

women are a complement to each other because there is no house/
family without a man and his wife. Both are essential to the development of any life.

The material conditions of most Black women would hardly lead them to
upset both economic and sexual arrangements that seem to represent some
stability in their lives. Many Black women have a good understanding of
both sexism and racism, but because of the everyday constrictions of their
lives, cannot risk struggling against them both.

The reaction of Black men to feminism has been notoriously negative.
They are, of course, even more threatened than Black women by the
possibility that Black feminists might organize around our own needs.
They realize that they might not only lose valuable and hardworking
allies in their struggles but that they might also be forced to change
their habitually sexist ways of interacting with and oppressing Black
women. Accusations that Black feminism divides the Black struggle are
powerful deterrents to the growth of an autonomous Black women's
movement. Still, hundreds of women have been active at different times
during the three-year existence of our group. And every Black woman
who came, came out of a strongly-felt need for some level of possibility
that did not previously exist in her life.

When we first started meeting early in 1974 after the NBFO first
eastern regional conference, we did not have a strategy for organizing, or
even a focus. We just wanted to see what we had. After a period of months
of not meeting, we began to meet again late in the year and started doing
an intense variety of consciousness-raising. The overwhelming feeling that
we had is that after years and years we had finally found each other.
Although we were not doing political work as a group, individuals continued their involvement in Lesbian politics, sterilization abuse and
abortion rights work, Third World Women's International Women's Day
activities, and support activity for the trials of Dr Kenneth Edelin, Joan
Little, and Inéz García. During our first summer when membership had
dropped off considerably, those of us remaining devoted serious discussion
to the possibility of opening a refuge for battered women in a Black community. (There was no refuge in Boston at that time.) We also decided

around that time to become an independent collective since we had serious disagreements with NBFO's bourgeois-feminist stance and their lack of a clear political focus.

We also were contacted at that time by socialist feminists, with whom we had worked on abortion rights activities, who wanted to encourage us to attend the National Socialist Feminist Conference in Yellow Springs. One of our members did attend and despite the narrowness of the ideology that was promoted at that particular conference, we became more aware of the need for us to understand our own economic situation and to make our own economic analysis.

In the fall, when some members returned, we experienced several months of comparative inactivity and internal disagreements which were first conceptualized as a Lesbian-straight split but which were also the result of class and political differences. During the summer those of us who were still meeting had determined the need to do political work and to move beyond consciousness-raising and serving exclusively as an emotional support group. At the beginning of 1976, when some of the women who had not wanted to do political work and who also had voiced disagreements stopped attending of their own accord, we again looked for a focus. We decided at that time, with the addition of new members, to become a study group. We had always shared our reading with each other, and some of us had written papers on Black feminism for group discussion a few months before this decision was made. We began functioning as a study group and also began discussing the possibility of starting a Black feminist publication. We had a retreat in the late spring which provided a time for both political discussion and working out interpersonal issues. Currently we are planning to gather together a collection of Black feminist writing. We feel that it is absolutely essential to demonstrate the reality of our politics to other Black women and believe that we can do this through writing and distributing our work. The fact that individual Black feminists are living in isolation all over the country, that our own numbers are small, and that we have some skills in writing, printing, and publishing makes us want to carry out these kinds of projects as a means of organizing Black feminists as we continue to do political work in coalition with other groups.

4. Black Feminist Issues and Projects

During our time together we have identified and worked on many issues of particular relevance to Black women. The inclusiveness of our politics makes us concerned with any situation that impinges upon the lives of women, Third World and working people. We are of course particularly committed to working on those struggles in which race, sex, and class are simultaneous factors in oppression. We might, for example, become involved in workplace organizing at a factory that employs Third World women or picket a hospital that is cutting back on already inadequate heath care to a Third World community, or set up a rape crisis center in a Black neighborhood. Organizing around welfare and daycare concerns might also be a focus. The work to be done and the countless issues that this work represents merely reflect the pervasiveness of our oppression.

Issues and projects that collective members have actually worked on are sterilization abuse, abortion rights, battered women, rape and health care. We have also done many workshops and educationals on Black feminism on college campuses, at women's conferences, and most recently for high school women.

One issue that is of major concern to us and that we have begun to publicly address is racism in the white women's movement. As Black feminists we are made constantly and painfully aware of how little effort white women have made to understand and combat their racism, which requires among other things that they have a more than superficial comprehension of race, color, and Black history and culture. Eliminating racism in the white women's movement is by definition work for white women to do, but we will continue to speak to and demand accountability on this issue.

In the practice of our politics we do not believe that the end always justifies the means. Many reactionary and destructive acts have been done in the name of achieving 'correct' political goals. As feminists we do not want to mess over people in the name of politics. We believe in collective process and a nonhierarchical distribution of power within our own group and in our vision of a revolutionary society. We are committed to a continual examination of our politics as they develop through criticism and self-criticism as an essential aspect of our practice. In her introduction to Sisterhood is Powerful Robin Morgan writes:

> I haven't the faintest notion what possible revolutionary role white heterosexual men could fulfill, since they are the very embodiment of reactionary-vested-interest-power.

As Black feminists and Lesbians we know that we have a very definite revolutionary task to perform and we are ready for the lifetime of work and struggle before us.

63.

DENISE RILEY

Born 1948, Carlisle, United Kingdom

A note on sex and 'the reclaiming of language'
1977

The 'Savage' is flying back home from the New Country
in native-style dress with a baggage of sensibility
to gaze on the ancestral plains with the myths thought up
and dreamed in her kitchens as guides

She will be discovered
as meaning is flocking densely around the words, seeking a way
any way in between the gaps, like a fertilisation

The work is
e.g. to write 'she' and for that to be a statement
of fact only, and not a strong image
of everything which is not-you, which sees you

The new land is colonised, though its prospects are empty

The 'Savage' weeps as, landing at the airport
she is asked to buy wood carvings, which represent herself

She's imagining her wife & how will she live her? when
the wife goes off to endless meetings in the rain
she'll say aah, I admire her spirit, bravo la petite
& when her belly swells into an improbable curve
the she-husband will think Yes, it was me who caused that,
and more generously, Biology, you are wonderful

She has ingested her wife
she has re-inhabited her own wrists
she is squatting in her own temples, the
fall of light on hair or any decoration
is re-possessed. 'She' is I.

There's nothing for it. Your 'father' and I.
Biologically, a lack. The child tries manfully
He calls it special seed but he gets confused at school

An unselfconscious wife is raised high as a flag over
    the playground and burns up

I heard the water freezing in a thousand launderettes
with a dense white shudder
I heard the roar of a thousand vacuum cleaners
stammer away into uncarpeted silence

today it is all grandiose domestic visions truly

in St Petersburg, now Leningrad, we have communal kitchens
the cooking is dreadful but we get to meet our friends

it's November, child, and time goes
in little bursts a warm room
clean and squeaky as an orange pip
in a wet landscape

64.

MAYA ANGELOU

Born 1928, St Louis, Missouri, United States of America
Died 2014, Winston-Salem, North Carolina, United States of America

Still I Rise

1978

You may write me down in history
With your bitter, twisted lies,
You may trod me in the very dirt
But still, like dust, I'll rise.

Does my sassiness upset you?
Why are you beset with gloom?
'Cause I walk like I've got oil wells
Pumping in my living room.

Just like moons and like suns,
With the certainty of tides,
Just like hopes springing high,
Still I'll rise.

Did you want to see me broken?
Bowed head and lowered eyes?
Shoulders falling down like teardrops,
Weakened by my soulful cries?

Does my haughtiness offend you?
Don't you take it awful hard
'Cause I laugh like I've got gold mines
Diggin' in my own backyard.

You may shoot me with your words,
You may cut me with your eyes,
You may kill me with your hatefulness,
But still, like air, I'll rise.

Does my sexiness upset you?
Does it come as a surprise
That I dance like I've got diamonds
At the meeting of my thighs?

Out of the huts of history's shame
I rise
Up from a past that's rooted in pain
I rise
I'm a black ocean, leaping and wide,
Welling and swelling I bear in the tide.

Leaving behind nights of terror and fear
I rise
Into a daybreak that's wondrously clear
I rise
Bringing the gifts that my ancestors gave,
I am the dream and the hope of the slave.
I rise
I rise
I rise.

65.

AUDRE LORDE

Born 1934, New York City, New York, United States of America
Died 1992, Christiansted, U.S. Virgin Islands

A Woman Speaks

1978

Moon marked and touched by sun
my magic is unwritten
but when the sea turns back
it will leave my shape behind.
I seek no favor
untouched by blood
unrelenting as the curse of love
permanent as my errors
or my pride
I do not mix
love with pity
nor hate with scorn
and if you would know me
look into the entrails of Uranus
where the restless oceans pound.

I do not dwell
within my birth nor my divinities
who am ageless and half-grown
and still seeking
my sisters

witches in Dahomey
wear me inside their coiled cloths
as our mother did
mourning.

I have been woman
for a long time
beware my smile
I am treacherous with old magic
and the noon's new fury
with all your wide futures
promised
I am
woman
and not white.

66.

SUSIE ORBACH

Born 1946, London, United Kingdom

from *Fat Is a Feminist Issue*

1978

Prologue

Obesity and overeating have joined sex as central issues in the lives of many women today. In the United States, 50% of women are estimated to be overweight. Every women's magazine has a diet column. Diet doctors and clinics flourish. The names of diet foods are now part of our general vocabulary. Physical fitness and beauty are every woman's goals. While this preoccupation with fat and food has become so common that we tend to take it for granted, being fat, feeling fat and the compulsion to overeat are, in fact, serious and painful experiences for the women involved.

Being fat isolates and invalidates a woman. Almost inevitably, the explanations offered for fatness point a finger at the failure of women themselves to control their weight, control their appetites and control their impulses. Women suffering from the problem of compulsive eating endure a double anguish: feeling out of step with the rest of society, and believing that it is all their own fault.

The number of women who have problems with weight and compulsive eating is large and growing. Owing to the emotional distress involved and the fact that the many varied solutions offered to women in the past have not worked, a new psychotherapy to deal with compulsive eating has had to evolve within the context of the movement for women's liberation. This new psychotherapy represents a feminist rethinking of traditional psychoanalysis.

A psychoanalytic approach has much to offer towards a solution to compulsive eating problems. It provides ways for exploring the roots of such problems in early experiences. It shows us how we develop our adult personalities, most importantly our sexual identity – how a female baby becomes a girl and then a woman, and how a male baby becomes a boy and then a man. Psychoanalytic insight helps us to understand what getting fat and overeating mean to individual women – by explaining their conscious or unconscious acts.

An approach based exclusively on classical psychoanalysis, without a feminist perspective is, however, inadequate. Since the Second World War, psychiatry has, by and large, told unhappy women that their discontent represents an inability to resolve the 'Oedipal constellation'. Female fatness has been diagnosed as an obsessive–compulsive symptom related to separation–individuation, narcissism and insufficient ego development.* Being overweight is seen as a deviance and anti–men. Overeating and obesity have been reduced to character defects, rather than perceived as the expression of painful and conflicting experiences. Furthermore, rather than attempting to uncover and confront women's bad feelings about their bodies or towards food, professionals concerned themselves with the problem of how to get the women thin. So, after the psychiatrists, analysts and clinical psychologists proved unsuccessful, experimental workers looked for biological and even genetic reasons for obesity. None of these approaches has had convincing, lasting results. None of them has addressed the central issues of compulsive eating which are rooted in the social inequality of women.

A feminist perspective to the problem of women's compulsive eating is essential if we are to move on from the ineffective blame–the–victim approach† and the unsatisfactory adjustment model of treatment. While psychoanalysis gives us useful tools to discover the deepest sources of emotional distress, feminism insists that those painful personal experiences derive from the social context into which female babies are born, and within which they develop to become adult women. The fact that

---

* See, for example: G. Bychowski, 'Neurotic Obesity', *The Psychology of Obesity*, ed. N. Kiell (Springfield, Illinois, 1973). Ludwig Binswanger, 'The Case of Ellen West', *Experience*, ed. Rollo May (New York, 1958).

† William Ryan, *Blame the Victim* (New York, 1971). This book shows how we come to blame the victims of oppression, rather than its perpetrators.

compulsive eating is overwhelmingly a woman's problem suggests that it has something to do with the experience of being female in our society. Feminism argues that being fat represents an attempt to break free of society's sex stereotypes. Getting fat can thus be understood as a definite and purposeful act; it is a directed, conscious or unconscious, challenge to sex-role stereotyping and culturally defined experience of womanhood.

Fat is a social disease, and fat is a feminist issue. Fat is *not* about lack of self-control or lack of will power. Fat *is* about protection, sex, nurturance, strength, boundaries, mothering, substance, assertion and rage. It is a response to the inequality of the sexes. Fat expresses experiences of women today in ways that are seldom examined and even more seldom treated. While becoming fat does not alter the roots of sexual oppression, an examination of the underlying causes or unconscious motivation that lead women to compulsive eating suggests new treatment possibilities. Unlike most weight-reducing schemes, our new therapeutic approach does not reinforce the oppressive social roles that lead women into compulsive eating in the first place. What is it about the social position of women that leads them to respond to it by getting fat?

The current ideological justification for inequality of the sexes has been built on the concept of the innate differences between women and men. Women alone can give birth to and breast-feed their infants and, as a result, a primary dependency relationship develops between mother and child. While this biological capacity is the only known genetic difference between men and women,* it is used as the basis on which to divide unequally women and men's labour, power, roles and expectations. The division of labour has become institutionalised. Woman's capacity to reproduce and provide nourishment has relegated her to the care and socialisation of children.

The relegation of women to the social roles of wife and mother has several significant consequences that contribute to the problem of fat. First, in order to become a wife and mother, a woman has to have a

* Dorothy Griffiths and Esther Saraga, 'Sex Differences in a Sexist Society.' Paper read at the International Conference on Sex-role Stereotyping, British Psychological Society, Cardiff, Wales, July 1977.

man. Getting a man is presented as an almost unattainable and yet essential goal. To get a man, a woman has to learn to regard herself as an item, a commodity, a sex object. Much of her experience and identity depends on how she and others see her. As John Berger says in *Ways of Seeing*:

> Men *act* and women *appear*. Men look at women. Women watch themselves being looked at. This determines not only most relations between men and women, but also the relation of women to themselves.*

This emphasis on presentation as the central aspect of a woman's existence makes her extremely self-conscious. It demands that she occupy herself with a self-image that others will find pleasing and attractive – an image that will immediately convey what kind of woman she is. She must observe and evaluate herself, scrutinising every detail of herself as though she were an outside judge. She attempts to make herself in the image of womanhood presented by billboards, newspapers, magazines and television. The media present women either in a sexual context or within the family, reflecting a woman's two prescribed roles, first as a sex object, and then as a mother. She is brought up to marry by 'catching' a man with her good looks and pleasing manner. To do this she must look appealing, earthy, sensual, sexual, virginal, innocent, reliable, daring, mysterious, coquettish and thin. In other words, she offers her self-image on the marriage marketplace. As a married woman, her sexuality will be sanctioned and her economic needs will be looked after. She will have achieved the first step of womanhood.

Since women are taught to see themselves from the outside as candidates for men, they become prey to the huge fashion and diet industries that first set up the ideal images and then exhort women to meet them. The message is loud and clear – the woman's body is not her own. The woman's body is not satisfactory as it is. It must be thin, free of 'unwanted hair', deodorised, perfumed and clothed. It must conform to an ideal physical type. Family and school socialisation teaches girls to groom themselves properly. Furthermore, the job is never-ending, for the image

* John Berger et al., *Ways of Seeing* (London, 1972), p.47.

changes from year to year. In the early 1960s, the only way to feel acceptable was to be skinny and flat chested with long straight hair. The first of these was achieved by near starvation, the second, by binding one's breasts with an ace bandage and the third, by ironing one's hair. Then in the early 1970s, the look was curly hair and full breasts. Just as styles in clothes change seasonally, so women's bodies are expected to change to fit these fashions. Long and skinny one year, petite and demure the next, women are continually manipulated by images of proper womanhood, which are extremely powerful because they are presented as the only reality. To ignore them means to risk being an outcast. Women are urged to conform, to help out the economy by continuous consumption of goods and clothing that are quickly made unwearable by the next season's fashion styles in clothes and body shapes. In the background, a ten billion dollar industry waits to remould bodies to the latest fashion. In this way, women are caught in an attempt to conform to a standard that is *externally* defined and constantly changing. But these models of femininity are experienced by women as unreal, frightening and unattainable. They produce a picture that is far removed from the reality of women's day-to-day lives.

The one constant in these images is that a woman must be thin. For many women, compulsive eating and being fat have become one way to avoid being marketed or seen as the ideal woman: 'My fat says "screw you" to all who want me to be the perfect mom, sweetheart, maid and whore. Take me for who *I* am, not for who I'm supposed to be. If you are really interested in *me*, you can wade through the layers and find out who I am.' In this way, fat expresses a rebellion against the powerlessness of the woman, against the pressure to look and act in a certain way and against being evaluated on her ability to create an image of herself.

Becoming fat is, thus, a woman's response to the first step in the process of fulfilling a prescribed social role which requires her to shape herself to an externally imposed image in order to catch a man. But a second stage in this process takes place after she achieves that goal, after she has become a wife and mother.

For a mother, everyone else's needs come first. Mothers are the unpaid managers of small, essential, complex and demanding organisations. They may not control the financial arrangements of this minicorporation or the major decisions on location or capital expenditure, but they do generally control the day-to-day operations. For her keep, the mother works an estimated ten hours a day (eighteen, if she has a second job outside the home) making sure that the food is purchased and prepared, the children's clothes, toys and books are in place, and that the father's effects are at the ready. She makes the house habitable, clean and comfy; she does the social secretarial work of arranging for the family to spend time with relatives and friends; she provides a baby-sitting and chauffeur-escort service for her children. As babies and children, we are all cared for. As adults, however, women are expected to feed and clean not only their babies but also their husbands, and only then, themselves.

In this role women experience particular pressure over food and eating. After the birth of each baby, breasts or bottle becomes a major issue. The mother is often made to feel insecure about her adequacy to perform her fundamental job. In the hospital the baby is weighed after each feed to see if the mother's breasts have enough milk. Pediatricians and baby-care books bombard the new mother with authoritative but conflicting advice about, for example, scheduled versus demand feeding, composition of the formula or the introduction of solid foods. As her children grow older, a woman continues to be reminded that her feeding skills are inadequate. To the tune of billions of dollars a year, the food industry counsels her on how, when and what she should feed her charges. The advertisements cajole her into providing nutritious breakfasts, munchy snacks, and whole-some dinners. Media preoccupation with good house-keeping and, particularly, with good food and good feeding, serves as a yardstick by which to measure the mother's ever-failing performance. This preoccupa-tion colonises food preparation so that the housewife is presented with a list of 'do's' and 'don'ts' so contradictory that it is a wonder that anything gets produced in the kitchen at all. It is not surprising that a woman quickly learns not to trust her own impulses, either in feeding her family or in listening to her own needs when she feeds herself.

During the period in her life which is devoted to child rearing, the woman is constantly making sure that others' lives run smoothly. She does this without thinking seriously that she is working at a full-time job. Her own experience of everyday life is as midwife to others' activities. While she is preparing her children to become future workers, and ena-bling her husband to be a more 'effective' producer, her role is to produce and reproduce workers. In this capacity she is constantly giving out without receiving the credit that would validate her social worth.

In a capitalist society everyone is defined by their job. A higher status is given to business*men*, academics and professionals than to production and service workers. Women's work in the home falls into the service and production category. Although often described as menial, deemed creative, dismissed as easy, or revered as god-given, women's work is seen as existing outside the production process and therefore devalued. Women as a group are allowed less expression than the men in their social class. However oppressed men are by a class society, they hold more power than women. Every man has to watch out for his boss. Every woman has to watch out lest her man not approve. The standards and views of the day are male. Women are seen as different from normal people (who are men), they are seen as 'other'.* They are not accepted as equal human beings with men. Their full identity is not supported by the society in which they grow up. This leads to confusion for women. Women are trapped in the role of an alien, yet delegated responsibility for making sure that others' lives are productive.

Since women are not accepted as equal human beings but are nevertheless expected to devote enormous energy to the lives of others, the distinctions between their own lives and the lives of those close to them may become blurred. Merging with others, feeding others, not knowing how to make space for themselves are frequent themes for women. Mothers are constantly giving out and feeding the world; everyone else's needs are primary. That they feel confusion about their own bodily needs is not surprising and there may be few ways of noting their personal concerns. A form of giving to and replenishing oneself is through food. 'I eat a lot because I'm always stoking myself up for the day's encounters. I look after my family, my mother and any number of people who pass in and out of my day. I feel empty with all this giving so I eat to fill up the spaces and give me sustenance to go on giving to the world.' The resulting fat has the function of making the space for which women crave. It is an attempt to answer the question, 'If I am constantly giving myself to everyone, where do I begin and end?' We want to look and be substantial.

* Simone de Beauvoir, *The Second Sex* (London, 1968).

We want to be bigger than society will let us. We want to take up as much space as the other sex. 'If I get bigger like a man then maybe I'll get taken seriously as is a man.'

What happens to the woman who does not fit the social role? Although the image of ideal sexual object and all-competent mother is socially pervasive, it is not only limiting and unattainable, but it also fails to correspond to the reality of many, many women's lives today. Most women today do still marry and have children. But many also continue to work outside the home after marriage, either to meet economic needs or in an attempt to break the limits of their social role. Women continually juggle with the many different aspects of their personalities which are developed and expressed at great cost against this unfriendly background. In this context, just as many women first become fat in an attempt to avoid being made into sexual objects at the beginning of their adult lives, so many women remain fat as a way of neutralising their sexual identity in the eyes of others who are important to them as their life progresses. In this way, they can hope to be taken seriously in their working lives outside the home. It is unusual for women to be accepted for their competence in this sphere. When they lose weight, that is, begin to look like a perfect female, they find themselves being treated frivolously by their male colleagues. When women are thin, they *are* treated frivolously: thin-sexy-incompetent worker. But if a woman loses weight, she herself may not yet be able to separate thinness from the packaged sexuality around her which simultaneously defines her as incompetent. It is difficult to conform to one image that society would have you fit (thin) without also being the other image (sexy female). 'When I'm fat, I feel I can hold my own. Whenever I get thin I feel I'm being treated like a little doll who doesn't know which end is up.'

We have seen how fat is a symbolic rejection of the limitations of women's role, an adaptation that many women use in the burdensome attempt to pursue their individual lives within the proscriptions of their social function. But in order to understand more about the way that overweight and, in particular, overeating, function in the lives of individual women, we must examine the process by which they are initially taught their social role. It is a complex and ironic process, for women are prepared for this life of inequality by other women who themselves suffer its limitations – their mothers. The feminist perspective reveals that compulsive eating is, in fact, an expression of the complex relationships between mothers and daughters.

If a woman's social role is to become a mother, nurturing – feeding the family in the widest possible sense – is the mother's central job. By and large, it is only within the family that a woman has any social power. Her competence as a mother and her ability to be an emotional support for her family defines her and provides her with a recognised context within which to exist. For a mother, a crucial part of the maternal role is to help her daughter, as her mother did before her, to make a smooth transition into the female social role. From her mother, the young girl learns who she herself is and can be. The mother provides her with a model of feminine behaviour, and directs the daughter's behaviour in particular ways.

But the world the mother must present to her daughter is one of unequal relationships, between parent and child, authority and powerlessness, man and woman. The child is exposed to the world of power relationships by a unit that itself produces and reproduces perhaps the most fundamental of these inequalities. Within the family, an inferior sense of self is instilled into little girls. While it is obvious that the growing-up process for girls and boys is vastly different, what may be less apparent is that to prepare her daughter for a life of inequality, the mother tries to hold back her child's desires to be a powerful, autonomous, self-directed, energetic and productive human being. From an early age, the young girl is encouraged to accept this rupture in her development and is guided to cope with this loss by putting her energy into taking care of others. Her own needs for emotional support and growth will be satisfied if she can convert them into giving to others.

Meanwhile, little boys are taught to accept emotional support without learning how to give this kind of nurturing and loving in return. Therefore, when a young woman finally achieves the social reward of marriage, she finds that it rarely provides either the nurture she still needs, or an opportunity for independence and self-development. To be a woman is to live with the tension of giving and not getting; and the mother and daughter involved in the process leading to this conclusion are inevitably bound up in ambivalence, difficulty and conflict.

67.

DENISE RILEY

Born 1948, Carlisle, United Kingdom

In 1970

The eyes of the girls are awash with violets
pansies are flowering under their tongues
they are grouped by the edge of the waves and are anxious to swim;
each one is on fire with passion to achieve herself.

68.

FADWA TUQAN

Born 1917, Nablus, Palestine
Died 2003, Nablus, Palestine

from *Difficult Journey – Mountainous Journey*
1978–1979

When I was young I was incapable of describing life as forcefully as a poet does. My world – the world of writing – was frightening and emotionally empty. I lived amidst thoughts sown in writing, but I was isolated from the world itself. As I matured into a woman, I was like a wounded animal, sterile in its cage. Although confined and deprived of a homeland, I was asked by my father to write political poetry. He wanted me to follow in the footsteps of my brother, Ibrahim, and publish for the good of the nation and its politics. Through writing, my father wanted me to respond to our national despair, but his demand made me miserable. I was unable to compose poetry; my inner voice was weak in protest against everything that had caused my silence. I was expected to create political poetry while the corrupt laws and customs insisted that I remain secluded behind a wall, not able to attend assemblies of men, not hearing the recurrent debates, not participating in public life. Oh, my nation, I want you to know the face behind the veil when I was forbidden to travel freely. I only knew Jerusalem because Ibrahim invited me there when he worked for the Palestine Broadcasting System. He wanted me to know a city other than Nablus, my birthplace.

The home environment in which I was raised did not nourish an interest in the outside world, but encouraged me, rather, to turn away from the struggle. Nevertheless, my father demanded that I realize the lofty aspirations he had for me. And yet, he never allowed me to establish a connection between his aspirations for me and my own inner emotions. For that reason, I was unable to compose poetry and instead sought refuge under a cover of tearful submission.

When we come of age, we are expected to concentrate our energies no matter what the personal cost, the obstacles and difficulties which preoccupy us. My father believed it was possible to solve any problem. My past had been deeply rooted in poetry, but my emotions had taken a very different direction from the course my father was urging me to follow. The poet must know the world before it can be healed through poetry. How else can the political issues be weighed? Where was I to find an intellectual atmosphere in which I could write political poetry? From the newspaper my father brought home at lunch every day? The newspaper is important, but it doesn't have the power to inspire poetry in the depths of one's soul. I was enslaved, isolated in my seclusion from the outside world, and my seclusion was imposed as a duty – I had no choice in the matter. The outside world was taboo for women of good families, and society didn't protest against that seclusion; it was not part of the political agenda.

My mother, as I recall, was one of the first members of the Society for the Welfare of Women. And yet, nothing changed for her. She did not • participate in social gatherings, and unlike other members of the Society, she was not allowed to travel to meetings. In fact, she was not allowed to travel at all unless accompanied by a member of the family. This women's organization was founded in Nablus in 1921 by Miriam Hashem, a teacher who died in 1947. Many outstanding people were members. In 1929, it became affiliated with the Arab Feminist Union, founded in Egypt by Huda Shaarawi. This affiliation stirred Palestinian women into being involved in their own political struggle.

The women in my family left the house only on rare occasions, such as family celebrations in the houses of relatives and close friends. Although my father permitted my mother to join Miriam Hashem's organisation, he restricted her activities to those associated with fundraising. If conferences were held in Egypt or in other cities in Palestine, my mother was not allowed to attend. Seclusion from the outside world deprived the home atmosphere, which women breathed, of any political or social consciousness.

Given the many prohibitions imposed on women, their movements in the home strongly resembled those of domesticated poultry who can come and go freely until they find fodder and then suffer constant temptation. But this particular domesticated poultry confined its energies to hatching the young. Women exhausted their lives with the big, copper cooking pots and gathering firewood for the stove in all seasons. As in other societies where the lives of women make no sense, the lives of Palestinian women, in every epoch and in every house, seemed devoid of significance. Such an environment had a stifling grip on me, which intensified as I approached sexual maturity.

My journey through life was filled with the misery of acute emotional and intellectual struggles. During the early years, I hated politics. I tried to realise my father's wishes in order to gain his love. I was not socially liberated but in my heart I justified rebellion and rejection. How could I possibly struggle for the sake of political liberation and for my own national convictions? Just as our society needed strong political action, so too did I need political activity. And while our cultural needs were not as pressing, we were deprived in this area as well.

I was conscious of my talent but I knew it could not mature except in society. This society created barriers to restrict me. The world of the harem stood between me and society. A spirit of impotence prevailed, and I could not write poetry. I was idle. I stopped exercising my poetic talents. In my difficult journey, I concealed the gift of my poetry. The strong awareness of what I had repressed and what I could potentially express left its traces on my spiritual and bodily existence. I became very thin and my brain felt fragmented. The weariness of my soul burdened all my limbs and during the night my body felt as if it had drowned.

Let me talk about the meaning of my life, its purpose and the particular port's anxiety which I bear. My afflictions tore me apart, but if my wretchedness increased my tears, it also expanded the sensitivity of my soul. I found relief when I thought of the wisdom of the ancient saying, 'If I am not for myself, who will be for me? And if I am only for myself, who am I?'

My commitment to life weakened as I remained secluded from the outside world. My soul was tormented because of this seclusion. My father's demands may have initiated my turmoil, but the pain always stayed with me, taking different forms throughout the journey of my life. Ultimately, at the source of my struggle was a tradition whose laws and customs constantly tested me. The process of maturing was a most painful experience in body and soul. I was oppressed, crushed; I felt bent out of shape. I could not participate in any aspect of life unless I pretended to be another person. I became more and more distant.

When I recovered, the words which intensified my feelings of subjugation and suppression also enriched the individuality and quality of my poetry. My work is existential, but it also penetrates the life of the harem which is narrow and constricted like a long-necked bottle. The talent, which I seemed initially to lack, had been blocked from view by this narrow long-necked bottle. My only bridge to society was the political poetry which I occasionally published in newspapers. I felt increasingly alienated and sensed that my poetic gifts were being plundered. I was aware of my ambition, but in those circumstances of seclusion, it appeared pathological. In the midst of my journey, my misery deepened, and one of my protectors, Nadim Salah, our family doctor, saved me from death and delivered me from my torture.

In 1948, during the Palestine War, my father died. With the loss of Palestine, my writing problems also ended. I began to write the nationalist poetry my father had always wished me to write. I began to devote myself to the nationalist cause, as had Ibrahim during his lifetime. I wrote poetry spontaneously and now with no complaints from the outside world. I was convulsed by the Palestine problem, the tragic situation of the refugees and the difficulties of the Arab world whose armies fought the war. I did not expect miracles from a politics which was then in its earliest stages, but I did not despair or abandon political activity. Politics gave me the will to persist in a struggle against the fragmentation and poverty of our war-torn nation. My immobility ended.

The Enclosed Environment of Women in Nablus During the 1930s and 1940s

Because of my family's status and position, my feelings about myself were strongly affected by the opinions of others. Even when I was angry at the outside world, my emotions were strongly affected by its views of me. My emotions were so volatile that I never questioned the need to disguise them. This disguise was my defence against criticism.

Men and women in Nablus have particular social customs which they impose by designating certain people as the city's 'watchdogs.' The authority these people enjoy does not stem from their special knowledge, but rather from their hateful pretentiousness. It has often been said that people from Nablus disapprove of everything. Unlike other citizens of Nablus, I do not impose on other people customs alien to their own, nor would I deprive anyone of free discussion. For the most part, however, people in Nablus are civil to one another without being especially warm or close.

During the 1930s and 1940s, I could not leave the house unless accompanied by another family member, such as my mother or aunt or sister or cousin. It was impossible to breathe freely during these visits. I was occasionally forced to join members of my family on their visits, although the atmosphere was hostile. I yearned for any situation in which my mother or the other women in my family would be allowed to go out more than once or twice a month. At the time, women were usually illiterate or had the most rudimentary skills of literacy. Their meagre education could be furthered only at the government high school (*Dar al-Muallimat*) in Jerusalem where they received a secondary school education.

However, there was a group of schoolteachers in Nablus and in other Palestinian cities who had a distinct social status. These women teachers distinguished themselves by their education and material possessions. They demanded and received deference from the common people. The women teachers had established a network of philanthropic societies which distributed pittances to people who were overwhelmed by what they considered extraordinary generosity. From these teachers, I learned the meaning of economic independence. In fact, my sisters and I began to support a woman enslaved by family and custom. This woman could not count on support from her family. Not that she was liberated from social customs and constraints. In fact, because her education was very limited, she could not change her personality and gain confidence in her own abilities and talents. In blind imitation of custom, she continued to consider male sponsorship and female subordination the rule. She believed that the power of men to make all the decisions in society was nothing more than brotherly compassion. But when the men in her family were unemployed, this woman was forced to turn to society for sustenance.

The situation for women teachers was not much better than the situation for other women in society, for they too had to abide by society's rules, which constrained their behaviour. The rules were shaped by arrogance, conceit, and pomposity. Despite their knowledge, these teachers did not have any special regard or appreciation for the books or articles published at the time. They were not cultured, nor did they engage in serious reading. Rather, the importance of this group stemmed from their fastidious dress. The money they earned as teachers enabled them to satisfy their desires for fashionable clothes. They never altered the rules and practices that existed among common people.

This educated class read in a destructive, hostile spirit. Only one woman was different. She alone possessed a craving for knowledge and culture. Sitt Fakhriya Hajawi was my former teacher in a school attended by the daughters of prosperous families in Nablus. She was very concerned with my life in and out of school. Sitt Fakhriya loved to read the newspaper to me or to read from the Egyptian journal *Al-Risala*. She was full of knowledge and would urge me to pursue my poetic journey. When I met her, I spoke to her about writing, reading, and about the structure of *qasida*. She paid me attention and I was happy.

With the exception of Sitt Fakhriya, I could not respect the privileged position of educated women. In turn, they made their negative feelings clear in unpleasant and haughty encounters with me. They would say sharply: 'Her brother, Ibrahim, composed the poetry and appended her name to it.' They directed their negative comments at me until Ibrahim's death. Their hostility was painful, and I was aware of the pain even though I was very young. Once I reached the age of puberty, I began to realise that every success achieved by a woman has its price both for her and her family. It is not even possible to laugh at the antics of clowns without being criticized. But I realised this only later; at the time, I merely suffered in silence.

During the 1930s and 1940s, I was secluded in female society. Because urban society strove for outward appearances which would distinguish it from village society, it maintained an isolated and inhospitable existence for women. But the breach between me and female society grew wider. While I kept my disdain secret, I could neither contribute to society nor accept anything from it. Female society was consumed by idle chatter. The chatter manifested the illiteracy of women who had no access to the beautiful and fertile writing appearing in the larger world around them. Unable to join in their illiteracy, I was forced into a breach with the society in which I was born.

I See, I Hear, I Suffer

I didn't show my father my emotions. My feelings toward him were almost neutral: I neither loathed nor loved him since I didn't matter to him. I felt for him only when he was sick, imprisoned, or banished for political reasons. His temper cast a shadow over us; in the morning we scarcely noticed it until it would explode like a storm. I was afraid he would die and abandon us. This outweighed any other feelings I had about him, feelings of alienation or indifference. I was not aware of the significance of this until I reached adolescence when I feverishly began to scrutinise my youth.

My burdens made me suffer. Seeing this, Ibrahim compensated for my father and always showed me great tenderness, affection, and goodness. When Ibrahim died, my father still imposed shackles on my life. But when my father passed on to the next world, I was freed from the frightening duty which had stifled my emotions and which I had endured for so many years. Even though I was sharply critical of his legacy I tried not to betray it. I considered his death an attack against the family itself. From that day on I was empowered. I no longer kept my distance from controversies: I saw, I heard, and I suffered. Earlier, I had written a *qasida* called 'Life', but my true feelings had been distant, absent.

The Narrow Long-Necked Bottle

I was much more attached to my aunt than to my mother, and my attachment to my paternal uncle, Hajj Hafiz, was stronger and deeper than my attachment to my father. Because of the warmth of his heart, his joking and laughing, I felt he truly loved me. My memories of my uncle continue to be clear and vivid, although my thoughts are fragmented and muddled. My uncle was involved in many enjoyable quarrels and controversies. One dispute between him and my father concerned my uncle's participation in family councils. The men of the city, considering my father too rigid in his views, would approach my uncle instead and meet constantly with him. I would often run to him during his meeting and he would take me in his arms and set me on his lap. My father would never do this.

During the first quarter of the year, the men of Nablus would celebrate the birthday of the Prophet Moses – Nabi Musa. The idea for this holiday began during the Ayyubid period in an effort to attract large numbers of Muslims to Jerusalem when many Christians were there celebrating Easter. This presumably would put Muslims on their guard against a surprise attack by the Crusaders. Muslim youth would arrive in the holy city in huge numbers from cities and villages all over Palestine. They would meet at the tomb of Nabi Musa, which is located between Jerusalem and Jericho. During the holiday, the young men of Nablus would go out with the religious dignitaries who were in charge of the rituals. The procession began with the religious men beating on drums and cymbals and singing popular songs. The parade continued to the city's limits, then turned to Jerusalem to join a procession of religious dignitaries of Hebron and Jerusalem. The singing continued throughout the Easter celebration.

In the Nabi Musa procession, just as in the procession of a bride and groom where the Quran in recited, the parade would stop in front of our house and look for the family 'jester.' The shouting and calls for my uncle would rise higher. My uncle would leave his office chamber to join the holiday procession near the government offices. The young men would mount him on their shoulders. They would all draw weapons. My uncle would wave his sword imploring the enthusiastic crowd to reply to his words: 'We are men of the mountain of light'. In the parade, orange-blossom water would drip from the pitchers or from long-necked bottles.

I was very proud of my uncle. Eventually, I recognized the reasons for his popularity. In 1925 the National Party was founded in Nablus to support the candidacy of Hajj Amin al-Husaini to the Supreme Muslim Council. Other parties, like the National Democratic Party, opposed the National Party in the elections. My uncle was one of the founders of the National Party. After his own success in the municipal elections, he distanced himself from party rivalries and from the factions in both the local council and the country. Of the two parties, the National was connected to Hajj Amin al-Husaini and the National Democratic was led by Raghib al-Nashashibi, mayor of Jerusalem. These two parties created damaging divisions in the country. Unlike my uncle, my father did not avoid this political battlefield. He belonged to various political organisations and was imprisoned several times by the British mandatory authorities. Still, my uncle continued to be more popular and prominent.

When my uncle died of diphtheria in 1927, at the age of fifty-two, I began my encounter with death. As if struck by lightning, I fell into confusion and a whirlpool of inconsolable sadness. For the first time, I experienced loss, and I grieved. Man's life is a chain of distinct losses, starting as a separation from the mother's breast and ending with his own death. My uncle's death deprived me of a loving guardian. After his death, he lay still, shrouded on a bed. I was confused by the lack of worry on his pale face, his unawareness of a crying family and friends. I concealed my sadness, trying not to think of the loss of the family member I felt closest to. We deceive ourselves in thinking that we can preserve the memory of the deceased by placing little stones on his grave. That ritual doesn't compensate for the loss. To tell children that it does is only to deceive them as they are forced to confront death. I hid my own grief and drew near to it only at night, crying myself to sleep.

I am not a philosopher. As a child, I reasoned simply as children do. But I was preoccupied by the dread which death inspires. I wondered about the external appearance of death since the dead seem absolutely isolated and indifferent. Even Julia, my childhood friend, who was distantly related to me, could not share my feelings of death for she, herself, died before my eyes in the seventeenth year of her life. She struggled alone and had to struggle alone, for no beholder can partake of another's death. When I think about Julia's death, I do not remember how she looked, but rather how I felt about her. I became angry when people said that death carries our loved ones to paradise in reward. The death of my uncle marked the end of my childhood. Julia's death appeared so unjustifiable that I thought only about death for a time. I was obsessed with the questions of why people died and why they left me. I was a child. I asked these questions simply and clearly.

Shaikha

Among my earliest memories are those of an aunt we called 'Shaikha.' I knew her as a mistress of intimidation, the person who controlled all the women in the family. She also reported on the activities and behaviour of the boys in the family, serving as a sort of police, surreptitiously transmitting accounts to my uncle.

Societies in which supervision is arbitrary and repressive engender dual reactions: submission and revolt. But these reactions, in turn, intensify the repressive power and create a hegemony in family and society. In my family, it was Shaikha who not only laid the foundation for this sort of power, but who also encompassed the qualities of submission and revolt.

When she was only sixteen, Shaikha returned to her father's house divorced from a marriage which had lasted a few months. She became a follower of the Sufi Order of Shaikh Abd al-Qadir al-Qilani. For Shaikha the religious order served as an escape from the frustrations of a failed marriage. In the religious community of this blind Egyptian sheikh, there was a polarization between female members who were divorced and those who were widows. The group assembled in the house of the treasurer who, with his wife, had the authority to dispense *baraka* and facilitate ritual purity. The shaikh proclaimed his *baraka* in a way that aggrandised his own importance. So doing, he deprived his followers of their own capacity to reason. By sharpening sensations with the fragrance of musk, the sheikh could convince his followers to see what was not visible, to hear what did not exist.

The account of the shaikh's *baraka* brings to mind a story about my old Turkish grandmother, Mother Aziza. One day she was present at one of the shaikh's demonstrations. In tears, she renounced what she saw and launched a devastating attack against the sheikh. From the day, an enmity was firmly established between Shaikha and my mother, whose modern outlook, especially on the subject of death, was at odds with Shaikha's religious piety. Shaikha attacked my mother, my brother Ahmad, and me for opposing her views.

As she aged and grew weaker, Shaikha was constantly engaged in praying, fasting, or proclaiming revelations. She would fast for three months – Rajab, Shaban and Ramadan – and pray and perform sacrifices at night. Her prayer beads were huge and always by her side. They consisted of a thousand individual beads, and as she touched each one she would pronounce one of the names of God. Her personality was like that string of prayer beads, displayed for public and private devotions; the beads were a concrete manifestation of her piety.

As a child, I used to love to watch people engaged in prayer especially because of the theatrics involved. I would often stop at the gate of the Al Bek Mosque facing our house in the old market area to watch the different ways in which the worshippers prayed. While their facial expressions were quite different, they all began at a speedy pace, then humbled themselves without paying attention to anything but God. My heart and spirit were moved as I watched the worshippers pray firmly and slowly.

I noticed the hand movements. They were raised behind the ears, then brought above the head and finally to the right side as prayers were whispered in undertones. Body movements began: bowing the torso to the front; raising the body and lifting the head to the sky, kneeling down, prostrating themselves while placing their hands on their legs. Raising two index fingers, the assembled group would testify to the existence of God. They would pronounce praises to God aloud and turn their heads from right to left.

Only much later did I discover why it was important to express religious submission through prayer. I learned of a continuity in religious rituals from the period of peasant paganism. All modern religions try to evoke a mysterious environment through their theatrics and expressions, which are similar to the devotions and activities of the early natural religions.

Shaikha's call to religious prayer was exaggerated and artificial. Occasionally, she seemed to imitate the rituals of dervishes. She would begin vehement, trembling motions, moving her head fiercely right and left while repeating Allah . . . Allah . . . Allah . . . Allah . . . , and so on. She pronounced the name rapidly, without pause, foaming at the mouth.

Because of Shaikha, my faith changed. Occasionally, it was said that her religious rigidity dissolved in gatherings of women visitors. I did not find that to be true. She loved to issue decrees to the women in the family and to censure them for religious impiety. Shaikha would insult people simply because they were poor or unsuccessful. Thus did Shaikha believe.

In most circumstances, she took the particular behaviour of individuals as a general commentary on all humanity. She would permit one of the girls in the family to become friendly with a relative, a school friend or a neighbourhood girl. Then seeing the two together in the courtyard she would fume with rage. This used to drive every school friend or neighbourhood companion away from the house. When I did Shaikha a favour or bought her a gift from the *suq*, she would insinuate that I was trying to buy her love. Even when she smiled or showed some gentleness her affection always stopped like a cold wall which cannot nourish green plants. In a way, I combined traits of my mother and those of Shaikha, and yet the two were very different. On the one hand, there was my mother's warmth, gentleness and softness, and on the other, Shaikha was like a desert without trees or water. She was a harsh goddess who aimed her breath at an invisible throne.

Proud and haughty, Shaikha was in control of an entire stratum of women who blindly obeyed her. This 'pious' Shaikha would lead the simple women by her example. She would sit with them during their children's illnesses. The women would hold pitchers of water while Shaikha stood near the sick babies reading passages from the Quran. The women believed Shaikha could purify and bless water as she exhaled into the pitchers. Given her devotion to God, this 'pious' Shaikha held an astonishing view of the upper class, which she expressed arrogantly: 'We are above and you are below. This is God's Wish.' During the 1930s and 1940s this view was commonly held by the classes which benefited from the established order. They legitimized their positions of authority through the name of God. One could always hear the words: 'Sayyids, ladies; at your service, Sayyids; at your service, ladies; at your service, sons of Sayyids.'

Ideas are effective as long as people accept them and do not revolt against them. We must reject Aristotle's saying 'that the slave resembles the beast' even though this idea was consistent with the venerated thought of Athenian society and not questioned at that time.

I remember what a woman once said to Shaikha: 'Honour us, O lady, with a visit during the holidays, for we visit you often and you do not visit us.' But Shaikha stared at her and said in her haughty way: 'Listen, you will visit us always and forever and we will not visit you in order to emphasise the significance of the day of our departure.' What has happened to the world! How inverted things are! The woman was ashamed and my heart was filled with sympathy for her. I left the room, rushed to my mother to tell her how Shaikha had shamed this poor woman. I was young. I did not understand the meaning of cruelty, but I distanced myself instinctively from Shaikha's views. My feelings overwhelmed me, and I fell ill.

Although it may have been unconscious, I considered pride improper. In my home, criticism of Shaikha's haughtiness was tolerated until it affected the family as a whole. Shaikha would say to us in utter simplicity: 'We are all Creations of the Lord and our fate is in God's hands,' but this harsh woman turned away from all else. It is not right to turn away from suffering in order to honour important men who hold esteemed social positions. Because she believed it was, God punished her and afflicted her with hostility to the poor. My mother told us about democracy, simply, and she could explain spontaneously how the demise of democracy affected all people at all social levels. My mother could teach us in a practical way the true meaning of the phrase, brotherly unity is no burden.

I saw Shaikha as a symbol of the hardness of society, and I did not find my efforts to destroy the symbol absurd. Ultimately, I was unable to put an end to Shaikha's religiosity and to convince her that her feelings were inhuman. She never could accept my beliefs that the true meaning of religion had been distorted and that God's attributes of love, mercy, and goodness had produced illiteracy and ignorance for most men and women. What Shaikha considered permissible and forbidden, proper and improper was a strange, soggy mixture. She would cry to me for help but considered me an apostate. 'Come on up, weak one. Buckle down. Submit more or you will enter Hell and so will your mother who sewed those disgraceful clothes for you.' Shaikha's views undermined any serenity I had in my childhood. Her simplicity confused my young mind. Peace returned only when I began to imagine that it was the god of Hell who visited with my mother. I imagined God himself as a harsh and fearful ruler without compassion.

Once, when I had raised my voice in song – 'How secure is the breath of fresh air for the beautiful beloved everywhere . . .' – Shaikha entered the room like a storm and said: 'Silence, close your mouth or you will perish and awaken in Hell. Hinkiyan . . . Hind . . . Surena . . .' My voice was suddenly broken; the song, broken and incomplete, stuck in my throat. Hind and Surena were professional singers in Nablus whom Shaikha called Hinkiyan or harpies, a term she derived from the Persian word for god.

Shaikha hurt me deeply during those days by condemning the desires I satisfied daily through music and dance. I regarded music and dance as desirable and liberating activities. I, alone, possessed the power to control music and dance; the world in which I lived did not. Shaikha could not impose her power over song, and I did not believe her when she said that song and dance were ugly.

My mother used to hum softly with her sad, tender voice. I would hum and sit on her lap listening attentively. Resting from time to time and comforting me – at family gatherings and with my friends – in warm soft light – she would make me content, which she loved to do as she would remind me of the words and music of a song. Singing delighted me and made me happy. To fulfil an ambition, my mother had learned to play the violin. But she was so devoted to that ambition that the instrument was forbiddcn in our house. Playing an instrument and singing represented outlets and then, at a later phase of my youthful journey, symbols of the sentimental yearnings I had suppressed. In harmony and song – both in listening and in practising – I found a release of tension. Like poetry, this release served as a means to realise my talents and liberate my imprisoned capacities.

One of the strongest of my depressing memories of Shaikha began in the girls' room. This room, in the front of the house, did not belong to her, for each of the upstairs rooms had a different name. She entered unexpectedly and came upon my older brother, Ahmad, who was answering some of my questions on poetic metre and form. Shaikha stopped silently and looked over our heads. Then she said to Ahmad reproachfully, 'Even you, then what more? For girls, words are opponents who collapse in battle.' Ahmad joked with her, using some meaningless words. Then he turned his attention once again to me and my questions about poetry.

'Even you . . .' A terrifying expression for me which Ahmad understood with indulgence and which made a loving impression on him. In contrast, Ibrahim, whom I always loved, was emancipated from family traditions and from Shaikha's harsh shackles. From that day on my attitude to Shaikha was completely hostile. I no longer hoped for anything different in the future. Shaikha was the nightmare of my childhood and adolescence, and she left her harsh traces on many years of my life.

Those who think little of their role in my life are often the ones who, in retrospect, penetrate it most deeply.

69.

AUDRE LORDE

Born 1934, New York City, New York, United States of America
Died 1992, Christiansted, U.S. Virgin Islands

The Master's Tools Will Never Dismantle the Master's House

1979

I agreed to take part in a New York University Institute for the Humanities conference a year ago, in 1978, with the understanding that I would be commenting upon papers dealing with the role of difference within the lives of American women: difference of race, sexuality, class and age. The absence of these considerations weakens any feminist discussion of the personal and the political.

It is a particular academic arrogance to assume any discussion of feminist theory without examining our many differences, and without a significant input from poor women, Black and Third World women, and lesbians. And yet, I stand here as a Black lesbian feminist, having been invited to comment within the only panel, 'The Personal and the Political', at this conference to commemorate the 30th anniversary of Simone de Beauvoir's *Second Sex*, where the input of Black feminists and lesbians is represented. What this says about the vision of this conference is sad, in a country where racism, sexism, and homophobia are inseparable. To read this programme is to assume that lesbian and Black women have nothing to say about existentialism, the erotic, women's culture and silence, developing feminist theory, or heterosexuality and power. And what does it mean in personal and political terms when even the two Black women who did present here were literally found at the last hour? What does it mean when the tools of a racist patriarchy are used to examine the fruits of that same patriarchy? It means that only the most narrow perimeters of change are possible and allowable.

The absence of any consideration of lesbian consciousness or the consciousness of Third World women leaves a serious gap within this conference and within the papers presented here. For example, in a paper on material relationships between women, I was conscious of an either/ or model of nurturing which totally dismissed my knowledge as a Black lesbian. In this paper there was no examination of mutuality between women, no systems of shared support, no interdependence as exists between lesbians and women-identified women. Yet it is only in the patriarchal model of nurturance that women who attempt to emancipate themselves pay perhaps too high a price for the results', as this paper states.

For women, the need and desire to nurture each other is not pathological but redemptive, and it is within that knowledge that our real power is rediscovered. It is this real connection which is so feared by a patriarchal world. Only within a patriarchal structure is maternity the only social power open to women.

Interdependency between women is the way to a freedom which allows the I to *be*, not in order to be used, but in order to be creative. This is a difference between the passive *be* and the active *being*.

Advocating the mere tolerance of difference between women is the grossest reformism. It is a total denial of the creative function of difference in our lives. Difference must be not merely tolerated, but seen as a fund of necessary polarities between which our creativity can spark like a dialectic. Only then does the necessity for interdependency become unthreatening. Only within that interdependency of different strengths, acknowledged and equal, can the power to seek new ways of being in the world generate, as well as the courage and sustenance to act where there are no charters.

Within the interdependence of mutual (nondominant) differences lies that security which enables us to descend into the chaos of knowledge and return with true visions of our future, along with the concomitant power to effect those changes which can bring that future into being. Difference is that raw and powerful connection from which our personal power is forged.

As women, we have been taught either to ignore our differences, or to view them as causes for separation and suspicion rather than as forces for change. Without community there is no liberation, only the most vulnerable and temporary armistice between an individual and her oppression. But community must not mean a shedding of our differences, nor the pathetic pretence that these differences do not exist.

Those of us who stand outside the circle of this society's definition of acceptable women; those of us who have been forged in the crucibles of difference – those of us who are poor, who are lesbians, who are Black, who are older – know that *survival is not an academic skill*. It is learning how to stand alone, unpopular and sometimes reviled, and how to make common cause with those others identified as outside the structures in order to define and seek a world in which we can all flourish. It is learning how to take our differences and make them strengths. *For the master's tools will never dismantle the master's house.* They may allow us temporarily to beat him at his own game, but they will never enable us to bring about genuine change. And this fact is only threatening to those women who still define the master's house as their only source of support.

Poor women and women of color know there is a difference between the daily manifestations of marital slavery and prostitution because it is our daughters who line 42nd Street. If white American feminist theory need not deal with the differences between us, and the resulting difference in our oppressions, then how do you deal with the fact that the women who clean your houses and tend your children while you attend conferences on feminist theory are, for the most part, poor women and women of color? What is the theory behind racist feminism?

In a world of possibility for us all, our personal visions help lay the groundwork for political action. The failure of academic feminists to recognize difference as a crucial strength is a failure to reach beyond the first patriarchal lesson. In our world, divide and conquer must become define and empower.

Why weren't other women of color found to participate in this conference? Why were two phone calls to me considered a consultation? Am I the only possible source of names of Black feminists? And although the Black panellist's paper ends on an important and powerful connection of love between women, what about interracial co-operation between feminists who don't love each other?

In academic feminist circles, the answer to these questions is often, 'We did not know who to ask.' But that is the same evasion of responsibility, the same cop-out, that keeps Black women's art out of women's exhibitions, Black women's work out of most feminist publications except for the occasional 'Special Third World Women's Issue' and Black women's texts off your reading lists. But as Adrienne Rich pointed out in a recent talk, white feminists have educated themselves about such an enormous amount over the past ten years, how come you haven't also educated yourselves about Black women and the differences between us – white and Black – when it is key to our survival as a movement?

Women of today are still being called upon to stretch across the gap of male ignorance and to educate men as to our existence and our needs. This is an old and primary tool of all oppressors to keep the oppressed occupied with the master's concerns. Now we hear that it is the task of women of color to educate white women – in the face of tremendous resistance – as to our existence, our differences, our relative roles in our joint survival. This is a diversion of energies and a tragic repetition of racist patriarchal thought.

Simone de Beauvoir once said, 'It is in the knowledge of the genuine conditions of our lives that we must draw our strength to live and our reasons for acting.'

Racism and homophobia are real conditions of all our lives in this place and time. I urge each one of us to reach down into that deep place of knowledge inside herself and touch that terror and loathing of any difference that lives there. See whose face it wears. Then the personal as the political can begin to illuminate all our choices.

70.

ANGELA CARTER

Born 1940, Eastbourne, United Kingdom
Died 1992, London, United Kingdom

The Tiger's Bride

1979

My father lost me to The Beast at cards.

There's a special madness strikes travellers from the North when they reach the lovely land where the lemon trees grow. We come from countries of cold weather; at home, we are at war with nature but here, ah! you think you've come to the blessed plot where the lion lies down with the lamb. Everything flowers; no harsh wind stirs the voluptuous air. The sun spills fruit for you. And the deathly, sensual lethargy of the sweet South infects the starved brain; it gasps: 'Luxury! more luxury!' But then the snow comes, you cannot escape it, it followed us from Russia as if it ran behind our carriage, and in this dark, bitter city has caught up with us at last, flocking against the windowpanes to mock my father's expectations of perpetual pleasure as the veins in his forehead stand out and throb, his hands shake as he deals the Devil's picture books.

The candles dropped hot, acrid gouts of wax on my bare shoulders. I watched with the furious cynicism peculiar to women whom circumstances force mutely to witness folly, while my father, fired in his desperation by more and yet more draughts of the firewater they call 'grappa', rids himself of the last scraps of my inheritance. When we left Russia, we owned black earth, blue forest with bear and wild boar, serfs, cornfields, farmyards, my beloved horses, white nights of cool summer, the fireworks of the northern lights. What a burden all those possessions must have been to him, because he laughs as if with glee as he beggars himself; he is in such a passion to donate all to The Beast.

Everyone who comes to this city must play a hand with the *grand seigneur*; few come. They did not warn us at Milan, or, if they did, we did not understand them – my limping Italian, the bewildering dialect of the region. Indeed, I myself spoke up in favour of this remote, provincial place, out of fashion two hundred years, because, oh irony, it boasted no casino. I did not know that the price of a stay in its Decembral solitude was a game with Milord.

The hour was late. The chill damp of this place creeps into the stones, into your bones, into the spongy pith of the lungs; it insinuated itself with a shiver into our parlour, where Milord came to play in the privacy essential to him. Who could refuse the invitation his valet brought to our lodging? Not my profligate father, certainly; the mirror above the table gave me back his frenzy, my impassivity, the withering candles, the emptying bottles, the coloured tide of the cards as they rose and fell, the still mask that concealed all the features of The Beast but for the yellow eyes that strayed, now and then, from his unfurled hand towards myself.

'La Bestia!' said our landlady, gingerly fingering an envelope with his huge crest of a tiger rampant on it, something of fear, something of wonder in her face. And I could not ask her why they called the master of the place, 'La Bestia' – was it to do with that heraldic signature? – because her tongue was so thickened by the phlegmy, bronchitic speech of the region I scarcely managed to make out a thing she said except, when she saw me: 'Che bella!'

Since I could toddle, always the pretty one, with my glossy, nut-brown curls, my rosy cheeks. And born on Christmas Day – her 'Christmas rose', my English nurse called me. The peasants said: 'The living image of her mother,' crossing themselves out of respect for the dead. My mother did not blossom long; bartered for her dowry to such a feckless spring of the Russian nobility that she soon died of his gaming, his whoring, his agonizing repentances. And The Beast gave me the rose from his own impeccable if outmoded buttonhole when he arrived, the valet brushing the snow off his black cloak. This white rose, unnatural, out of season, that now my nervous fingers ripped, petal by petal, apart as my father magnificently concluded the career he had made of catastrophe.

This is a melancholy, introspective region; a sunless, featureless landscape, the sullen river sweating fog, the shorn, hunkering willows. And a cruel city; the sombre piazza, a place uniquely suited to public executions, under the beetling shadow of that malign barn of a church. They used to hang condemned men in cages from the city walls; unkindness comes naturally to them, their eyes are set too close together, they have thin lips. Poor food, pasta soaked in oil, boiled beef with sauce of bitter herbs. A funereal hush about the place, the inhabitants huddled up against the cold so you can hardly see their faces. And they lie to you and cheat you, innkeepers, coachmen, everybody. God, how they fleeced us!

The treacherous South, where you think there is no winter but forget you take it with you.

My senses were increasingly troubled by the fuddling perfume of Milord, far too potent a reek of purplish civet at such close quarters in so small a room. He must bathe himself in scent, soak his shirts and underlinen in it; what can he smell of, that needs so much camouflage?

I never saw a man so big look so two-dimensional, in spite of the quaint elegance of The Beast, in the old-fashioned tailcoat that might, from its looks, have been bought in those distant years before he imposed seclusion on himself; he does not feel he need keep up with the times. There is a crude clumsiness about his outlines, that are on the ungainly, giant side; and he has an odd air of self-imposed restraint, as if fighting a battle with himself to remain upright when he would far rather drop down on all fours. He throws our human aspirations to the godlike sadly awry, poor fellow; only from a distance would you think The Beast not much different from any other man, although he wears a mask with a man's face painted most beautifully on it. Oh, yes, a beautiful face; but one with too much formal symmetry of feature to be entirely human: one profile of his mask is the mirror image of the other, too perfect, uncanny. He wears a wig, too, false hair tied at the nape with a bow, a wig of the kind you see in old-fashioned portraits. A chaste silk stock stuck with a pearl hides his throat. And gloves of blond kid that are yet so huge and clumsy they do not seem to cover hands.

He is a carnival figure made of papier mâché and crêpe hair; and yet he has the Devil's knack at cards.

His masked voice echoes as from a great distance as he stoops over his hand and he has such a growling impediment in his speech that only his valet, who understands him, can interpret for him, as if his master were the clumsy doll and he the ventriloquist.

The wick slumped in the eroded wax, the candles guttered. By the time my rose had lost all its petals, my father, too, was left with nothing.

'Except the girl.'

Gambling is a sickness. My father said he loved me yet he staked his daughter on a hand of cards. He fanned them out; in the mirror, I saw wild hope light up his eyes. His collar was unfastened, his rumpled hair stood up on end, he had the anguish of a man in the last stages of debauchery. The draughts came out of the old walls and bit me, I was colder than I'd ever been in Russia, when nights are coldest there.

A queen, a king, an ace. I saw them in the mirror. Oh, I know he thought he could not lose me; besides, back with me would come all he had lost, the unravelled fortunes of our family at one blow restored. And would he not win, as well, The Beast's hereditary palazzo outside the city; his immense revenues; his lands around the river; his rents, his treasure chest, his Mantegnas, his Giulio Romanos, his Cellini saltcellars, his titles . . . the very city itself.

You must not think my father valued me at less than a king's ransom; but, at *no more* than a king's ransom.

It was cold as hell in the parlour. And it seemed to me, child of the severe North, that it was not my flesh but, truly, my father's soul that was in peril.

My father, of course, believed in miracles; what gambler does not? In pursuit of just such a miracle as this, had we not travelled from the land of bears and shooting stars?

So we teetered on the brink.

The Beast bayed; laid down all three remaining aces.

The indifferent servants now glided smoothly forward as on wheels to douse the candles one by one. To look at them you would think that nothing of any moment had occurred. They yawned a little resentfully; it was almost morning, we had kept them out of bed. The Beast's man brought his cloak. My father sat amongst these preparations for departure, staring on at the betrayal of his cards upon the table.

The Beast's man informed me crisply that he, the valet, would call for me and my bags tomorrow, at ten, and conduct me forthwith to The Beast's palazzo. Capisco? So shocked was I that I scarcely did 'capisco'; he repeated my orders patiently, he was a strange, thin, quick little man who walked with an irregular, jolting rhythm upon splayed feet in curious, wedge-shaped shoes.

Where my father had been red as fire, now he was white as the snow that caked the window-pane. His eyes swam; soon he would cry.

'"Like the base Indian," he said; he loved rhetoric. "One whose hand,/ Like the base Indian, threw a pearl away/Richer than all his tribe . . ." I have lost my pearl, my pearl beyond price.'

At that, The Beast made a sudden, dreadful noise, halfway between a growl and a roar; the candles flared. The quick valet, the prim hypocrite, interpreted unblinking: 'My master says: If you are so careless of your treasures, you should expect them to be taken from you.'

He gave us the bow and smile his master could not offer us and they departed.

I watched the snow until, just before dawn, it stopped falling; a hard frost settled, next morning there was a light like iron.

The Beast's carriage, of an elegant if antique design, was black as a hearse and it was drawn by a dashing black gelding who blew smoke from his nostrils and stamped upon the packed snow with enough sprightly appearance of life to give me some hope that not all the world was locked in ice, as I was. I had always held a little towards Gulliver's opinion, that horses are better than we are, and, that day, I would have been glad to depart with him to the kingdom of horses, if I'd been given the chance.

The valet sat up on the box in a natty black and gold livery, clasping, of all things, a bunch of his master's damned white roses as if a gift of flowers would reconcile a woman to any humiliation. He sprang down with preternatural agility to place them ceremoniously in my reluctant hand. My tear-beslobbered father wants a rose to show that I forgive him. When I break off a stem, I prick my finger and so he gets his rose all smeared with blood.

The valet crouched at my feet to tuck the rugs about me with a strange kind of unflattering obsequiousness yet he forgot his station sufficiently to scratch busily beneath his white periwig with an oversupple index finger as he offered me what my old nurse would have called an 'old-fashioned look', ironic, sly, a smidgen of disdain in it. And pity? No pity. His eyes were moist and brown, his face seamed with the innocent cunning of an ancient baby. He had an irritating habit of chattering to himself under his breath all the time as he packed up his master's winnings. I drew the curtains to conceal the sight of my father's farewell; my spite was sharp as broken glass.

Lost to The Beast! And what, I wondered, might be the exact nature of his 'beastliness'? My English nurse once told me about a tiger-man she saw in London, when she was a little girl, to scare me into good behaviour, for I was a wild wee thing and she could not tame me into submission with a frown or the bribe of a spoonful of jam. If you don't stop plaguing the nursemaids, my beauty, the tiger-man will come and take you away. They'd brought him from Sumatra, in the Indies, she said; his hinder parts were all hairy and only from the head downwards did he resemble a man.

And yet The Beast goes always masked; it cannot be his face that looks like mine.

But the tiger-man, in spite of his hairiness, could take a glass of ale in his hand like a good Christian and drink it down. Had she not seen him do so, at the sign of The George, by the steps of Upper Moor Fields when she was just as high as me and lisped and toddled, too. Then she would sigh for London, across the North Sea of the lapse of years. But, if this young lady was not a good little girl and did not eat her boiled beetroot, then the tiger-man would put on his big black travelling cloak lined with fur, just like your daddy's, and hire the Erl-King's galloper of wind and ride through the night straight to the nursery and –

Yes, my beauty! GOBBLE YOU UP!

How I'd squeal in delighted terror, half believing her, half knowing that she teased me. And there were things I knew that I must not tell her. In our lost farmyard, where the giggling nursemaids initiated me into the mysteries of what the bull did to the cows, I heard about the waggoner's daughter. Hush, hush, don't let on to your nursie we said so; the waggoner's lass, hare-lipped, squint-eyed, ugly as sin, who would have taken her? Yet, to her shame, her belly swelled amid the cruel mockery of the ostlers and her son was born of a bear, they whispered. Born with a full pelt and teeth; that proved it. But, when he grew up, he was a good shepherd, although he never married, lived in a hut outside the village and could make the wind blow any way he wanted to besides being able to tell which eggs would become cocks, which hens.

The wondering peasants once brought my father a skull with horns four inches long on either side of it and would not go back to the field where their poor plough disturbed it until the priest went with them; for this skull had the jaw-bone of a *man*, had it not?

Old wives' tales, nursery fears! I knew well enough the reason for the trepidation I cosily titillated with superstitious marvels of my childhood on the day my childhood ended. For now my own skin was my sole capital in the world and today I'd make my first investment.

We had left the city far behind us and were now traversing a wide, flat dish of snow where the mutilated stumps of the willows flourished their ciliate heads athwart frozen ditches; mist diminished the horizon, brought down the sky until it seemed no more than a few inches above us. As far as eye could see, not one thing living. How starveling, how bereft the dead season of this spurious Eden in which all the fruit was blighted by cold! And my frail roses, already faded. I opened the carriage door and tossed the defunct bouquet into the rucked, frost-stiff mud of the road. Suddenly a sharp, freezing wind arose and pelted my face with a dry rice of powdered snow. The mist lifted sufficiently to reveal before me an acreage of half-derelict facades of sheer red brick, the vast mantrap, the megalomaniac citadel of his palazzo.

It was a world in itself but a dead one, a burned-out planet. I saw The Beast bought solitude, not luxury, with his money.

The little black horse trotted smartly through the figured bronze doors that stood open to the weather like those of a barn and the valet handed me out of the carriage on to the scarred tiles of the great hall itself, into the odorous warmth of a stable, sweet with hay, acrid with horse dung. An equine chorus of neighings and soft drummings of hooves broke out beneath the tall roof, where the beams were scabbed with last summer's swallows' nests; a dozen gracile muzzles lifted from their mangers and turned towards us, ears erect. The Beast had given his horses the use of the dining room. The walls were painted, aptly enough, with a fresco of horses, dogs and men in a wood where fruit and blossom grew on the bough together.

The valet tweaked politely at my sleeve. Milord is waiting.

Gaping doors and broken windows let the wind in everywhere. We mounted one staircase after another, our feet clopping on the marble.

Through archways and open doors, I glimpsed suites of vaulted chambers opening one out of another like systems of Chinese boxes into the infinite complexity of the innards of the place. He and I and the wind were the only things stirring; and all the furniture was under dust sheets, the chandeliers bundled up in cloth, pictures taken from their hooks and propped with their faces to the walls as if their master could not bear to look at them. The palace was dismantled, as if its owner were about to move house or had never properly moved in; The Beast had chosen to live in an uninhabited place.

The valet darted me a reassuring glance from his brown, eloquent eyes, yet a glance with so much queer superciliousness in it that it did not comfort me, and went bounding ahead of me on his bandy legs, softly chattering to himself. I held my head high and followed him; but, for all my pride, my heart was heavy.

Milord has his eyrie high above the house, a small, stifling, darkened room; he keeps his shutters locked at noon. I was out of breath by the time we reached it and returned to him the silence with which he greeted me. I will not smile. He cannot smile.

In his rarely disturbed privacy, The Beast wears a garment of Ottoman design, a loose, dull purple gown with gold embroidery round the neck that falls from his shoulders to conceal his feet. The feet of the chair he sits in are handsomely clawed. He hides his hands in his ample sleeves. The artificial masterpiece of his face appals me. A small fire in a small grate. A rushing wind rattles the shutters.

The valet coughed. To him fell the delicate task of transmitting to me his master's wishes.

'My master –'

A stick fell in the grate. It made a mighty clatter in that dreadful silence; the valet started; lost his place in his speech, began again.

'My master has but one desire.'

The thick, rich, wild scent with which Milord had soaked himself the previous evening hangs all about us, ascends in cursive blue from the smoke of a precious Chinese pot.

'He wishes only –'

Now, in the face of my impassivity, the valet twittered, his ironic composure gone, for the desire of a master, however trivial, may yet sound unbearably insolent in the mouth of a servant and his role of go-between clearly caused him a good deal of embarrassment. He gulped; he swallowed, at last contrived to unleash an unpunctuated flood.

'My master's sole desire is to see the pretty young lady unclothed nude without her dress and that only for the one time after which she will be returned to her father undamaged with bankers' orders for the sum which he lost to my master at cards and also a number of fine presents such as furs, jewels and horses –'

I remained standing. During this interview, my eyes were level with those inside the mask that now evaded mine as if, to his credit, he was ashamed of his own request even as his mouthpiece made it for him. Agitato, molto agitato, the valet wrung his white-gloved hands.

'Desnuda –'

I could scarcely believe my ears. I let out a raucous guffaw; no young lady laughs like that! my old nurse used to remonstrate. But I did. And do. At the clamour of my heartless mirth, the valet danced backwards with perturbation, palpitating his fingers as if attempting to wrench them off, expostulating, wordlessly pleading. I felt that I owed it to him to make my reply in as exquisite a Tuscan as I could master.

'You may put me in a windowless room, sir, and I promise you I will pull my skirt up to my waist, ready for you. But there must be a sheet over my face, to hide it; though the sheet must be laid over me so lightly that it will not choke me. So I shall be covered completely from the waist upwards, and no lights. There you can visit me once, sir, and only the once. After that I must be driven directly to the city and deposited in the public square, in front of the church. If you wish to give me money, then I should be pleased to receive it. But I must stress that you should give me only the same amount of money that you would give to any other woman in such circumstances. However, if you choose not to give me a present, then that is your right.'

How pleased I was to see I struck The Beast to the heart! For, after a baker's dozen heartbeats, one single tear swelled, glittering, at the corner of the masked eye. A tear! A tear, I hoped, of shame. The tear trembled for a moment on an edge of painted bone, then tumbled down the painted cheek to fall, with an abrupt tinkle, on the tiled floor.

The valet, ticking and clucking to himself, hastily ushered me out of the room. A mauve cloud of his master's perfume billowed out into the chill corridor with us and dissipated itself on the spinning winds.

A cell had been prepared for me, a veritable cell, windowless, airless, lightless, in the viscera of the palace. The valet lit a lamp for me; a narrow bed, a dark cupboard with fruit and flowers carved on it bulked out of the gloom.

'I shall twist a noose out of my bed linen and hang myself with it,' I said.

'Oh, no,' said the valet, fixing upon me wide and suddenly melancholy eyes. 'Oh, no, you will not. You are a woman of honour.'

And what was *he* doing in my bedroom, this jigging caricature of a man? Was he to be my warder until I submitted to The Beast's whim or he to mine? Am I in such reduced circumstances that I may not have a lady's maid? As if in reply to my unspoken demand, the valet clapped his hands.

'To assuage your loneliness, madame . . .'

A knocking and clattering behind the door of the cupboard; the door swings open and out glides a soubrette from an operetta, with glossy, nut-brown curls, rosy cheeks, blue, rolling eyes; it takes me a moment to recognize her, in her little cap, her white stockings, her frilled petticoats. She carries a looking glass in one hand and a powder puff in the other and there is a musical box where her heart should be; she tinkles as she rolls towards me on her tiny wheels.

'Nothing human lives here,' said the valet.

My maid halted, bowed; from a split seam at the side of her bodice protrudes the handle of a key. She is a marvellous machine, the most delicately balanced system of cords and pulleys in the world.

'We have dispensed with servants,' the valet said. 'We surround ourselves, instead, for utility and pleasure, with simulacra and find it no less convenient than do most gentlemen.'

This clockwork twin of mine halted before me, her bowels churning out a settecento minuet, and offered me the bold carnation of her smile. Click, click – she raises her arm and busily dusts my cheeks with pink, powdered chalk that makes me cough; then thrusts towards me her little mirror.

I saw within it not my own face but that of my father, as if I had put on his face when I arrived at The Beast's palace as the discharge of his debt. What, you self-deluding fool, are you crying still? And drunk, too. He tossed back his grappa and hurled the tumbler away.

Seeing my astonished fright, the valet took the mirror away from me, breathed on it, polished it with the ham of his gloved fist, handed it back to me. Now all I saw was myself, haggard from a sleepless night, pale enough to need my maid's supply of rouge.

I heard the key turn in the heavy door and the valet's footsteps patter down the stone passage. Meanwhile, my double continued to powder the air, emitting her jangling tune but, as it turned out, she was not inexhaustible; soon she was powdering more and yet more languorously, her metal heart slowed in imitation of fatigue, her musical box ran down until the notes separated themselves out of the tune and plopped like single raindrops and, as if sleep had overtaken her, at last she moved no longer. As she succumbed to sleep, I had no option but to do so, too. I dropped on that narrow bed as if felled.

Time passed but I do not know how much; then the valet woke me with rolls and honey. I gestured the tray away but he set it down firmly beside the lamp and took from it a little shagreen box, which he offered to me.

I turned away my head.

'Oh, my lady!' Such hurt cracked his high-pitched voice! He dextrously unfastened the gold clasp: on a bed of crimson velvet lay a single diamond earring, perfect as a tear.

I snapped the box shut and tossed it into a corner. This sudden, sharp movement must have disturbed the mechanism of the doll; she jerked her arm almost as if to reprimand me, letting out a rippling fart of gavotte. Then was still again.

'Very well,' said the valet, put out. And indicated it was time for me to visit my host again. He did not let me wash or comb my hair. There was so little natural light in the interior of the palace that I could not tell whether it was day or night.

You would not think The Beast had budged an inch since I last saw him; he sat in his huge chair, with his hands in his sleeves, and the heavy air never moved. I might have slept an hour, a night, or a month, but his sculptured calm, the stifling air remained just as it had been. The incense rose from the pot, still traced the same signature on the air. The same fire burned.

Take off my clothes for you, like a ballet girl? Is that all you want of me?

'The sight of a young lady's skin that no man has seen before –' stammered the valet.

I wished I'd rolled in the hay with every lad on my father's farm, to disqualify myself from this humiliating bargain. That he should want so little was the reason why I could not give it; I did not need to speak for The Beast to understand me.

A tear came from his other eye. And then he moved; he buried his cardboard carnival head with its ribboned weight of false hair in, I would say, his arms; he withdrew his, I might say, hands from his sleeves and I saw his furred pads, his excoriating claws.

The dropped tear caught upon his fur and shone. And in my room for hours I hear those paws pad back and forth outside my door.

When the valet arrived again with his silver salver, I had a pair of diamond earrings of the finest water in the world; I threw the other into the corner where the first one lay. The valet twittered with aggrieved regret but did not offer to lead me to The Beast again. Instead, he smiled ingratiatingly and confided: 'My master, he say: invite the young lady to go riding.'

'What's this?'

He briskly mimicked the action of a gallop and, to my amazement, tunelessly croaked: 'Tantivy! tantivy! a-hunting we will go!'

'I'll run away, I'll ride to the city.'

'Oh, no,' he said. 'Are you not a woman of honour?'

He clapped his hands and my maidservant clicked and jangled into the imitation of life. She rolled towards the cupboard where she had come from and reached inside it to fetch out over her synthetic arm my riding habit. Of all things. My very own riding habit, that I'd left behind me in a trunk in a loft in that country house outside Petersburg that we'd lost long ago, before, even, we set out on this wild pilgrimage to the cruel South. Either the very riding habit my old nurse had sewn for me or else a copy of it perfect to the lost button on the right sleeve, the ripped hem held up with a pin. I turned the worn cloth about in my hands, looking for a clue. The wind that sprinted through the palace made the door tremble in its frame; had the north wind blown my garments across Europe to me? At home, the bear's son directed the winds at his pleasure; what democracy of magic held this palace and the fir forest in common? Or, should I be prepared to accept it as proof of the axiom my father had drummed into me: that, if you have enough money, anything is possible?

'Tantivy,' suggested the now twinkling valet, evidently charmed at the pleasure mixed with my bewilderment. The clockwork maid held my jacket out to me and I allowed myself to shrug into it as if reluctantly, although I was half mad to get out into the open air, away from this deathly palace, even in such company.

The doors of the hall let the bright day in; I saw that it was morning. Our horses, saddled and bridled, beasts in bondage, were waiting for us, striking sparks from the tiles with their impatient hooves while their stablemates lolled at ease among the straw, conversing with one another in the mute speech of horses. A pigeon or two, feathers puffed to keep out the cold, strutted about, pecking at ears of corn. The little black gelding who had brought me here greeted me with a ringing neigh that resonated inside the misty roof as in a sounding box and I knew he was meant for me to ride.

I always adored horses, noblest of creatures, such wounded sensitivity in their wise eyes, such rational restraint of energy at their high-strung hindquarters. I lirruped and hurrumphed to my shining black companion and he acknowledged my greeting with a kiss on the forehead from his soft lips. There was a little shaggy pony nuzzling away at the *trompe l'oeil* foliage beneath the hooves of the painted horses on the wall, into whose saddle the valet sprang with a flourish as of the circus. Then The Beast, wrapped in a black fur-lined cloak, came to heave himself aloft a grave grey mare. No natural horseman he; he clung to her mane like a shipwrecked sailor to a spar.

Cold, that morning, yet dazzling with the sharp winter sunlight that wounds the retina. There was a scurrying wind about that seemed to go with us, as if the masked, immense one who did not speak carried it inside his cloak and let it out at his pleasure, for it stirred the horses' manes but did not lift the lowland mists.

A bereft landscape in the sad browns and sepias of winter lay all about us, the marshland drearily protracting itself towards the wide river. Those decapitated willows. Now and then, the swoop of a bird, its irreconcilable cry.

A profound sense of strangeness slowly began to possess me. I knew my two companions were not, in any way, as other men, the simian retainer and the master for whom he spoke, the one with clawed forepaws who was in a plot with the witches who let the winds out of their knotted handkerchiefs up towards the Finnish border. I knew they lived according to a different logic than I had done until my father abandoned me to the wild beasts by his human carelessness. This knowledge gave me a certain fearfulness still; but, I would say, not much . . . I was a young girl, a virgin, and therefore men denied me rationality just as they denied it to all those who were not exactly like themselves, in all their unreason. If I could see not one single soul in that wilderness of desolation all around me, then the six of us – mounts and riders, both – could boast amongst us not one soul, either, since all the best religions in the world state categorically that not beasts nor women were equipped with the flimsy, insubstantial things when the good Lord opened the gates of Eden and let Eve and her familiars tumble out. Understand, then, that though I would not say I privately engaged in metaphysical speculation as we rode through the reedy approaches to the river, I certainly meditated on the nature of my own state, how I had been bought and sold, passed from hand to hand. That clockwork girl who powdered my cheeks for me; had I not been allotted only the same kind of imitative life amongst men that the doll-maker had given her?

Yet, as to the true nature of the being of this clawed magus who rode his pale horse in a style that made me recall how Kublai Khan's leopards went out hunting on horseback, of that I had no notion.

We came to the bank of the river that was so wide we could not see across it, so still with winter that it scarcely seemed to flow. The horses lowered their heads to drink. The valet cleared his throat, about to speak; we were in a place of perfect privacy, beyond a brake of winter – bare rushes, a hedge of reeds.

'If you will not let him see you without your clothes –'

I involuntarily shook my head –

'– you must, then, prepare yourself for the sight of my master, naked.'

The river broke on the pebbles with a diminishing sigh. My composure deserted me; all at once I was on the brink of panic. I did not think that I could bear the sight of him, whatever he was. The mare raised her dripping muzzle and looked at me keenly, as if urging me. This river broke again at my feet. I was far from home.

'You,' said the valet, 'must.'

When I saw how scared he was I might refuse, I nodded.

The reed bowed down in a sudden snarl of wind that brought with it a gust of the heavy odour of his disguise. The valet held out his master's cloak to screen him from me as he removed the mask. The horses stirred.

The tiger will never lie down with the lamb; he acknowledges no pact that is not reciprocal. The lamb must learn to run with the tigers.

A great, feline, tawny shape whose pelt was barred with a savage geometry of bars the colour of burned wood. His domed, heavy head, so terrible he must hide it. How subtle the muscles, how profound the tread. The annihilating vehemence of his eyes, like twin suns.

I felt my breast ripped apart as if I suffered a marvellous wound.

The valet moved forward as if to cover up his master now the girl had acknowledged him, but I said: 'No.' The tiger sat still as a heraldic beast, in the pact he had made with his own ferocity to do me no harm. He was far larger than I could have imagined, from the poor, shabby things I'd seen once, in the Czar's menagerie at Petersburg, the golden fruit of their eyes dimming, withering in the far North of captivity. Nothing about him reminded me of humanity.

I therefore, shivering, now unfastened my jacket, to show him I would do him no harm. Yet I was clumsy and blushed a little, for no man had seen me naked and I was a proud girl. Pride it was, not shame, that thwarted my fingers so; and a certain trepidation lest this frail little article of human upholstery before him might not be, in itself, grand enough to satisfy his expectations of us, since those, for all I knew, might have grown infinite during the endless time he had been waiting. The wind clattered in the rushes, purled and eddied in the river.

I showed his grave silence my white skin, my red nipples, and the horses turned their heads to watch me, also, as if they, too, were courteously curious as to the fleshly nature of women. Then The Beast lowered his massive head; Enough! said the valet with a gesture. The wind died down, all was still again.

Then they went off together, the valet on his pony, the tiger running before him like a hound, and I walked along the river bank for a while. I felt I was at liberty for the first time in my life. Then the winter sun began to tarnish, a few flakes of snow drifted from the darkening sky and, when

I returned to the horses, I found The Beast mounted again on his grey mare, cloaked and masked and once more, to all appearances, a man, while the valet had a fine catch of waterfowl dangling from his hand and the corpse of a young roebuck slung behind his saddle. I climbed up on the black gelding in silence and so we returned to the palace as the snow fell more and more heavily, obscuring the tracks that we had left behind us.

The valet did not return me to my cell but, instead, to an elegant, if old-fashioned boudoir with sofas of faded pink brocade, a jinn's treasury of Oriental carpets, tintinnabulation of cut-glass chandeliers. Candles in antlered holders struck rainbows from the prismatic hearts of my diamond earrings, that lay on my new dressing table at which my attentive maid stood ready with her powder puff and mirror. Intending to fix the ornaments in my ears, I took the looking glass from her hand, but it was in the midst of one of its magic fits again and I did not see my own face in it but that of my father; at first I thought he smiled at me. Then I saw he was smiling with pure gratification.

He sat, I saw, in the parlour of our lodgings, at the very table where he had lost me, but now he was busily engaged in counting out a tremendous pile of banknotes. My father's circumstances had changed already; well-shaven, neatly barbered, smart new clothes. A frosted glass of sparkling wine sat convenient to his hand beside an ice bucket. The Beast had clearly paid cash on the nail for his glimpse of my bosom, and paid up promptly, as if it had not been a sight I might have died of showing. Then I saw my father's trunks were packed, ready for departure. Could he so easily leave me here?

There was a note on the table with the money, in a fine hand. I could read it quite clearly. 'The young lady will arrive immediately.' Some harlot with whom he'd briskly negotiated a liaison on the strength of his spoils? Not at all. For, at that moment, the valet knocked at my door to announce that I might leave the palace at any time hereafter, and he bore over his arm a handsome sable cloak, my very own little gratuity, The Beast's morning gift, in which he proposed to pack me up and send me off.

When I looked at the mirror again, my father had disappeared and all I saw was a pale, hollow-eyed girl whom I scarcely recognized. The valet asked politely when he should prepare the carriage, as if he did not doubt that I would leave with my booty at the first opportunity while my maid, whose face was no longer the spit of my own, continued bonnily to beam.

I will dress her in my own clothes, wind her up, send her back to perform the part of my father's daughter.

'Leave me alone,' I said to the valet.

He did not need to lock the door, now. I fixed the earrings in my ears. They were very heavy. Then I took off my riding habit, left it where it lay on the floor. But, when I got down to my shift, my arms dropped to my sides. I was unaccustomed to nakedness. I was so unused to my own skin that to take off all my clothes involved a kind of flaying. I thought The Beast had wanted a little thing compared with what I was prepared to give him; but it is not natural for humankind to go naked, not since first we hid our loins with fig leaves. He had demanded the abominable. I felt as much atrocious pain as if I was stripping off my own underpelt and the smiling girl stood poised in the oblivion of her balked simulation of life, watching me peel down to the cold, white meat of contract and, if she did not see me, then so much more like the market place, where the eyes that watch you take no account of your existence.

And it seemed my entire life, since I had left the North, had passed under the indifferent gaze of eyes like hers.

Then I was flinching stark, except for his irreproachable tears.

I huddled in the furs I must return to him, to keep me from the lacerating winds that raced along the corridors. I knew the way to his den without the valet to guide me.

No response to my tentative rap on his door.

Then the wind blew the valet whirling along the passage. He must have decided that, if one should go naked, then all should go naked; without his livery, he revealed himself, as I had suspected, a delicate creature, covered with silken moth-grey fur, brown fingers supple as leather, chocolate muzzle, the gentlest creature in the world. He gibbered a little to see my fine furs and jewels as if I were dressed up for the opera and, with a great deal of tender ceremony, removed the sables from my shoulders. The sables thereupon resolved themselves into a pack of black, squeaking rats that rattled immediately down the stairs on their hard little feet and were lost to sight.

The valet bowed me inside The Beast's room.

The purple dressing gown, the mask, the wig, were laid out on his chair; a glove was planted on each arm. The empty house of his appearance was ready for him but he had abandoned it. There was a reek of fur and piss; the incense pot lay broken in pieces on the floor. Half-burned sticks were scattered from the extinguished fire. A candle stuck by its own grease to the mantelpiece lit two narrow flames in the pupils of the tiger's eyes.

He was pacing backwards and forwards, backwards and forwards, the tip of his heavy tail twitching as he paced out the length and breadth of his imprisonment between the gnawed and bloody bones.

He will gobble you up.

Nursery fears made flesh and sinew; earliest and most archaic of fears, fear of devourment. The beast and his carnivorous bed of bone and I, white, shaking, raw, approaching him as if offering, in myself, the key to a peaceable kingdom in which his appetite need not be my extinction.

He went still as stone. He was far more frightened of me than I was of him.

I squatted on the wet straw and stretched out my hand. I was now within the field of force of his golden eyes. He growled at the back of his throat, lowered his head, sank on to his forepaws, snarled, showed me his red gullet, his yellow teeth. I never moved. He snuffed the air, as if to smell my fear; he could not.

Slowly, slowly he began to drag his heavy, gleaming weight across the floor towards me.

A tremendous throbbing, as of the engine that makes the earth turn, filled the little room; he had begun to purr.

The sweet thunder of this purr shook the old walls, made the shutters batter the windows until they burst apart and let in the white light of the snowy moon. Tiles came crashing down from the roof; I heard them fall into the courtyard far below. The reverberations of his purring rocked the foundations of the house, the walls began to dance. I thought: 'It will all fall, everything will disintegrate.'

He dragged himself closer and closer to me, until I felt the harsh velvet of his head against my hand, then a tongue, abrasive as sandpaper. 'He will lick the skin off me!'

And each stroke of his tongue ripped off skin after successive skin, all the skins of a life in the world, and left behind a nascent patina of shining hairs. My earrings turned back to water and trickled down my shoulders; I shrugged the drops off my beautiful fur.

71

MARIAMA BÂ

Born 1929, Dakar, Senegal
Died 1981, Dakar, Senegal

from *So Long a Letter*
1979

My own crisis came three years after yours. But unlike your case, the source was not my family-in-law. The problem was rooted in Modou himself, my husband.

My daughter Daba, who was preparing for her *baccalauréat*, often brought some of her classmates home with her. Most of the time it was the same young girl, a bit shy frail, made noticeably uncomfortable by our style of life. But she was really beautiful in this her adolescent period, in her faded but clean clothes! Her beauty shone, pure. Her shapely contours could not but be noticed.

I sometimes noticed that Modou was interested in the pair. Neither was I worried when I heard him suggest that he should take Binetou home in the car – 'because it was getting late,' he would say.

Binetou was going through a metamorphosis, however. She was now wearing very expensive off-the-peg dresses. Smilingly, she would explain to my daughter: 'Oh, I have a sugar-daddy who pays for them.'

Then one day, on her return from school, Daba confided to me that Binetou had a serious problem: 'The sugar-daddy of the boutique dresses wants to marry Binetou. Just imagine. Her parents want to withdraw her from school, with only a few months to go before the *bac*, to marry her off to the sugar-daddy'

'Advise her to refuse,' I said.

'And if the man in question offers her a villa, Mecca for her parents, a car, a monthly allowance, jewels?'

'None of that is worth the capital of youth.'

'I agree with you, Mum. I'll tell Binetou not to give in; but her mother is a woman who wants so much to escape from mediocrity and who regrets so much her past beauty, faded in the smoke from the wood fires, that she looks enviously at everything I wear; she complains all day long.'

'What is important is Binetou herself. She must not give in.'

And then, a few days afterwards, Daba renewed the conversation, with its surprising conclusion.

'Mum! Binetou is heartbroken. She is going to marry her sugar-daddy. Her mother cried so much. She begged her daughter to give her life a happy end, in a proper house, as the man has promised them. So she accepted.'

'When is the wedding?'

'This coming Sunday, but there'll be no reception. Binetou cannot bear the mockery of her friends'.

And in the evening of this same Sunday on which Binetou was being married off I saw come into my house, all dressed up and solemn, Tamsir, Modou's brother, with Mawdo B and his local *Imam*. Where had they come from, looking so awkward in their starched *boubous*? Doubtless, they had come looking for Modou to carry out an important task that one of them had been charged with. I told them that Modou had been out since morning. They entered laughing, deliberately sniffing the fragrant odour of incense that was floating on the air. I sat in front of them, laughing with them. The *Imam* attacked:

'There is nothing one can do when Allah the almighty puts two people side by side'.

'True, true', said the other two in support.

A pause. He took a breath and continued: 'There is nothing new in this world'.

'True, true', Tamsir and Mawdo chimed in again.

'Some things we may find to be sad are much less so than others . . .'

I followed the movement of the haughty lips that let fall these axioms, which can precede the announcement of either a happy event or an unhappy one. What was he leading up to with these preliminaries that rather announced a storm? So their visit was obviously planned.

Does one announce bad news dressed up like that in one's Sunday best? Or did they want to inspire confidence with their impeccable dress?

I thought of the absent once. I asked with the cry of a hunted beast: 'Modou?'

And the *Imam*, who had finally got hold of a leading thread, held tightly on to it. He went on quickly, as if the words were glowing embers in his mouth: 'Yes, Modou Fall, but, happily, he is alive for you, for all of us, thanks be to God. All he has done is to marry a second wife today. We have just come from the mosque in Grand Dakar where the marriage took place.'

The thorns thus removed from the way, Tamsir ventured: 'Modou sends his thanks. He says it is fate that decides men and things: God intended him to have a second wife, there is nothing he can do about it. He praises you for the quarter of a century of marriage in which you gave him all the happiness a wife owes her husband. His family, especially myself, his elder brother, thank you. You have always held us in respect. You know that we are Modou's blood.'

Afterwards there were the same old words, which were intended to relieve the situation: 'You are the only one in your house, no matter how big it is, no matter how dear life is. You are the first wife, a mother for Modou, a friend for Modou.'

Tamsir's Adam's apple danced about in his throat. He shook his left leg, crossed over his folded right leg, His shoes, white Turkish slippers, were covered with a thin layer of red dust, the colour of the earth in which they had walked. The same dust covered Mawdo's and the *Imam*'s shoes.

Mawdo said nothing. He was reliving his own experience. He was thinking of your letter, your reaction, and you and I were so alike. He was being wary. He kept his head lowered, in the attitude of those who accept defeat before the battle.

I acquiesced under the drops of poison that were burning me: 'A quarter of a century of marriage', 'a wife unparalleled'. I counted backwards to determine where the break in the thread had occurred from which everything had unwound. My mother's words came back to me: 'too perfect . . .' I completed at last my mother's thought with the end of the dictum: '. . . to be honest'. I thought of the first two incisors with a wide gap between them, the sign of the primacy of love in the individual. I thought of his absence, all day long. He had simply said: 'Don't expect me for lunch.' I thought of other absences, quite frequent these days, crudely clarified today yet well hidden yesterday under the guise of trade union meetings. He was also on a strict diet, 'to break the stomach's egg', he would say laughingly, this egg that announced old age.

Every night when he went out he would unfold and try on several of his suits before settling on one. The others, impatiently rejected, would slip to the floor. I would have to fold them again and put them back in their places; and this extra work, I discovered, I was doing only to help him in his effort to be elegant in his seduction of another woman.

I forced myself to check my inner agitation. Above all, I must not give my visitors the pleasure of relating my distress. Smile, take the matter lightly, just as they announced it. Thank them for the humane way in which they have accomplished their mission. Send thanks to Modou, 'a good father and a good husband', 'a husband become a friend'. Thank my family-in-law, the *Imam*, Mawdo. Smile. Give them something to drink. See them out, under the swirls of incense that they were sniffing once again. Shake their hands.

How pleased they were, all except Mawdo, who correctly judged the import of the event.

Alone at last, able to give free rein to my surprise and to gauge my distress. Ah! yes, I forgot to ask for my rival's name so that I might give a human form to my pain.

My question was soon answered. Acquaintances from Grand Dakar came rushing to my house, bringing the various details of the ceremony. Some of them did so out of true friendship for me; others were spiteful and jealous of the promotion Binetou's mother would gain from the marriage.

'I don't understand.' They did not understand either the entrance of Modou, a 'personality', into this extremely poor family.

Binetou, a child the same age as my daughter Daba, promoted, to the rank of my co-wife, whom I must face up to. Shy Binetou! The old man who bought her the new off-the-peg dresses to replace the old faded ones was none other than Modou. She had innocently confided her secrets to her rival's daughter because she thought that this dream, sprung from a brain growing old, would never become reality. She had told everything: the villa, the monthly allowance, the offer of a future trip to Mecca for her parents. She thought she was stronger than the man she was dealing with. She did not know Modou's strong will, his tenacity before an obstacle, the pride he invests in winning, the resistance that inspires new attempts at each failure.

Daba was furious, her pride wounded. She repeated all the nicknames Binetou had given her father: old man, pot-belly, sugar-daddy! . . . the person who gave her life had been daily ridiculed and he accepted it. An overwhelming anger raged inside Daba. She knew that her best friend was sincere in what she said. But what can a child do, faced with a furious mother shouting about her hunger and her thirst to live?

Binetou, like many others, was a lamb slaughtered on the altar of affluence. Daba's anger increased as she analysed the situation: 'Break with him, mother! Send this man away. He has respected neither you nor me. Do what Aunty Aissatou did; break with him. Tell me you'll break with him. I can't see you fighting over a man with a girl my age'.

I told myself what every betrayed woman says: if Modou was milk, it was I who had had all the cream. The rest, well, nothing but water with a vague smell of milk.

But the final decision lay with me. With Modou absent all night (was he already consummating his marriage?), the solitude that lends counsel enabled me to grasp the problem.

Leave? Start again at zero, after living twenty-five years with one man, after having borne twelve children? Did I have enough energy to bear alone the weight of this responsibility, which was both moral and material?

Leave! Draw a clean line through the past. Turn over a page on which not everything was bright, certainly, but at least all was clear. What would now be recorded there would hold no love, confidence, grandeur or hope. I had never known the sordid side of marriage. Don't get to know it! Run from it! When one begins to forgive, there is an avalanche of faults that comes crashing down, and the only thing that remains is to forgive again, to keep on forgiving. Leave, escape from betrayal! Sleep without asking myself any questions, without straining my ear at the slightest noise, waiting for a husband I share.

I counted the abandoned or divorced women of my generation whom I knew.

I knew a few whose remaining beauty had been able to capture a worthy man, a man who added fine bearing to a good situation and who was considered 'better, a hundred times better than his predecessor'. The misery that was the lot of these women was rolled back with the invasion of the new happiness that changed their lives, filled out their cheeks, brightened their eyes. I knew others who had lost all hope of renewal and whom loneliness had very quickly laid underground.

The play of destiny remains impenetrable. The cowries that a female neighbor throws on a fan in front of me do not fill me with optimism, neither when they remain face upwards, showing the black hollow that signifies laughter, nor when the grouping of their white backs seems to say that 'the man in the double trousers' is coming towards me, the promise of wealth. 'The only thing that separates you from them, man and wealth, is the alms of two white and red cola nuts', adds Farmata, my neighbour.

She insists: 'There is a saying that discord here may be luck elsewhere. Why are you afraid to make the break? A woman is like a ball; once a ball is thrown, no one can predict where it will bounce. You have no control over where it rolls, and even less over who gets it. Often it is grabbed by an unexpected hand . . .'

Instead of listening to the reasoning of my neighbour, a *griot* woman who dreams of the generous tips due to the go-between, I looked at myself in the mirror. My eyes took in the mirror's eloquence. I had lost my slim figure, as well as ease and quickness of movement. My stomach protruded from beneath the wrapper that hid the calves developed by the impressive number of kilometers walked since the beginning of my existence. Suckling had robbed my breasts of their round firmness. I could not delude myself: youth was deserting my body.

Whereas a woman draws from the passing years the force of her devotion, despite the ageing of her companion, a man, on the other hand, restricts his field of tenderness. His egoistic eye looks over his partner's shoulder. He compares what he had with what he no longer has, what he has with what he could have.

I had heard of too many misfortunes not to understand my own. There was your own case, Aissatou, the cases of many other women, despised, relegated or exchanged, who were abandoned like a worn-out or out-dated *boubou*.

399

To overcome distress when it sits upon you demands strong will. When one thinks that with each passing second one's life is shortened, one must profit intensely from this second; it is the sum of all the lost or harvested seconds that makes for a wasted or a successful life. Brace oneself to check despair and get it into proportion! A nervous breakdown waits around the corner for anyone who lets himself wallow in bitterness. Little by little, it takes over your whole being.

Oh, nervous breakdown! Doctors speak of it in a detached, ironical way, emphasizing that the vital organs are in no way disturbed. You are lucky if they don't tell you that you are wasting their time with the ever-growing list of your illnesses – your head, throat, chest, heart, liver – that no X-ray can confirm. And yet what atrocious suffering is caused by nervous breakdowns!

And I think of Jacqueline, who suffered from one. Jacqueline, the Ivorian, had disobeyed her Protestant parents and has married Samba Diack, a contemporary of Mawdo Bâ's, a doctor like him, who, on leaving the African School of Medicine and Pharmacy, was posted to Abidjan. Jacqueline often came round to see us, since her husband often visited our household. Coming to Senegal, she found herself in a new world, a world with different reactions, temperament and mentality from that in which she had grown up. In addition, her husband's relatives – always the relatives – were cool towards her because she refused to adopt the Muslim religion and went instead to the Protestant church every Sunday.

A black African, she should have been able to fit without difficulty into a black African society, Senegal and the Ivory Coast both having experienced the same colonial power. But Africa is diverse, divided. The same country can change its character and outlook several times over, from north to south or from east to west.

Jacqueline truly wanted to become Senegalese, but the mockery checked all desire in her to co-operate. People called her *gnac*, and she finally understood the meaning of this nickname that revolted her so.

Her husband, making up for lost time, spent his time chasing slender Senegalese women, as he would say with appreciation, and did not bother to hide his adventures, respecting neither his wife nor his children. His lack of precautions brought to Jacqueline's knowledge the irrefutable proof of his misconduct: love notes, cheque stubs bearing the names of the payees, bills from restaurants and for hotel rooms. Jacqueline cried; Samba Diack 'lived it up'. Jacqueline lost weight; Samba Diack was still living fast. Jacqueline complained of a disturbing lump in her chest, under her left breast; she said she had the impression that a sharp point had pierced her there and was cutting through her flesh right to her very bones. She fretted. Mawdo listened to her heart: nothing wrong there, he would say. He prescribed some tranquillizers. Eagerly, Jacqueline took the tablets, tortured by the insidious pain. The bottle empty, she noticed that the lump remained in the same place; she continued to feel the pain just as acutely as ever.

She consulted a doctor from her own country, who ordered an electro-cardiogram and various blood tests. Nothing to be learned from the electric reading of the heart, nothing abnormal found in the blood. He too prescribed tranquillizers, big, effervescent tablets that could not allay poor Jacqueline's distress.

She thought of her parents, of their refusal to consent to her marriage. She wrote them a pathetic letter, in which she begged for their forgiveness. They sent their sincere blessing but could do nothing to lighten the strange weight in her chest.

72.

ADRIENNE RICH

Born 1929, Baltimore, Maryland, United States of America
Died 2012, Santa Cruz, California, United States of America

from *Compulsory Heterosexuality and Lesbian Existence*
1980

Woman identification is a source of energy, a potential springhead of female power, curtailed and contained under the institution of heterosexuality. The denial of reality and visibility to women's passion for women, women's choice of women as allies, life companions, and community, the forcing of such relationships into dissimulation and their disintegration under intense pressure have meant an incalculable loss to the power of all women *to change the social relations of the sexes, to liberate ourselves and each other.* The lie of compulsory female heterosexuality today afflicts not just feminist scholarship, but every profession, every reference work, every curriculum, every organizing attempt, every relationship or conversation over which it hovers. It creates, specifically, a profound falseness, hypocrisy, and hysteria in the heterosexual dialogue, for every heterosexual relationship is lived in the queasy strobe light of that lie. However we choose to identify ourselves, however we find ourselves labeled, it flickers across and distorts our lives.*

The lie keeps numberless women psychologically trapped, trying to fit mind, spirit, and sexuality into a prescribed script because they cannot look beyond the parameters of the acceptable. It pulls on the energy of such women even as it drains the energy of 'closeted' lesbians – the energy exhausted in the double life. The lesbian trapped in the 'closet,' the woman

---

* See Russell and van de Ven, p. 40: 'Few heterosexual women realize their lack of free choice about their sexuality, and few realize how and why compulsory heterosexuality is also a crime against them.'

imprisoned in prescriptive ideas of the 'normal' share the pain of blocked options, broken connections, lost access to self-definition freely and powerfully assumed.

The lie is many-layered. In Western tradition, one layer – the romantic – asserts that women are inevitably, even if rashly and tragically, drawn to men; that even when that attraction is suicidal (e.g., *Tristan and Isolde*, Kate Chopin's *The Awakening*), it is still an organic imperative. In the tradition of the social sciences it asserts that primary love between the sexes is 'normal'; that women *need* men as social and economic protectors, for adult sexuality, and for psychological completion; that the heterosexually constituted family is the basic social unit; that women who do not attach their primary intensity to men must be, in functional terms, condemned to an even more devastating outsiderhood than their outsiderhood as women. Small wonder that lesbians are reported to be a more hidden population than male homosexuals. The Black lesbian-feminist critic Lorraine Bethel, writing on Zora Neale Hurston, remarks that for a Black woman – already twice an outsider – to Choose to assume still another 'hated identity' is problematic indeed. Yet the lesbian continuum has been a life line for Black women both in Africa and the United States.

> Black women have a long tradition of bonding together . . . in a Black/women's community that has been a source of vital survival information, psychic and emotional support for us. We have a distinct Black woman-identified folk culture based on our experiences as Black women in this society; symbols, language and modes of expression that are specific to the realities of our lives. . . . Because Black women were rarely among those Blacks and females who gained access to literary and other acknowledged forms of artistic expression, this Black female bonding and Black woman-identification has often been hidden and unrecorded except in the individual lives of Black women through our own memories of our particular Black female tradition.*

Another layer of the lie is the frequently encountered implication that women turn to women out of hatred for men. Profound skepticism, caution,

---

* Bethel, "'This infinity of Conscious Pain,'" *op. cit.*

and righteous paranoia about men may indeed be part of any healthy woman's response to the misogyny of male-dominated culture, to the forms assumed by 'normal' male sexuality, and to *the failure even of 'sensitive' or 'political' men to perceive or find these troubling*. Lesbian existence is also represented as mere refuge from male abuses, rather than as an electric and empowering charge between women. One of the most frequently quoted literary passages on lesbian relationship is that in which Colette's Renée, in *The Vagabond*, describes 'the melancholy and touching image of two weak creatures who have perhaps found shelter in each other's arms, there to sleep and weep, safe from man who is often cruel, and there to taste *better than any pleasure, the bitter happiness of feeling themselves akin, frail and forgotten* [emphasis added].'* Colette is often considered a lesbian writer. Her popular reputation has, I think, much to do with the fact that she writes about lesbian existence as if for a male audience; her earliest 'lesbian' novels, the Claudine series, were written under compulsion for her husband and published under both their names. At all events, except for her writings on her mother, Colette is a less reliable source on the lesbian continuum than, I would think, Charlotte Brontë, who understood that while women may, indeed must, be one another's allies, mentors, and comforters in the female struggle for survival, there is quite extraneous delight in each other's company and attraction to each others' minds and character, which attend a recognition of each others' strengths.

By the same token, we can say that there is a *nascent* feminist political content in the act of choosing a woman lover or life partner in the face of institutionalized heterosexuality.† But for lesbian existence to realize this political content in an ultimately liberating form, the erotic choice must deepen and expand into conscious woman identification – into lesbian feminism.

The work that lies ahead, of unearthing and describing what I call here 'Lesbian existence,' is potentially liberating for all women. It is work that must assuredly move beyond the limits of white and middle-class Western

---

* Dinnerstein, the most recent writer to quote this passage, adds ominously: 'But what has to be added to her account is that these "women enlaced" are sheltering each other not just from what men want to do to them, but also from what they want to do to each other' (Dinnerstein, p. 103). The fact is, however, that woman-to-woman violence is a minute grain in the universe of male-against-female violence perpetuated and rationalized in every social institution.

† Conversation with Blanche W. Cook, New York City, March 1979.

Women's Studies to examine women's lives, work, and groupings within every racial, ethnic, and political structure. There are differences, moreover, between 'lesbian existence' and the 'lesbian continuum,' differences we can discern even in the movement of our own lives. The lesbian continuum, I suggest, needs delineation in light of the 'double life' of women, not only women self-described as heterosexual but also of self-described lesbians. We need a far more exhaustive account of the forms the double life has assumed. Historians need to ask at every point how heterosexuality as institution has been organized and maintained through the female wage scale, the enforcement of middle-class women's 'leisure,' the glamorization of so-called sexual liberation, the withholding of education from women, the imagery of 'high art' and popular culture, the mystification of the 'personal' sphere, and much else. We need an economics which comprehends the institution of heterosexuality, with its doubled workload for women and its sexual divisions of labor, as the most idealized of economic relations.

The question inevitably will arise: Are we then to condemn all heterosexual relationships, including those which are least oppressive? I believe this question, though often heartfelt, is the wrong question here. We have been stalled in a maze of false dichotomies which prevents our apprehending the institution as a whole: 'good' versus 'bad' marriages; 'marriage for love' versus arranged marriage; 'liberated' sex versus prostitution; heterosexual intercourse versus rape; *Liebeschmerz* versus humiliation and dependency. Within the institution exist, of course, qualitative differences of experience; but the absence of choice remains the great unacknowledged reality, and in the absence of choice, women will remain dependent upon the chance or luck of particular relationships and will have no collective power to determine the meaning and place of sexuality in their lives. As we address the institution itself, moreover, we begin to perceive a history of female resistance which has never fully understood itself because it has been so fragmented, miscalled, erased. It will require a courageous grasp of the politics and economics, as well as the cultural propaganda, of heterosexuality to carry us beyond individual cases or diversified group situations into the complex kind of overview needed to undo the power men everywhere wield over women, power which has become a model for every other form of exploitation and illegitimate control.

73.

ASSOCIATION OF AFRICAN WOMEN FOR RESEARCH AND DEVELOPMENT (AAWORD)

Founded in Dakar, Senegal in December 1977 by African women researchers

A Statement on Genital Mutilation

1980

In the last few years, Western public opinion has been shocked to find out that in the middle of the 20th Century thousands of women and children have been 'savagely mutilated' because of 'barbarous customs from another age'. The good conscience of Western society has once again been shaken. Something must be done to help these people, to show public disapproval of such acts.

There have been press conferences, documentary films, headlines in the newspapers, information days, open letters, action groups – all this to mobilize public opinion and put pressure on governments of the countries where genital mutilation is still practised.

This new crusade of the West has been led out of the moral and cultural prejudices of Judaeo-Christian Western society: aggressiveness, ignorance or even contempt, paternalism and activism are the elements which have infuriated and then shocked many people of good will. In trying to reach their own public, the new crusaders have fallen back on sensationalism, and have become insensitive to the dignity of the very women they want to 'save'. They are totally unconscious of the latent racism which such a campaign evokes in countries where ethnocentric prejudice is so deep-rooted. And in their conviction that this is a 'just cause', they have forgotten that these women from a different race and a different culture are also *human beings*, and that solidarity can only exist alongside self-affirmation and mutual respect.

This campaign has aroused three kinds of reaction in Africa

1) the highly conservative, which stresses the right of cultural differ-ence and the defence of traditional values and practices whose supposed aim is to protect and elevate women; this view denies Westerners the right to interfere in problems related to culture;
2) which, while condemning genital mutilation for health reasons, considers it premature to open the issue to public debate;
3) which concentrates on the aggressive nature of the campaign and considers that the fanaticism of the new crusaders only serves to draw attention away from the fundamental problems of the eco-nomic exploitation and oppression of developing countries, which contribute to the continuation of such practices.

Although all these reactions rightly criticize the campaign against genital mutilation as imperialist and paternalist, they remain passive and defensive. As is the case with many other issues, we refuse here to confront our cultural heritage and to criticize it constructively. We seem to prefer to draw a veil of modesty over certain traditional practices, whatever the consequences may be. However, it is time that Africans realized they must take a position on all problems which concern their society, and to take steps to end any practice which debases human beings.

AAWORD, whose aim is to carry out research which leads to the liberation of African people and women in particular, *firmly condemns* genital mutilation and all other practices – traditional or modern – which oppress women and justify exploiting them economically or socially, as a serious violation of the fundamental rights of women.

AAWORD intends to undertake research on the consequences of genital mutilation for the physical and mental health of women. The results of these studies could be used as the basis of an information and educational campaign, and could help to bring about legislation on all aspects of this problem.

However, as far as AAWORD is concerned, the fight against genital mutilation, although necessary, should not take on such proportions that the wood cannot be seen for the trees. Young girls and women who are mutilated in Africa are usually among those who cannot even satisfy their basic needs and who have to struggle daily for survival. This is due to the exploitation of developing countries, manifested especially through the impoverishment of the poorest social classes. In the context of the present world economic crisis, tradition, with all of its constraints, becomes more than ever a form of security for the peoples of the Third World, and especially for the 'wretched of the earth'. For these people, the modern world, which is primarily Western and bourgeois, can only represent aggression at all levels – political, economic, social and cultural. It is unable to propose viable alternatives for them.

Moreover, to fight against genital mutilation without placing it in the context of ignorance, obscurantism, exploitation, poverty, etc., without questioning the structures and social relations which perpetuate this situation, is like 'refusing to see the sun in the middle of the day'. This, however, is precisely the approach taken by many Westerners, and is highly suspect, especially since Westerners necessarily profit from the exploitation of the peoples and women of Africa, whether directly or indirectly.

Feminists from developed countries – at least those who are sincerely concerned about this situation rather than those who use it only for their personal prestige – should understand this other aspect of the problem. They must accept that it is a problem for *African women*, and that no change is possible without the conscious participation of African women. They must avoid ill-timed interference, maternalism, ethnocentrism and misuse of power. These are attitudes which can only widen the gap between the Western feminist movement and that of the Third World.

African women must stop being reserved and shake themselves out of their political lethargy. They must make themselves heard on all national and international problems, defining their priorities and their special role in the context of social and national demands.

On the question of such traditional practices as genital mutilation, African women must no longer equivocate or react only to Western interference. They must speak out in favour of the total eradication of all these practices, and they must lead information and education campaigns to this end within their own countries and on a continental level.

The Lusaka Regional Conference on the Integration of Women in Development (3–7 December 1979) ought to provide an occasion to denounce these practices and to recommend to the governments of the region to take steps to suppress them in the context of a global strategy for improving the situation of women.

At the World Mid-Decade Conference on Women at Copenhagen (July 1980), the African delegations should not let themselves be diverted by those who want to confuse 'the wood with the trees'. The women's question is a political problem; the African delegations have a duty to place it firmly within the context of the demand for a new international order.

74.

ERNA BRODBER

Born 1940, St Mary Parish, Jamaica

from *Jane and Louisa Will Soon Come Home*
1980

The One-Sided Drum

But I need to be cleansed.

Have you ever seen a new sucker trying to grow out of a rotten banana root? My whole chest was that rotten banana root and there were two suckers. Alexander Richmond knew that I was rotting. I told him to touch me but he wouldn't. Just looked strange and sent me to my mother. I was rotting.

– You are eleven now and soon something strange will happen to you. When it does go and tell your Aunt. – I needed cleansing.

Not all trees let you climb them step by step. Not all trees have branches by their roots. Some trees you have to climb by wrapping your feet around them and hauling yourself up by your chest and your belly. The coconut tree is one such tree. I could no longer climb the coconut tree.

I was strange and everybody knew it. The boys knew it. They kept daring me to hug myself. They knew that I was hard and soft, putty and wood, a rotting trunk and growing suckers. I was not quite alone though, thank God: Janey and Louise were changing too, or so *I* saw when they came to stay with us that summer when we were eleven. Thank God for that; but it wasn't enough for I was getting much stranger than they and much more rotten. They shared the summer and the hurricane with me, they shared the change with me, but I faced 'it' alone.

We had known that 'it' would come one day but never thought seriously of, nor discussed its happening to us, though we knew all about its happening

410

to other people. We knew who was having 'it' and who had just had 'it'. We could tell when any of our women folk were about to have 'it'. We knew that when they sat down and made themselves whispers one to the other, they were talking about 'it'. We knew when Sister got 'it'. We were pushed away, she began to do things that had to be done in secret and joined their whisper circle. 'It' was a hidey-hidey thing! It made you a whisper.

It had never happened to Aunt Alice though. She never left us but you see, Aunt Alice was old and never married. She could not make the whisper circle. She had never been like Baba's mother, Cousin B, the whisper circle, like the women. She had no need to push us away. She stayed with us. We didn't want to leave Aunt Alice. We didn't want to be like them and never thought that we would have to be like them. Like those others.

Those others were whispers and echoes. Baba's mother, Cousin B, they were echoes. You heard from them, you heard of them. At times they were nothing but rumours. You saw the doctor's kit and carpenter's tools, the alabaster doll and its lemonade set that they sent but you never saw them. 'It' cut them off from everybody. 'It' spoilt your life if you weren't careful! Yet 'it' gave you power, the power of a duppy that could send presents that nobody else could buy. A hollow duppy with no toes. 'Its' wood ants and termites dug toys and fancy Christmas cards out of you. A chute without dimension, a hollow without name or face, a hollow that pulled innocent girls in, an instrument as hollow and one-sided as a drum, and like a drum, its message reverberated loud and very clear but it carried no physical form nor even image of one. That is you. That's what 'it' makes you.

'It' made me powerful too and in a strange way. 'It' gave me powers over them. I was the centre of attraction. They spent energy to get me clean. Was I taking my hot water baths? Was I learning to wash and cook? Did I remember to wear my rubber-soled shoes to school? I mustn't forget to wear a slip and I must remember to let Aunt Becca know if 'it' came again. I was being given corrupting powers.

'It' corrupted Mass Stanley.

– You getting big Nellie. Hmmmm. Can't see you no more. You leave out the ole man gaan find young man now. But you watch out for the rascal them. –

That hurt for it wasn't true and Mass Stanley knew it and we never did lie to each other. He only wanted to let 'it' come between us. He knew very well that there were no young men. Mass Stanley if nobody else knew, for he watched us carefully when he wasn't thinking things he didn't want to think. We were his life. He knew more than anybody else that Baba and Errol and Barry had gone off to High School and I only saw them on holidays. He knew too that even when I saw them, they didn't see me. Baba never did see me anyway but Barry and Errol had been different. We had been friends. Now they pretended that they didn't see me. Pretended that I didn't know how to catch janga or to play cricket. And when they looked at me, they looked at me strangely. Mass Stanley knew all that so he shouldn't be pretending too.

Only Egbert was still nice and warm. His rolly-polly black pepper hair still smelt of warm wood smoke. He was not in it but his grandfather was. Egbert didn't let 'it' bother him but his grandfather did for him. Now he was always wanting to know what we were doing in the kitchen as if I had not helped his grandson boil hog feeding all my life. He had taken to hearing my mother calling me as soon as I arrived at his house. He let 'it' spoil Egbert for me:

– Don't let your father see you doing that with me. I don't able him come talk to me – Egbert had said. That hurt me deep deep down in those places that 'its' erosions had made most tender.

And 'it' came again in all its fullness.

The circle tightened 'round my feet: I must have some dirty un-named thing in me that could make even Egbert dirty.

– She has something in her – they said Anything could happen to her now. We must ship this one out with the sun. Go eena Kumbla. –

– She had something in her – Aunt Becca said. She had said it too of Baba but in a different way. I have the devil in me and only Aunt Becca knows how to deal with it. I surrendered. I told her. I told her that 'it' had come again and Aunt Khaki used 'it' to seduce me. I have 'it' in me and Aunt Becca Pinnock has no children of her own. I must go to Town with 'it' and her and Teacher Pinnock to his promotion.

The circle narrowed, the distance was complete. Go eena Kumbla for you need to be cleaned and preserved like peppers in a kilner jar. Go eena Kumbla. I went with Aunt Becca and the sun.

75.

ANGELA DAVIS

Born 1944, Birmingham, Alabama, United States of America

from *Women, Race & Class*

1981

The Legacy of Slavery: Standards for a New Womanhood

Proportionately, more Black women have always worked outside their homes than have their white sisters.* The enormous space that work occupies in Black women's lives today follows a pattern established during the very earliest days of slavery. As slaves, compulsory labor overshadowed every other aspect of women's existence. It would seem, therefore, that the starting point for any exploration of Black women's lives under slavery would be an appraisal of their role as workers.

The slave system defined Black people as chattel. Since women, no less than men, were viewed as profitable labor-units, they might as well have been genderless as far as the slaveholders were concerned. In the words of one scholar, 'the slave woman was first a full – time worker for her owner, and only incidentally a wife, mother and homemaker.'† Judged by the evolving nineteenth-century ideology of femininity, which emphasized women's roles as nurturing mothers and gentle companions and house-keepers for their husbands, Black women were practically anomalies.

Though Black women enjoyed few of the dubious benefits of the ideology of womanhood, it is sometimes assumed that the typical female slave was a houseservant – either a cook, maid, or mammy for the children in

---

* See W. E. B. DuBois, 'The Damnation of Women,' Chapter VII of *Darkwater* (New York: Harcourt, Brace and Howe, 1920).
† Kenneth M. Stampp, *The Peculiar Institution: Slavery in the Antebellum South* (New York: Vintage Books, 1956), p. 343.

the 'big house'. Uncle Tom and Sambo have always found faithful companions in Aunt Jemima and the Black Mammy – stereotypes which presume to capture the essence of the Black woman's role during slavery. As is so often the case, the reality is actually the diametrical opposite of the myth. Like the majority of slave men, slave women, for the most part, were field workers. While a significant proportion of border-state slaves may have been houseservants, slaves in the Deep South – the real home of the slaveocracy – were predominantly agricultural workers. Around the middle of the nineteenth century, seven out of eight slaves, men and women alike, were field workers.*

Just as the boys were sent to the fields when they came of age, so too were the girls assigned to work the soil, pick the cotton, cut the cane, harvest the tobacco. An old woman interviewed during the 1930s described her childhood initiation to field work on an Alabama cotton plantation:

> We had old ragged huts made out of poles and some of the cracks chinked up with mud and moss and some of them wasn't. We didn't have no good beds, just scaffolds nailed up to the wall out of poles and the old ragged bedding throwed on them. That sure was hard sleeping, but even that felt good to our weary bones after them long hard days' work in the field. I 'tended to the children when I was a little gal and tried to clean house just like Old Miss tells me to. Then as soon as I was ten years old, Old Master, he say, 'Git this here nigger to that cotton patch.'†

Jenny Proctor's experience was typical. For most girls and women, as for most boys and men, it was hard labor in the fields from sunup to sundown. Where work was concerned, strength and productivity under the threat of the whip outweighed considerations of sex. In this sense, the oppression of women was identical to the oppression of men.

But women suffered in different ways as well, for they were victims of sexual abuse and other barbarous mistreatment that could only be inflicted

---

* Ibid., p. 31; p. 49; p. 50; p. 60.
† Mel Watkins and Jay David, editors, *To Be a Black Woman: Portraits in Fact and Fiction* (New York: William Morrow and Co., Inc., 1970), p. 16. Quoted from Benjamin A. Botkin, editor, *Lay My Burden Down: A Folk History of Slavery* (Chicago: University of Chicago Press, 1945).

on women. Expediency governed the slave-holders' posture toward female slaves: when it was profitable to exploit them as if they were men, they were regarded, in effect, as genderless, but when they could be exploited, punished and repressed in ways suited only for women, they were locked into their exclusively female roles.

When the abolition of the international slave trade began to threaten the expansion of the young cotton-growing industry, the slaveholding class was forced to rely on natural reproduction as the surest method of replenishing and increasing the domestic slave population. Thus a premium was placed on the slave woman's reproductive capacity. During the decades preceding the Civil War, Black women came to be increasingly appraised for their fertility (or for the lack of it): she who was potentially the mother of ten, twelve, fourteen or more became a coveted treasure indeed. This did not mean, however, that as mothers, Black women enjoyed a more respected status than they enjoyed as workers. Ideological exaltation of motherhood – as popular as it was during the nineteenth century – did not extend to slaves. In fact, in the eyes of the slaveholders, slave women were not mothers at all; they were simply instruments guaranteeing the growth of the slave labor force. They were 'breeders' – animals, whose monetary value could be precisely calculated in terms of their ability to multiply their numbers.

Since slave women were classified as 'breeders' as opposed to 'mothers', their infant children could be sold away from them like calves from cows. One year after the importation of Africans was halted, a South Carolina court ruled that female slaves had no legal claims whatever on their children. Consequently, according to this ruling, children could be sold away from their mothers at any age because 'the young of slaves . . . stand on the same footing as other animals.'*

As females, slave women were inherently vulnerable to all forms of sexual coercion. If the most violent punishments of men consisted in floggings and mutilations, women were flogged and mutilated, as well as raped. Rape, in fact, was an uncamouflaged expression of the slaveholder's economic mastery and the overseer's control over Black women as workers.

---

* Barbara Wertheimer, *We Were There: The Story of Working Women in America* (New York: Pantheon Books, 1977), p. 109.

The special abuses inflicted on women thus facilitated the ruthless economic exploitation of their labor. The demands of this exploitation caused slaveowners to cast aside their orthodox sexist attitudes except for purposes of repression. If Black women were hardly 'women' in the accepted sense, the slave system also discouraged male supremacy in Black men. Because husbands and wives, fathers and daughters were equally subjected to the slavemasters' absolute authority, the promotion of male supremacy among the slaves might have prompted a dangerous rupture in the chain of command. Moreover, since Black women as workers could not be treated as the 'weaker sex' or the 'housewife', Black men could not be candidates for the figure of 'family head' and certainly not for 'family provider'. After all, men, women and children alike were all 'providers' for the slaveholding class.

In the cotton, tobacco, corn and sugar-cane fields, women worked alongside their men. In the words of an ex-slave:

> The bell rings at four o'clock in the morning and they have half an hour
> to get ready. Men and women start together, and the women must work
> as steadily as the men and perform the same tasks as the men.*

Most slaveowners established systems of calculating their slaves' yield in terms of the average rates of productivity they demanded. Children, thus, were frequently rated as quarter hands. Women, it was generally assumed, were full hands – unless they had been expressly assigned to be 'breeders' or 'sucklers', in which case they sometimes ranked as less than full hands.†

Slaveowners naturally sought to ensure that their 'breeders' would bear children as often as biologically possible. But they never went so far as to exempt pregnant women and mothers with infant children from work in the fields. While many mothers were forced to leave their infants lying on the ground near the area where they worked, some refused to leave them unattended and tried to work at the normal pace with their babies

---

* Ibid., p. III. Quoted from Lewis Clarke, *Narrative of the Sufferings of Lewis and Milton Clarke, Sons of a Soldier of the Revolution* (Boston: 1846), p. 127.
† Stampp, op. cit., p. 57.

on their backs. An ex-slave described such a case on the plantation where he lived:

> One young woman did not, like the others, leave her child at the end of the row, but had contrived a sort of rude knapsack, made of a piece of coarse linen cloth, in which she fastened her child, which was very young, upon her back; and in this way carried it all day, and performed her task at the hoe with the other people.*

On other plantations, the women left their infants in the care of small children or older slaves who were not able to perform hard labor in the fields. Unable to nurse their infants regularly, they endured the pain caused by their swollen breasts. In one of the most popular slave narratives of the period, Moses Grandy related the miserable predicament of slave mothers:

> On the estate I am speaking of, those women who had sucking children suffered much from their breasts becoming full of milk, the infants being left at home. They therefore could not keep up with the other hands: I have seen the overseer beat them with raw hide, so that the blood and milk flew mingled from their breasts.†

Pregnant women were not only compelled to do the normal agricultural work, they could also expect the floggings workers normally received if they failed to fulfill their day's quota or if they 'impudently' protested their treatment.

> A woman who gives offense in the field, and is large in a family way, is compelled to lie down over a hole made to receive her corpulency, and

---

* Charles Ball, *Slavery in the United States: A Narrative of the Life and Adventures of Charles Ball, a Black Man* (Lewistown, Pa.: J. W. Shugert, 1836), pp. 150–151. Quoted in Gerda Lerner, editor, *Black Women in White America: A Documentary History* (New York: Pantheon Books, 1972), p. 48.
† Moses Grandy, *Narrative of the Life of Moses Grandy: Late a Slave in the United States of America* (Boston: 1844), p. 18. Quoted in E. Franklin Frazier, *The Negro Family in the United States* (Chicago: University of Chicago Press, 1969. First edition: 1939).

is flogged with the whip or beat with a paddle, which has holes in it; at every stroke comes a blister. One of my sisters was so severely punished in this way, that labor was brought on, and the child was born in the field. This very overseer, Mr Brooks, killed in this manner a girl named Mary. Her father and mother were in the field at that time.*

On those plantations and farms where pregnant women were dealt with more leniently, it was seldom on humanitarian grounds. It was simply that slaveholders appreciated the value of a slave child born alive in the same way that they appreciated the value of a newborn calf or colt.

When timid attempts at industrialization were made in the pre-Civil War South, slave labor complemented – and frequently competed with – free labor. Slaveowning industrialists used men, women and children alike, and when planters and farmers hired out their slaves, they found women and children in as great demand as men.†

Slave women and children comprised large proportions of the work forces in most slave-employing textile, hemp and tobacco factories . . . Slave women and children sometimes worked at 'heavy' industries such as sugar refining and rice milling . . . Other heavy industries such as transportation and lumbering used slave women and children to a considerable extent.‡

Women were not too 'feminine' to work in coal mines, in iron foundries or to be lumberjacks and ditchdiggers. When the Santee Canal was constructed in North Carolina, slave women were a full fifty percent of the labor force.§ Women also worked on the Louisiana levees, and many of the Southern railroads still in use today were constructed, in part, by female slave labor.¶

The use of slave women as substitutes for beasts of burden to pull trams

---

* Ibid.
† Robert S. Starobin, *Industrial Slavery in the Old South* (London, Oxford, New York: Oxford University Press, 1970), pp. 165ff.
‡ Ibid., pp. 164–165.
§ Ibid., p. 165.
¶ Ibid., pp. 165–166.

in the Southern mines* is reminiscent of the horrendous utilization of white female labor in England, as described in Karl Marx's *Capital*:

> In England women are still occasionally used instead of horses for hauling canal boats, because the labor required to produce horses and machines is an accurately known quantity, while that required to maintain the women of the surplus population is below all calculation.†

Like their British counterparts, the Southern industrialists made no secret of the reasons motivating them to employ women in their enterprises. Female slaves were a great deal more profitable than either free workers or male slaves. They 'cost less to capitalize and to maintain than prime males'.

Required by the masters' demands to be as 'masculine' in the performance of their work as their men, Black women must have been profoundly affected by their experiences during slavery. Some, no doubt, were broken and destroyed, yet the majority survived and, in the process, acquired qualities considered taboo by the nineteenth-century ideology of womanhood. A traveler during that period observed a slave crew in Mississippi returning home from the fields and described the group as including:

> . . . forty of the largest and strongest women I ever saw together; they were all in a simple uniform dress of a bluish check stuff; their legs and feet were bare; they carried themselves loftily, each having a hoe over the shoulder, and walking with a free, powerful swing like chasseurs on the march.

While it is hardly likely that these women were expressing pride in the work they performed under the ever-present threat of the whip, they must

---

* 'Iron works and mines also directed slave women and children to lug trams and to push lumps of ore into crushers and furnaces.' Ibid., p. 166.
† Karl Marx, *Das Kapital, Kritik der politischen Ökonomie*, Erster Band (Berlin, D.D.R.: Dietz Verlag, 1965), pp. 415–416: 'In England werden gelegentlich statt der Pferde immer noch Weiber zum Ziehn usw. bei den Kanalbooten verwandt, weil die zur Produktion von Pferden und Maschinen erheischte Arbeit ein mathematisch gegebenes Quantum, die zur Erhaltung von Weibern der Surplus-population dagegen unter aller Berechnung steht.' Translation: *Capital*, Vol. 1 (New York: International Publishers, 1968), p. 391.

have been aware nonetheless of their enormous power – their ability to produce and create. For, as Marx put it, 'labor is the living, shaping fire; it represents the impermanence of things, their temporality.' It is possible, of course, that this traveler's observations were tainted by racism of the paternalistic variety, but if not, then perhaps these women had learned to extract from the oppressive circumstances of their lives the strength they needed to resist the daily dehumanization of slavery. Their awareness of their endless capacity for hard work may have imparted to them a confidence in their ability to struggle for themselves, their families and their people.

[. . .]

Education and Liberation: Black Women's Perspective

Millions of Black people – and especially the women – were convinced that emancipation was 'the coming of the Lord'.*

> This was the fulfillment of prophecy and legend. It was the Golden Dawn, after chains of a thousand years. It was everything miraculous and perfect and promising.†

> There was joy in the South. It rose like perfume – like a prayer. Men stood quivering. Slim, dark girls, wild and beautiful with wrinkled hair, wept silently; young women, black, tawny, white and golden, lifted shivering hands, and old and broken mothers, black and gray, raised great voices and shouted to God across the fields and up to the rocks and the mountains.‡

> A great song arose, the loveliest thing born this side of the seas. It was a new song . . . and its deep and plaintive beauty, its great cadences and

---

* DuBois, *Black Reconstruction in America*, Chapter V.
† Ibid., p. 122.
‡ Ibid., p. 124.

wild appeal wailed, throbbed and thundered on the world's cars with a message seldom voiced by man. It swelled and blossomed like incense, improvised and born anew out of an age long past and weaving into its texture the old and new melodies in word and in thought.*

Black people were hardly celebrating the abstract principles of freedom when they hailed the advent of emancipation. As that '. . . great human sob shrieked in the wind and tossed its tears upon the sea – free, free, free',† Black people were not giving vent to religious frenzy. They knew exactly what they wanted: the women and the men alike wanted land, they wanted the ballot and '. . . they were consumed with desire for schools.'‡

Like the young slave child Frederick Douglass, many of the four million people who celebrated emancipation had long since realized that 'knowledge unfits a child to be a slave.'§ And like Douglass' master, the former slaveholders realized that '. . . if you give a nigger an inch, he will take an ell. Learning will spoil the best nigger in the world.'¶ Master Hugh's proscription notwithstanding, Frederick Douglass secretly continued his pursuit of knowledge. Soon he could write all the words from *Webster's Spelling-Book*, further perfecting his skill by examining the family Bible and other books in the clandestinity of the night. Of course, Frederick Douglass was an exceptional human being who became a brilliant thinker, writer and orator. But his desire for knowledge was by no means exceptional among Black people, who had always manifested a deep-seated urge to acquire knowledge. Great numbers of slaves also wanted to be 'unfit' for the harrowing existence they led. A former slave interviewed during the 1930s, Jenny Proctor recalled the *Webster's Spelling-Book* which she and her friends had surreptitiously studied.

None of us was 'lowed to see a book or try to learn. They say we git smarter than they was if we learn anything, but we slips around and gits

* Ibid.
† Ibid.
‡ Ibid., p. 123.
§ Douglass, op. cit., p. 79.
¶ Ibid.

hold of that Webster's old blue-back speller and we hides it till 'way in the night and then we lights a little pine torch, and studies that spelling book. We learn it too. I can read some now and write a little too.*

Black people learned that emancipation's 'forty acres and a mule' was a malicious rumor. They would have to fight for land; they would have to fight for political power. And after centuries of educational deprivation, they would zealously assert their right to satisfy their profound craving for learning. Thus, like their sisters and brothers all over the South, the newly liberated Black people of Memphis assembled and resolved that education was their first priority. On the first anniversary of the Emancipation Proclamation, they urged the Northern teachers to make haste and

> . . . to bring their tents with them, ready for erection in the field, by the roadside, or in the fort, and not to wait for magnificent houses to be erected in time of war . . .†

The mystifying powers of racism often emanate from its irrational, topsy-turvy logic. According to the prevailing ideology, Black people were allegedly incapable of intellectual advancement. After all, they had been chattel, naturally inferior as compared to the white epitomes of humankind. But if they really were biologically inferior, they would have manifested neither the desire nor the capability to acquire knowledge. Ergo, no prohibition of learning would have been necessary. In reality, of course, Black people had always exhibited a furious impatience as regards the acquisition of education.

The yearning for knowledge had always been there. As early as 1787, Black people petitioned the state of Massachusetts for the right to attend Boston's free schools.‡ After the petition was rejected, Prince Hall, who was the leader of this initiative, established a school in his own home.§ Perhaps the most stunning illustration of this early demand for education

---

* Watkins and David, op. cit., p. 18.
† Aptheker, *A Documentary History*, Vol. 1, p. 493.
‡ Ibid., p. 19.
§ Ibid.

was the work of an African-born woman who was a former slave. In 1793 Lucy Terry Prince boldly demanded an audience before the trustees of the newly established Williams College for Men, who had refused to admit her son into the school. Unfortunately, the racist prejudices were so strong that Lucy Prince's logic and eloquence could not sway the trustees of this Vermont institution. Yet she aggressively defended her people's desire for – and right to – education. Two years later Lucy Terry Prince successfully defended a land claim before the highest court of the land, and according to surviving records, she remains the first woman to have addressed the Supreme Court of the United States.*

Seventeen ninety-three was also the year an ex-slave woman, who had purchased her freedom, established a school in the city of New York which was known as Katy Ferguson's School for the Poor. Her pupils, whom she recruited from the poorhouse, were both Black and white (twenty-eight and twenty respectively)† and were quite possibly both boys and girls. Forty years later the young white teacher Prudence Crandall steadfastly defended Black girls' right to attend her Canterbury, Connecticut, school. Crandall persistently taught her Black pupils until she was dragged off to jail for refusing to shut down her school.‡ Margaret Douglass was another white woman who was imprisoned in Norfolk, Virginia, for operating a school for Black children.§

The most outstanding examples of white women's sisterly solidarity with Black women are associated with Black people's historical struggle for education. Like Prudence Crandall and Margaret Douglass, Myrtilla Miner literally risked her life as she sought to impart knowledge to young Black women.¶ In 1851, when she initiated her project to establish a Black teachers' college in Washington, DC, she had already instructed Black children in Mississippi, a state where education for Blacks was a criminal offense. After Myrtilla Miner's death, Frederick Douglass described his own incredulousness when she first announced her plans to him. During

---

* Wertheimer, op. cit., pp. 35–36.
† Lerner, *Black Women in White America*, p. 76
‡ See Chapter 2.
§ Foner, *The Life and Writings of Frederick Douglass*, Vol. 4, p. 553 (note 16).
¶ Ibid., pp. 371ff.

their first meeting he wondered about her seriousness in the beginning, but then he realized that

> ... the fire of enthusiasm lighted in her eye and that the true martyr spirit flamed in her soul. My feelings were those of mingled joy and sadness. Here I thought is another enterprise – wild, dangerous, desperate and impracticable, and destined only to bring failure and suffering. Yet I was deeply moved with admiration by the heroic purpose of the delicate and fragile person who stood or rather moved to and fro before me.*

It was not long before Douglass recognized that none of the warnings he issued to her – and not even the stories of the attacks on Prudence Crandall and Margaret Douglass – could shake her determination to found a college for Black women teachers.

> To me the proposition was reckless almost to the point of madness. In my fancy I saw this fragile little woman harassed by the law, insulted in the street, a victim of slaveholding malice and possibly beaten down by the mob.†

In Frederick Douglass' opinion, relatively few white people outside the anti-slavery activists would sympathize with Myrtilla Miner's cause and support her against the mob. This was a period, he argued, of diminishing solidarity with Black people. Moreover,

> ... the District of Columbia (was) the very citadel of slavery, the place most watched and guarded by the slave power and where humane tendencies were more speedily detected and sternly opposed.‡

In retrospect, however, Douglass confessed that he did not really understand the depth of this white woman's individual courage. Despite the grave risks, Myrtilla Miner opened her school in the fall of 1851, and

---

* Ibid., p. 372.
† Ibid.
‡ Ibid., p. 371.

within a few months her initial six students had grown to forty. She taught her Black students passionately over the next eight years, simultaneously raising money and urging congressmen to support her efforts. She even acted as a mother to the orphan girls whom she brought into her home so that they might attend the school.*

As Myrtilla Miner struggled to teach and as her pupils struggled to learn, they all fought evictions, arson attempts and the other misdeeds of racist stone-throwing mobs. They were supported by the young women's families and abolitionists such as Harriet Beecher Stowe, who donated a portion of the royalties she received from the sale of *Uncle Tom's Cabin*.†
Myrtilla Miner may have been 'frail', as Frederick Douglass observed, but she was definitely formidable, and was always able, at lesson time, to discover the eye of that racist storm. Early one morning, however, she was abruptly awakened by the odor of smoke and raging flames, which soon consumed her schoolhouse. Although her school was destroyed, the inspiration she provided lived on, and eventually Miner's Teachers College became a part of the District of Columbia public educational system.‡
'I never pass the Miner Normal School for colored girls,' so Frederick Douglass confessed in 1883,

> . . . without a feeling of self reproach that I could have said aught to quench the zeal, shake the faith, and quail the courage of the Noble woman by whom it was founded and whose name it bears.§

Sisterhood between Black and white women was indeed possible, and as long as it stood on a firm foundation – as with this remarkable woman and her friends and students – it could give birth to earthshaking accomplishments. Myrtilla Miner kept the candle burning that others before her, like the Grimke sisters and Prudence Crandall, had left as a powerful legacy. It could not have been a mere historical coincidence that so many of the white women who defended their Black sisters in the most dangerous of

* Ibid.
† Flexner, op. cit., p. 99.
‡ Ibid., pp. 99–101.
§ Foner, op. cit., Vol. 4, p. 373

situations were involved in the struggle for education. They must have understood how urgently Black women needed to acquire knowledge – a lamp unto their people's feet and a light unto the path toward freedom.

Black people who did receive academic instruction inevitably associated their knowledge with their people's collective battle for freedom. As the first year of Black schooling in Cincinnati drew to a close, pupils who were asked 'What do you think *most* about?' furnished these answers:

> 1st. We are going . . . to be good boys and when we get a man to get the poor slaves from bondage. And I am sorrow to hear that the boat of Tiskilwa went down with two hundred poor slaves . . . it grieves my heart so that I could faint in one minute. (seven year old)
>
> 2nd . . . What we are studying for is to try to get the yoke of slavery broke and the chains parted asunder and slave holding cease for ever . . . (twelve year old)
>
> 3rd . . . Bless the cause of abolition . . . My mother and step-father, my sister and myself were all born in slavery. The Lord did let the oppressed go free. Roll on the happy period that all nations shall know the Lord. We thank him for his many blessings. (eleven year old)
>
> 4th . . . This is to inform you that I have two cousins in slavery who are entitled to their freedom. They have done everything that the will requires and now they won't let them go. They talk of selling them down the river. If this was your case what would you do? . . . (ten year old)*

The last surviving answer came from a sixteen-year-old attending this new Cincinnati school. It is an extremely fascinating example of the way the students gleaned a contemporary meaning from world history that was as close to home as the desire to be free.

> 5th. Let us look back and see the state in which the Britons and Saxons and Germans lived. They had no learning and had not a knowledge of letters. But now look, some of them are our first men. Look at King Alfred and see what a great man he was. He at one time did not know his a,b,c, but before his death he commanded armies and nations. He

* Aptheker, *A Documentary History*, Vol. 1, pp. 157–158.

was never discouraged but always looked forward and studied the harder. I think if the colored people study like King Alfred they will soon do away the evil of slavery. I can't see how the Americans can call this a land of freedom where so much slavery is.*

As far as Black people's faith in knowledge was concerned, this sixteen-year-old child said it all.

This unquenchable thirst for knowledge was as powerful among the slaves in the South as among their 'free' sisters and brothers in the North. Needless to say, the anti-literacy restrictions of the slave states were far more rigid than in the North. After the Nat Turner Revolt in 1831, legislation prohibiting the education of slaves was strengthened throughout the South. In the words of one slave code, '. . . teaching slaves to read and write tends to dissatisfaction in their minds, and to produce insurrection and rebellion.'† With the exception of Maryland and Kentucky, every Southern state absolutely prohibited the education of slaves.‡ Throughout the South, slaveholders resorted to the lash and the whipping post in order to counter their slaves' irrepressible will to learn. Black people wanted to be educated.

> The poignancy of the slaves' struggle for learning appeared everywhere. Frederika Bremer found a young woman desperately trying to read the Bible. 'Oh, this book,' she cried out to Miss Bremer. 'I turn and turn over its leaves and I wish I understood what is on them. I try and try; I should be so happy if I could read, but I can not.'§

Susie King Taylor was a nurse and teacher in the first Black regiment of the Civil War. In her autobiography she described her persistent efforts to educate herself during slavery. White children, sympathetic adults, as well as her grandmother, assisted her to acquire the skills of reading and

---

* Ibid.
† William Goodell, *The American Slave Code* (New York: American and Foreign Anti-Slavery Society, 1853), p. 321. Quoted in Elkins, op. cit., p. 60.
‡ Ibid.
§ Genovese, Roll, Jordan, Roll, p. 565.

writing.* Like Susie King's grand-mother, numerous slave women ran great risks as they imparted to their sisters and brothers the academic skills they had secretly procured. Even when they were compelled to convene their schools during the late hours of the night, women who had managed to acquire some knowledge attempted to share it with their people.†

These were some of the early signs – in the North and South alike – of that post-emancipation phenomenon which DuBois called 'a frenzy for schools'.‡ Another historian described the ex-slaves' thirst for learning in these words:§

> With a yearning born of centuries of denial, ex-slaves worshipped the sight and sound of the printed word. Old men and women on the edge of the grave could be seen in the dark of the night, poring over the Scripture by the light of a pine knot, painfully spelling out the sacred words.

According to yet another historian,

> [M]any educators reported that they found a keener desire to learn among the Negro children of the Reconstruction South than among white children in the North.¶

About half of the volunteer teachers who joined the massive educational campaign organized by the Freedman's Bureau were women. Northern white women went South during Reconstruction to assist their Black sisters who were absolutely determined to wipe out illiteracy among the millions of former slaves. The dimensions of this task were herculean: according to DuBois, the prevailing illiteracy rate was 95 percent.** In the histories chronicling the Reconstruction Era and in the historical accounts

---

* Lerner, *Black Women in White America*, pp. 27ff. and pp. 99ff.
† Ibid., pp. 32ff.
‡ DuBois, *Black Reconstruction in America*, p. 123
§ Lerone Bennett, *Before the Mayflower* (Baltimore: Penguin Books, 1969), p. 181.
¶ Foster, op. cit., p. 321.
** DuBois, *Black Reconstruction in America*, p. 638.

of the Women's Rights Movement, the experiences of Black and white women working together in the struggle for education have received sparse attention. Judging, however, from the articles in the *Freedman's Record*, these teachers undoubtedly inspired each other and were themselves inspired by their students. Almost universally mentioned in the white teachers' observations was the former slaves' unyielding commitment to knowledge. In the words of a teacher working in Raleigh, North Carolina, '[i]t is surprising to me to see the amount of suffering which many of the people endure for the sake of sending their children to school.'* Material comfort was unhesitatingly sacrificed for the furtherance of educational progress:

> A pile of books is seen in almost every cabin, though there be no furniture except a poor bed, a table and two or three broken chairs.†

As teachers, the Black and white women seem to have developed a profound and intense mutual appreciation. A white woman working in Virginia, for example, was immensely impressed by the work of a Black woman teacher who had just emerged from slavery. It '. . . seems almost a miracle', this white woman exclaimed, that '. . . a colored woman, who had been a slave up to the time of the Surrender, would succeed in a vocation to her so novel . . . '‡ In the reports she authored, the Black woman in question expressed sincere – though by no means servile – gratitude for the work of her 'friends from the North'.§

By the time of the Hayes Betrayal and the overthrow of Radical Reconstruction, the accomplishments in education had become one of the most powerful proofs of progress during that potentially revolutionary era. Fisk University, Hampton Institute and several other Black colleges and universities had been established in the post-Civil War South.¶ Some 247,333 pupils were attending 4,329 schools – and these were the building blocks for the South's first public school system, which would benefit Black and

---

* Lerner, *Black Women in White America*, p. 102.
† Ibid., p. 103.
‡ Ibid.
§ Ibid., pp. 104–105.
¶ Franklin, op. cit., p. 308.

white children alike. Although the post-Reconstruction period and the attendant rise of Jim Crow education drastically diminished Black people's educational opportunities, the impact of the Reconstruction experience could not be entirely obliterated. The dream of land was shattered for the time being and the hope for political equality waned. But the beacon of knowledge was not easily extinguished – and this was the guarantee that the fight for land and for political power would unrelentingly go on.

> Had it not been for the Negro school and college, the Negro would, to all intents and purposes, have been driven back to slavery . . . His reconstruction leadership had come from Negroes educated in the North, and white politicians, capitalists and philanthropic teachers. The counter-revolution of 1876 drove most of these, save the teachers, away. But already, through establishing public schools and private colleges, and by organizing the Negro church, the Negro had acquired enough leadership and knowledge to thwart the worst designs of the new slave drivers.*

Aided by their white sister allies, Black women played an indispensable role in creating this new fortress. The history of women's struggle for education in the United States reached a true peak when Black and white women together led the post-Civil War battle against illiteracy in the South. Their unity and solidarity preserved and confirmed one of our history's most fruitful promises.

* DuBois, *Black Reconstruction in America*, p. 667.

76.

AUDRE LORDE

Born 1934, New York City, New York, United States of America
Died 1992, Christiansted, U.S. Virgin Islands

from *The Uses of Anger: Women Responding to Racism*
1981

Anger is an appropriate reaction to racist attitudes, as is fury when the actions arising from those attitudes do not change. To those women here who fear the anger of women of Color more than their own unscrutinized racist attitudes, I ask: Is the anger of women of Color more threatening than the woman-hatred that tinges all aspects of our lives?

It is not the anger of other women that will destroy us but our refusals to stand still, to listen to its rhythms, to the substance, to tap that anger as an important source of empowerment.

I cannot hide my anger to spare you guilt, nor hurt feelings, nor answering anger; for to do so insults and trivializes all our efforts. Guilt is not a response to anger; it is a response to one's own actions or lack of action. If it leads to change then it can be useful, since it is then no longer guilt but the beginning of knowledge. Yet all too often, guilt is just another name for impotence, for defensiveness destructive of communication; it becomes a device to protect ignorance and the continuation of things the way they are, the ultimate protection for changelessness.

Most women have not developed tools for facing anger constructively. CR groups in the past, largely white, dealt with how to express anger, usually at the world of men. And these groups were made up of white women who shared the terms of their oppressions. There was usually little attempt to articulate the genuine differences between women, such as those of race, color, age, class, and sexual identity. There was no apparent need at that time to examine the contradictions of self, woman as oppressor. There was work on expressing anger, but very little on anger directed against each other. No tools were developed to deal with other women's anger except to avoid it, deflect it, or flee from it under a blanket of guilt.

I have no creative use for guilt, yours or my own. Guilt is only another way of avoiding informed action, of buying time out of the pressing need to make clear choices, out of the approaching storm that can feed the earth as well as bend the trees. If I speak to you in anger, at least I have spoken to you: I have not put a gun to your head and shot you down in the street; I have not looked at your bleeding sister's body and asked, 'What did she do to deserve it?' This was the reaction of two white women to Mary Church Terrell's telling of the lynching of a pregnant Black woman whose baby was then torn from her body. That was in 1921, and Alice Paul had just refused to publicly endorse the enforcement of the Nineteenth Amendment for all women – by refusing to endorse the inclusion of women of Color, although we had worked to help bring about that amendment.

The angers between women will not kill us if we can articulate them with precision, if we listen to the content of what is said with at least as much intensity as we defend ourselves against the manner of saying. When we turn from anger we turn from insight, saying we will accept only the designs already known, deadly and safely familiar. I have tried to learn my anger's usefulness to me, as well as its limitations.

For women raised to fear, too often anger threatens annihilation. In the male construct of brute force, we were taught that our lives depended upon the good will of patriarchal power. The anger of others was to be avoided at all costs because there was nothing to be learned from it but pain, a judgment that we had been bad girls, come up lacking, not done what we were supposed to do. And if we accept our powerlessness, then of course any anger can destroy us.

But the strength of women lies in recognizing differences between us as creative, and in standing to those distortions which we inherited without blame, but which are now ours to alter. The angers of women can transform difference through insight into power. For anger between peers births change, not destruction, and the discomfort and sense of loss it often causes is not fatal, but a sign of growth.

My response to racism is anger. That anger has eaten clefts into my living only when it remained unspoken, useless to anyone. It has also served me in classrooms without light or learning, where the work and history of Black women was less than a vapor. It has served me as fire in the ice zone of uncomprehending eyes of white women who see in my experience and the experience of my people only new reasons for fear or guilt. And my anger is no excuse for not dealing with your blindness, no reason to withdraw from the results of your own actions.

When women of Color speak out of the anger that laces so many of our contacts with white women, we are often told that we are 'creating a mood of hopelessness,' 'preventing white women from getting past guilt,' or 'standing in the way of trusting communication and action.' All these quotes come directly from letters to me from members of this organization within the last two years. One woman wrote, 'Because you are Black and Lesbian, you seem to speak with the moral authority of suffering.' Yes, I am Black and Lesbian, and what you hear in my voice is fury, not suffering. Anger, not moral authority. There is a difference.

To turn aside from the anger of Black women with excuses or the pretexts of intimidation is to award no one power – it is merely another way of preserving racial blindness, the power of unaddressed privilege, unbreached, intact. Guilt is only another form of objectification. Oppressed peoples are always being asked to stretch a little more, to bridge the gap between blindness and humanity. Black women are expected to use our anger only in the service of other people's salvation or learning. But that time is over. My anger has meant pain to me but it has also meant survival, and before I give it up I'm going to be sure that there is something at least as powerful to replace it on the road to clarity.

What woman here is so enamored of her own oppression that she cannot see her heelprint upon another woman's face? What woman's terms of oppression have become precious and necessary to her as a ticket into the fold of the righteous, away from the cold winds of self-scrutiny?

I am a lesbian woman of Color whose children eat regularly because I work in a university. If their full bellies make me fail to recognize my commonality with a woman of Color whose children do not eat because she cannot find work, or who has no children because her insides are rotted from home abortions and sterilization; if I fail to recognize the lesbian who chooses not to have children, the woman who remains closeted because her homophobic community is her only life support, the woman

433

who chooses silence instead of another death, the woman who is terrified lest my anger trigger the explosion of hers; if I fail to recognize them as other faces of myself, then I am contributing not only to each of their oppressions but also to my own, and the anger which stands between us then must be used for clarity and mutual empowerment, not for evasion by guilt or for further separation. I am not free while any woman is unfree, even when her shackles are very different from my own. And I am not free as long as one person of Color remains chained. Nor is any one of you.

I speak here as a woman of Color who is not bent upon destruction, but upon survival. No woman is responsible for altering the psyche of her oppressor, even when that psyche is embodied in another woman. I have suckled the wolf's lip of anger and I have used it for illumination, laughter, protection, fire in places where there was no light, no food, no sisters, no quarter. We are not goddesses or matriarchs or edifices of divine forgiveness; we are not fiery fingers of judgment or instruments of flagellation; we are women forced back always upon our woman's power. We have learned to use anger as we have learned to use the dead flesh of animals, and bruised, battered, and changing, we have survived and grown and, in Angela Wilson's words, we *are* moving on. With or without uncolored women. We use whatever strengths we have fought for, including anger, to help define and fashion a world where all our sisters can grow, where our children can love, and where the power of touching and meeting another woman's difference and wonder will eventually transcend the need for destruction.

For it is not the anger of Black women which is dripping down over this globe like a diseased liquid. It is not my anger that launches rockets, spends over sixty thousand dollars a second on missiles and other agents of war and death, slaughters children in cities, stockpiles nerve gas and chemical bombs, sodomizes our daughters and our earth. It is not the anger of Black women which corrodes into blind, dehumanizing power, bent upon the annihilation of us all unless we meet it with what we have, our power to examine and to redefine the terms upon which we will live and work; our power to envision and to reconstruct, anger by painful anger, stone upon heavy stone, a future of pollinating difference and the earth to support our choices.

We welcome all women who can meet us, face to face, beyond objectification and beyond guilt.

77.

RIGOBERTA MENCHÙ

Born 1959, Laj Chimel, Guatemala

from *I, Rigoberta Menchù*
1983

Women and political commitment. Rigoberta renounces marriage and motherhood

'We have kept our identity hidden because we have resisted'
— Rigoberta Menchú

I still haven't approached the subject – and it's perhaps a very long subject – of women in Guatemala. We have to put them into categories, anyway: working-class women, peasant women, poor *ladino* women, and bourgeois women, middle-class women. There is something important about women in Guatemala, especially Indian women, and that something is her relationship with the earth – between the earth and the mother. The earth gives food and the woman gives life. Because of this closeness the woman must keep this respect for the earth as a secret of her own. The relationship between the mother and the earth is like the relationship between husband and wife. There is a constant dialogue between the earth and the woman. This feeling is born in women because of the responsibilities they have, which men do not have.

That is how I've been able to analyse my specific task in the organization. I realize that many *compañeros*, who are revolutionaries and good *compañeros*, never lose the feeling that their views are better than those of any women in charge of them. Of course, we mustn't dismiss the great value of those *compañeros*, but we can't let them do just whatever they like. I have a responsibility, I am in charge, and they must accept me for what I am. But in this respect I've met serious problems when handing out tasks to those *compañeros*, and I've often found it upsetting having to assume this role. But I really believed that I could contribute, and that they should respect me. All the same, it was difficult for me to say: 'Listen, *compañero*, these tasks are for you; and you, *compañero*, these are your defects, what are we going to do about them?' It doesn't mean you dominate a man, and you mustn't get any sense of satisfaction out of it. It's simply a question of principle. I have my job to do just like any other *compañero*. I found all this very difficult and, as I was saying, I came up against revolutionary *compañeros*, *compañeros* who had many ideas about making a revolution, but who had trouble accepting that a woman could participate in the struggle not only in superficial things but in fundamental things. I've also had to punish many *compañeros* who try to prevent their women taking part in the struggle or carrying out any task. They're sometimes willing to let them participate but only within certain limits. They start saying: 'Oh no, not that. No, not here. No.' Well, we've had to talk seriously with these *compañeros* to solve that problem.

My mother, of course, didn't know all these ideas, all these theories about the position of women. But she knew all these things in practice. I learned a lot from my mother but I also learned a lot from other people, especially when I had the opportunity of talking to women who aren't from our country. We discussed the organization of women and we came to the conclusion that many women so often take other people's problems upon themselves and push their own to one side. This doesn't do us any good. It shows us that we must solve our problems ourselves and not ask someone else to come and solve them, otherwise it's dishonest. No-one will solve our problems for us.

The Indian women who have a clear political vision and participate in the leadership of the organization are realizing this. We're seeing change, revolution, taking power, but this isn't the profound change within society. We women *compañeras* came to the conclusion (because for a time we thought of creating an organization for women) that it was paternalistic to say there should be an organization for women when in practice women work and are exploited as well. Women work picking coffee and cotton, and on top of that, many women have taken up arms and even elderly women are fighting day and night; so it isn't possible to say that now we're setting up an organization so that women can rebel, work or study women's problems. It won't always be like this, of course. That is just the situation we're facing at the moment. Perhaps in the future, when there's a need for it, there will be a women's organization in Guatemala. For the time being, though, we think that it would be feeding *machismo* to set up an organization for women only, since it would mean separating women's work from men's work. Also we've found that when we discuss women's problems, we need the men to be present, so that they can contribute by giving their opinions of what to do about the problem. And so that they can learn as well. If they don't learn, they don't progress. Our struggle has shown us that many *compañeros* have clear ideas, but if they don't follow in the footsteps of their woman, they'll never have the clarity that she has, and they'll be left behind. What is the point of educating women if men aren't there to contribute to the apprenticeship and learn as well? By creating an organization for women we would be presenting the system which oppresses us with another weapon. We don't want that. We must fight as equals. If a *compañero* is asked a question about *machismo*, he must be able to give a wide balanced view of women, and a woman must be able to do the same for men, because the two have been studying the problem together.

That has been my experience anyway. I'm not married, but I've taken part in important discussions where we've talked about the problem of men and women, in a mixed group. We think that this is the right path to follow. Naturally, we can't say that this alone will do away with *machismo*, because it wouldn't be true. In all revolutionary countries, socialist countries, wherever you care to name, *machismo* still exists. The whole world is afflicted with this sickness. It's part of society. Part of it we can improve, and part of it we can wipe out. But perhaps it's not possible to solve the problem entirely.

There is something else we are discovering in Guatemala to do with intellectuals and illiterate people. We've learned that we haven't all got the ability of an intellectual: an intellectual is perhaps quicker and able to make finer syntheses. But nevertheless, others of us have perhaps the same ability for other things. Before, everyone used to think that a leader had to be someone who knew how to read, write and prepare documents. And our leaders fell into that trap for a time, and said: 'I am a leader, it's my job to lead and yours to fight.' Well, in every process there are certain exchanges which have to be made. That is not unusual. I think that every movement has gone through the process whereby an opportunist arrives, feels that he is worth more than the others and abuses their confidence. At one time, many of our leaders would come from the capital to see us in the *finca* and say: 'You peasants are stupid, you don't read or study.' And the peasants told them: 'You can go to Hell with your books. We know you don't make a revolution with books, you make it through struggle.'

And that was why we decided to learn many things, and rightly so, because, remember, that now everything was in our hands. We had to make big sacrifices. And so, we peasants have learned to direct our struggle ourselves, and *that* we owe to our understanding of our situation. A leader must be someone who's had practical experience. It's not so much that the hungrier you've been, the purer your ideas must be, but you can only have a real consciousness if you've really lived this life. I can say that in my organization most of the leaders are Indians. There are also some *ladinos* and some women in the leadership. But we have to erase the barriers which exist between ethnic groups, between Indians and *ladinos*, between men and women, between intellectuals and non intellectuals, and between all the linguistic areas.

The situation we are in means that our women don't get married because they're expecting something happy, a lovely family, pleasure, or something different from what they already have. No, not at all. They know that a very hard life awaits them. Although for us marriage is something joyful (because the concept our ancestors had was that our race must not die out and we must follow our traditions and customs as they did), at the same time it is something very painful, knowing that when you get married you'll have the responsibility of bringing up your children, and not only of looking after them, but worrying, trying to make do, and hoping they live. In Guatemala, it's unusual for a family not to see some of their young children die.

Well, in my case, I analysed my ideas about not getting married with some of my *compañeros*. I realized that what I said wasn't crazy, that it wasn't some personal mad idea, but that our whole situation makes women think very hard before getting married, because who will look after the children, who will feed them? As I was saying before, we're used to living in a community, among up to ten or eleven brothers or sisters. But there are also cases of women who are left alone because all their brothers and sisters go off and get married, so they're sometimes forced to get married because they know how hard it will be for them by themselves. But knowing that I had to multiply the seed of our ancestors and, at the same time, rejecting marriage . . . that was a crazy idea. I thought I was alone in feeling like this, but when I discussed it with other women, they saw the whole thing of getting married in the same way I did. It is terrible to know that such a hard life awaits you, with so much responsibility to make sure your children live. You can't think any other way in Guatemala: when you get engaged or married, you immediately think of the many children you're going to have. I've been in love many times but it was precisely because of that fear that I didn't jump into marriage. But the time came when I saw clearly – it was actually when I'd begun my life as a revolutionary – that I was fighting for a people and for many children who hadn't anything to eat. I could see how sad it would be for a revolutionary not to leave a seed, because the seed which was left behind would enjoy the fruits of this work in the future. But I thought of the risks of having a child. It would be much easier for me to die, at any time or place, if I weren't leaving anyone behind to suffer. That would be sad, because although my community would take care of my child, of my seed, no other person can give a child the love his mother can, however much that person looks after and cares for the child. I was very confused about all this because so many dedicated *compañeros* said they would be there on the day of victory, but I knew that they could give their lives at any time and would no longer be there. All this horrified me and gave me a lot to think about.

I was engaged once but I wasn't sure, because, well, the idea our ancestors had – and it's ours too – is that you don't only look for happiness for yourself but also for your family. I was very confused. Society and so many other things wouldn't leave me alone, I always had a heavy heart.

And then when my parents died, I felt what a daughter feels for a father and mother when they die, and even more so because of the way they died. That's when I decided, although I can't say that it's a final decision because I am open to life. My idea is, though, that there will be time enough after our victory; but at the moment I wouldn't feel happy having a *compañero* and giving myself to him while so many of our people are not thinking of their own personal happiness and haven't a single moment to rest. This gave me a lot to think about. As I said, I am human and I am a woman so I can't say that I reject marriage altogether, but I think my primary duty is to my people and then to my personal happiness. I know many *compañeros* who have devoted themselves without reservation to the struggle, without thinking of personal happiness. And I know *compañeros* who've gone through bitter moments, who have troubles and worries, but who, nevertheless, are in the struggle and carry on. It could be that I renounced marriage because of the harsh experience of having seen so many friends die. This not only frightens me, it puts me in a panic, because I don't want to be a widow, or a tortured mother. I'm restricted by so many things. It's not just not wanting a child. Many little things have made me think about renouncing all this. I know that our men have suffered too, because many *compañeros* had to give their children away so they could carry on the struggle, or they've had to leave their women in other places, not because they don't want marriage but because they feel it is their duty to fight for their people.

The conclusion I came to was that, while we have so many problems, we shouldn't look for more. There are married women in the struggle, however, who contribute as much as I do, *compañeras* who have five or six children and do magnificent work. Being afraid of all that is a certain trauma I have. I'm even more afraid when I think that if I had a *compañero*, I'd probably love him very much and I wouldn't want it to be for only a week or two because after that he wouldn't be there. While I don't have this problem, I won't look for it. But, as I said, I'm open to life. It doesn't mean that I reject everything because I know that things come in their time and when you do things calmly, they work much better.

As I said, I was engaged once. At one time he wanted a lot of things in life; a nice house for his children and a peaceful life. But I didn't think like that. We'd known each other since we were children, but unfortunately he left our village and had to go to the city. He became a factory worker, and then really turned into a *compañero* with good work prospects who thought differently from the way I and my village thought. So, when I became a revolutionary I had to choose between two things – the struggle or my *compañero*. I came to all sorts of conclusions because I loved this *compañero* and I could see the sacrifices he made for me. It was a more open engagement than was usual for people of my culture. Well, there I was between these two things – choosing him or my people's struggle. And that's what I chose, and I left my *compañero* with much sadness and a heavy heart. But I told myself that I had a lot to do for my people and I didn't need a pretty house while they lived in horrific conditions like those I was born and grew up in. Well, that's when we went our separate ways. I told him that it wasn't right for me to stay with him because he had other ideas and we'd never understand each other, since he wanted one thing and I'd always go on wanting another. Then I went on with our struggle and now I'm on my own. But, as I said, there'll be a time when things will be different, when we'll all be happy, perhaps not with nice houses, but at least we won't see our lands running with blood and sweat.

78.

LIZ LOCHHEAD

Born 1947, Motherwell, United Kingdom

Everybody's Mother
1984

Of course everybody's mother always and
so on . . .

Always never
loved you enough
or too smothering much.

Of course you were the Only One, your
mother
a machine
that shat out siblings, listen

everybody's mother
was the original Frigid-
aire Icequeen clunking out
the hardstuff in nuggets, mirror-
slivers and ice-splinters that'd stick
in your heart.

Absolutely everybody's mother
was artistic when she was young.

Everybody's mother
was a perfumed presence with pearls, remote
white shoulders when she
bent over in her ball dress
to kiss you in your crib.

Everybody's mother slept with the butcher
for sausages to stuff you with.

Everybody's mother
mythologised herself. You got mixed up
between dragon's teeth and blackmarket stockings.

Naturally
she failed to give you
Positive Feelings
about your own sorry
sprouting body (it was a bloody shame)

but she did
sit up all night sewing sequins
on your carnival costume

so you would have a good time

and she spat
on the corner of her hanky and scraped
at your mouth with sour lace until you squirmed

so you would look smart

And where
was your father all this time?
Away
at the war, or in his office, or anyway conspicuous for his
Absence, so

what if your mother did
float around above you
big as a barrage balloon
blocking out the light?

Nobody's mother can't not never do nothing right.

79.

VALERIE AMOS AND PRATIBHA PARMAR

Valerie Amos: born 1954, Georgetown, Guyana
Pratibha Parmar: born 1955, Nairobi, Kenya

from *Challenging Imperial Feminism*
1984

Our task here is to begin to identify the ways in which a particular tradition, white Eurocentric and Western, has sought to establish itself as the only legitimate feminism in current political practice. We seek to address ourselves in very broad terms, to the theoretical and consequently political limitations of Euro-American feminism and the ways such analyses inform and distort white women's political practice. In challenging such feminist writings we not only look at the ways in which analyses of racism have been significantly lacking from that work but equally importantly we look at the ways in which we as Black women have been made 'visible' in such writings and the terms in which our experiences have been explained.

The growth of the Black feminist movement in Britain in the last decade has forced the question of the centrality of Black women's oppression and exploitation onto the political and theoretical agendas. The political energy of Black women who have organized at the grassroots within our communities against the myriad of issues engendered by the racism of the British state has inspired and pointed to the urgent need to challenge many of the theoretical conceptualizations and descriptions of Black and Third World women existing within white feminist literature.

bell hook's argument (1982) that racism in the women's movement in the USA has acted to exclude the participation of Black women is equally applicable to the British situation:

From a Black female perspective, if white women are denying the existence of Black women, writing 'feminist' scholarship as if Black women are not part of the collective group of American women, or discriminating against Black women, then it matters less that North America was colonised by white patriarchal men who institutionalised a radically imperialistic social order, than that white women who purport to be feminists support and actively perpetuate anti-Black racism.

It is our aim in this article to critically examine some of the key theoretical concepts in white feminist literature, and discuss their relevance or otherwise for a discussion and development of Black feminist theory.

It would be naïve of us to suggest in any way that the white women's movement is a monolithic structure or organization, indeed we recognize that it is a variety of groups with a diversity of interests and perspectives.

However, our concern here is to show that white, mainstream feminist theory, be it from the socialist feminist or radical feminist perspective, does not speak to the experiences of Black women and where it attempts to do so it is often from a racist perspective and reasoning.

In terms of practice, while there are a broad range of issues and demands that white feminists are engaged in, we believe there is a particular kind of implicit consensus amongst these women about the issues which are thought to be important to organize around. The limitations of the movement are expressed in the issues which are identified as priorities: they are issues which in the main have contributed to an improvement in the material situation of a small number of white middle-class women often at the expense of their Black and working class 'sisters', e.g. short term gains such as equal opportunities and job sharing. The power of sisterhood stops at the point at which hard political decisions need to be made and political priorities decided. In the same way that the Labour movement has lamented the supposed lack of involvement of Black people in their struggles so white women have condemned Black women for not engaging in the struggles they have identified as important – the colonial heritage marches on.

This unconscious consensus has been successful in excluding large numbers of Black women from participating in any meaningful way. A further element contributing to Black women's exclusion is due to the fact that very often women's oppression is seen in a straightforward and non-contradictory way, where women organizing as women is seen as positive, regardless of the context. An example of such reasoning taken to its extreme is when some white feminists have applauded Maggie Thatcher as Prime Minister as a positive female image. Such uncritical acceptance of the virtues of strong female images serves only to further alienate Black women whose experience at the hands of the British state demands a more responsible political response.

Our starting point then is the oppressive nature of the women's movement in Britain both in terms of its practice and the theories which have sought to explain the nature of women's oppression and legitimize the political practices which have developed out of those analyses. In describing the women's movement as oppressive we refer to the experiences of Black and working-class women of the movement and the inability of feminist theory to speak to their experience in any meaningful way.*

In arguing that most contemporary feminist theory does not begin to adequately account for the experience of Black women we also have to acknowledge that it is not a simple question of their absence, consequently the task is not one of rendering their visibility.

On the contrary we will have to argue that the process of accounting for their historical and contemporary position does, in itself, challenge the use of some of the central categories and assumptions of recent mainstream feminist thought (Carby, 1982). This work has already begun; Black women are not only making history but rewriting it.

The publication in recent years of a number of books by Black feminists in the US marks the beginning of a systematic documentation of Black women's individual and collective histories. Dominant among these are the rediscovery of ourselves; our place in the Black movement; the boundaries of our sisterhood with white feminists (Lewis and Parmar, 1983).

These are important areas for us Black women, for our experience is

* Some attempts have been made to look at both racism and feminism. For example Jenny Bourne in her essay (1983) 'Toward an anti-racist feminism' attempts to locate anti racist practice within a (white) feminist context. However Jenny Bourne's essay fails adequately to address contemporary debates within feminism and ignores the contribution of black feminists to the broader debates around issues of racism, feminism, class and sexuality.

the shared experience of Black people but it is also the shared experience of women within different class contexts. Our political responses have been and will continue to be shaped by that duality, the range of political options available to us will depend on the social context in which we experience that dualism. To date, the majority of work available by Black women addresses itself to the situation in the USA or to the situation in the Third World countries from which our ancestors are drawn. Although comparisons can be made between Britain and the USA and although it is important to draw on the histories of the communities and countries of the Third World which have contributed to our world view, it is important that Black women in Britain locate their experiences within the context of what is happening to Black people here.

There is little recognition in the women's movement of the ways in which the gains made by white women have been and still are at the expense of Black women. Historically white women's sexuality has been constructed in oppositional terms to that of Black women (Davis 1982, Ware 1983). And it is to this history that white women refer as their starting point, it is with this history that they seek to come to terms but in an uncritical way – the engagement with it is essentially selective. The 'herstory' which white women use to trace the roots of women's oppression or to justify some form of political practice is an imperial history rooted in the prejudices of colonial and neo-colonial periods, a 'herstory' which suffers the same form of historical amnesia of white male historians, by ignoring the fundamental ways in which white women have benefitted from the oppression of Black people. What forms of contemporary feminist and socialist theories share is an inability to adequately deal with the contradictions inherent in gender and class relations within the context of a racist society. 'Race and sex are social realities which at particular historical moments structure class relations in as much as class relations structure them' (Lewis and Parmar, 1983).

Thus the perception white middle-class feminists have of what they need liberating from has little or no relevance to the day to day experience of the majority of Black women in Britain and the ways in which they determine the political choices which have to be made. Nowhere is this more apparent than in the oppositional terms in which women's liberation and Black people's liberation has been and still is posed. In her analysis of the women's suffrage movement in the USA and the Abolition of Slavery Campaigns, Angela Davis pointed to the opportunistic and racist arguments of some white women who made simplistic comparisons between the position of Black men and white women in nineteenth-century America (Davis, 1982). One such woman, Elizabeth Cady Stanton, wrote in 1865:

> The representation of women of the nation have done their uttermost for the last 30 years to secure freedom for the negroes and as long as he was the lowest in the scale of being we were willing to press his claims but now, as the celestial gate to civil rights is slowly moving on its hinges, it becomes a serious question whether we had better stand aside and see 'sambo' walk into the kingdom first (Davis, 1982).

This line of reasoning was not only limited to the USA; the movement for female emancipation in Britain was closely linked to theories of racial superiority and Empire.

It would appear that although feminists and indeed Marxists invoke the spectre of history/herstory at will in an attempt to locate the articulation of class and gender oppression, at the point at which that very history is called into question and challenges the bases of their analyses there is a curious kind of amnesia. The past is invoked at will, but differentially, to make sense of the range of political options open to socialists and feminists.*

Few white feminists in Britain and elsewhere have elevated the question of racism to the level of primacy, within their practical political activities or in their intellectual work. The women's movement has unquestioningly been premised on a celebration of 'sisterhood' with its implicit assumption that women qua women have a necessary basis for unity and solidarity; a sentiment reflected in academic feminist writings which is inevitably influenced by the women's movement and incorporates some of its assumptions.

---

* There have been a range of debates around socialism and feminism which have ignored the issue of race. See for example Rowbotham, Segal and Wainwright (1979) and Sargent (1981) which has only one essay on 'The Incompatible Menage a Trois.'

While one tendency has been for Black women to have either remained invisible within feminist scholarship or to have been treated purely as women without any significance attached to our colour and race, another tendency has been the idealization and culturalism of anthropological works. Often we have appeared in cross cultural studies which under the guise of feminist and progressive anthropology, renders us as 'subjects' for 'interesting' and 'exotic' comparison. For instance, the book *Women United Women Divided* looked at women's solidarity in cross cultural perspectives and 'discovered' that solidarity was no unitary concept. The authors defined feminist consciousness and then proceeded to judge other cultural situations to see if they are feminist or not. While acknowledging that there are problems about uncritically accepting women as a universal category, this is purely on the basis of 'differential relations in class and status hierarchies as well as factors such as age and kinship affiliation.' There is no apology for, nay awareness even, of the contradictions of white feminists as anthropologists studying village women in India, Africa, China for evidence of feminist consciousness and female solidarity. Furthermore, one wonders why they find it easier to study middle-class women in India and their organizations to prove that 'these women organize to protect class privilege in activities that complement their husbands' objective positions in the class hierarchy' than to study or examine the class position of the majority of the white women in the women's organizations in Western Europe; to examine how these women have different interests and power according to their class, age, race and sexuality and organize accordingly to protect their interests. By adopting the research methods and frameworks of white male academics much academic feminist writing fails to challenge their assumptions, repeats their racial chauvinism and is consequently of less use to us.

One such assumption is that pre-capitalist economies equal backwardness in both a cultural and ideological sense and in fact are responsible for the continued oppression of women in these societies. It is further implied that it is only when Third World women enter into capitalist relations will they have any hope of liberation:

> There can be little doubt that on balance the position of women in imperialist, i.e. advanced capitalist societies is, for all its implications

more advanced than in the less developed capitalist and non capitalist societies. In this sense the changes brought by imperialism to Third World societies may, in some circumstances have been historically progressive (Molyneux, 1981).

The above analysis falsely assumes that imperialism necessarily brings capitalist relations and is parallel to the resurgence of development theories in neo-marxist literature that argue that imperialism is progressive for 'underdeveloped' nations (Warren, 1980; for critique see Sivanandan, 1982).

Furthermore, when Black and Third World women are being told that imperialism is good for us, it should be of no great surprise to anyone when we reject a feminism which uses Western social and economic systems to judge and make pronouncements about how Third World women can become emancipated. Feminist theories which examine our cultural practices as 'feudal residues' or label us 'traditional', also portray us as politically immature women who need to be versed and schooled in the ethos of Western feminism. They need to be continually challenged, exposed for their racism and denied any legitimacy as authentic feminists.

References

Carby, Hazel (1982) 'White Women Listen! Black Feminism and the Boundaries of Sisterhood' in Centre for Contemporary Cultural Studies (1982).

Davis, Angela (1982) *Women, Race and Class* London: Women's Press.

Lewis, Gail and Parmar, Pratibha (1983) 'Review Essay of American Black Feminist Literature' *Race and Class* vol 25 Autumn 1983.

Molyneux, Maxine (1981) 'Socialist Societies Old and New: Progress Towards Women's Emancipation' *Feminist Review* no 8, pp. 1–34.

Sivanandan, A. (1982) 'Capitalism, Highest Stage of Imperialism. Warren and the Third World' *Race and Class* no. 24 1982.

Ware, Veronica (1983) 'Imperialism, Racism and Violence Against Women' *Emergency* no 1, winter 83/4.

Warren, Bill (1980) *Imperialism, Pioneer of Capitalism* London: New Left Books.

80.

BELL HOOKS

Born 1952, Hopkinsville, Kentucky, United States of America

from *Feminist Theory: From Margin to Center*
1984

A central tenet of modern feminist thought has been the assertion that 'all women are oppressed.' This assertion implies that women share a common lot, that factors like class, race, religion, sexual preference, etc. do not create a diversity of experience that determines the extent to which sexism will be an oppressive force in the lives of individual women. Sexism as a system of domination is institutionalized, but it has never determined in an absolute way the fate of all women in this society. Being oppressed means the *absence of choices*. It is the primary point of contact between the oppressed and the oppressor. Many women in this society do have choices (as inadequate as they are); therefore exploitation and discrimination are words that more accurately describe the lot of women collectively in the United States. Many women do not join organized resistance against sexism precisely because sexism has not meant an absolute lack of choices. They may know they are discriminated against on the basis of sex, but they do not equate this with oppression. Under capitalism, patriarchy is structured so that sexism restricts women's behavior in some realms even as freedom from limitations is allowed in other spheres. The absence of extreme restrictions leads many women to ignore the areas in which they are exploited or discriminated against; it may even lead them to imagine that no women are oppressed.

81.

TONI MORRISON

Born 1931, Lorain, Ohio, United States of America
Died 2019, New York City, New York, United States of America

A Knowing So Deep

1985

I think about us, Black women, a lot. How many of us are battered and how many are champions. I note the strides that have replaced the tiptoe; I watch the new configurations we have given to personal relationships, wonder what shapes are forged and what merely bent. I think about the sisters no longer with us, who, in rage or contentment, left us to finish what should never have begun: a gender/racial war in which everybody would lose, if we lost, and in which everybody would win, if we won. I think about the Black women who never landed who are still swimming open-eyed in the sea. I think about those of us who did land and see how their strategies for survival became our maneuvers for power.

I know the achievements of the past are staggering in their everyday-ness as well as their singularity. I know the work undone is equally staggering, for it is nothing less than to alter the world in each of its parts: the distribution of money, the management of resources, the way families are nurtured, the way work is accomplished and valued, the penetration of the network that connects these parts. If each hour of every day brings fresh reasons to weep, the same hour is full of cause for congratulations: Our scholarship illuminates our past, our political astuteness brightens our future, and the ties that bind us to other women are in constant repair in order to build strength in this present, now.

I think about us, women and girls, and I want to say something worth saying to a daughter, a friend, a mother, a sister – my self. And if I were to try, it might go like this:

Dear Us:

You were the rim of the world – its beginning. Primary. In the first shadow the new sun threw, you carried inside you all there was of startled and startling life. And you were there to do it when the things of the world needed words. Before you were named, you were already naming.

Hell's twins, slavery and silence, came later. Still you were like no other. Not because you suffered more or longer, but because of what you knew and did before, during, and following that suffering. No one knew your weight until you left them to carry their own. But you knew. You said, 'Excuse me, am I in the way?' knowing all the while that you were the way. You had this canny ability to shape an untenable reality, mold it, sing it, reduce it to its manageable, transforming essence, which is a knowing so deep it's like a secret. In your silence, enforced or chosen, lay not only eloquence but discourse so devastating that 'civilization' could not risk engaging in it lest it lose the ground it stomped. All claims to prescience disintegrate when and where that discourse takes place. When you say 'No' or 'Yes' or 'This and not that,' change itself changes.

So the literature you live and write asks and gives no quarter. When you sculpt or paint, organize or refute, manage, teach, nourish, investigate or love, you do not blink. Your gaze, so lovingly unforgiving, stills, agitates and stills again. Wild or serene, vulnerable or steel trap; you are the touchstone by which all that is human can be measured. Porch or horizon, your sweep is grand.

You are what fashion tries to be – original and endlessly refreshing. Say what they like on channel X, you are the news of the day. What doesn't love you has trivialized itself and must answer for that. And anybody who does not know your history doesn't know their own and must answer for that too.

You did all right, girl. Then, at the first naming, and now at the renaming. You did all right. You took the hands of the children and danced with them. You defended men who could not defend you. You turned grandparents over on their sides to freshen sheets and white pillows. You made meals from leavings, and leaving you was never a real separation because nobody needed your face to remember you by. And all along the way you had the best of company – others, we others, just like you. When you cried, I did too. When we fought, I was afraid you would break your fingernails or split a seam at the armhole of your jacket. And you made me laugh so hard the sound of it disappeared – returned, I guess, to its beginning when laughter and tears were sisters too.

There is a movement in the shadow of a sun that is old now. There, just there. Coming from the rim of the world. A disturbing disturbance that is not a hawk nor stormy weather, but a dark woman, of all things. My sister, my me – rustling, like life.

82.

DONNA HARAWAY

Born 1944 Denver, Colorado, United States of America

from *A Cyborg Manifesto: Science, Technology, and Socialist-Feminism in the Late Twentieth Century*

1985

The cyborg is a creature in a postgender world; it has no truck with bisexuality, pre-oedipal symbiosis, unalienated labor, or other seductions to organic wholeness through a final appropriation of all the powers of the parts into a higher unity. In a sense, the cyborg has no origin story in the Western sense – a 'final' irony since the cyborg is also the awful apocalyptic *telos* of the 'West's' escalating dominations of abstract individuation, an ultimate self untied at last from all dependency, a man in space. An origin story in the 'Western', humanist sense depends on the myth of original unity, fullness, bliss and terror, represented by the phallic mother from whom all humans must separate, the task of individual development and of history, the twin potent myths inscribed most powerfully for us in psychoanalysis and Marxism. Hilary Klein has argued that both Marxism and psychoanalysis, in their concepts of labor and of individuation and gender formation, depend on the plot of original unity out of which difference must be produced and enlisted in a drama of escalating domination of woman/nature. The cyborg skips the step of original unity, of identification with nature in the Western sense. This is its illegitimate promise that might lead to subversion of its teleology as Star Wars.

The cyborg is resolutely committed to partiality, irony, intimacy, and perversity. It is oppositional, utopian, and completely without innocence. No longer structured by the polarity of public and private, the cyborg defines a technological polis based partly on a revolution of social relations in the *oikos*, the household. Nature and culture are reworked; the one can no longer be the resource for appropriation or incorporation by the other.

456

The relationships for forming wholes from parts, including those of polarity and hierarchical domination, are at issue in the cyborg world. Unlike the hopes of Frankenstein's monster, the cyborg does not expect its father to save it through a restoration of the garden – that is, through the fabrication of heterosexual mate, through its completion in a finished whole, a city and cosmos. The cyborg does not dream of community on the model of the organic family, this time without the oedipal project. The cyborg would not recognize the Garden of Eden; it is not made of mud and cannot dream of returning to dust. Perhaps that is why I want to see if cyborgs can subvert the apocalypse of returning to nuclear dust in the manic compulsion to name the Enemy. Cyborgs are not reverent; they do not re-member the cosmos. They are wary of holism, but needy for connection – they seem to have a natural feel for united-front politics, but without the vanguard party. The main trouble with cyborgs, of course, is that they are the illegitimate offspring of militarism and patriarchal capitalism, not to mention state socialism. But illegitimate offspring are often exceedingly unfaithful to their origins. Their fathers, after all, are inessential.

I will return to the science fiction of cyborgs at the end of this essay, but now I want to signal three crucial boundary breakdowns that make the following political-fictional (political-scientific) analysis possible. By the late twentieth century in U.S. scientific culture, the boundary between human and animal is thoroughly breached. The last beachheads of uniqueness have been polluted if not turned into amusement parks: language, tool use, social behavior, mental events – nothing really convincingly settles the separation of human and animal. And many people no longer feel the need for such a separation; indeed, many branches of feminist culture affirm the pleasure of connection of human and other living creatures. Movements for animal rights are not irrational denials of human uniqueness; they are a clear-sighted recognition of connection across the discredited breach of nature and culture. Biology and evolutionary theory over the past two centuries have simultaneously produced modern organisms as objects of knowledge and reduced the line between humans and animals to a faint trace re-etched in ideological struggle or professional disputes between life and social science. Within this framework, teaching modern Christian creationism should be fought as a form of child abuse.

Biological-determinist ideology is only one position opened up in scientific culture for arguing the meanings of human animality. There is much room for radical political people to contest the meanings of the breached boundary. The cyborg appears in myth precisely where the boundary between human and animal is transgressed. Far from signaling a walling off of people from other living beings, cyborgs signal disturbingly and pleasurably tight coupling. Bestiality has a new status in this cycle of marriage exchange.

The second leaky distinction is between animal-human (organism) and machine. Pre-cybernetic machines could be haunted; there was always the specter of the ghost in the machine. This dualism structured the dialogue between materialism and idealism that was settled by a dialectical progeny, called spirit or history, according to taste. But basically machines were not self-moving, self-designing, autonomous. They could not achieve man's dream, only mock it. They were not man, an author to himself, but only a caricature of that masculinist reproductive dream. To think they were otherwise was paranoid. Now we are not so sure. Late twentieth-century machines have made thoroughly ambiguous the difference between natural and artificial mind and body, self-developing and externally designed, and many other distinctions that used to apply to organism and machines. Our machines are disturbingly lively, and we ourselves frighteningly inert.

Technological determination is only one ideological space opened up by the reconceptions of machine and organism as coded texts through which we engage in the play of writing and reading the world. 'Textualization' of everything in poststructuralist, postmodernist theory has been damned by Marxists and socialist-feminists for its utopian disregard for the lived relations of domination that ground the 'play' of arbitrary reading. It is certainly true that postmodernist strategies, like my cyborg myth, subvert myriad organic wholes (for example, the poem, the primitive culture, the biological organism). In short, the certainty of what counts as nature – a source of insight and promise of innocence – is undermined, probably fatally. The transcendent authorization of interpretation is lost, and with it the ontology grounding 'Western' epistemology. But the alternative is not cynicism or faithlessness, that is, some version of abstract existence, like the accounts of technological determinism destroying 'man' by the 'machine' or 'meaningful political action' by the 'text.' Who cyborgs will be is a radical question; the answers are a matter of survival. Both chimpanzees and artifacts have politics (de Waal 1982; Winner 1980), so why shouldn't we?

The third distinction is a subset of the second: the boundary between physical and nonphysical is very imprecise for us. Pop physics books on the consequences of quantum theory and the indeterminacy principle are a kind of popular scientific equivalent to Harlequin romances as a marker of radical change in American white heterosexuality: they get it wrong, but they are on the right subject. Modern machines are quintessentially microelectronic devices: they are everywhere and they are invisible. Modern machinery is an irreverent upstart god, mocking the Father's ubiquity and spirituality. The silicon chip is a surface for writing; it is etched in molecular scales disturbed only by atomic noise, the ultimate interference for nuclear scores.

Writing, power, and technology are old partners in Western stories of the origin of civilization, but miniaturization has changed our experience of mechanism. Miniaturization has turned out to be about power; small is not so much beautiful as preeminently dangerous, as in cruise missiles. Contrast the TV sets of the 1950s or the news cameras of the 1970s with the TV wristbands or hand-sized video cameras now advertised. Our best machines are made of sunshine; they are all light and clean because they are nothing but signals, electromagnetic waves, a section of a spectrum, and these machines are eminently portable, mobile – a matter of immense human pain in Detroit and Singapore. People are nowhere near so fluid, being both material and opaque. Cyborgs are ether, quintessence.

The ubiquity and invisibility of cyborgs are precisely why these Sunshine Belt machines are so deadly. They are as hard to see politically as materially. They are about consciousness – or its simulation. They are floating signifiers moving in pickup trucks across Europe, blocked more effectively by the witch-weavings of the displaced and so unnatural women of the antinuclear Greenham Women's Peace Camp, who read the cyborg webs of power so very well, than by the militant labor of older masculinist politics, whose natural constituency needs defense jobs. Ultimately the 'hardest' science is about the realm of greatest boundary confusion, the realm of pure number, pure spirit, C³I, cryptography, and the preservation of potent secrets. The new machines are so clean and light. Their engineers are sun-worshippers mediating a new scientific revolution associated with the night dream of postindustrial society. The diseases evoked by these clean machines are 'no more' than the minuscule coding changes of an antigen in the immune system, 'no more' than the experience of stress. The nimble fingers of 'Oriental' women, the old fascination of little Anglo-Saxon Victorian girls with doll's houses, women's enforced attention to the small take on quite new dimensions in this world. There might be a cyborg Alice taking account of these new dimensions. Ironically, it might be the unnatural cyborg women making chips in Asia and spiral dancing in Santa Rita jail whose constructed unities will guide effective oppositional strategies.

So my cyborg myth is about transgressed boundaries, potent fusions, and dangerous possibilities, which progressive people might explore as one part of needed political work. One of my premises is that most American socialists and feminists see deepened dualisms of mind and body, animal and machine, idealism and materialism in the social practices, symbolic formulations, and physical artifacts associated with 'high technology' and scientific culture. From *One-Dimensional Man* (Marcuse 1964) to *The Death of Nature* (Merchant 1980), the analytic resources developed by progressives have insisted on the necessary domination of technics and recalled us to an imagined organic body to integrate our resistance. Another of my premises is that the need for unity of people trying to resist worldwide intensification of domination has never been more acute. But a slightly perverse shift of perspective might better enable us to contest for meanings, as well as for other forms of power and pleasure in technologically mediated societies.

From one perspective, a cyborg world is about the final imposition of a grid of control on the planet, about the final abstraction embodied in a Star Wars apocalypse waged in the name of defense, about the final appropriation of women's bodies in a masculinist orgy or war (Sofia 1984). From another perspective, a cyborg world might be about lived social and bodily realities in which people are not afraid of their joint kinship with animals and machines, not afraid of permanently partial identities and contradictory standpoints. The political struggle is to see from both perspectives at once because each reveals both dominations and possibilities unimaginable from the other vantage point. Single vision produces worse illusions than double vision or many-headed monsters. Cyborg unities are monstrous and illegitimate; in our present political circumstances, we could hardly hope for more potent myths for resistance and recoupling. I like to imagine LAG, the Livermore Action Group, as a kind of cyborg society, dedicated to realistically converting the laboratories that most fiercely embody and spew out the tools of the technological apocalypse, and committed to building a political form that actually manages to hold together witches, engineers, elders, perverts, Christians, mothers, and Leninists long enough to disarm the state. Fission Impossible is the name of the affinity group in my town. (Affinity: related not by blood but by choice, the appeal of one chemical nuclear group for another, avidity.)

83.

ANGELA DAVIS

Born 1944, Birmingham, Alabama, United States of America

Let Us All Rise Together: Radical Perspectives on Empowerment For Afro-American Women

1987

The concept of empowerment is hardly new to Afro-American women. For almost a century, we have been organized in bodies that have sought collectively to develop strategies illuminating the way to economic and political power for ourselves and our communities. During the last decade of the nineteenth century, after having been repeatedly shunned by the racially homogeneous women's rights movement, Black women organized their own Club Movement. In 1895 – five years after the founding of the General Federation of Women's Clubs, which consolidated a club movement reflecting concerns of middle-class White women – one hundred Black women from ten states met in the city of Boston, under the leadership of Josephine St Pierre Ruffin, to discuss the creation of a national organization of Black women's clubs. As compared to their White counterparts, the Afro-American women issuing the call for this national club movement articulated principles that were more openly political in nature. They defined the primary function of their clubs as an ideological as well as an activist defense of Black women – and men – from the ravages of racism. When the meeting was convened, its participants emphatically declared that, unlike their White sisters, whose organizational policies were seriously tainted by racism, they envisioned their movement as one open to all women:

Our woman's movement is woman's movement in that it is led and directed by women for the good of women and men, for the benefit of *all* humanity, which is more than any one branch or section of it. We want, we ask the active interest of our men, and, too, we are not drawing the color line; we are women, American women, as intensely interested in all that pertains to us as such as all other American women; we are not alienating or withdrawing, we are only coming to the front, willing to join any others in the same work and cordially inviting and welcoming any others to join us.*

The following year, the formation of the National Association of Colored Women's Clubs was announced. The motto chosen by the Association was 'Lifting As We Climb.'†

The nineteenth-century women's movement was also plagued by classism. Susan B. Anthony wondered why her outreach to working-class women on the issue of the ballot was so frequently met with indifference. She wondered why these women seemed to be much more concerned with improving their economic situation than with achieving the right to vote.‡ As essential as political equality may have been to the larger campaign for women's rights, in the eyes of Afro-American and White working-class women it was not synonymous with emancipation. That the conceptualization of strategies for struggle was based on the peculiar condition of White women of the privileged classes rendered those strategies discordant with working-class women's perceptions of empowerment. It is not surprising that many of them told Ms Anthony, 'Women want bread, not the ballot.'§ Eventually, of course, working-class White women, and Afro-American women as well, reconceptualized this struggle, defining the vote not as an end in itself – not as the panacea that would cure all the ills related to gender-based discrimination – but rather as an important weapon in the continuing fight for higher wages, better working conditions, and an end to the omnipresent menace of the lynch mob.

---

* Gerda Lerner, *Black Women in White America* (New York: Pantheon Books, 1972), p. 443.
† These clubs proliferated the progressive political scene during this era. By 1916 – twenty years later – 50,000 women in 28 federations and over 1000 clubs were members of the National Association of Colored Women's Clubs. See Paula Giddings's discussion of the origins and evolution of the Black Women's Cub Movement in When and Where I Enter (New York: William Morrow, 1984), Chapter IV–VI.
‡ Miriam Schneir, ed., Feminism: The Essential Historical Writings (New York: Vintage, 1972), pp.138–142.
§ Ibid.

Today, as we reflect on the process of empowering Afro-American women, our most efficacious strategies remain those that are guided by the principle used by Black women in the club movement. We must strive to 'lift as we climb.' In other words, we must climb in such a way as to guarantee that all of our sisters, regardless of social class, and indeed all of our brothers, climb with us. This must be the essential dynamic of our quest for power – a principle that must not only determine our struggles as Afro-American women, but also govern all authentic struggles of dispossessed people. Indeed, the overall battle for equality can be profoundly enhanced by embracing this principle.

Afro-American women bring to the women's movement a strong tradition of struggle around issues that politically link women to the most crucial progressive causes. This is the meaning of the motto, 'Lifting As We Climb.' This approach reflects the often unarticulated interests and aspirations of masses of women of all racial backgrounds. Millions of women today are concerned about jobs, working conditions, higher wages, and racist violence. They are concerned about plant closures, homelessness, and repressive immigration legislation. Women are concerned about homophobia, ageism, and discrimination against the physically challenged. We are concerned about Nicaragua and South Africa. And we share our children's dream that tomorrow's world will be delivered from the threat of nuclear omnicide. These are some of the issues that should be integrated into the overall struggle for women's rights if there is to be a serious commitment to the empowerment of women who have been rendered historically invisible. These are some of the issues we should consider if we wish to lift as we climb.

During this decade we have witnessed an exciting resurgence of the women's movement. If the first wave of the women's movement began in the 1840's, and the second wave in the 1960's, then we are approaching the crest of a third wave in the final days of the 1980's. When the feminist historians of the twenty-first century attempt to recapitulate the third wave, will they ignore the momentous contributions of Afro-American women, who have been leaders and activists in movements often confined to women of color, but whose accomplishments have invariably advanced the cause of white women as well? Will the exclusionary policies of the mainstream women's movement – from its inception to the present – which have often compelled Afro-American women to conduct their struggle for equality outside the ranks of that movement, continue to result in the systematic omission of our names from the roster of prominent leaders and activists of the women's movement? Will there continue to be two distinct continuums of the women's movement, one visible and another invisible, one publicly acknowledged and another ignored except by the conscious progeny of the working-class women – Black, Latina, Native American, Asian, and white – who forged that hidden continuum? If this question is answered in the affirmative, it will mean that women's quest for equality will continue to be gravely deficient. The revolutionary potential of the women's movement still will not have been realized. The racist-inspired flaws of the first and second waves of the women's movement will have become the inherited flaws of the third wave.

How can we guarantee that this historical pattern is broken? As advocates and activists of women's rights in our time, we must begin to merge that double legacy in order to create a single continuum, one that solidly represents the aspirations of all women in our society. We must begin to create a revolutionary, multiracial women's movement that seriously addresses the main issues affecting poor and working-class women. In order to tap the potential for such a movement, we must further develop those sectors of the movement that are addressing seriously issues affecting poor and working-class women, such as jobs, pay equity, paid maternity leave, federally subsidized child care, protection from sterilization abuse, and subsidized abortions. Women of all racial and class backgrounds will greatly benefit from such an approach.

For decades, white women activists have repeated the complaint that women of color frequently fail to respond to their appeals. 'We invited them to our meetings, but they didn't come.' 'We asked them to participate in our demonstration, but they didn't show.' 'They just don't seem to be interested in women's studies.'

This process cannot be initiated merely by intensified efforts to attract Latina women or Afro-American women or Asian or Native American women into the existing organizational forms dominated by white women of the more privileged economic strata. The particular concerns of women of color must be included in the agenda.

An issue of special concern to Afro-American women is unemployment. Indeed, the most fundamental prerequisite for empowerment is the ability to earn an adequate living. At the height of its audacity, the Reagan government boasted that unemployment had leveled off, leaving only(!) 7.5 million people unemployed. These claims came during a period in which Black people in general were twice as likely to be unemployed as white people, and Black teenagers almost three times as likely to be unemployed as white teenagers.* We must remember that these figures do not include the millions who hold part-time jobs, although they want and need full-time employment. A disproportionate number of these underemployed individuals are women. Neither do the figures reflect those who, out of utter frustration, have ceased to search for employment, nor those whose unemployment insurance has run out, nor those who have never had a job. Women on welfare are also among those who are not counted as unemployed.

At the same time that the Reagan administration attempted to convey the impression that it had successfully slowed the rise of unemployment, the AFL-CIO estimated that 18 million people of working age were without jobs. These still-critical levels of unemployment, distorted and misrepresented by the Reagan administration, are fundamentally responsible for the impoverished status of Afro-American women, the most glaring evidence of which resides in the fact that women, together with their dependent children, constitute the fastest-growing sector of the 4 million homeless people in the United States. There can be no serious discussion of empowerment today if we do not embrace the plight of the homeless with an enthusiasm as passionate as that with which we embrace issues more immediately related to our own lives.

The United Nations declared 1987 to be the Year of Shelter for the Homeless. Although only the developing countries were the initial focus of this resolution, eventually it became clear that the United States is an 'undeveloping country.' Two-thirds of the 4 million homeless in this country are families, and 40 percent of them are Afro-American.† In some urban areas, as many as 70 percent of the homeless are Black. In New York City, for example, 60 percent of the homeless population are Black, 20 percent Latino, and 20 percent white.‡ Presently, under New York's

---

* Children's Defense Fund, *Black and White Children in America: Key Facts* (Washington, D.C.: Author, 1985), pp. 21–22.
† *WREE-VIEW*, Vol. 12, nos. 1 & 2, January–April, 1987.
‡ Ibid.

Work Incentive Program, homeless women and men are employed to clean toilets, wash graffiti from subway trains, and clean parks at wages of sixty-two cents an hour, a mere fraction of the minimum wage.* In other words, the homeless are being compelled to provide slave labor for the government if they wish to receive assistance.

Black women scholars and professionals cannot afford to ignore the straits of our sisters who are acquainted with the immediacy of oppression in a way many of us are not. The process of empowerment cannot be simplistically defined in accordance with our own particular class interests. We must learn to lift as we climb.

If we are to elevate the status of our entire community as we scale the heights of empowerment, we must be willing to offer organized resistance to the proliferating manifestations of racist violence across the country. A virtual 'race riot' took place on the campus of one of the most liberal educational institutions in this country not long ago. In the aftermath of the World Series, white students at the University of Massachusetts, Amherst, who were purportedly fans of the Boston Red Sox, vented their wrath on Black students, whom they perceived as a surrogate for the winning team, the New York Mets, because of the predominance of Black players on the Mets. When individuals in the crowd yelled 'Black bitch' at a Black woman student, a Black man who hastened to defend her was seriously wounded and rushed unconscious to the hospital. Another one of the many dramatic instances of racist harassment to occur on college campuses during this period was the burning of a cross in front of the Black Students' Cultural Center at Purdue University.† In December 1986, Michael Griffith, a young Black man, lost his life in what amounted to a virtual lynching by a mob of White youths in the New York suburb of Howard Beach. Not far from

---

* Ibid.
† The incidence of racial violence on college campuses has increased significantly since this speech was delivered in the summer of 1987. 'Reports of racist acts at U.S. colleges and universities have been piling up at an increased pace for several years, and now, fresh incidents and controversies seem to arrive almost daily' ('Racism, A Stain on Ivory Towers', *The Boston Daily Globe*, 2/28/88, p.1). In response to these incidents, students have organized themselves to improve the racial climate on their campuses. For example, in March 1988, a coalition of multiracial, domestic and international students at Hampshire College in Amherst, Massachusetts, demonstrated the seriousness of their concerns by staging a building takeover and demanding specific correctives.

Atlanta, civil rights marchers were attacked on Dr Martin Luther King's birthday by a mob led by the Ku Klux Klan. An especially outrageous instance in which racist violence was officially condoned was the acquittal of Bernhard Goetz, who, on his own admission, attempted to kill four Black youths because he *felt* threatened by them on a New York subway.

Black women have organized before to oppose racist violence. In the nineteenth century the Black Women's Club Movement was born largely in response to the epidemic of lynching during that era. Leaders like Ida B. Wells and Mary Church Terrell recognized that Black women could not move toward empowerment if they did not radically challenge the reign of lynch law in the land. Today, Afro-American women must actively take the lead in the movement against racist violence, as did our sister-ancestors almost a century Ago. We must lift as we climb. As our ancestors organized for the passage of a federal antilynch law – and indeed involved themselves in the woman suffrage movement for the purpose of securing that legislation – we must today become activists in the effort to secure legislation declaring racism and anti-Semitism as crimes. Extensively as some instances of racist violence may be publicized at this time, many more racist-inspired crimes go unnoticed as a consequence of the failure of law enforcement to specifically classify them as such. A person scrawling swastikas or 'KKK' on an apartment building may simply be charged – if criminal charges are brought at all – with defacing property or malicious mischief. Recently, a Ku Klux Klanner who burned a cross in front of a Black family's home was charged with 'burning without a permit.' We need federal and local laws against acts of racist and anti-Semitic violence. We must organize, lobby, march, and demonstrate in order to guarantee their passage.

As we organize, lobby, march, and demonstrate against racist violence, we who are women of color must be willing to appeal for multiracial unity in the spirit of our sister-ancestors. Like them, we must proclaim: We do not draw the color line. The only line we draw is one based on our political principles. We know that empowerment for the masses of women in our country will never be achieved as long as we do not succeed in pushing back the tide of racism. It is not a coincidence that sexist-inspired violence – in particular, terrorist attacks on abortion clinics – has reached a peak during the same period in which racist violence has proliferated dramatically.

Violent attacks on women's reproductive rights are nourished by these explosions of racism. The vicious antilesbian and antigay attacks are a part of the same menacing process. The roots of sexism and homophobia are found in the same economic and political institutions that serve as the foundation of racism in this country and, more often than not, the same extremist circles that inflict violence on people of color are responsible for the eruptions of violence inspired by sexist and homophobic biases. Our political activism must clearly manifest our understanding of these connections.

We must always attempt to lift as we climb. Another urgent point on our political agenda – for Afro-American and for all progressive women – must be the repeal of the Simpson-Rodino Law. The Simpson-Rodino Law is a racist law that spells repression for vast numbers of women and men who are undocumented immigrants in this country. Camouflaged as an amnesty program, its eligibility restrictions are so numerous that hundreds of thousands of people stand to be prosecuted and deported under its provisions. Amnesty is provided in a restricted way only for those who came to this country before 1982. Thus, the vast numbers of Mexicans who have recently crossed the border in an attempt to flee intensified impoverishment bred by the unrestricted immigration of U.S. corporations into their countries are not eligible. Salvadorans and other Central Americans who have escaped political persecution in their respective countries over the last few years will not be offered amnesty. We must organize, lobby, march, and demonstrate for a repeal of the Simpson-Rodino Law.* We must lift as we climb.

When we as Afro-American women, when we as women of color, proceed to ascend toward empowerment, we lift up with us our brothers of color, our white sisters and brothers in the working class, and, indeed, all women who experience the effects of sexist oppression. Our activist agenda must encompass a wide range of demands. We must call for jobs and for the unionization of unorganized women workers, and, indeed, unions must be compelled to take on such issues as affirmative action, pay equity, sexual harassment on the job, and paid maternity leave for women. Because Black and Latina women are AIDS victims in disproportionately

* Unfortunately, the Simpson-Rodino bill was signed into law on November 6, 1987, with employer sanctions taking effect on June 1, 1988.

469

large numbers, we have a special interest in demanding emergency funding for AIDS research. We must oppose all instances of repressive mandatory AIDS testing and quarantining, as well as homophobic manipulations of the AIDS crisis. Effective strategies for the reduction of teenage pregnancy are needed, but we must beware of succumbing to propagandistic attempts to relegate to young single mothers the responsibility for our community's impoverishment.

In the aftermath of the Reagan era, it should be clear that there are forces in our society that reap enormous benefits from the persistent, deepening oppression of women. Members of the Reagan administration include advocates for the most racist, antiworking class, and sexist circles of contemporary monopoly capitalism. These corporations continue to prop up apartheid in South Africa and to profit from the spiraling arms race while they propose the most vulgar and irrational forms of anti-Sovietism – invoking, for example, the 'evil empire' image popularized by Ronald Reagan – as justifications for their omnicidal ventures. If we are not afraid to adopt a revolutionary stance – if, indeed, we wish to be radical in our quest for change – then we must get to the root of our oppression. After all, *radical* simply means 'grasping things at the root.' Our agenda for women's empowerment must thus be unequivocal in our challenge to monopoly capitalism as a major obstacle to the achievement of equality.

I want to suggest, as I conclude, that we link our grass-roots organizing, our essential involvement in electoral politics, and our involvement as activists in mass struggles to the long-range goal of fundamentally transforming the socioeconomic conditions that generate and persistently nourish the various forms of oppression we suffer. Let us learn from the strategies of our sisters in South Africa and Nicaragua. As Afro-American women, as women of color in general, as progressive women of all racial backgrounds, let us join our sisters – and brothers – across the globe who are attempting to forge a new socialist order – an order which will reestablish socioeconomic priorities so that the quest for monetary profit will never be permitted to take precedence over the real interests of human beings. This is not to say that our problems will magically dissipate with the advent of socialism. Rather, such a social order should provide us with the real opportunity to further extend our struggles, with the assurance that one day we will be able to redefine the basic elements of our oppression as useless refuse of the past.

84.

GLORIA ANZALDÚA

Born 1942, Rio Grande Valley, Texas, United States of America
Died 2004, Santa Cruz, California, United States of America

from *Borderlands*

1987

Cultural Tyranny

Culture forms our beliefs. We perceive the version of reality that it com-municates. Dominant paradigms, predefined concepts that exist as unquestionable, unchallengeable, are transmitted to us through the cul-ture. Culture is made by those in power – men. Males make the rules and laws; women transmit them. How many times have I heard mothers and mothers-in-law tell their sons to beat their wives for not obeying them, for being *bociconas* (big mouths), for being *callejeras* (going to visit and gossip with neighbors), for expecting their husbands to help with the rearing of children and the housework, for wanting to be something other than housewives?

The culture expects women to show greater acceptance of, and com-mitment to, the value system than men. The culture and the Church insist that women are subservient to males. If a woman rebels she is a *mujer mala*. If a woman doesn't renounce herself in favor of the male, she is selfish. If a woman remains a *virgen* until she marries, she is a good woman. For a woman of my culture there used to be only three directions she could turn: to the Church as a nun, to the streets as a prostitute, or to the home as a mother. Today some of us have a fourth choice: entering the world by way of education and career and becoming self-autonomous persons. A very few of us. As a working-class people our chief activity is to put food in our mouths, a roof over our heads and clothes on our backs. Educating our children is out of reach for most of us. Educated or not, the onus is still on woman to be a wife/mother – only the nun can escape motherhood. Women are made to feel total failures if they don't marry and have children. '*Y cuando te casas, Gloria? Se te va a pasar el tren.' Y yo les digo, 'Pos si me caso, no va ser con un hombre.' Se quedan calladitas. Sí, soy hija de la Chingada*. I've always been her daughter. *No 'tés chingando.*

Humans fear the supernatural, both the undivine (the animal impulses such as sexuality, the unconscious, the unknown, the alien) and the divine (the superhuman, the god in us). Culture and religion seek to protect us from these two forces. The female, by virtue of creating entities of flesh and blood in her stomach (she bleeds every month but does not die), by virtue of being in tune with nature's cycles, is feared. Because, according to Christianity and most other major religions, women is carnal, animal, and closer to the undivine, she must be protected. Protected from herself. Woman is the stranger, the other. She is man's recognized nightmarish pieces, his Shadow-Beast. The sight of her sends him into a frenzy of anger and fear.

La gorra, el rebozo, la mantilla are symbols of my culture's 'protection' of women. Culture (read males) professes to protect women. Actually it keeps women in rigidly defined roles. It keeps the girlchild from other men – don't poach on my preserves, only I can touch my child's body. Our mothers taught us well, '*Los hombres nomás quieren una cosa*'; men aren't to be trusted, they are selfish and are like children. Mothers made sure we didn't walk into a room of brothers or fathers or uncles in nightgowns or shorts. We were never alone with men, not even those of our own family.

Through our mothers, the culture gave us mixed messages: *No voy a dejar que ningún pelado desgraciado maltrate a mis hijos.* And in the next breath it would say, *La mujer tiene que hacer lo que le diga el hombre.* Which was it to be – strong, or submissive, rebellious or conforming?

Tribal rights over those of the individual insured the survival of the tribe and were necessary then, and, as in the case of all indigenous peoples in the world who are still fighting off intentional, premeditated murder (genocide), they are still necessary.

Much of what the culture condemns focuses on kinship relationships. The welfare of the family, the community, and the tribe is more important than the welfare of the individual. The individual exists first as kin – as sister, as father, as *padrino* – and last as self.

In my culture, selfishness is condemned, especially in women; humility and selflessness, the absence of selfishness, is considered a virtue. In the past, acting humble with members outside the family ensured that you would make no one *envidioso* (envious); therefore he or she would not use witchcraft against you. If you get above yourself, you're an *envidiosa*. If you don't behave like everyone else, *la gente* will say that you think you're better than others, *que te crees grande*. With ambition (condemned in the Mexican culture and valued in the Anglo) comes envy. *Respeto* carries with it a set of rules so that social categories and hierarchies will be kept in order: respect is reserved for *la abuela, papá, el patrón*, those with power in the community. Women are at the bottom of the ladder one rung above the deviants. The Chicano, *mexicano*, and some Indian cultures have no tolerance for deviance. Deviance is whatever is condemned by the community. Most societies try to get rid of their deviants. Most cultures have burned and beaten their homosexuals and others who deviate from the sexual common. The queer are the mirror reflecting the heterosexual tribe's fear: being different, being other and therefore lesser, therefore sub-human, in-human, non-human.

Half and Half

There was a *muchacha* who lived near my house. *La gente del pueblo* talked about her being *una de las otras*, 'of the Others.' They said that for six months she was a woman who has a vagina that bled once a month, and that for the other six months she was a man, had a penis and she peed standing up. They called her half and half, *mita' y mita'*, neither one nor the other but a strange doubling, a deviation of nature that horrified, a work of nature inverted. But there is a magic aspect in abnormality and so-called deformity. Maimed, mad, and sexually different people were believed to possess supernatural powers by primal cultures magico-religious thinking. For them, abnormality was the price a person had to pay for her or his inborn extraordinary gift.

There is something compelling about being both male and female, about having an entry into both worlds. Contrary to some psychiatric tenets, half and halfs are not suffering from a confusion of sexual identity, or even from a confusion of gender. What we are suffering from is an absolute despot duality that says we are able to be only one or the other. It claims that human nature is limited and cannot evolve into something better. But I, like other queer people, am two in one body, both male and female. I am the embodiment of the *hieros gamos:* the coming together of opposite qualities within.

Fear of Going Home: Homophobia

For the lesbian of color the ultimate rebellion she can make against her native culture is through her sexual behavior. She goes against two moral prohibitions: sexuality and homosexuality. Being lesbian and raised Catholic, indoctrinated as straight, I *made the choice to be queer* (for some it is genetically inherent). It's an interesting path, one that continually slips in and out of the white, the Catholic, the Mexican, the indigenous, the instincts. In and out of my head. It makes for *loquería*, the crazies. It is a path of knowledge – one of knowing (and of learning) the history of oppression of our *raza*. It is a way of balancing, of mitigating duality.

In a New England college where I taught, the presence of a few lesbians threw the more conservative heterosexual students and faculty into a panic. The two lesbian students and we two lesbian instructors met with them to discuss their fears. One of the students said, 'I thought homophobia meant fear of going home after a residency'.

And I thought, how apt. Fear of going home. And of not being taken in. We're afraid of being abandoned by the mother, the culture, *la Raza*, for being unacceptable, faulty, damaged. Most of us unconsciously believe that if we reveal this unacceptable aspect of the self our mother/culture/ race will totally reject us. To avoid rejection, some of us conform to the values of the culture, push the unacceptable parts into the shadows. Which leaves only one fare – that we will be found out and that the Shadow-Beast will break out of its cage. Some of us take another route. We try to make ourselves conscious of the Shadow-Beast, stare at the sexual lust and lust for power and destruction we see on its face, discern among its features the undershadow that the reigning order of heterosexual males project on our Beast. Yet still others of us take it another step: we try to waken the Shadow-Beast inside us. Not many jump at the chance to confront the Shadow-Beast in the mirror without flinching at her lidless serpent eyes, her cold clammy moist hand dragging us underground, fangs bared and hissing. How does one put feathers on this particular serpent? But a few of us have been lucky – on the face of the Shadow-Beast we have seen not lust but tenderness; on its face we have uncovered the lie.

Intimate Terrorism: Life in the Borderlands

The world is not a safe place to live in. We shiver in separate cells in enclosed cities, shoulders hunched, barely keeping the panic below the surface of the skin, daily drinking shock along with our morning coffee, fearing the torches being set to our buildings, the attacks in the streets. Shutting down. Woman does not feel safe when her own culture, and white culture, are critical of her; when the males of all races hunt her as prey.

Alienated from her mother culture, 'alien' in the dominant culture, the woman of color does not feel safe within the inner life of her Self. Petrified, she can't respond, her face caught between *los intersticios*, the spaces between the different worlds she inhabits.

The ability to respond is what is meant by responsibility, yet our cultures take away our ability to act – shackle us in the name of protection. Blocked, immobilized, we can't move forward, can't move backwards. That writhing serpent movement, the very movement of life, swifter than lightning, frozen.

We do not engage fully. We do not make full use of our faculties. We abnegate. And there in front of us is the crossroads and choice: to feel a victim where someone else is in control and therefore responsible and to blame (being a victim and transferring the blame on culture, mother, father, ex-lover, friend, absolves me of responsibility), or to feel strong, and, for the most part, in control.

My Chicana identity is grounded in the Indian woman's history of resistance. The Aztec female rites of mourning were rites of defiance protesting the cultural changes which disrupted the equality and balance between female and male, and protesting their demotion to a lesser status, their denigration. Like *la Llorona*, the Indian woman's only means of protest was wailing.

So *mamá, Raza*, how wonderful, *no tener que render cuentas a nadie*. I feel perfectly free to rebel and to rail against any culture. I fear no betrayal on my part because, unlike Chicanas and other women of color who grew up white or who have only recently returned to their native cultural roots, I was totally immersed in mine. It wasn't until I went to high school that I 'saw' whites. Until I worked on my master's degree I had not gotten within an arm's distance of them. I was totally immersed *en lo mexicano*, a rural, peasant, isolated, *mexicanismo*. To separate from my culture (as from my family) I had to feel competent enough on the outside and secure enough inside to live life on my own. Yet in leaving home I did not lose touch with my origins because *lo mexicano* is in my system. I am a turtle, wherever I go I carry 'home' on my back.

Not me sold out my people but they me. So yes, though 'home' permeates every sinew and cartilage in my body, I too am afraid of going home. Thought I'll defend my race and culture when they are attacked by non-*mexicanos, conozco el malestar de mi cultura*. I abhor some of my culture's ways, how it cripples its women, *como burras*, our strengths used against us, lowly *burras* bearing humility with dignity. The ability to serve, claim the males, is our highest virtue. I abhor how my culture makes *macho* caricatures of its men. No, I do not buy all the myths of the tribe into which I was born. I can understand why the more tinged with Anglo blood, the more adamantly my colored and colorless sisters glorify their colored culture's values – to offset the extreme devaluation of it by the white culture. It's a legitimate reaction. But I will not glorify those aspects of my culture which have injured me and which have injured me in the name of protecting me.

So, don't give me your tenets and your laws. Don't give me your luke-warm gods. What I want is an accounting with all three cultures – white, Mexican, Indian. I want the freedom to carve and chisel my own face, to staunch the bleeding with ashes, to fashion my own gods out of my entrails. And if going home is denied me then I will have to stand and claim my space, making a new culture – *una cultura mestiza* – with my own lumber, my own bricks and mortar and my own feminist architecture.

85.

LEE MARACLE

Born 1950, Vancouver, Canada, member of the Stó:Lō Nation

from *I am Woman*

1988

The Women's Movement

A good number of non-white women have addressed the women's movement and decried the fact that we are outside the women's movement. I have never felt outside of that movement, except when I denied my own womanhood during my misguided youth. White women can hardly be expected to take responsibility for that. But then, I have never felt that the women's movement was centred or defined by women here in North America.

That the white women of North America are racist and that they define the movement in accordance with their own narrow perspective should not surprise us. White people define everything in terms of their own people, and then very magnanimously open the door to a select number of others. They let us in the door as we prove ourselves to be civilized. Such is the nature of racism. If we don't escape learning it, can we expect that they should?

We are part of a global movement of women in the world, struggling for emancipation. Women worldwide will define the movement, and we are among them. Until white women can come to us on our own terms, we ought to leave the door closed. Do we really want to be a part of a movement that sees the majority as the periphery and the minority as the centre?

I heard a white woman the other day talk about herself as a lesbian and refer to non-white women as minorities. That is the madness, the psychosis, of racism; the mistress accords herself distinction as a certain type of woman while erasing the womanhood of other peoples. For me, Audre Lorde most properly represents the women's movement in North America. The women's movement is all about the liberation of humanity from the yoke of domination. It is all about the fight against racism and sexism and their effects on our consciousness, no matter what colour we are. It is all about the struggle for unity between oppressed women and men.

There are some white women who truly wish to struggle with the effect that racism has had on their consciousness. That puts them at my doorstep, around my kitchen table. It does not inspire me to enter the master's wife's home, thank you very much. I do not have to urge white women to deal with their racism. The emancipation of non-white women of the world is taking care of that. The red-neck practices of the so-called feminist movement are already becoming history in some circles.

Some women accuse me of being angry and bitterly resentful about the life that this society handed me. You miss the real point. I write about racism to free my mind. Racism is the poison that crippled my tree. It also bent yours in all kinds of crazy directions. A talk, an intimate talk, between an ex-racist and an ex-victim of racism is not apt to be pretty.

Sojourner Truth told you already, 'Ain't I a woman.' She asked the white feminist movement on our behalf, a hundred years ago, and the white women of North America have yet to face the answer. She served up the question; we need do no more.

The world is a dark world. It is an impoverished world. It is a world fighting for its survival. It is not concerned about CanAmerica's definition of 'women's issues.' It is a world at war. Sojourner Truth properly reflects the world of today.

The women of the world are re-writing history with their bodies. White women of CanAmerica are a footnote to it all. I am not in the habit of concerning myself with footnotes. I am concerned about us, though. White women figure too largely in our minds. Let us stop chasing them and challenging their humanity at every turn. Let us begin by talking to each other about ourselves. Let us cleanse the dirty shack the racism left us. Let us deal with our men-folk and the refuse of patriarchy they borrowed from white men.

I represent the future of women in North America, just as any other woman does. That white women only want to hear from me as a Native and not as a voice in the women's movement is their loss. Embodied in my truth is the brilliance of hundreds of Native women who faced the worst that CanAmerica had to offer and deal with it. Embodied in my brilliance is the great sea of knowledge that it took to overcome the paralysis of a colonized mind. I did not come to this clearing alone. Hundreds walked alongside me – Black, Asian and Native women whose tide of knowledge was bestowed upon me are the key to every CanAmerican's emancipation.

Audre Lorde and I were destined to be close. The combined knowledge of African ex-slaves and colonized Natives in North America is going to tear asunder the holy citadel of patriarchy. Who can understand the pain of this land better than a Native woman? Who can understand the oppression that capitalism metes out to working people better than a Black woman?

The road to freedom is paved with the intimate knowledge of the oppressed.

86.

JUDITH PLASKOW

Born 1947, Brooklyn, New York, United States of America

from *Standing Again at Sinai: Judaism
from a Feminist Perspective*
1990

It's Feminist, But Is It Jewish?

For many people – from secular feminists to observant Jews –
the notion of a feminist Judaism is an oxymoron. Feminists often see
Judaism as irredeemably patriarchal, attachment to it as incomprehensible and retrogressive. Jews often perceive feminism as an alien
philosophy, at odds with Jewish self-understanding in important
ways. On either view, Jewish feminists dwell in a state of self-
contradiction that can be escaped only by choosing between aspects of
our identity.

This either/or view of Jewish feminism is well illustrated by an incident
at a Jewish theology conference I attended several years ago, at which a
prominent left-wing Orthodox rabbi told a moral tale for the benefit of
the feminists present. In the Bialystok Ghetto, he said, women were the
primary gunrunners because they could pass as non-Jews more easily than
men. In the last days of the Ghetto, the women staged a brief rebellion,
refusing to hand over the guns they had smuggled and arguing that it was
better to join the Partisans in the forest than to make a last, fruitless stand
against the Nazis. But the women finally surrendered the weapons when
the men insisted, he continued, because as Jews first and women second,
they realized they needed to remain in solidarity with their men. 'What
would you have done?' he asked us. 'Which side are you on?' His

480

underlying question hung unasked in the ensuing silence: 'Are you a feminist or are you a Jew?'

[. . .]

The process of coming to write this book has been for me a gradual
process of refusing the split between a Jewish and a feminist self. I am
not a Jew in the synagogue and a feminist in the world. I am a Jewish
feminist and a feminist Jew in every moment of my life. I have increasingly come to realize that in setting up Judaism and feminism as conflicting
ideologies and communities, I was handing over to a supposedly monolithic Jewish tradition the power and the right to define Judaism for the
past and for the future. 'Judaism' was a given that I could fit myself into
or decide to reject. It was not a complex and pluralistic tradition involved
in a continual process of adaption and change – a process to which I and
other feminist Jews could contribute. Like the wicked child of the Passo-
ver Seder, I was handing over Judaism to *them*, denying my own power
as a Jew to help shape what Judaism will become.

I am no longer willing to relinquish that power. I reject the rabbi's
dilemma of whether to hand over the guns to the men and be a Jew or keep
the guns and be a woman who denies my people. As I intuited when I first
heard his story but now see more clearly, the choice is a false one. The women
of the Bialystok Ghetto were acting as Jews, but they understood the meaning of Jewish action differently from the men. Had they held to their position,
the story would have had a different ending – but still a Jewish one. Perhaps
some of the inhabitants of the Ghetto might have survived instead of all of
them being destroyed. The rabbi's moral tale may thus be read as having a
different lesson from the one he intended. When Jewish feminists allow
Judaism and feminism to be defined by others in oppositional ways, then we
are stuck with two 'givens' confronting each other, and we are fundamentally
divided. When, however, we refuse to sever or choose between different
aspects of our identity, we create a new situation. If we are Jews not despite
being feminists but *as feminists*, then Judaism will have to change – we will
have to work to change it – to make a whole identity possible. This change,
moreover, may lead to new life for us and for the tradition.

The commitment that underlines this book is precisely a commitment to creating a new Jewish situation, to making a feminist Judaism a reality. Since I assume this commitment but do not defend it elsewhere in the text, my decision to remain within a patriarchal tradition requires some explanation. The important decisions we make in our lives are seldom rooted in rational calculation or easily analyzable, so the sources of this commitment are difficult for me to articulate. Especially in the American context where religious traditions are often viewed as selections in a great smorgasbord from which we pick and choose, the place of upbringing, community, and identity in adult religious decisions is often neglected or devalued. For me, the move toward embracing a whole Jewish/feminist identity did not grow out of my conviction that Judaism is 'redeemable,' but out of my sense that sundering Judaism and feminism would mean sundering my being. Certainly, I did not become a feminist Jew by adding up columns of sexist and nonsexist passages in the Bible and tradition and deciding the nonsexist side had won. Judaism is, I shall argue, a deeply patriarchal tradition. To change it will require a revolution as great as the transition from biblical to rabbinic Judaism precipitated by the destruction of the Second Temple. I do not believe there is some nonsexist 'essence' of Judaism in the name of which I struggle, nor do I believe that success is assured.

The factors that make up my commitment to change, and particularly to religious change, are more complex and intertwining. First, from childhood, I have been drawn to and fascinated by questions of ultimate truth and meaning so that I cannot put aside the peculiar difficulties of religious sexism to struggle against male domination on some less charged ground – even the ground of Jewish secularism. Second, if Judaism is patriarchal, I do not believe there is any *non*patriarchal space to which I can go to create a new religion. It is true that women who move outside traditional religions dispense with the need to deal with certain arguments and institutions that drain feminist energy. Still, as I see it, the creativity, imagination, and risks involved in creating a feminist Judaism (or Christianity) are in many ways similar in nature and substance to the work and risks involved in creating a purely feminist spirituality.

These are arguments for Judaism by default, however, and they would not be sufficient, were it not that I find value and meaning in Judaism and in my own Jewish identity, and that Judaism has been an important and nourishing part of my life. Many Jewish feminists, alienated by the sexism of the tradition, are making their way back to Judaism because of anti-Semitism in the women's movement. Learning about anti-Semitism had a profound effect on my sense of Jewish identity as I early immersed myself in literature about the Holocaust. And growing up as part of a minority in American culture contributed to my sense of connection to Judaism and to my sense of Jewish loyalty. But I never experienced minority status as simply negative; it came to me as both burden and gift. It gave me a different lens for looking at the world, the lens of the outsider who has access to questions the majority does not see. Moreover, anti-Semitism, while it reverberated with the central Jewish experience of slavery in the land of Egypt, was never the whole of my Jewish identity. Judaism was also lighting candles on Friday night and observing the cycle of the year; it was the stories of my ancestors, the words of the prophets calling us to justice and social engagement – the ethical monotheism we learned about in religious school and in which I deeply believed.

In *Beyond God the Father*, Mary Daly talks about the fact that feminists always live and work 'on the boundaries' of particular institutions in our patriarchal world. I have chosen to work with other Jewish feminists on the boundary of Judaism because that is where the different aspects of my identity most fully come together. In 1980, when I taught a course on Jewish feminist theology at the first National Havurah Summer Institute, it was my first opportunity to grapple with issues of theology and spirituality in a Jewish feminist context. Talking with other Jewish feminists about our relation to tradition, I felt it as a coming home. Out of that Institute, several women started B'not Esh, an ongoing Jewish feminist spirituality collective that has tried to create a space in which feminist Judaism is a reality. I have found in that collective a community of vision and struggle that I believe has much to offer toward the transformation of the wider Jewish community as well as the transformation of our society and our world.

87.

JUDITH BUTLER

Born 1956, Cleveland, Ohio, United States of America

from *Gender Trouble*

1990

What is the prohibitive law that generates the corporeal stylization of gender, the fantasied and fantastic figuration of the body? We have already considered the incest taboo and the prior taboo against homosexuality as the generative moments of gender identity, the prohibitions that produce identity along the culturally intelligible grids of an idealized and compulsory heterosexuality. The disciplinary production of gender effects a false stabilization of gender in the interests of the heterosexual construction and regulation of sexuality within the reproductive domain. The construction of coherence conceals the gender discontinuities that run rampant within heterosexual, bisexual, and gay and lesbian contexts in which gender does not necessarily follow from sex, and desire, or sexuality generally, does not seem to follow from gender – indeed, where none of these dimensions of significant corporeality express or reflect one another. When the disorganization and disaggregation of the field of bodies disrupt the regulatory fiction of heterosexual coherence, it seems that the expressive model loses its descriptive force. That regulatory ideal is then exposed as a norm and a fiction that disguises itself as a developmental law regulating the sexual field that it purports to describe.

According to the understanding of identification as an enacted fantasy or incorporation, however, it is clear that coherence is desired, wished for, idealized, and that this idealization is an effect of a corporeal signification. In other words, acts, gestures, and desire produce the effect of an internal core or substance, but produce this *on the surface* of the body, through the play of signifying absences that suggest, but never reveal, the organizing principle of identity as a cause. Such acts, gestures, enactments, generally construed, are *performative* in the sense that the essence or identity that they otherwise purport to express are *fabrications* manufactured and sustained through corporeal signs and other discursive means. That the gendered body is performative suggests that it has no ontological status apart from the various acts which constitute its reality. This also suggests that if that reality is fabricated as an interior essence, that very interiority is an effect and function of a decidedly public and social discourse, the public regulation of fantasy through the surface politics of the body, the gender border control that differentiates inner from outer, and so institutes the 'integrity' of the subject. In other words, acts and gestures, articulated and enacted desires create the illusion of an interior and organizing gender core, an illusion discursively maintained for the purposes of the regulation of sexuality within the obligatory frame of reproductive heterosexuality. If the 'cause' of desire, gesture, and act can be localized within the 'self' of the actor, then the political regulations and disciplinary practices which produce that ostensibly coherent gender are effectively displaced from view. The displacement of a political and discursive origin of gender identity onto a psychological 'core' precludes an analysis of the political constitution of the gendered subject and its fabricated notions about the ineffable interiority of its sex or of its true identity.

88.

BIKINI KILL

Punk band formed in October 1990, Olympia, Washington,
United States of America

Riot Grrrl Manifesto

1991

BECAUSE us girls crave records and books and fanzines that speak to US that WE feel included in and can understand in our own ways.

BECAUSE we wanna make it easier for girls to see/hear each other's work so that we can share strategies and criticize-applaud each other.

BECAUSE we must take over the means of production in order to create our own meanings.

BECAUSE viewing our work as being connected to our girlfriends-politics-real lives is essential if we are gonna figure out how what we are doing impacts, reflects, perpetuates, or DISRUPTS the status quo.

BECAUSE we recognize fantasies of Instant Macho Gun Revolution as impractical lies meant to keep us simply dreaming instead of becoming our dreams AND THUS seek to create revolution in our own lives every single day by envisioning and creating alternatives to the bullshit christian capitalist way of doing things.

BECAUSE we want and need to encourage and be encouraged in the face of all our own insecurities, in the face of beergutboyrock that tells us we can't play our instruments, in the face of 'authorities' who say our bands/zines/etc are the worst in the US and

BECAUSE we don't wanna assimilate to someone else's (boy) standards of what is or isn't.

BECAUSE we are unwilling to falter under claims that we are reactionary 'reverse sexists' AND NOT THE TRUEPUNKROCKSOULCRUSADERS THAT WE KNOW we really are.

BECAUSE we know that life is much more than physical survival and are patently aware that the punk rock 'you can do anything' idea is crucial to the coming angry grrrl rock revolution which seeks to save the psychic and cultural lives of girls and women everywhere, according to their own terms, not ours.

BECAUSE we are interested in creating non-hierarchical ways of being AND making music, friends, and scenes based on communication + understanding, instead of competition + good/bad categorizations.

BECAUSE doing/reading/seeing/hearing cool things that validate and challenge us can help us gain the strength and sense of community that we need in order to figure out how bullshit like racism, able-bodieism, ageism, speciesism, classism, thinism, sexism, anti-semitism and hetero-sexism figures in our own lives.

BECAUSE we see fostering and supporting girl scenes and girl artists of all kinds as integral to this process.

BECAUSE we hate capitalism in all its forms and see our main goal as sharing information and staying alive, instead of making profits of being cool according to traditional standards.

BECAUSE we are angry at a society that tells us Girl = Dumb, Girl = Bad, Girl = Weak.

BECAUSE we are unwilling to let our real and valid anger be diffused and/or turned against us via the internalization of sexism as witnessed in girl/girl jealousism and self defeating girltype behaviors.

BECAUSE I believe with my wholeheartmindbody that girls constitute a revolutionary soul force that can, and will change the world for real.

89.

NAWAL EL SAADAWI

Born 1931, Kafr Tahlah, Egypt

from *Writing and Freedom*

1992

From the moment the world of writing opened itself before me, I started to follow a route that was drastically different from the one preordained for me before birth. The history of enslavement dating back to pharaonic times had not only laid out the path I should follow from cradle to grave, but had also created the authorities to make sure that I did. It thus provided the authority of the father and husband in the small family, the authority of the state, the legal system, social institutions, the authority of religion and Shari'a, and finally the authority of international legitimacy.

These authorities took the shape of a pyramid. At the top, you would find what we today call the New World Order, the *New York Times* and CNN, while at the bottom there would be the local governments, local television, prisons, censorship and literary criticism.

As a child I discovered that writing was the only means by which I could breathe. But the government, the patriarchal and religious authorities, the propaganda in the media, as well as the teachings of the Faculty of Medicine (which I joined to please my father), all said to me, 'There is no connection between writing and the act of breathing in a woman.' My experience in life, however, has confirmed the very close connection between writing and the entry of air into my lungs. These hierarchical authorities joined forces and, like an iron fist, pushed me into the conjugal bed, under the illusion of love and the 'scientific' ideas, derived from Freud, that women must create babies and not ideas. At one stage of my life I produced babies and more than once in my life I was married to the brim. Yet, instead of feeling the air enter my lungs, I felt suffocated.

The more a woman dedicates herself to the institution of marriage, the more suffocated she is bound to feel. I looked up the word 'dedication' in the inherited dictionary of enslavement, and I found it connected with the devotion of slaves to their masters. It's a term that implies the act of getting lost in others, of self-denial and self-sacrifice, terms that come under the category of death or of self-destruction.

But creativity and writing are quite the opposite. They involve keeping the self alive, rather than destroying it. They mean the realization of self and its denial.

And thus I discovered the contradiction between marital devotion and self-fulfilment in a woman's life, since marriage dictates that a woman's identity dissolve into that of her husband or into those of her children (after all, the children are the rightful property of the husband and his name is written on them). Thus the man of letters is blessed with a wife who cooks his food, washes his trousers, and offers him tea, while he sits to write down the story of his love for another woman. On the other hand, the woman of letters is blessed with a husband who turns her life into misery and scolds her all the time for having neglected to cook, wash or sweep the floors, or for having allowed the children to scream out loud while he slept. The creative man has a wife who delights in his success and feels happier as he becomes more successful. The creative woman has a husband who gets depressed when she succeeds, and gets increasingly more depressed as she becomes more successful.

If the creative woman has the courage to suppress part of her brain, she may save herself from the depression of husbands, and may be able to avoid losing herself in the sacred women's kingdom inside the house. She will be able then to go out on the streets, demonstrating along with others and shouting 'God . . . nation . . . and king' (or whoever occupies the position of a king). But she may also find herself required to identify completely with the king or the president. If she is not willing to do that, a huge wooden gate will open up before her, leading her into prison.

While in prison in 1981, I tried day and night to discover the crime I had committed, never having been affiliated to any political party, never having committed adultery, never having carried an illegitimate child, and never having insulted anyone. After eighty days and nights in my cell, I discovered that my only crime was having been unable to lose myself in the self of the president. In ancient Egypt, the pharaoh considered himself divine, and all other selves were required to dissolve completely into his. Losing oneself has been the virtue most highly appreciated from the days of the pharaohs until now. But dissolving is the opposite of creativity. Writing means expressing my self. It means that my self will not dissolve in any other self, be it my husband, God or the president.

Writing means surviving and denying death. If it had not been for writing, all prophets, gods and pharaohs would have disappeared forever. If it had not been for the discovery of printing, we would not have known anything about those who had died. But for the Torah, the Bible and the Qur'an, we would not have Moses, Jesus or Muhammad.

Writing has the power to give life to the dead. This is why writing has become the only way I can survive. I often wonder how people who do not write manage to survive or endure life. My mother died leaving not a trace. I am one of the nine children she had given birth to. None of us carried her name. My father also died, leaving behind no mark except for his name in mine, written on my books. With the translation of my books into several languages, my father's name has become known, while my mother's has disappeared forever.

On the other hand, I feel better off than the English writer Virginia Woolf, who took on her husband's name and was known by it. A woman should use her own name on her works and not that of her father or husband. If I had to choose between my father's name and my husband's, I would certainly prefer my father's, since it is at least permanent. The husband's name may change with a change of circumstances. This is particularly true in our country. When a husband happens to fall in love with another woman, all he need do is open his mouth and utter the words 'You're divorced', three times, upon which his wife packs her bags and leaves. In the eyes of the law and Shari'a, she has become a divorced woman.

I consider myself lucky that I have never taken the name of any husband and never signed my books except with my father's name and that of my paternal grandfather, El Saadawi – the name of a man who is a total stranger to me, since he died before I was born. He died of bilharzia, poverty and enslavement, the triple chronic disease afflicting our peasants from the days of the pharaohs until the present. There are times when my name is shortened to my grandfather's name, El Saadawi. This is how this strange man gets his name imprinted on me and on the covers of my books.

Nothing consoles me more than the thought that at least on doomsday, I will be able to shed that strange name and carry my mother's. When I was a little girl, my father once told me that on doomsday people would be called by their mothers' names. I asked him why this was so, and he said that maternity was certain. So I asked, 'Is paternity not certain, then?' I saw the pupil of his eye quiver slightly, and a long silence followed. He gave my mother a look wavering between doubt and certainty.

My mother knew no man other than my father. How could she have, if she never left the house or, more precisely, never left the kitchen? After giving birth to her ninth child, she became pregnant with the tenth. She had an abortion.

One day while she slept, she dreamt of my father with another woman. Her grief made the milk freeze in her breast, forming a cancerous tumour. She died very young. My maternal grandmother used to sing to herself in the bathroom a song that went: 'Trusting a man is like trusting that water would stay in a sieve.' She used to pour water over the sieve and watch it disappear to the last drop. She would smack her lips in distress. When her husband came home late at night, she would smell the other woman in his underwear. In the morning, he would lecture her on the love of the homeland.

After the death of my grandfather, I became very sceptical of any man who chanted the song of patriotism. If he moved from the love of the motherland to the love of the peasants or labourers, my suspicions increased. If he went beyond that and held a rosary in his hand, my skepticism was confirmed beyond doubt.

Whenever I met a man who was full of religious words and clichés, and who held the rosary in his hand, I would immediately smell a rat. If this man happened to be the head of the state, the problem moved from the domain of the personal to the public. And if he happened to be my husband, the disaster would still be unmitigated, because I would then have to choose between writing and living in the Garden of Eden.

I have always chosen writing, Eden being rather out of reach, and its delights designed for the gratification of men. Prominent among these delights is the presence of fair young virgins. But I am a woman of dark skin. I have long lost my virginity and am at the moment in the menopausal phase (to use the language of the system). In paradise, a woman like me will have none other than her husband. What a disaster! To have my husband chasing me in life and after death!

That is why I have always chosen writing. I came to realize, even as a child, that I was not going to have the same fate as my mother, my grandmother or, for that matter, any other woman. Why I had this conviction is not totally clear to me. One reason may have been that I saw my father's great admiration for the Prophet, and I wanted to get my father's admiration. One day I dreamt I became a prophet and my father looked at me admiringly. When, in the morning, I told my grandmother about that dream, she just hit her chest in disbelief. She heated some water for me to cleanse myself of the guilt. A woman could never be a prophet, she told me.

That day I took up my pen and jotted down angry words on the page. My brother, who failed his exams every year, could become a prophet, while I, who succeeded every year, could not. My anger was directed at a power I did not know. My grandmother said it was God who preferred my brother, though he failed his exams every year.

There is certainly a connection between creativity and anger. The little girl is taught to conceal her anger and draw an angelic smile on her face. But no connection exists between angels and creativity. That is why in Arabic we have the expressions 'the demon of poetry' and 'the demon of art'.

I began to voice my anger against all authorities from the bottom up, starting with the authority of my father. My father, noticing a frown rather than a smile on my face, told me that frowning made girls lose their femininity. So I had to choose between femininity and writing. I chose writing.

In the dead of the night, I hugged my anger the way the woman carrying an illegitimate child hugged her secret. I told my mother that if a woman did not become angry at injustice, she would not be human. She told me that being human was better than being a woman. My grandmother raised her hand to her chin and said defiantly, 'I bet you won't find anyone to marry you. Obeying your father is obeying God.'

In obedience to my father, I joined the Faculty of Medicine and put on the angelic white coat. For years I lived with the stool and urine of patients, the rules of the Ministry of Health and the guidelines of the general director and the minister. When my father died, I was free of my promise and started to live to please no one but myself.

Creativity only begins when man is free from the wish to please others.

90.

WINONA LADUKE

Born 1959, California, United States of America,
member of the Anishinaabe Nation

from *Mothers of our Nations: Indigenous Women Address the World*

1995

The Earth is our Mother. From her we get our life, and our ability to live. It is our responsibility to care for our Mother, and in caring for our Mother, we care for ourselves. Women, all females, are the manifestation of Mother Earth in human form. We are her daughters, and in my cultural instructions we are to care for her. I am taught to live in respect for Mother Earth [. . .]

While I am from one nation of indigenous peoples, there are an estimated 500 million indigenous peoples or some 5,000 nations of indigenous peoples worldwide [. . .] We are not populations nor minority groups. We are peoples and nations of peoples. Under international law we meet the criteria of nation states, with each having a common economic system, language, territory, history, culture, and governing institutions – conditions which indicate nations of peoples. Despite this fact, indigenous people are not allowed to participate in the United Nations.

Nations of indigenous peoples are not represented at the United Nations. Most decisions are made by the 180 or so member states. Those states, by and large, have been in existence for only 200 years or less, while most indigenous nations, with few exceptions, have been in existence for thousands of years [. . .]

This is the centerpiece of the problem. Decision-making is not made by those who are affected – people who live on the land – but the corporations with interests entirely different from that of the land and the people or the women of the land . . . And we clearly, as women and as indigenous peoples, demand and will recover that right – the right of self-determination, to determine our own destiny and that of our future generations.

The origins of this problem lie with the predatory/prey relationship that industrial society has developed with the Earth and, subsequently, the people of the Earth. This same relationship exists vis-à-vis women. We collectively find that we are often in the role of the prey to a predator society whether through sexual discrimination, exploitation, sterilization, absence of control over our bodies, or being the subjects of repressive laws and legislation in which we have no voice. This occurs on an individual level, but equally and more significantly on a societal level. It is also critical to point out at this time most matrilineal societies, societies in which government and decision-making are largely controlled by women, have been obliterated from the face of the Earth by colonialism and industrialism. The only matrilineal societies that exist in the world today are those of indigenous nations. Yet we also face obliteration [. . .]

What befalls our Mother Earth, befalls her daughters – the women who are the mothers of our nations. Simply stated, if we no longer bear children, and if our bodies are wracked with poisons, we will have accomplished little in the way of determining our destiny or improving our conditions. These problems, reflected in our health and well-being, are the result of historical processes and are inherently resulting in a decline of the status of women. We need to challenge these processes if we want to be ultimately in charge of our own destinies, our own self-determination, and the future of the Earth, our Mother.

I call on you to support the struggle of indigenous peoples of the world for recognition as peoples who have self-determination. I ask you to look into the Charter of the United Nations, which states that 'all peoples have the right to self-determination. By virtue of that right, they may freely determine their political status and freely pursue their economic, social and political development.' 'All peoples' should be construed to mean that indigenous peoples have that right, too. Accord us the same rights as all other nations of peoples, and through that process, allow us to protect our ecosystems, their inherent biodiversity, human cultural diversity, and the last remaining matriarchal governments in the world.

This is not a struggle for women of the dominant society in so-called 'first world' countries to have equal pay and equal status if that pay and status continues to be based on a consumption model that is unsustainable. It is a struggle to recover our status as Daughters of the Earth. In that is our strength and security, not in the predator, but in the security of our Mother, for our future generations. In that, we can insure our security as the Mothers of Our Nations.

91.

ARWA SALIH

Born 1951, Cairo, Egypt
Died 1997, Cairo, Egypt

from *The Stillborn*

1996

1. The End of Bourgeois Love Is Death

In bourgeois society, our lives – our most private relationships – have become a form of organized slavery. Love will always be a pretty dream until we put an end to possession and the logic of cowardice and coercion in relationships, relationships that would surely die if they ever breathed the air of freedom. Love is only possible as the exercise of free will between free individuals. The 'realists' will laugh and wink but the contemptible truth of love and marriage in our society gives us no choice but to dream.

2. An Interlude on Innocence

In the spectacle of the (Egyptian) intellectual's relations with women, ghosts from another time and place haunt the living. Though money and social capital are absent from the intellectual's theatre of action, exploitation is still the name of the game. The bourgeois logic of buying and selling (capitalism), which is at least governed by laws, turns into a game with no rules, a game in which everything is allowed and winner takes all, a con man's game actually (and a secondary symptom of capitalism).

The young woman who accepts a date with an intellectual doesn't dare hope for a fancy outing, or even a not-so-fancy one. You'll find her heading for a decrepit cafe where her young intellectual will buy her a glass of bitter boiled tea and sell her a bunch of 'progressive' dreams that cost him nothing but a string of his cheapest merchandise talk. Talk about 'justice' that he himself is no longer quite sure he believes in; the kind of talk that a sheltered and oppressed petty-bourgeois girl desperately longs to hear. Or she might be an upper-middle-class girl looking for a bit of danger (all the better for him as she's sure to taste of the considerable cost that went into her upbringing).

And so our young man talks about justice, and the hypocrisy of social values, and a lot of other things besides. But the most important thing – the real purpose of it all – is the talk of 'free love' – love liberated of money and of responsibility of any sort, love raised on 'personal responsibility' with no social consequences whatsoever. Our intrepid intellectual plunges into this particular theme with a persistence that he sometimes lacks in other, no less momentous matters. Of course his 'personal responsibility' is to be borne by one party alone. It's a fairy tale in a society built on relentless interference in the private lives of individuals (marriage and divorce, personal-status laws, etc.). The truth is that there is only *social responsibility* and society always calls to account those who sign on the state's dotted line. Otherwise, personal responsibility is just a favourite subject of private and often malicious gossip about such-and-such couple. The gatherings at which this gossip transpires represent society's moral authority, and so of course they judge (i.e. condemn) one party alone: the woman, the party who is always magically transformed by all the talk about 'personal responsibility' into a whore (our Arab intellectuals excel at this type of miraculous transmutation). As for the man, his personal responsibility becomes an affirmation of his virility, and he struts and preens for all comers (literally and not jokingly). There was, in what we call our 'backward' values, a finer conception of manhood, one that was based in a rich legacy of ethical striving. Our generation simply dropped the nobility of the ideal and kept the backwardness.

And so free love ends up being free-ride love. But what of it? Just another idea in the archive of grand and inspiring ideas that become clichés in the cafes of the Egyptian intellectual. This one is neither more nor less noble than any of the other ones they've cheapened. Whether they like to admit it or not, it's one of the cornerstones of their vast hollowness. Death does not spare this most intimate and private part of them, the core of human identity. And yet how proud they are of their 'realism'!

Being a man, the intellectual requires innocence in a woman. But innocence that doesn't allow for any kind of comprehension of the ways of the world isn't much more than a form of idiocy (and in this the 'not innocent' woman has the advantage). Our friend considers it his right to exploit her. His logic is that since she's accepted exploitation, she deserves it. Her innocence – as experience always shows him – is a fragile thing. And there's more. If this fool can't himself understand the 'complexity' of his precious soul, how can he possibly hand it over to her, the stupid one? She must be content with his precious body. If he's a determined reformed romantic, he'll be sure to set her straight.

There is a secondary issue here, nonetheless an important one. Washed-out intellectuals adore smashing idols of every kind: creativity, success, fame. They love it so much that not being able to do some smashing slays them with frustration. Proving that 'everything is false and worthless' is an endless need for them; they are like punctured water-skins that must haemorrhage water. This is also how they judge women (they know them inside out, of course). Women are only good for one of two things: either to be a stupid wife (not worthy of her man) or a crafty slut (not worthy of her man either). Any other 'type' of woman is a mythical creature. A completely unsurprising paradox follows. When the Egyptian intellectual fantasizes about 'woman', he is an incurable romantic. The creature of his imagination is the little goddess of literary endeavour, healing all wounds and compensating for all losses and betrayals (and there are many indeed). She embraces and enfolds, she offers the comfort and security that is to be found in her arms alone. On top of this, she is – of course – very beautiful. Her eyes are black or hazel or green but they are always wide. She has perfect breasts imported from Europe, firm and round and supple; they bounce up and down like rubber balls (the favoured description of novelists). Of course this exalted goddess is not one iota more of a real person than the slut or the clumsy wife. She too lives in a notional prison that endlessly reproduces the triangle of goddess, wife and whore. She is forced to conform to his taxonomy whether she likes it or not. Between the coarseness of the reality and the fantasy, experience can build no bridges. It can never be enriching, because instead of being something that connects two people to each other in a continuous dialogue, it's a one-way street inside one person's head, his head; a street that's blocked between cruel ideation on one end, and fantasies of escape and transgression on the other.

For the intellectual, a woman's 'morals' are synonymous with her sexual behaviour. She might well be a predatory beast – society will neither object to this nor punish her for it. In fact, this is exactly the horrible revenge that women often take on men in general. She fulfils his expectations of her: she makes him her prey. She's definitely not a 'rebel', she's a pragmatist, exactly like him. Society itself teaches women how to circumvent its morals – morals that are precise and consistent and logical because we drink them with our mother's milk. This is how duplicity becomes 'logical' and 'natural'. Oppression teaches her to be cunning and humiliation teaches her malice and hate. It's her arsenal in the battle for 'survival of the smartest', which is the real battle being waged in the real world (not some silly struggle between vice and virtue). And so she's treated by society (and by men in particular) like a despicable creature, incapable of nobility. She's taught to debase herself and she learns to despise weakness and modesty and sincerity, and to admire aggressiveness and vulgarity and power. She learns how to see men as prey, how to turn them into prey, because this is the real 'social contract', the law of the world she lives in.

(And slaves continue to reproduce slaves – people who are incapable of facing the world naked of everything but their freedom to choose. Their legacy is a poison, a manufactured epidemic.)

When this finishing school for girls is run by intellectuals, you'll find the most dangerous type of woman of all. T. S. Eliot once wrote something to the effect that women invest in their upper regions so as to double the value of their nether parts. These are women who surely learnt about life in our finishing school. They're really good at holding forth on 'pressing' social issues with their sights set much further down. And yet our society demands that women alone blush with shame.

92

MARILYN DUMONT

Born 1955, Olds, Canada, of Cree/Métis ancestry

Memoirs of a Really Good Brown Girl
1996

You are not good enough, obviously not good enough.
The chorus is never loud or conspicuous,
just there.

Carefully dressed, hair combed like I am going to the doctor, I follow my older sister, we take the shortcut by the creek, through the poplar and cottonwood trees, along sidewalks, past the pool hall, hotel, variety store, the United Church, over the bridge, along streets until we reach the school pavement. It is at this point that I sense my sister's uneasiness; no obvious signs, just her silence, she is holding my hand like she holds her breath, she has changed subtly since we left home. We enter a set of doors which resemble more a piece of machinery than a doorway, with metal handles, long glass windows and iron grates on the floor, the halls are long and white, our feet echo as we walk. I feel as though I've been wrapped in a box, a shoebox where the walls are long and manila gloss, it smells of paper and glue, there are shuffling noises I've never heard before and kids in the rooms we pass by. We enter a room from what seems like the back door, rows of small tables lined up like variety cereal boxes, other small faces look back vacant and scared next to the teacher's selling smile. (I have learned that when whites smile that fathomless smile it's best to be wary). I am handed over to the teacher. Later I will reflect upon this exchange between my older sister and the teacher as the changing of the guard, from big sister to teacher, and before that, when I was even younger, from mother to big sister.

This is my first day of a school and I stand alone; I look on. Most of the kids know what to do, like they've all been here before, like the teacher is a friend of the family. I am a foreigner, I stay in my seat, frozen, afraid to move, afraid to make a mistake, afraid to speak, they talk differently than I do. I don't sound the way they do, but I don't know how to sound any different, so I don't talk, don't volunteer answers to questions the teacher asks. I become invisible.

I don't glisten with presence, confidence, glisten with the holiness of Ste. Anne whose statue I see every year at the pilgrimage, her skin translucent, as if the Holy Ghost is a light and it shines out through her fluorescent skin, as if a sinless life makes your skin a receptacle of light.

The other kids have porcelain skin like Ste. Anne too, but unlike her, they have little blond hairs growing out of small freckles on their arms, like the kind of freckles that are perfectly placed on the noses of the dolls I got each Christmas. In fact, the girls in my class look like my dolls: bumpy curls, geometric faces, crepe-paper dresses, white legs and patent shoes.

My knees are scarred, have dirt ground in them from crawling under fences, climbing trees, riding skid horses and jumping from sawdust piles. I remember once. When I was a flower girl for my brother's wedding. I was taken home to the city by my brother's white fiancée and she 'scrubbed the hell out of me.' All other events that took place on that visit are diminished by the bathtub staging, no other event was given as much time or attention by her. I was fed and watered like a lamb for slaughter. I was lathered, scrubbed, shampooed, exfoliated, medicated, pedicured, manicured, rubbed down and moisturized. When it was over, I felt that every part of my body had been hounded of dirt and sin and that now I, like Ste. Anne, had become a receptacle of light.

My skin always gave me away. In grade one, I had started to forget where I was when a group of us stood around the sink at the back of the class washing up after painting and a little white girl stared at the colour of my arms and exclaimed, 'Are you ever brown!' I wanted to pull my short sleeves down to my wrists and pretend that I hadn't heard her, but she persisted, 'Are you Indian?' I wondered why she had chosen this ripe time to ask me and if this was the first she'd noticed.

How could I respond? If I said yes, she'd reject me: worse, she might tell the other kids my secret and then they'd laugh and shun me. If I said no, I'd be lying, and when they found out I was lying, they'd shun me.

I said 'No,' and walked away.

I just watched and followed; I was good at that, good at watching and following. It was what I did best, I learned quickly by watching. (Some learning theories say that native kids learn best by watching, because they're more visual. I always knew that I learned by watching to survive in two worlds and in a white classroom.) I only needed to be shown something once and I remembered it. I remembered it in my fibre.

I lived a dual life; I had white friends and I had Indian friends and the two never mixed and that was normal. I lived on a street with white kids, so they were my friends after school. During school I played with the Indian Kids. These were kids from the other Indian families who were close friends with my parents. At school my Indian friends and I would play quite comfortably in our own group, like the white kids did in theirs.

I am looking at a school picture, grade five, I am smiling easily. My hair is shoulder length, curled, a pageboy, I am wearing a royal blue dress. I look poised, settled, like I belong. I won an award that year for most improved student. I learned to follow really well.

I am in a university classroom; an English professor corrects my spoken English in front of the class. I say, 'really good.' He says, 'you mean, really well, don't you?' I glare at him and say emphatically, 'No, I mean really good.'

93.

M. A. JAIMES GUERRERO

Born 1946, Arizona, United States of America, member of the
Juaneño Band of Mission Indians, Acjachemen Nation

from *Civil Rights versus Sovereignty: Native American Women in Life and Land Struggles*

1997

This essay explores conflicts between civil rights and sovereignty in the liberation struggles of American indigenous peoples. Understanding these conflicts is crucial in locating the position of native women in relation to both patriarchal tribal structures and to the United States, which I define here as an advanced colonial/capitalist state. An overview of the historical legal disenfranchisement of native peoples and two contemporary court cases involving women's loss of tribal status demonstrate that it is insufficient to view the U.S. solely as an advanced capitalist state. To fully comprehend the struggles of native peoples, and specifically native women, we must also understand the U.S. as an advanced colonial state, because territorial colonization remains integral to the relationship between the state and native peoples.

I wish to argue in this essay that the mainstream feminist movement has been ineffective and inconsistent when faced with the issues of land rights and sovereignty (feminism versus 'indigenism'). The movement's reluctance to grapple with questions of indigenism makes solidarity politics among native women and white women difficult and also makes some native women reluctant to claim feminism. Any feminism that does not address land rights, sovereignty, and the state's systematic erasure of the cultural practices of native peoples, or that defines native women's participation in these struggles as non-feminist, is limited in vision and exclusionary in practice.

For the purposes of this discussion, 'land rights' need to be understood in a context of culture and territoriality. This context differs from what we traditionally understand as proprietary rights. Similarly, tribal sovereignty must be understood in its cultural context, one that reflects a self-determination and self-sufficiency traditionally predicated on reciprocity rather than individual ownership. Here, too, this context differs from the Eurocentric construction of sovereignty from which the political concept is derived. These definitions are crucial in theorizing the nature of the U.S. polity and its racially subordinated populations, in this instance, native peoples.

Neither mainstream feminism nor the notion of proprietary rights enables an understanding of native peoples' histories of organizing – histories in which native women have played important roles at local, regional, and even international levels. In addition to clouding and erasing these histories, the contradictory location in which native women find themselves – both inside and outside the tribe – has no place in these inherited paradigms. Yet the success of Indian women can be seen in our reemergence as visible leaders and activists and through our positions in tribal governance.* 'We have always been inspired by the traditions of matrilineal societies, and matrifocal spheres of female power continue to be handed down to younger generations. But despite a rich tradition of female power bases, and despite some women's contemporary roles as leaders, these are troubled times for native women – times when sexism in Indian politics compounds, and is compounded by, racism and sexism in the U.S. polity. Indian women are sometimes forced to choose between loyalty to their male-controlled tribal groups and loyalty to other 'third world' women in the patriarchal hierarchy, subjected as it were to a 'trickle-down patriarchy.'† Yet it is these

---

* G.M. Bataille and K.M. Sands, *American Indian Women: Telling Their Lives* (Lincoln: University of Nebraska Press, 1984). In addition, see Rayna Green, ed., *Native American Women: A Contextual Bibliography*, (Bloomington: Indiana University Press, 1983), and her latest book, *Women in American Indian Society* (New York: Chelsea House Publishers, 1992).

† M.A. Jaimes and Theresa Halsey, 'American Indian Women: At the Center of Indigenous Resistance in Contemporary North America,' in *The State of Native America*, Jaimes, ed., (Boston: South End Press, 1992), pp. 311–44. The term 'trickle-down patriarchy' actually came from a review of 'Once Upon a Conquest: The Legacy of Five Hundred Years of Survival and Resistance,' by Elliot, in *Labyrinth*, (Oct. 1992): 2–3.

colonizing practices which themselves prefigure the kinds of strategies of resistance that native women employ.

Civil Rights versus Sovereignty

In this section, I argue that the legal apparatus of the U.S. government plays a central role in defining critical questions regarding liberation struggles for gender equality, while simultaneously charting an agenda for the rights of tribal peoples and their communities. It is in the context of this advanced stage of American colonialism that issues of 'civil rights versus sovereignty' and 'feminism versus indigenism' gain critical importance.

As traditionally communal peoples, native women organize their liberation struggles against American colonization from the premise of collective human rights – a practice that some of us refer to as *indigenism.** This practice diverges radically from the priorities and sociopolitical agendas of the white, middle-class women's movement, some of which are individualist rather than communal in orientation. As long as class hierarchy and an elitist leadership prevail, and as long as the ideological schisms and differences surrounding various definitions of 'feminism' continue to be grounded in a Eurocentric worldview, the struggles of native women will be subordinated within feminist agendas. In addition, traditional indigenous peoples, both women and men, often resist socialist/communist as well as socialist/feminist resolutions to our subordination by the nation state. This is so in spite of the valuable Marxist-Leninist work on labor theory that has been so important to understanding our contemporary experience of advanced colonization. One reason for the persistent critique by native people of these progressive movements is that the Eurocentric paradigm continues to be perpetuated at the expense of the universal indigenist worldview.

I am suggesting here that the struggle between Indian nations and the American state over questions of sovereignty and incorporation into the

* Ward Churchill, 'I am Indigenist: notes on the Ideology of the Fourth World,' in *Struggle for the Land: Indigenous Resistance to Genocide, Ecocide and Expropriation in Contemporary America*, (ME: Common Courage Press, 1992/93). See also M. A. Jaimes, 'Native American Identity and Survival: Indigenism and Environmental Ethics,' in *Issues in Native American Culture: Critical Institutions*, Vol. 2, ed. Peter Lang, 1995.

U.S. polity are most visible when one examines the contradictions that emerge over the tribal status of native women. Civil rights and sovereignty, moreover, are fundamentally gendered issues and practices because patriarchy operates both inside and outside the tribe to define belonging (the tribal status) of native women. These two patriarchal structures can, in concert, literally determine whether native women's claims to membership within tribes are honored or ignored.

[. . .]

Native American Women in Life and Land Struggles

[. . .] This essay has illuminated how native women's resistance – and survival – is grounded in an indigenous heritage of self-determination only partially reflected in our contemporary sociopolitical leadership. Indigenism is thriving as a liberation movement inspired by our Indian cosmologies. It differs markedly from any feminism that limits the scope of our experiences and liberation struggles by defining them solely in terms of sexism. One can understand why the struggle for self-determination is simultaneously a struggle against patriarchy and a struggle for a land base that is ecologically safe and whole. As we enter the twenty-first century, native women continue to organize in multiple ways: as activities struggling against patriarchal tribal leaders; as political organizers against U.S. advanced colonization; and as writers, poets, artists, teachers, and scholars all working for the restoration of traditional indigenous rights. Native American women in North America will likely become even more visible in the fight for our people's rights and for the rights of indigenous women. Our resistance will continue to be transformative and visionary. Our long heritage includes not only the many courageous survivors of colonialist disempowerment, but our ancestors in Spirit as well as in struggle. It is in this Spirit and tradition that native women engage in indigenous liberation movements against colonization. We seek to build alliances and coalitions with other colonized groups, including third-world feminists, ecofeminists, gays and lesbians, and all other disenfranchised and dispossessed peoples, regardless of gender.

94.

CAROL ANN DUFFY

Born 1955, Glasgow, United Kingdom

Little Red-Cap

1999

At childhood's end, the houses petered out
into playing fields, the factory, allotments
kept, like mistresses, by kneeling married men,
the silent railway line, the hermit's caravan,
till you came at last to the edge of the woods.
It was there that I first clapped eyes on the wolf.

He stood in a clearing, reading his verse out loud
in his wolfy drawl, a paperback in his hairy paw,
red wine staining his bearded jaw. What big ears
he had! What big eyes he had! What teeth!
In the interval, I made quite sure he spotted me,
Sweet sixteen, never been, babe, waif, and bought me a drink,

my first. You might ask why. Here's why. Poetry.
The wolf, I know, would lead me deep into the woods,
away from home, to a dark tangled thorny place
lit by the eyes of owls. I crawled in his wake,
my stockings ripped to shreds, scraps of red from my blazer
snagged on twig and branch, murder clues. I lost both shoes

but got there, wolf's lair, better beware. Lesson one that night,
breath of the wolf in my ear, was the love poem.
I clung till dawn to his thrashing fur, for
What little girl doesn't dearly love a wolf?
Then I slid from between his heavy matted paws
And went in search of a living bird – white dove –

which flew, straight, from my hands to his hope mouth.
One bite, dead. How nice, breakfast in bed, he said,
licking his chops. As soon as he slept, I crept to the back
of the lair, where a whole wall was crimson, gold, aglow with books.
Words, words were truly alive on the tongue in the head,
warm, beating, frantic, winged; music and blood.

But then I was young – and it took ten years
in the woods to tell that a mushroom
stoppers the mouth of a buried corpse, that birds
are the uttered thought of trees, that a greying wolf
howls the same old song at the moon, year in, year out,
season after season, same rhyme, same reason. I took an axe

to a willow to see how it wept. I took an axe to a salmon
to see how it leapt. I took an axe to the wolf
as he slept, one chop, scrotum to throat, and saw
the glistening, virgin white of my grandmother's bones.
I filled his old belly with stones. I stitched him up.
Out of the forest I come with my flowers, singing, all alone.

95.

BELL HOOKS

Born 1952, Hopkinsville, Kentucky, United States of America

from *Feminism is for Everybody*

2000

Everywhere I go I proudly tell folks who want to know who I am and what I do that I am a writer, a feminist theorist, a cultural critic. I tell them I write about movies and popular culture, analyzing the message in the medium. Most people find this exciting and want to know more. Everyone goes to movies, watches television, glances through magazines, and everyone has thoughts about the messages they receive, about the images they look at. It is easy for the diverse public I encounter to understand what I do as a cultural critic, to understand my passion for writing (lots of folks want to write, and do). But feminist theory – that's the place where the questions stop. Instead I tend to hear all about the evil of feminism and the bad feminists: how 'they' hate men; how 'they' want to go against nature – and god; how 'they' are all lesbians; how 'they' are taking all the jobs and making the world hard for white men, who do not stand a chance.

When I ask these same folks about the feminist books or magazines they read, when I ask them about the feminist talk they have heard, about the feminist activists they know, they respond by letting me know that everything they know about feminism has come into their lives thirdhand, that they really have not come close enough to feminist movement to know what really happens, what it's really about. Mostly they think feminism is a bunch of angry women who want to be like men. They do not even think about feminism as being about rights – about women gaining equal rights. When I talk about the feminism I know – up close and personal – they willingly listen, although when our conversations end, they are quick to tell me I am different, not like the 'real' feminists who hate men, who are angry. I assure them I am as a real and as radical a

510

feminist as one can be, and if they dare to come closer to feminism they will see it is not how they have imagined it.

Each time I leave one of these encounters, I want to have in my hand a little book so that I can say, read this book, and it will tell you what feminism is, what the movement is about. I want to be holding in my hand a concise, fairly easy to read and understand book; not a long book, not a book thick with hard to understand jargon and academic language, but a straightforward, clear book – easy to read without being simplistic. From the moment feminist thinking, politics, and practice changed my life, I have wanted this book. I have wanted to give it to the folk I love so that they can understand better this cause, this feminist politics I believe in so deeply, that it is the foundation of my political life.

I have wanted them to have an answer to the question 'what is feminism?' that is rooted neither in fear or fantasy. I have wanted them to have this simple definition to read again and again so they know: 'Feminism is a movement to end sexism, sexist exploitation, and oppression.' I love this definition, which I first offered more than 10 years ago in my book *Feminist Theory: From Margin to Center*. I love it because it so clearly states that the movement is not being anti-male. It makes it clear that the problem is sexism. And that clarity helps us remember that all of us, female and male, have been socialized from birth on to accept sexist thought and action. As a consequence, females can be just as sexist as men. And while that does not excuse or justify male domination, it does mean that it would be naïve and wrongminded for feminist thinkers to see the movement as simplistically being for women against men. To end patriarchy (another way of naming the institutionalized sexism) we need to be clear that we are all participants in perpetuating sexism until we change our minds and hearts, until we let go sexist thought and action and replace it with feminist thought and action.

Males as a group have and do benefit the most from patriarchy, from the assumption that they are superior to females and should rule over us. But those benefits have come with a price. In return for all the goodies men receive from patriarchy, they are required to dominate women, to exploit and oppress us, using violence if they must to keep patriarchy intact. Most men find it difficult to be patriarchs. Most men are disturbed by hatred and fear of women, by male violence against women, even the men who perpetuate this violence. But they fear letting go of the benefits. They are not certain what will happen to the world they know most intimately if patriarchy changes. So they find it easier to passively support male domination even when they know in their minds and hearts that is wrong. Again and again men tell me they have no idea what it is feminists want. I believe them. I believe in their capacity to change and grow. And I believe that if they knew more about feminism they would no longer fear it, for they would find in feminist movement the hope of their own release from the bondage of patriarchy.

It is for these men, young and old, and for all of us, that I have written this short handbook, the book I have spent more than 20 years longing for. I had to write it because I kept waiting for it to appear, and it did not. And without it there was no way to address the hordes of people in this nation who are daily bombarded with anti-feminist backlash, who are being told to hate and resist a movement that they know very little about. There should be so many little feminist primers, easy to read pamphlets and books, telling us all about feminism, that this book would be just another passionate voice speaking out on behalf of feminist politics. There should be billboards; ads in magazines; ads on buses, subways, trains; television commercials spreading the word, letting the world know more about feminism. We are not there yet. But this is what we must do to share feminism, to let the movement into everyone's mind and heart. Feminist change has already touched all our lives in a positive way. And yet we lose sight of the positive when all we hear about feminism is negative.

When I began to resist male domination, to rebel against patriarchal thinking (and to oppose the strongest patriarchal voice in my life – my mother's voice), I was still a teenager, suicidal, depressed, uncertain about how I would find meaning in my life and a place for myself. I needed feminism to give me a foundation of equality and justice to stand on. Mama has come around to feminist thinking. She sees me and all her daughters (we are six) living better lives because of feminist politics. She sees the promise and hope in the feminist movement. It is that promise and hope that I want to share with you in this book, with everybody.

Imagine living in a world where there is no domination, where females and males are not alike or even always equal, but where a vision of mutuality is the ethos shaping our interaction. Imagine living in a world where we can all be who we are, a world of peace and possibility. Feminist revolution alone will not create such a world; we need to end racism, class elitism, imperialism. But it will make it possible for us to be fully self-actualized females and males able to create beloved community, to live together, realizing our dreams of freedom and justice, living the truth that we are all 'created equal.' Come closer. See how feminism can touch and change your life and all our lives. Come closer and know firsthand what the feminist movement is all about. Come closer and you will see: feminism is for everybody.

96.

INCITE! WOMEN, GENDER NON-CONFORMING, AND TRANS PEOPLE OF COLOR AGAINST VIOLENCE

Formed in 2000, Santa Cruz, California, United States of America

Gender Violence and the Prison Industrial Complex

2001

We call social justice movements to develop strategies and analysis that address both state AND interpersonal violence, particularly violence against women. Currently, activists/movements that address state violence (such as anti-prison, anti-police brutality groups) often work in isolation from activists/movements that address domestic and sexual violence. The result is that women of color, who suffer disproportionately from both state and interpersonal violence, have become marginalized within these movements. It is critical that we develop responses to gender violence that do not depend on a sexist, racist, classist, and homophobic criminal justice system. It is also important that we develop strategies that challenge the criminal justice system and that also provide safety for survivors of sexual and domestic violence. To live violence-free lives, we must develop holistic strategies for addressing violence that speak to the intersection of all forms of oppression.

The anti-violence movement has been critically important in breaking the silence around violence against women and providing much-needed services to survivors. However, the mainstream anti-violence movement has increasingly relied on the criminal justice system as the front-line approach toward ending violence against women of color. It is important to assess the impact of this strategy:

1. Law enforcement approaches to violence against women MAY deter some acts of violence in the short term. However, as an overall strategy for ending violence, criminalization has not worked. In fact, [...] mandatory arrest laws for domestic violence have led to decreases in the number of battered women who kill their partners in self-defense, but they have not led to a decrease in the number of batterers who kill their partners. Thus, the law protects batterers more than it protects survivors.

2. The criminalization approach has also brought many women into conflict with the law, particularly women of color, poor women, lesbians, sex workers, immigrant women, women with disabilities, and other marginalized women. For instance, under mandatory arrest laws, there have been numerous incidents where police officers called to domestic incidents have arrested the woman who is being battered. Many undocumented women have reported cases of sexual and domestic violence, only to find themselves deported. A tough law and order agenda also leads to long punitive sentences for women convicted of killing their batterers. Finally, when public funding is channeled into policing and prisons, budget cuts for social programs, including women's shelters, welfare and public housing, are the inevitable side effect. These cutbacks leave women less able to escape violent relationships.

3. Prisons don't work. Despite an exponential increase in the number of men in prisons, women are not any safer, and the rates of sexual assault and domestic violence have not decreased. In calling for greater police responses to and harsher sentences for perpetrators of gender violence, the anti-violence movement has fueled the proliferation of prisons which now lock up more people per capita in the U. S. than any other country. During the past fifteen years, the numbers of women, especially women of color in prison has skyrocketed. Prisons also inflict violence on the growing numbers of women behind bars. Slashing, suicide, the proliferation of HIV, strip searches, medical neglect and rape of prisoners has largely been ignored by anti-violence activists. The criminal justice system, an institution of violence, domination, and control, has increased the level of violence in society.

4. The reliance on state funding to support anti-violence programs has increased the professionalization of the anti-violence movement and alienated it from its community-organizing, social justice roots. Such reliance has isolated the anti-violence movement from other social justice movements that seek to eradicate state violence, such that it acts in conflict rather than in collaboration with these movements.

5. The reliance on the criminal justice system has taken power away from women's ability to organize collectively to stop violence and has invested this power within the state. The result is that women who seek redress in the criminal justice system feel disempowered and alienated. It has also promoted an individualistic approach toward ending violence such that the only way people think they can intervene in stopping violence is to call the police. This reliance has shifted our focus from developing ways communities can collectively respond to violence.

In recent years, the mainstream anti-prison movement has called important attention to the negative impact of criminalization and the build-up of the prison industrial complex. Because activists who seek to reverse the tide of mass incarceration and criminalization of poor communities and communities of color have not always centered gender and sexuality in their analysis or organizing, we have not always responded adequately to the needs of survivors of domestic and sexual violence.

1. Prison and police accountability activists have generally organized around and conceptualized men of color as the primary victims of state violence. Women prisoners and victims of police brutality have been made invisible by a focus on the war on our brothers and sons. It has failed to consider how women are affected as severely by state violence as men. The plight of women who are raped by INS officers or prison guards, for instance, has not received sufficient attention. In addition, women carry the burden of caring for extended family when family and community members are criminalized and warehoused. Several organizations have been established to advocate for women prisoners; however, these groups have frequently been marginalized within the mainstream anti-prison movement.

2. The anti-prison movement has not addressed strategies for addressing the rampant forms of violence women face in their everyday lives, including street harassment, sexual harassment at work, rape, and intimate partner abuse. Until these strategies are developed, many women will feel shortchanged by the movement. In addition, by not seeking alliance with the anti-violence movement, the anti-prison movement has sent the message that it is possible to liberate communities without seeking the well-being and safety of women.

3. The anti-prison movement has failed to sufficiently organize around the forms of state violence faced by LGBTI communities. LGBTI street youth and trans people in general are particularly vulnerable to police brutality and criminalization. LGBTI prisoners are denied basic human rights such as family visits from same sex partners, and same sex consensual relationships in prison are policed and punished.

4. While prison abolitionists have correctly noted that rapists and serial murderers comprise a small percentage of the prison population, we have not answered the question of how these cases should be addressed. The inability to answer the question is interpreted by many anti-violence activists as a lack of concern for the safety of women.

5. The various alternatives to incarceration developed by anti-prison activists have generally failed to provide sufficient mechanism[s] for safety and accountability for survivors of sexual and domestic violence. These alternatives often rely on a romanticized notion of communities, which have yet to demonstrate their commitment and ability to keep women and children safe or seriously address the sexism and homophobia that [are] deeply embedded within them.

We call on social justice movements concerned with ending violence in all its forms to:

1. Develop community-based responses to violence that do not rely on the criminal justice system AND which have mechanisms to ensure safety and accountability for survivors of sexual and domestic violence. Transformative practices emerging from local communities

should be documented and disseminated to promote collective responses to violence.

2. Critically assess the impact of state funding on social justice organizations and develop alternative fundraising strategies to support these organizations. Develop collective fundraising and organizing strategies for anti-prison and anti-violence organizations. Develop strategies and analysis that specifically target state forms of sexual violence.

3. Make connections between interpersonal violence, the violence inflicted by domestic state institutions (such as prisons, detention centers, mental hospitals, and child protective services), and international violence (such as war, military base prostitution, and nuclear testing).

4. Develop analyses and strategies to end violence that do not isolate individual acts of violence (either committed by the state or individuals) from their larger contexts. These strategies must address how entire communities of all genders are affected in multiple ways by both state violence and interpersonal gender violence. Battered women prisoners represent an intersection of state and interpersonal violence and as such provide an opportunity for both movements to build coalitions and joint struggles.

5. Put poor/working class women of color at the center of their analysis, organizing practices, and leadership development. Recognize the role of economic oppression, welfare 'reform,' and attacks on women workers' rights in increasing women's vulnerability to all forms of violence and locate anti-violence and anti-prison activism alongside efforts to transform the capitalist economic system.

6. Center stories of state violence committed against women of color in our organizing efforts.

7. Oppose legislative change that promotes prison expansion, criminalization of poor communities and communities of color and thus state violence against women of color, even if these changes also incorporate measures to support victims of interpersonal gender violence.

8. Promote holistic political education at the everyday level within our communities, specifically how sexual violence helps reproduce

the colonial, racist, capitalist, heterosexist, and patriarchal society we live in as well as how state violence produces interpersonal violence within communities.

9. Develop strategies for mobilizing against sexism and homophobia WITHIN our communities in order to keep women safe.

10. Challenge men of color and all men in social justice movements to take particular responsibility to address and organize around gender violence in their communities as a primary strategy for addressing violence and colonialism. We challenge men to address how their own histories of victimization have hindered their ability to establish gender justice in their communities.

11. Link struggles for personal transformation and healing with struggles for social justice.

We seek to build movements that not only end violence, but that create a society based on radical freedom, mutual accountability, and passionate reciprocity. In this society, safety and security will not be premised on violence or the threat of violence; it will be based on a collective commitment to guaranteeing the survival and care of all peoples.

97

HILARY MANTEL

Born 1952, Glossop, United Kingdom

from *Giving Up the Ghost*
2003

A short time later I was vomiting a good deal. I had finished the course of anti-depressants, but felt no more cheerful, and my GP did what you do when someone says she is vomiting: send her to a psychiatrist. I should like to say I protested, but I was willing enough. I thought perhaps I was a fascinating case. I had been tested for anaemia, but I wasn't iron-deficient. No one seemed to be able to think of another disorder to test me for, and if my body was not the problem it must be my mind that was acting up; I could believe this, and wanted my mind fixed. 'Psychosomatic' was the buzzword. Properly understood, the term suggests a subtle inter-action between mind and body, between the brain and the endocrine system. Improperly understood, it means, 'it's all in the mind' – that is to say, your symptoms are invented. You've nothing better to do with your time. You're seeking attention.

Dr G, the psychiatrist, was remote and bald. He had as much chance of understanding a girl like me as he had of rising from his desk and skimming from the window on silver pinions. He soon diagnosed my problem: stress, caused by overambition. This was a female complaint, one which people believed in, in those years, just as the Greeks believed that women were made ill by their wombs cutting loose and wandering about their bodies. I had told Dr G, in response to his questions about my fam-ily, that my mother was a fashion buyer in a large department store; it was true, for at the end of the sixties she had reinvented herself as a blonde, bought herself some new clothes and taken up a career. Oh really, said Dr G: how interesting. Thereafter, he referred to her place of work as 'the dress shop'. If I were honest with myself, he asked, wouldn't I rather have a job in my mother's dress shop than study law? Wouldn't the dress shop, when all's said and done, be more in my line?

I saw Dr G once a week. He must have obtained reports about me from my tutors, for he said, conscientious, hm, it says you're *very* conscientious.

Was I? I only turned in the work asked for. Didn't other people bother?

'And a *mind for detail*,' Dr G said, 'you have that.' I tried to imagine the other kind of law student, the kind who favoured the broad-brush approach, who took on the law of trusts, for example, with a grand generalist's sweep and dash. 'Tell me,' said Dr G, 'if you were a doctor, what kind would you be?'

I said politely that to be a psychiatrist must be interesting. No, pick something else, he said, something less close to home. I'd often thought, I said, that GPs had a challenging job, the variety of people and problems, the need for quick thinking – but no, I could see by his face that wasn't the answer required. Dr G sat back in his chair. I see you as a medical researcher, he said, one of those quiet invaluable people in the back room, unseen, industrious, unsung – a mind for detail, you see. And wasn't it the same, he asked, with law? If I did go on with my studies, wouldn't the niche for me be in a solicitor's office, conveying clients' houses – wasn't it just what people needed, at such a stressful time in their lives, to have the services of someone *very conscientious*, like me?

I could see her: a clerk very conscientious and quiet and dull, who wore snuff-coloured garb and filed herself in a cabinet every night and whose narrow heart fluttered when anyone mentioned a flying freehold or an ancient right of way. But you're not *looking* at me, I thought. I was quite thin; nausea was wearing me away. I left G's consulting room and stood on the pavement to consider this new version of myself. I felt as if I had been dealt a dull blow, but I didn't know which part of me ached.

The next time I went to Dr G's office I sat and wept. It was as if a dam had burst. I must have worked through a box of tissues, and no doubt it was his upset-girl ration for the whole month. Dr G spoke gently to me; said gravely he had not known that things were so bad. I had better have some stronger pills. And maybe a spell in the university clinic? I trucked off there, with my textbooks. At least now my husband would be able to study in peace for his finals, I wasn't easy company; I was labouring under a violent sense of injustice that may have seemed unreasonable to the people around me; I was angry, tearful and despairing, and I still had pains in my legs.

I think, in retrospect, that it would have been better if I had denied that I had pains in my legs, if I had taken it all back, or brightly said that I was well now. But because I didn't, the whole business began to spiral out of control. I still believed that honesty was the best policy; but the brute fact was, I was an invalid now, and I wasn't entitled to a policy, not a policy of my own. I feared that if I didn't tell the strict truth, my integrity would be eroded; I would have nothing then, no place to stand. The more I said that I had a physical illness, the more they said I had a mental illness. The more I questioned the nature, the reality of the mental illness, the more I was found to be in denial, deluded. I was confused; when I spoke of my confusion, my speech turned into a symptom. No one ventured a diagnosis: not out loud. It was in the nature of educated young women, it was believed, to be hysterical, neurotic, difficult, and out of control, and the object was to get them back under control, not by helping them examine their lives, or fix their practical problems – in my case, silverfish, sulking, family, poverty, cold – but by giving them drugs which would make them indifferent to their mental pain – and in my case, indifferent to physical pain too.

The first line of medication, in those days, were the group of drugs called tricyclic anti-depressants – which I had already sampled – and also what were then called 'minor tranquillisers'; the pills marketed as Valium were the most famous example of the type. Highly popular in those days among overworked GPs, the minor tranquillisers are central nervous system depressants. They impair mental alertness and physical co-ordination. They dull anxiety. They are habit-forming and addictive.

The anti-depressants didn't seem to be having much effect on me – or not the wanted effects, anyway, only the effects of making me unable to grapple with the written word, of making print slide sideways and fall out of the book. It didn't seem as if I would be able to sit my finals, Dr G said, but never mind: in view of my good work record, the university would grant me an aegrotat degree. Did I understand *aegrotat*? It meant 'he is sick'.

I muttered 'he, not she?' It would have been much healthier for me if I had stopped muttering, and kept smiling.

Valium, however, did work; it worked to damage me. Some people, given tranquillisers of this type, experience what is called a 'paradoxical reaction'. Instead of being soothed, they are enraged. One day I sat by the hearth at Roebuck Road and imagined myself starting fires – not in my own chimney, but fires in the houses of strangers, fires in the streets. Somewhere along the line, I seemed to have been damaged; I imagined myself doing damage, in my turn. I knew these thoughts were not rational, but I was obliged to entertain them; day by day I smouldered in a sullen fury, and when I saw a carving knife I looked at it with a new interest. I agreed to the clinic because I thought that, if I were to act on my impulses, someone would see me and stop me – before, at least, it got to arson and stabbing, and the deaths of strangers who had never harmed me at all.

After a day or two in the clinic I felt a little calmer. No one saw me as a danger; the danger was all in my own head. At first I came and went; I would go back to Roebuck Road during the day and do the cleaning. One day I went down to town to buy myself a nightdress. But because my vision was blurred, I misread the label, and came back with a size 16 instead of a size 10. 'Look at this monster garment!' I cried gaily to the nurses: I was having one of my less murderous days, and trying to lighten the tone. 'Look what I bought!'

My nightdress, I found, was viewed in a grave light. Why had I bought it? It was a mistake, I said, you see I . . . Didn't you hold it up? they asked me. Well, no, I, I just liked the pattern, I . . . Didn't you remember what size you were? Did you feel you didn't know? Yes, I know my size, but you see, my eyesight, it's misty, it's because of the drugs I . . . oh, never mind.

But they wouldn't drop the topic. It was obviously characteristic of mad girls to buy big nightdresses. Every time I spoke I dug myself into a deeper hole.

Dr G came to see me. Well, and what was I doing with myself now that I was free from my struggles with my textbooks? I have written a story, I offered brightly. It was a long story – that is to say, a short story, but long as these things go. Short but long, said Dr G. Hm. And what was it about? A changeling, I said. A woman who believes her baby has been taken away, and a substitute provided in its place. I see, said Dr G, and where and when did this occur? In rural Wales, I said, funnily enough.

(I'd never been to Wales.) I don't have to say the date, but it feels like the early 1920s. I mean, judging by their furniture and clothes. Does it? Said Dr G. It's a time well before social insurance, anyway, I said. The doctor won't come up the mountain to see them because they can't pay. I see, said Dr G. And how does it end? Oh, badly.

If you didn't respond to the first wave of drugs – if they didn't fix you, or you wouldn't take them – the possibility arose that you were not simply neurotic, hypochondriacal and a bloody nuisance, but heading for a psychotic breakdown, for the badlands of schizophrenia, a career on a back ward. To head off this disaster, doctors would prescribe what were then called the major tranquillisers, a group of drugs intended to combat thought disorder and banish hallucinations and delusions.

The next time I saw Dr G he forbade me to write: or – more precisely – he said, 'I don't *want* you writing.' He put more energy into this statement than any I had heard him make. He seemed as remote as ever, and yet inexpressibly angry. 'Because –' he added; and broke off. He was not going to impart to me what came after 'because'.

I said to myself, if I think of another story I will write it. In fact, I didn't think of another story for quite some years – not a story of the long but short type – and when I did I sent it to *Punch* and what I got back was not a malediction but a cheque. The changeling too paid off, in time, in a novel published in 1985; the setting was not rural Wales, nor the 1920s, but the present day in a prosperous and dull Midlands town. The novel contained mad people, but no one suggested its author was mad. It's different, somehow, when you've received money for your efforts; once you've got an agent, and professionalized the whole thing.

The first drug I was given was called Fentazine. That would do the job, Dr G thought.

Do you know about akathisia? It is a condition that develops as a side-effect of anti-psychotic medication, and the cunning thing about it is that it looks, and it feels, exactly like madness. The patient paces. She is unable to stay still. She wears a look of agitation and terror. She wrings her hands; she says she is in hell.

And from the inside, how does it feel? Akathisia is the worst thing I have ever experienced, the worst single, defined episode of my entire life – if I discount my meeting in the secret garden. No physical pain has ever matched that morning's uprush of killing fear, the hammering heart. You are impelled to move, to pace in a small room. You force yourself down into a chair, only to jump out of it. You choke; pressure rises inside your skull. Your hands pull at your clothing and tear at your arms. Your breathing becomes ragged. Your voice is like a bird's cry and your hands flutter like wings. You want to hurl yourself against the windows and the walls. Every fibre of your being is possessed by panic. Every moment endures for an age and yet you are transfixed by the present moment, stabbed by it; there is no sense of time passing, therefore no prospect of deliverance. A desperate feeling of urgency – a need to act – but to do what, and how? – throbs through your whole body, like the pulses of an electric shock.

You run out into the corridor. A man is standing there, gazing dolefully towards you. It is your GP, the man at the Student Health Service, the man with the rimless glasses and the polished brogues. The tension rises in your throat. Speech is dragged and jerked out of you, your ribs heaving. You think you are screaming but you are only whispering. You whisper that you are dying, you are damned, you are already being dipped into hell and you can feel the flames on your face.

And the answer to this? Another anti-psychotic. An injection of Largactil knocked me into insensibility. I lay with my face in the pillow as the drug took effect, and sank into darkness; as I ceased to panic and fight, the hospital sheets dampened, and wrapped around me like ropes.

After I woke up, I was maintained on Largactil, to combat my madness. It was not a friendly drug; it made my throat jump and close, as if someone were hanging me. This is how a mad person appears to the world – lips trembling, speech fumbling and jerky. You can say, this is the drugs you know, this is not me; I am quite all right, inside myself. They say, yes dear, of course you are; have you taken your pill?

But then it was the end of term, the end of the year. My course of studies was over. The university's responsibility was ended. I was discharged from the clinic. I went home, and was sane. The drugs wore off; no longer twitched and jumped. I could have passed for normal in any company. My legs didn't seem to ache so much; I had more abdominal pain, but I knew better than to mention it. For a time I claimed to be well.

But it was not so easy to shake off the events of the last year. The problem was the names of those drugs I had 'needed', spelled out like evil charms in my medical notes. Fentazine, Largactil, Stelazine. If I set foot in a GP's surgery – as I did, when I grew increasingly sick – I ran the risk of being prescribed a dose of them that would knock an elephant off its feet. Then there was my old friend Valium, which I knew I shouldn't go near: not unless I wanted to be arrested.

So when in time I went back to a doctor, I said I had backache, nausea, vomiting, that I was too tired to move. My GPs – to a man, and a woman – suggested a test to see if I was anaemic. I never was. They had no other suggestions; except perhaps some Valium: and a little spell away might do me good? By the time I was twenty-four I had learned the hard way that whatever my mental distress – and it does distress one, to be ignored, invalidated, and humiliated – I must never, ever go near a psychiatrist or take a psychotropic drug. My vision blurred, in those days, entirely without the help of the anti-depressants. Sometimes there were gaps in the world: I complained one day that the front door had been left open, but the truth was that I just couldn't see the door. Sometimes it seemed that some rustling, suspicious activity was going on, at the left side of my head, but I couldn't put a name to what it was. I couldn't put a name to lots of things, my speech came out muddled: I called a clock's hands its fingers, and a chair's arms its sleeves.

I was all right if I stuck with abstractions, ideas, images. And some days I was half well. I had a job, but I needed a pursuit, I thought. I went to the library and got out a lot of books about the French Revolution. I made some notes and some charts. I went to a bigger library and got more books and began to break down the events of 1789–94 so that I could put them into a card index. I was *very conscientious* and with *a mind for detail*. If you had been having a revolution you would certainly – at such a stressful time in your life – have needed the services of someone as conscientious as me. I began to read about the old regime, its casual cruelties, its heartless style. I thought, but I know this stuff. By nature, I knew about despotism: the unratified decisions, handed down from the top, arbitrarily enforced: the face of strength when it moves in on the weak.

98.

ANNE ENRIGHT

Born 1962, Dublin, Ireland

from *Making Babies*

2004

Breeding

Growing up in Ireland, we didn't need aliens – we already had a race of higher beings to gaze deep into our eyes and force us to have babies against our will: we called them priests. It is great being Catholic. A loopy Protestant, on the other hand, has to make it up as she goes along. And no one makes it up better than your American Protestant, driven mad by all that sky. In the 1980s, while we were fighting for contraception and abortion, they were fighting for the future of the human race. I am talking about those people who are forced to carry alien foetuses against their knowledge or will. In 1994 it was said that the alien breeding programme had already affected 'up to two million' carefully selected Americans. What I want to know is – who was counting? How do you get on this programme? And why do you have to be white to qualify?

Not that I am smug about being Irish, Catholic and obliged to give birth in a field – personally I would rather see a flying saucer than a vision of the Virgin Mary, I think it would be less frightening. The alien breeding programme that leaves strange bruises around the genitals of middle America, though spooky, may just have been preferable to the vicious fight in Ireland over who owns your insides. 'Get your rosaries off our ovaries,' was the battle cry as we voted, over and over, for or against abortion, while the pro-life louts hung around the Dublin streets with their short hair and jars full of dead body. I used to live in the centre of town and passed them on my way to the shops, waving their grim placards. Instead of spitting or shouting, I would amuse myself by imagining shafts of light with small putty-coloured creatures floating in them; creatures with rubbery fingers and blank, shiny eyes. Because nothing looks more like a foetus, of course, than your average small grey from beyond the Horsehead Nebula.

Never mind the folk legends, the *National Enquirer,* or trash paranoia on the Internet, for easy reference aliens in America can be sorted into two types – boys' aliens and girls' aliens. The boys' aliens are the ones that everyone knows about. They fly around the place in different-shaped craft, many of which could turn on a dime. They come from big mother ships that are so big you just couldn't say how big they are. These crafts appear over long roads and in big skies; they glow strangely and don't do a lot – a few scorch marks in the grass, a crop circle, some mutilated cattle. The CIA know all about boys' aliens, the radar blips and the pilot's black box, because boys can not only verify their aliens scientifically, they also suspect other boys of conspiring to cover this proof up.

Girls do not deal in proof. Girls' aliens happen under the skin. Girls' aliens make you fall in love; they manifest themselves in the things that you have forgotten, until you remember it, all in a rush. Despite the fact that girls not only meet the aliens, but also have their babies, they do not remember their impregnation, except under hypnotic regression. How can Hollywood get it so wrong? There are no tentacles, and no one speaks English – aliens have no need of mere speech. There are enough transcripts of these women weeping as they recover the details of their alien abduction for us to arrive at a reasonably consistent anatomy. We're talking three fingers here, not five, or none, or six. Aliens have no knuckles, no knees, and no muscular structure. They have difficulty walking. Their mouths never open when they speak. Above all, aliens never ever have sexual organs and a pregnant alien is a contradiction in terms.

Things move fast in the alien business. Abductees are so up in the nature of the beasts that float them out of their cars or beds on shafts of light that, though distressed, they are never old-fashioned. 'There was just this usual grey crap,' says one woman, recovering her first memory of being on board an alien craft. Still, they are surprisingly hard to describe. At the borders of conscious memory, when they are walking around our planet, aliens may use strange props, something slightly 'off': a stetson hat of unnatural size, a miner's lamp, or a false moustache pinned beneath a non-existent grey nose. The silver suits of the fifties are well gone, as are the space-bitches of the sixties: 'I am Lamxhia and I need your earth sperm.' When you're on the ship these days, with your clothes in a heap on the floor, lying on a one-legged table with your ankles in (optional) stirrups, there are only two types of alien – small greys and tall greys. Small greys move you around despite your protests and the fact that your legs don't work, and when they have attended to all those little surgical details, taking tissue, scraping out eggs, putting in foetuses or nasal implants or the small implant that goes in the back of your calf, then it's time for the tall grey to come in, wave them off, and gaze deep into your eyes. This is the moment when it all makes sense. Aliens' eyes are large, lanceolate and black, they are non-reflective and have no pupils. It is a terrifying thing to look into an alien's eyes, but, against your will, you may find yourself saturated with emotion and a sense of meaning; helpless with love.

Abductees are 94 per cent Caucasian, 75 per cent female and they have 1.9 children. All of them arrive at the hypnotherapist's office seeking help, frightened and distressed, with a story about missing time. They saw something strange at the foot of the bed, they saw something strange at the side of the road – then it's two hours later and they are in the wrong place with no idea how they got there. They are heading south on the wrong highway and the tank is still full of gas. They wake with the sheets awry and a husband who is sleeping too soundly. They arrive for work two hours late with their blouse on the wrong way around. (You see? It's happened to you.)

What they remember, eventually, is a hidden reproductive history. Men may have their sperm mechanically harvested, in a sudden access of unwelcome pleasure, but it is the women (mostly) who get pregnant. The pregnancy will subsequently disappear, with no evidence of a miscarriage. Sometimes the hymen is left unbroken. Where does the foetus go? On the spaceship, victims might see rows of jars with something growing in them; whole walls or rooms full of them. They might remember, like Debbie Tomey, being spreadeagled on a table with 'a terrible pressure within her loins', shouting, 'It's not fair! It's mine! It's mine!' They might remember later – years later – meeting a slender, hybrid daughter with ivory skin, no eyebrows, and sparse, cotton-coloured hair.

One of the main practitioners in the field of hypnotic regression is Budd Hopkins, the New York artist who stumbled into the aliens business when an article he wrote for the *Village Voice*, SANE CITIZEN SEES UFO IN NEW JERSEY, won him a postbag of frightened people who wanted to know what had happened to them after they, too, saw a strange light in the sky. He is now experienced in the techniques of hypnotic regression, or assisted imagination – 'Let's *allow* it to start getting dark in the room . . . I want you to *get the feeling* of getting into your bed.' His abductees have group therapy sessions to deal with their sense of isolation, helplessness and overwhelming anger. They are now abducted so regularly, they don't know what to do any more. Their children are abducted, their parents are abducted, and their grandparents feel a bit off-colour.

Budd seems like a nice man – like many other regression therapists who investigate alien abduction. Many are handsome in a rugged kind of way and admit to being brought up as 'strict materialists'. They really do want to do something. They really don't know what is going on. Their world view has been exploded by a series of highly distressed women whom only they can help. The women's sincerity, the weirdness of their accounts, the fact that they are so normal (read stupid), convinces them that 'she couldn't be making it all up'. How, for example, could you make up the detail about a small grey trying on your shoes? Speaking as some-one who makes things up for a living, who can spot a 'strict materialist' from five hundred paces, I think the shoes are a nice detail, as is the green elevator shaft with eyes, and the man in blue striped pyjamas.

Nine of Hopkins's abductees were tested blind by an independent psy-chologist who found them to be 'of above average intelligence', with a 'considerable richness of inner life', which is tied to a 'risk of being over-whelmed by the urgency of their impulses'. They suffer from lowered self-esteem and relative egocentricity. Under stressful conditions 'at least six of the nine showed a potential for more or less transient psychotic experiences . . . with confused and disordered thinking that can be bizarre, peculiar, or very primitive and emotionally charged'. These people are not pathological liars, paranoid schizophrenics or hysteroid characters subject to fugue states and/or multiple personalities. They are normal. They are not making it up – at least, they don't know that they are making it up. Perhaps you could say that the story is making them up instead.

Time was, people who suffered childhood sexual abuse were accused of 'making it all up'. As many as 35 per cent of abductees were also abused, yet they are 'making up' something else entirely. As therapist John Mack (Ph.D.) points out, regression therapy moves through dissociative strategies and false memories to approach the real facts of a patient's past. The difference with his patients is that some of them have a *false* memory of sexual abuse, which in fact covers the real story of alien abduction. It is only of limited use asking whether this man should be in jail.

Whatever the facts, there is a considerable amount at stake here: the word 'hysteric' is as charged and as complicated as the women it tries to identify. Besides, what about all those, to quote one abductee, 'Baby things. Baby here. Baby there. Baby everything. Everything is babies. Oh, God, I mean like babies, OK?'

The first foetus to star in a movie was the one in *2001: A Space Odyssey*, a star child, the first of a new hybrid race. I wonder if the actor was ever born.

The first female protagonist of a Hollywood science fiction film was Sigourney Weaver in *Alien* – a film so saturated with reproductive anxiety it still makes you check for something stirring in your guts. (Is that a tapeworm, or was it just wind?)

Look at a copy of the *National Geographic*, a magazine that will always exist in 1973, and there it is – between a photo essay on the birth of a distant galaxy and an article about breast decoration among the Nuba, floats the foetus, 'the world within'. It drifts free, like an astronaut on his umbilical cable; glowing, weightless; with pads for fingers, and plum-like, radioactive eyes. The foetus sees nothing, knows everything. It does not eat, or speak – the mouth is a bare line – but it seems to smile. It lives in water. It is a different life form. The foetus has no capacity for wonder. There is something blank and mean-spirited about it, perhaps. It lurks. It is all potential. We do not know if it means us as well.

As Julia Kristeva says, quoting Mallarme, ' "What is there to say concerning childbirth?" I find that question much more pungent than Freud's well-known "What does a women want?" Indeed, what does it mean to give birth to a child? Psychoanalysts do not talk much about it.'

What is it like being pregnant? 'It is like having an alien inside you,' a women said to me, many years ago. 'No really, it is.' She had three.

We do not choose, sometimes, to be occupied by this other creature, and this is one reason why women find pregnancy unsettling. It is assumed that our bodies will 'know', even if we don't, what pregnancy is like and what it is for; that we are, on some cellular level, wise, or even keen on the reproductive game. But I do not know how such cellular knowledge might happen, or where it might inhere.

A woman probably does know what she wants when she says, 'I want a baby,' because a baby is, first and foremost, an act of the imagination (unless it is an act of fourteen tequilas after the office do). But there are many cases of women who do not know that they are pregnant until they go into labour. There are cases of women who 'know' that they are pregnant, but who are not. In discussions about reproductive choice, it seems to me that we do not know what we are talking about, or that different people are talking about different things, and the experience of pregnancy, because it is so difficult to describe, is skipped or ignored.

In Ireland the imagination is still held in high regard. 'Making things up' is a normal and often social activity. This has its drawbacks, of course. There are always the priests, some of them abusive – and the babies. In Ireland we have babies all the time. Easy-peasy. We have them just like that.

'I think you should forget about aliens,' says Gerry, my friend. 'All that nonsense. Have a baby instead.'

And I say, 'Watch the skies.'

99.

MARY DALY

Born 1928, Schenectady, New York, United States of America
Died 2010, Gardner, Massachusetts, United States of America

from *Amazon Grace: Re-calling the Courage to Sin Big*
2006

The extent and depth of damage inflicted by phallocracy on Self-consciousness is ineffable and unfathomable. To begin to See this, and then to Name it and Act consistently with this Seeing and Naming, women may require an experience of great shocks which can move us into a state of shock. Our Foresister Susan B. Anthony believed this. In 1870 she wrote:

> So while I do not pray for anybody or any party to commit outrages, still I do pray, and that earnestly and constantly, for some terrific shock to startle the women of this nation into a self-respect which will compel them to see the abject degradation of their present position; which will force them to break their yoke of bondage, and give them faith in themselves, which will make them proclaim their allegiance to women first; which will enable them to see that man can no more feel, speak, or act for women than could the old slaveholder for his slave.

In the first decade of this century Susan B. Anthony's prayer of 1870 might seem to have been partially answered. G. W. Bush and his sordidly sub-missive Environmental Protection Agency delivered a 'terrific shock' to this nation by abandoning all attempts at denying that climate change is real, ongoing, and man-made, and then, without missing a beat, continuing to insist on NO CHANGE in US policy that would deal with this horrendous threat. Bush & company even suggested that we can 'adapt' and rely upon 'voluntary efforts' to reduce US emissions of carbon dioxide and other air pollutants.

The 'shock' of this ongoing travesty is experienced not only by some women, of course, but also by some men, many of whom have been outstanding opponents of environmental destruction. So how does this connect with Susan B. Anthony and her prayer for a shock that would startle women, specifically? To work our way toward an answer to this complex question, consider the implications of the fact that the successive heads of the EPA appointed by G.W. have conveniently functioned as token torturers of our Sister the Earth and her nonhuman and human inhabitants.

What feelings and thoughts does this simple fact elicit in a woman who identifies as a Feminist and who cares profoundly about the fate of the Earth and its inhabitants? There is a sense of disappointment and horror. But often this is blended with a bland, matter-of-fact, sophisticated acceptance of 'reality': 'Of course,' says our bland feminist, 'they're Bush appointees, so what can you expect?'

Over a quarter of a century ago I published in *Gyn/Ecology* an analysis of assimilation, psychic numbing, token tortures, and the state of total tokenism. It may be that in the expanding state of total tokenism in this century most women have become incapable of experiencing great shocks. Perhaps the worse the shocks women have had to endure, the greater our susceptibility to psychic numbing. In the early twenty-first century the media's portrayals of everyday atrocities against women and nature all over the globe have given heightened meaning to Hannah Arendt's expression 'the banality of evil.'

This observation leads to the thought that in the state of shock we are knocked into an unshockable state.

The self-contradiction and dilemma attached to the condition of 'shock' would seem to put a damper on Susan's famous prayer for a 'terrific shock.' Was she praying for the wrong thing? Not exactly; I believe that her use of the word 'shock' is an indication that she was on the trail of Something Big.

Although Susan could not then adequately articulate the Wondrous Positively Shocking Reality which can hurl us beyond the self-contradiction, she intuited its existence. Indeed, her heroic life is itself a manifestation of this Reality.

The dilemma arises from hearing and saying the word *shock* only from a foreground perspective. Shocks that are caused by the deadbeat daddies of daddyland are simply not Terrific enough. Since they are mere foreground phenomena, they inevitably keep us stuck in a maze of contradictions. The 'outrages' of fatherland, no matter how hideous and destructive, cannot of themselves be the answer to Susan's prayer. They cannot Shock us Out of the phallocentric foreground and into the Magnificent and Infinitely Shocking Background. For this, something Other is needed.

The Shock of Be-ing

All Wild creatures and Other realities participate in Be-ing, by which I mean 'Ultimate/Intimate Reality, the constantly Unfolding Verb of Verbs which is intransitive, having no object that limits its dynamism.' The Terrific Shock of encountering and Realizing Be-ing is utterly unlike the foreground shocks which keep us imprisoned and circling the masters' mazes. The Shock of meeting Be-ing is simple and direct. It is absolutely surprising and joyous. It is Self-transformative and changes Everything. It is unforgettable. It opens pathways that go on and on. It makes one Realize how Lucky she is. The Prayer that comes to mind is 'Thank you! Thank you!'

Be-ing manifests in natural creatures. A clover blossom announces: 'I am.' The girl or woman sitting on the grass who just 'happens' to Hear these words is astonished but not afraid. The simplicity and naturalness of the event – its ordinariness – does not conflict with its extraordinariness. It simply Is, and subtly everything changes.

This means that the women who has met the ontologically articulate clover blossom (or pebble or blade of grass or tree or piece of ice in the snow) gradually is enabled also to meet the foreground shocks in a different way. Having encountered Background Reality that is everywhere in nature, Be-Speaking in the Chorus of Be-ing, she becomes more Adventurous. She is surrounded by Natural Friends, as she follows her own path. She is a creator. When it is necessary she confronts the evil foreground world, taking on the attackers and oppressors of women and nature with confidence and Daring.

She is aided always, all ways by Amazon Grace, which manifests as an ontological experience.

100.

WANGARI MUTA MAATHAI

Born 1940, Nyeri, Kenya
Died 2011, Nairobi, Kenya

from *Unbowed*

2006

Another tributary of knowledge consisted of the women themselves, who brought the urgency of the situation home to me. By the early 1970s, I was a member of the National Council of Women of Kenya (NCWK). The NCWK was founded in 1964 as an umbrella organization to unify women's groups, both large and small, throughout Kenya, with membership drawn from urban and rural areas. The leadership consisted of women who were successful in their business, professional, or religious lives and they gave one another moral support in whatever sphere they were involved.

At a seminar organized by the NCWK, a woman researcher presented the results of a study she had done, which found that children in the central region of Kenya were suffering from diseases associated with malnutrition. This was an eye-opener for me, since that is where I come from and I knew from personal experience that the central region was one of the most fertile in Kenya. But times had changed. Many farmers had converted practically all of their land into growing coffee and tea to sell in the international market. These 'cash crops' were occupying land previously used to produce food for people to eat.

Consequently, women were feeding their families processed foods like white bread, maize flour, and white rice, all of which are high in carbohydrates but relatively low in vitamins, proteins, and minerals. Cooking these foods consumed less energy than the foods I had eaten as a child, and this made them attractive and practical, because available firewood for cooking was limited due to deforestation in the region. Instead, women were using as fuel materials left over from the harvest, such as corn stems and husks. This shortage of firewood, the researcher concluded, was lead-ing directly to malnutrition as people's diets changed in response. The most vulnerable were children and the elderly.

These facts troubled me, not least because they seemed so contrary to my experiences as a child – when there was more than enough food, the food itself was nutritious and wholesome, people were healthy and strong, and there was always enough firewood to cook with. I remembered how the colonial administration had cleared the indigenous forests and replaced them with plantations of exotic trees for the timber industry. After inde-pendence, Kenyan farmers had cleared more natural forests to create space to grow coffee and tea. Until now, however, I had not fully appreciated the multiple costs of these activities.

Although the leadership of the NCWK was generally elite and urban, we were concerned with the social and economic status of the majority of our members, who were poor, rural women. We worried about their access to clean water and firewood, how they would feed their children, pay their school fees, and afford clothing, and we wondered what we could do to ease their burdens. We had a choice: We could either sit in an ivory tower wondering how so many people could be so poor and not be work-ing to change their situation, or we could try to help them escape the vicious cycle they found themselves in. This was not a remote problem for us. The rural areas were where our mothers and sisters still lived. We owed it to them to do all we could.

At the same time, women in other countries throughout the world were recognizing the need to make changes in their own communities and bring their perspectives and experiences to the global arena, and their political leaders were giving them increasing space to do so. In June 1975, to coincide with the International Women's Year, 133 governments and about 4,000 women from around the world gathered in Mexico City for the first UN conference on women.

In the two years leading up to the women's conference, at both the Environment Liaison Centre and the NCWK, we were asking ourselves what our agenda should be for Mexico City. The NCWK held a number of seminars at which we heard from various constituencies, including women from the rural areas. These women confirmed what the researcher's study had suggested. They didn't have enough wood for fuel or fencing, fodder for their livestock, water to cook with or drink, or enough for themselves or their families to eat.

As I sat listening to the women talk about water, energy, and nutrition, I could see that everything they lacked depended on the environment. These women were laying out their agenda. When the representatives of the NCWK returned from the Mexico City conference (I was unable to go because there were not sufficient funds), they carried the same message: We needed to do something about water and energy. The conference participants had also concluded that the world needed to address the realities of rural women, their poverty, the overall lack of development, and the state of the environment that sustained them.

It suddenly became clear. Not only was the livestock industry threatened by a deteriorating environment, but I, my children, my students, my fellow citizens, and my entire country would pay the price. The connection between the symptoms of environmental degradation and their causes – deforestation, devegetation, unsustainable agriculture, and soil loss – were self-evident. Something had to be done. We could not just deal with the manifestations of the problems. We had to get to the root causes of those problems.

Now, it is one thing to understand the issues. It is quite another to do something about them. But I have always been interested in finding solutions. This is, I believe, a result of my education as well as my time in America: to think of what can be done rather than worrying about what cannot. I didn't sit down and ask myself, 'Now let me see; what shall I do?' It just came to me: 'Why not plant trees?' The trees would provide a supply of wood that would enable women to cook nutritious foods. They would also have wood for fencing and fodder for cattle and goats. The trees would offer shade for humans and animals, protect watersheds and bind the soil, and, if they were fruit trees, provide food. They would also heal the land by bringing back birds and small animals and regenerate the vitality of the earth.

AFRICAN FEMINIST FORUM

Formed in 2006, Accra, Ghana

The Charter of Feminist Principles for African Feminists
2006

Preamble: Naming Ourselves as Feminists

We define and name ourselves publicly as Feminists because we celebrate our feminist identities and politics. We recognize that the work of fighting for women's rights is deeply political, and the process of naming is political too. Choosing to name ourselves Feminist places us in a clear ideological position. By naming ourselves as Feminists we politicise the struggle for women's rights, we question the legitimacy of the structures that keep women subjugated, and we develop tools for transformatory analysis and action. We have multiple and varied identities as African Feminists. We are African women; we live here in Africa and even when we live else-where, our focus is on the lives of African women on the continent. Our feminist identity is not qualified with 'Ifs,' 'Buts,' or 'Howevers': We are Feminists. Full Stop.

Our Understanding of Feminism and Patriarchy

As African feminists our understanding of feminism places patriarchal social relations structures and systems which are embedded in other oppressive and exploitative structures at the center of our analysis. Patri-archy is a system of male authority which legitimizes the oppression of women through political, social, economic, legal, cultural, religious and military institutions. Men's access to, and control over, resources and rewards within the private and public sphere derives its legitimacy from the patriarchal ideology of male dominance. Patriarchy varies in time and space, meaning that it changes over time, and varies according to class, race, ethnic, religious and global-imperial relationships and structures. Furthermore, in the current conjectures, patriarchy does not simply change according to these factors, but is inter-related with and informs relationships of class, race, ethnic, religious, and global–imperialism. Thus to challenge patriarchy effectively also requires challenging other systems of oppression and exploitation, which frequently mutually support each other.

Our understanding of patriarchy is crucial because it provides for us, as feminists, a framework within which to express the totality of oppressive and exploitative relations which affect African women. Patriarchal ideology enables and legitimizes the structuring of every aspect of our lives by establishing the framework within which society defines and views men and women and constructs male supremacy. Our ideological task as feminists is to understand this system and our political task is to end it. Our focus is fighting against patriarchy as a system rather than fighting individual men or women. Therefore, as feminists, we define our work as investing individual and institutional energies in the struggle against all forms of patriarchal oppression and exploitation.

Our Identity as African Feminists

As Feminists who come from/work/live in Africa, we claim the right and the space to be Feminist and African. We recognize that we do not have a homogenous identity as feminists – we acknowledge and celebrate our diversities and our shared commitment to a transformatory agenda for African societies and African women in particular. This is what gives us our common feminist identity.

Our current struggles as African Feminists are inextricably linked to our past as a continent – diverse pre-colonial contexts, slavery, colonization, liberation struggles, neo-colonialism, globalization, etc. Modern African States were built off the backs of African Feminists who fought alongside men for the liberation of the continent. As we craft new African

States in this new millennium, we also craft new identities for African women, identities as full citizens, free from patriarchal oppression, with rights of access, ownership and control over resources and our own bodies and utilizing positive aspects of our cultures in liberating and nurturing ways. We also recognize that our pre-colonial, colonial and post-colonial histories and herstories require special measures to be taken in favour of particular African women in different contexts.

We acknowledge the historical and significant gains that have been made by the African Women's Movement over the past forty years, and we make bold to lay claim to these gains as African feminists: they happened because African Feminists led the way, from the grassroots level and up; they strategised, organized, networked, went on strike and marched in protest, and did the research, analysis, lobbying, institution building and all that it took for States, employers and institutions to acknowledge women's personhood.

As African feminists, we are also part of a global feminist movement against patriarchal oppression in all its manifestations. Our experiences are linked to that of women in other parts of the world with whom we have shared solidarity and support over the years. As we assert our space as African feminists, we also draw inspiration from our feminist ancestors who blazed the trail and made it possible to affirm the rights of African women. As we invoke the memory of those women whose names are hardly ever recorded in any history books, we insist that it is a profound insult to claim that feminism was imported into Africa from the West. We reclaim and assert the long and rich tradition of African women's resistance to patriarchy in Africa. We henceforth claim the right to theorize for ourselves, write for ourselves, strategise for ourselves and speak for ourselves as African feminists.

Individual Ethics

As individual feminists, we are committed to and believe in gender equality based on feminist principles which are:

- The indivisibility, inalienability and universality of women's human rights.

- The effective participation in building and strengthening progressive African feminist organizing and networking to bring about transformatory change.
- A spirit of feminist solidarity and mutual respect based on frank, honest and open discussion of difference with each other.
- The support, nurture, and care of other African feminists, along with the care for our own well-being.
- The practice of non-violence and the achievement of non-violent societies.
- The right of all women to live free of patriarchal oppression, discrimination and violence.
- The right of all women to have access to sustainable and just livelihoods as well as welfare provision, including quality health care, education, water and sanitation.
- Freedom of choice and autonomy regarding bodily integrity issues, including reproductive rights, abortion, sexual identity and sexual orientation.
- A critical engagement with discourses of religion, culture, tradition and domesticity with a focus on the centrality of women's rights.
- The recognition and presentation of African women as the subjects not the objects of our work, and as agents in their lives and societies.
- The right to healthy, mutually respectful and fulfilling personal relationships.
- The right to express our spirituality within or outside of organized religion.
- The acknowledgement of the feminist agency of African women which has a rich Herstory that has been largely undocumented and ignored.

Institutional Ethics

As feminist organisations we commit to the following:

- Advocating for openness, transparency, equality and accountability in feminist-led institutions and organisations.

- Affirming that being a feminist institution is not incompatible with being professional, efficient, disciplined and accountable.
- Insisting on and supporting African women's labour rights, including egalitarian governance, fair and equal remuneration and maternity policies.
- Using power and authority responsibly, and managing institutional hierarchies with respect for all concerned. We believe that feminist spaces are created to empower and uplift women. At no time should we allow our institutional spaces to denigrate into sites of oppression and undermining of other women.
- Exercising responsible leadership and management of organisations whether in a paid or unpaid capacity and striving to uphold critical feminist values and principles at all times.
- Exercising accountable leadership in feminist organisations taking into consideration the needs of others for self-fulfillment and professional development. This includes creating spaces for powersharing across generations.
- Women's organizations and networks should be led and managed by women. It is a contradiction of feminist leadership principles to have men leading, managing and being spokespersons for women's organizations.
- Feminist organisations as models of good practice in the community of civil society organizations, ensuring that the financial and material resources mobilised in the name of African women are put to the service of African women and not diverted to serve personal interests. Systems and structures with appropriate Codes of Conduct to prevent corruption and fraud, and to manage disputes and complaints fairly, are the means of ensuring institutionalized [transparency] within our organizations.
- Striving to inform our activism with theoretical analysis and to connect the practice of activism to our theoretical understanding of African feminism.
- Being open to critically assessing our impact as feminist organizations, and being honest and proactive with regards to our role in the movement.

- Opposing the subversion and/or hijacking of autonomous feminist spaces to serve right wing, conservative agendas.
- Ensuring that feminist non-governmental or mass organisations are created in response to real needs expressed by women that need to be met, and not to serve selfish interests, and accountable income generating.

Feminist Leadership

As leaders in the feminist movement, we recognize that feminist agency has popularized the notion of women as leaders. As feminist leaders we are committed to making a critical difference in leadership, based on the understanding that the quality of women's leadership is even more important than the numbers of women in leadership. We believe in and commit ourselves to the following:

- Disciplined work ethics guided by integrity and accountability at all times.
- Expanding and strengthening a multi-generational network and pool of feminist leaders across the continent.
- Ensuring that the feminist movement is recognised as a legitimate constituency for women in leadership positions.
- Building and expanding our knowledge and information base on an ongoing basis, as the foundation for shaping our analysis and strategies and for championing a culture of learning beginning with ourselves within the feminist movement.
- Nurturing, mentoring and providing opportunities for young feminists in a non-matronising manner.
- Crediting African women's labour, intellectual and otherwise in our work.
- Creating time to respond in a competent, credible and reliable manner to other feminists in need of solidarity and support whether political practical or emotional.
- Being open to giving and receiving peer reviews and constructive feedback from other feminists.

102.

JOANNE ARNOTT

Born 1960, Winnipeg, Canada, of Métis descent

Change Herself
2007

first my single woman's
scrawny form takes on
roundness among the angles,
my single woman's mind explores
the meaning in being more –

where my borders are
and the center of balance
pulled by unrelenting change,
secrets pulled from convert muscle
secrets leap with energy and blood
through opened channels,
flush about my being,
tumble out of disturbed flesh,
and materialize in dreams –

labour intensifies the process
labour, the real shakedown –
birth
is terrifying
for i cannot say no to the infant,
but to say yes
is to lay the mind open
to the whole of my unabsorbed life
stashed away in my body

103.

SARA AHMED

Born 1969, Salford, United Kingdom

from *Feminist Killjoys (And Other Willful Subjects)*

2010
*A note on this article.**

What is my story? Like you, I have many. One way of telling my feminist story would be to begin with a table. Around the table, a family gathers. Always we are seated in the same place: my father one end, myself the other, my two sisters to one side, my mother to the other. Always we are seated this way, as if we are trying to secure more than our place. A childhood memory, yes. But it is also memory of an everyday experience in that quite literal sense of an experience that happened every day. An intense everyday: my father asking questions, my sisters and me answering them, my mother mostly silent. When does intensity become tension?

We begin with a table. Around this table, the family gathers, having polite conversations, where only certain things can be brought up. Someone says something you consider problematic. You are becoming tense; it is becoming tense. How hard to tell the difference between what is you and what is it! You respond, carefully, perhaps. You say why you think what they have said is problematic. You might be speaking quietly, but you are beginning to feel 'wound up,' recognising with frustration that you are being wound up by someone who is winding you up. In speaking up or speaking out, you upset the situation. That you have described what was said by another as a problem means you have created a problem. You become the problem you create.

To be the object of shared disapproval, those glances that can cut you up, cut you out. An experience of alienation can shatter a world. The

---

* This paper is dedicated to all feminist killjoys. You know who you are!

family gathers around the table; these are supposed to be happy occasions. How hard we work to keep the occasion happy, to keep the surface of the table polished so that it can reflect back a good image of the family. So much you are not supposed to say, to do, to be, in order to preserve that image. If you say, or do, or be anything that does not reflect the image of the happy family back to itself, the world becomes distorted. You become the cause of a distortion. You are the distortion you cause. Another dinner, ruined. To become alienated from a picture can allow you to see what that picture does not and will not reflect.

Becoming a feminist can be an alienation from happiness (though not just that, not only that: oh the joy of being able to leave the place you were given!). When we feel happiness in proximity to the right objects, we are aligned; we are facing the right way. You become alienated – out of line with an affective community – when you do not experience happiness from the right things. The gap between the affective value of an object and how we experience an object can involve a range of affects, which are directed by the modes of explanation we offer to fill this gap.

If we are disappointed by something that is supposed to make us happy, we generate explanations of why that thing is disappointing. We can be disappointed without ever being happy. Think of the wedding day, imagined as 'the happiest day of your life' before it even happens! What happens *when* the day happens, *if* happiness does not happen? In her classic *The Managed Heart*, Arlie Russell Hochschild explores how if the bride is not happy on the wedding day, and feels 'depressed and upset,' then she is experiencing an 'inappropriate affect,' or is being affected inappropriately. You have to save the day by feeling right: 'sensing a gap between the ideal feeling and the actual feeling she tolerated, the bride prompts herself to be happy'.* The capacity to 'save the day' depends on the bride being able to make herself be affected in the right way, or at least being able to persuade others that she is being affected in the right way. To correct our feelings is to become disaffected from a former affection: the bride makes herself happy by stopping herself from being miserable. We learn from this example that it is possible not to inhabit fully one's own happiness,

---

* Arlie Russell Hochschild, *The Managed Heart: Commercialization of Human Feeling* (Berkeley: University of California Press, 2003) 59–61.

or even to be alienated from one's happiness, if the former affection remains lively, persisting as more than just memory, or if one is made uneasy by the very necessity of having to make oneself feel a certain way.

You cannot always close the gap between how you do feel and how you should feel. Behind the sharpness of this 'cannot' is a world of possibility. Does activism act out of this gap, opening it up, loosening it up? Not to close the gap between what you do feel and what you should feel might begin as or with a sense of disappointment. Disappointment can involve an anxious narrative of self-doubt (why am I not made happy by this; what is wrong with me?), or a narrative of rage, where the object that is 'supposed' to make us happy is attributed as the cause of disappointment. Your rage might be directed against it, or spill out toward those that promised you happiness through the elevation of such objects as good. We become strangers, or affect aliens, in such moments.

Affect aliens are those who experience alien affects. You are unseated by the table of happiness. If you lose your seat what happens? Activism is often a matter of seats. The word 'dissidence' for instance derives from the Latin *dis* – 'apart' + *sedere* 'to sit.' The dissident is the one who sits apart. Or the dissident is the one who would be unseated by taking up a place at the table: your seat is the site of disagreement. In *Queer Phenomenology* I was too obsessed with tables to notice the queerness of the chair. But I did suggest then that if we begin with the body that loses its chair, the world we describe might be quite different.*

To be unseated by the table of happiness might be to threaten not simply that table, but what gathers around it, what gathers on it. When you are unseated, you can even get in the way of those who are seated, those who want more than anything to keep their seats. To threaten the loss of the seat can be to kill the joy of the seated. How well we recognize the figure of the feminist killjoy! How she makes sense! Let's take the figure of the feminist killjoy seriously. One feminist project could be to give the killjoy back her voice. Whilst hearing feminists as killjoys might be a form of dismissal, there is an agency that this dismissal rather ironically reveals. We can respond to the accusation with a 'yes.'

* Sara Ahmed, *Queer Phenomenology: Orientations, Objects, Others* (Durham, NC: Duke University Press, 2006) 138.

The figure of the feminist killjoy makes sense if we place her in the context of feminist critiques of happiness, of how happiness is used to justify social norms as social goods (a social good is what causes happiness, given happiness is understood as what is good). As Simone de Beauvoir described so astutely 'it is always easy to describe as happy a situation in which one wishes to place [others].'* Not to agree to stay in the place of this wish might be to refuse the happiness that is wished for. To be involved in political activism is thus to be involved in a struggle against happiness. Even if we are struggling for different things, even if we have different worlds we want to create, we might share what we come up against. Our activist archives are thus unhappy archives. Just think of the labor of critique that is behind us: feminist critiques of the figure of 'the happy housewife;' Black critiques of the myth of 'the happy slave'; queer critiques of the sentimentalisation of heterosexuality as 'domestic bliss.' The struggle over happiness provides the horizon in which political claims are made. We inherit this horizon.

To be willing to go against a social order, which is protected as a moral order, a happiness order is to be willing to cause unhappiness, even if unhappiness is not your cause. To be willing to cause unhappiness might be about how we live an individual life (not to choose 'the right path' is readable as giving up the happiness that is presumed to follow that path). Parental responses to coming out, for example, can take the explicit form not of being unhappy about the child being queer but of *being unhappy about the child being unhappy*.† Even if you do not want to cause the unhappiness of those you love, a queer life can mean living with that unhappiness. To be willing to cause unhappiness can also be how we immerse ourselves in collective struggle, as we work with and through others who share our points of alienation. Those who are unseated by the tables of happiness can find each other.

So, yes, let's take the figure of the feminist killjoy seriously. Does the feminist kill other people's joy by pointing out moments of sexism? Or does she expose the bad feelings that get hidden, displaced, or negated under public signs of joy? Does bad feeling enter the room when somebody expresses anger

---

* Simone de Beauvoir, *The Second Sex*, trans. by H.M. Parshley (London: Vintage Books, 1997) 28.
† See, for example: Nancy Garden, *Annie on My Mind* (New York: Farrar, Straus & Giroux, 1982) 191.

about things, or could anger be the moment when the bad feelings that circulate through objects get brought to the surface in a certain way? The feminist subject 'in the room' hence 'brings others down' not only by talking about unhappy topics such as sexism but by exposing how happiness is sustained by erasing the signs of not getting along. Feminists do kill joy in a certain sense: they disturb the very fantasy that happiness can be found in certain places. To kill a fantasy can still kill a feeling. It is not just that feminists might not be happily affected by what is supposed to cause happiness, but our failure to be happy is read as sabotaging the happiness of others.

We can consider the relationship between the negativity of the figure of the feminist killjoy and how certain bodies are 'encountered' as being negative. Marilyn Frye argues that oppression involves the requirement that you show signs of being happy with the situation in which you find yourself. As she puts it, 'it is often a requirement upon oppressed people that we smile and be cheerful. If we comply, we signify our docility and our acquiescence in our situation.' To be oppressed requires that you show signs of happiness, as signs of being or having been adjusted. For Frye 'anything but the sunniest countenance exposes us to being perceived as mean, bitter, angry or dangerous'.*

To be recognized as a feminist is to be assigned to a difficult category and a category of difficulty. You are 'already read' as 'not easy to get along with' when you name yourself as a feminist. You have to show that you are not difficult through displaying signs of good will and happiness. Frye alludes to such experiences when she describes how: 'this means, at the very least, that we may be found to be "difficult" or unpleasant to work with, which is enough to cost one's livelihood.'† We can also witness an investment in feminist unhappiness (the myth that feminists kill joy because they are joyless). There is a desire to believe that women become feminists *because* they are unhappy. This desire functions as a defense of happiness against feminist critique. This is not to say that feminists might not be unhappy; becoming a feminist might mean becoming aware of *just how much* there is to be unhappy about. Feminist consciousness could be understood as consciousness

---

* Marilyn Frye, *The Politics of Reality: Essays in Feminist Theory* (Trumansburg, New York: The Crossing Press, 1983).
† Frye, 2–3.

of unhappiness, a consciousness made possible by the refusal to turn away. My point here would be that feminists are read as being unhappy, such that situations of conflict, violence, and power are read as *about* the unhappiness of feminists, rather than being what feminists are unhappy *about*.

Political struggles can take place over the causes of unhappiness. We need to give a history to unhappiness. We need to hear in unhappiness more than the negation of the 'un.' The history of the word 'unhappy' might teach us about the unhappiness of the history of happiness. In its earliest uses, unhappy meant to cause misfortunate or trouble. Only later, did it come to mean to feel misfortunate, in the sense of wretched or sad. We can learn from the swiftness of translation from causing unhappiness to being described as unhappy. We must learn.

The word 'wretched' has its own genealogy, coming from wretch, meaning a stranger, exile, banished person. Wretched in the sense of 'vile, despicable person' was developed in Old English and is said to reflect 'the sorry state of the outcast.' Can we rewrite the history of happiness from the point of view of the wretch? If we listen to those who are cast as wretched, perhaps their wretchedness would no longer belong to them. The sorrow of the stranger might give us a different angle on happiness not because it teaches us what it is like or must be like to be a stranger, but because it might estrange us from the very happiness of the familiar.

Phenomenology helps us explore how the familiar is that which is not revealed. A queer phenomenology shows how the familiar is not revealed to those who can inhabit it. For queers and other others the familiar is revealed to you, because you do not inhabit it. To be 'estranged from' can be what enables a 'consciousness of.' This is why being a killjoy can be a knowledge project, a world-making project.

A feminist call might be a call to anger, to develop a sense of rage about collective wrongs. And yet, it is important that we do not make feminist emotion into a site of truth: as if it is always clear or self-evident that our anger is right. When anger becomes righteous it can be oppressive; to assume anger makes us right can be a wrong. We know how easily a politics of happiness can be displaced into a politics of anger: the assumption of a right to happiness can convert very swiftly into anger toward others (immigrants, aliens, strangers) who have taken the happiness assumed 'by right' to be ours. It is precisely that we cannot defend ourselves against such defensive use of emotion that would be my point. Emotions are not always just, even those that seem to acquire their force in or from an experience of injustice. Feminist emotions are mediated and opaque; they are sites of struggle, and we must persist in struggling with them.*

After all, feminist spaces are emotional spaces, in which the experience of solidarity is hardly exhaustive. As feminists we have our own tables. If we are unseated by the family table, it does not necessarily follow that we are seated together. We can place the figure of the feminist killjoy alongside the figure of the angry Black woman, explored so well by Black feminist writers such as Audre Lorde† and bell hooks.‡ The angry black woman can be described as a killjoy; she may even kill feminist joy, for example, by pointing out forms of racism within feminist politics. She might not even have to make any such point to kill joy. Listen to the following description from bell hooks: 'a group of white feminist activists who do not know one another may be present at a meeting to discuss feminist theory. They may feel bonded on the basis of shared womanhood, but the atmosphere will noticeably change when a woman of color enters the room. The white woman will become tense, no longer relaxed, no longer celebratory.'§

It is not just that feelings are 'in tension,' but that the tension is located somewhere: in being felt by some bodies, it is attributed as caused by another body, who comes to be felt as apart from the group, as getting in

---

* For early work on feminist emotion see: Alison Jaggar, 'Love and Knowledge: Emotion in Feminist Epistemology,' in Ann Garry and Marilyn Pearsall (eds.), *Women, Knowledge and Reality: Explorations in Feminist Philosophy* (New York: Routledge, 1996) 166–190; and Elizabeth Spelman, 'Anger and Insubordination,' in Ann Garry and Marilyn Pearsall (eds.), *Women, Knowledge and Reality: Explorations in Feminist Philosophy* (New York: Routledge, 1989) 263–274. For an important argument about the need to separate injustice from the experience of pain and hurt see: Lauren Berlant, 'The Subject of True Feeling: Pain, Privacy and Politics' in Sara Ahmed, Celia Lury, Jane Kilby, Maureen McNeil, and Beverley Skeggs (eds.), *Transformations: Thinking Through Feminism* (London: Routledge, 2000) 33–47. For further discussion of feminism and emotion see the final chapter, 'Feminist Attachments,' which considers wonder, hope and anger as feminist emotions in: Sara Ahmed, *The Cultural Politics of Emotion* (Edinburgh: Edinburgh University Press, 2004).
† See Audre Lorde, *Sister Outsider: Essays and Speeches* (Trumansburg, New York: The Crossing Press, 1984).
‡ See bell hooks, *Feminist Theory: From Margin to Centre* (London: Pluto Press, 2000).
§ hooks, 56.

the way of its enjoyment and solidarity. The body of color is attributed as the cause of becoming tense, which is also the loss of a shared atmosphere. As a feminist of color you do not even have to say anything to cause tension! The mere proximity of some bodies involves an affective conversion. We learn from this example how histories are condensed in the very intangibility of an atmosphere, or in the tangibility of the bodies that seem to get in the way. Atmospheres might become shared if there is agreement in where we locate the points of tension.

A history can be preserved in the very stickiness of a situation. To speak out of anger as a woman of color is then to confirm your position as the cause of tension; your anger is what threatens the social bond. As Audre Lorde describes: 'When women of Color speak out of the anger that laces so many of our contacts with white women, we are often told that we are "creating a mood of helplessness," "preventing white women from getting past guilt," or "standing in the way of trusting communication and action."'* The exposure of violence becomes the origin of violence. The woman of color must let go of her anger for the white woman to move on.

The figure of the angry black woman is a fantasy figure that produces its own effects. Reasonable, thoughtful arguments are dismissed as anger (which of course empties anger of its own reason), which makes you angry, such that your response becomes read as the confirmation of evidence that you are not only angry but also unreasonable! To make this point in another way, the anger of feminists of color is attributed. You might be angry *about* how racism and sexism diminish life choices for women of color. Your anger is a judgement that something is wrong. But then in being heard as angry, your speech is read as motivated by anger. Your anger is read as unattributed, as if you are against x because you are angry rather than being angry because you are against x. You become angry at the injustice of being heard as motivated by anger, which makes it harder to separate yourself from the object of your anger. You become entangled with what you are angry about because you are angry about how they have entangled you in your anger. In becoming angry about that entanglement, you confirm their commitment to your anger as the truth 'behind' your speech, which is what blocks your anger, stops it from getting through. You are blocked by not getting through.

* Lorde, 131.

Some bodies become blockage points, points where smooth communication stops. Consider Ama Ata Aidoo's wonderful prose poem, *Our Sister Killjoy*, where the narrator Sissie, as a black woman, has to work to sustain the comfort of others. On a plane, a white hostess invites her to sit at the back with 'her friends,' two black people she does not know. She is about to say that she does not know them, and hesitates. 'But to have refused to join them would have created an awkward situation, wouldn't it? Considering too that apart from the air hostess's obviously civilized upbringing, she had been trained to see the comfort of all her passengers.'*

Power speaks here in this moment of hesitation. Do you go along with it? What does it mean not to go along with it? To create awkwardness is to be read as being awkward. Maintaining public comfort requires that certain bodies 'go along with it.' To refuse to go along with it, to refuse the place in which you are placed, is to be seen as causing trouble, as making others uncomfortable. There is a political struggle about how we attribute good and bad feelings, which hesitates around the apparently simple question of who introduces what feelings to whom. Feelings can get stuck to certain bodies in the very way we describe spaces, situations, dramas. And bodies can get stuck depending on the feelings with which they get associated.

Getting in the Way

A killjoy: the one who gets in the way of other people's happiness. Or just the one who is in the way – you can be in the way of *whatever*, if you are already perceived as being in the way. Your very arrival into a room is a reminder of histories that 'get in the way' of the occupation of that room. How many feminist stories are about rooms, about who occupies them, about making room? When to arrive is to get in the way, what happens, what do you do? The figure of the killjoy could be rethought in terms of the politics of willfulness. I suggested earlier that an activist archive is an unhappiness archive, one shaped by the struggles of those who are willing to struggle against happiness. We might redescribe this struggle in terms of those who are willing to be willful. An unhappiness archive is a willfulness archive.

* Ama Ata Aidoo, *Our Sister Killjoy* (Harlow: Longman, 1997) 10.

Let's go back: let's listen to what and who is behind us. Alice Walker describes a 'womanist' in the following way: 'A black feminist or feminist of color . . . Usually referring to outrageous, audacious, courageous or *willful* behavior. Wanting to know more and in greater depth than is considered "good" for one . . . Responsible. In charge. Serious.'* Julia Penelope describes lesbianism as willfulness: 'The lesbian stands against the world created by the male imagination. What **willfulness** we possess when we claim our lives!'† Marilyn Frye's radical feminism uses the adjective willful: 'The willful creation of new meaning, new loci of meaning, and new ways of being, together, in the world, seems to be in these mortally dangerous times the best hope we have'.‡ Willfulness as audacity, willfulness as standing against, willfulness as creativity.

We can make sense of how willfulness comes up, if we consider a typical definition of willfulness: 'asserting or disposed to assert one's own will against persuasion, instruction, or command; governed by will without regard to reason; determined to take one's own way; obstinately self-willed or perverse' (OED). To be called obstinate or perverse because you are not persuaded by the reason of others? Is this familiar to you? Have you heard this before? When you are charged with willfulness it is as if your being is an insistence on being, a refusal to give way, to give up, to give up your way. Can what we are charged with become a charge in Alice Walker's sense, a way of being in charge? If we are charged with willfulness, we can accept and mobilize this charge.

We have to become willful, perhaps, to keep going the way we are going, if the way you are going is perceived to be 'the wrong way.' We all know the experience of 'going the wrong way' in a crowd. Everyone seems to be going the opposite way than the way you are going. No one person has to push or shove for you to feel the collective momentum of the crowd as a pushing and shoving. For you to keep going you have to push harder than any of those individuals who are going the right way. The body 'going the wrong way' is the one that is experienced as 'in the way' of the will

---

* Ama Ata Aidoo, *Our Sister Killjoy* (Harlow: Longman, 1997) 10.
† Julia Penelope, *Call Me Lesbian: Lesbian Lives, Lesbian Theory* (Berkeley, CA: Crossing Press, 1992) 42.
‡ Marily Frye, *Willful Virgin: Essays in Feminism, 1976–1992* (Berkeley, CA: Crossing Press, 1992) 9.

that is acquired as momentum. For some bodies mere persistence, 'to continue steadfastly,' requires great effort, an effort that might appear to others as stubbornness or obstinacy, as insistence on going against the flow. You have to become insistent to go against the flow; you are judged to be going against the flow because you are insistent. A life paradox: you have to become what you are judged as being.

It is crucial that we don't assume that willfulness is simply about lonely individuals going against the tide of the social. At the same time, we can note how the social can be experienced as a force: you can feel a force most directly when you attempt to resist it. It is the experience of 'coming up against' that is named by willfulness, which is why a willful politics needs to be a collective politics. The collective here is not assumed as a ground. Rather, willfulness is a collecting together, of those struggling for a different ground for existence. You need to be supported when you are not going the way things are flowing. This is why I think of a feminist queer politics as a politics of tables: tables give support to gatherings, and we need support when we live our lives in ways that are experienced by others as stubborn or obstinate.

A flow is an effect of bodies that are going the same way. To go is also to gather. A flow can be an effect of gatherings of all kinds: gatherings of tables, for instance, as kinship objects that support human gatherings. How many times have I had the experience of being left waiting at a table when a straight couple walks into the room and is attended to straight away! For some, you have to become insistent to be the recipient of a social action, you might have to announce your presence, wave your arm, saying: 'Here I am!' For others, it is enough just to turn up because you have already been given a place at the table *before you take up your place*. Willfulness describes the uneven consequences of this differentiation.

An attribution of willfulness involves the attribution of negative affect to those bodies that get in the way, those bodies that 'go against the flow' in the way they are going. The attribution of willfulness is thus effectively a charge of killing joy. Conversations are also flows; they are saturated. We hear this saturation as atmosphere. To be attributed as willful is to be the one who 'ruins the atmosphere.' A colleague says to me she just has to open her mouth in meetings to witness eyes rolling as if to say, 'oh here she goes.' My experience as a feminist daughter in a conventional family taught me a great deal about rolling eyes. You already know this. However you speak, the one who speaks up as a feminist is usually viewed as 'causing the argument,' as the one who is disturbing the fragility of peace. To be willful is to provide a point of tension. Willfulness is stickiness: it is an accusation that sticks.

If to be attributed as willful is to be the cause of the problem, then we can claim that willfulness as a political cause. Queer feminist histories are full of self-declared willful subjects. Think of the Heterodoxy Club that operated in Greenwich Village in the early 20th century, a club for unorthodox women. They described themselves as 'this little band of willful women,' as Judith Schwarz reveals in her wonderful history of this club.* A heterodoxy is 'not in agreement with accepted beliefs, or holding unorthodox opinions.' To be willful is to be willing to announce your disagreement, and to put yourself behind a disagreement. To enact a disagreement might even mean to become disagreeable. Feminism we might say is the creation of some rather disagreeable women.

Political histories of striking and of demonstrations are histories of those willing to put their bodies in the way, to turn their bodies into blockage points that stop the flow of human traffic, as well as the wider flow of an economy. When willfulness becomes a style of politics, it means not only being willing not to go with the flow, but also *being willing to cause its obstruction*. One could think of a hunger strike as the purest form of willfulness: a body whose agency is expressed by being reduced to obstruction, where the obstruction to others is self-obstruction, the obstruction of the passage into the body. Histories of willfulness are histories of those who are willing to put their bodies in the way.

Political forms of consciousness can also be thought of as willfulness: not only is it hard to speak about what has receded from view, but you have to be willing to get in the way of that recession. An argument of second-wave feminism (one shared with Marxism and Black politics) that I think is worth holding onto is the argument that political consciousness is achieved: raising consciousness is a crucial aspect of collective political work. Raising consciousness is difficult as consciousness is consciousness of what

---

* Judith Schwarz, *Radical Feminists of Heterodoxy* (Chicago, IL: New Victoria Publishers, 196) 103.

recedes. If the point of a recession is that it gives some the power to occupy space (occupation is reproduced by the concealment of the signs of occupation), then raising consciousness is a resistance to an occupation.

Take the example of racism. It can be willful even to name racism: as if the talk about divisions is what is divisive. Given that racism recedes from social consciousness, it appears as if the ones who 'bring it up' are bringing it into existence. We learned that the very talk of racism is experienced as an intrusion from the figure of the angry black women: as if it is her anger about racism that causes feminist estrangement. To recede is to go back or withdraw. To concede is to give way, to yield. People of color are often asked to concede to the recession of racism: we are asked to 'give way' by letting it 'go back.' Not only that: more than that. We are often asked to embody a commitment to diversity. We are asked to smile in their brochures. The smile of diversity is a way of not allowing racism to surface; it is a form of political recession.

Racism is very difficult to talk about as racism can operate to censor the very evidence of its existence. Those who talk about racism are thus heard as creating rather than describing a problem. The stakes are indeed very high: to talk about racism is to occupy a space that is saturated with tension. History is saturation. One of the findings of a research project I was involved with on diversity was that because racism saturates everyday and institutional spaces, people of color often make strategic decisions *not to use* the language of racism.* If you already pose a problem, or appear 'out of place' in the institutions of whiteness, there can be 'good reasons' not to exercise what is heard as a threatening vocabulary.† Not speaking about racism can be a way of inhabiting the spaces of racism. You minimize the threat you already are by softening your language and appearance, by keeping as much distance as you can from the figure of the angry person of color. Of course, as we know, just to walk into a room can be to lose that distance, because that figure gets there before you do.

When you use the very language of racism you are heard as 'going on about it,' as 'not letting it go.' It is as if talking about racism is what keeps it going.

---

* Sara Ahmed, Shona Hunter, Sevgi Kilic, Elaine Swan, and Lewis Turner, 'Race, Diversity and Leadership in the Learning and Skills Sector', (PDF) Unpublished Report, 2006.
† Nirmal Puwar, *Space Invaders: Race, Gender and 'Bodies out of Place'* (Oxford: Berg, 2004).

104.

JEANETTE WINTERSON

Born 1959, Manchester, United Kingdom

from *Why Be Happy When You Could Be Normal?*

2011

This Is The Road

I decided to apply to read English at the University of Oxford because it was the most impossible thing I could do. I knew no one who had been to university and although clever girls were encouraged to go to teacher training college, or to take their accountancy exams, Oxford and Cambridge were not on the list of things to do before you die.

The Equal Pay Act had become law in Britain in 1970, but no woman I knew got anything like equal pay – or believed that she should.

In the industrial north of England traditional kinds of blue-collar employment were strong – factory work, manufacture, mining, and men held the economic power.

The women held together the family and the community, but the invisibility of women's contribution, not measured or paid for, or socially rewarded, meant that my world was full of strong able women who were 'housewives' and had to defer to their men. My mother did it to my father. She held him in contempt (and that wasn't fair), but she called him the head of the household (and that wasn't true). That marital/domestic pattern was repeated everywhere I looked.

Few women I knew had professional or managerial jobs and those who did were unmarried. Most of my female teachers at school were unmarried. Mrs Ratlow was a widow, and she was head of English, but she still did all the cooking and cleaning for her two sons, and she never took holidays because she said – and I will never forget it: 'When a woman alone is no longer of any interest to the opposite sex, she is only visible where she has some purpose.'

It is quite a quote, and should have made her a feminist, but she had no time for feminism as a movement. She adored men, even though the lack of one rendered her invisible in her own eyes – the saddest place in the township of invisible places a woman can occupy. Germaine Greer had published *The Female Eunuch* in 1970 but none of us had read it.

We were not sophisticated. We were northerners. We didn't live in a big city like Manchester, and feminism seemed not to have reached us.

'Battleaxe' has always been a word used both for and against the strong northern working-class woman. That cleaver image split our identity too. Northern women were tough, and reckoned that way in the home and in popular comedy – all the seaside postcards were drawings of weedy little men and dominating women – and in the drunken working men's clubs, stage acts like Les Dawson dressed up in headscarves and aprons, parodying, but also celebrating, the formidable women the men loved, feared, and were dependent upon. Yet those women who were supposed to stand at the door waiting to whack their men with a rolling pin had no economic clout. And when they had, they hid it.

The women I knew who ran their own small businesses, like the market stall I worked on, or the fish and chip shop that supplied me with many of my meals, pretended it was their husband's enterprise, and that they just worked there.

When we had our one and only sex education lesson at school it was not about sex at all, but sexual economics. We should pay our own way, because that was the modern thing to do, but we should give the boy the money beforehand, so that he could be seen to pay. We were only talking bus fares and cinema tickets, but later, when we managed the household budget, we should make sure he knew that everything was his. Male pride, I think the teacher called it. I thought it was the stupidest thing I had ever heard; a flat earth theory of social relations.

The only women who were contentedly living the life they wanted without pretending socially were the pair who ran the sweet shop, but they had to pretend sexually, and weren't able to be openly gay. People laughed at them, and one wore a balaclava.

I was a woman. I was a working-class woman. I was a woman who wanted to love women without guilt or ridicule. Those three things formed the basis of my politics, not the unions; or class war as understood by the male Left.

The Left has taken a long time to fully include women as independent and as equals – and no longer to enfold women's sexuality into a response to male desire. I felt uncomfortable and sidelined by what I knew of left-wing politics. And I wasn't looking to improve the conditions of my life. I wanted to change my life out of all recognition.

*

In the late 1970s, Margaret Thatcher appeared, talking about a new culture of risk and reward – one where you could achieve, one where you could be anything you wanted to be, if you would only work hard enough and be prepared to abandon the safety nets of tradition.

I had already left home. I was already working evenings and weekends to get through school. I had no safety net.

Thatcher seemed to me to have better answers than the middle-class men who spoke for the Labour Party, and the working-class men who campaigned for a 'family' wage, and wanted their women at home.

I had no respect for family life. I had no home. I had rage and courage. I was smart. I was emotionally disconnected. I didn't understand gender politics. I was the ideal prototype for the Reagan/Thatcher revolution.

I sat my Oxford entrance exam, coached by Mrs Ratlow, got an interview and bought a coach ticket to Oxford.

I had applied to St Catherine's because it had a new modern feel, because it was a mixed college, and because it had been formed out of the St Catherine's Society – a kind of sad satellite of the established Oxford colleges, founded for students too poor to attend Oxford proper.

But now it was Oxford proper. And maybe I could go there.

I got off the bus in Oxford and asked my way to St Catherine's. I felt like Jude the Obscure in Thomas Hardy's novel, and I was determined not to hang myself.

I had no idea that there could be such a beautiful city, or places like the colleges, with quadrangles and lawns, and that sense of energetic quiet that I still find so seductive.

I had been given overnight accommodation, and meals were provided in college, but I was too intimidated by the confidence of the other candidates to go in and eat with them.

I was unable to speak clearly during my interviews because for the first time in my life I felt that I looked wrong and sounded wrong. Everybody else seemed relaxed, though I am sure that was not true. They certainly had better clothes and different accents. I knew I was not being myself, but I didn't know how to be myself there. I hid the self that I was and had no persona to put in its place. A few weeks later I heard that I had not been given a place.

I was in despair. Mrs Ratlow said we must look at other options; to me, there were no other options. I was not interested in options; I was interested in Oxford.

So I came up with a plan.

I had passed my driving test at last, sold the Mini I didn't really own, and bought a road-legal Hillman Imp that cost me £40. The doors didn't work, but it had a good engine. As long as you were prepared to wriggle in through the glass flap at the back, you could go quite a long way.

Janey said she would come with me, so we took my tent and set off to Oxford, travelling at 50 mph, the Imp's maximum speed, with frequent stops to add petrol, oil, water and brake fluid. We had two eggs with us in case the radiator leaked. In those days you could easily repair a radiator by dropping a broken egg into it, just as a fan belt could be replaced with a nylon stocking, and a snapped clutch cable with two bolts and a can of Tizer (holes in either end of can, bolts tied either end of snapped cable, bolts plus cable dropped into each end of can – you will find that with a bit of clunking, you can now depress the clutch).

Janey's family had a camp-site book and we looked up cheap camping at a golf club outside Oxford.

It took us about nine hours to get there but we had our bacon and beans and we were happy.

The next day I had an appointment to see the senior tutor and one of the English fellows – the other, fortunately for me, was away.

I had the usual problem of not being able to speak at all and then babbling like . . . Under stress I am a cross between Billy Budd and the Donkey in *Shrek*.

I spread my hands in despair and saw that the palms were covered in oil. The Imp had a leak.

So there was nothing for it but to explain at *Shrek*-speed about the Hillman Imp, and the tent, and the market stall where I worked, and a little bit about the Apocalypse and Mrs Winterson, and English Literature in Prose A–Z . . .

They already had a letter from Mrs Ratlow open on the desk. I don't know what she said, but Mrs Oliphant was mentioned.

'I want to be a better writer than her.'

'That shouldn't be too hard – though she did write a very good ghost story called –'

'*The Open Door*. I've read that. It's scary.'

For some reason Mrs Oliphant was on my side.

The senior tutor explained that St Catherine's was a progressive college, only founded in 1962, committed to bringing in pupils from state schools, and one of the few mixed colleges.

'Benazir Bhutto is here. Margaret Thatcher studied Chemistry at Somerville, you know.'

I didn't know and I didn't know who Benazir Bhutto was either.

'Would you like there to be a woman prime minister?'

Yes . . . In Accrington women couldn't be anything except wives or teachers or hairdressers or secretaries or do shop work. 'Well, they can be librarians, and I thought of doing that, but I want to write my own books.'

'What kind of books?'

'I don't know. I write all the time.'

'Most young people do.'

'Not in Accrington they don't.'

There was a pause. Then the English fellow asked me if I thought that women could be great writers. I was baffled by the question. It had never occurred to me.

'It's true they mostly come at the beginning of the alphabet – Austen, Brontës, Eliot . . .'

'We study those writers of course. Virginia Woolf is not on the syllabus though you will find her interesting – but compared to James Joyce . . .'

It was a reasonable introduction to the prejudices and pleasures of an Oxford degree course.

I left St Catherine's and walked down Holywell Street to Blackwell's bookshop. I had never seen a shop with five floors of books. I felt dizzy, like too much oxygen all at once. And I thought about women. All these books, and how long had it taken for women to be able to write their share, and why were there still so few women poets and novelists, and even fewer who were considered to be important?

I was so excited, so hopeful, and I was troubled too, by what had been said to me. As a woman would I be an onlooker and not a contributor? Could I study what I could never hope to achieve? Achieve it or not, I had to try.

And later, when I was successful, but accused of arrogance, I wanted to drag every journalist who misunderstood to this place, and make them see that for a woman, a working-class woman, to want to be a writer, to want to be a good writer, and to believe that you were good enough, that was not arrogance; that was politics.

Whatever happened that day worked out for me; I was given a place, deferred for a year.

And that took me straight to Margaret Thatcher and the 1979 election. Thatcher had the vigour and the arguments and she knew the price of a loaf of bread. She was a woman – and that made me feel that I too could succeed. If a grocer's daughter could be prime minister, then a girl like me could write a book that would be on the shelves of English Literature in Prose A–Z.

I voted for her.

It is commonplace now to say that Thatcher changed two political parties: her own, and the left-wing Labour opposition. It is less often remembered that Reagan in the US and Thatcher in the UK broke forever the post-war consensus – and that consensus had lasted for over thirty years.

Spin back to 1945, and whether you were on the Left or the Right in Britain or Western Europe, rebuilding societies after the war could not happen using the outdated and discredited neo-liberal economics of the free market – unregulated labour, unstable prices, no provision for the sick or the old or the unemployed. We were going to need housing, plenty of jobs, a welfare state, nationalisation of utilities and transport.

It was a real advance in human consciousness towards collective responsibility; an understanding that we owed something not only to our flag or to our country, to our children or our families, but to each other. Society. Civilisation. Culture.

That advance in consciousness did not come out of Victorian values or philanthropy, nor did it emerge from right-wing politics; it came out of the practical lessons of the war, and – *and this matters* – the superior arguments of socialism.

Britain's economic slow-down in the 1970s, our IMF bail-out, rocketing oil prices, Nixon's decision to float the dollar, unruly union disputes, and a kind of existential doubt on the Left, allowed the Reagan/Thatcher 1980s Right to skittle away annoying arguments about a fair and equal society. We were going to follow Milton Friedman and his pals at the Chicago School of Economics back to the old free market laissez-faire, and dress it up as a new salvation.

Welcome TINA – There Is No Alternative.

In 1988, Thatcher's Chancellor of the Exchequer, Nigel Lawson, called the post-war consensus, the 'postwar delusion'.

I did not realise that when money becomes the core value, then education drives towards utility or that the life of the mind will not be counted as a good unless it produces measurable results. That public services will no longer be important. That an alternative life to getting and spending will become very difficult as cheap housing disappears. That when communities are destroyed only misery and intolerance are left.

I did not know that Thatcherism would fund its economic miracle by selling off all our nationalised assets and industries.

I did not realise the consequences of privatising society.

I am driving under the viaduct and past the Factory Bottoms. As I drive past the Elim Pentecostal Church I see my dad coming out in his overalls. He's been painting. My foot lifts off the accelerator and I nearly stop. I want to say goodbye, but I don't because I can't. Did he see me? I don't know. I look in the mirror. He's going home. I am going away.

Out now, through Oswaldtwistle, past the dog-biscuit factory. There are some kids waiting by the side door for the broken bits of pink and green bone-shaped biscuits. Only one of them has a dog in tow.

I am in my Morris Minor van – successor to the Imp – loaded up with a bicycle and a trunk of books, a small suitcase of clothes and a pack of sardine sandwiches, and twenty gallons of petrol in tins because no one has told me that you can buy petrol on the motorway. As the dynamo on the Minor is faulty, I dare not switch off the engine, so I have to pull up on the hard shoulder of the motorway, run round and fill up with fuel, and set off again. I don't care.

I am going to Oxford.

105

RACHEL CUSK

Born 1967, Saskatoon, Canada

from *Aftermath: On Marriage and Separation*

2012

Call yourself a feminist, my husband would say to me, disgustedly, in the raw bitter weeks after we separated. He believed he had taken the part of woman in our marriage, and seemed to expect me to defend him against myself, the male oppressor. He felt it was womanly to shop and cook, to collect the children from school. Yet it was when I myself did those things that I often felt most unsexed. My own mother had not seemed beautiful to me in the exercise of her maternal duties: likewise they seemed to threaten, not enhance, her womanliness. In those days we lived in a village in the flat Suffolk countryside; she seemed to spend a great deal of time on the telephone. The sound of her voice talking as though to itself was mesmerising. To me her phrases sounded scripted, her laughter slightly artificial. I suspected her of using a special voice, like an actress. Who was she, this woman on the telephone? My mother was someone I knew only from the inside; I shared her point of view, seemed to dwell within her boredom or pleasure or irritation. Her persona was where I lived, unseeing. How could I know what my mother was? How could I see her? For her attention felt like the glance of some inner eye that never looked at me straight, that took its knowledge from my own private knowledge of myself.

It was only when she was with other people that, as a child, I was able to notice her objectively. Sometimes she would have a female friend round to lunch and then all at once there it would be, my mother's face. Suddenly I could see her, could compare her to this other woman and find her better or worse, could see her being liked or envied or provoked, could know her particular habits and her atmosphere, which were not those of this other. At such times her persona, my dwelling-place, was inaccessible to me, darkened, like an empty house. If I knocked at the door I was curtly – sometimes roughly – despatched. Her body, usually so extensive, so carelessly ubiquitous, seemed to have been packed up and put away. And she too was locked out, relieved for a while of the business of being herself. Instead she was performing; she was pure story, told badly or well.

Her friends were generally mothers too, women whose geography I recognized, the sense of an enigma that lay all around their masks of make-up and talk like open countryside around a city. You could never get out into that countryside but you knew it was there. She did have one friend, Sally, who was different from the others. At the time I didn't understand why, but now I do: Sally didn't have children. She was a large woman, a wit, though her face was sad. You could walk around in the sadness of her mouth and eyes; it was open to everyone. She came once when my mother had made a chocolate cake, for which she tried to give Sally the recipe. Sally said, 'If I made that cake I'd just eat the whole thing in one sitting.' I had never heard of a woman eating a whole cake. It struck me as a tremendous feat, like weightlifting. But I could tell that my mother didn't like this remark. In some obscure sense Sally had given the game away. Not knowing any better, she had opened up a chink in the tall wall of womanhood, and given me a rare glimpse of what was on the other side.

*

Of certain parts of life there can be no foreknowledge – war, for instance. The soldier going to war for the first time does not know how he will behave when confronted by an armed enemy. He does not know this part of himself. Is he killer or coward? When confronted he will respond, yet he doesn't know in advance what his response will be.

My husband said that he wanted half of everything, including the children. No, I said. What do you mean no, he said. This was on the telephone. I looked out of the window at the garden, a rectangle among other urban rectangles, the boundaries prowled by cats. Lately our garden had become overgrown. The beds were drowning in weeds. The grass was long, like hair. But no matter how disorderly it became the grid would be undisturbed: the other rectangles would hold their shape regardless.

You can't divide people in half, I said.

They should be with me half the time, he said.

They're my children, I said. They belong to me.

In Greek drama, to traduce biological human roles is to court the change that is death, the death that is change. The vengeful mother, the selfish father, the perverted family, the murderous child – these are the bloody roads to democracy, to justice. The children belong to me: once I would have criticized such a sentiment severely, but of certain parts of life there can be no foreknowledge. Where had this heresy gestated? If it was part of me, where had it lived for all those years, in our egalitarian household? Where had it hidden itself? My mother liked to talk about the early English Catholics forced to live and worship in secrecy, sleeping in cupboards or underneath the floorboards. To her it seemed extraordinary that the true beliefs should have to hide themselves. Was this, in fact, a persecuted truth, and our own way of life the heresy?

I said it again: I couldn't help myself. I said it to my friend Eleanor, that the children belonged to me. Eleanor has a job, is often away for weeks at a time; her husband takes over when she's not there, putting their children to bed, handing them over to the nanny in the morning. Eleanor pursed her mouth and disapprovingly shook her head a little. Children belong just as much to their fathers as their mothers, she said. I said to my friend Anna, who has no job and four children, the children belong to me. Anna's husband works long hours. She manages the children largely alone, as I now do. Yes, she said, they're your children. You're the one they need. They should be your number one priority.

It has existed in a kind of banishment, my flesh history with my daughters. Have I been, as a mother, denied? The long pilgrimage of pregnancy with its wonders and abasements, the apotheosis of childbirth, the sacking and slow rebuilding of every last corner of my private world that motherhood has entailed – all unmentioned, willfully or casually forgotten as time has passed, the dark ages on which I now feel the civilisation of our family has been built. And I was part of that pact of silence, in a way: it was a condition of the treaty that gave me my equality, that I would not invoke the primitivism of the mother, her innate superiority, that voodoo in the face of which the mechanism of equal rights breaks down. My own mother once wept at the supper table, wildly accusing us of never having thanked her for giving birth to us. And we joked about it later, cruel teenaged sophisticates. We felt uneasy, and rightly so: we had been unjustly blamed. Wasn't it my father who should have thanked her, for giving form and substance, continuance, to himself? Instead his own contribution, his work, ran parallel to hers: it was she who had to be grateful to him, superficially at least. For years he had gone to the office and come back again, regular as a Swiss train, as authorised as she was illicit. The rationality of this behaviour was what irrationalised hers, for her womanhood was all imposition and cause, all profligacy, was a kind of problem to which his work was the solution. How could she expect gratitude for what no one seemed to think of as a gift? Through her we all of us served the cause of life: she was the exacting representative of our dumb master, nature. She gave, as nature gives, but we were not going to survive in nature on mere gratitude. We had to tame, to cultivate her gifts; and increasingly, we ourselves took all the credit for the results. We were in league with civilisation.

Like God, my father expressed himself through absence: it was easier, perhaps, to be grateful to someone who wasn't there. He too seemed to obey the call of civilisation, to recognise it when it spoke. As rational beings we allied ourselves with him, against the paganism of my mother, her cycles of emotion, her gaze forever dwelling on what was done and past or on the relieving blankness of what was yet to come. These qualities seemed to be without origin: they belonged neither to motherhood nor to herself, but to some eternal fact that arose out of the conjunction of the two. I knew, of course, that once upon a time she had had her own reality, had lived as it were in real time. In the wedding photograph that stood on the mantelpiece, her slenderness was always arresting. There she stood in white, the sacrificial victim: a narrow-waisted smiling beauty, as compact as a seed. The key, the genius of it all, seemed to lie in how little of her there was. In the finely graven lines of her beauty our whole sprawling future was encrypted. That youthful beauty was gone now, all used up, like the oil that is sucked out of the earth for the purpose of combustion. The world has grown hectic, disorganised, wasteful on oil. Sometimes, looking at that photograph, my family seemed like the bloated product of my mother's beauty.

But for me the notion of a woman's beauty had somewhere in the course of things become theoretical, like the immigrant's notion of home. And in the generational transition between my mother and myself a migration of sorts had indeed occurred. My mother may have been my place of birth, but my adopted nationality was my father's. She had aspired to marriage and motherhood, to being desired and possessed by a man in a way that would legitimise her. I myself was the fruit of those aspirations, but somehow, in the evolution from her to me, it had become my business to legitimise myself. Yet my father's aspirations – to succeed, to win, to provide – did not quite fit me either: they were like a suit of clothes made for someone else, but they were what was available. So I wore them and felt a little uncomfortable, a little unsexed, but clothed all the same. Cross-dressed I met with approval, for a good school report, a high grade. I got into Oxford, my sister to Cambridge, immigrants to the new country of sexual equality achieving assimilation through the second generation.

One is formed by what one's parents say and do; and one is formed by what one's parents are. But what happens when what they say and what they are don't match? My father, a man, advanced male values to us, his daughters. And my mother, a woman, did the same. So it was my mother who didn't match, who didn't make sense. We belong as much to our moment in history as to our parents: I suppose it would have been reprehensible, in Britain in the late twentieth century, for her to have told us not to worry about our maths, that the important thing was to find a nice husband to support us. Yet her own mother had probably told her precisely that. There was nothing, as a woman, she could bequeath us; nothing to pass on from mother to daughter but these adulterated male values. And of that forsaken homeland, beauty, which now lay so despoiled – as the countryside around our Suffolk home was in the years of my growing up despoiled, disfigured by new roads and houses that it pained my oversensitive eyes to look at – of beauty, a woman's beauty, of the place I had come from I knew nothing at all. I didn't know its manners or its customs. I didn't speak its language. In that world of femininity where I had the right to claim citizenship, I was an alien.

*

Call yourself a feminist, my husband says. And perhaps one of these days I'll say to him, yes, you're right. I shouldn't call myself a feminist. You're right. I'm so terribly sorry.

And in a way, I'll mean it. What is a feminist, anyway? What does it mean, to call yourself one? There are men who call themselves feminists. There are women who are anti-feminist. A feminist man is a bit like a vegetarian: it's the humanitarian principle he's defending, I suppose. Sometimes feminism seems to involve so much criticism of female modes of being that you could be forgiven for thinking that a feminist is a woman who hates women, hates them for being such saps. Then again, the feminist is supposed to hate men. She is said to scorn the physical and emotional servitude they exact. Apparently she calls them *the enemy*.

In any case, she wouldn't be found haunting the scene of the crime, as it were; loitering in the kitchen, in the maternity ward, at the school gate. She knows that her womanhood is a fraud, manufactured by others for their own convenience; she knows that women are not born but made. So she stays away from it, the kitchen, the maternity ward, like the alcoholic stays away from the bottle. Some alcoholics have a fantasy of modest social drinking: they just haven't been through enough cycles of failure yet. The woman who thinks she can choose femininity, can toy with it like the social drinker toys with wine – well she's asking for it, asking to be undone, devoured, asking to spend her life perpetrating a new fraud, manufacturing a new fake identity, only this time it's her equality that's fake. Either she's doing twice as much as she did before, or she sacrifices her equality and does less than she should. She's two women, or she's half a woman. And either way she'll have to say, because she chose it, that she's enjoying herself.

So I suppose a feminist shouldn't get married. She shouldn't have a joint bank account or a house in joint names. Perhaps she shouldn't have children either, girl children whose surname is not their mother's but their father's, so that when she travels abroad with them they have to swear to the man at passport control that she *is* their mother. No, I shouldn't have called myself a feminist, because what I said didn't match with what I was: just like my mother, only the other way around.

What I lived as feminism were in fact the male values my parents, among others, well-meaningly bequeathed me – the cross-dressing values of my father, and the anti-feminine values of my mother. So I am not a feminist. I am a self-hating transvestite.

106.

JACQUELINE ROSE

Born 1949, London, United Kingdom

Mothers

2014

Matilda the Musical, adapted from Roald Dahl, opens with what might be described as the paradox of maternal recognition. A troupe of hideously grimacing children sing 'My Mummy says I'm a miracle' in such a way as to suggest that they are monsters while Matilda, who really is miraculous in that she has magic powers, fails to be recognised by her parents. Her mother, unaware that she was pregnant until very near the point of delivery, neither wanted a baby nor knew what to do with one; her father was expecting a boy (he persists in calling Matilda 'boy' till almost the end of the play). They both hate their daughter for her gifts, and have nothing but contempt for the love of reading into which she pours her unhappiness and through which she escapes it. Matilda is special, we are repeatedly told. She needs to be seen. She is eventually adopted by a schoolteacher, Jenny Honey, an orphan whose mother died in childbirth (in the book, when she was two), who recognises her unique qualities. The implication is that Jenny can save Matilda because she herself was denied, and therefore knows, what Matilda is looking for. Failed mothers are everywhere – overinvested, neglectful, dead. Just how high the stakes are can be gauged by the immense difficulty Dahl had in completing his story. In the first version, Matilda herself didn't survive.

In the book he makes a point of stating which of these forms of parental failure is worse: parents 'who take no interest in their children . . . of course are far worse than the doting ones', although the venom he directs at the latter is pretty intense. It's clear that to be seen by a mother is a mixed blessing either way. Too much and you will be a monster. Not enough and again the chances are you will enter a not fully human world. The genius of Dahl's story is to make something very difficult and very strange – Matilda is nothing if not strange – seem easy and obvious. A mother, as most writing on mothers seems to concur, must be there for her baby. This process will only kick in if she recognises the baby as her own, but not as 'His Majesty the Baby', to use Freud's famous formula, not as a narcissistic object, a mirror that simply reflects her own idealised image back onto her ('My mummy says I'm a miracle'). Instead her task is to recognise who the baby is for her or himself, even though what that may mean is something neither of them can know in advance. Perhaps it's because this uncertainty is hard to tolerate that 'His Majesty the Baby' continues to wield such power. During the grand royal tour in April this year, we were given a daily dose, as Prince George was credited with, among other things, having quelled any remnants of republicanism in Australia. Proffered as a role model for mothers all over the world, the Duchess of Cambridge must also turn her baby into a king. The challenge will be to stop him becoming a monster or a nobody (or, most likely, a bit of both).

The subject of mothers is thick with idealisations, one of the earliest and foremost targets of feminist critique. Expecting mothers to be perfect is not unrelated to the drive to perfection that characterises an 'overinvested' or 'narcissistic' mother's relationship to her baby. Or to put it another way, if you are asking mothers to be perfect, why wouldn't they pass that impossible demand on to their children? Any mother who obeys this diktat could be said to be perversely fulfilling the requirements of her role. Perfection breeds perfection, lives stopped in time, fawning over themselves (it is surely no coincidence that perfection is also the false promise of consumer objects, which is why every disappointing purchase leads to another). Once again Dahl is making a profound point. Bringing up a child to believe it is a miracle is a form of cruelty, albeit at the opposite pole from neglect. How can such a child find a place in the world, when the only person it will be able to see will be her or himself? This is the opposite of saying that all children are miracles, a proposition which recognises each child as unique while placing every individual child on a par with every other. It also has nothing to do with what Winnicott, and many analysts after him, term 'primary maternal preoccupation', which refers to the form of attention a mother, in the very earliest stages, bestows on a baby, something many mothers may well recognise without accepting its punishing intensifier, the version of motherhood into which it is so effortlessly folded: that a mother must live only for her child – a mother is a mother and nothing else.

The question then is how to acknowledge a new birth as the event it is, without immediately divesting the newborn of her or his humanity. 'Every infant born,' Adrienne Rich writes in Of Woman Born (1976), her meditation on being a mother, 'is testimony to the intricacy and breadth of possibilities inherent in humanity.' The rest of the book relentlessly charts the way motherhood as an institution crushes that dream. For Hannah Arendt, in a passage Rich seems to be alluding to, every new birth is the supreme anti-totalitarian moment. In Arendt's view, freedom is identical with the capacity to being. Over beginning, she writes, 'no logic, no cogent deduction can have any power because its chain presupposes, in the form of a premise, a new beginning'. Totalitarian terror is therefore needed 'lest with the birth of each new human being a new beginning arise and raise its voice in the world'.

In *The Years*, written on the eve of fascism, Virginia Woolf treads similar ground. She is commenting on the dire consequences of parental exclusivity, on the damage it does to the social fabric – which was on the point of being rent beyond repair – to think it right to put your child, your family, before everyone else. She is also suggesting that, while England takes pride in its difference from Nazi Germany, there might even so be a link between the overweening egoism of the bourgeois family and the autocracy of statehood (a point central to *Three Guineas*, which she was writing at the same time). At a family gathering in the mid-1930s – this final section of the novel is called 'Present Day' – North, the now grown-up grandson of Colonel Pargiter, watches as people inquire after each other's children:

> My boy – my girl . . . they were saying. But they're not interested in other people's children, he observed. Only in their own; their own property; their own flesh and blood, which they would protect with the unsheathed claws of the primeval swamp, he thought . . . how then can we be civilised?

Protecting with unsheathed claws is an image commonly used to describe a mother lioness with her cubs. In their different but connected ways, Rich, Arendt and Woolf are all describing how, at the core of human nurture and in its name, the intricacy and breadth of human possibility can be sidelined or quashed before it has even begun. And the ones expected to realise this deadly template of absolute devotion and blindness – all in the guise of nourishing the world's future – are mothers.

There was a time when becoming a mother could signal a woman's entry into civic life. In ancient Greece, a woman was maiden, bride and then, after childbirth, mature female, which allowed her to enter the community of women and participate in religious ceremonies. Established in her household as a mother, a woman gained new economic and affective power (she had ceased to be an object of exchange). She could fulfil her destiny only by becoming a mother, but according to one account of Greek motherhood, in doing so she became more rather than less engaged in the polity. Having a child ushered the woman on a path that led to something other than motherhood itself – an idea which modern times seem progressively to have lost. This version of motherhood expanded horizons. It gave women a voice. In Euripides' *The Suppliant Women*, Aethra pleads with her son Theseus to be allowed to speak on behalf of the Argive mothers whose fallen sons lie unburied. When he objects, 'You do not belong to them,' she replies: 'Shall I say something, my son, that brings honour to you and the city?' Defying him in the name of a cross-national community of mothers, she makes her case in terms of women's contribution to the civic good: if he ignores their plea, the city over which he rules will be destroyed. Aethra is drawing on the authority owing to her as mother of the Athenian king. She speaks for women on behalf of the state. Women are citizens and civic membership is something they possess. The fact that women on the Greek stage also had the ability to destroy the polis simply bears witness to the power that mothers could wield over the fate of nations. Clytemnestra, around whose death the royal household rebuilds itself, failed to destroy it; Medea, who murders her children by Jason as well as Glauce, Jason's new princess bride, succeeded by thus wiping out any future progeny of Corinth. In Greek literature, mothers only ever kill sons, never daughters. Infanticide is therefore a political act through which an enraged mother deprives her spouse, in the words of the French scholar Nicole Loraux, 'of the arrogant tranquillity of a father whose sons would perpetuate his name and lineage'.*

* *Mothers in Mourning* (1998).

Motherhood was part of the public stage in another sense. According to Plutarch, the only exceptions to the rule against naming the dead on Sparta's tombstones were men who fell in battle and women who died in childbirth: the woman, the producer of the future citizens of the city state, bore childbirth 'just as the warrior bears the enemy's assault, by struggling against pain: giving birth is a battle.' 'Not just a symmetry,' Loraux writes, 'it is more like an act of exchange or at the very least the presence of war at the heart of childbirth.'* Could it be, Jean-Pierre Vernant suggests to Loraux in conversation, that 'giving birth is the most accomplished test of a woman's virility?' In which case, the act that is seen as supremely defining of a woman, as the acme of femininity, is also the moment when she leaves her femininity behind. The equation also works in the other direction, with men becoming women, as the wounded soldier's pain is compared by Loraux, after Euripides, to the agonies of childbirth: 'Fortune and misfortune of the warrior: to break all limits, including that of the virility he ostensibly embodies, in order to suffer like a woman.' From which, Loraux concludes, we shouldn't be in too much of a hurry to charge Greek thought with misogyny.

Motherhood, as Lauren Hackworth Petersen and Patricia Salzman-Mitchell insist in their collection of essays on mothering in the ancient world, was no less an 'uncontested territory' then than it is today. Instances abound of women cherished only as nurturers. In one version of the mother as warrior, the embryo is permanently at war with the uterus, which, to be born, it must defeat. According to Diogenes of Apollonia and some Pythagoreans, the father was sole generator, the woman a mere vehicle for the foetus she must nourish and then release: 'a stranger for a stranger' in Aeschylus' phrase. There are few testimonies from the women themselves, who 'left little trace of their own existence' (many examples are taken of necessity from their funeral urns). But why in modern times is the participation of mothers in political and public life seen as the exception – Great Britain lagging behind the rest of Europe and the US? Why are mothers not seen as an essential part of a contested polity? Why are they exhorted to make their stand in the boardroom – to 'lean in', as the ghastly imperative of Sheryl Sandberg's bestseller has it – as if being the props of neoliberalism were the most mothers could aspire to, the

* In 'Le lit, la guerre', *L'Homme* 21, January–March 1981.

highest form of social belonging they could expect. Today we are witnessing what Angela McRobbie has described as a 'neoliberal intensification of mothering': perfectly turned out middle-class, mainly white mothers, with their perfect jobs, perfect husbands and marriages, whose permanent glow of self-satisfaction is intended to make all the women who don't conform to that image – because they are poorer or black or their lives are just more humanly complicated – feel like total failures.* This has the added advantage of letting a government whose austerity policy has disproportionately targeted women and mothers completely off the hook.

'Parenthood is not a transition,' Rachel Cusk writes in *A Life's Work: On Becoming a Mother*, 'but a defection, a political act.' She is describing the way motherhood can leave women stranded on the far shore of any viable political life, but it's also possible to read her sentence as a demand that the isolation of mothers be recognised as a disenfranchisement and hence as a fully political fact. Much praised, much hated on its publication in 2001, her book provides a visceral account of the loss of any sense of social personhood, of herself as a woman in the world, which followed the birth of her first baby. But perhaps it is because she charts that collapse so bloodily that she can at the same time see the heightened emotional link to the world's wider stage that motherhood offers: 'In motherhood, I have experienced myself as both more virtuous and terrible, and more implicated in the world's virtue and terror, than I could from the anonymity of childlessness have thought possible.' This is just one reason why any discourse that dwells solely on the virtue of mothers and motherhood is such a con, since, among other things, it is asking women to conspire in cutting the world off from self-knowledge. If we are all capable of virtue and terror, then no one culture, certainly not Western culture, can claim a monopoly on virtue, and the capacity for terror can't conveniently be projected onto everyone else. 'I do not see the mother with her child as either more morally credible or more morally capable than any other woman,' Adrienne Rich, once more way ahead of the game, writes in *Of Woman Born*.

For the same reason, Denise Riley concluded in *War in the Nursery* (1983), her pathbreaking study of maternal social policy after the Second

---

* I was led to these examples, as well as to Loraux's article, by Petersen and Salzman-Mitchell's anthology.

World War, that feminism has nothing to gain from a validation of mother-hood in the name of female creativity or power. Women who are mothers are not better or more creative than women who aren't. They have just chosen to do things differently, to live other lives. This isn't to say that motherhood can't be experienced as creative or that being a mother doesn't give you another take on the world. It is simply to warn of the ease with which such ideas slip out of women's own grasp and into the imperative mode: 'Be good!' – a demand, a trap. Women like Rich and Cusk, and also Rozsika Parker and Lisa Baraitser, who lay bare the complex run of emotions to which motherhood gives rise, are issuing a political corrective, sourced in but reaching far beyond the domain of motherhood itself. The idea of maternal virtue is a myth that serves no one, neither mothers nor the world for whose redemption it is intended. Or to put it more simply, no woman who has ever been a mother can believe for a second that she is only ever nice (virtue and terror both).

One of the most striking characteristics of discourse on mothering is that the idealisation doesn't let up as reality makes the ideal harder for mothers to meet. If anything, it seems to intensify. This isn't quite the same as saying that mothers are always to blame, although the two propositions are surely linked. As austerity and inequality increase – the Conservatives are promis-ing that if they win the 2015 election, austerity will continue well into their second term – more and more children will fall into poverty. More and more families will be fighting a rearguard action to protect their children from inexorable social decline. Social unrest is likely to increase. In this context, as in so many moments of social crisis, focusing on mothers is a perfect diversionary tactic, not least because it so effectively deflects what might be far more disruptive forms of social critique. Mothers always fail: the point of most of the writing I have mentioned so far is to make that not catastrophic but normal, to allow failure to be seen as part of the task. But in so far as mothers are seen as the *fons et origo* of the world, there is nothing easier than to make social deterioration look like something which it's the sacred duty of mothers to prevent (a socially upgraded version of the tendency in families to blame mothers for everything).

The first measure proposed by Tony Blair's government in 1997 was a cut in benefits to single mothers. This so obviously contradicted the supposed humanitarian ethos of New Labour that he had to back down immediately. But his move was symptomatic of the way lone mothers are singled out for punishment. In troubled times, the most vulnerable are always the easiest targets. But might there also be a connection between the demand for singular devotion on the part of mothers and the hostility which single mothers – even if they aren't single by choice and even if they are obeying that injunction to the letter – have historically incurred?

A single mother stands as a glaring rebuke to the ideal. Throughout the 1980s and 1990s, the number of single mothers in this country rose faster than at any other time in history, seemingly unaffected by an increasingly strident Conservative rhetoric of blame. The most pervasive image was of an unemployed teenager who had deliberately got herself pregnant in order to claim benefits, although as Pat Thane and Tanya Evans point out in *Sinners? Scroungers? Saints?*, their study of twentieth-century unmarried motherhood, she was 'very rarely to be found'. Over the past century, single mothers have variously been accorded one or other, or all three, of those epithets, the first and last stringing them between opprobrium and holiness (neither of this world), the second more prosaically casting them as objects of moral contempt. The single mother, it seems, was the original 'scrounger', the term which allows a cruelly unequal society to turn its back on those it has thrown on the scrapheap. This manipulative, undeserving mother was the perfect embodiment of the 'dependency' culture, an idea which is being revived today in order to justify an ever more thorough dismantling of the welfare state. It is also worth noting how far her vulnerability and her needs, not to speak of those of the children for whom she has sole responsibility, seem to count against her – lone parents, especially unmarried mothers, are still today one of the poorest groups in Britain.

As if genuine neediness – being, or having once been, a baby – is what this Conservative rhetoric most hates. Perhaps when right-wing politicians wrinkle their noses at scroungers, asylum seekers and refugees, it is their own vaguely remembered years of dependency that they are trying, and instructing us, to repudiate. The one who most loudly proclaims the ideal of iron-clad self-sufficiency must surely have the echo of the baby in the nursery hovering in the back of his or her – mostly his – head. The complaint that so many of the present cabinet went to Eton – where life is already nicely regimented – as if there were no life before schooling, while true and worth making, would also be something of a decoy. There is a feminist point to be made here. The problem for everyone, but especially for men, to cite Rich again, is that 'all human life on the planet is born of woman' (the first line of her book). 'There is much to suggest,' she continues, 'that the male mind has always been haunted by the force of the idea of *dependence on a woman for life itself*' (her italics).

It is then immensely reassuring to register the occasions when women organise against the forms of prejudice and social exclusion directed at them. *Sinners? Scroungers? Saints?* is also a history of the pioneering National Council for the Unmarried Mother and Her Child, set up in 1918 to support such women and still active today (renamed the National Council for One-Parent Families in 1970, known since 2007 as Gingerbread). The story includes moments of unlikely solidarity. A midwife working during the First World War explains to the executive of the Prince of Wales Fund, a charity that had decided not to support unmarried mothers, how the 'respectable married woman' she had attended the previous day had been happy to 'wash herself and leave her child unwashed' so that the midwife could go to plead the cause of unmarried mothers. A report on mother and baby hostels set up during the Second World War – another moment when unmarried mothers were the object of moral panic – describes the way the matrons turned desolate premises into havens for 'utterly friendless girls' who may never have known a home or 'whose parents set their own petty respectability above the ordinary decencies of human relationships'. The girls would leave the hostels 'with a great deal more confidence than they had when they arrived'. The report was never published.

Note too the sexual undertow (these girls are not 'respectable'). One of the great wartime fears was that single girls would become pregnant by black American servicemen, with dire consequences both for the nation and, potentially, for the servicemen themselves: 'Any English girl who walks out, however harmlessly, with a coloured American soldier,' a lady-in-waiting to Queen Mary, the queen mother, wrote to Violet Markham in 1942, 'should be made to understand that she will very probably cause his death.' Her remark manages to express in one breath solicitude for the girl and the soldier and raw prejudice against the idea of 'mixed marriages'. During the First World War, Markham had been secretary to an official investigation into suggested 'immorality' among servicewomen stationed in France.

It is another common assumption that a single mother is a woman who puts her sex life ahead of her social responsibility. Manipulative or sexual, she exhibits either too much self-control or not enough (what is never mentioned in relation to teenage pregnancies is the possibility of child abuse and rape). Behind the idea of maternal virtue, therefore, another demand and/or reproach. A mother is a woman whose sexual being must be invisible. She must save the world from her desire – a further projection that allows the world to conceal from itself the unmanageable nature of all human sexuality, and its own voraciousness. Even in the years leading up to the 1960s, when there was more sympathy for the predicament of single mothers, the basic assumption was there. 'Innocent' girls could get into trouble and deserved understanding 'provided that they did not flaunt their transgressions'. Nor is the childless woman immune from sexual taint. 'Surely,' one journalist said recently, expressing a common attitude to the declining birth rate in 21st-century France, 'a woman who refuses to be a mother enjoys lovemaking rather too much?'

In this context, ancient Greece and Rome are again refreshing. Cleopatra, deemed the most desirable of women, was the mother of four children, one, she claimed, by Julius Caesar and the three youngest by Mark Antony, something most representations of Cleopatra conspire not to remember or talk about (no one I have mentioned this to had the faintest idea she was a mother). In fact the silence began with Octavian in a bid to prevent his conflict with Mark Antony being seen as a civil war, with his offspring potentially in arms against hers in a battle for the keys of the city state. Venus was referred to as mater amoris or 'mother of love' (how, one might ask, do you mother eros other than incestuously, which might be the whole point?). Genevieve Lively, in her essay on mothers and lovers in ancient Rome, in Petersen and Salzman-Mitchell's anthology, cites the description of Venus in the Aeneid that follows her dismissive response to Aeneas' account of his woes: 'She spoke, and as she turned away, her rosy neck gleamed, while from her head her heavenly hair breathed a divine fragrance, her robes slipped down to her feet and in her step she was revealed as a true goddess.' This is breathless and brutal: her sexuality, her body, is exposed as the naked truth of her cruelty towards her son, who only now fully recognises her as his mother. But other images are less damning. The Terra Mater, a panel of the Ara Pacis in Rome dated 13-9 bce, shows the mother goddess and her two children with her garment slipping gently from her shoulders (as this is a sculpture the exposure stops there). She is therefore also Venus and her sensuality is part of her tenderness towards the two boys cavorting on her lap.

At a gathering of British psychoanalysts, students and academics organised by John Forrester in the 1980s the French psychoanalyst Jean Laplanche asked why there are no artistic representations of the erotic pleasure a mother gains in breastfeeding her child. Behind that question was another one. Why does the psychoanalytic representation of the infant focus on the baby's sexual impulses towards the mother and remain mostly silent on those of the mother towards her child? For Laplanche this was the question since, for him, the infant's inability to decipher the mother's unconscious sexuality – the point being that, as is the way with all sexuality, she cannot decipher it herself – will precipitate the child's lifelong endeavour to read a world that makes no sense. (I was delighted a short while later to come across Liberale da Verona's two studies of a woman with head tilted back and eyes closed, her child at her breast in Vienna.)

Laplanche was right about the psychoanalytic literature which, in a move that could be seen as un-Freudian, tends to make erotic desire in the mother-baby pair almost exclusively the province of the infant. A rare exception is Helene Deutsch, who describes birth and after as a more or less continuous erotic exchange of bodily organs and pleasures: 'In coitus,' she writes in 'The Psychology of Woman in Relation to the Functions of Reproduction', 'the penis becomes the breast while in lactation the breast becomes the penis' (the mind boggles). Mostly however, the idea of motherhood brings the idea of woman as a subject of sexual desire to a standstill. Mothering, it seems, is one of the ways our culture purifies itself of the sexuality that in most cases still brings motherhood about. Even if, as Rachel Bowlby argues in *A Child of One's Own*, advances in reproductive technology mean we are approaching a time when we will no longer be able to assume that children come 'from two parents, of two sexes, who once had sex'.

Against what is all this a defence? What are all these pious, oversexualised, punitive or simply dotty versions of motherhood covering for? Elisabeth Badinter argues in *The Conflict* that things are getting worse. In response to economic crisis, and what she sees as a crisis of identity between the sexes, a new eco-maternalism, an updated ecological version of the maternal instinct as 'innate, essential, eternal, non-negotiable' in the words of one commentator, is driving women back into the home (French women come in for special praise for bucking the trend). Badinter blames a 'sacred alliance' of reactionaries and a new 'essentialist feminism' with mother nature at its core. Central to this project is breastfeeding, and central to that is La Leche League. Formed by American mothers to promote breastfeeding in 1956, the LLL, as it is known, had 17,000 trained group leaders by 1981; by 1990 its book, *The Womanly Art of Breast-feeding*, had sold more than two million copies. According to Badinter, the breastfeeding rate in the US rose from 38 per cent in the late 1940s to 60 per cent by the mid-1980s, and reached 75 per cent by 2011 (a rise for which LLL can presumably take some, if not all, the 'credit'). 'I am the milk of your breasts, you shall have no other form of infant nutrition in your house' is one of the pronouncements on the website Alternamoms that takes its cue from the 'ten commandments' of the LLL. When Courtney Love opened her concert on US Mothers' Day this year with the words: 'Happy Mother's Day. I got flowers for mine with a note saying, "Thanks for not breastfeeding,"' she may or may not have been fully aware of what she was talking about.

The Conflict is not Badinter's first excursion into this domain. *Mother Love*, her original critique of the maternal instinct, was published in 1981. When her editor invited Bruno Bettelheim to contribute a preface, he replied:

> I've spent my whole life working with children whose lives have been destroyed because their mothers hated them . . . Which demonstrates that there is no maternal instinct – of course there isn't . . . This book will only serve to free women from their feelings of guilt, the only restraint that means some children are saved from destruction, suicide, anorexia etc. I don't want to give my name to suppressing the last buttress that protects a lot of unhappy children from destruction.

The vitriol of this statement takes us close to the heart of the matter. There is no maternal instinct, he agrees with Badinter, which is why so many children are doomed. (We didn't know when he said this how Bettelheim himself treated the children in his care.) There is also only the mother, so no fathers, no social deprivation, and therefore outside the nursery – the mother-baby bond – no world. Only guilt will secure a mother to her child. Bettelheim has invented a listen-with-mother version of Freud's account of the superego which lashes the poor, defenceless ego to its allotted social role. For Freud, this meant acknowledging the oppressive and self-defeating nature of civilisation's highest commands. The last thing analysis should do is join in. For Bettelheim, on the other hand, mothers must be driven by guilt into a role which, by his own account, is false. Children must be saved from hatred at any price. And since he will not give his name to Badinter's book even though he thinks she is right, the price includes suppressing the truth. Hatred is therefore the guilty party (something of a tautology). What is being asked of mothers – the demand behind all demands, as one might say – is a hate-free world.

When Winnicott wrote 'Hate in the Counter-Transference', he must have known he was breaking taboos. When he listed the 18 reasons a mother has to hate her baby, he must have known he was pushing hard against the ideal ('The mother hates her infant from the word go'). The last and most often cited in his list ('He excites her but frustrates – she mustn't eat him or trade in sex with him') is another of the rare instances in psychoanalytic writing where a mother is allowed to be sexually aroused by her baby. Winnicott's essay has become an ur-text for women seeking to shatter the cliché of benign, devoted motherhood, a weapon to be wielded on behalf of maternal ambivalence as it struggles to be recognised. Ambivalence doesn't, however, seem quite right to me, at least not as something to be 'managed' or as contributing to the creativity of a mother's task, a reparative move often made in such discussions, as if the only way to deal with maternal ambivalence is by giving it with one hand and taking it back with the other (which is oddly in tune with its nature).

In Winnicott's vocabulary, the Kleinian concept of reparation doesn't figure. He is talking about something else, something so acutely painful it can only be felt at the risk of effacing itself. He is talking about a form of hatred which, against all her better 'instincts', as one might say, the mother needs to know she is feeling, and to stay with, if the infant is to have any chance of experiencing, other than by means of a violent ejection, true affect in her or himself. The alternative is masochism. Winnicott is therefore making a political point: 'If, for fear of what she may do, she cannot hate appropriately when hurt by her child she must fall back on masochism, and I think it is this that gives rise to the false theory of a natural masochism in women.' The baby, he writes, 'needs hate to hate'. Sentimentality, he concludes, 'is useless for parents'. This has lost none of its pertinence today. 'What we have, for the most part,' Daisy Waugh writes in *I Don't Know Why She Bothers: Guilt-Free Motherhood for Thoroughly Modern Women*, 'is a repressive sentimentality, a smiling acceptance of female martyrdom, which teeters, at times, beyond martyrdom into a sort of approved, mass-culture masochism.' But Waugh's insights are trounced by her breeziness, which makes you feel that mothers have only themselves to blame – that 'thoroughly modern' in the title is the give-away.

Winnicott's argument doesn't mean that the mother doesn't love her baby. As Alison Bechdel puts it in her cartoon-strip drama, *Are You My Mother?*, 'The mother loves the baby too. But this is the point. Hate is a part of love.' Bechdel's book, published in 2012, narrates her quest to reach some kind of mutual recognition with her mother. Her bestselling *Fun Home* (2006), subtitled 'A Family Tragicomic', focused on her relationship with her father, the director of a funeral parlour – hence 'fun home' – who had homosexual relations as a young man and at the age of 44 committed suicide. (As well as being turned into a musical, *Fun Home* was removed from a public library in Missouri after residents objected to its contents.) *Are You My Mother?* is a type of Winnicott primer. The chapter from which the quote about love/hate is taken is called 'Hate', others – 'True and False Self' and 'The Use of an Object' – are lifted straight from Winnicott's writing. Bechdel tells us his life story, lays his 18 reasons out on the page (reminding us that he was 'revolutionary' for using 'he or she' and 'his or her' decades before anyone else). She also graphically pursues him into the bedroom of his second marriage, where he and his wife discuss the oddity of sex (Bechdel is not alone in assuming that only this marriage was consummated). 'I want him,' the narrator says at one point during therapy, 'to be my mother.'

'Hate in the Counter-Transference' should be compulsory reading for anyone involved with today's government-sponsored talking cures (cognitive behavioural therapy and the like). Winnicott was addressing psychoanalysts who cannot bear the strain of acutely disturbed patients. Only an analyst in touch with 'his own fear and hate' will be of use to such a patient; only such an analyst will be responding to the patient's – as opposed to the analyst's – own needs (in that way of thinking, CBT, with its questionnaires and instant results, is therapy designed to protect the therapist by getting hatred out of the room as fast as it can). For Winnicott, the analyst must place her or himself 'in the position of the mother of an infant unborn or newly born'. This is not, in my understanding, how most analysts think of themselves (although Micheal Balint's idea of analysis as fostering the birth of a 'new beginning' gets close). Winnicott is presenting us with a choice. We can go for the therapeutic quick fix, the full-frontal political assault on any traces of dependency, to be smoked out like rats in the basement. We can opt for hatred of hatred (Bettleheim's problem, I would say). Or we can take as a model for our social as well as psychological well-being the complex, often painful reality of motherhood. This isn't quite the same as suggesting mothers should rule the world, but it is close. What qualifies mothers for this task is that they aren't in flight from the anguish of what it means to be human. Not that mothers are the only ones who ever have access to that insight.

Are You My Mother? is full of writers. Alongside Winnicott, they are mostly but not exclusively women: Rich, Woolf, but also Emily Dickinson and Sylvia Plath. The book is a textual collage. It is through fierce verbal and textual contestation that the narrator's struggle with her mother takes place: 'Language was our field of contest.' When Alison was 11, her mother 'took over' writing her diary entries on the eve of Rosh Hashanah, the day 'when the deeds of humanity are open for review', 'the righteous are inscribed' and 'the wicked blotted out' (Alison doesn't appear to see a problem in her mother thus assigning herself the place of divine writ and punishment). Alison's mother is a dedicated reader, has an MA, is a qualified teacher, and was an amateur actress. As a young woman, she had attended Roe v. Wade demonstrations in support of abortion rights. None of this means, however, that she can tolerate her daughter's lesbianism. When Alison, now at university, plucks up the courage to write and tell her, she replies: 'Couldn't you just get on with your work? You are young, you have talent, you have a mind.' The response echoes Mrs Winterson's: 'Why be happy when you could be normal?' The tragedy for Alison is that her mother can't see the link between her daughter's right to mental freedom, no less the result of women's struggle, and her right to freedom in the sexual choices of her life. In fact they are alternatives: 'You have a mind.'

Alison's mother suffered depression as a young woman. Psychoanalysis was not an option for her. We could say that psychoanalysis, like feminism, came too late: 'By the time *The Feminine Mystique* was published in 1963, Mom was stuck at home with two small children,' She is part of a generation whose destiny was above all to become mothers and who found themselves, after a devastating war, under the harshest obligation to be happy and fulfilled in that role. Could it be that, however much they encouraged their own daughters' independence, however much they urged their daughters to live their own unlived lives, they were also silently obeying an injunction against experiencing the full range of their emotions? And that what they demanded of their daughters was that they protect them from their own raging hearts? If that is the case Winnicott's 1949 essay would not have come out of nowhere, but would be his response to the suffocating psychic legacy which the aftermath of the war was in danger of passing on to its children. For, to stay inside his vocabulary, the child of such a mother will be a false self, compliant not just with her mother's demands – which is how he mostly describes it – but with the mother's hidden inner world, a world seen in cloying tunnel vision, in which the mother is flailing without knowing it. Unless the daughter manages to shatter the carapace that binds her to a mother who, through no fault of her own, was never given the chance to understand her own mettle, to realise what – in all senses of the term – she was truly made of. Bechdel's answer to her own question – Are You My Mother? – is finally affirmative. But the path to understanding is littered with images, lifted from her dreams and nightmares, of cracking ice, shattered glass and kicked-in walls. 'It only occurs to me now as I am writing this book about my mother,' Alison muses as she lies with a patch over one eye, 'that perhaps I had scratched my cornea to punish myself for "seeing" the truth about my family.' Has Bechdel chosen to be a graphic artist to make us see?

Perhaps, then we should be asking a slightly different question: not what a mother is or should be, but what version of motherhood might make it possible for a mother to listen to her child? For if Western culture in our times, especially in America and Europe, has repeatedly conspired to silence the inner life of the mother by laying on her the weight of its own impossible and most punishing ideals, if the term 'mothers' is a trigger for a willed self-perfection that crushes women as mothers, then how can mothers be expected to hear their children's cry – the cry not of wailing babies, which is hard enough, but the cry of protest and plaint? How can they bear to watch their child cast off the yoke of false mental safety, turning on its head what was meant to be the psychic legacy of their own version of motherhood?

For me this has always been the best way to think about the relationship between Sylvia Plath and her mother, which is not quite the same as the excessive closeness or osmosis through which it has often been analysed. In *Are You My Mother?* Alison reads Woolf but not Plath, her mother more or less the reverse (as if, between mother and daughter the one has to exclude the other). This leaves a gaping hole between the two writers, at least on the subject of mothers. Plath's 1962 verse drama, *Three Women*, her voice meditation set in a maternity ward, was inspired by *The Waves*. When Aurelia, Plath's mother, lectured on Plath after her death, she interspersed her memory of her daughter with lines like these from the First Voice, the only one of the three who ends up with her baby (the Second miscarries, the Third abandons her newborn child):

> What did my fingers do before they held him?
> What did my heart do with its love?

And these:

> I shall meditate upon normality.
> I shall meditate upon my little son.
> I do not will him to be exceptional.
> It is the exception that interests the devil.

She left out lines like these:

> There is no miracle more cruel than this.
> I am the centre of an atrocity.
> What pains, what sorrow must I be mothering?
> Can such innocence kill and kill? It milks my life.

The point being that Plath didn't shy from putting atrocity, cruelty and murderousness in the midst of a mother's love: 'The world conceives/Its end and runs towards it, arms held out in love.' But her own mother couldn't stand it. A mother censors a daughter's representation of mothering, shutting down the world of thought. If it was just a question of cramping her daughter's style, then, however poignant this story, it would be easy to blame Plath's mother and turn away. But the implications surely reach beyond the tragedy of this famous case. What do we expect when society continues to believe it has the right to trample over the mental lives of mothers?

'If Freud had been less preoccupied with Oedipus and more observant of Medea when he remarked that "aggression forms the basis of every relation of affection and love among people,"' Loraux writes in *Mothers in Mourning*, 'he would certainly not have added: "with the single exception, perhaps, of the mother's relation to her male child."' The great theorist of Oedipus, she elaborates, was blind to the strand in Greek tragic thinking in which wrath against the spouse triumphs over physical intimacy with the child. It perhaps goes without saying that Freud was probably recounting his own memories, however reliable, and/or describing something he longed to be true – that is, not for the first or last time, he was talking about himself. But even this reading of Medea is uncertain. In other versions of the tale, some written before Euripides, Medea doesn't murder her children: hatred of Medea drives the Corinthians to kill them, or the relatives of Creon kill them in revenge after Medea has murdered Creon and fled to Athens, or she puts her children through a rite designed to make them immortal in the course of which they die. Even in Euripides' drama, what drives Medea to kill is not, or not only, her sexual rage against their father, but equally the loss of his love for their children which condemns them to an uncertain future. Her cry is for justice and her famous diatribe on the pains of mothering the lament of a mother whose greatest fear is that she and her children will be homeless and stateless (hence her plea to Creon to delay her expulsion from the city). Only in their final confrontation after the murder, when Jason accuses her of being 'stung by thoughts of sex' ('And you believe it justified/to kill them for the sake of sex?'), does she return: 'Do you suppose such troubles to be trivial for a woman?' For the most part it isn't sex that Medea has on her mind but survival. Although she is finally given all the assurances she seeks, she doesn't believe them. She kills her children to save them from a worse fate: 'I swear, there is no way that I shall leave/my boys among my enemies so they/can treat them with atrocity.'

It is interesting, therefore, that it is the image of sexual frenzy that has most popularly attached itself to Medea and that what gets lost in translation is any trace of the reasons a mother might have for thinking there is no longer any place in the world for her child. That is certainly the reality confronted by Veronique Olmi's narrator in her bestselling rewrite of Medea from 2001, *Bord de mer* (the translated title, *Beside the Sea*, loses the pun *mer/mère*, by the sea/mother at the edge), who, before murdering her two sons on a visit to the seaside, goes quietly mad and dreams of spending her life in bed with her children watching the TV: 'Holding on to the remote, we'd have switched the world off as soon as it fucked up.' 'What woman,' Rich asks in her chapter 'Violence: The Heart of Maternal Darkness', 'has not dreamed of "going over the edge"?' Despite being criticised for including this chapter, which starts with its own story of a mother who murdered the two youngest of her eight children in a Chicago suburb in 1974, Rich chose to include it in the 1995 reprint of her book.

But it is Christa Wolf's 1996 retelling which is, for me, the true feminist text. In this version, Medea doesn't kill her children, or Glauce, or her brother Absyrtus whom, in another strand of the legend, she murdered before fleeing her original home of Colchis with Jason. If all this is laid at her door by the citizens of Corinth it's because she has uncovered the city's ugly secret: Creon's killing of Glauce's sister in order to keep his succession out of the grasp of his wife, who after the killing goes silent and progressively mad (Medea's father had similarly murdered Absyrtus, whom he saw as a rival for the succession). 'Either I'm out of my mind,' Medea muses in her first soliloquy, 'or their city is founded on a crime.' This makes Medea into a psychoanalyst – the allusions are explicit – as she slowly persuades the ailing Glauce that she knows the truth, saw the deed. Medea taught me, Glauce reflects, that 'there is no thought I must forbid myself to have.'

Medea's true crime is to have shattered a myth of collective innocence. She is a scapegoat: 'They're looking for a woman who will tell them they are not guilty of anything.' Worse, by exposing the crime, she risks plunging the whole nation into sorrow: 'Someone must grieve.' Compare, one last time, Adrienne Rich: 'We know too much at first hand [of] the violence which over centuries we have been told is the way of the world, but which we exist to mitigate and assuage.' In Wolf's version, it is because Medea assuages nothing that she is indicted of all crimes. It is because she knows the city is built on the corpses of children that she is hounded out of Corinth. Wolf has written a parable of Germany in the 20th century. In *On the Natural History of Destruction*, his account of the silence that followed the Allied bombing of German cities at the end of the war, W.G. Sebald writes of the 'well-kept secret of the corpses built into the foundations of our state'. Above all Wolf has turned Medea into the story of what happens when a woman is held responsible for the ills of the world. Medea 'has no need of our doubt, of our endeavours to do her justice', she writes in her prelude: 'We must venture into the darkest core of our misjudgement – of her and of ourselves – simply walk in, with one another, behind one another, while the crash of collapsing walls sounds in our ears.'

To conclude. When I was preparing to adopt my daughter, I would try to seduce my social worker with obscenely large red cherries which would sit in their bowl, I liked to think, as a flagrant riposte to, and distraction from, her steely, unrelenting inquisition (the adoption process takes the idea of a fault-finding mission to a new height). I remember thinking later that the two things the whole process could never prepare you for and which made it as useless as it was invasive were, first, the worry – the OMG of every scratch and fall, at once absurd and wholly in tune with the fragility of life – and the joy. In the famous story, Tiresias is struck blind by Juno for having revealed that a woman's sexual pleasure is greater than a man's. As I was reading the outpourings of all these recent books on motherhood, it occurred to me that we need a version of this story for mothers, a version in which, without any need to deny everything else talked about here, the acute pleasure of being a mother would be neither a guilty secret, nor something enviously co-opted by bullies – 'You *will* be happy!' – but instead would be allowed to get on quietly with its work of making the experience of motherhood more than worth it.

107.

CHIMAMANDA NGOZI ADICHIE

Born 1977, Enugu, Nigeria

from *We Should All Be Feminists*

2014

We spend too much time teaching girls to worry about what boys think of them. But the reverse is not the case. We don't teach boys to care about being likeable. We spend too much time telling girls that they cannot be angry or aggressive or tough, which is bad enough, but then we turn around and either praise or excuse men for the same reasons. All over the world, there are so many magazine articles and books telling women what to do, how to be and not to be, in order to attract or please men. There are far fewer guides for men about pleasing women.

I teach a writing workshop in Lagos and one of the participants, a young woman, told me that a friend had told her not to listen to my 'feminist talk'; otherwise she would absorb ideas that would destroy her marriage. This is a threat – the destruction of a marriage, the possibility of not having a marriage at all – that in our society is much more likely to be used against a woman than against a man.

Gender matters everywhere in the world. And I would like today to ask that we should begin to dream about and plan for a different world. A fairer world. A world of happier men and happier women who are truer to themselves. And this is how to start: we must raise our daughters differently. We must also raise our sons differently.

*

We do a great disservice to boys in how we raise them. We stifle the humanity of boys. We define masculinity in a very narrow way. Masculinity is a hard, small cage, and we put boys inside this cage.

We teach boys to be afraid of fear of weakness, of vulnerability. We teach them to mask their true selves, because they have to be, in Nigerian-speak, *a hard man*.

In secondary school, a boy and a girl go out, both of them teenagers with meagre pocket money. Yet the boy is expected to pay the bills, always, to prove his masculinity. (And we wonder why boys are more likely to steal money from their parents.)

What if both boys and girls were raised *not* to link masculinity and money? What if their attitude was *not* 'the boy has to pay', but rather, 'whoever has more should pay'?

Of course, because of their historical advantage, it is mostly men who *will* have more today. But if we start raising children differently, then in fifty years, in a hundred years, boys will no longer have the pressure of proving their masculinity by material means.

But by far the worst thing we do to males – by making them feel they have to be hard – is that we leave them with *very* fragile egos. The *harder* a man feels compelled to be, the weaker his ego is.

And then we do a much greater disservice to girls, because we raise them to cater to the fragile egos of males.

We teach girls to shrink themselves, to make themselves smaller.

We say to girls, 'You can have ambition, but not too much. You should aim to be successful but not too successful, otherwise you will threaten the man. If you are the breadwinner in your relationship with a man, pretend that you are not, especially in public, otherwise you will emasculate him.'

But what if we question the premise itself? Why should a woman's success be a threat to a man? What if we decide to simply dispose of that word – and I don't know if there is an English word I dislike more than this – *emasculation*.

A Nigerian acquaintance once asked me if I was worried that men would be intimidated by me.

I was not worried at all – it had not even occurred to me to be worried, because a man who would be intimidated by me is exactly the kind of man I would have no interest in.

Still, I was struck by this. Because I am female, I'm expected to aspire to marriage.

I am expected to make my life choices always keeping in mind that marriage is the most important. Marriage can be a good thing, a source of joy, love and mutual support. But why do we teach girls to aspire to marriage, yet we don't teach boys to do the same?

I know a Nigerian woman who decided to sell her house because she didn't want to intimidate a man who might want to marry her.

I know an unmarried woman in Nigeria who, when she goes to conference, wears a wedding ring because she wants her colleagues to - according to her – 'give her respect'.

The sadness in this is that a wedding ring will indeed automatically make her seem worthy of respect, while not wearing a wedding ring would make her easily dismissible – and this is in a modern workplace.

I know young women who are under so much pressure – from family, from friends, even from work – to get married that they are pushed to make terrible choices.

Our society teaches a woman at a certain age who is unmarried to see it as a deep personal failure. While a man at a certain age who is unmarried has not quite come around to making his pick.

It is easy to say, 'But women can just say no to all this.' But the reality is more difficult, more complex. We are all social beings. We internalize ideas from our socialization.

Even the language we use illustrates this. The language of marriage is often a language of ownership, not a language of partnership.

We use the word *respect* for something a woman shows a man, but not often for something a man shows a woman.

Both men and women will say, 'I did it for peace in my marriage.'

When men say it, it is usually about something they should not be doing anyway. Something they say to their friends in a fondly exasperated way, something that ultimately proves to them their masculinity – 'Oh, my wife said I can't go to clubs every night, so now, for peace in my marriage, I go only on weekends.'

When women say 'I did it for peace in my marriage,' it is usually because they have given up a job, a career goal, a dream.

We teach females that in relationships, compromise is what a woman is more likely to do.

We raise girls to see each other as competitors – not for jobs or accomplishments, which in my opinion can be a good thing, but for the attention of men.

We teach girls that they cannot be sexual beings in the way boys are. If we have sons, we don't mind knowing about their girlfriends. But our daughters' boyfriends? God forbid. (But we of course expect them to bring home the perfect man for marriage when the time is right.)

We police girls. We praise girls for virginity but we don't praise boys for virginity (and it makes me wonder how exactly this is supposed to work out, since the loss of virginity is a process that usually involves two people of opposite genders).

Recently a young woman was gang-raped in a university in Nigeria, and the response of many young Nigerians, both male and female, was something like this: 'Yes, rape is wrong, but what is a girl doing in a room with four boys?'

Let us, if we can, forget the horrible inhumanity of that response. These Nigerians have been raised to think of women as inherently guilty. And they have been raised to expect so little of men that the idea of men as savage beings with no self-control is somehow acceptable.

We teach girls shame. *Close your legs. Cover yourself.* We make them feel as though by being born female, they are already guilty of something. And so girls grow up to be women who cannot say they have desire. Who silence themselves. Who cannot say what they truly think. Who have turned pretence into an art form.

I know a woman who hates domestic work, but she pretends that she likes it, because she has been taught that to be 'good wife material', she has to be – to use that Nigerian word – *homely*. And then she got married. And her husband's family began to complain that she had changed. Actually, she had not changed. She just got tired of pretending to be what she was not.

The problem with gender is that it prescribes how we *should* be rather than recognizing how we are. Imagine how much happier we would be, how much freer to be our true individual selves, if we didn't have the weight of gender expectations.

108.

AMAL MOUSSA

Born 1971, Tunis, Tunisia

Love Me

2015

I carry me on my fingertips.
I carry me on the galloping of my vision.
I wrap myself with a swaddling of my skin.
I embrace me longing for myself.
I bless my flowing, my gushing.
I cradle me in my chest.
I glove these budding hands with poetry.

I claim revelation,
my engravings are on stone.
My image carries water to thirst,
and bait to fishermen' nets.
I spend the time of the tolling
of evening bells
sculpting.
I sleep in my own shade.
I wear my Bedouin nature
to spite cities.

I stroll within me
when I weary myself.
I enter a garden
that does not entice myself against me.
I love my impossible self,
the one whose feet
the earth does not know.

109.

MAGGIE NELSON

Born 1973, San Francisco, California, United States of America

from *The Argonauts*

2015

2011, the summer of our changing bodies. Me, four months pregnant, you six months on T. We pitched out, in our inscrutable hormonal soup, for Fort Lauderdale, to stay for a week at the beachside Sheraton in monsoon season, so that you could have top surgery by a good surgeon and recover. Less than twenty-four hours after we arrived, they were snapping a sterile green hat on your head – a 'party hat,' the nice nurse said – and wheeling you away. While you were under the knife, I drank gritty hot chocolate in the waiting room and watched Diana Nyad try to swim from Florida to Cuba. She didn't make it that time, even in her shark cage. But you did. You emerged four hours later, hilariously zonked from the drugs, trying in vain to play the host while slipping in and out of consciousness, your whole torso more tightly bound than you've ever managed yourself, a drain hanging off each side, two pouches that filled up over and over again with blood stuff the color of cherry Kool-Aid.

To save money over the week, we cooked our food in the hotel bathroom on a hot plate. One day we drove to a Sport Chalet and bought a little tent to set up on the beach because the beachside cabanas cost too much money to rent. While you slept I ambled down to the beach and set up the tent, then tried to read Sedgwick's *A Dialogue on Love* inside. But it was like a nylon sweat lodge in there, and neither I nor the four-month-old fetus could tolerate it. I had started showing, which was delightful. Maybe there would be a baby. One night we splurged in our sober way and had eight-dollar virgin strawberry daiquiris at the infinity pool, which was stocked with Europeans on cheap vacation packages. The air was hot and lavender with a night storm coming in. There was always a storm coming in. Frat brothers and sorority sisters thronged every fried fish joint on the boardwalk. The crowds were loud and repulsive and a little scary but we were protected by our force field. On our third day, we drove to the second-largest mall in the world and walked for hours, even though I was dizzy and exhausted from early pregnancy and the suffocating heat and you were just barely over the lip of the Vi-codin. At the mall I went into Motherhood Maternity and tried on clothes with one of those gelatin strap-on bellies they have so you can see what you'll look like as you grow big. Wearing the strap-on belly, I tried on a fuzzy white wool sweater with a bow at the sternum, the kind that makes your baby look like a present. I bought the sweater and ended up wearing it back at home all winter. You bought some loungy Adidas pants that look hot on you. Over and over again we emptied your drains into little Dixie cups and flushed the blood stuff down the hotel toilet. I've never loved you more than I did then, with your Kool-Aid drains, your bravery in going under the knife to live a better life, a life of wind on skin, your nodding off while propped up on a throne of hotel pillows, so as not to disturb your stitches. 'The king's sleep,' we called it, in homage to our first pay-per-view purchase of the week, *The King's Speech*.

Later, from our Sheraton Sweet Sleeper Bed, we ordered *X-Men: First Class*. Afterward we debated: assimilation vs. revolution. I'm no cheerleader for assimilation per se, but in the movie the assimilationists were advocating nonviolence and identification with the Other in that bastardized Buddhist way that gets me every time. You expressed sympathy for the revolutionaries, who argued, *Stay freaky and blow 'em up before they come for you, because no matter what they say, the truth is they want you dead, and you're fooling yourself if you think otherwise.*

PROFESSOR: I can't stop thinking about the others out there, all those minds that I touched. I could feel them, their isolation, their hopes, their ambitions. I tell you we can start something incredible, Erik. We can help them.

ERIK LEHNSHERR: Can we? Identification, that's how it starts. And ends with being rounded up, experimented on, and eliminated.

PROFESSOR: Listen to me very carefully, my friend: killing Shaw will not bring you peace.

ERIK LEHNSHERR: Peace was never an option.

We bantered good-naturedly, yet somehow allowed ourselves to get polarized into a needless binary. That's what we both hate about fiction, or at least crappy fiction – it purports to provide occasions for thinking through complex issues, but really it has predetermined the positions, stuffed a narrative full of false choices, and hooked you on them, rendering you less able to see out, to *get* out.

While we talked we said words like *nonviolence, assimilation, threats to survival, preserving the radical.* But when I think about it now I hear only the background buzz of our trying to explain something to each other, to ourselves, about our lived experiences thus far on this peeled, endangered planet. As is so often the case, the intensity of our need to be understood distorted our positions, backed us farther into the cage.

Do you want to be right or do you want to connect? ask couples' therapists everywhere.

Deleuze / Parnet

The aim is not to answer questions, it's to get out, to get out of it.

Flipping channels on a different day, we landed on a reality TV show featuring a breast cancer patient recovering from a double mastectomy. It was uncanny to watch her performing the same actions we were performing – emptying her drains, waiting patiently for her unbinding – but with opposite emotions. You felt unburdened, euphoric, reborn; the woman on TV feared, wept, and grieved.

Our last night at the Sheraton, we have dinner at the astoundingly overpriced 'casual Mexican' restaurant on the premises, Dos Caminos. You pass as a guy; I, as pregnant. Our waiter cheerfully tells us about his family, expresses delight in ours. On the surface, it may have seemed as though your body was becoming more and more 'male,' mine, more and more 'female.' But that's not how it felt on the inside. On the inside, we were two human animals undergoing transformations beside each other, bearing each other loose witness. In other words, we were aging.

Many women describe the feeling of having a baby come out of their vagina as taking the biggest shit of their lives. This isn't really a metaphor. The anal cavity and vaginal canal lean on each other; they, too, are the sex which is not one. Constipation is one of pregnancy's principal features: the growing baby literally deforms and squeezes the lower intestines, changing the shape, flow, and plausibility of one's feces. In late pregnancy, I was amazed to find that my shit, when it would finally emerge, had been deformed into Christmas tree ornament-type balls. Then, all through my labor, I could not shit at all, as it was keenly clear to me that letting go of the shit would mean the total disintegration of my perineum, anus, and vagina, all at once. I also knew that if, or when, I could let go of the shit, the baby would probably come out. But to do so would mean *falling forever, going to pieces.*

In perusing the Q&A sections of pregnancy magazines at my ob/gyn's office before giving birth, I learned that a surprising number of women have a related but distinct concern about shit and labor (either that, or the magazine editors are making it up, as a kind of projective propaganda):

Q: If my husband watches me labor, how will he ever find me sexy again, now that he's seen me involuntarily defecate, and my vagina accommodate a baby's head?

This question confused me; its description of labor did not strike me as exceedingly distinct from what happens during sex, or at least some sex, or at least much of the sex I had heretofore taken to be good.

No one asked, *How does one submit to falling forever, to going to pieces.* A question from the inside.

In current 'grrrl' culture, I've noted the ascendancy of the phrase 'I need X like I need a dick in my ass.' Meaning, of course, that X is precisely what you *don't* need (dick in my ass = hole in my head = fish with a bicycle, and so on). I'm all for girls feeling empowered to reject sexual practices that they don't enjoy, and God knows many straight boys are all too happy to stick it in any hole, even one that hurts. But I worry that such expressions only underscore the 'ongoing absence of a discourse of female anal eroticism ... the flat fact that, since classical times, *there has been no important and sustained Western discourse in which women's anal eroticism* | Sedgwick | *means.* Means anything.'

Sedgwick did an enormous amount to put women's anal eroticism on the map (even though she was mostly into spanking, which is not precisely an anal pursuit). But while Sedgwick (and Fraiman) want to make space for women's anal eroticism to *mean*, that is not the same as inquiring into how it *feels.* Even ex-ballerina Toni Bentley, who knocked herself out to become the culture's go-to girl for anal sex in her memoir *The Surrender,* can't seem to write a sentence about ass-fucking without obscuring it via metaphor, bad puns, or spiritual striving. And Fraiman exalts the female anus mostly for what it is not: the vagina (presumably a lost cause, for the sodomite).

I am not interested in a hermeneutics, or an erotics, or a metaphorics, of my anus. I am interested in ass-fucking. I am interested in the fact that the clitoris, disguised as a discrete button, sweeps over the entire area like a manta ray, impossible to tell where its eight thousand nerves begin and end. I am interested in the fact that the human anus is one of the most innervated parts of the body, as Mary Roach explained to Terry Gross in a perplexing piece of radio that I listened to while driving Iggy home from his twelve-month vaccinations. I checked on Iggy periodically in the rearview mirror for signs of a vaccine-induced neuromuscular break-down while Roach explained that the anus has 'tons of nerves. And the reason is that it needs to be able to discriminate, by feel, between solid, liquid, and gas and be able to selectively release one or maybe all of those. And thank heavens for the anus because, you know, really a lot of grati-tude, ladies and gentlemen, to the human anus.' To which Gross replied: 'Let's take a short break here, then we'll talk some more. This is *Fresh Air*.'

A few months after Florida: you always wanting to fuck, raging with new hormones and new comfort in your skin; me vaulting fast into the unfuckable, not wanting to dislodge the hard-won baby seed, falling through the bed with dizziness whenever I turned my head – *falling forever* – all touch starting to sicken, as if the cells of my skin were indi-vidually nauseated.

That hormones can make the feel of wind, or the feel of fingers on one's skin, change from arousing to nauseating is a mystery deeper than I can track or fathom. The mysteries of psychology pale in comparison, just as evolution strikes me as infinitely more spiritually profound than Genesis.

Our bodies grew stranger, to ourselves, to each other. You sprouted coarse hair in new places; new muscles fanned out across your hip bones. My breasts were sore for over a year, and while they don't hurt anymore, they still feel like they belong to someone else (and in a sense, since I'm still nursing, they do). For years you were stone; now you strip your shirt off whenever you feel like it, emerge muscular, shirtless, into public spaces, go running – swimming, even.

Via T, you've experienced surges of heat, an adolescent budding, your sexuality coming down from the labyrinth of your mind and disseminating like a cottonwood tree in a warm wind. You like the changes, but also feel them as a sort of compromise, a wager for visibility, as in your drawing of a ghost who proclaims, *Without this sheet, I would be invisible.* (Visibility makes possible, but it also disciplines: disciplines gender, disciplines genre.) Via pregnancy, I have my first sustained encounter with the pendulous, the slow, the exhausted, the disabled. I had always presumed that giving birth would make me feel invincible and ample, like fisting. But even now – two years out – my insides feel more quivery than lush. I've begun to give myself over to the idea that the sensation might be forever changed, that this sensitivity is now mine, ours, to work with. Can fragility feel as hot as bravado? I think so, but sometimes struggle to find the way. Whenever I think I can't find it, Harry assures me that we can. And so we go on, our bodies finding each other again and again, even as they – we – have also been *right here*, all along.

For reasons almost incomprehensible to me now, I cried a little when our first ultrasound technician – the nice, seemingly gay Raoul, who sported a little silver sperm-squiggle pin on his white coat – told us at twenty weeks that our baby was a boy, without a shadow of a doubt. I guess I had to mourn something – the fantasy of a feminist daughter, the fantasy of a mini-me. Someone whose hair I could braid, someone who might serve as a femme ally to me in a house otherwise occupied by an adorable boy terrier, my beautiful, swaggery stepson, and a debonair butch on T.

But that was not my fate, nor was it the baby's. Within twenty-four hours of hearing the news, I was on board. Little Agnes would be little Iggy. And I would love him fiercely. Maybe I would even braid his hair! As you reminded me on the drive home from our appointment, *Hey, I was born female, and look how that turned out.*

Despite agreeing with Sedgwick's assertion that 'women and men are more like each other than chalk is like cheese, than ratiocination is like raisins, than up is like down, or than 1 is like o,' it took me by surprise that my body could make a male body. Many women I know have reported something of the same, even though they know this is the most ordinary of miracles. As my body made the male body, I felt the difference between male and female body melt even further away. I was making a body with a difference, but a girl body would have been a different body too. The principal difference was that the body I made would eventually slide out of me and be its own body. Radical intimacy, radical difference. Both in the body, both in the bowl.

I kept thinking then about something poet Fanny Howe once said about bearing biracial children, something about how you become what grows inside you. But however 'black' Howe might have felt herself becoming while gestating her children, she also remained keenly aware that the outside world was ready and waiting – and all too willing – to reinforce the color divide. She is of her children, and they are of her. But they know and she knows they do not share the same lot.

This divide provoked in Howe the sensation of being a double agent, especially in all-white settings. She recalls how, at gatherings in the late '60s, white liberals would openly converse 'about their fear of blacks, and their judgments of blacks, and I had to announce to them that my husband and children were black, before hastily departing.' This scene was not limited to the '60s. 'This event has been repeated so many times, in multiple forms, that by now I make some kind of give-away statement after entering a white-only room, one way or the other, that will warn the people there "which side I am on,"' Howe says. 'On these occasions, more than any others, I feel that my skin is white but my soul is not, and that I am in camouflage.'

Harry lets me in on a secret: guys are pretty nice to each other in public. Always greeting each other 'hey boss' or nodding as they pass each other on the street.

Women aren't like that. I don't mean that women are all backstabbers or have it in for each other or whatnot. But in public, we don't nod nobly at one another. Nor do we really need to, as that nod also means *I mean you no violence.*

Over lunch with a fag friend of ours, Harry reports his findings about male behavior in public. Our friend laughs and says: *Maybe if I looked like Harry, I'd get a 'hey boss' too!*

When a guy has cause to stare at Harry's driver's license or credit card, there comes an odd moment during which their camaraderie as two dudes screeches to a halt. The friendliness can't evaporate on a dime, however, especially if there has been a longish prior interaction, as one might have over the course of a meal, with a waiter.

Recently we were buying pumpkins for Halloween. We'd been given a little red wagon to put our pumpkins in as we traipsed around the field. We'd haggled over the price, we'd oohed and ahed at the life-size mechanical zombie removing his head. We'd been given freebie minipumpkins for our cute baby. Then, the credit card. The guy paused for a long moment, then said, 'This is her card, right?' – pointing at me. I almost felt sorry for him, he was so desperate to normalize the moment. I should have said yes, but I was worried I would open up a new avenue of trouble *(never the scofflaw* – yet I know I have what it takes to put my body on the line, if and when it comes down to it; this knowledge is a hot red shape inside me). We just froze in the way we freeze until Harry said, 'It's my card.' Long pause, sidelong stare. A shadow of violence usually drifts over the scene. 'It's complicated,' Harry finally said, puncturing the silence. Eventually, the man spoke. 'No, actually, it's not,' he said, handing back the card. 'Not complicated at all.'

Every other weekend of my pregnant fall – my so-called golden trimester – I traveled alone around the country on behalf of my book *The Art of Cruelty*. Quickly I realized that I would need to trade in my prideful self-sufficiency for a willingness to ask for help – in lifting my bags in and out of overhead compartments, up and down subway steps, and so on. I received this help, which I recognized as great kindness. On more than one occasion, a service member in the airport literally saluted me as I shuffled past. Their friendliness was nothing short of shocking. *You are holding the future; one must be kind to the future* (or at least a certain image of the future, which I apparently appeared able to deliver, and our military ready to defend). So this is the seduction of normalcy, I thought as I smiled back, compromised and radiant.

But the pregnant body in public is also obscene. It radiates a kind of smug autoeroticism: an intimate relation is going on – one that is visible to others, but that decisively excludes them. Service members may salute, strangers may offer their congratulations or their seats, but this privacy, this bond, can also irritate. It especially irritates the antiabortionists, who would prefer to pry apart the twofer earlier and earlier – twenty-four weeks, twenty weeks, twelve weeks, six weeks . . . The sooner you can pry the twofer apart, the sooner you can dispense with one constituent of the relationship: *the woman with rights.*

For all the years I didn't want to be pregnant – the years I spent harshly deriding 'the breeders' – I secretly felt pregnant women were smug in their complaints. Here they were, sitting on top of the cake of the culture, getting all the kudos for doing exactly what women are supposed to do, yet still they felt unsupported and discriminated against. Give me a break! Then, when I wanted to be pregnant but wasn't, I felt that pregnant women had the cake I wanted, and were busy bitching about the flavor of the icing.

I was wrong on all counts – imprisoned, as I was and still am, by my own hopes and fears. I'm not trying to fix that wrongness here. I'm just trying to let it *hang out.*

Place me now, like a pregnant cutout doll, at a 'prestigious New York university,' giving a talk on my book on cruelty.

During the Q&A, a well-known playwright raises his hand and says: *I can't help but notice that you're <u>with child</u>, which leads me to the question – how did you handle working on all this dark material [sadism, masochism, cruelty, violence, and so on] in your <u>condition</u>?*

Ah yes, I think, digging a knee into the podium. Leave it to the old patrician white guy to call the lady speaker back to her body, so that no one misses the spectacle of that wild oxymoron, *the pregnant woman who thinks.* Which is really just a pumped-up version of that more general oxymoron, *a woman who thinks.*

As if anyone was missing the spectacle anyway. As if a similar scene didn't recur at nearly every location of my so-called book tour. As if when I myself see pregnant women in the public sphere, there isn't a kind of drumming in my mind that threatens to drown out all else: *pregnant, pregnant, pregnant,* perhaps because the soul (or souls) in utero is pumping out static, static that disrupts our usual perception of an other as a *single* other. The static of facing not one, but also not two.

During irritating Q&As, bumpy takeoffs and landings, and frightful faculty meetings, I placed my hands on my risen belly and attempted silent communion with the being spinning in the murk. Wherever I went, there the baby went, too. Hello, New York! Hello, bathtub! And yet babies have a will of their own, which becomes visible the first time mine sticks out a limb and makes a tent of my belly. During the night he gets into weird positions, forcing me to plead, *Move along, little baby! Get your foot off my lungs!* And if you are tracking a problem, as I was, you may have to watch the baby's body develop in ways that might harm him, with nothing you can do about it. Powerlessness, finitude, endurance. You are making the baby, but not *directly*. You are responsible for his welfare, but unable to control the core elements. You must allow him to unfurl, you must feed his unfurling, you must hold him. But he will unfurl as his cells are pro-grammed to unfurl. You can't reverse an unfolding structural or chromosomal disturbance by ingesting the right organic tea.

Why do we have to measure his kidneys and freak out about their size every week if we've already decided we are not going to take him out early or do anything to treat him until after he's born? I asked the doctor rolling the sticky ultrasound shaft over my belly for seemingly the thousandth time. *Well, most mothers want to know as much as possible about the condition of their babies,* she said, avoiding my eyes.

Truth be told, when we first started trying to conceive, I had hoped to be done with my cruelty project and onto something 'cheerier,' so that the baby might have more upbeat accompaniment in utero. But I needn't have worried – not only did getting pregnant take much longer than I'd wanted it to, but pregnancy itself taught me how irrelevant such a hope was. Babies grow in a helix of hope and fear; gestating draws one but deeper into the spiral. It isn't cruel in there, but it's dark. I would have explained this to the playwright, but he had already left the room.

After the Q&A at this event, a woman came up to me and told me that she just got out of a relationship with a woman who had wanted her to hit her during sex. *She was so fucked up,* she said. *Came from a background of abuse. I had to tell her I couldn't do that to her, I could never be that person.* She seemed to be asking me for a species of advice, so I told her the only thing that occurred to me: I didn't know this other woman, so all that seemed clear to me was that their perversities were not compatible.

Even identical genital acts mean very different things to different people. | Sedgwick | This is a crucial point to remember, and also a difficult one. It reminds us that there is difference right where we may be looking for, and expecting, communion.

At twenty-eight weeks, I was hospitalized for some bleeding. While discussing a possible placental issue, one doctor quipped, 'We don't want that, because while that would likely be OK for the baby, it might not be OK for you.' By pressing a bit, I figured out that she meant, in that particular scenario, the baby would likely live, but I might not.

Now, I loved my hard-won baby-to-be fiercely, but I was in no way ready to bow out of this vale of tears for his survival. Nor do I think those who love me would have looked too kindly on such a decision – a decision that doctors elsewhere on the globe are mandated to make, and that the die-hard antiabortionists are going for here.

Once, I was riding in a cab to JFK, passing by that amazingly over-packed cemetery along the Brooklyn-Queens Expressway (Calvary?). My cabdriver gazed out wistfully at the headstones packed onto the hill and said, *Many of those graves are the graves of children. Likely so,* I returned with a measure of fatigued trepidation, the result of years of fielding unwanted monologues from cabdrivers about how women should live or behave. *It is a good thing when children die,* he said. *They go straight to Paradise, because they are the innocents.*

During my sleepless night under placental observation, this monologue came back to me. And I wondered if, instead of working to fulfill the dream of worldwide enforced childbearing, abortion foes could instead get excited about all the innocent, unborn souls going straight from the abortion table to Paradise, no detour necessary into this den of iniquity, which eventually makes whores of us all (not to mention Social Security recipients). Could that get them off our backs once and for all?

Never in my life have I felt more pro-choice than when I was pregnant. And never in my life have I understood more thoroughly, and been more excited about, a life that began at conception. Feminists may never make a bumper sticker that says IT'S A CHOICE *AND* A CHILD, but of course that's what it is, and we know it. We don't need to wait for George Carlin to spill the beans. We're not idiots; we understand the stakes. Sometimes we choose death. Harry and I sometimes joke that women should get way beyond twenty weeks – maybe even up to two days after birth – to decide if they want to keep the baby. (Joke, OK?)

I have saved many mementos for Iggy, but I admit to tossing away an envelope with about twenty-five ultrasound photos of his in-utero penis and testicles, which a chirpy, blond ponytailed technician printed out for me every time I had an ultrasound. *Boy, he's sure proud of his stuff,* she would say, before jabbing Print. Or, *He really likes to show it off!*

Just let him wheel around in his sac, for Christ's sake, I thought, grimly folding the genital triptychs into my wallet, week after week. Let him stay oblivious – for the first and last time, perhaps – to the task of performing a self for others, to the fact that we develop, even in utero, in response to a flow of projections and reflections ricocheting off us. Eventually, we call that snowball a self *(Argo).*

I guess the cheery way of looking at this snowball would be to say: Subjectivity is keenly relational, and it is strange. *We are for another, or by virtue of another.* In my final weeks, I walked every day in the Arroyo Seco, listing aloud all the people who were waiting on earth to love Iggy, hoping that the promise of their love would eventually be enough to lure him out.

As my due date neared, I confided in Jessica, the woman who would be assisting our birth, that I was worried I wouldn't be able to make milk, as I had heard of women who couldn't. She smiled and said, *You've made it already.* Seeing me unconvinced, she said, *Want me to show you?* I nodded, shyly lifting a breast out of my bra. In one stunning gesture, she took my breast into her hand-beak and clamped down hard. A bloom of custard-colored drops rose in a ring, indifferent to my doubts.

According to Kaja Silverman, the turn to a paternal God comes on the heels of the child's recognition that the mother cannot protect against all harm, that her milk – be it literal or figurative – doesn't solve all problems. As the human mother proves herself a separate, finite entity, she disappoints, and gravely. In its rage at maternal finitude, the child turns to an all-powerful patriarch – God – who, by definition, cannot let anyone down. 'The extraordinarily difficult task imposed upon the child's primary caretaker not only by the culture but also by Being itself is to induct it into relationality by saying over and over again, in a multitude of ways, what death will otherwise have to teach it: "This is where you end and others begin."

'Unfortunately, this lesson seldom "takes," and the mother usually delivers it at enormous cost to herself. Most children respond to the partial satisfaction of their demands with extreme rage, rage that is predicated on the belief that the mother is withholding something that is within her power to provide.'

I get that if the caretaker does not teach the lesson of the 'me' and the 'not-me' to the child, she may not make adequate space for herself. But why does the delivery of this lesson come at such an enormous cost? What is the cost? Withstanding a child's rage? Isn't a child's rage something we should be able to withstand?

Silverman also contends that a baby's demands on the mother can be 'very flattering to the mother's narcissism, since it attributes to her the capacity to satisfy her infant's lack, and so – by extension – her own. Since most women in our culture are egoically wounded, the temptation to bathe in the sun of this idealization often proves irresistible.' I have seen some mothers use their babies to fill a lack, or soothe an egoic wound, or bathe in the sun of idealization in ways that seemed pathological. But for the most part those people were pathological prior to having a baby. They would have had a pathological relation to carrot juice. Remnant Lacanian that she is, Silverman's aperture does not seem wide enough to include an enjoyment that doesn't derive from filling a void, or love that is not merely balm for a wound. So far as I can tell, most worthwhile pleasures on this earth slip between gratifying another and gratifying oneself. Some would call that an ethics.

Silverman does imagine, however, that this cycle could or should change: 'Our culture should support [the mother] by providing enabling representations of maternal finitude, but instead it keeps alive in all of us the tacit belief that [the mother] *could* satisfy our desires if she really *wanted to*.' What would these 'enabling representations' look like? Better parts for women in Hollywood movies? Books like this one? I don't want to represent anything.

At the same time, every word that I write could be read as some kind of defense, or assertion of value, of whatever it is that I am, whatever viewpoint it is that I ostensibly have to offer, whatever I've lived. *You know so much about people from the second they open their mouths. Right away you might know that you might want to keep them out.* That's part of the horror of speaking, of writing. There is nowhere to hide. When you try to hide, the spectacle can grow grotesque. Think of Joan Didion's preemptive attempt, in *Blue Nights*, to quash any notion that her daughter Quintana Roo's childhood was a privileged one. '"Privilege" is a judgment. "Privilege" is an opinion. "Privilege" is an accusation. "Privilege" remains an

Eileen
Myles

area to which – when I think of what [Quintana] endured, when I consider what came later – I will not easily cop.' These remarks were a pity, since her account of 'what came later' – Quintana's death, on the heels of the death of Didion's beloved husband – underscores Didion's more interesting, albeit disavowed subject, which is that economic privilege does not protect against all suffering.

I am interested in offering up my experience and performing my particular manner of thinking, for whatever they are worth. I would also like to cop easily to my abundant privilege – except that the notion of privilege as something to which one could 'easily cop,' as in 'cop to once and be done with,' is ridiculous. Privilege *saturates*, privilege *structures*. But I have also never been less interested in arguing for the rightness, much less the righteousness, of any particular position or orientation. *What other reason is there for writing than to be traitor to one's own reign, traitor to one's own sex, to one's class, to one's majority? And to be traitor to writing.*

Deleuze /
Parnet

Afraid of assertion. Always trying to get out of 'totalizing' language, i.e., language that rides roughshod over specificity; realizing this is another form of paranoia. Barthes found the exit to this merry-go-round by reminding himself that 'it is language which is assertive, not he.' It is absurd, Barthes says, to try to flee from language's assertive nature by 'add[ing] to each sentence some little phrase of uncertainty, as if anything that came out of language could make language tremble.'

My writing is riddled with such tics of uncertainty. I have no excuse or solution, save to allow myself the tremblings, then go back in later and slash them out. In this way I edit myself into a boldness that is neither native nor foreign to me.

At times I grow tired of this approach, and all its gendered baggage. Over the years I've had to train myself to wipe the *sorry* off almost every work e-mail I write; otherwise, each might begin, Sorry for the delay, Sorry for the confusion, Sorry for *whatever. One only has to read interviews with outstanding women to hear them apologizing.* But I don't intend to denigrate the power of apology: I keep in my *sorry* when I really mean it. And certainly there are many speakers whom I'd like to see do more trembling, more unknowing, more apologizing.

Monique
Wittig

FATEMEH SHAMS

Born 1983, Mashhad, Iran

Acid-Throwing

2016

How I wish it were possible that I could remove my
    face
and put it in place of your burned face
and then forever turn a mirror
toward you.

EILEEN MYLES

Born 1949, Boston, Massachusetts, United States of America

Acceptance Speech
2016

First I want to say this feels incredible. To be female, to run and run and run to not see any end in sight but maybe have a feeling that there's really no outside to this endeavor this beautiful thing. You know we don't have a single female on any of our bills. And what about two women, two women loving. Or even more. A lot of women. A lot of money. Is there a message that I failed to receive that the face of woman cannot be on our money. And what about that house I just won. that white one. When I sit there and if I sit there and I've got to tell you I'm not sure I want to sit there. Some of you might remember my first campaign yes that was back in 1992. Few men have run for twenty-four years. Twenty-five by the time I stand and take the oath in January to serve my country. I did not quit I stand here with you on this beautiful rapturous day sunny day in New York to turn around, to look back and look at all that we've won. But I'm getting ahead of myself. Let's get back to that house. That white house. We often hear these words even as an explanation of what metonym means. Are you familiar with this term. Yes I promise you poetic presidency. The white house speaks is a metonym. Certainly that white house we speak of is not the whole government. Like Fred Moten says it is incomplete. But it has come to be a symbol of it. And I think two things. I think whiteness, I think of the whiteness of the house and I think of house-ness. It houses the government. Now that I have won it offers to house me now. I now officially make that white house a home-less shelter. It is a complete total disgrace that we have people without homes living on the streets of America. I have lived with them. Not for long periods of time but in the same way that I am the first president who knows what women feel because I am a woman, I am one, I have also eaten chicken with the homeless. I ate at the Bowery mission. Very rubbery, very chewy chicken. Those chicken were not happy when they lived and they are no happier being chewed on dead at the Bowery mission, and the chewers are not happy either, no. So here's the future good food at the white house for all the homeless in America. You know who the homeless are. They are military men and women. Who fought our pointless wars, who came home after each stupid greedy war we have waged and they got less. Is there a GI bill for veterans of Iraq and Afghanistan. I'm not sure but I don't think so. Can they buy a house. Who can buy a house. Under Myles they have bought the white house. That is my gift. The white house will house the mentally ill, out patiented during the great president Reagan, meaning he threw them out of the house, the mentally ill, thrown out of the American house, and the alcoholics who do not have free and abundant and available treatment? Cause this country breaks our hearts. We will habit them too. We will occupy all government buildings and memorials housing and holding and loving the homeless and the sick and the starving. We'll do what the statue says. you know liberty. We will take buildings and we will build buildings and our culture our new America will begin to live. Our government needs to be in the business of living not dying, what else is a government for. The government will become more departmental and take you in, you and your wonderful needs. We'll start with the Department of Women. Obviously to say women matter and do matter so much and a lot we need a distinct place in the government to specifically focus on female concerns which is parity mainly, reforming congress so that if America is increasingly diverse in a multitude of ways our congress must represent those groups percentage wise that's smart don't you think. So if most of the people in America are female so should be our government right. America is not a department store. We want to do more in our country than shop online and at the mall. Let's face it everyone is home shopping and yelling each other at their computers. The malls are falling apart. The malls are pretty much gone. Let them go. We want to make real departments for who we really are. Not shopping. We will be stalwart, we will be strong. Let's go. Let's go out. we are out there now. We are here on the highline. Yes.

That's the way it works under Myles. Early on I described a department of culture. We will have that. We will have art in America, not just the magazine, just for starters we will multiply the budget of the NEA by tenfold. We will bring back CETA, that was like an art workers program we had in the eighties but we will call it SEE THE . . . SEE THE . . . what I don't know. I just got elected, I haven't worked everything out but just think of the possibilities. SEE THE sky, SEE THE river over there, SEE THE Whitney, a lot of people will be walking around appreciating and we will pay them. There will also be the HEAR THE program, the SMELL THE program. That's probably what you're going to do early on with all those you know recovering veterans who don't have to live on the streets. Get them in on the SEE THE, SMELL THE, HEAR THE programs. We're going to massively fund libraries, open twenty-four hours, and they will not be filled with homeless people because they will have homes, so the libraries will be filled with people reading and watching movies, and going into the conversation rooms and having conversations and so on. All education will be free, trains will be free. Cars will eventually be banned. Cars are stupid. No more pumping oil, no more fracking. Everything will be driven by the sun, or else be plugged in electrically. Electric something. There'll be lots of free food. A lot of archery. Everyone will be a really good shot. We'll get good at aiming, intentions, not killing. Oh yeah and we'll send a lot of masseuses to Israel and Palestine. Everyone needs a good rub. No more pesticides, here, anywhere, lots of small farmers, an amazing number of stand up comedians, and lots of rehearsal spaces and available musical instruments and learning centers for people like myself who would like to play something, perhaps a guitar. Nobody would be unemployed. Everyone would be learning Spanish, or going to the sex center for a while having ejaculation contests, or just looking at porn for a while and going out into the yard and helping the farmers improve the crops. Just gardening. Helping the flowers. Distributing the flowers. SEE THE flowers. When in doubt always just being a SEE THE person for a while. There'll be a whole lot of people encouraging people to SEE THE. We want the SEE THE to thoroughly come back. There'd be an increase in public computers, like water, like air, have we stopped the oil and the fracking early enough to protect the water and air, we hope so but there will be a decrease in private computers with an enhanced desire to be here, exactly here where we are, which some would argue is there on the computer which of course would be allowed but being here would be cool, some people meditating, other people just walking around, smiling feeling good about themselves, living shamelessly and glad. Guns would be buried. Guns would be in museums and people would increasingly not want to go there. Gun museums would die. What was that all about. Money would become rare. I would have a radio show as your president and also I might be on television and also I just might want to talk to you. In the tradition of American Presidents like Fiorello LaGuardia the little Flower I would be president Edward Myles, the woman, changing my name, very often, would probably be good I would like that and I would write a new poem for you each week. I might just walk around saying it and eventually you would forget I was the president. I would go to the gym. There are people who like to manage things just like there are people who like to play cards and the managers would change often enough and they would keep the parks clean, America increasingly turning into one big park, one big festival of existence with unmarked toilets and nightly daily events and free surfing lessons and free boards, just put it back when you're done and a good bed for everyone, I just slept in the best bed last night and I slept on the plane sleep is great nobody would be short of sleep everyone would be well slept, chaotic and loving hearted and have all the time in the world to not kill, to love and be president everyone take your turn and dance. Dance now. I love my fellow citizens. It is good to win. Thank you. I feel like I had a bad dream last night that like the head of the FBI decided to steal the election by making shit up about me because I am female but that wasn't true and we are really here undeluded, un mucked up. Wide awake in America for once. See the see the see all of your fabulous beauty and your power and your hope. Thanks for your vote. And I love you so much thanks.

112

TRAMA DI TERRE

Founded in 1997, Imola, Bologna, Italy

Manifesto for a Migrant Feminism
2016

Male violence [against] women has no colour, no religion, no culture – it crosses all patriarchal societies because it needs to maintain the power imbalance between men and women. But there are forms of violence which are imported with migration, and affect mainly migrant women, putting their lives and bodies at stake, when they are not in a position where they can enforce their own rights.

Today we suffer the consequences of 'neutral' anti-racist policies which have been favouring cultural rights [over] women's rights, strengthening the patriarchate within some migrant communities. We need to defend secularism not only against Catholic fundamentalists but against every kind of interference in the public sphere and in women's self-determination by every religion in this country.

Interculturalism is an intricate process that has to be built day after day through dialogue and conflict as well. It may fail if we don't have a strong focus on the protection of women's rights and individual liberties. That's why we prefer talking about GENDER INTERCULTURALISM.

For migrant women the current immigration law [entails] a double black-mailing: it makes them more exploitable in labour, and it ties them down to their husbands' documents in case of family reunification. Therefore, for foreign women the residence permit can become an instrument of patriarchal control in the hands of violent employers and family members.

Women asylum-seekers and women refugees have survived many different forms of male violence – gender discrimination, domestic violence, traffic for sexual exploitation, difficult access to education and efficient social services, abuse related to traditional practices such as forced marriage (including early marriage), genital mutilations, corrective rape; situations which are exacerbated by the ever-increasing religious fundamentalism and by war.

Due to the absence of humanitarian corridors, migrants are forced to travel in a total lack of safety. Travelling poses an even greater risk for women, as they are exposed to systematic rape, also used as a blackmail to exploit them economically and sexually.

In transit and arrival countries, women find even more violence. In the absence of gender-sensitive policies, the public-funded so-called 'reception' centres (*centri d'accoglienza*) are often the scene of sexist abuse, while outside these centres, in addition to the growing race/gender intersectional discrimination, there is the institutional violence of economic and social policies which are strengthening poverty and inequality and therefore affecting migrant women's lives in a double way.

In the current context of daily episodes of sexist and racist violence, it becomes more important; reporting the abuse suffered by migrant women and women asylum-seekers, and supporting them in the realization of their life projects. Therefore, we call to fight for a new Migrant Feminism, taking into account the class/status differences which affect deeply women's possibility of self-determination, and fighting against the rising fundamentalism and fascism.

113

MARIA ALYOKHINA

Born 1988, Moscow, USSR

from *Riot Days*

2017

let's go

The time came. The church was 200 meters away. Or 300. Me in my Cossack hat, the girls in Orthodox headscarves – we walked towards the church as if we were floating. The entrance loomed up ahead.

> *'To secure unhindered entry into the place of worship, the accused wore clothes fully in keeping with the requirements of such places of worship; thus, under the guise of ordinary visitors, they entered the church.'*

An empty square in front of the church. There are no beggars. I don't think the beggars were against sitting there, but the propriety of the church wouldn't allow them.

church for the wealthy

Amid the clicks of cameras, tourists taking photos, we approached the iron gates of the metal detector.

'Put your backpacks on the table and open them, girls.' The morning faces of the guards are fatigued and lazy. I open my backpack.

One by one.

How do you smuggle an electric guitar into a secured tourist site? We had tried out various methods over the course of the previous month. First, the guards had demanded that I leave the guitar – in the case or out – under the window by the entrance. Then we decided to try out an enormous hiking backpack and a man who spoke perfect English, smuggling the guitar inside the church with the help of both.

'Knives?'

'No.'

'Proceed.'

everything, but the knives

I close my backpack without glancing up and go in. The main thing is that they don't find the guitar. Petya had the guitar.

'Young man! Wait a moment.'

In our plan, Petya was the foreigner, the man who spoke perfect English.

'What's in your backpack?'

'Nothing special,' he answered in English.

Usually, Russian security guards get completely flustered by charming foreigners. It worked. The amp was also in that backpack.

nothing special

We left the cold weather outside the church. It was 11 a.m. The cathedral was nearly empty, except for people in green uniforms tending the devotional candles.

'We have to act like ordinary girls in church.'

What do ordinary girls do in church?

'No idea.'

We decided to go up to one of the women tending the candles and ask where it would be best to light one.

'Where can we place our candles?'

While she explained the procedure for lighting our candles, which we didn't in fact have, I looked behind her and saw the low barrier surrounding the altar and the green carpet leading towards the altar gates.

The carpet is the same colour as her uniform, I thought.

'Thank you,' Nadya said.

green carpet to the altar

We walked around the edge of the church and reached a corner. The guards seemed alarmed. There was no time to lose.

We went up to the low barrier guarding the altar. Katya was the first to hop over. Because she's Katya. She just hops over and she's off. Nadya hopped after her, and then everyone else followed. I thought, I'm wearing this uncomfortable coat that weighs a ton, I'm going to get stuck on something, I'll fall and bring the whole barrier down – it's an accident waiting to happen. How am I going to jump around in this heavy thing? It is long, almost to my ankles. Why the hell did I wear this damn thing to an action? What was I thinking, – putting it on at a time like this?

And then I hopped over, too. I was the last one to jump, just as the candle-tender was running up to me looking a bit freaked out.

'The careful planning and coordinated actions of the performance allowed the group to carry out their criminal intentions in their entirety.'

We needed to plug the guitar into the amp. Katya was responsible for that, for the guitar. She threw off her outer clothing and started taking the guitar out of the case. The security guards considered this to be particularly non-Orthodox.

the guitar is an un-orthodox instrument

'Ms Samutsevich, carrying out her criminal role, with the knowledge and assent of all the participants, took out an electric guitar.'

621

The security guards grabbed Katya. She managed to distract them all, and this bought us 40 seconds to do our performance. 40 seconds of crime.

40 seconds

'what was the music like?'
'goodness me, I don't know how to describe it'
'was it church music?'
'no, certainly not!'
'you mean to say it was not church music?'
'absolutely not'
'what did the instrument sound like?'
*'I don't know what to compare it to, but it wasn't at all
Orthodox'*
'what are Orthodox sounds'
'I can't answer that!'

judge: 'you are obliged to answer the question'

We scramble up the stairs towards the altar, dropping our backpacks by the Holy Gates. They symbolize the gates to heaven. Women are only allowed to stand on the green walkway before the gates – the soleas – if they are cleaning women. Or brides. In Russia, there are no women priests. In Russia, there is Pussy Riot.

We shed our clothes. The outer layers.

We put on our balaclavas.

'Alyokhina was wearing a blue mask. She wore a dress that was somewhere between pink and red, green tights, and a bra that was falling from her shoulders.'

I remember: I open my mouth to sing and everything around me – the whole church – seems to freeze. It is motionless. The sound dies away.

There is only the echo of our uncoordinated screaming and shouting. Too many eyes on the icons.

time stood still

The security guards try to catch us.

'Alyokhina's dress was longer than the others', and she had to kick her legs higher.'

It looked like some bizarre folk dance: he runs up to you, you run backwards; he runs again, you run in a different direction.

'Voice answered voice; word answered word,'
the candle-tender said during the trial.

Almost a compliment.
It was the most absurd prayer.

'We tried to get them off the ambo. They wouldn't leave, they resisted and ran back up again, then fell to their knees and started crossing themselves. This was humiliating and offensive to me.'

Two men take my hands and lead me to the exit. The balaclava slips sideways and restricts my breathing. It's unclear who is leading whom. The church is still frozen, until one small figure, an old woman, starts to move. She screams, 'Girls! Girls! What are you doing? You're ruining yourselves!' We kept walking, and I thought, What, am I now ruining myself?
They took us to the exit and let us go.

We stood there, looking at the street.
Not a single police car. Katya was waiting for us by the entrance.
We started to run. And I thought, Where are we running to?

Why are we running, if there's no one after us?
Who are we running from?
Why can't we just walk to wherever we're going?
The security guards stayed on the job. There were no cops in sight.

why are we running?

Why are we running, then?

114

DEBORAH LEVY

Born 1959, Johannesburg, South Africa

from *The Cost of Living*
2018

There is a photograph I have kept of my mother in her late twenties. She is sitting on a rock at a picnic with friends. Her hair is wet because she's just had a swim. There is a kind of introspection in her expression that I now relate to the very best of her. I can see that she is close to herself in this random moment. I'm not sure that I thought introspection was the best of her when I was a child and teenager. What do we need dreamy mothers for? We do not want mothers who gaze beyond us, longing to be elsewhere. We need her to be of this world, lively, capable, entirely present to our needs.

Did I mock the dreamer in my mother and then insult her for having no dreams?

As the vintage story goes, it is the father who is the hero and the dreamer. He detaches himself from the pitiful needs of his women and children and strides out into the world to do his thing. He is expected to be himself. When he returns to the home that our mothers have made for us, he is either welcomed back into the fold, or becomes a stranger who will eventually need us more than we need him. He tells us some of what he has seen in his world. We give him an edited version of the living we do every day our mothers live with us in this living and we blame her for everything because she is near by. At the same time, we try not to collude with myths about her character and purpose in life. All the same, we need her to feel anxiety on our behalf – after all, our everyday living is full of anxiety. If we do not disclose our feelings to her, we mysteriously expect her to understand them anyway. And if she moves beyond us, comes close to being a self that is not at our service, she has transgressed from the mythic, primal task of being our protector and nurturer. Yet, if she comes too close, she suffocates us, infecting our fragile courage with her contagious anxiety. When our father does the things he needs to do in the world, we understand it is his due. If our mother does the things she needs to do in the world, we feel she has abandoned us. It is a miracle she survives our mixed messages, written in society's most poisoned ink. It is enough to drive her mad.

> I believe that always, or almost always, in all childhoods and in all the lives that follow them, the mother represents madness. Our mothers always remain the strangest, craziest people we've ever met.
>
> Marguerite Duras, *Practicalities*

When I was a teenager, most arguments with my mother were about clothes. She was baffled by what it was inside myself that I was expressing outside of myself. She could no longer reach or recognize me. And that was the whole point. I was creating a persona that was braver than I actually felt. I took the risk of being mocked on buses and in the streets of the suburbs in which I lived. The secret message that lurked in the zips of my silver platform boots was that I did not want to be like the people doing the mocking. Sometimes we want to unbelong as much as we want to belong. On a bad day, my mother would ask me, 'Who do you think you are?' I had no idea how to answer that question when I was fifteen, but I was reaching for the kind of freedom that a young woman in the 1970s did not socially possess. What else was there to do? To become the person someone else had imagined for us is not freedom – it is to mortgage our life to someone else's fear.

If we cannot at least imagine we are free, we are living a life that is wrong for us.

My mother was braver in her life than I have ever been. She escaped from the upper-class WASP family she loved and married a penniless Jewish historian. She became involved with him in the struggle for human rights in the South Africa of her generation. Clever, glamorous and witty, she never made it to university in her early twenties. No one thought it necessary to tell her she had an abundance of talent. Women of her class were expected to marry as soon as they left home, or after their first job. This was supposed to be a nominal job and not a serious career. My mother was taught to type, to learn shorthand and to wear clothes that pleased her male bosses. She wished she had been a less skilled secretary, but it was her fast typing that fed and clothed her children when my father became a political prisoner. She gave me a hard time, beyond the call of a dutiful daughter, but I can now see that I did not want to let her be herself, for better or worse.

A year after I moved with my daughters into the apartment on the hill, my mother became fatally sick. I lay awake all night waiting for a call from the hospital, each hour marked by the call of the various birds on my bird clock. The nightingale sang just before midnight, as if it were perched in the boughs of the dripping tree in the car park. She always said that when she died, she wanted her body to be carried to the peak of a mountain and then devoured by birds.

In the last few weeks of her dying, she was unable to eat or to drink water. However, I discovered that she was able to lick and swallow a particular brand of ice lolly. It came in three flavours – lime was her favourite, then strawberry, last of all the dreaded orange. Winter was not the best time for this particular ice lolly to be stocked in the shops, but I had found a supply of them in the freezer of my local newsagent, owned by three Turkish brothers. They often sold mushrooms in a box that was placed on the lid of this long, low freezer, which was positioned in the middle of the shop. Also placed on its lid were lottery tickets, reduced-price cleaning products, cans of fizzy drinks, shoe polish, batteries and pastries. Inside this freezer were the ice lollies that were my mother's only comfort during her dying. At the time I was so devastated from my shipwrecked marriage and my mother's diagnosis of cancer, both happening within a year of each other, I was unable to explain to the brothers why I bought ice lollies every day in February. I arrived grim-faced, eyes always wet, my bicycle parked outside. Without saying a single word, I began to move the mushrooms, lottery tickets, reduced-price cleaning products, cans of fizzy drinks, shoe polish, batteries and pastries to one side of the freezer. Then I'd slide the door open and search for the lollies – triumphant when I found the lime, good if I found strawberry, acceptable when I found the orange. I'd always buy two and then cycle to the hospital down the hill where my mother was dying.

*

I would sit by her bed and hold the ice lolly to her lips, pleased to hear her ooh and aah with pleasure. She was always insatiably thirsty. There was a fridge in her room but not a freezer, so the second lolly would melt, but my ritual was to always buy two. Looking back on this, I don't know why I didn't buy all the lollies in the newsagent and put them in my own freezer, but somehow it never occurred to me at this difficult time. And then one day, a terrible thing happened in the lolly scheme of things. As usual, I cycled to the newsagent, whooshed everything that was resting on the lid of the freezer aside, and, watched by the baffled Turkish brothers, slid open the freezer door. It turned out there was a fourth flavor. The brothers had run out of lime, strawberry and even the dreaded orange. I looked up from the freezer, straight into the kind brown eyes of the youngest brother.

'Why have you only got bubblegum flavor?' I started to shout – why would anyone bother to make a bubblegum ice lolly, never mind sell it? What was the point and could they urgently stock up on the other flavours, particularly the lime?

The brother did not shout back. He just stood in baffled silence while I angrily purchased two bubblegum-flavoured lollies. It felt like a catastrophe as I cycled to the hospital, and actually it was a catastrophe because they were more or less the only things keeping her alive for another day.

I tried a few other shops on the way to the hospital, but none of them stocked the brand that was easy to swallow. So I sat by my skeletal mother's bed, unwrapped the bubblegum ice lolly and moved it to her lips. She licked it, grimaced, tried it again and then shook her head. When I told her how I had raved and ranted like a lunatic in the shop, these tiny sounds came out of her mouth, her chest moving up and down. I knew she was laughing and it is one of my favourite memories of our last days together. That night when I was reading a book by her bed, I glanced in remorse at the bubblegum lolly melting into a pink blob in the basin. I wasn't really reading, just skimming the page, but it was comforting to be near her. When the doctor came into the room to do her last rounds, my mother lifted her thin hand and somehow managed to make the tiny voice she had at this time sound imperious and commanding: 'Arrange for some light. My daughter is reading in the dark.'

[. . .]

When a woman has to find a new way of living and breaks from the societal story that has erased her name, she is expected to be viciously self-hating, crazed with suffering, tearful with remorse. These are the jewels reserved for her in the patriarchy's crown, always there for the taking. There are plenty of tears, but it is better to walk through the black and bluish darkness than reach for those worthless jewels.

115

EILEEN MYLES

Born 1949, Boston, Massachusetts, United States of America

Transmission

2018

I'm overcome
by the cruelty
of nature
no I mean
I'm with
it. And each little capacity
it has
can't be transferred
I mean
a spruce
can't give
its oils to you
can it.
But that's how
it grows
in the ab
sence of
technology
my thoughts
grow. My thoughts
grow among
trees
but I don't
help them
though

I'm for them.
I'm for my
dog & inci
dentally
I feed
her but I
don't see
her much.
Joe does.
Joe is
my friend
& also
a dog father
I don't
help mountains
Mountains
help me
I know
the planet
is old
& splashy
Sleep helps
me. Time
helps
me. My mother
helped
me. And
now she
is gone. She
also hurt
me so it's
good that
she's gone.
I can grow
different
in the

day or
three decades
in which
I've got
left
I can
grow towards
the mountains
sit in solidarity
with prisoners
or go
to jail. I'm not joking
I can
push different
I want
to say
something
about my cunt.
Because
That's
what you
ask. But
I am
alone. No
mother
no phone
just a notebook
& a cunt
& my thoughts.
I don't
even think
my thoughts.
you do.

116.

LOLA OLUFEMI

Born 1996, London, United Kingdom

from *Feminism, Interrupted*
The answer to sexual violence is not more prisons

2020

For example, in what sense could we produce knowledge about women in prison? . . . This is not merely a question about how we have to rethink knowledge but about how we rethink an abolitionist politics that start from the position of those women on the underside of capital but does not put them in another cage. – Gina Dent *

'Upskirting', the practice of taking unauthorised photographs under a person's clothing without their permission, became a criminal offence punishable by up to two years in prison on 12 April 2019. Spearheaded by Gina Martin, the campaign to introduce the bill focused heavily on the 'no-brainer' nature of criminalising this offence. Gina tells the story of having indecent images taken of her at a festival and calling the police, only to be told that, as the act was not a criminal offence, nothing could be done. She did the first thing that many of us are taught to do when things go wrong – turn to the police. Everything about the world we live in tells us that the police are there to protect us and prisons force the criminal to reflect on their actions, deter them from committing other crimes and remind them that nobody is above the law. Here, the wrong-doer, the thief, the rapist, the abuser *deserves* punishment – deserves to experience the pain and suffering that they have put others through. But what about the woman with insecure immigration status for whom calling

---

* Angela Davis and Gina Dent, 'Prison as a Border: A conversation on Gender, Globalisation and Punishment,' *Signs 26*, no. 4 (summer):1235–42.

the police might mean deportation? What about the women from communities for whom police presence has meant the unexplained deaths in custody of their family members? What about sex workers who face sexual violence and harassment from police officers themselves? Realising that the police and law enforcement do not equal safety for everyone is the first step to rethinking ideas about justice.

The idea that justice is served when criminals go to prison is relatively new. In the sixteenth and seventeenth century, 'criminals' were punished using public tools of humiliation, which including whipping, the ducking stool and the pillory. They were killed in public executions. Ironically, prisons were introduced in order to make punishment more 'humane'. They were popularised in the eighteenth century and rarely used; some convicts were shipped to British colonies and required to perform hard labour.* The history of prisons is inseparable from the history of British imperial endeavour. Because of the increased securitisation of our everyday lives, it can seem like prisons and the police have existed forever. We see adverts to join the police force on the London Underground; we see police officers roaming the streets. We learn about the police force in school, and in popular media. Their presence subtly reaffirms the importance of their role in maintaining order. But order for whom and at what cost?

Any mother, sister, aunt, cousin, friend who has lost someone to the prison system knows that prisons eat people up. People are removed from society and subjected to inhumane conditions, stifling any chance for them to reintegrate into society once they have been released – countless studies prove that many ex-prisoners go on to re-offend due to lack of employment, housing and social prospects. But the idea that prisons equal justice and that the law is fairly applied is so insidious that mainstream feminist movements turn to these forces as a response to sexual and gendered violence. If we can only imagine justice being served in one way, then carceral responses to sexual violence seem like common sense. The logic is as follows: if we make a law about it, the problem will go away or at the very least, the frequency of the problem will decrease because criminals will know that they can no longer get away with it. But the problem with sexual violence is that no amount of retribution can stem the consequences of an

* https://howardleague.org/history-of-the-penal-system (last accessed 05/2019).

invasion of bodily autonomy. We know that the majority of rapists in the world are not in prison, nor will they ever be. They are walking among us, they are our family members, our friends, they hold government positions; they make the laws they claim will hold others to account.

Whether or not prison brings peace of mind to individual victims, it does not prevent that same violence from being enacted on somebody else. Prison provides an individualistic response to harm – it locates the problem in the body of the 'bad' person rather than connecting patterns of harm to the conditions in which we live. A feminist conceptualisation of justice recognises that the world is organised in ways that expose some women to disproportionate levels of violence. Ironically, the more that liberal feminists invite law enforcement into our homes, schools and civic life looking for protection, the more we place women on the margins (poor, black, trans, disabled) in danger. The majority of women in prison have been victims of domestic violence.* Many reported committing crimes in order to support their abusive partner's drug habits and being trapped in abusive relationships. Criminalising domestic violence means more women in prison. Criminalising sex work means more women in prison. Criminalising drug use means more women in prison – more vulnerable women who fall through the cracks. In 2017, TV licence evasion was the most common offence for which women were convicted, the crime accounts for 30 per cent of all 'female' prosecutions.† Women are being sent to prison for things as arbitrary as being unable to repay fines.

But it's not enough to argue that because the 'wrong' kind of people end up in prison we should rethink it. We must rethink the prison system and work to abolish it because feminism demands the abolition of systems and structures that make it impossible for us to live collectively. Prison obscures the causes of social ills; it sweeps violence under the rug and affirms the idea that it is inevitable. In a society that produces 'criminals', we all bear responsibility for transforming the structures that make this label possible.

---

* www.prisonreformtrust.org.uk/PressPolicy/News/vw/1/ItemID/494 (last accessed 05/2019).
† www.refinery29.com/en-gb/2019/07/237240/tv-licence-evasion-women (last accessed 09/2019).

Getting to the root

In 2017, it was estimated that 20 per cent of women in the UK experienced some type of assault, attempted rape happened roughly 11 times every hour and that 90 per cent of those who were raped knew the perpetrator prior to the offence.* No amount of legislation or prison sentences can undo the idea that takes root in every young girl's mind as soon as she recognises that she is vulnerable: *I am not safe*. Prisons do nothing for women clutching their keys in the dark on their way home. Surely, a feminist future is one without the need to protect ourselves from harm. A feminist future is a future without sexual violence of any kind. Getting there requires us to stop considering solutions to harm after it has happened and instead turn our attention to thinking about how to prevent harm.

In the UK, the majority of known instances of sexual harassment, assault and rape are carried out by men against women.† Anyone who refuses to naturalise aggression, domination and violence in men's bodies, understands that these traits have more to do with enforcement of gender as a system than individual action. Gendered violence is a systemic problem that requires a collective response. It is crucial that we disrupt normative masculinity and the systems it is predicated on before they become cemented in the bodies of individuals. There are a number of ways men might be held accountable, ones that recognise the failure of punitive solutions to change cycles of violence. By refusing to pathologise men's behaviour, feminist responses can also recognise that anybody is capable of harm; the perpetration of sexual violence is not exclusive to men. Oppressive ideas of sex and sexuality come to define every single one of our interactions, no matter who we are.

Carceral responses to sexual violence fail to address the root causes of the problem. Putting an offender in jail does nothing to reshape the logic of sexual and gendered violence, nor does it signal that the act itself was

---

* https://rapecrisis.org.uk/get-informed/about-sexual-violence/statistics-sexual-violence (last accessed 05/2019).
† www.ons.gov.uk/aboutus/transparencyandgovernance/freedomofinformationfoi/ rapestatisticsbygenderofvictimandperpetrator (last accessed 05/2019).

an injustice. Simply criminalising sexual offences will not bring about the wholesale transformation of society that feminism seeks. It simply pushes out the undesirables, filters them from society and then reintroduces them without the means or resources to stop them reoffending.

Abolition feminism

When we speak of prison abolition, the fear of a world without order springs to mind. The idea is that without prisons, without institutions that enforce law and order, there would be no way of keeping us safe. But the logic of prison abolition asks us to interrogate who 'we' are and why we place our safety in opposition to those we imagine place us in danger. Who are *they*? The 'bad' people who become defined by their criminality or the violence they have enacted and can never escape it? Why is it easier to organise a society around the idea that some people deserve to be disappeared into the prison system, while others deserve freedom and the ability to live, work and build a life? The idea that prisons keep those on the outside 'safe' presupposes that they are effective in catching 'bad guys' and putting them away. A belief in prisons presupposes that they are racially neutral, efficient deterrents – that they help rehabilitate criminals and put right the injustice suffered by victims.

Developed by leading pioneers, activists and scholars including Angela Davis, Gina Dent and Ruth Gilmore, abolition feminism asks us to focus on the root causes of the problems that plague our society. Abolition feminism is a feminist theory and practice that seeks a world beyond prisons, offering grassroots solutions to the problems of racism, inadequate mental health support, domestic violence and organising for economic, racial and gender justice. Abolition feminism recognises the harm that prisons do, and how they lead to unnecessary and unavoidable death. It does not trust the state to deliver us justice. Instead of being preoccupied with the question of reform, it cuts right through to the heart of violence. It organises to build a world where prisons are not necessary. This means tackling the issues that put people in prison in the first place: racism, borders, drug use, petty fines. It argues for culturally competent, fully funded mental health services where they were most needed and for decriminalisation of sex work and drug use. It trains mental health professionals and community members to intervene in violent situations and deescalate them before a 'crime' is committed. It is attentive to the concerns of communities, seeking to expand benefit, housing, social services, healthcare and education systems, engaging in political education and instilling a radical feminist ethos into every single person that comes into our care and protection. It campaigns against prison expansion, stop and search and mandatory conviction targets, fights the gutting of vital youth services, as well as overt and covert methods of criminalisation.

Abolition begins with an end to prison expansion, a fight against the privatisation of prisons and the immediate release of all political prisoners. Abolition feminism begins at home – it resists the desire to catastrophise (*what do we do with all the murderers?*) and realises that murder is not only uncommon in many contexts but is also entirely avoidable. It focuses on how we might create the conditions to transform the relations that cause crime in the first place. It asks us to identify the areas where our communities are sick and suffering and to propose solutions that do not involve detention, restriction, sectioning, policing. It asks us not to call 999 on somebody who is vulnerable and could be helped in another way and recognises that prisons merely wrap dirty gauze around dirty wounds; they reinfect our society every moment they stay open.

Prison expansion

In November 2016, the British government released a white paper that stated its commitment to create 10,000 new prison places, through the construction of six megaprisons and five new 'residential centres' for women. Corporate Watch stated that five of those were to be completed by 2020. Despite the government abandoning some of these plans, it remains vital to explore how women offenders and victims are mobilised in debates around prison expansion. Gender has become central to the justification of the building and expansion of our Prison Island. There are reports that the Scottish government is considering building a new prison to hold non-binary people in order to '[increase] the protections against discrimination on the basis of a person's gender identity.'*

While this plan may appear to some a sensitive move on the part of the government to respond to conversations about gender in society, for critical feminists, it provides further justification to divorce feminism from the state apparatus and put forward a new vision for what justice could look like. There is no such thing as a socially conscious prison. Prisons are by their very nature, oppressive. The things that we care about – sexual assault, rape, domestic violence – are used by the state to justify harsher prison sentences and the expansion of the prison industrial complex around the world. The advocates of this expansion do not care about ending violence; they care about prisons as for-profit entities and as places where the labour of prisoners can be exploited. If we know that the existence of prisons has no real impact on rates for reoffending, that abuse, self-harm and suicide are rife in prisons† and that, in the cases of sexual assault and rape, individuals are very unlikely to go to prison in the first place, it becomes clear that the safety that carceral thinking sells us is a lie.

Feminists fight back

In 2017, Sisters Uncut occupied the Visitors Centre of Holloway Prison and held a week long festival of community events to highlight the potential of the space to be used as a vehicle for community building and care. When they occupied Holloway, they did not know what the space could be, but they entered with the hope of reclamation. A member of Sisters Uncut told me:

> We wanted to show that safe spaces for the community are needed for our learning, healing, and support. That it's possible to create a transformative space even in a place so historically saturated in violence . . . During the occupation, the whole space was decorated with home-made bunting and

* https://corporatewatch.org/new-non-binary-prison-in-scotland (last accessed 05/2019).
† www.guardian.com/society/2019/jan/31/prison-figures-reveal-rise-in-deaths-assaults-and-self-harm (last accessed 05/2019).

curtains, tablecloths, cushions with slogans 'CARE NOT CAGES', and 'SAFETY IS A RIGHT' knitted onto the covers, and a pink banner that said 'This is a political occupation' in sparkling letters. Much of the decor was purple and green, the Sisters colours. Not just the physical space, but the whole atmosphere was transformed. The smell of delicious food being cooked throughout the day, sitting and eating meals together, painting each other's nails or drawing and craft-making with the kids; it was no doubt a very different vibe from the old visitors centre.

The work of reclaiming the space did not end when the festival ended. Sisters Uncut are calling for private property developers that now own the land that the prison is built on to commit to building genuinely affordable housing and a women's building after its demolition. Sisters Uncut oppose prisons in disguise, so-called 'residential women's centres' funded by the state that seek to put a glossier face on incarceration. They want the site of the largest women's prison in Europe, to become something else – another place for women to come together.

We are trying to arrange meetings with Peabody, who own the land now, to find out what their plans are so far for the women's centre and to present them with our own plans of our vision for the space . . . I am worried about Peabody's interpretation of 'women's centre', and hope that we can apply pressure both as local community stakeholders through building that relationship with Peabody and also publicly, by writing articles and creating media around the site with actions and demos . . . In June 2018, the MOJ announced that they were 'scrapping' plans to build 5 women's prisons. However, with this same announcement came one instead about opening 5 'residential centres'. While we don't have much information on the location of these new centres or how they will be run, a project that is still run and funded by the MOJ and within a system wherein vulnerable people are criminalised before being provided with support services does nothing to dismantle the framework of criminal justice and punishment.

Activist efforts are also at risk of being co-opted by the state. Prisons under another name do not spell freedom. In the UK, groups like Empty

Cages, CAPE, Women in Prison and INQUEST have furthered the fight for prison abolition. They spread information, skill share and work directly with communities affected by the prison industrial complex in the UK. They expose the increasingly privatised nature of the prison industry, the prevalence of the school to prison pipeline, and the fact that the UK has the most privatised prison system in Europe, with 11.6 per cent of the total prison population being held in a private prison.* But prison as a profit-making endeavour is not new – state-owned prisons have always been moneymakers. Private companies provide the food and maintenance services that keep prisons going. There are 14 private prisons in the UK, which hold one fifth of all UK prisoners and are run by three companies: G4S Justice Services, SodexoJustice Services and Serco Custodial Services. Private prisons mean that corporations can generate profit from those in prisons, putting them to work to produce goods that can be bought and sold on the outside. This bolsters the intricate systems, networks and relationships between prisons, the police, the probation service, courts and all of the companies that profit from the movement and containment of individuals.

If corporations can make money from prisoners, then incarceration is just another mode through which the logic of capital structures the way society is ordered. This for-profit motive is aided by globalisation: private companies build prisons around the world, reproducing colonial era style methods of extraction and labour production. There are American owned prisons in Australia, Kenya and South Africa. Perhaps the most dangerous part of prison is the fact that we do not really know what happens on the inside. Whether prisoners' labour is exploited or not, whether they are left with little to do to stimulate their mind or aid the process of 'rehabilitation' – prisons are a private endeavour; they seek to isolate and insulate. They cut off connection.

Feminism and transformative justice

The principles of transformative justice offer us a challenge. Instead of relying on the law, prison and police to rectify the harm committed by an

* www.prisonabolition.org/what-is-the-prison-industrial-complex (last accessed 05/2019).

individual, we undergo a process of community accountability. A group of friends, a church, an organisation come together and design a process to hold an individual to account without sending them away. This process might look like: community service, reflective practice, reaffirming commitment to values and practices, meditation, finding methods to cope with rage and shame, therapy, mental health support and trauma-centred programmes designed to identify the root causes of behaviour. In the case of sexual violence, often the criminal justice system can re-traumatise victims, asking them to rehash evidence of the violence inflicted upon them, subjecting them to cross-examination and to the scrutiny of the public.

A transformative justice approach would not only be attentive to the needs of survivors and victims, it would lift the burden of proof that lay with them. What transformative justice offers, is the specificity that rectifying instances of harm may require. It is not a broad-brush approach but rather a tailor-made process designed for specific individuals. Perhaps one of the most chilling realisations is that for some offences, there can be no adequate punishment. No punishment can completely undo the multi-layered consequences of harm – so crafting methods of harm reduction and prevention is not only a feminist response to crime; it is the only response that does not reproduce the violence it seeks to eradicate. When prison abolition is referred to as 'utopian' it signals to the public imagination that we do not currently possess the resources to make that vision a reality. Not only is this untrue, it stifles our ability to take the necessary steps towards prison abolition. Across the world, activist groups are preventing the building of new prisons and forging links between those on the inside and those on the outside. Abolitionist work is happening all around us, we only have to look for it.

Justice means everyone. If feminist work is justice work, it must be able to stand up to the complexities of our lives. We are too messy to be divided into 'good' and 'bad' people, the former deserving of freedom and the latter deserving of cruelty. Feminism seeks to give us back the ability to care and relate to one another in ways we have yet to imagine. Feminism responds to urgency, and prisons pose one of the most urgent questions of our time: What kind of world would we like to live in?

Permissions Credits

We are grateful to the following for permission to reproduce copyright material:

Alice Walker for an epigraph from *The Color Purple*, Phoenix, 1983. Reproduced by permission of David Higham Associates.

Christine de Pizan for an extract on from *The Book of the City of Ladies*, translated by Rosalind Brown-Gran, Penguin Classics, copyright © 1999 by Rosalind Brown-Gran. Reprinted with permission of Penguin Books Limited.

Olympe de Gouges for an extract from 'Declaration of the Rights of Woman' from *Women in Revolutionary Paris, 1789-1795: Selected Documents, Translated with Notes and Commentary*, edited and translated by Darline Gay Levy, Harriet Branson Applewhite, and Mary Durham Johnson, University of Illinois Press, 1980, pp.87-96, copyright © 1979 by the Board of Trustees of the University of Illinois. Used with permission of the University of Illinois Press.

Tarabai Shinde for extracts from *A Comparison Between Women and Men: Tarabai Shinde and the Critique of Gender Relations in Colonial India*, translated by Rosalind O'Hanlon, copyright © 1994 by Oxford University Press. Reproduced with permission of Oxford University Press India.

Kishida Toshiko for 'Daughters in Boxes' from *In The Modern Murasaki: Writing by Women of Meiji Japan*, translated Rebecca L. Copeland and Aiko Okamoto MacPhail, Columbia University Press, 2006, pp.62-71, copyright © 2006. Reproduced with permission of the publisher.

Francisca Senjorinha da Motta Diniz for 'Equality of Rights' from *Emancipating the Female Sex: The Struggle for Women's Rights in Brazil, 1850-1940*, translated June Edith Hahner. Duke University Press, 1990.

Permissions Credits

Chia-lin Pao Tao for 'A Song: Promoting Women's Rights', from *Waiting for the Unicorn: Poems and Lyrics of China's Last Dynasty, 1644-1911*, translated by Chia-lin Pao Tao, edited by Irving Yucheng Lo and William Schultz. Bloomington, IN: Indiana University Press, 1986, 400-401. Reprinted with permission.

Nadezhda Teffi for an extract from the play 'The Woman Question' from *An Anthology of Russian Women's Writing 1777-1992*, translated and edited by Catriona Kelly, Oxford University Press 1994, pp.175-180. Selection, translations and editorial material © 1994 by Catriona Kelly. Reproduced with permission of the Licensor through PLSclear.

Rosa Luxemburg for 'Women's Suffrage and Class Struggle' from 'Selected Political Writings of Rosa Luxemburgs' translated by Rosmarie Waldrop, *Monthly Review Press*, 1971, pp.216-222. Reproduced with permission of the publisher and conveyed through Copyright Clearance Center.

Anna Akhmatova for the poem 'Sister I have Come to Take Your Place' from *An Anthology of Russian Women's Writing 1777-1992*, translated and edited by Catriona Kelly, Oxford University Press, 1994. Selection, translations and editorial material © 1994 by Catriona Kelly. Reproduced with permission of the Licensor through PLSclear.

A. Alexandra Kollontai for extracts from 'Sexual Relations and the Class Struggle' and 'The Labour of Women in the Evolution of the Economy' from *Selected Writings*, translated by Alix Holt, Allison & Busby, copyright © 1977. Reproduced with permission of the Susan Schulman Literary Agency LLC.

Rakhshanda Jalil for 'Man and Woman' from *A Rebel and Her Cause the Life and Work of Rashid Jahan*, first published in India in 2014 by Women Unlimited in association with Indira Gandhi National Centre for the Arts, pp.160-165. Reproduced with permission.

Ding Ling for 'Thoughts on March 8' from *I Myself am a Woman. Selected Writings of Ding Ling*, ed. Tani Barlow with Gary J Borge, Beacon Press, 1989. Permission conveyed through Copyright Clearance Center, Inc.

Huda Shaarawi for an extract from 'Pan-Arab Feminism', in *Opening the Gates*, 2nd ed, Indiana University Press, 2004. Reproduced with permission of the publisher and conveyed through Copyright Clearance Center.

Permissions Credits

Claudia Jones for 'An End to the Neglect of the Problems of the Negro Women', originally published in *Political Affairs*, June 1949, National Women's Commission, C.P.U.S.A. Reproduced with permission of International Publishers.

Susan Sontag for extracts from *Reborn*, Penguin, copyright © 2008, The Estate of Susan Sontag. Preface copyright © 2008 by David Rieff. Reproduced with permission of Penguin Books Limited.

Doris Lessing for an extract from *The Golden Notebook*, Fourth Estate, 2013, copyright © 1962, 1972 by Doris Lessing. Reproduced with permission of HarperCollins Publishers Ltd.

Sylvia Plath for the poem 'Daddy' published in *Collected Poems of Sylvia Plath, Faber & Faber Ltd*, copyright © 1960, 1965, 1971, 1981 by the Estate of Sylvia Plath. Reproduced with permission of the publisher.

Betty Friedan for *The Feminine Mystique*, copyright © 1963 by Betty Friedan. Reproduced with permission of The Orion Publishing Group, London and Curtis Brown, Ltd. All rights reserved.

Shulamith Firestone for an extract from *The Dialectic of Sex*, Verso, 2015, copyright © Shulamith Firestone, 1970, 2015. Reproduced with permission of the publisher.

Germaine Greer for an extract from *The Female Eunuch*, HarperCollins, copyright © 1970, 1971 by Germaine Greer. Reproduced with permission of HarperCollins Publishers Ltd.

Alice Walker for the poem '"Women of Colour" have Rarely Had the Opportunity to Write About Their Love Affairs' from *Collected Poems*, The Women's Press, 1991. Reproduced with permission of David Higham Associates.

Audre Lorde for the poems 'Who Said it was Simple' and 'Love Poem' from *The Collected Poems of Audre Lorde*, WW Norton, 2002. Reproduced with permission of Abner Stein.

Rabbi Rachel Adler for 'The Jew Who Wasn't There: Halacha and the Jewish Woman' *Response: A Contemporary Jewish Review*, Summer 1973, https://jwa.org/media/jew-who-wasnt-there-halacha-and-jewish-woman. Reproduced with permission of the author.

Jan Morris for an extract from *Conundrum*, Faber & Faber, 2018, copyright © 1974 by Jan Morris. Reproduced with permission of the publisher.

Mariarosa Dalla Costa for an extract from 'A General Strike' published in *Women and the Subversion of the Community: A Mariarosa Dalla Costa Reader*, copyright © 2019 by PM Press. Reproduced with permission of PM Press.

Silvia Federici for an extract from *The New York Wages For Housework Committee: History, Theory, Documents, 1972-1977*, edited with Arlen Austin. Reproduced with permission of the author.

An extract from 'Of Woman Born' from *Of Woman Born: Motherhood as Experience and Institution* by Adrienne Rich, W.W. Norton, copyright © 1986, 1976 by W. W. Norton & Company, Inc. Reproduced with permission of W. W. Norton & Company, Inc.

Ursula K. Le Guin for 'The Space Crone' published in *Dancing At the Edge of the World*, Grove Press, 1997, pp.3-6, copyright © 1989 by Ursula K. Le Guin. Used with permission of Grove/Atlantic, Inc. Any third party use of this material, outside of this publication, is prohibited.

Andrea Dworkin for an extract from *Our Blood*, HarperCollins, 1976, pp.45-46. Reproduced with permission of Elaine Markson Literary Agency.

Denise Riley for the poem 'In 1970' and an extract from 'A note on sex and the "reclaiming of language"' from *Selected Poems 1976-2016*, Picador, 2019. Reproduced with permission of the author.

Maya Angelou for the poem 'Still I Rise' from *And Still I Rise*, Virago Press, 1978, 1986, copyright © 1978 by Maya Angelou. Reproduced with permission of Little, Brown Book Group.

Susie Orbach for an extract from *Fat is a feminist Issue*, Arrow Books, 2016, copyright © 2016 by Susie Orbach. Reproduced with permission of the Random House Group.

Fadwa Tuqan for 'Difficult Journey - Mountainous Journey' published in *Opening the Gates: An Anthology of Arab Feminist Writing*, translated by Donna Robinson Divine, 1990. Reproduced with permission of the translator;

Permissions Credits

Audre Lorde for extracts from 'The Master's Tools Will Never Dismantle the Master's House' and 'The Uses of Anger: Women Responding to Racism' from *Sister Outsider*, Penguin, 2019. Reproduced with permission of Abner Stein.

Angela Carter for an extract from *The Bloody Chamber*, Penguin, 1995, copyright © The Estate of Angela Carter. Reproduced with permission of the Estate c/o Rogers, Coleridge & White Ltd., 20 Powis Mews, London W11 1JN.

Mariama Bâ for an extract from *So Long a Letter*, translated by Modupé Bodé-Thomas Heinemann, 2008, pp.36-34, copyright © 1980 by Nouvelles Editions Africaines de Sénégal; © 1981 English translation by Modupé Bodé-Thomas. Reproduced with permission of Pearson Education Ltd.

An extract from 'Compulsory Heterosexuality and Lesbian Existence' from *Blood, Bread, and Poetry: Selected Prose 1979-1985* by Adrienne Rich, copyright © 1985 by Adrienne Rich. Reproduced with permission of W. W. Norton & Company, Inc.

AAWORD for 'A Statement on Genital Mutilation' from *Cambridge University Press Feminist Reader*, Vol 3, ed. Harris and Hughes, 2013. Reproduced with permission of the Licensor through PLSclear.

Rigoberta Menchu for an extract from *I, Rigoberta Menchu: An Indian Woman in Guatemala*, translated by Ann Wright, Verso, copyright © 1984. Reproduced with permission of the publisher.

Liz Lochhead for the poem 'Everybody's Mother' from *Dreaming Frankenstein and Collected Poems 1967-1984*, Polygon, 2003. Reproduced with permission of the Licensor through PLSclear;

Valerie Amos and Pratibha Parmar for 'Challenging Imperial Feminism' published in *Feminist Review*, No.17, Autumn 1984, Sage Publications Ltd. Permission conveyed through Copyright Clearance Center, Inc.;

bell hooks for an extract from *Feminist Theory: From Margin to Center*, Routledge, 2015, copyright © 2000 by Gloria Watkins. Reproduced with permission of Taylor and Francis Group, LLC, a division of Informa plc, and conveyed through Copyright Clearance Center.

Permissions Credits

Toni Morrison for 'A Knowing So Deep' first printed in *Essence,* 1985, copyright © 1985 by the Estate of Chloe A. Morrison. Reproduced with permission of ICM Partners.

Donna Haraway for an extract from *Simians, Cyborgs and Women: The Reinvention of Nature,* first published by Free Association Books Ltd, copyright © 1991 by Donna J. Haraway. Reproduced with permission via CM Foreign Rights Agency.

Gloria Anzaldúa for an extract from *Borderlands, La Frontera, The New Mestiza,* copyright © 1987, 1999. Aunt Lute Books. Reproduced with permission of the publisher.

Judith Plaskow for the introduction to *Standing Again At Sinai: Judaism from a Feminist Perspective,* Bravo, 1991, pp.ix-xv, copyright © 1990 by Judith Plaskow. Used with permission of HarperCollins Publishers.

Judith Butler for an extract from *Gender Trouble,* Routledge, 2007. Permission conveyed through Copyright Clearance Center, Inc.

Winona LaDuke for an extract from *Mothers of Our Nations: Indigenous Women Address the World,* 1995. Reproduced with permission.

Arwa Salih for an extract from *The Stillborn: Notebooks of a Woman from the Student-Movement Generation in Egypt* by Arwa Salih, translated by Samah Selim, Seagull Books 2017. Reproduced with permission of Seagull Books.

Marilyn Dumont for 'Memoirs of a Really Good Brown Girl' from *A Really Good Brown Girl,* copyright © 1996, 2015. Reproduced with permission from Brick Books.

M. A. Jaimes Guerrero for an extract from 'Civil Rights versus Sovereignty: Native American Women in Life and Land Struggles' from *Feminist Genealogies, Colonial Legacies, Democratic Futures,* Routledge, 1997, copyright © 1997. Reproduced by permission of Taylor and Francis Group, LLC, a division of Informa plc, and conveyed through Copyright Clearance Center.

Carol Ann Duffy for the poem 'Little Red-Cap' from *The World's Wife,* Picador, 1999. Reproduced with permission of the Licensor through PLSclear.

bell hooks for an extract from *Feminism is for Everybody: Passionate Politics,* Routledge, copyright © 2015 by Gloria Watkins. Reproduced with permission of Taylor and Francis Group, LLC, a division of Informa plc, and conveyed through Copyright Clearance Center.

An extract from 'Gender Violence and the Prison Industrial Complex' INCITE, https://incite-national.org/. Reproduced with permission from INCITE! National.

Hilary Mantel for an extract from *Giving up the Ghost*, Fourth Estate, copyright © 2003 by Hilary Mantel. Reprinted with permission of HarperCollins Publishers Ltd.

Anne Enright for an extract from *Making Babies*, Vintage, copyright © Anne Enright. Reproduced by permission of the author c/o Rogers, Coleridge & White Ltd., 20 Powis Mews, London W11 1JN.

Mary Daly for an extract from *Amazon Grace*, Palgrave Macmillan, 2006. Reproduced with permission of the Licensor through SNCSC.

Wangari Muta Maathai for an extract from Unbowed: My Autobiography, Arrow Books, 2008, copyright © 2006 by Wangari Muta Maathai, Repdouced with permission of The Random House Group Limited.

An extract from 'The Charter of Feminist Principles for African Feminist', AWDF, 2006. Reproduced with permission of The African Women's Development Fund, www.awdf.org.

Joanne Arnott for the poem 'Change Yourself', from *Mother Time: Poems New and Selected*, 2007. Published with permission from Ronsdale Press.

Sarah Ahmed for 'Conclusion 2. A Killjoy Manifesto' from *Living a Feminist Life*, copyright © 2017, Duke University Press. All rights reserved. Republished with permission of the copyright holder. www.dukeupress.edu.

Jeanette Winterson for an extract from *Why Be Happy When You Could Be Normal?* Vintage, 2012, copyright © 2011 by Jeanette Winterson. Reproduced with permission of The Random House Group Limited.

Rachel Cusk for an extract from *Aftermath*, Faber & Faber Ltd, pp.6-14, copyright © 2014. Reproduced with permission of the publisher.

Permissions Credits

Jacqueline Rose for an extract from *Mothers*, London Review of Books, Vol 36, Issue 12, 19/06/2014, pp.17-22. https://www.lrb.co.uk/v36/n12/jacqueline-rose/mothers. Reproduced with permission of London Review of Books and the author.

Chimamanda Ngozi Adichie for an extract from *We Should All Be Feminists*, Fourth Estate, copyright © 2014 by Chimamanda Ngozi Adichie. Reproduced with permission of HarperCollins Publishers Ltd.

Amel Moussa for the poem 'Love Me' translated by Khaled Mattawa, originally published in *The poetry of Arab Women*, *Banipal Magazine of Modern Arab Literature*, No. 3, October, 1998. Reproduced with permission of Banipal Publishing and Khaled Mattawa.

Maggie Nelson for *The Argonauts*, Melville House, 2016, pp.99-12, copyright © 2016. Reproduced with permission of the publisher, Melville House Ltd. Originally published in the US by Graywolf Press.

Fatemeh Shams for the poem 'Acid-Throwing', translated by Dick Davis in *When They Broke Down the Door*, Mage Publishers, 2016, p.93. Reproduced with permission of the publisher.

Eileen Myles for an extract from 'Acceptance Piece' and the poem 'Transmission', published in *Evolution*, pp.113-117, 201-204, copyright © 2018 by Eileen Myles. Used with permission of Grove/Atlantic, Inc. Any third party use of this material, outside of this publication, is prohibited.

Associazione Trama di Terre for the 'Manifesto for Migrant Feminism', Trama di Terre, 2016. Reproduced with permission.

Maria Alyokhina for an extract from *Riot Days*, Allen Lane, 2017, Penguin Books 2018, copyright © 2017 by Maria Alyokhina. Reproduced with permission of the Penguin Group Ltd.

Deborah Levy for extracts from *The Cost of Living*, Penguin Books, 2019. Reproduced with permission of Penguin Books Ltd.

Lola Olufemi for a chapter from *Feminism, Interrupted*, Pluto Press, 2020. Reproduced with permission of the Licensor through PLSclear.

In some instances we have been unable to trace the owners of copyright material, and we would appreciate any information that would enable us to do so.

Acknowledgements

I began at the shoreline. I thought feminism came in waves. But when I waded into them for this anthology, I was quickly swept out to open water. As I read and read, I felt like I was diving, as far as I could go, only to find that the places I was reaching gave onto gardens upon gardens under the sea. For helping me find them, I thank Katherine Angel, Shrabani Basu, Clem Cecil, Sara Collins, Richard Drayton, David Edgerton, Hannah Elsisi, Paula Erizanu, Katrina Forrester, Nell Gifford, Anne Goldgar, Toby Green, Jo Heygate, Vincent Hirribarren, Susan James, Rehana Kapadia, Kate Kirkpatrick, Laura Gowing, Louise Gray, Deborah Levy, Olivia Laing, Anna Lee, Suzannah Lipscomb, Stephen Lovell, Catherine Mayer, Rana Mitter, Hannah Murphy, Katharina Oke, Susie Orbach, Rachel Scott, Hélène Seppain, Sophie Smith, Adam Sutcliffe, Susannah Trefgarne, Anna Vaux, Alex von Tunzelman, and Abigail Woods.

For extending the confines of my knowledge and pointing me in new directions, I am indebted to the editors, translators, and commentators who have brought so much feminist writing into anglophone publishing, especially anthologisers before me, for their own beautiful maps of the territory – Breanne Fahs, Sharon M. Harris, Linda K. Hughes, Tiffany K. Wayne, and Penny A. Weiss.

I am grateful to my students at King's College London whose insights and multiple perspectives schooled me not only in feminist theory but also in feminist practice, as we sat, together, with the discomforts of the present and the past. My colleagues at King's, especially in the Department of History, have sustained me with their collegiality. King's has been a spiritual home for this project, and it has provided a physical refuge, too. I could not have carved out the time nor the mental space away from my children, had I not had a room of my own in which to work. Through the long evenings and weekends at the office, my most constant companions were the security staff at King's. I thank them for their unfailing cheer, especially Isabel Agbahwe for the stories and the laughter that we shared on the night shift. We missed our children and praised our mothers and sisters; hers were in Nigeria and mine were a bus ride away.

Colleagues in London more broadly, and further afield, have nourished me with their wisdom and feedback, and I thank especially Richard Bourke, Annabel Brett, Angus Gowland, Niall O'Flaherty, Joanne Paul, Quentin Skinner, Gareth Stedman Jones, Georgios Varouxakis, Waseem Yaqoob, and the forum where so many of our conversations take place – The Institute of Historical Research. I thank the participants in my Guardian Masterclasses on the history of feminism for their smart ruminations, and Kirsty McCusker-Delicado and her crack team for organising these joyous events.

Christine Mathias and Alice Taylor each read the introduction. I cannot thank them enough for their astute comments, and for urging me to come clean. I am also grateful to Rhian Jones, for her meticulous research assistance.

When Maria Bedford asked me whether I would be interested in compiling an anthology of feminists for Penguin Classics, I blithely said yes. Neither of us fathomed the vastness of the task nor the agonies of indecision, but as we pored over texts and tried to keep track of the variables, I could not have hoped for a more sympathetic or judicious editor – and the cake was always delicious. Thank you for saying yes; thank you for saying no. The whole team at Penguin has been a pleasure to work with; shout-outs to Alice Bloch for getting the texts together, Rachel Thorne for the massive job of clearing permissions, Stephanie Barrett and absolutely heroic Rebecca Lee for their soothing, patient copyediting through a global pandemic, and Micca Wright and Corina Romonti for their marketing and publicity magic.

Sarah Chalfant and Alba Ziegler-Bailey are the agents of dreams. Immediately, dazzlingly present when I need them, I love being under their wing – and thank them and everyone at The Wylie Agency. I could not have better guidance.

At home, and on green hills, Vladimir Eatwell has loved me, brought me tea, talked everything through, and looked after our daughters when I could not. Dora and Ada rooted for me, even when they wanted me all to themselves – their smiles and duvet occupations and probing thoughts spur me on. My own mum, Sandra Dawson, who showed me early on how to be strong and open at the same time, has read and cared at more drops of the hat than I can count. Rebecca Dawson has been a sister in every sense of the word. I have a father and brother, too, Henry and Tom, and they have buoyed me up with their jaunty spirits and sweet tunes.

Rebecca was pregnant when I was pulling this book together, and I found that I could not deliver it until beloved baby Joan had made it safely into the world. Darlings, I dedicate these pages to you.

Books are always co-created, one way or another, but this one is especially so. Most of all, I salute the feminist writers inside and outside these covers, for changing the world.